© 2022 Deb McQuilkin all rights reserved. Pre-publication edition, not for distribution outside the Columbia International University community.

ISBN: 9798359993302

No part of this book may be reproduced to transmitted in any form or any means, electronic or mechanical except as permitted in writing. Requests for reprints may be addressed in writing to djmcquilkin@gmail.com

Excerpts from *Introduction to Biblical Ethics* come from McQuilkin's earlier manuscripts so as not to confuse writings with his later co-author Paul Copan. Citations are provided for content similar or partially quoted in the 2014 edition. For further study the reader is encouraged to examine the most current version of *An Introduction to Biblical Ethics*.

Excerpts taken from *Five Views of Sanctification* by Melvin E. Dieter, Anthony A. Hoekema, Stanley M. Horton, J. Robertson McQuilkin, and John F. Walvoord. Copyright © 1987 by Zondervan. Used by permission of HarperCollins Christian Publishing. www.harpercollinschristian.com. The rights to *Five Smooth Stones, Life in the Spirit and Living the Life 1 & 2* originally published by Lifeway are returned to Robertson's widow, Deb.

Scripture unless otherwise noted is in the English Standard Version. Scripture quotations are from the ESV® Bible (The Holy Bible, English Standard Version®), copyright © 2001 by Crossway, a publishing ministry of Good News Publishers. Used by permission. All rights reserved. The ESV text may not be quoted in any publication made available to the public by a Creative Commons license. The ESV may not be translated into any other language.

In this early edition of *Transformed*, diverse sources and previous publishers were used. Style guides differ in their rules for capitalization of pronouns for God. Your forbearance is requested in the inconsistencies of capitalization of the pronouns for God in this edition.

Robertson McQuilkin (1927-2016) was one of the 20th century's greatest missionary statesmen. With his brilliant mind, he was also a homemaker, writer, conference speaker, ethicist, and theologian. He was President of Columbia Bible College from 1968 to 1990. Prior to serving as President, he and his first wife, Muriel were missionaries in Japan for twelve years from 1956-1968. McQuilkin is perhaps best known for his resignation in 1990 from the presidency of CBC (now Columbia International University) to care for Muriel until the slow ravages of Alzheimer's took her in 2003. To his astonishment, that decision which he considered easy and unremarkable, continues to reverberate throughout the evangelical world. That story is now a classic entitled *A Promise Kept*.

His theological and practical expositions come in the form of the books *Understanding and Applying the Bible, Introduction to Biblical Ethics (IBE), The Great Omission, Five Views of Sanctification, Five Smooth Stones, Life in the Spirit and Living the Life 1 & 2 and A Promise Kept*. His journal publications abound, and his sermons often quoted.

This devotional is a collection of excerpts from those publications, private writings, and sermon notes. They include God's truth that transcends time and context. McQuilkin believed in the power of story. God's story in the lives of people. Some consider him one of the 20th century's great storytellers. Those stories are threaded throughout this devotional. Many are his own life example, offered to assist us to see how to live or not live the Christian life. Through these stories, illustrations of principles of Christian living weave throughout this devotional. Each offering a nugget of practical biblical and theological truth that is just enough to ponder and apply for that day. Some of these daily reading may feel academic, but do not be misled. By the end of a year, if one is serious about applying as well as knowing principles of Christian living, growth toward the God-intended life will occur. It is that *life* for which we all yearn.

McQuilkin married his second wife, Deb, in 2005. They were married for eleven years until his death at 89 years old. Deb serves as the editor of this collection, having scoured through computer notes, published writing and through years of listening in loving support for his ongoing ministry. It was her work as Associate Professor at the University of South Carolina that prepared her for this task of assimilating his life's work into a daily reader to benefit us all. Deep gratitude is expressed for Robertson's loving friends, colleagues, and the women God brought into Deb's life who served as proof-readers. Their capable and detailed assistance is priceless. Any grammatical mistakes remaining are hers alone.

McQuilkin's life verse, evident through his writings, is 2 Corinthians 3:18 *"But we all, with unveiled face beholding as in a mirror the glory of the Lord, are transformed into the same image from glory to glory, even as from the Lord the Spirit." (ASV)* May this be so for us!

2 Corinthians 3:18

But we all, with unveiled face beholding as in a mirror the glory of the Lord, are being transformed from one degree of likeness to another.

Introduction to Time with God

Perhaps these daily devotionals will provide a start for your quiet time, transforming your life by the Spirit in obedience through God's Word. We touch on many different aspects of a life changed in its core to become more intimate with God, the Creator of the universe, who has a will and plan for each life. Some of these snippets are personal, some are stories as examples and each is based on Scripture. We will not be the same, I offer my own stories only as an example of God's dealing with one man. My desire is that it will stimulate you to *"love and good deeds"*- and to walk in ever increasing *"oneness with God"*.

I began having a personal quiet time following my surrender to Christ at age 12, but reading the Bible was more like eating sawdust; and praying—well, was God listening at all? I tried to keep that morning appointment with Him, but more often than not I skipped it in favor of more sleep or breakfast. Finally, at age 21, I told the Lord I would read the Word daily whether it had meaning for me or not, just as an act of obedience. Things didn't change except that I kept that promise faithfully, week after weary week, eating sawdust. Then one morning I realized I had changed. I couldn't get along without that time with God. In fact, the Bible had come alive to me. It's been that way ever since. Commitment may be the key.

I have a set appointment with the Lord every morning at 6:00 a.m. Why morning? Well, David said God would hear his voice every morning (Ps. 5:3). Jesus set a powerful example by praying early in the morning, and a friend of mine once said he couldn't see tuning your violin after the concert was over! Some say they just aren't morning people; but it is important to have a set time or other things will crowd out your time with God. The enemy will see to that! I prefer early morning because there aren't many interruptions at 6:00 a.m. Besides, I want to tune my violin before the concert! To be honest, I anticipate those daily encounters with my lover and when an emergency aborts the schedule, I feel a loneliness of soul.

I set aside an hour, but often it runs over a little. Many Korean pastors say for them 4 hours is necessary. For myself, I can hardly unwind and settle my restless mind in 15 minutes. One thing is sure, a hasty salute toward heaven is not sufficient for building a meaningful relationship with God. The goal is companionship, not dutiful routine.

First, I sing aloud a couple of hymns or choruses, that tunes my heart. He doesn't care about my lack of solo quality! The Bible contains many commands to sing, so as I sing through the hymnal, if I don't know the melody I just make up a tune as I go along. Fortunately, I'm alone!

After tuning my soul with song, I turn to the Bible. I use a different translation each time I read through the Bible to keep it fresh and gain new insights. I read consecutively through each book, the way the author wrote it and intended it to be read, in context, in continuity. I often pause before reading and ask the Spirit to speak to me through His Word.

My goal is to hear from the Lord, not cover territory! Though I usually read a chapter, I may read more or less— reading till there's been a real soul-connection. To make that connection, to hear the voice of the Spirit, I read reflectively, pausing at any passage that speaks to me in my present situation—encouragement, conviction of sin, a guiding principle, a fresh vision of God's goodness or greatness—whatever. I may pray this back to the Lord with thanksgiving, or with a petition to change me. Often I use the passage to pray on behalf of those for whom I intercede that day.

As I read I underline passages that speak to me and return to them over and over: first, when I finish my passage for the day, then again at the beginning of my reading the following day, and finally, when I've finished that book I go back and read the underlined passages for the entire book. They become friends to guide my life. I do a couple of other things with those passages. When a passage comes through with an especially powerful impact I go back and ink them in, making the "type" boldface. Finally, at a later time, I may take those special messages, type them out on 3-by-5 inch cards, and rotate them on my "refrigerator collection" so they can speak to me again and again.

This is not a prescriptive pattern, yet this sets me in a lifestyle of choosing Jesus first, growing in His word, and walking in ever greater intimacy with Him-connecting with the one I love. Commitment is key to all relationships, day in and day out. Over three quarters of a century, a loving oneness develops. Whereas life seems empty without spending one-on-one time with the One I love most. How about you? Will you join us as we grow together?

January 1
REMEMBER...FORGET
Isaiah 46.9-11

"Remember not the former things, nor consider the things of old. Behold, I am doing a new thing; now it springs forth, do you not perceive it? I will make a way in the wilderness and rivers in the desert. The wild beasts will honor me, the jackals and the ostriches, for I give water in the wilderness, rivers in the desert, to give drink to my chosen people, the people whom I formed for myself that they might declare my praise." (Isaiah 43:18-21)

Remember! That is what we are doing for this New Year celebration. We look back and remember. Why should we recall the past? To focus on God's great actions in our behalf. It will help us to "know that He alone is God...and there are no others." Today, celebrating years of God's faithfulness, what are your memories that exalt God? As you review those memories, how do they cause people to stand in awe of your God?

For me, I remember...A college student in Japan who brought so many fellow students to church that my children were amazed. I remember ping-pong dendo and all the trips the young people took together. I remember the many baptisms. Then came the day we had a call to return to America to lead Columbia International University. God told me from his Book that I should ask the church family for guidance. I was fearful they wouldn't agree that this was God's call. But I remember how the church gathered around and confirmed God's call. And how God blessed that decision in prospering his work in Columbia to send out thousands of messengers to the ends of the earth. Another memory that shines the spotlight on God. As you reflect on your past, what are your memories that bring him glory? We obey the prophet and remember to give God the credit and point out his glorious power to others. BUT then he says, "forget it!" Remember, look back, celebrate God, but then turn around and face the future. Why? Because God wants to do something altogether new, something awesome, something greater than the past. How is that possible? And what exactly does he have in mind for you?

Rivers in the desert. What are the rivers he plans for you? The "new thing?" Surely anyone with a dried up, barren experience of God can even today have rivers of God's blessing in your desert. He wants to flood you with his Holy Spirit, so you'll grow and flourish in your own spirit and bear a bumper crop of fruit. You'll bear "Jesus fruit," his character reproduced in your words and actions so the people in your life will see it and get hungry for what you have. That's the new thing he intends for you.

How can that happen? WHY would he do such a thing? *"I have formed you for myself,"* he says. You belong to him, not to yourself. When you deliberately acknowledge that every day, he's free to take over and flood out through you. And what will happen? He tells us, *"...in order to declare his praise!"* Why, that's the same purpose as the "remembering," isn't it? And when we remember today his past blessing, then don't keep dwelling on that but turn to look for the new thing he intends, we will surely *"declare his praise"* in new ways and with new power.

I don't know what he has in mind for you, but I do know he wants to do a new thing. And he will reveal it to those who are wholly his and seeking, searching for new ways to bring him great glory. Pray and pray together until he tells you what that is and then trust him to do that new thing, to flood out from you to a dried-up, parched, dying world.

January 2
Aim Well
2 Corinthians 3:18

"We all . . . are being transformed into the same image" (2 Corinthians 3:18, NKJV).

"Blessed are those who aim at nothing for verily they shall hit it!" states a popular proverb. We need to know what we're aiming at-in our jobs, marriages, responsibilities, and our relationship with God. As we enter a new year, what is your goal in life? What do you want to accomplish? I want to . . . "survive with sanity," "build a good marriage with successful children," "make a bundle," "become like Jesus," "maintain good health and happiness," or perhaps "be filled with the Spirit." None of those objectives are bad, though some are more worthy than others. If we want our goals in life to fit together and not compete, we've got to set an ultimate purpose that brings all the others together. Paul gives us a good goal: "*We all . . . are being transformed into the same image*" (2 Corinthians 3:18, NKJV).

To be like Jesus! Now there's an objective that will purify and focus all our other goals. But why did God choose such a lofty plan for us? God created us based on His design. We're designed in some mysterious sense as models of the God who created us. God created us, but we rebelled against His purpose. We call that rebellion the fall. We became a fallen or broken model of God. Because of the fall, we can't always act like Jesus. We fail to have His attitude about people or His kind of relationship with the Father. But God has a reconstruction program to take us-broken models of Himself-and re-make us into His likeness. Before we come to know Jesus, we are all on the downward spiral away from God. His purpose is to turn us around and spiral us up toward ever greater likeness to Jesus: "*We all . . . are being transformed into the same image*." Before God could transform us, He had to get our attention and reveal Himself to us. So we examine the Spirit's role in revealing God to humanity; "*God created man in his own image, in the image of God he created him; male and female he created them.*" (Genesis 1:27)

If you wanted to know what God expects of you or plans for you, how would you find out? Jesus is our model of what God is like. He is our standard. He is our goal. We don't know much about Jesus apart from the Bible. Besides, the Bible teaches us not only about Jesus but also about God and what He expects of us. The Bible is God's revelation of His will for us; it's our only sure road map for life.

How can I know the Bible is reliable? (See 2 Timothy 3:16-17; Matthew 5:17-18). Some folks say, "Try it and see for yourself." That's good common-sense advice, but the "what works is true" test won't do to prove the validity of the Bible. What if my attempts to follow the Bible don't seem to work all that well? I try to do what I think the Bible teaches and everything comes unglued. Does that mean the instruction manual is unreliable, that it led me astray? Or does it mean I misread it and must study it more carefully? The bottom line is this: Jesus fully trusted the Scriptures. And I'm not smarter than He! We have to lay a solid foundation. Some folks are impatient with foundation laying. They want to get on with the exciting truths about how to experience the God intended life. They are like the home builder who's so excited about the Jacuzzi for the second-floor master bedroom that he neglects laying a solid foundation. Too bad for the Jacuzzi and its occupant if the foundation is poor! We need to be sure of our foundation and our goal.

January 3
God's Nature
Mathew 22.37

"Jesus replied: Love the Lord your God with all your heart and with all your soul and with all your mind." (Matthew 22.37).

What do you like best about Jesus? His nature is love. Love—not getting but giving. How much? Total self-giving. Other-oriented, not self-oriented. That's #1 in his model for us.

Number one then, is loving God. But there's more. Jesus continued with number two: loving the others in our life. As a son of Eve, we are not naturally that way. I work to fulfill me, not you. I sacrifice anything to protect me, provide for me, yes, even entertain me. But Jesus loved his neighbor, not **as** himself, but more than he loved himself. Love. Maybe we get close to loving our spouse and children that way, but our friends? Even broader, my neighbor? Why can't I love you that way? Love on God's standard. If we consider Satan's anti-image of God to this self-giving, covetousness, then, reigns. To get more than to give. Love.

Is there anything else you like about the Jesus model? How about holiness? What if he were corrupt, untrustworthy, filled with lust? In the anti-image there is also pride. And there's a dilemma here. How could humility be part of the character of the King of Kings? Humility? But that also is his model for us. Philippians 2:3-8: *"Do nothing out of selfish ambition or vain conceit. Rather, in humility value others above yourselves, not looking to your own interests but each of you to the interests of the others. In your relationships with one another, have the same mindset as Christ Jesus: Who, being in very nature God, did not consider equality with God something to be used to his own advantage; rather, he made himself nothing by taking the very nature of a servant, being made in human likeness. And being found in appearance as a man, he humbled himself by becoming obedient to death— even death on a cross!"*

Jesus sets a high standard, indeed. How different were Eve in the lush garden of Eden, and Jesus in the desert! Eve with a perfect heredity, Jesus with a deplorable ancestry. Yet Jesus prevailed. He is our model. Ever so briefly then, that's the Bible's standard for the God-intended life. In a word, Jesus.

What is a picture of that standard: Victory— Overcoming all conscious, deliberate rejection of the known will of God. Yet it's not just victory over temptation that God plans. The life he intends for you is far more than that. He wants the positive, He wants you to feel like Jesus, to think like Jesus, to choose like Jesus, to act like Jesus.

Christ-like life. Feeling, thinking, acting more and more like Jesus. But even that is not the ultimate, remember, He planned to restore the image ON PURPOSE. He created, redeemed and sanctifies us in order that we might have loving oneness with Him. Lovers to become truly one must be compatible, right? Therefore, we were created God-compatible. Loving oneness with God is the goal of it all. Joy filled companionship.

January 4
Love for Me or You?
Matthew 22:39

"You shall love your neighbor as yourself." (Matthew 22:39)

My 9-year-old granddaughter Natasha, and I set off at dusk down a rural road. On the first curve we met a pickup truck with its lights still off. "Look at that!" I said, "That's illegal! He could be arrested for that."

"But maybe his lights don't work, and he's trying to get to the garage to have them fixed."

"Fat chance! There's no garage out here in the country."

"Well, maybe he just forgot. He's probably had a hard day and is trying to get home quickly to his family."

"Some excuse," I grumped. Then I had a bright idea. I decided to notice as many bad things as I could as we drove along and comment on each. Sure enough, Natasha had an excuse for every bad behavior that I called to her attention. She made up a good motive for every bad action just as creatively and persistently as we might rationalize our own behavior.

Who are some people or groups of people you regularly rail against, at least in your mind?

Do you find yourself justifying your animosity toward these people? How?

Because I love myself unconditionally, I'm not very critical toward myself; I always have a good reason for my error or delinquency. "Love covers a multitude of sins" (1 Pet. 4:8). If I don't love someone, it's easy to find fault; to assign blame; to ascribe evil intent; and yes, even to hate.

Imagine that a friend slights you in a meeting. Your thoughts might sound like this:

He meant exactly what he said.… He said it because he doesn't like me.….He always says that kind of thing. …. Or He said it because that's the way he is.

Now apply the same responses to yourself when you say something that offends someone: I didn't mean it the way he took it.… I meant well; my motive was good.… I slipped.… I wasn't myself.… or It's just the way I am. Maybe your answers are like mine: I respond favorably to myself because I love me!

1 John 2:9 says: *"The one who says he is in the light but hates his brother is in the darkness until now."*

As long as we hate, we will never see good qualities in another person, just as I refused to give the truck driver the benefit of the doubt. Hate also blinds us to another person's need. We will never be sensitive to physical, emotional, or spiritual needs if we view others with hatred.

We find that a lack of love is the root of all other sins, of breaking all the other nine of the ten commandments. We don't love God with all our heart, soul, mind, and strength because we're in love with ourselves. Jesus identified the second greatest: *"Love your neighbor as yourself"* (Matt. 22:39). Would we violate the laws against adultery, stealing, lying, and coveting if we truly loved the other person? Self-absorption, self-protection, prejudice, an unsympathetic response to a hurting person, the failure to witness—certainly a lack of love lies behind these attitudes and actions.

Since Jesus was God incarnate, His very nature was love, and He taught His disciples that love should be the distinguishing mark of His followers: *"Love one another as I have loved you."* (John 15:12) Only through the constant filling of the Holy Spirit can we love others the way Christ intended.

January 5
Unplugged
Luke 8:49-53, Mark 9:17-19, 22-24, Mark 4:37-40

"I will put my trust in him." (Hebrews 2:3)

Think for a moment about how we unplug from the energizing power of the Holy Spirit. There are three ways that can happen to become unplugged from yielding.

Ignorance of God's standard. There is a story of the young lady in the doctor's office. She was seven months pregnant and nonchalantly, to me, a perfect stranger-- or so I thought-- mentioned she was planning a wedding. To the man who had fathered her baby, I hope. She was blinded by the prevailing culture. But was she really ignorant of God's standard? She told me she'd heard me preach once. And when I told her the church I belonged to, she said, "Oh, that's where I attend!" If she attended very often, she wasn't ignorant of God's standard, I'm sure. So maybe she wasn't ignorant of God's will, but of God's judgment on sin? Or maybe she had struggled with temptation and was ignorant of God's provision to overcome temptation? At any rate, she seemed ignorant of all God has for us in the God-intended life.

How about you? After reading so far, you can't plead ignorance, can you? So more often the power disconnect is rebellion. Have you ever heard the old hymn—"Have thine own way, Lord"? When my oldest sister was a toddler, her mother found her in her tiny rocking chair, rocking her doll and sweetly singing, "I have my own way, Lord." And believe me, she did! That was long before Frank Sinatra sang his most famous song, "I did it my way." That's one sure way to unplug. Paul teaches us, "Do not grieve the Spirit." grieve, it will quench the Spirit, we are taught. No more power flow.

But for most true believers, more often than deliberate rebelling to unplug, is…spiritual… Drift. The most common way for the sin-barrier to drift in, to get the "yield" prong unplugged with slow drifting is rationalization. Oh, it's not so bad, everyone does it, or that's just the way I am. Or I figure out a way to re-interpret the plain teaching of Scripture. The ways of rationalization are infinite—Satan will see to that.

But more often the drift comes, not through deliberate rebellion, but through neglect of the weapons the Spirit has provided—prayer, Bible study, fellowship and accountability with other believers. When I feel the cloud drifting in and the personal relationship with my traveling Companion grows dim, neglect of what the Spirit provides is usually the culprit.

Whatever means the Great Deceiver uses to blow that cloud of separation between you and your inside Companion—ignorance, rebellion, or drift-- the "yield" plug must be kept tight. Shouldn't we check the connection every day? That's to be yielded.

And the other prong of the faith-connection…Trust unplugged. How do we get "trust" unplugged? Three video clips from the Bible demonstrate how we unplug the Trust prong of faith. Watch them!

a) Luke 8:49-53-They doubted God because they knew better-
b) Mark 9:17-19, 22-24 They doubted God's power, and
c) Mark 4:37-40-They doubted God's care.

And so it is with us—

- a) "God, I know you want me to go that way, but I'm not so sure. I think I know a better way." Or…
- b) "God, you're powerful but this one may be too hard for you. I'm hopeless, nothing but failure." Or…
- c) "God, you're smart enough, you're strong enough, but do you really care about me that much?"

Unplug! Shorted out! No Spirit power flow. We are dissing God! His very character is maligned.

Yield and trust. Notice an important difference between yielding and trusting. Yield *can* be once-for-all. No need to ever deliberately say "no," to unplug. Of course, if you do say "no," you need to make that yield choice again. But trust usually isn't in full bloom in an instant of decision. It seems to need grow-time. The more you companion with a friend, the more you trust him or her, right? And so it is with the Spirit, faith grows as you stay tight with him. And that's the God-intended life.

January 6
Transforming Pain
1 Peter 2

"For what credit is there if, when you sin and are harshly treated, you endure it with patience? But if you do what is right and suffer for it, you patiently endure it, this finds favor with God. For you have been called for this purpose, since Christ also suffered for you, leaving you an example for you to follow in his steps." (1 Peter 2:20b-21)

What if there were a way to change the sea of trouble engulfing you today into still waters of joy and peace? What if there were a way for that very pain to transform you into all God ever intended? There is! And that's our theme today: transforming pain.

For example, how could a good God with all power allow a doctor and nurse, who had for a quarter century been dispensing life to the very lost people of Yemen, to be gunned down at the hospital entrance?

Puzzled, distressed, we turn to the Bible for answers. Because the greatest pain is meaningless suffering. Still, there IS meaning to our suffering. That glorious truth Scripture highlights by its stories from Genesis to Revelation.

As I grow older and the troubles of my family and friends grow greater, I return over and over to what the Bible has to say is the meaning of our suffering. I was delighted to discover the first pastor of the First Church at Jerusalem, Peter, refers to all our questions about pain. He answers….Whose suffering does he address? What kind of suffering? Where does it come from? Why does God permit it? How may we make it transforming? And when does relief come?

First then; whose suffering does Peter address? Astonishingly, Jesus' suffering and yours are intertwined throughout. Everyone suffers.

Another strange thing confronts us when we ask…Where does this suffering come from? The number one culprit, we like to think, is our great enemy, Satan. And he IS the source of both devouring temptation AND persecution. Your adversary, the devil, prowls about like a roaring lion, seeking someone to devour (1 Peter 5:8) Perhaps we think, "Millions in the world suffer persecution and Peter speaks reassurance to them." And the reassurance IS for those who are persecuted for Christ's sake. But that isn't all Satan does to devour us. He tempts us to sin, he creates all kinds of human suffering. But he's not the only source, nor, perhaps, the chief source of our suffering. Our human condition is often the source of pain. *"Beloved, I urge you as aliens and strangers to abstain from fleshly lusts, which wage war against the soul." (1 Peter 2:11)* see also (1 Peter 4:12).

Did you notice? Both temptation and opposition are part of the daily environment of every one of us. We live in a fallen world where bad things happen to Christians just as to anyone else. If Christians had no suffering, everyone would want to become a "Christian" – and for all the wrong reasons!

But if you ask the why question when trouble comes, you're in good company: David asked it constantly. Even Jesus asked "Why?" Of course, there's a good "why" and a bad "why'". The bad why is accusing God. God, you're not smart enough—I know a better way. Or, God, you're not strong enough to handle this problem. Or, God, you are smart enough and strong enough, but you don't care that much about me. It's the why of unbelief.

But the why of faith—that's different. Why did you let this happen, God, what is your purpose in this? How can I use this pain for your glory? Why does God send it or permit it? Many possible reasons but always two: my growth, his glory. How can these two reasons for pain transform your suffering?

January 7
How can I Know for Sure?
2 Timothy 3:16-17

"All Scripture is inspired by God and is profitable for teaching, for rebuking, for correcting, for training in righteousness, so that the man of God may be complete, equipped for every good work." (2 Timothy 3:16-17)

How can I know for sure? A contemporary individual, immersed from birth in a postmodern culture, would answer that question unequivocally: you can't! In fact, you can't know anything for sure. The only reality is a combination of whatever is out there and my perception of it, so my reality and yours can never be the same. You might object, "Wait a minute. That may be the way secular professors, entertainers, politicians, and the media think, but Bible believers are different!" Don't be too sure. How often from our own pulpits and in evangelical articles and books do we hear that the intuitive approach to reality is just as valid as, if not more valid than, the outmoded intellectual approach? Some Christian leaders think our guide shouldn't be so much what we think but how we feel.

In this devotional we will take the Word of God as our text. I didn't always see it that way. Raised in a Christian home, I felt called to ministry and enrolled in a leading evangelical seminary. It was there the problems in Scripture, endlessly spotlighted and analyzed by the critics, began to erode my faith. Finally, I slipped my moorings and bravely launched out into the dark sea of agnosticism. It was a lonely business, denying the validity of anything that lacked the credentials of scientific—that is, physical—evidence. It turned out that little of importance rests on that basis—things like human relationships, especially love.

In the end I began to return to faith. But still the shadows of doubt lurked around the fringes of my mind, sometimes with great insistence. Finally, I said to myself, In or Out, McQuilkin. How can you teach a Book you're not all that sure of? So I took my Bible and tent, went to a lonely beach, and camped out with the intent to get the matter settled one way or the other before I left. I read the Gospels once, twice, three times. I still knew all of the problems, but as I read that old story again, the person of Jesus Christ loomed large—over me, over the critics, over history. I couldn't explain Him on any naturalistic assumption. Finally, on the third day as I stood gazing out over the Pacific, it seemed there was a hand on my shoulder, and a strong, gentle voice said, "Little brother, are you smarter than I?"

In an instant all of the lights came on. "Oh no, no!" I cried. "I'm not smarter than You. And none of these critics are smarter than You!" From that moment as I embraced Jesus with my mind, He became my authority. Whatever He taught about the Bible, I accepted. I'm not smarter than Jesus, and He said not one letter of God's Word will fail (see Matt. 5:18). Whatever He said about salvation, about heaven and hell, I believed.

Soon 2 Timothy 3:16-17 became a life theme for me: *"All Scripture is inspired by God and is profitable for teaching, for rebuking, for correcting, for training in righteousness, so that the man of God may be complete, equipped for every good work."* What to believe, what not to believe, how to behave, how not to behave—that covers just about everything! And if God breathed it out—the literal meaning of inspired—I'd better trust it. If He breathed it out, I'd better obey it. What about you? What do you believe? Is the Bible inspired by God and does Scripture equip us for Christian living? Does the Word will accomplish what God intends? Did the writers of Scripture speak from God as directed by the Holy Spirit?

How can we know for sure? Because God said it!

January 8
True Worship
Mark 12:19-30

"God spoke to him, saying, 'I am the God of Abraham, and the God of Isaac, and the God of Jacob'?" (Mark 12:26b)

When a Bible scholar asked Jesus what was the most important thing, the ultimate, He replied, borrowing from Moses, "You shall love the Lord your God with all your heart, with all your soul, with all your mind, with all your strength. This is the BIG ONE, this is the great commandment." Then he added, the whole teaching of our Scriptures hangs on this. Sounds like you might say, "A person's chief end is to love God and be loved of Him forever." It is so beautiful. If you truly love a person you will glorify them, keep the spotlight ceaselessly on the true worth of the beloved. If you truly love a person and he is God, you will honor and glorify Him so highly you will worship him, you will bow down in humble adoration, you will sing to high heaven. So to glorify and worship God doesn't automatically lead to love, but love, to truly love, will always bring praise and worship.

To worship Him "in spirit" is to love Him with all your heart. To pursue a lifetime of loving intimacy with Him. But it's not just a worship in spirit, it is a tight connection spirit-to-spirit.

What God is looking for, said Jesus, is people who will worship Him not only with that intimate, love-intoxicated inner connection, in spirit, but also "in truth." No fakery.

The proof of love is not in how loud you sing but in how well you obey. Sing your heart out to Jesus. Enjoy the rush of corporate celebration. But above all, to truthfully worship is to obey: that's how we most truly spotlight His worth. That's how the people who watch, see and understand our God's true value. He is seeking those who worship in truth. Ungodly choices give the lie as to who God truly is.

If you love me, Jesus said, you will--what? Feel that affection deeply? Say and sing it with fervor? But of course. Yet what he *said* was, "if you love me you will keep my commandments." That's to worship in truth. Our whole lives demonstrating His worth, extolling His virtue. "Godly" we call it--in some small way, a god-like life. That's to worship.

There is a church bulletin where it reads, following the order of worship, "Our worship has ended, now our service begins." No, no! "Our corporate worship in words has ended and our worship in action—service—begins." That would be nearer the truth--true worship, that is. To worship in truth is to worship God with our lives as we put his glory on display. True worship is to love with intense passion and to express that love with words of adoration. Sing your heart out! But to love is to obey. That is true worship, the kind God still seeks.

Worship flowing from love begins on the inside, then, in spirit and becomes visible and audible in obedience, praise, thanksgiving. So "worship in truth," is to have our lives so in alignment with His that truth is demonstrated, but it also includes, even prior to that, truth in our thinking. Truth can never be found apart from revelation, God making known to us what we cannot bring up from inside ourselves alone. Truth (revelation) flows from the outside into a trusting, loving heart. Thus both "spirit" and "truth" are needed. Some Christians study truth but do not allow it to penetrate the motives, values, priorities of the heart. And we can also ignore feeding on truth, and worship then becomes a heart filled with empty words, and that projects a distorted image of God. Ponder anew where you can better worship- in spirit, loving Him with all your heart or in truth, that penetration of the values, motives and priorities which offer the world a right view of who God is.

January 9
Filled
Ephesians 5:18

"Therefore, brothers, pick out from among you seven men of good repute, full of the Spirit and of wisdom…" (Acts 6:3b)

How specifically does Christ enable us to overcome, to grow, to succeed? How does He enable us to have a pattern of success in place of the old pattern of failure? Does He displace our personalities with His? The beauty and glory of God's victory in our humanity is that He does not by-pass or replace us. Rather, He renews the new person after the likeness of God Himself (Col 3:10). As we shall see, this renewing work is primarily accomplished through the various means of grace that God provides, in the use of which we cooperate with Him.

But because God in us is not an impersonal resident force or influence in our lives but a person, the new life is one of delightful personal companionship. Like a good friend, His presence does wonderful things for us. He comforts us when we are discouraged and sensitizes our moral judgment through giving us understanding of His Book. His very presence galvanizes our will when we are weak; His counsel clarifies issues when we are confused. He works within us to change our thought patterns and outside us to control our circumstances for our long-term good.

Scripture speaks of each member of the Trinity living in us, but because the agent for effecting God's purposes in this world is the Holy Spirit, most of the teaching in the New Testament on normal Christian living focuses on the work of the Holy Spirit. The person who is in covenant relationship with God is said to have been baptized by the Spirit into the body of Christ, to have been born of the Spirit, to be indwelt by the Spirit, to walk in the Spirit, to bear the fruit of the Spirit, and to have been sealed by the Spirit. Of all these analogies, the most common is the idea of being filled with the Spirit. What does this picture language mean literally?

A tank may be empty, half-full, or full, and some Bible teachers refer to the filling of the Holy Spirit almost in such material terms. But we speak of a person, not a force, much less a liquid. Others use physical/figurative ideas similar to being full-blooded genetically or full of alcohol in their system and may be so affected by it that they have little control over themselves. This notion is better than the material concepts of fullness and has the advantage of an apparent biblical analogy: *"Don't be drunk with wine but be filled with the Spirit"* (Eph. 5:18, author's paraphrase). There are many parallels between the effects of drunkenness and God-intoxication, no doubt, but we are left in the realm of the figurative and still do not know what the expression means literally

The important question is about the present – "Are you filled with the Spirit?" In this sense the expression seems to indicate a state or condition. This use of the expression must also be valid because we are commanded to be filled continually with the Spirit (Ephesians 5:18). One problem is that many take the state to refer primarily to a subjective feeling, similar, perhaps, to our expression, "filled with joy." Scripture does promise us a life of awareness of God's presence.

Another biblical use of the expression seems to refer to a personal characteristic. When we say that a man is full of pride, sin*ful*, we mean that he or she is characterized by pride or sin. Used in this sense, the expression "filled with the Spirit" would mean that the person was characterized by Godlikeness, by God's being the predominant person or the pervasive influence in one's life. This must have been the meaning when people in Scripture were said to be Spirit-filled (e.g., Acts 6:3). Others could watch them and tell that their lives were characterized above all else by their association with God and by the results of that association. If someone were to describe what characterizes you, what would they say? What would you want them to say?

January 10
Nothing before God
Matthew 10:37

"Whoever loves father or mother more than me is not worthy of me, and whoever loves son or daughter more than me is not worthy of me." (Matthew 10:37)

To "have" a god is to ascribe to someone or something attributes that belong only to God or to relate to someone or something as the ultimate—to seek above all else, to trust above all else, to love above all else, to serve and obey above all else is to treat as God. To make something central in life, the pivot or ultimate reference point, is to "have a god." To yield ultimate allegiance to or to consider someone or something as the ultimate happiness or most desirable object, even to fear above all else is to "have a god." Notice that the first commandment does not say that we should have no other gods.

Actually, the rest of Scripture teaches that there are no other gods in reality; there is only one God. And yet this command prohibits having other gods before the true God. It is quite legitimate to have other loves, loyalties, and ambitions. But none of these loves and loyalties can come before God or we have broken the ultimate relationship and violated the supreme commandment. It is not the one who loves his father, mother, son, or daughter who is unworthy of the Lord Jesus, but the one who loves someone else more than him. *"Whoever loves father or mother more than me is not worthy of me, and whoever loves son or daughter more than me is not worthy of me."* (Matthew 10:37).

God is the ultimate reality, the fundamental fact, the integrating factor of the universe. Therefore, to be rightly aligned with him is the most important relationship in human existence. To be in alignment with reality and truth is life; to be out of alignment is destruction and death. To leave God out of the equation of life or to diminish his role is like seeking to build a skyscraper without mathematics or to bake a cake without flour.

When I arrived in Japan it grieved me deeply to see people call earnestly on gods who are not gods. But before long, I was among those who enjoyed photographing "quaint oriental customs." On one occasion an earnest Japanese Christian was giving us a guided tour of a famous shrine. "What is your reaction to places like this?" I inquired. "The same as all Japanese. I'm just sightseeing." "But," I responded, "some of these people really worship these idols. How do you feel about that?" "Oh, I think it's comical, an interesting custom." Let us remind ourselves that God does not consider the worship of anything else an interesting custom.

One's trust and obedience, allegiance or love may be quite legitimate and never demand a special, conscious evaluation until the loves or loyalties come into conflict. Then one's god stands revealed. At the point of choice, which love or loyalty we put before the other will determine who or what our true god is. What is most valuable to me? What do I hold to be most irreplaceable? What would I be lost without? What do I think of with most intensity in the long stretches of my thoughts? What is my incentive for living? What gives my work meaning and purpose? This I worship. Money and things can be sought above all else. A friend, a mate, a child, or a parent can be loved above all else. One can seek pleasure or fame above all else. One's love of country, a hero or leader, a philosophy or ideology can be an idol. Even something as abstract as art, education, or service can usurp the place of God. The most common idol of all is self. Today sift through your priorities and determine what threatens God's place in your life.

January 11
Forgiveness
Matthew 6:15

"If you don't forgive people, your Father will not forgive your wrongdoing" (Matt. 6:15).

George is puzzled. His older sister, Helen, is still holding him accountable for something he did a half century ago. He doesn't have the vaguest idea what it could have been, and she won't tell him. That grudge has totally poisoned the relationship. And she's considered the more spiritual of the two! Apparently, Helen has decided whatever George did is so grievous an offense that no amount of love can cover it. It's unforgivable. What a dangerous place to be.

Forgiveness is one of the most significant ways we show love for Christ and for others, and it may be the most difficult thing you are ever asked to do. The term forgive has objective and subjective meanings. The most basic meaning is the idea of letting the guilty party off the hook, not holding him accountable, not making her pay her just dues. That's the objective meaning of forgiveness. But to forgive also has a subjective nuance. To forgive is to let go of the inner animosity you've held. It's important to identify the meaning we have in mind because one is required of us always, the other only sometimes.

We shouldn't have animosity toward another person to begin with even if they have wronged us. God doesn't forgive most people in the sense of pardoning; there must be payment for sin, and His Son made that payment for all of us on the cross. Even so, God doesn't remit the guilt—forgive in the objective sense. But God never hated the person, felt vindictive, or exulted in the person's downfall as we sometimes do. We are called to relinquish those ugly inner emotions. However, we may experience innocent emotions that are not so easily dismissed, such as hurt and fear. A woman who has been raped is not expected to feel no pain or fear of her assailant, and certainly she can't be expected to forget what was done to her, although the ministry of the Spirit can heal the hurt and fear. But letting go of all hatred, all vengeance, all desire for the offender to pay— that we are obligated to do. Always.

I didn't. I was the object of a five-year attack by a member of the board to which I was responsible. It was unjust and carried out in a sneaky way, but when the matter was resolved, my cause vindicated before all, I never sought revenge. In fact, I didn't even hold it against Sal. After all, he felt he was being faithful, standing for the right. That's the problem with church fights: both sides feel they're serving God in what they do. I recognized that and forgave in both senses—didn't try to hold him accountable, didn't hold animosity against him. Or did I? Several years passed. I was reading of Christ's plea for His Father to forgive those who crucified Him, and Sal came to mind. I'd forgiven him as best I knew how, but would I ask God to forgive him? "No, Lord," I objected, "I won't hold him accountable, but don't You let him off the hook. You're for justice, right? He needs to get straightened out before someone else gets hurt." I wrestled with God until finally I admitted my forgiveness hadn't reached the deepest level if I were to be like Jesus. So I prayed, "It's OK, Lord, You can let him off. To his own master he stands or falls. I trust You to do right, and I trust You to take care of the outcome." At last, I'd forgiven. That's the subjective sense of the word, the kind of forgiveness that's always required of me.

Are you holding on to resentment? Who do you resent today? Confess your unwillingness to forgive and ask God to help you relinquish any animosity or desire for retribution.

January 12
Objective Forgiveness
Matthew 18:22

"Then Peter came up and said to him, "Lord, how often will my brother sin against me, and I forgive him? As many as seven times?" Jesus said to him, "I do not say to you seven times, but seventy-seven times." (Matthew 18:21-22)

What about objective forgiveness, not holding someone accountable for what they have done? When the offense is personal and the offender has asked for forgiveness and when I'm not in a responsible position to see that he or she does right or is punished, I'm required to forgive in the objective sense as well as the subjective sense. Jesus said, "If your brother sins, rebuke him, and if he repents, forgive him" (Luke 17:3). This means I don't require payment and don't seek punishment. And remember, making a person pay doesn't have to be sending a bill demanding cash. It can be holding the offense over a person, never letting them forget, subtly hinting at their failure. These means of holding someone accountable are sure signs of unforgiveness.

On the other hand, if I am responsible in some way to see that justice is done, that a person behaves, if I'm officially responsible, then I can't always forgive in this objective sense. Parents may need to discipline the child, the judge must pass sentence, or the church needs to discipline the cheating spouse. But if I am not responsible to hold the person accountable, I need to let it go. Usually I'm not responsible to see justice served; I have no official role of supervision. In those circumstances if the person asks forgiveness, I'm required to do it.

Peter asked Jesus how many times he was obligated to forgive someone. Jesus answered, "70 times seven" (Matt. 18:22). Then He told a cautionary parable about a slave who asked his master to forgive his debt. The master complied with his request and forgave his debt. But the slave then refused to have mercy on a fellow slave who owed him money, instead having him thrown in jail. When the master heard about it, he had the slave thrown in jail as well. Jesus concluded, "So My heavenly Father will also do to you if each of you does not forgive his brother from his heart" (v. 35). Jesus' teaching shows that we are required to forgive others; it's a command.

If the person doesn't ask for forgiveness, I'm not required to cancel the debt, just as God doesn't. Even so, I may choose to do so, just as Jesus and Stephen prayed for the forgiveness of those who were killing them (see Luke 23:34; Acts 7:60). And killing is a fairly heavy offense! Of course, we have no record of whether their prayers were answered, but they were not demanding justice from God, just pleading mercy for the offender.

The heart of forgiveness leads to another facet of the problem that confuses sensitive Christians. Subjective forgiveness is closely linked with love. In fact, it's love that makes such forgiveness possible. So when earnest people overreach in the matter of forgiveness, claiming that we must always forgive no matter what the offense, no matter the lack of repentance, they ask us to be more spiritual than God. What they should be saying is that we are to love a person no matter what the offense, no matter whether they repent. We are *always* obligated to love and forgive subjectively. We are *sometimes* obligated to forgive objectively.

A nephew of mine once appeared in court at a parole hearing. The man who brutally killed his sister was making his second appeal for parole, and family members were present to oppose the parole. Had they not forgiven? Yes, but they felt he was a danger to others. One of her brothers struggled for years to let the offense go until finally, weeping, God met him and gave him the gift of forgiveness, washing away the anger and bitterness. But still he was responsible to hold accountable a violent, hardened criminal. Is there any response that reveals an unforgiving spirit? Now is the time to get rid of that poisonous root. Turn over this hurt to God and ask Him to enable you to forgive as He has forgiven you.

January 13
Forgiven
Micah 7:19

"He will again have compassion on us; he will tread our iniquities underfoot. You will cast all our sins into the depths of the sea." (Micah 7:19)

Carmen was distressed. Young, attractive, and intelligent, she had accumulated quite a load of sin. She had drugged and slept with people across Europe, searching for meaning. And there she found Christ and the incredible joy of sins forgiven. From then on, she testified, she never had another twinge of guilt. But after becoming a Christian, she had slipped, and now she didn't feel God would forgive such a sin.

I spoke to Carmen about the certainty of God's forgiveness, but she continued to struggle. Then one day she came to see me, radiant and filled with joy. She told me she had once again been reviewing her big failure and agonizing before God when He said to her, "What sin are you talking about?" It was on her mind but not His!

Does God forget our sins? Micah 7:19 gives this reassuring picture of God's forgiveness. "You will cast all our sins into the depths of the sea." Do you believe God has literally forgotten your sins?

The problem with taking this poetic expression to mean that our sins are literally obliterated from God's mind is that such a view seems to contradict God's omniscience. Does He literally forget some things? Perhaps, but maybe we're safer in saying that He judicially forgets, declaring the debt paid on the basis of Jesus' blood and no longer holding us accountable.

Does God relinquish His animosity? To say God feels no animosity raises the issue of love. God's nature is love (see 1 John 4:8), and He loves us with an everlasting love (see Jer. 31:3). He cannot feel or act contrary to His nature. God loves not only those He has forgiven but also those He hasn't forgiven. Nevertheless, the Bible tells us that God also gets angry; He was angry with Moses, David, and the children of Israel, for example. But unlike our anger, God's anger is righteous—untainted by the flesh and therefore devoid of selfishness, ego, or pettiness. His intention is always redemptive in dealing with people. So when He gets angry, it's because someone is harming herself and others by living contrary to His law and His will. God holds no hostility or bitterness toward anyone, forgiven or unforgiven. We can set aside the idea that God relinquishes His animosity when He forgives our sin. He never had any to begin with!

Does God cancel our debt of sin? Any hope we have of success in the Christian life is based on this solid foundation: God has canceled our debt; He no longer holds us accountable. Paul explained, "He erased the certificate of debt, with its obligations, that was against us and opposed to us, and has taken it out of the way by nailing it to the cross" (Col. 2:14). Though God may at times discipline us (see Heb. 12:7; Rev. 3:19), we will never face any condemnation by the Judge at the final bar of justice. We are forgiven! Hallelujah!

The problem is, like Carmen, many of us find it difficult to forgive ourselves. And that can be almost as spiritually crippling as not accepting God's forgiveness. In fact, it may boil down to the same thing, for in continuing to carry the guilt load, we defame Jesus' sacrifice, treating the cross as if it were not a sufficient payment for our sin. Some people hobble through life with this dysfunctional sense of hope, never soaring free in the consciousness of sins forgiven.

Others, on the other hand, are cavalier about their sins, feeling no guilt or pain for sins against the Savior. How is it with you? Be very honest in your assessment because all future growth and victory depend on your response to

God's forgiveness. Embrace His forgiveness, and there is hope for a life of spiritual transformation and freedom.

Pray and express sorrow for any sins in your life and ask forgiveness. If God has already forgiven you, ask Him to help you forgive yourself. One of the many marvelous blessings of being a believer is experiencing God's forgiveness of all our transgressions of the law.

January 14
Grace and Knowledge
2 Peter 3:17-18

"You therefore, beloved, knowing this beforehand, take care that you are not carried away with the error of lawless people and lose your own stability. But grow in the grace and knowledge of our Lord and Savior Jesus Christ." (2 Peter 3:17-18)

The consistent teaching of the New Testament about the Christian life is growth. We're to grow in all ways, but Peter commands us to grow in two specific things: grace and knowledge. A grace is a gift given to one who hasn't earned it. It's something you can't get no matter how hard you work, like salvation. When we grow "in grace" we receive more and more Holy Spirit power for godly living. The Spirit's bank of grace is infinite, to be sure, but my capacity to receive His gifts is limited. I need to grow in appropriating more and more the resources the Spirit makes available.

We're commanded to grow also in "the knowledge of our Lord Jesus Christ". I must grow in understanding what the will of God is. Sin can be unintentional for two distinct reasons, unconscious or involuntary. I know well enough it's wrong to be impatient and I don't plan to "lose it." But suddenly I find myself upset over the way someone speaks to me. I need God's enabling grace. On the other hand, I keep discovering racial prejudices that are buried so deep I had no idea they were there. I need knowledge—of myself and of God's view of right and wrong.

Should there be a third category, "bondage"? Although I can't find that separate variety of sin in Scripture, it seems that chemical dependency does fall in a different category. Is it ignorance? No. Is it involuntary? Not exactly, though it may seem so to the tippler. Is it unconscious? Certainly not. We call it an addiction, and that it is. My problem with creating a separate category is that soon our contemporaries will dump all sorts of things into the "addiction" bin where you're trapped and there's not much hope of getting out. The truth is all sin is addictive! A particular pattern of failure gets an ever-tighter grip on a person till it seems uncontrollable. But is it? The Bible offers a way out and it's the same for those unyielding sins binding us as for sins with a lesser grip, though it may be a greater challenge, the conflict may be more intense.

So, for two reasons I hesitate to create a third category: Scripture doesn't make room for a condition for which one is less responsible than with other sins, and the way of deliverance is the same for deliberate and addictive sin. One more thing to notice before we turn the spotlight on ourselves. The temptation to involuntary sin, once we succumb to it, becomes voluntary. I may be caught off guard by a tempting image on TV but if I keep watching, it's conscious sin, deliberate and defiant. The same is true of unconscious sins—falling short of God's holiness. The moment it becomes conscious I can make some choices and the sin shifts categories. When I realize that a scenario I'm running on myself is actually an ego trip and don't cry out to God for deliverance, that ego trip becomes conscious and deliberate. Thus, whenever the unconscious rises to the level of consciousness I'm responsible to deal with it as a matter of choice. I may not win instant victory, but at that point I join the battle, or a rebellious spirit stands exposed.

It may not be easy to judge clearly in our own lives. But usually, down deep, we really do know the difference between deliberate and unconscious sin, if we will only resist the temptation to rationalize and make excuses for our attitudes and behavior.

Are you aware of any defects in your Christian life, things you struggle with, things you need to change? Maybe you've called them "habitual sins," meaning the temptation is always at you and you go down in defeat more often than you'd like others to know about. Why not create three lists, (Deliberate Choices, Unintentional-involuntary, and Unintentional-unconscious) in your private journal, being very honest and very thorough. Once you've been honest about it, you can choose to quit or start pleading for God's resources (graces) to overcome.

January 15
Putting out the Fire
John 15:1-17

"I am the vine; you are the branches. Whoever abides in me and I in him, he it is that bears much fruit, for apart from me you can do nothing." (John 15:5)

The Spirit of God is a gentleman. He won't force His way on you. Any kind of "no" will "quench" the Spirit, put out the fire of passion, stop the flow of power. Whenever I take back control of my life I'm shutting off his free flow of life. How can you tell? He seems more distant, close companionship seems to have slipped away, service for God lacks power, temptations begin to win out, I'm beginning to spiral down. Here are some ways I've "quenched" the Spirit: a) neglect my devotional life, b) watch a typical TV drama, sitcom, talk show, c) rationalize some failure instead of acknowledging it, d) refuse to forgive someone who hurt me, e) flip through a magazine with sexy pictures, f) say "yes" to too many people and get overloaded, g) nurse my bruised ego, self-pity, h) let my mind dwell on how someone else has it better than I have, i) listen to a song that promotes this-world's values.

In your relationship with God have you ever been quite sure you were *not* filled with the Spirit? Reflect on my list and check any that may have contributed to your drift out of a tight relationship with the Spirit.

Perhaps it was simply that you chose against God's will, saying "no" to something he wanted you to do or stop doing. That will cause the fire of the Spirit to die back instantly. Be very honest. Perhaps you could list in the margin (or in your journal), what you know or what you suspect the culprit may have been. Or is, indeed, even now.

There's another expression used of our relationship to the Spirit. The Holy Spirit is a person with feelings—it's quite possible to make him sad. "Do not grieve the Spirit of God," Paul says (Ephesians 4:30). Then he tells us exactly the kind of thing that will make the Spirit sad: unwholesome talk, bitterness, rage and anger, brawling, slander, malice (vv. 29-32).

One meaning of being filled with the Spirit, then, is to yield full control to Him. Are you a Spirit-filled Christian in that sense? There's no place else to begin. Here's my prayer response to this wonderful promise of Holy Spirit fullness:

Holy Spirit of God, thank you, thank you for allowing me to have a personal relationship with you. I really do want you to be the controlling partner in that relationship and I reaffirm today that you are indeed Lord of my life. I'm truly sorry for the ways I've made you sad. Please forgive me. And give me strength to always say "yes" to you in the small things as well as the major choices I make. Let me ever be filled with your presence and power.

Perhaps you'd like to write out your own prayer response in your journal, making sure once again that the connection is tight, that, so far as you have anything to do with it, you're filled with the Spirit.

The first—and most important—outward evidence of filling up on the Spirit is to produce Spirit fruit. But what does the picture-word "fruit" (of the Spirit) mean literally? Fruit, of course, is the product of a plant or tree, but it also is the evidence of what's inside, what kind of plant or tree it is. It's also evidence of the health of the tree. If we have become "Jesus plants," are alive and healthy, we'll produce Jesus fruit. And everyone in my life is a fruit inspector—they can tell what's on the inside by what comes out. *"By their fruit you shall know them,"* said Jesus (Matthew 7:20).

Jesus never intended us to have a few little shriveled "fruits," just enough to prove we're alive and what kind of "tree" we are. He promises a bumper crop—lots of Jesus' characteristics. You might call it "full," a full crop. He told us about it Himself in Scripture's most complete chapter on fruit, John 15:1-17. Why don't you check out the harvest you produce? A few shriveled fruit or a bumper crop? What is on the inside that is evidenced on the outside?

January 16
Our Companion in the Battle
Romans 8:26-27

"Likewise the Spirit helps us in our weakness. For we do not know what to pray for as we ought, but the Spirit himself intercedes for us with groanings too deep for words. And he who searches hearts knows what is the mind of the Spirit, because the Spirit intercedes for the saints according to the will of God." (Romans 8:26,27)

Every battle plan for overcoming the enemies of your soul that have most successfully assaulted needs to be custom designed for you. And it may change for each stage of life, whether the temptations and uncertainties of youth, the frustrations and failed dreams of middle years or the regrets and anxieties of age. Where are you today in your spiral up toward likeness to Jesus? It's time now for the Big Assignment. Don't let the brevity of today fool you; it may be the most demanding of all!

It's time to write out your own battle plan for overcoming the failure that most grieves the Holy Spirit and embarrasses you. This is for real, not just an assignment to be fulfilled. Create a strategic plan you'll use for a lifetime! Before you begin, however, pause and ask the Holy Spirit for wisdom. You'll need it! The secret of success in the Christian life, including consistent success in overcoming temptation, does not ultimately depend on a technique, a strategy, or your own activity. Ultimately, it is the Holy Spirit within who is the overcomer. But the indwelling powerful One does not displace your personality with His. Rather, He is a personal companion, living in you to...

- ➤ strengthen you when you falter
- ➤ remind you of truth from His Word when your focus is blurred
- ➤ point out the enemy when you're under attack
- ➤ comfort you
- ➤ lift you up when you fall
- ➤ forgive you when you fail
- ➤ guide you when you're confused
- ➤ sensitize your moral judgment by His Word to discern right from wrong
- ➤ strengthen your will when you waver

Glorious as that is, it's not all He does! He prays for us when our prayers fall short (Romans 8:26,27): *Likewise the Spirit helps us in our weakness. For we do not know what to pray for as we ought, but the Spirit himself intercedes for us with groanings too deep for words. And he who searches hearts knows what is the mind of the Spirit, because the Spirit intercedes for the saints according to the will of God*), and as we rely on him, he enables us to pray effectively. It is God the Spirit who gave us his Word and the Church and it is he who enables us to understand and appropriate that Word in the face of testing and to live in the kind of relationship with other Christians that will make us overcomers together.

That's the glorious Spirit of the living God! Hallelujah! Celebrate!

January 17
Ultimate Purpose
Matthew 22:37-40

"And he said to him, "You shall love the Lord your God with all your heart and with all your soul and with all your mind. This is the great and first commandment. And a second is like it: You shall love your neighbor as yourself. On these two commandments depend all the Law and the Prophets."(Matthew 22:37-40)

I was speaking to a group of collegians and seminarians on "Living Godly in a Post-modern World." Actually, it was a series, called by some, "The Victorious Christian Life." But my purpose was to reformat the original biblical truth about life in the Spirit into the thought forms and vocabulary of the post-modern. I told again the story of a God who transcends the generations, the unchanging reality, who is out to re-write ***your*** story:

- ➤ From a loser, striving vainly to fill up on self, without much hope of finding any significance in your life-story, to a winner, every day more like Jesus in attitudes and actions.
- ➤ From a purposeless story of flitting shadows to empowered participation in the mega-story of the ages. You ***can*** make a difference!

Is that all? Is that the whole story? Are godliness of life and power in ministry the goal of life? What would you say is the ultimate purpose of your existence?

If you memorized the Westminster Catechism as a child, as I did, perhaps you completed that ". . . to glorify God and enjoy him forever." If, on the other hand, you're not so much rooted in past theologies as in contemporary experiences, perhaps you completed the sentence, ". . .to worship God." But think about it. It's quite possible to glorify someone you despise, as any press agent can tell you; and it's quite possible to worship someone you fear and loathe as multitudes do. But put it the other way around, if I love someone supremely I won't be able to honor them, praise them, glorify them too much. And if that "someone" is God, worship will be the natural overflow of a heart full of love. No, our chief end is to love God and be loved of him forever.

How do I get the temerity to re-write the great theologians of old? By going back a little farther, looking a little higher. Jesus Christ himself spelled out our goal and I've just followed his lead. In Matthew 22:37-40, Jesus dips into the Old Testament and quotes the Shema, affirming it to be the foundation of his own teaching, not just of "Moses." The first and greatest of all the stated will of God, said Jesus, is to *love God* with all our being. In fact, if the second-ranked command *to love your neighbor is* added to the first, all the revealed will of God hangs suspended on these two commands.

And loving intimacy with God is the ultimate love relationship. "Knowing God" isn't merely an academic pursuit, for the concept of knowing God traces back to the Hebrew concept used of sexual union. When a man "knew" a woman or a woman "knew" a man, God considered them married, the most intimate of all human relationships. No wonder Israel is the wife of Jehovah; no wonder the church is the bride of Christ.

So the ultimate goal of transformation and empowerment is to re-write your story from an isolated, alienated loner—to a tight connection with the ultimate lover. That's what God is after, always has been, always will be. Does this sound familiar? Actually it's the concept that the purpose of creation and redemption, creating us God-compatible and restoring that compatibility, is for the purpose of making possible loving oneness with God. No wonder we can call this, "Beyond victory!"

January 18
In Christ
Romans 8

"….like a branch that is thrown away and withers; such branches are picked up, thrown into the fire and burned" (Jn 15.6)

Is there a life filled so full of good things that it overflows? Have you discovered God's own guarantee of a life overflowing with love and joy, of effective service to God and others (John 15)? And the plan was not to provide this fulfillment for some special cadre of super saints, but for everyone who is "in Christ." Yet how that life may be experienced seems to elude many.

But the Bible starts with bad news about you. In fact, it says that apart from Christ you are "*like a branch that is thrown away and withers; such branches are picked up, thrown into the fire and burned"* (Jn 15.6). This passage (Jn 15.2,6) causes us to ask, " was this 'branch' in Christ and then got cut off?" Or "was this person safe in Christ but was merely disciplined?" Or "was he never in Christ at all?" I suggest that the passage is figurative, an allegory, and thus should not be treated as a literal doctrinal statement. To fit the vine-and-branch analogy Jesus was simply saying that people who do not live an authentic Christian life should not consider themselves joined to him, that people who do belong to him will give evidence of it in attitudes and action. It seems clear that those who are not "in Christ" are in bad trouble. And this is the consistent witness of Scripture.

But we don't like this bad news. We like it so little we have re-written our hymns. We used to sing with the ex-slave trader, John Newton, "Amazing grace how sweet the sound that saved a wretch like me." Now we sing of how it saved "someone like me." We can't even bring ourselves to identify with the self-pronounced wretched Paul. But the Bible is clear that without Christ I am a worm, a worthless wretch. Indeed, a withered branch fit for burning. We don't like to hear it put that way. Oh, I am an image bearer of the glorious God, to be sure, spoiled and damaged though the likeness is. But the bad news I must confront first is that I am a hell deserving sinner.

The law always precedes the Gospel. Paul understood this. The most glorious description of our salvation, of what it means to be "*in Christ*" (Romans 3-8) follows hard after the very bad news of humankind's moral rottenness and total lostness apart from Christ (Romans 1-3). First the bad news, then the good.

And the good news is good indeed. In fact, when God regenerates or re-creates a person, the transformation is so radical you could compare it to a birth (John 3). The transformation is so radical you could liken it to death (Romans 6). One other biblical expression used to identify this new being is to describe a person as now being "in Christ." Thus, whoever is in Christ is a new creation, all is new (II Cor 5.17).

This is the first meaning of being "in Christ." It describes the relationship into which one enters by faith at initial salvation, what takes place when God re-creates or does what is called regeneration. What Christ himself teaches us about abiding in him in John 15 includes regeneration, but his teaching goes far beyond that basic entry "into Christ." There are three corollary teachings that spotlight, from different angles, the rich meaning of that initial salvation which Paul describes as being "in Christ."

Twice he speaks of being "baptized into Christ" (Rom 6:3 and Gal 3:27). To be baptized into something (in the spiritual use of the term), is to be joined to, to become a part of; it is the initial uniting. So, one who is "in Christ" is one who has been united to him in a bonding relationship.

A second line of teaching is the idea that Christ is in us (2 Cor 13:5). Both the expressions "you in Christ" and "Christ in you" could have a literal or physical meaning. The Father, Son and Holy Spirit in some mysterious and special sense come into and "take up their abode" within us (Jn 14:15-24).

A third line of teaching that helps us understand some of the glorious implications of that relationship is the entire eighth chapter of Romans. It begins with the proclamation: *"...there is now no condemnation for those who are in Christ Jesus!"*--to be in him is to be safe in him (8:1). To be in Christ is to be free from the domineering authority of sin and resultant death (vs 2). To be in Christ is to have an infused power to think and live like him (vs 4-6). To be in Christ is to have peace with God (vs 6,7). To be in Christ is to have the Holy Spirit within (vs 9). It is to be alive--eternally alive (vs 10, 11). To be in Christ makes me a beloved child of God and, indeed, an heir (vs 15-17). To be in Christ means that God the Spirit, God the Son, and God the Father are active in my behalf, that they even work all the circumstances of life toward an assured destiny of likeness to him and that nothing--absolutely nothing--can ever separate me from God's love (vs 24-39). All of this -- and more -- comes the moment I am united with him by faith.

January 19
Promise Keepers
Ecclesiastes 5: 4 & 5

"When you vow a vow to God, do not delay paying it, for he has no pleasure in fools. Pay what you vow. It is better that you should not vow than that you should vow and not pay."(Ecclesiastes 5: 4 & 5)

"Almost all women stand by their men, very few men stand by their women." The distinguished oncologist lived constantly with dying people and that was his verdict. I felt a deep surge of anger when he told me. What's wrong with those men? But then the light began to dawn. Perhaps that explains the startling experience I was having. Why would hundreds of people--many I had never met--write of the high impact my simple decision had made on them? Perhaps some of those men were tempted, and some of those women wondered what might happen to them if they should fall to Alzheimer's or some other dread disease. But hadn't I simply done the normal thing? I really had no choice in the matter, did I?

It's been a decade since that day in Florida when Muriel told the couple riding with us the same story she had told us five minutes earlier. Funny, I thought; that's never happened before. But it happened again. Occasionally. Three years later, when she was hospitalized to check out heart palpitations, a young doctor called me to one side and said, "You may need to think about the possibility of Alzheimer's." I was incredulous. These young doctors are so presumptuous. And insensitive. Muriel could do almost anything she had ever done. True, we had stopped entertaining in our home--no small loss for the president of a thriving seminary and Bible college. And she was having uncommon difficulty producing a portrait of me which the Board had requested to hang by the splendid portrait of my predecessor which she had painted earlier. But Alzheimer's? I had hardly heard the name. Still, the dread of a living death began to lurk about the fringes of my consciousness.

When her memory deteriorated further and she lost other basic skills, we went to a neurologist friend who gave her the full battery of tests and, by elimination, diagnosed her as having Alzheimer's. But there was some question. There was none of the typical physical deterioration, so we went to Duke with the conviction I should get the best second opinion available. We would accept the verdict and not chase around the country after every new miracle treatment we might hear about. Go standard. Little did I know the day was coming when we would be urged--on average, once a week--to pursue every variety of treatment under the sun. And some over the sun! Vitamins, demons, chemicals, this guru, that healer, the other clinic. How could I even check them all out, let alone pursue them? I was grateful to friends who made suggestions, however, because each was an expression of love. But for us, we would trust the Lord to work a miracle in Muriel if he so desired and work a miracle in me if he didn't.

About this time I made the decision that when the day came Muriel needed me full-time, she would have me. I hoped that wouldn't be necessary till I reached retirement and could survive financially, but at 57 that seemed problematical. I told the Board of Trustees and advised them to start planning for my successor

But the decision was firm and it didn't take any heavy duty thought. It was a matter of integrity. Hadn't I promised, 37 years before, "...in sickness and in health...till death do us part?"

It wasn't some kind of grim duty to which I stoically bowed, however. It was only fair--she had cared for me for almost four decades with marvelous devotion; now it was my turn. And such a partner she was! If I cared for her for 40 years I would never be out of her debt. As the country song has it, "I can fly higher than the eagle because you are the wind under my wings."

But how could I walk away from the responsibility of a ministry God has blessed so signally during our 22 years at Columbia Bible College and Seminary? Not easily. So many dreams fulfilled beyond our imagination, but so many dreams yet on the drawing board. And the peerless team God has brought together--a team not just of highly competent professionals, but of dear friends--how could I bear to leave them? Resignation was painful; but not difficult. Because whatever Columbia needs, it does not need a part-time, distracted leader. Better to step aside and let God's choice leader step in while the momentum is surging. As I told our students, "If Columbia does not continue to grow in strength and influence after I leave, I have been one sorry leader." How is it with you? What promise is difficult? Solomon exhorts us in Ecclesiastes 5:4-5: *"When you vow a vow to God, do not delay paying it, for he has no pleasure in fools. Pay what you vow."*

January 20
The Gift
1 Corinthians 13

"If I speak in the tongues of men and of angels, but have not love, I am a noisy gong or a clanging cymbal. And if I have prophetic powers, and understand all mysteries and all knowledge, and if I have all faith, so as to remove mountains, but have not love, I am nothing. If I give away all I have, and if I deliver up my body to be burned, but have not love, I gain nothing." (1 Corinthians 13:1-3)

I write this in the throes of Alzheimer's. Muriel, my wife, can't comprehend much, nor express many thoughts, and those not for sure. But she knows whom she loves and lives in happy oblivion to almost everything else. Tough and resilient as ever, she doesn't know why nothing works, nothing at all. But she will not let it get her down. She doesn't remember any more how greatly gifted she was, how effective in mothering and in ministry. And that's a blessing. It also gives a clue as to the other reason for my decision to resign from a dynamic ministry just when it was orbiting higher than ever.

She is such a delight to me. I don't <u>have</u> to care for her, I <u>get</u> to. She is teaching me so much about love, God's love. She picks flowers outside--anyone's--and fills the house with them. Lately she has begun to pick them inside, too. Someone had given us the most beautiful Easter Lily I've seen, two stems with four or five lilies on each, with more to come. One day I came into the kitchen to do the dishes or get dinner and there on the windowsill over the sink was a vase with a stem of lilies in it. I've learned to "go with flow" and not correct irrational behavior. After all, it is just that--irrational. She means no harm and doesn't understand what should be done, nor would she remember a rebuke. Nevertheless, <u>I</u> did the irrational--I told her how disappointed I was, how the lilies would soon die, the buds would never bloom, and <u>please</u> do not break off the other stem.

The next day or youngest son, soon to leave for India, came from Houston for a visit and we were sitting on the porch swinging on the old swing he had made as a Christmas gift long years ago. I had told Kent of my stupid rebuke of his mother and how bad I felt about it. About that time, she comes to the door with a gift of love for me-- she gently laid the other stem of lilies on the table with a gentle smile and turned back into the house. I said simply, "thank you." Kent said, "You're doing better, Dad!"

I began to think about God. We work so hard at bringing our gifts to him, messing up his best intentions, ruining the beauty of his plans, and he just smiles and says, "thank you." No hassle, no put-down. He accepts it for what it is--a gift of love. Perhaps our communication with him is similar to Muriel's and mine, too. We make such beautiful, carefully crafted prayers and maybe a lot of it is just nonsense. But he is good--much better than I with Muriel--in figuring out what we mean and what would be good for us. He says such beautiful, wise things to us in his Book, and we only half comprehend. But we think we've got it all together.

Recently the dentist needed to have Muriel open and shut her mouth often to test the new crown. But when he said, "please open" she would clench her teeth. The more he pled with her, the tighter she clenched. I tried, but to no avail. She knew she wasn't pleasing us, so she tried harder-how she wanted to please. But she got it all backwards. I love her so. Just like God loves us.

And she loves me. She can't speak in sentences, now, only words and often words that don't make sense--"no" when she means "yes,' for example. But she can say one sentence. And she says it often: "I love you." During the two years the Board arranged for a companion to stay in our home so I could travel and go daily to the office, it became increasingly difficult to keep her at home. As soon as I would leave home, she would take out after me. With me, she was content; without me she was distressed, sometimes terror stricken. The walk to school is a mile round-trip. She would make that trip as many as ten times a day--ten miles at high speed. Sometimes at night when I would help her undress, I would find bloody feet. When I told our doctor, he wept.

So the decision to lay down my public responsibilities and go on a retirement income three years early was not difficult. I had promised her 42 years before and I keep my word. Besides, it's only fair--she cared for me so faithfully for so long. But it's much, much more. She is the joy of my life as I watch her brave descent into oblivion and discern daily new manifestations of the kind of person she is, the Muriel I always loved.

January 21
So Much More
Romans 8:9

"You, however, are not in the flesh but in the Spirit, if in fact the Spirit of God dwells in you. Anyone who does not have the Spirit of Christ does not belong to him." (Romans 8:9)

The standard for living the Christian life is high. Very high. Yet the provision for living that life is higher still. Who does God provide to enable us to life that life? Why the Spirit!

The other day I was with a group of friends and acquaintances for dinner in a restaurant. One in the group talked a lot. But he always turned away from me and spoke animatedly to those on the other side of him. I couldn't hear a word he said! You can imagine how I felt. I wonder how the Holy Spirit feels when we sit at table with the Father, the Son, and the Spirit and talk only to others, listen only to the others and ignore the Spirit?

But the Spirit doesn't want just a piece of our time, a piece of us, he wants to fill us up with himself. *"Be filled with the Spirit."* (Eph 5:18) This is not a suggestion, a recommendation. It's a command.

What does it mean to be filled with the Spirit? Well, some say it means an ecstatic feeling. You feel full. And it's true that it was said of Jesus, "At that time he was full of joy in the Holy Spirit." But the filling of the Spirit is one of the major themes of the New Testament and that's about the only text I know that identifies the experience as a feeling. So we enlightened usually say it means to give full control of our lives over to him. And it is true that in a few cases that seems to be the evidence of being full of the Spirit. But in almost all the references to being filled, the evidence is one of two things: power in ministry or Christ-like character. The gifting of the Spirit. The fruit of the Spirit.

So, if you ask me if I'm filled with the Spirit, I'd have to know which kind of filling you have in mind. An ecstatic feeling? Well, sometimes. Fully yielded to him? Well, as best I know, yes. The visible evidence? The gifts, the fruit? I don't know. You tell me. You're the fruit inspector. That's why, in Scripture, we never find anyone saying "I, filled with the Spirit." It's always "he" or 'they,' filled with the Spirit. But whatever it means to be filled, that's what I want. Don't you?

Then, the Spirit does something else. Transforming. Here is the Spirit at work taking a saint and making us ever more saintly. He not only births us into the family, He sets about renovating, transforming us in our core being. That's what 2 Corinthians 3:18 means: *"we are being transformed from one degree of His likeness to another.* And part of that transforming is to empower us to overcome temptation.

Rom 8:13 &14 is a conundrum for many: *"for if you are living according to the [impulses of the] flesh, you are going to die. But if [you are living] by the [power of the Holy] Spirit you are habitually putting to death the sinful deeds of the body, you will [really] live forever."*(Amp) When I taught, one assignment was to write a personal battle strategy for overcoming temptation. It turned out to be the most talked-about part of the course. Years later I've heard from former students who wrote to tell me of the life-transforming impact of that assignment. How is it with you? Do you have a battle strategy for overcoming temptation in your life?

When I was a student at Columbia International University, I looked in mirror. I saw a man with two great struggles- my tongue and my temper-T&T. And I discovered the Spirit has given me three weapons to use in the battle: Prayer, Scripture, the Church. And, further, that there is both a defensive use and an offensive use of each.

I began to pray daily, earnestly. I didn't just say, "Lord, help me be Christ like today," I prayed "Lord, you know I have a short fuse and a loose tongue. Please, please give me victory today." That was my defense. And the offensive? A quick prayer when temptation looms: "Spirit of God, please tie my tongue, keep me from saying what this jerk deserves." Or maybe there's only time to say, "help, Lord!"

Then the weapon of the Word. As my defense, I *"hid God's word in my heart, that I might not sin…"* What did I do? Memorize! James 3 about what God has to say about a short fuse and a loose tongue.

And what of the church? I did find strength in the larger body of Christ. And what a help to take the initiative, the offensive, in seeking out my prayer partner in the hour of testing or defeat.

So what has been the outcome? Certainly not all I wish, but you wouldn't recognize me for the same man I was. The Spirit is at work as the overcomer. He transforms me into ever greater likeness to Jesus.

January 22
The Grand Celebration
Revelation 19:6-9

""Then I heard what seemed to be the voice of a great multitude, like the roar of many waters and like the sound of mighty peals of thunder, crying out, "Hallelujah! For the Lord our God the Almighty reigns. Let us rejoice and exult and give him the glory, for the marriage of the Lamb has come, and his Bride has made herself ready, it was granted her to clothe herself with fine linen, bright and pure"— for the fine linen is the righteous deeds of the saints. And the angel said to me, "Write this: Blessed are those who are invited to the marriage supper of the Lamb." And he said to me, "These are the true words of God." Then I fell down at his feet to worship him, but he said to me, "You must not do that! I am a fellow servant with you and your brothers who hold to the testimony of Jesus. Worship God." For the testimony of Jesus is the spirit of prophecy." (Revelation 19:6-9)

In our new church plants in Japan, we took the Spirit's gifting seriously. Every new believer was expected to minister. Their task was to seek how God might use them. Our task was to help them discover the Spirit's gifting, help develop that gift, and then to deploy the gift, making sure they were provided an outlet to use the gift to the full.

Result? In that church of believers fresh from Buddhism and Shintoism with no experience of church, within five years they had participated in planting 4 other churches, leading, teaching, preaching, deploying the gifts God was giving.

There's a side benefit to discovering, developing, and deploying your gift. If you don't, it not only cripples the church by that much, it cripples YOU. You can't experience the God-intended life in its fullness without discovering, developing and using your gift. Since so few do that, many churches are limping along, trying to fulfill all the purposes of the church with 10% of the body-parts functioning. Gifting. Then…

There's one more activity of the Spirit reaching out through you. That activity is sending. The Spirit wants to send every believer to witness by life and word, to seek the redemption of the world. The astonishing fact that the redemption the Spirit enabled the Son to purchase in his death and resurrection he now intends to complete through the likes of us! Incredible!

But that isn't all. There's still the final activity yet awaiting: consummation *"If the Spirit of him who raised Jesus from the dead is living in you, he who raised Christ from the dead will also give life to your mortal bodies through his Spirit who lives in you."* (Rom 8:11)

At the close of his book of Revelation, He gives the invitation: *"The Spirit and the bride say, 'come'!"* And that's my invitation to you today.

As we have thought for a few minutes about God's provision for living the life he intends, for spiraling up to be more and more like Jesus, how is it with you and the Holy Spirit? Let us pause and ask the Spirit's forgiveness for our neglect, if need be, and give thanks for this greatest gift.

January 23
The Lordship of Christ
Matthew 7:21

"Not everyone who says to me, 'Lord, Lord,' will enter the kingdom of heaven, but only the one who does the will of my Father who is in heaven." (Matthew 7:21)

"Do you remember me?" The bright-eyed teen looked at me eagerly. I couldn't bring myself to say "no," so I stalled: "Are you from Birmingham?" I knew there was a large group from Birmingham at the youth conference, and the leader had told me a remarkable story of how God had moved in the local high school all year long. The whole campus was transformed, starting with a couple of girls in an early morning prayer meeting. Dozens had come to Christ.

The seventeen-year-old must have decided to let me off the hook when she heard "Birmingham," so she continued, "Do you remember last year, the night after that last meeting of the conference when we sat on that stone wall over there?" It all came back to me. "Oh, yes, Debbie, I remember."

That night she had talked despondently of a failed Christian life. "I didn't respond to the invitation to consecrate my life to the Lord," she'd said, "because I'm sick and tired of doing it over and over. Nothing ever comes of it. I go forward in a meeting and everything changes. It's really great. For two weeks. Then it's boom, back to the same miserable failure again. What's wrong with me?"

"I really don't know, Debbie. Tell me, who's in the driver's seat of your life?"

"Jesus is...." She paused, then added, "most of the time."

"Oh, no," I said. "It doesn't work that way. You don't let him drive down the road to the first intersection and then grab the wheel when you think He's turning the wrong direction. I think this is what you're saying." On a piece of paper I wrote two words: "No" and "Lord." "Well, yes, sometimes I do say that." "But you can't," I said.

Debbie bristled a little, "But I do!"

"But you can't," I insisted. "What does 'Lord' mean?" "Savior?" she asked.

"The Savior is Lord, but what does the word 'Lord' mean?"

A few more guesses and she gave up. "Well," I tried again, "How about 'king?' What does king mean?"

"That's easy. A king is the big boss."

"Do you say 'no' to the king?"

"Well, it wouldn't be healthy."

"Right," I said. "And Jesus is King of all kings, Lord of all lords. You can't say 'no' to Him! It's either 'yes, Lord' or 'no, Jesus.' 'No' cancels out the meaning of 'lord.'" I tore the paper in half, with 'no' on one piece and 'Lord' on the other. "Which will it be?" I asked. "'No' or 'Lord'?" She dropped her head and long hair covered her face as she wrestled with the choice. Minutes passed. Finally she threw her head back, tears streaming down her face.

She reached out to take the paper with 'Lord' written on it, but I pulled it away.

"How long do you want Him to be Lord, Debbie?" I asked.

"Oh," she said, "I want him to be Lord forever!" In that moment she was filled with the Spirit of God. And then he began to overflow into the lives of those around her until a whole high school was transformed.

If a high school teen can experience the full resources of the Spirit for living the life and ministering with power, how about a mature Christian? The exciting thing is this: the resources God provides for living the abundant life of promise are not gifts sent UPS from a distant Omnipotence; the resource is himself, God in person coming to live with us. And it's no halfway measure—he intends to fill us full of himself.

Being filled with the Spirit isn't optional, as Debbie discovered, it's commanded: "Be filled with the Spirit" (Ephesians 5:18). But what does it mean to be "filled" with the Spirit? After all, He isn't a liquid or impersonal force. Do you sometimes wish the Bible didn't use so much picture language, that it would just tell you straight out what it means? Like "full"— when you get right down to it, what does it look like to be "filled with the Spirit"? What actually happens? What does it feel like? The Bible never defines it for us. We may not be able to describe "full" precisely, but it's a wonderful picture word. There's excitement in it, a completeness, a satisfaction, and a mystery. Are you filled full?

January 24
The Bible
2 Timothy 3:16-17

"...be diligent to present yourself approved to God as a workman who does not need to be ashamed, handling accurately the word of truth." (2 Tim. 2:15)

How important is it to understand the Bible? Is it possible?

Church history indicates that understanding the Bible is very important, yet very difficult to do. The enormous energies devoted to explaining the Bible show the great importance of understanding the Bible. On the other hand, the division of the church into so many denominations bears witness to the fact that we are far from agreement on what the Bible means. If it is *God's* Word, revealing *His* will, nothing could be of greater importance than understanding it. If the Bible was given to reveal the truth and not to hide it, God must intend that we understand it. If we do not, the fault must lie with us, not with Him. If we do not understand His communication, it is imperative that we determine the reason.

Some people do not understand the Bible because they do not believe it is true, or at least, they do not believe that all parts of it are true. Others do not understand it because they are unwilling to obey it. Still others misunderstand the communication because they are unwilling to work hard at searching out the meaning. For those people who go astray in their understanding of the Bible, there are several words from God: *"All Scripture is inspired by God and profitable for teaching, for reproof, for correction, for training in righteousness; that the man of God may be adequate, equipped for every good work."* (2 Tim. 3:16-17)

God's Word is to be trusted and obeyed. The one who does not trust it, or is not prepared to obey it, cannot expect to fully understand what God is saying. *"Be diligent to present yourself approved to God as a workman who does not need to be ashamed, handling accurately the word of truth.."* (2 Tim. 2:15)

It is not enough simply to trust and obey; one must be prepared to work diligently to understand Scripture.

But the right attitude or approach to the Bible is not all that is necessary for understanding its meaning. Do a good attitude and a commitment to hard work alone enable a person to build a beautiful piece of furniture? No, for there is a right way and a wrong way to build. Furthermore, certain skills must be developed before a person, though using the right method, can build properly. So it is with understanding the Bible. One must not only have the right attitude and approach; he must also use good methods and develop skill in their use.

The methods one chooses for biblical interpretation will depend on one's presuppositions about the nature of the Bible. Then, we turn to the portion of Bible study which is examining the practical skills necessary to put the principles into practice. Through this method of study the student should be able to gain the knowledge and develop the skills necessary for determining and applying the appropriate meaning of Scripture so that the Christian is thoroughly equipped for every good work. [1]

The basic presupposition about the Bible that distinguishes believers from unbelievers is that the Bible is God's revelation of Himself and of His will for us. Although Christians are united in that basic affirmation, the implications of the statement are viewed in very different ways. Does it consist of infallible propositions? Is it the record of certain acts of God? Is it an inspired record? Is there revelation outside Scripture? Our views here will dictate how we handle the text. Our minds are not empty when we read or listen to Scripture; what we hear is already partly predetermined by what is already in our thinking. May we study God's word faithfully!

January 25
Beautiful Feet
Romans 10:8-21

"And that message is the very message about faith that we preach: If you openly declare that Jesus is Lord and believe in your heart that God raised him from the dead, you will be saved. For it is by believing in your heart that you are made right with God, and it is by openly declaring your faith that you are saved." (Romans 10:.8-10)

A frightened jailer who had just been rescued from suicide and execution, cried out, "What shall I do to be saved?" and was told, "Believe on the Lord Jesus Christ and you will be saved." A successful young businessman asked, "What shall I do to inherit eternal life?" and was told, "Sell what you have, give it to the poor and follow Jesus." A group of awe-struck Jews called out to a nondescript, uneducated bunch of street-preachers, "What must we do?" They were told, "Repent and be baptized."

What did these answers have in common? They were all addressed to particular people in specific historical settings and were never intended to give a theological explanation of how all people in all circumstances are to be saved from sin. But there is a summary statement which is intended to give a more comprehensive, theological definition of saving faith: Romans 10:.8-10*:" And that message is the very message about faith that we preach: If you openly declare that Jesus is Lord and believe in your heart that God raised him from the dead, you will be saved. For it is by believing in your heart that you are made right with God, and it is by openly declaring your faith that you are saved."*

First, one must confess Jesus as Lord. You must be willing to go public with your acknowledgment that you are no longer lord of your life, but that Jesus is Lord. Secondly *fall*, you must believe from the heart that God raised

---

[1] *Understanding and Applying the Bible,* Robertson McQuilkin, (2014), Moody Press, 15-17.

Jesus from the dead. In other words, the saving faith of Paul's theology is not in some undefined deity or disembodied philosophical concept, it is in a person, an historical person, a person who through his power over death demonstrated publicly that he is the Savior. His resurrection validates all his claims and as history it is a verifiable fact, not a myth or philosophical abstraction. Thus, reliance on the Savior raised from the dead, and acknowledgment of his absolute authority is what Paul says is "trusting in him" (Rom 10:11) or "calling on him" (vs 13).

That's how a person gets saved. But how does he get lost? And who is lost? Paul doesn't tell us in this passage, but he has already told us in chapter 3: "*All have sinned and short of the glory of God*" and chapter 6, "*The wages of sin is death...*" But, he says here, "*whoever calls on the name of the Lord, will be saved.*"

Are there no other ways to life? Are there not, as the Japanese say, "Many paths to the summit of Mount Fuji?"

It is no accident that Paul says, whoever calls on the <u>name.</u> In other words, not just any name will do. Peter said the same thing, "Neither is there salvation in any other..."(Acts 4.12). Increasing numbers are saying that people are not saved only on the merits of Christ, as Peter and Paul said, but they are saved without knowing about him. They are saved when they are obedient to the light they do have. But Peter said, in the same way Paul says in this passage, "there is none other <u>name</u> under heaven, given among men whereby we must be saved." Note that he didn't say, no other person. When you name a <u>name</u> there is no ambiguity, no leeway for conjecture. Christ taught the same thing: "I am the way, the truth, and the life." (Jn 14.6). But now we are told people can have the life without going the way or knowing the truth. Jesus seemed to be saying something else: "No one comes to the Father except by <u>me.</u>" In this passage Paul says that saving "faith comes from hearing the message, and the message is heard through the word of <u>Christ</u>" (vs 17). If God chose not to profer hope or describe another way out, how much more should we refrain!

January 26
The Dream
Romans 10:14-17

"How then will they call on him in whom they have not believed? And how are they to believe in him of whom they have never heard? And how are they to hear without someone preaching? And how are they to preach unless they are sent? ......So faith comes from hearing, and hearing through the word of Christ." (Romans10:14-17)

In my dream I found myself on an island. Sheep island. The sheep were scattered and lost. I learned that there is a forest fire sweeping across from the opposite side. All are doomed to destruction unless there is a way of escape. A glance at my official map tells us there IS indeed a bridge to the mainland. A single bridge, a narrow bridge, built at awful cost. And our job is to get the sheep across. There are many shepherds herding the found sheep and those within easy access to the bridge. But the bulk of the sheep are far distant, the shepherds seeking them few. Those who are near the fire, know they are in trouble and are frightened. Those at a distance are peacefully grazing, enjoying life. But still are lost and doomed.

Some shepherd--or more likely a hireling--often can't tell the difference in good times--near the bridge whispers the hope that there is another way out. Maybe the chasm is narrow somewhere and the particularly strong sheep at least has a chance to save himself. Or maybe the current is gentle, the stream shallow further downstream and the courageous at least, can make it across. Or maybe, wouldn't it be great--maybe this isn't an island at all. Maybe it's a peninsula and great multitudes of sheep are already safe. At any rate, surely the owner would have provided some alternate route. They relax and go about other business.

Of course there are problems with this: why would the owner have gone to such terrible expense to build the bridge? Especially since it is a narrow bridge and many of the sheep refuse to cross it even when they know about it? As I mused, a voice behind me said, "But there is a greater reason than the logic of it, my friend. Look at your map. This is the main reason. Logic alone can lead in many directions." So I looked again and carved on the old, rugged bridge was this inscription: "I am the bridge. No sheep escapes to safety but by me." And then I noticed a notation from the first under-shepherd, Peter, which read, "For neither is there salvation in any other. For there is no other way from the island to the mainland whereby a sheep may be saved."

Do you believe that people without Christ are lost? Do you care? Does your life demonstrate that you believe and care? Some say a person must actively reject the gospel to be lost. Paul seemed to be saying something different. Re-read Romans 10:14-17. *How then will they call on him in whom they have not believed? And how are they to believe in him of whom they have never heard? And how are they to hear without someone preaching? And how are they to preach unless they are sent? ......So faith comes from hearing, and hearing through the word of Christ.*" When new Christians in Japan asked about the final destination of their ancestors, I responded in the words of Abraham who was debating with God the same issue of righteous people being condemned along with the unrighteous, "*Shall not the judge of all the earth do right?*" (Gen 18.25).

Does that mean that <u>every</u>one who lacks knowledge is lost? The Scripture does not directly address this question. So I cannot affirm on the basis of Scripture that every person in every time and place who has not heard of Christ will be lost, but neither can I affirm from Scripture that <u>any</u>one will be. One position, based on the clear teaching of Scripture that all have sinned and the result is death and that faith in Christ, (indeed in the name of Jesus Christ from Nazareth, crucified and risen) is the only way of salvation, one interprets that to mean that all who do not call on that name are lost. The result of that teaching is to put world evangelization at the top of one's priority, to obey the great commission, to find Paul's teaching in this passage life-transforming. Not a bad result.

January 27
Super Saint?
Matthew 4:19

"And he said to them, "Follow me, and I will make you fishers of men." (Matthew 4:19)

Last week I heard a word from beyond the grave. I was searching through a file of developing chapel themes when I discovered a note requesting that I speak on a particular theme. The note was from Charlie. He wrote the note in response to a prayer I had written. Charlie said he wanted me to finish it up and he suggested a verse that did so. I read the verse and what Charlie had in mind became even more mysterious. It was Christ's word to Peter, hinting at the way he would die. Charlie had cardiac disease, so he had a thirty-year hint of the way he would die, too. I wonder if my son Bob did? I wonder if you do? But John did not say that Jesus was telling Peter merely the manner of death he would die, but this he said -he would glorify God.

Will your death glorify God? Some do and some don't. Charlie thought the answer to that question lies in one's obedience to the command which follows. Jesus told Peter about death and then he told him about life: follow me. Peter wanted to know about the other fellow. Don't we all? Jesus said, that is none of your business. Your business is simple. Follow me.

If we follow Jesus, where will he go? Perhaps the same way Charlie went. Let me read you a portrait of Charlie: *"I always thank my God for you because of his grace given you in Christ Jesus. For in him you have been enriched in every way—with all kinds of speech and with all knowledge— God thus confirming our testimony about Christ among you. Therefore you do not lack any spiritual gift as you eagerly wait for our Lord Jesus Christ to be revealed. He will also keep you firm to the end, so that you will be blameless on the day of our Lord Jesus Christ. God is faithful, who has called you into fellowship with his Son, Jesus Christ our Lord."* (1 Corinthians 1:4-9)

A portrait of Charlie? Some super saint? It was written to the worst bunch of failures in any church described for us in the New Testament! How could Paul write this to the Corinthians?

Why is Paul so thankful for the stumbling, bumbling saints of Corinth? Because of their excellent track record? Because of the grace that was given them. Everything outside of hell is the grace of God, so certainly everyone in Christ is in grace. That's where we begin in following Jesus: we enter into His grace. The Corinthians had. Charlie began there. Have you?

Where does he lead us, then, once we enter the relationship? A Spirit-enriched life--enriched in every way (vs 5). High octane, super high octane. The working of the Holy Spirit brings a supernatural quality of life and supernatural effectiveness in ministry. This effect of the Spirit's his work is confirmation that we are truly "in Christ" (vs. 6). As a group, the local congregation, the body in concert will have all the gifts and abilities needed to accomplish God's purposes in the world (vs 7). If all the members function as designed, that is.

We produce fruit- we are blameless on that day (vs 8). We are spiritually strong. What does that mean? A growing, adult Christian. Our mind is in process of renewal, our heart inflamed with passion for God, we are an authentic reproduction of the original. No one can point the finger, blameless. Not some rare super-saint, just the plain old normal Spirit-enriched Christian life of following Jesus.

If you are a genuine Christian, truly in Christ, you will have, in increasing measure, these two Spirit-signs of God at work: fruit and gifts, what you are and what you do. But, you may say, it isn't happening in MY life. At least not at any measurable rate of speed. How does it happen? How can one follow Jesus? By what manner of death will you glorify the Lord? It may depend on how well you follow Jesus. Not all do follow closely.

January 28
Two-Legged Race
1 Corinthians 4:1-9

"For who makes you different from anyone else? What do you have that you did not receive? And if you did receive it, why do you boast as though you did not?" (1 Corinthians 4:7)

God has made full provision for success in the Christian life. You might even say the victorious Christian life, but how do we appropriate such a life? Through God's resources, not our own. Why is Paul so thankful for the stumbling, bumbling saints of Corinth? Because of their excellent track record? Because of the <u>grace</u> that was <u>given</u> them. Everything outside of hell is the grace of God, so certainly everyone <u>in Christ</u> is in grace. That's where we begin in following Jesus: we enter into His grace. The Corinthians had. Have you?

It is required of stewards that they be found faithful.......... Then each one will receive his commendation from God.(1 Corinthians 2:4 & 5b)

Living successfully is a process: the first step is that we are called into fellowship--not merely correct doctrine, happy experience, good feeling. Relationship! Called into fellowship. That is the goal of creation. This starts at birth into God's family, consummated at translation into His very presence. The second coming is a strong motivation.

The lordship of Jesus covers everything in a right relationship with God. Jesus is Lord of everything--every person, every event. So you can trust him. You'd be foolish not to. And he is MY Lord, so I must obey him. The mystery is solved. One is tower is "trust," the other "obey." The two towers of the Christian life, the foundation and the pinnacle; the two elements in a right relationship with God the two hands of the Christian life: yield and trust. By these we lay hold of God. Jesus is Lord of all, so you can trust him, Jesus is <u>my</u> Lord, so <u>I</u> <u>must</u> obey him. Trust and obey for there's no other way to have victory in Jesus but to trust and obey: two steps left, then two right. Remember, you can't hop into the Kingdom on one leg and you can't hop in victory. It's a two-legged race!

We live in a society in which it is cool to be detached, uncommitted, it is not cool to get hot, involved, committed. But what are the danger signs of the uncommitted: Do you use the term "spiritual" as a put down of those who seem to be more concerned about things of the Spirit than material things? Do you say, "Accept me as I am" and mean approve me as I am because I am no hypocrite and I intend honestly to stay as I am? Have your expectations for success in the Christian life failed and you have concluded that anyone who seems to have succeeded is faking it?

And the most dangerous: if you feel free in a self-oriented life, that very feeling is a flashing red danger signal. If you truly belong to Jesus and slip into self-oriented thinking, doing your own thing, fighting to be free of obligations to others, or whatever direction the self-orientation may take, the first and all-pervasive evidence of your belonging to Jesus will be misery and inner strife. A corpse doesn't feel pain, but to a sick person, the pain may just be his salvation.

If there are danger signs, what should a person do? Don't worry, be happy, we're told. Well, there is only one way to be free and strong and happy, and it's a two-legged race: trust and obey. Which of these 2 legs is not strong in your life? Are you weak in the trust department? Not sure of God's care and adequacy? Or is your obedience weak? It is difficult to move forward on one leg. Commit to exercise both for happy journey on the way and a strong finish at the end!

January 29
The Spirit Inside
John 16:7

"Nevertheless, I tell you the truth: it is to your advantage that I go away, for if I do not go away, the Helper will not come to you. But if I go, I will send him to you." (John 16:7)

Today we examine the operation of the Spirit in the process of redeeming fallen humanity. He brought about the birth, ministry, death, and resurrection of Jesus. This activity of the Spirit is redeeming. In the mid-eighties I became computer-dependent in my writing. I was satisfied with the way my old computer worked-after all, it used to be state-of-the-art. But increasingly I experienced difficulties. Gradually I found my computer could "talk" with fewer and fewer other computers. It couldn't read what other people sent me, but the Internet was designed for speedy new models, not for my Noah's ark. I upgraded, but it wasn't enough. I needed a new model altogether. Dressing up the old one wasn't good enough.

Our experience with the Spirit resembles my situation with the computer. We humans were originally created God-compatible-we could communicate with Him. At least our first ancestor, Adam, could. But a breakdown occurred. I tried self-improvement-reprogramming my mind to think more like God so I could understand what He was saying in His Word-but it didn't work. I needed to be an altogether new model, a new creation (1 Cor. 2:14).

That's exactly what the Holy Spirit provides-a new creation. My body and brain is the same, but when He recreated me He put a new spirit within me. The inner workings of the new me are different from the old me. The new me is made God-compatible. We call this change regeneration. It represents so radical a transformation; the Bible calls it "a new birth" (1 Peter 1:3). Most of us, however, underestimate the potential in the new model. We don't tap into the resources the Holy Spirit has provided by making us new (2 Cor. 5:17).

If you've been born again, the Spirit has already made you into something altogether new. Not only does the Spirit re-make us into new models, He begins a new personal relationship with us. His names hint at the personal aspect of our relationship. He is called Comforter and Counselor.

Descriptions of His activity, such as convicting of sin and teaching us all things also point to the Spirit's personal ministry in our lives. Can you think of any other names or activities of the Spirit that focus on your personal relationship with Him?

Perhaps you considered names or activities such as the indwelling Spirit, Guide, Helper, walking with the Spirit, or being filled with the Spirit. Actually, the list is very long. The Holy Spirit is God's provision for Christian living. You might associate indwelling with the moment of salvation when the Spirit enters the new believer's life. His ultimate goal is not merely to make us like Jesus in attitude and behavior. The Spirit is making us like Jesus so we can have a love relationship with the Father-a relationship like the one Jesus has. The new relation is the beginning of an eternity of growing intimacy in our companionship with God. We can relate to God in several ways.

People often speak of how wonderful joining the apostolic band and walking the roads of Galilee with Jesus would have been. But Jesus said another relationship is better: having the Holy Spirit living inside (John 16:7). Your relationship of immediate companionship with God in heaven will be something like Adam and Eve knew in the garden of Eden.

These are the activities of the Spirit in history and in bringing you into a love relationship with God. These activities take us from the moment of creation to our return to fellowship. The Spirit immediately begins to transform us into likeness to Jesus. *"But I tell you the truth: it is for your good that I am going away. Unless I go away, the Counselor will not come to you; but if I go, I will send him to you."* (John 16:7)

It is about beginning the sanctification process, being made holy. The activity of the Spirit is transforming What can a believer expect from life in the Spirit? The only way to hint at the depth and height and breadth of the meaning is to say, "full". What does the word full bring to your mind? Total- all-absorbing -comprehensive -dominant -unlimited -unrestrained -extending to all parts -suffused- satisfying-complete -bountiful -abundant!

Now imagine any of those words describing your relationship with God! That kind of glorious relationship can be yours, not as a one-time event, but as a daily experience. Full! Why not close today's reading by thanking Him for all He has done, is doing, and will do?

January 30
Paradox
1 John 1:8 & 3:8-9

John says some puzzling things, *"If we say we have no sin, we deceive ourselves, and the truth is not in us."* (1 John 1:8) then he adds in chapter 3," *The one who does what is sinful is of the devil, because the devil has been sinning from the beginning.....No one who is born of God will continue to sin, because God's seed remains in them; they cannot go on sinning, because they have been born of God."* (1 John 3:8-9).

This is one reason we tend to go to an extreme is that the Bible itself emphasizes both sides of the truth about our Christian experience. Consider the verse above for example. The two passages seem contradictory, don't they? However, two truths, are clear: 1) If you think you can have an experience that will remove all possibility of failure, and eliminate spiritual combat, you are badly deceived. And 2) If you think you can live as you please continuing in deliberate sin and still be OK with God, you are even more deceived.

Joe was way out of alignment with God. He'd gotten into drugs and partying quite naturally-his parents were alcoholics. When he came to Christ the change was dramatic. But he had a long way to go. Although he was fun to be with, outgoing and smart, he didn't sound much like Jesus and he sure didn't act like Him! Joe did, however, have one characteristic I've never quite seen in anyone else. Like many, he found admitting he was wrong or seeing what God expected of him difficult; but once he saw it, he changed. Period.

When he finally saw, for example, that he shouldn't spend all his time out talking to everyone else, but needed to spend some of his time at home with his wife and children, he just changed. He rearranged his entire life pattern to do right. In one area after another, Joe would finally see the truth, accept it, and spiral up a notch into greater likeness to Jesus. The Bible calls it the fruit of the Spirit.

When we make the big turnaround, yielding to God's will and trusting Him to work, the Holy Spirit begins to change us. We become more like Jesus in our attitudes, in our view of things, in our goals and ambitions, in our responses and behavior. Consequently, we get closer and closer to Him in daily companionship (2 Corinthians 3:18). The more we know Him, the more we love Him; the more we love Him, the more we want to be with Him; the more we're with Him the more we want to be like Him ; the more we change to be like Him, the better we know Him, the more we love Him-the spiral continues toward likeness to Christ and a greater love relationship with God.

The ultimate goal God has in mind for you isn't merely a change in character to resemble Jesus. God intends for you to be like Jesus in another way, in your intimate love relationship with the Father. That's the grand climax of your existence as a redeemed human being. What does it mean to be best friends here and now, and how do we experience that intimacy? Why not spend a few minutes now and reflect on your attitude toward deliberate sin – are you arrogant in choosing to go your own way? and secondly how you get to be good friends with someone and what helps the friendship grow? That translates to our relationship with Jesus- knowing Him, wanting to be with Him, becoming like Him, loving Him more….

January 31
My Value
Psalm 139:13-18

"For you created my inmost being; you knit me together in my mother's womb. I praise you because I am fearfully and wonderfully made; your works are wonderful, I know that full well. My frame was not hidden from you when I was made in the secret place, when I was woven together in the depths of the earth. Your eyes saw my unformed body; all the days ordained for me were written in your book before one of them came to be. How precious to me are your thoughts, God! How vast is the sum of them! Were I to count them, they would outnumber the grains of sand— when I awake, I am still with you." (Psalm 139:13-18)

You may live with the acute realization of your own finitude and fallenness, but the contemporary assures us that you cannot be truly free and fulfilled if you put a low value on self. A low self-image will ruin it all. But "low" and "high"--who decides? Where is the price list? We need a reality check, for only recognizing true value will liberate and open the way to fulfillment. An inflated view or a deflated view, distorting reality, will surely tie you up tighter than ever and shut out the possibility of fulfillment. But if you measure your worth by what you own, how much fun you are having, and how successful people recognize you to be, you've given in to the world's value system and have doomed yourself to bondage and unfulfillment because those things--no matter how abundant--cannot liberate us nor fill us up. If a therapist persuades me that I really am significant, no matter what those around think about me, such counsel can be permanently liberating only if it's true. And the truth is that we are worth a lot!

* You are a designer brand. You are valuable not because of what you own or have done but because of how God designed you. He created you on his pattern. You have his insignia stamped on you. You are an image bearer of the Infinite One and that's impressive, no matter what others may think of you.

*You have a very high sticker price. God himself valued you so highly he paid an outrageous price to buy you back from your slave-holder, your bondage to stuff, fun, and an inflated self-image. You are of infinite worth to God, not for your achievements or possessions, but because he invested in you the life of his own Son.

Those values are shared by all believers, but you have a value no one else shares. You have a unique destiny. God not only created you to bear his family likeness, he not only purchased you with the life of his only Son, but he did so on purpose. He has a purpose for you, something he wants to accomplish on earth through you. No matter how the world or the church may evaluate your contribution, the grand Designer valued you enough to plan your unique role to bring him the greatest possible honor.

That's why I'm proud to be a homemaker. I try to be the best cook, housekeeper, gardener, and nurse I know how. I'm not the best at any of those, to be sure, but I give it my best because it's my assignment, God's purpose for me. And I greatly enjoy it, never fret about what I'd rather be doing, about what might have been. Much less compare my "value" to others with higher callings and greater gifts.

And there's something more. Worth is often judged by the company a person keeps--royalty, skid row--whatever. And you are a member of high society--the highest! Incredible as it may seem, God has planned your life around him, uninterrupted companionship with the greatest Lover who ever lived.

Talk about self-worth! If that knowledge of who you are in Christ doesn't liberate and fill life to the full, what will?

Created on the pattern of God, not a monkey.

Purchased by the most precious commodity this world has ever known, the blood of God.

Living a life planned by the master Designer of the planets, the suns, and every atom.

A constant companion of the King of Kings. Indeed, theology can liberate and fill a person full.

February 1
Inspiring the Word
2 Kings 23:2-3

He read in their hearing all the words of the Book of the Covenant, which had been found in the temple of the Lord. The king stood by the pillar and renewed the covenant in the presence of the Lord-to follow the Lord and keep his commands, regulations and decrees with all his heart and all his soul, thus confirming the words of the covenant written in this book. Then all the people pledged themselves to the covenant. (2 Kings 23:2-3)

The Bible claims to be inspired by God, and that makes me curious. Exactly what did the Holy Spirit do to the Bible authors? How did He make sure they wrote what He wanted to say? Since He doesn't tell us, we try to figure it out. Some conclude the Spirit must have dictated the Bible to the authors like executives dictate to their secretaries. He obviously did dictate parts of the Bible; for example, when He gave the Ten Commandments to Moses. However, I do not believe much of Scripture was dictated in that way.

Some of the Bible comes from historical research, as in the case of the Gospel of Luke and the Book of Acts, as Doctor Luke himself tells us . n the human side, the experiences and writing style of each author are evident throughout Scripture. But in some mysterious way those authors were inspired by the Holy Spirit, so that what they wrote was consistently called, "the Word of God."

Though we may not know how the Spirit carried out this activity, we know from Scripture itself that He so guided the writing process that the human authors, using their own experiences and vocabulary, wrote what the divine Author wanted communicated. This cannot be said of any other book, no matter how helpful it is. Other books may be called "inspired" in the sense that they inspire the reader, but none can be said to be God-breathed as is Scripture. The Bible alone carries that guarantee. That's why we can trust it.

Since the Bible does not define inspiration, we might be tempted to take the option of calling it a mystery and letting it go at that! My son Kent, well-versed in the creation story of Genesis, first encountered an alternative view of human origins in the third grade. His righteous indignation ran so hot that he conducted his own inquisition at the lunch hour. Going down the line of little people waiting to be fed, he asked each one, "Do you believe the monkey business?" When he reached his best friend Darwin, his friend replied, " Of course I do ." (He seemed to live up to the name his parents gave him!) Kent then leveled his accusation: "Then you don't believe the Bible ." Darwin replied, " Oh yes I do, I just don't believe the part about creation ." With the wisdom of his advanced years, untutored by any elder, Kent responded, "Well, how do you choose which part to believe? If you are uncertain about the reliability of the Bible, how would you answer Kent's question, "How do you choose which part to believe?"

I remember hearing W. A. Criswell, pastor of First Baptist Church of Dallas for more than half a century, thunder, "They tell me the Book is inspired in parts and I'm inspired to pick the parts!" Eight-year old Kent and the 80-year-old pastor each identified the key issue. If I do what Jesus Christ never did and affirm error in Scripture, then I put myself over Scripture. By deciding what to accept and what not to accept as trustworthy, I must sit in judgment on the Book; I consider my inspiration superior to the inspiration of Scripture. In that way I would reduce the inspiration of Scripture to the size of my intellect, and that's not a very impressive "revelation!" Paul assures us that *"All Scripture is inspired by God."* (1 Timothy 3:16)

The Bible helps us in the following ways :
- It describes God's character so we may know Him
- It tells us how to become a child of God
- It gives us moral direction for our lives
- It assures us of our final destination.

The Holy Spirit gave us a fully reliable revelation of God's will for us. What a magnificent gift! He unveiled the character and purposes of God. We can know God! Knowing Him we will surely love Him. Love leads us to obedience as we seek to conform our wills to that of the Father.

This is my prayer response as I think about the inspiration of the Word. Pray along with me or voice your own prayer concerning the Bible.

Father, thank You for the good gift of Your Spirit who has revealed all the truth I need to know You, to love You, to please You. Thank You that the Bible is reliable. Help me to understand it more clearly and obey its teachings more.

February 2
Living Purposefully
John 15

"No longer do I call you servants,[a] for the servant does not know what his master is doing; but I have called you friends, for all that I have heard from my Father I have made known to you." (John 15:15)

Today begin by reading John 15. Then let's start with a quiz: What is the ultimate purpose of life? To serve God well? Win souls and evangelize the world? To be holy, Christlike? To glorify God? To worship God?

Would you exclude me from the fold of orthodoxy if I said none of the above? Oh, to be sure, we are called to pursue all the above, but is there no ***ultimate*** goal, no integrating purpose? Most of us seem to act as if the one we chose to concentrate on is the ultimate, the integrating purpose of life. And our choice is often influenced by the most recent religious trend. Think about it ...

Historically, the natural tendency of Christians seems to have been to make service to God the chief end, the purpose of human existence. Christ himself came to do the Father's work, didn't he? (Jn 5:19). In light of the final denouement, said Paul, work very hard. In fact, always abound in the work of the Lord (I Cor 15.58). The Reformers broadened the narrower focus of "the work of the Lord" to include every vocation as God's work and from that came what was to be called the "Protestant work ethic."

But the "work of the Lord" was narrowed again, especially in America with the advent of the great evangelists from Finney on through Moody to Graham. The ultimate goal is to win people to Christ. And in the Nineteenth and Twentieth centuries, a large segment of the church said, "Not just any lost souls, but primarily those who have never heard the gospel." So the greatest missionary movement of church history was born. Since God so loved the whole world that he gave his son, we ought to be about doing the same- giving ourselves, our sons and daughters to reach the whole world. If world-wide redemption is God's purpose and we are his chosen means to accomplish that, how can anything other than world missions be paramount, the chief purpose at least of the church?

Some have been uneasy with that definition of "ultimate purpose" and have pointed out that it isn't so much what we do as who we are, what we become. Isn't being holy, becoming like Christ the focus of the Epistles? That goal, among Protestants, gave birth, in the 17th and 18th centuries, to pietism, in the 19th century to the holiness movements with their "higher" (or "deeper") life teaching and in the 20th century to the emphases of some Pentecostal and Charismatic groups. Being godly, that's what life is about -so they say. But there is more to life than this, and we will consider it over the next few days. Take a few minutes and consider how you live- what you consciously or unconsciously prioritize as your integrating purpose of life.

February 3
The Chief End of Man
John 15:8-10

"By this my Father is glorified, that you bear much fruit and so prove to be my disciples. As the Father has loved me, so have I loved you. Abide in my love. If you keep my commandments, you will abide in my love, just as I have kept my Father's commandments and abide in his love. " (John 15:8-10)

We can relate to the two emphases we considered yesterday as the purpose of life- service to God and evangelism. Let's consider another purpose of life. Could it be found in John 15:8-10?

Many of my friends, direct descendants of Westminster, say, "Stop! Holiness and evangelism aren't man's chief end. It is the glory of God!" I know about that. My mother raised me to believe that the Sabbath was made for going to church in the morning and evening and memorizing the Westminster Catechism in the afternoon. I also know from personal experience that a person can work frenetically for God, throw his life away on some distant mission field, and pursue godliness unremittingly, all for the wrong reasons. For example, perhaps I'm driven to do these things for my own benefit, in time or eternity. Or, at best, I may pursue these goals to please someone else–my parents, the keepers of my tradition, or, at a higher level, the salvation of lost people. But if I keep my focus on God, pursuing his honor, his joy, that could purify all the tireless activity, all that cultivation of godliness. So, yes, God's glory does seem to trump holiness and faithful service as the ***chief*** end. Or does it?

In the latter part of the 20th Century, perhaps enhanced by post-modern influences, God's people began to feel that "the glory of God" could be too intellectual, too impersonal. What is missing is the spirit of worship, the internal response of the human spirit. The spiritual, if you please. The term, "worship," mutated from it's earlier breadth of meaning, all that spotlights in word or action the worth of God, to a special emphasis on music. And, toward the end of the century, to worship was to enjoy an experience of contemporary music led by a worship team.

Some, with greater theological finesse, have tried to rescue the worship juggernaut from missing the mark by pointing out that worship is at least one of the best ways to glorify God. And if the motive of worship is to glorify God it won't end up as no more than an exciting experience, an emotional high. On this account, "worship" and "glorify" reinforce, maybe even define one another. But still....could your ultimate purpose be more? What are your top three defining purposes in life?

February 4
Loving God
Matthew 22:37

"And he said to him, "You shall love the Lord your God with all your heart and with all your soul and with all your mind." (Matthew 22:37)

This issue of our ultimate purpose for life is so important let's consider it one more time.

"Daddy, why does God want us to brag on him?" The night before, our six-year-old Kent had been reprimanded for showing off to the guests. Apparently that got him mulling over what he'd been taught about glorifying God. Why did that kid always have to turn things into theological issues? I stumbled around and told him it wasn't so much the glory for himself God was after, but that we get things straight. If we don't recognize him for who he is and ourselves for who we truly are, we will self-destruct. He loves us too much to let that happen.

Well, it's not a worthless response, is it? To be out of alignment with reality is always destructive. Maybe the Westminster divines were onto something–"Man's chief end is to glorify God..." That focus would certainly be a corrective for our natural tendencies.

Through the decades I've contemplated Kent's question and finally decided to investigate. To my astonishment, as I reviewed the hundreds of biblical references to God's glory, I could find only a scant handful in which it was God who was asking for it. The answer to Kent's question about why God asks us to brag on him seemed to be, he doesn't! At least, not that much. His prophets demanded it often as essential to rightly relating to God, his people enjoined one another to get on with it, to be sure, but what was it God himself was most after?

How do I get the temerity to question the received wisdom? On pretty high authority, actually. When the question about human destiny was put by a theologian to an itinerant preacher, he did not respond that the glory of God, even expressed in glorious worship, is the chief thing God is after. He said in Matthew 22:37 (author's translation): *The way to true life, the greatest of all God's demands, the ultimate purpose of your life, that on which all the other commands hang suspended is to **love** the Lord your God.* Then he appended, from another Old Testament passage, a corollary love command, one that makes visible the ultimate command, *"and love on your neighbor the same way you love on yourself."*

The problem with making "glorifying God" the ultimate is that we can glorify someone we despise. Ask any press agent, any serving a dictator. One can worship a god he fears or loathes, as millions do. But if you love a person deeply, it's impossible to stop honoring them, bragging on them at every opportunity. If I love a person, and that person is God, I'll want to worship him, put his glories on display in all I say or sing. Or do. The flow must be that direction. Glory and worship, holiness and service may flow from other sources, but love is the only fountainhead from which all the others will surely flow.

February 5
The Motive
John 17:11

"And I am no longer in the world, but they are in the world, and I am coming to you. Holy Father, keep them in your name, which you have given me, that they may be one, even as we are one." (John 17:11)

It's a motive question. All we do flows from one of three motives, or a combination of them: love for God, love for others, and love for self. Love for self usually wins out in any competition of loves, even in religious activity. The altruistic, especially the regenerated altruist, may act sometimes out of love for others. But God calls us to love him above all. And not just with our hearts (our affections); not just with our souls (the choices we make); not just with our minds (our intellectual endeavor); but with, indeed, all of these to the maximum–with all our strength. Once this order is in place, loving God above all else, passionately and unconditionally we will pursue his glory, not our own, and we will do so in worship, in service, in the pursuit of holiness.

Why have I wrestled a lifetime with the question of the ultimate purpose of life? Is it an attempt to love God with my mind in search of theological precision? Not really, at least not primarily. What I hold consciously as my ultimate purpose does shape my mind, to be sure, and drives my actions; but above all, it defines my relationships.

Go back to the beginning. Why did God create us in his likeness? To prove his creative capabilities? Was it not the overflow of his love-nature (I John 4:8,16) to create a being to join the Father, the Son, and the Spirit in their circle of love? But for lovers to be one, they must be compatible. So he created us God-compatible. He wanted to "walk with us in the cool of the evening." We blew it, of course, became morally dysfunctional, out of sync with our ultimate lover, estranged. More– we divorced. And it is we who took the initiative in the divorce proceedings. But his nature did not change, and he reached out. To do what? Rescue the ones he loved from eternal banishment? Yes, but so much more. He wanted to restore the God-compatibility. "Regeneration," we call it, and "sanctification." To what end? Is **that** the end, the ultimate? No, no. To be one with him, to share in a passionate, intimate love relationship-- that was his goal.

This ultimate plan of God is so incredible I can't understand it, let alone explain it. But an intimate conversation between the Son and the Father astonishes us with what he had in mind. The seventeenth chapter of John has been so pre-empted by the ecumenical movement to teach unity among believers–important as that is–that we may miss the point of what he was saying to the Father in John 17:11; *"My prayer for all of them is that they will be one, just as you and I are one, Father–that just as you are in me and I am in you, so they will be in us....so that they may be one, as we are–I in them and you in me, all being perfected into one."*

Astonishing! The only way to describe what God is after is to say that he has designed a relationship so intimate the only way to explain it is to say that in some mysterious way it's like the relationship between the Father and the Son.

February 6
Accountability
John 13:34-35

"A new commandment I give to you, that you love one another: just as I have loved you, you also are to love one another. By this all people will know that you are my disciples, if you have love for one another." (John 13:34-35)

To really grow spiritually it takes more than a teacher teaching and a hearer listening. Ideally, for mind renovation and behavioral change to take place, accountability to another person or persons is essential. Small group and personal mentoring are sub-authentic if they end in teaching/learning, let alone if they end in no more than warm fellowship and encouragement. Accountability within the group or in the mentoring relationship should be a part of the relationship if true growth and discipleship are to take place.

There is an important part of discipleship that must be present in a congregation whether or not that ideal of personal accountability structures are provided. We call it church discipline. The church must faithfully deal with sin in its members if spiritual growth is to take place. How this is to be accomplished is so important and we must note that any serious attempt to "make disciples" must include holding all members accountable. When a member fails in moral dereliction (as in the church of Corinth) it not only means the sinning person becomes ever less a true disciple of Christ, his failure, unchecked by the body, affects all other members. This is a major theme of Paul in both letters to the church at Corinth. Again, it is obvious that one who teaches heresy is not a true disciple. But it must be emphasized that his teaching also holds back the rest of the body from advancing in discipleship, in right thinking and right behavior. Responsibility relationships in the congregation, however, go far beyond those two "disciplinable" behaviors – unrepented moral dereliction and teaching heresy. We must hold one another to the highest standards of Christian behavior, not just in those major matters that demand church discipline. For true growth in discipleship ALL that Jesus taught is included (Matthew 28:18). And for that we really do need one another.

It won't do merely to proclaim the truths of holiness from the pulpit. In some structured relationship-small group or one-on-one- all of us, including leaders, need to have accountability partners. That's what "small group", "mentoring", "pastoring" are all about! When we are to take action and how it is to be done have everything to do with success in the making of disciples.

My seat mate on the flight into Atlanta turned out to be a high-ranking Air Force officer who had just returned from his third tour of duty in Viet Nam. He had flown over 300 sorties over North Viet Nam and had returned unscathed. The average hit on American planes was one every 12 sorties! I asked if it were scary when the ground to air guided missile came after him. "No," he replied, "those big ones are easy to evade. They are the size of a telephone pole. When they come up you just dive and they miss you."

"What about air-to-air missiles from behind where you can't see them?" I asked.

"Oh, that's why we always fly in pairs. Your buddy alerts you. If he fails, you are dead meat."

So, I concluded, he wasn't the ace I thought, he just had a good buddy. That's why he came home safe every time. And so it is with church. The big ones you may be able to dodge on your own. But those that slip up from behind, you need a faithful buddy.

Family solidarity is the least experienced of the God-designed purposes for his church, at least in American congregations. Most churches do not have a program to monitor, let alone proactively care for members' spiritual, emotional, physical, and material welfare. And that's sad because what's a family for? And family was Gods' design, the blood ties of Calvary binding us closer than human blood ties. Who can be your wing man, looking for the incoming attacks that can bring you down?

February 7
I am the Truth
John 14:6

"I am the way, the truth and the life. No one comes to the Father except through me." (John 14:6)

The most grievous reputation theft is to steal God's. At one time I was astounded to realize how grave a sin my grumbling was as I reflected on the fact that complaining was a capital offense for many Israelites (see Num. 11:1). Complaining about my circumstances steals glory from God. In fact, when I complain, I'm telling people my God isn't smart enough to know my best interests, isn't strong enough to handle this situation, or doesn't care about me. In making these insinuations, I've damaged His reputation. Only thanksgiving and praise will restore the luster.

Take a few minutes and list your current gripes, particularly things you've complained about to others. Confess those words as the sin they are. If there's a need to restore God's reputation with the one you spoke to, make plans to do that. Pause now and by faith thank God for the good He intends by allowing those circumstances that plague you so. They may not be good; in fact, they may be evil. But God intends good for you by sending them, permitting them, or redirecting the evil purpose an enemy may have had. Thank Him! Praise will restore your tranquility and God's honor. Acknowledge that God's glory transcends your circumstances.

Yet what about our own reputation as well as God's? As we consider another aspect of the ninth commandment: *"Do not give false testimony against your neighbor"* (Exodus 20:16). Giving false testimony means lying. Strictly speaking, the ninth commandment prohibits only perjury, deliberately making a false statement in a court of law. Perjury is especially serious because it threatens the integrity of the courts by which justice is secured. Yet, as with each of the Ten Commandments, there are deeper implications. "Do not lie to one another" (Col. 3:9; also see Lev. 19:11) is a pervasive command in Scripture, and the law itself identifies many varieties of lying, in addition to perjury: dealing falsely; gossip; breaking a contract; and above all, swearing falsely in God's name (see Lev. 19:11-12,16).

The psalmist's love for God's Word bred in him a godly aversion to anything false. He wrote: *I hate and abhor falsehood, but I love Your instruction."* (Psalm 119:163)

The Bible reminds us that falsehood includes not only what we say about others, but also what we say about God and what we say about ourselves. We cross the commandments about stealing (reputations), lying (is this really true?), and God's glory when we embellish details in our thoughts and speech. *"Finally, brothers, whatever is true, whatever is honorable, whatever is just, whatever is pure, whatever is lovely, whatever is commendable, if there is any excellence, if there is anything worthy of praise, think about these things."*

How bad a sin is deception? For the Christian, every word and act either affirms the truth of God or denies God. In other words, to the extent we conform to reality in what we do and say, to that extent we conform to the ultimate reality, God. To the extent we do not conform, to that extent we tell lies about God, we profane his reputation. When we do this knowingly or deliberately, we sin the more grievously. So the basic evil of deception is that it denies the character of God who is truth (Heb. 6:18). Jesus said, *"I am the truth"* (John 14:6). He also said the word of God is the embodiment of truth (John 17:17). God is utterly reliable. This is the foundation of a coherent universe.

February 8
Freedom
Romans 7 & 8

...the power of the life-giving Sprit has freed you, through Christ Jesus, from the power of sin...God destroyed sin's control over us...us, who no longer follow our sinful nature... If your sinful nature controls your mind, there is death...For the sinful nature is always hostile to God. It never did obey God's laws, and it never will. That's why those who are still under the control of their sinful nature can never please God. But you are not controlled by your sinful nature. You are controlled by the Spirit if you have the Spirit of God living in you...you have no obligation whatsoever to do what your sinful nature urges you to do. For if you keep on following it, you will perish. But if through the power of the Holy Spirit you turn from it and its evil deeds, you will live...overwhelming victory is ours through Christ (Romans 8:2,3,4,6,8,9,12,13,37).

The distinguished professor was holding forth on Romans 7:14-25, declaiming that Paul intended to describe the normal experience of every believer. Ever feel like that? Maybe you felt trapped in a lock box of dark expectations. Our professor did. In the midst of his disquisition a student raised his hand. "Professor," he asked, "did Paul never get out of Romans 7 into Romans 8?" Romans 8—that grand symphony of hope, that glorious treasure-trove of Holy Spirit empowerment!

The student might just as well have asked if Paul ever really left Romans 6- *"Our old sinful selves were crucified with Christ so that sin might lose its power in our lives. We are no longer slaves to sin. For when we died with Christ we were set free from the power of sin...Sin is no longer your master... Now you are free from sin, your old master. .. now you are free from the power of sin and have become slaves of God."* (Romans 6:6,7,14,18,22)

Did Paul never get out of Romans 7? The professor raised himself to his considerable full height, pacing back and forth in front of the class. "Well," he said, "Maybe he did. But when he got right with God he got back in again!"

Some hold that the Romans 7 experience is normative, like our professor, others that it is a flashback to Paul's pre- conversion days, and still others teach that it represents a time of spiritual defeat in Paul's life, a time, by the way, unreported elsewhere. My own position is that we ask chapter 7 the wrong question. Maybe it isn't either/or, but just a graphic testimony of spiritual conflict that fits many a situation. Maybe yours?

But Romans 6 and 8 are very real promises of break-out from hopelessness and defeat into freedom and fulfilment. And how important that we discover and experience that fulness of life in the Spirit! Because if we don't, instead of spiraling up toward ever greater likeness to Jesus and ever closer companionship with him, we spiral down ever further from the image in which we were created and ever greater distance from a tight relationship with God. Hope slips away, darkness enfolds.

Apparently that was the experience of our professor. What demons of darkness warred within we'll never know.. But as a tragic parable of life and death, we are reminded that hopelessness brings death in one form or another. Paul said so, repeatedly. Then he concluded: "Oh wretched man that I am! Who will deliver me?" Would that our professor had "gotten out of Romans 7" before he continues down the dark road to utter despondency. For there is a way out — "I thank God through Jesus Christ our Lord!"(Rom 7:25).

Of course, hope is built on a solid foundation: forgiven! declared right! transformed! an intimate relationship of love! We know all that, it's just elemental, right? Or is it? We must understand the profound implications of each of those initiating elements in our salvation, implications for living out the life today. Otherwise, it's just dead doctrine.

Hope is born with the experience of forgiveness, justification, regeneration, and indwelling, but that hope is still in its infancy. *"So let us stop going over the basics of Christianity again and again. Let us go on instead and become mature in our understanding"* (Hebrews 6:1 NLB). That will be our aim: growing up to full maturity. Freed up and filled full!

Yes, there is hope, a hope that will never lead to shame. Thank God who always causes us to triumph in Christ!

February 9
Racism
Galatians 5:14

"For the whole law is fulfilled in one word: You shall love your neighbor as yourself." (Galatians 5:14)

Pride is a root cause of racism. And such a foolish pride, based on physical characteristics for which one has no responsibility. Probably pride of race, however, is based on cultural differences more than on the purely physical differences. We generalize from the very real, profound, and wide-ranging differences in culture to assume that the highly visible physical differences are an indispensable part of the group's distinctives. Since people naturally prefer to associate with those whom they understand and with whom they agree, segregation in one form or another seems inevitable. Which natural affinity grouping may be legitimate and which is sinful thus becomes an abiding dilemma. It is the task of the Christian and the church to work at solving this dilemma with wisdom, compassion, and courage. Pride says, "Our way is the best way," and then concludes that all other ways are inferior.

Ignorance extends this judgment to identify cultural patterns with skin color, and the observed behavior of some is generalized to characterize all in the group. "All Indians march in single file . . . at least the one I saw did." So pride and the ignorance of faulty logic combine to divide and hurt.

In addition to pride and ignorant generalizing, fear is a major cause of racial and class strife, fear of the unknown. Patterns of segregation increase the ignorance of what the other group is really like, and the prior decision to view whatever it *is* like as inferior to "our way" creates an atmosphere of fear in which imagination has more influence than reality. Another fear is that of being hurt by "the enemy," either through his deliberate antagonism or through being deprived of some real or potential benefit because of him. When one's person, possessions, or position is put in jeopardy by someone else, fear, whether reasonable or not, begins to determine behavior. Fear can cause a member of a powerless minority to be just as racist in attitudes and actions as those who have the power to impose injustice. Thus pride and fear often combine with ignorance to produce the full range of attitudes and actions of racism, from inadequate love, through hatred and violence, to structured injustice and killing.

Some, like the late Tom Skinner, former leading black evangelical spokesman, say American racial problems are a white problem. There are at least two differing emphases among those who hold this view. Some hold that black and white are today reaping the whirlwind from the winds generated by America's slaveholding forefathers. White attitudes and black behavior patterns, both destructive to the black, were created during 250 years of American slavery.

Later studies discount this and point to present social structures and personal attitudes as the problem.[5] This view sees high potential in African Americans but a potential from which most African-Americans are permanently barred by a tightly woven social fabric that begins with poverty and poor education leading to unemployment, low-paying jobs, and crime.

The conclusion reached by most American academic, media, and political leaders is that society, particularly white majority society, is responsible to change the environment. But another conclusion from the same theory of social conditioning holds the black person primarily responsible for his own deliverance; at least deliverance cannot be won without his participation. Charles Silberman, a strong advocate of black causes, holds this position: "The Negro will be unable to compete on equal terms until he has been able to purge from his mind all sense of white superiority and black inferiority—until he really believes, with all his being, that he is a free man, and acts accordingly. In this sense, therefore, only the Negro can solve the Negro problem.... If all discrimination were to end immediately, that alone would not materially improve the Negro's position. The unpleasant fact is that too many Negroes are unable—and unwilling—to compete in an integrated society."7

Whatever the perceptions and misperceptions, how did we get into the terrible impasse of blacks locked into ghettos of poverty, crime, unemployment, and disintegrating families, while white Christians don't consider it a major problem? White Americans rated racism thirty-first among the problems facing the nation.... Yet blacks, in the same survey, said racism was the number one problem facing America.9

These grave black problems will not be fully solved by human wisdom and political actions, not only because of their vast complexity, but because the root problem is sin. Therefore, the church alone holds the solution, but the church has failed.

Note that we have dealt with America's most severe racial problem, but that the principles involved apply equally to Jews, Native Americans, Hispanics, and all other ethnic groups who have been wrongly discriminated against. We must, however, work aggressively for unity in the body of Christ and labor together for the advance of Christ's kingdom in which there is no barrier between white and black, high class and low class, male and female, rich and poor. Another evidence of racism in the church was the paternalistic, if not colonialist attitudes and relationships of many missionaries in the past. This has been replaced, in some instances, by a new racism, a nationalism that has given birth to antiwhite attitudes among some church leaders in non-Western nations. Either type of racism is unworthy of those who are called Christian.

The principles enunciated for racism in the American church apply just as much to the far more common worldwide problem of classism or making unchristian discrimination on the basis of a person's social status. Tribal warfare across the continent of Africa, for example, and the caste system, which holds hundreds of millions of Indians in abject bondage, make the evil of racism in North America pale by comparison. Yet we are responsible, not for the sins of others, but for our own. And measured by the pain inflicted, racism in the United States is a grievous personal and social ill. [2] What can you do to love better?

---

[2] *Introduction to Biblical Ethics* (IBE), Robertson McQuilkin, (2014), Inter-Varsity Press, 358-359.

February 10
Responsibility in Race Relations
Galatians 3:26-28

"...for in Christ Jesus you are all sons of God, through faith. For as many of you as were baptized into Christ have put on Christ. There is neither Jew nor Greek, there is neither slave nor free, there is no male and female, for you are all one in Christ Jesus." (Galatians 3:26-28)

Political action is necessary, but only a cure of the spirit can bring about a lasting solution. Only the transforming work of Christ in the human heart is adequate to the sin problem. But the problem remains: Racism has infected the church with the same virus. In fact, sometimes the strain within the church seems more virulent and less subject to cure than outside. How can the church cleanse and heal its own members and then become God's instrument to cleanse and heal society?

The New Birth. New people alone can build a new society. But church membership does not bring this about automatically. The most severe racial problems have been in the southern states and in South Africa where the incidence of born-again church members is high. Historically, black Christians, under far greater provocation, have overcome racial prejudice more than white, though this seems to be changing. How does one get Christians to behave like Christians?

Teaching. The church has the responsibility to teach the truth that we are all one in Christ Jesus (Gal. 3:26-28; Eph. 2:11-14; 4:3-4; Col. 3:10-11). But since attitudes are so enculturated as to be unconscious, the church must apply this truth rigorously, pointing out the insidious outcroppings of racial prejudice and God's hatred of this sin against the unity of his body.

Personal Relations. Teaching must be activated in the personal relationship of differing races on the job, in the community, in the home, and in the church. The loving fellowship intended by the Father among members of his family must be lived out. "Teaching" includes spiritual supervision, of course, so that members of the church are disciplined in living what is taught.

Truly new people who are taught and disciplined in Scripture, sensitive to the Holy Spirit, and obedient to the Lord of the church can make a difference. Differing races of people of this kind can build godly personal relations and wake a culture-bound church. The awakened, free church can influence its community to build a more just and merciful society.

Structure and Program. The church must not only teach and help individuals find the right way, it must eliminate every direct or indirect church policy of racial discrimination.

Affirmative Action. It would be absurd to insist that all who speak different languages must belong to the same local congregation when more than one language group has a church. There are other "languages" as well — cultural and theological. Ways of worship differ radically, and doctrinal issues are important to people. Must all be forced into the same local congregation when more than one type of fellowship is available? Does "affirmative action" mean that Scripture requires every African American church, for example, to aggressively recruit whites until there is a racial balance equivalent to society at large? I believe this goes beyond any biblical mandate. On the other hand, though churches and other groups tend to develop along lines of cultural compatibility, this does not give license for any church to put formal or informal impediments to full participation by anyone, regardless of race, social status, or any other nonmoral characteristic.[3]

---

[3] IBE (2014), 111.

February 11
Hierarchy of Sin
Matthew 5:19

"Therefore whoever relaxes one of the least of these commandments and teaches others to do the same will be called least in the kingdom of heaven, but whoever does them and teaches them will be called great in the kingdom of heaven." (Matthew 5:19)

Some have held that before God there is no difference among sins. All sins are equally vile and there is no legitimate gradation of guiltiness among sins. This curious notion probably originated in a misunderstanding of Christ's meaning in the Sermon on the Mount. Not only is murder wrong, he taught, but anger is wrong in itself, whether or not it leads to murder; it is in the same category of evil, in the same family of sins. Christ never intended to teach that the first beginning of sinful thought and its mature manifestation in action were equally heinous. The notion is a terrifying one. It is intended to reinforce the sinfulness of sin, but in actual fact it has the opposite effect. If it is as wrong to desire a woman as to take her by force, why not act on your impulses? You are no more guilty. The rest of mankind would plead with the one holding such a doctrine: If you covet my possessions, please keep it at that level and do not take them; if you hate me or fail to love me as Christ does, please keep it at that level and do not assault or kill me.

There is a biblical hierarchy of both virtue and sin. Love for God takes precedence over love for my neighbor. Those who sin without knowledge are to be punished on the judgment day with less severity than those who sin with knowledge (Luke 12:47-48). In the Old Testament where specific punishments were prescribed by God, there was a gradation from capital punishment down to a slight fine. There are "least commandments" (Matt. 5:19) and "weightier matters" (Matt. 23:23). Some insults, for example, are worse than others, and to speak in wrath is worse than merely feeling it (Matt. 5:22).

To hold that all sins are of equal gravity in the sight of God finds no confirmation in either the Old Testament or the New Testament. It is true that one who breaks the least commandment is guilty of the whole in the sense that he has become a lawbreaker (James 2:10). He is no longer an innocent person. It is also true that the least sin separates from a holy God. In this way, it could be said that all sins are equally sin. But it can never be said on biblical grounds that all sins are equally sinful.

Not all sinners will receive the same punishment. For example, those who have sinned deliberately for a lifetime against great light certainly will receive far greater condemnation than those who had no gospel light and died in childhood. Karl Marx and Adolf Hitler will give an account for their rejection of biblical truth they learned so well in their youth.

The notion that all sins are equally sinful does not tend to make guilt heavier on sins of the spirit, like selfishness, as much as it tends to make light the guilt of more heinous violations. Criminal law and church discipline must be based on the biblical view that there is a great difference among sins and that they should be punished accordingly.

To say there is a great difference in the weight of various sins does not mean that our view of that variation is accurate. In the nature of the subject—sin—we could almost assume in advance that fallen human evaluation will go astray. For example, in the sight of God, which would be the graver sin: a ghetto child who steals a loaf of bread to feed his crippled mother, or a university professor who delights in destroying the faith of hundreds of freshmen? Yet which would be punished in the courts of our land if found guilty of such activity? Sins against God are lightly thought of, even by Christians, but from God's point of view they are the most worthy of judgment. So it is that God alone may evaluate the level of guilt. But far be it from any just judge to assign to Anne Frank and Adolf Hitler the same level of punishment.

Having said all this, however, let us remember that the slightest falling short of God's glorious character brings separation from God, suffering, death, and hell. Let us remember that the least of all my sin would nail Jesus to the cross as the price of love to set me free. In contrast to murder, what is so terrible about eating a piece of fruit? And yet it was enough to rob heaven of its glory and damn the whole race.

As we have examined what Scripture has to say about the nature and results of sin, where it comes from and what it leads to, we may feel as if we have been sounding the depths of some vast and unfathomable cesspool. We have been probing the edges of some horror of impenetrable darkness. And why is the holy Word of God so full of this foul subject? In order to know God and become like him, it is not enough to love righteousness. We must hate sin. To induce this hatred, God strips sin of all its guises and fully reveals its hideous reality. But there is a prior reason for this grim revelation—against this dark background the splendor of his glorious grace stands revealed. Only when the hideous pollution of our corrupt nature is known will we seek cleansing. And only with this reality pressed upon us will we be willing to acknowledge how utterly hopeless and how helpless we are and run for refuge to the mighty Savior. [4]

What sin might you be excusing? Anger? Yelling? Adultery? Pornography? Fear? Surely not murder, yet perhaps gossip or the destruction of reputations? There is a hierarchy of sin, and the consequences are proportional. Why not admit it, commit to change now and be set free from guilt and separation from God?

---

[4] IBE (2014), 110.

February 12
Things Muriel Taught Me About Love
Ephesians 4:32

"Be kind to one another, tenderhearted, forgiving one another, as God in Christ forgave you." (Ephesians 4:32)

I once knew a girl. She didn't try to draw me to her, she just did. And, not only me, but too many other males! The first thing that caught my eye was her pretty face, but soon I discovered she had a delightful personality to go with it—vivacious, full of laughter, talented in art and music, smart. Best of all she was an exuberant lover of God. I loved that woman. But I wasn't too good at expressing it. So she taught me. In fact, she taught me many things about love and that's what I want to tell you about—the six things Muriel taught me about love.

My parents were of the old school that didn't believe in expressing affection, especially publicly. I never saw my parents embrace, for example. I'm pretty sure they did, however. Well—I'm here! But when I brought Muriel home to visit, Mother ridiculed her mushy ways—forever hugging and saying she loved me. Right out in front of family, yet!

The first thing Muriel taught me about love, then, was that it needs to be *expressed*. Passionately, frequently-like Solomon and the sun-browned Shulamite. They were forever talking love. And the Holy Spirit thought their love talk so good he chose to make a book of Scripture composed of it. We call it the Song of Songs, that is, the best of all songs. Love talk.

But love expressed verbally or even physically may not be genuine love. It might be lust or some other desire to get what one wants. The motive for love-talk can be to get, not to give. In Scripture we find the term "love" more often a verb than a noun. A verb describing action more than a noun describing a feeling. Muriel spent thirty-five years demonstrating her love for me by her actions. In fact, she seemed to live for me. Certainly not for herself. Oblivious to her own rights or desires or even her own welfare. She taught me that love, to be genuine, must be acted out 24/7, love demonstrated. But above all she lived to bring my goals to fruition.

Paul instructed us on how to love our mates. Husbands, love your wives as Christ loved the church. And how did Christ love his church—you, that is? And gave himself up for it. (Eph 5.25) To love, then is to *lay down life*—dreams, ambitions, rights, pleasures-- if need be—for the best interests of one's mate.

How do you measure love? What thermometer do you use to measure the heat of it, what sonar to plumb the depth of it, what scales to find the weight of it? There is a way, says Jesus: love is proved by the sacrifice it makes. Greater love, said Jesus, has no one than this, than one lay down one's life for a friend. (Jn 15.13) You may have genuine love without making a sacrifice for the one loved, but it would be unproved. Maybe I'm acting lovingly because of all the benefits I get out of the relationship. But sacrifice—ah, there's the proof. I've discovered that happy homes are those where each lives for the welfare of the other.

The next thing Muriel taught me about love is what to do when communication breaks down. Love *forgives*. Muriel bragged on me so outrageously I wasn't even aware there was anything in me to forgive. She never let on there could be any improvement. Till one day. We'd been reading a how-to article on marriage–for ministry purposes, of course. The author suggested each write out a list of things in the other they would change if they could and then exchange the lists. We decided to give it a try before suggesting it to others. I listed 3 or 4 minor matters and ran out. But there she sat scribbling away. I was incredulous. She filled the page! That gave me just an inkling there might be some need for honest evaluation and change. I don't remember the outcome. I hope there was change. But I'm not so sure.

February 13
More things Muriel taught me about love
Ecclesiastes 5:4

"When you make a vow to God, ...pay it; for he has no pleasure in fools. Pay what you have vowed." (Ecclesiastes 5:4)

I once had an interesting experience with Ephesians 5. A couple came to me for marriage counsel. They were in constant conflict. I said, "Well, let's turn to Ephesians 5." The wife burst out, "No need! My husband reads it to me every night." I didn't ask, I'll guarantee he didn't read about husbands loving your wives as Christ loved the church.

So when the student men's organization asked me to speak to them on marriage relationships. I spoke on partnering. "You talk things over, you seek consensus, you postpone the decision. That's the way of love". No more than 5 times in 35 years did I pull rank and say, "Well, honey, someone has to call this shot and I guess I'm the designated player." Those were not very exciting ideas for budding male chauvinists, but they must have liked it anyway because they invited me to return and repeat it the following year so they could invite their friends to hear it.

Muriel mobilized all her superlative creativity and inexhaustible energy to make my work succeed and, doing that, taught me to do the same for her dreams. And that will tighten any marriage. Married love is a full *partnership*—Muriel taught me that.

My counsel to young men who wanted a perfect marriage. You can tell it wasn't hard to love that woman. But in 1978 that bright light in my life began to dim. I noticed it while in Florida. She told the same story twice within ten minutes. She was 55 years old. They call that kind of Alzheimer's "early onset." One of four over eighty years of age experience Alzheimer's, but 55? But still Muriel taught me about love. She would speed walk back and forth from our home on campus to my office just to be with me. One night she had bloody feet. When I told our doctor about it, he just paused, with tears in his eyes; "Such love" he commented. Love is companionship. But it takes intentionality.

The sixth thing Muriel taught me about love is that it *endures*. In America, seven of ten couples in which one spouse gets a terminal illness, split, I'm told. God doesn't like that. David asked the question about who is God's companion, who is accepted by him? His answer: *"Those who keep their promises no matter how much it may cost"* (Ps 15.4). And what does God abhor? David's son Solomon tells us: *"When you make a vow to God, ...pay it; for he has no pleasure in fools. Pay what you have vowed."* (Ecclesiastes 5:4) God loves promise keepers, doesn't have much use for promise breakers.

It's a matter of integrity, of commitment. Commitment to God... and to one another. Love feelings may blaze up and die down, but commitment is the bond that holds. Of course, commitment without the warm feelings isn't much fun!

So, I think when he looks at your love affair and hears your incessant love talk, he says, That's good. But when he sees you acting out that love in living for the other, sacrificing self-interest if need be, he says, That's real good. When he hears you humbly pleading for forgiveness, he says That's so good. When he sees you partnering—each working hard to advance the goals of the other, he says, I like that. When he sees your constant intentional companionship, I believe he says, That's good. And when he sees it holding tight in the tough times, he says, That's real good.

February 14
Love
John 17:21

"that they may all be one, just as you, Father, are in me, and I in you, that they also may be in us, so that the world may believe that you have sent me." (John 17:21)

The last few days we considered the story of what Muriel has taught me about love. She could hardly teach me anything, could she, as she lay abed those ten years with no awareness of anything from Alzheimer's? Yes, she could--the most important thing of all about love, in fact.

One day I was speaking about the seven things Muriel taught me about love. A single woman said afterward; "You tricked me!" "I set you up, didn't I?" I replied. "Yes, you did and I'll be eternally grateful."

You see, I've been telling you a parable. It must be an OK parable, because the Bible itself incessantly tells the same parable; marriage is designed to mirror our relationship with God. In the Old Testament it was Israel, God's wife; in the New Testament our mirror is the Church, Christ's bride.

Here's how Muriel taught me the seventh–and most important thing–about love. Once during those 12 years she lay abed, I was looking at her lying quietly asleep, thinking of how loveable she is to me, about how I love her now more than ever and about how the heartache is she can't love me back, I thought, "Lord, is that the way it is with you and me? You pouring out your love on me by day and by night, caring for me, protecting me, providing for me, longing for my constant companionship, and all you get in return are a few grunts when things don't please me?" How sad. For HIM! Sad because love for him is the ultimate purpose of life.

Where did I get that idea? Why from Matthew 22:37:

"*You shall love the Lord your God with all your heart and with all your soul and withall your mind. This is the great and first commandment.*"

This is the first, the greatest. Why? We are created to be God-compatible.

Redemption? Save us from hell? Yes, because he loves us so. But so much more. Remake us in our God-likeness, godliness? Yes, but to what end? God-compatible so you can be one with him! I may not be able to understand or describe it, but I can illustrate it and the illustration is so incredible it will blow you away. Or it should. In John 17 we have the record of the Son's conversation with the Father. Now there's as intimate a love relationship as you could get, right? God the Father and his Son. Problem is, the passage has been co-opted by the ecumenical movement to teach unity among believers—important as that is—that we may miss the point. And what a point! Listen in on their conversation with fresh ears. John 17:21:

My prayer for all of them is that they will be one, just as you and I are one, Father—that just as you are in me and I am in you, so they will be in us…so that they may be one, as we are—I in them and you in me, all being perfected into one.

Wouldn't you want that kind of love affair with God? Lord, I want to love you just the way Muriel taught me:
- By telling you of my love throughout each day,
- Demonstrating it by living wholly for your welfare, not fixating on my own
- By partnering with you to advance your cause in my generation, on my watch

- By companioning with you all day long, sharing your joys as well as my own, sharing your hurts, not just dumping on you about mine
- And by holding steady till death do us… unite as one forever!

February 15
Outrageous Love
John 3:16

"For God so loved the world, that he gave his only Son, that whoever believes in him should not perish but have eternal life." (John 3:16)

Dad, I have terrible news. Bob has been badly hurt in a diving accident. Please pray." My daughter-in-law's voice at the other end of the line was quiet, and though she was in control, terror lurked around the fringes of her words.

I sat at my desk, stunned. I cried out to God to spare my son. Bob had just made a fresh commitment of his life. I thought of the conversation only three days earlier when he told me, "Dad, it's time for me to stop circling the harbor and launch out to sea." He was reaching the summit of his career as a photo-journalist, his marriage to Susan was idyllic, I had just received another of those exquisitely crafted love letters he periodically wrote me. What a terrible time to die. "Please, God," I cried. I felt so helpless; dared I even hope?

Ten minutes later the phone rang again. "Dad, Bob's with Jesus …" Hot tears flowed as if to wash away the pain, and friends gathered to embrace me, but the wound was too deep to be healed. Sons are meant to bury their fathers, not fathers their sons.

In those days I began to think about a father's love. I would do anything to protect my son. If given a choice, how gladly I would have taken his place. I would never choose to let him go, not for anyone. Yet God did just that. He chose to give His son for me. That's how much God loved me. I was not a family member, not even friend. An enemy. And, unlike me, God did not have two sons left. His only son. For me. Outrageous love.

I had always thought of Jesus' love as supreme. And perhaps it was. And yet…. and yet…it is one thing to give up one's own life, but the life of your beloved son? I began to feel a little of the pain of the brokenhearted Father. I wrote;

Father,
What was YOUR Gethsemane?
And when…
And where…
Did you decide,
Against all heart and reason,
To abandon your beloved one?
And that for me—
Oh, worthless substitute!

Like the piercings of a sword
We hear the cry,
"My God, my God, why
Have you forsaken me?"
"What love," we say.
And yet…. And yet…
Was not the Savior's piteous lament
A mere echo
Of that broken-hearted cry
Reverberating down the endless
Corridors of heaven,
"My Son, my Son,
My beloved Son,
Why have I forsaken you?"

No greater human love,
Christ taught, than when one
Gives his life.
But Father's love explodes
Beyond the reach of
Highest, deepest, and most untamed
Flight of human thought—
God gave not life, but SON.
His ONLY Son.
For me…

Parents may give a son or daughter for love of country; a: firefighter in a rescue that fails. But for an enemy? Yet "God has shown us how much He loves us-it was while we were still sinners that Christ died for us" (Rom. 5:1).

February 16
Purity
Matthew 5:27-28

"You have heard that it was said, 'You shall not commit adultery.' But I say to you that everyone who looks at a woman with lustful intent has already committed adultery with her in his heart." (Matthew 5:27-28)

What purpose did God have in mind when He thought of marriage? God isn't married. Angels don't marry. Not even many animal varieties couple for life. Eagles do, but we don't read any commands of God's binding them to it. So why us?

God explained His purpose for marriage in the very beginning: *"It is not good for the man to be alone"* (Gen. 2:18). Man alone is incomplete; he needs a companion to complete him (see Gen. 2:18-25; Matt. 19:3-6). So the first purpose of marriage is fellowship, oneness, and wholeness in a love relationship. No surprise since God is love! But that's not all. As soon as God got the first couple up and running, He gave His first command: have children (see Gen. 1:28). Animals do that too, of course, but with a major difference. Scripture gives a pattern of the home, a network of relationships in which parents are fully responsible for the care of their children. Procreation is in the context of family. Procreation, then, is a second purpose of marriage. But there's another purpose in marriage that is even more foundational. *"Wives, submit to your own husbands as to the Lord, for the husband is the head of the wife as Christ is the head of the church."* Ephesians 5:22-23

In light of this verse, what purpose of marriage is suggested in these verses? As illustrated in these verses, the marriage relationship is used throughout Scripture to instruct us about God's desired relationship with people. So this is a purpose of marriage: to help us understand and reflect the relationship God desires to have with His people. God is love, and from the overflow of this love among Father, Son, and Spirit came the creation of a being on the same pattern, designed to love and to be loved as in the divine model.

What do we find are the characteristics of marriage that are revealed by a comparison with the divine-human relationship? You probably list things like love, submission, and faithfulness. The divine-human relationship is eternal, whereas the marriage relationship is not. But the more we learn of one relationship, the more we are able to understand the other.

The holiness of the relationship among the members of the Trinity reflects the purity that is to characterize an earthly marriage. From the beginning God intended for marriage to be between a man and a woman for life.

The man said: *"This one, at last, is bone of my bone and flesh of my flesh; this one will be called "woman," for she was taken from man. This is why a man leaves his father and mother and bonds with his wife, and they become one flesh."* Genesis 2:23-24 Scripture insists that this one-flesh bond must remain inviolate. The seventh commandment reads, *"Do not commit adultery"* (Ex. 20:14), and the Old Testament emphasizes teaching against adultery second only to teaching against idolatry. In the New Testament both Christ and the apostles emphasized marital fidelity. Paul included sexual sins in every one of his many lists of sins, and in most cases they headed the list and received the greatest emphasis. For example, he wrote in Colossians 3:5, "Put to death what belongs to your worldly nature: sexual immorality, impurity, lust, evil desire, and greed, which is idolatry."

Jesus not only quoted the seventh commandment but also included sexual desire under this command—as mental adultery: *"You have heard that it was said, 'Do not commit adultery.' But I tell you, everyone who looks at a woman to lust for her has already committed adultery with her in his heart"* (Matt. 5:27-28). The end result of violating this command? Hell (see vv. 29-30)! It seems that Jesus took this commandment pretty seriously. So must we.

Purity, then, from God's viewpoint, extends beyond physical infidelity. The safeguard of the pure marriage relationship He designed begins in the mind, in the desires of the heart, Jesus said. Can you,…are you… safeguarding your heart?

February 17
Maximum Impact
Acts 2:41

"Those who accepted his message were baptized, and about three thousand were added to their number that day." (Acts 2:41)

The apostles were filled with the Spirit on the day of Pentecost and 3,000 people were converted (Acts 2:41). I'd call 3,000 responses really full. Yet a few weeks later they had a special need-their leaders had been arrested and threatened. They did the only thing to do; they called a prayer meeting and prayed for courage to witness in the face of persecution. Once again they were filled with the Spirit (Acts 4:31) and as a result proclaimed the word with boldness. Amazing! Spirit-filled people were filled! The same pattern is common throughout Acts- Spirit-filled people are said to be filled again. How can that be? Remember, filled is a picture word. I get the picture of a great schooner plowing through the ocean with sails full of wind when suddenly a gust of wind sweeps down and the schooner surges ahead under really full sail . So it is with the wind of the Spirit. (In both the Hebrew and Greek, the word spirit means "breath" or "wind.")

When we practice surrendered, obedient faith, we will experience the movement of the Spirit. The Spirit moves in with wisdom, courage, and words that just weren't naturally there. You know God is at work and others can tell, too. Before I preach I always ask the Spirit to move with power. I've been at it a long time. If I rely on myself I can explain Scripture and tell stories. People will listen and say nice things, but nothing of eternal value will happen if the Spirit doesn't act. When the Spirit works, I watch in wonder as God transforms lives. When I write, I'm always grateful to note any small amount of "fruit" God gives. But once in a while the words flow almost uninvited out of my computer like they're on fire. When published, the work seems to take on a life of its own. When I read it later I say, "Where'd that come from? Did I write that?" The Spirit had been working that day, and the result wasn't just my work. I wish it happened always. I wish every time I write or speak lives would be changed. I do not want to glorify myself. Rather I long to be filled permanently with the Spirit, so people will know for sure God is at work and give Him the credit .

Do you have some gift working at a minimal level? Can you tell God is at work through you, but it's not full throttle so that other people can tell? Ask Him to fill you. Open your heart to the wind of the Spirit and trust Him to empower and use you. Begin the habit of asking Him, at the time of special opportunity or challenge, to completely empower you so that He may get the glory.

As we've seen, the picture word *full* seems to have three different emphases. A person is full when, in his or her relationship with the Spirit, the Spirit is in full control. Second, a person is full when plenty of evidence shows the Spirit at work-a miracle quality of life (fruit) or a miracle impact in ministry (gifts). People can see it. The third emphasis is more elusive, as feelings always are. Do you feel full?

Full can also speak of a personal relationship-the kind of thing that defies scientific analysis. How do you analyze a relationship? Like a good marriage, the outward evidence, such as a home and children, may be obvious, but the feelings are more mysterious. A relationship includes moments of shared ecstasy and shared agony, a deep and constant sense of well-being and surges of passionate love. So it is living in a deep relationship with the Spirit. If you're filled with the Spirit you'll have joy, confidence, or peace when there's no earthly reason to have any peace at all. Your affection for God will be filled with passion-an excited sense of anticipation when you worship Him, a rush of pleasure when you think about His love for you. You may not sustain an emotional high; but you will have moments of uninhibited ecstasy, especially in devotional times alone with Him. But also, unexpectedly in the midst of a busy day the wind of the Spirit may blow in gale strength. I can't explain it, but we can feel it.

If you can't remember anything out of the ordinary in your relationship with God and you are thirsty for a full surge of awareness of God's presence, why not pause right now and tell Him so? But don't leave it there. Tell Him how much you love Him, how grateful you are for Him, for His constant companionship, and for all the wonderful blessings He floods into your life . Ask Him to fill you up with Himself. Pause now and write out in your journal either the description of your experience of fullness, the prayer for fullness, or both.

February 18
Transforming Love
Exodus 34:6-7

"The LORD passed before him and proclaimed, "The LORD, the LORD, a God merciful and gracious, slow to anger, and abounding in steadfast love and faithfulness, keeping steadfast love for thousands,[a] forgiving iniquity and transgression and sin….."(Exodus 34:6-7)

In the Old Testament, love speaks of a spontaneous feeling that impels to self-giving. This was true both for God and man. When man "loved" God, it meant "to have pleasure in God, striving impulsively after him, seeking God for his own sake." From God's side, the warm, strong feeling of affection that characterizes a healthy parent-child relationship is taken as a picture of how God the Father relates to Israel, his son. Love is the foundation of the covenant relationship. If the legal, covenantal aspect of the relationship is strong in the father-son analogy, the passionate loving-kindness of a good marriage is strong in the picture of God the husband and Israel the wife. The climactic revelation of this love relationship is seen in the prophet Hosea and his well-loved harlot-wife. The same analogy of father-son, bridegroom-bride continues in the New Testament, focusing on the warm affection and unfailing bonds between two who love each other deeply.

But the internal aspect of love is more than a feeling. It is a characteristic of life, a disposition. Old Testament scholars seem to have a problem in translating another Hebrew word, *chesded.* Some translations speak of *loving-kindness* (KJV), some of *steadfast love* (ASV, RSV), some of *constant love* (TEV, Today's English Version). Indeed, the love of God is steadfast, unfailing—a basic disposition that never changes and that controls all that he does. This has to do with commitment. God's kind of love is not a sometime thing, tentative and sporadic. It does not run out. His covenantal love is from youth to old age, from generation to generation, from age to age, from eternity to eternity. This unending love is faithful through all kinds of circumstances, even rejection. Biblical love, then, is not a passing emotion, but a way of life, a disposition, a relationship of permanent commitment to the welfare of another.

There is yet another element in the internal aspect of biblical love: loving feelings motivate. In fact, it is not too much to say that love is the only motive. At the root of every choice, every action a person takes, lies love. It may be purely from love of self that a person takes action, or it may be other-love. But always love is the dynamic that propels, the catalyst that transforms thought into action.

Some speak of the glory of God as a motive. But strictly speaking, glory is not a motive. If I seek my wife's glory, for example, my motive may be my own glory. If she is highly thought of, I will be more praiseworthy for having caught her and kept her. Of course, I may seek to put her in the best light before others because I love her, not me. But the *motive* is not *her* glory. The motive is *my* love, one way or the other. In the same way, the great commission is said to be a motive. But I may obey any command of God because I love me—it is the smart thing to do. A pastor may work himself into an ulcer to build his own reputation on earth or in heaven. I may give generously for the impression it will make on others or witness for fear of the consequences if I do not. Thus, I may seek my own glory because I love me. Or I may be totally indifferent to how people think of me. I may prefer pleasure. Or money. But money, pleasure, honor do not motivate; they are the means by which I may seek my own fulfillment. The same is true of seeking God's fulfillment, or my neighbor's. The basic drive, the mainspring, the motive of all human action is love.

Bible treats self-love and other-love and how the conflict between them may be resolved. But at this point it is important to identify how biblical love is a feeling, a disposition, and a motive.

Our focus on the internal aspects of love is immediately shifted to the external by the term *motive.* Motivated to what? To act. So we now turn from love as an inner response to love as a description of how a love-motivated person behaves.

The Bible emphasizes what love does more than how love feels. This is no doubt why those who translated the Hebrew Old Testament into Greek chose the colorless agape over the strong, vibrant eros and the warm, affectionate philia. Agape had this going for it: It emphasized choice, action. The others did not. Eros (not to be restricted to contemporary definitions of erotic or sexually oriented affections) was so passionate as to be compared with intoxication. There was no choice, no will, no freedom for the man seized by the tyrannical omnipotence of eros. But agape referred to a free and decisive act determined by the subject himself, not by the drawing power of the object, as in the case of passionate eros or warm, but duty-bound philia. The primary characteristic of biblical love is action.

In the New Testament, as in the Old, loving is often linked with obeying—the outward response of an inward condition of love. We are commanded to love. "You shall love the LORD your God. . . . You shall love your neighbor as yourself" (Lev. 19:18; Deut. 6:5; Matt. 22:37-39). "If you love me, you will keep my commandments" (John 14:15). "For this is the love of God, that we keep his commandments" (1 John 5:3; 2 John 6). The first question Scripture asks is not, How do you feel about this person? but, rather, What choices must you make concerning this person? What commitment will you fulfill? How can you better promote their best? How can you reflect [5]the unwavering love of God in this relationship? The answer to this transforms the most mundane life!

---

[5] IBE (2014), 32.

February 19
Lying
John 14:6

"Jesus said to him, "I am the way, and the truth, and the life. No one comes to the Father except through me." (John 14:6)

Quantified estimates of lying range from 2 per day to 200! Perhaps some lie about lying. Regardless, lying is prevalent. The basic evil of deception is that it denies the character of God who is truth (Heb. 6:18). Jesus said, *"I am the truth"* (John 14:6). He also said the word of God is the embodiment of truth (John 17:17). God is utterly reliable. This is the foundation of a coherent universe.

If God may be described as *"the truth,"* Satan may be described as *"the father of lies"* (John 8:44). He is the original lie incarnate, and his use of deceit is for the purpose of destruction. It is ideally designed to achieve that end, for every break with reality is inherently destructive. Destruction is what every liar achieves and finally experiences, first in himself, then in his relationships, and finally in the judgment he receives from a holy God.

There is no more sure method to destroy character than to deceive. But are there in fact no biblical exceptions to the law against deception? Before examining the biblical texts, let us review two important facts.

The basic sin is deception, not merely the deliberate verbal expression of falsehood. Words can be in conformity to facts and still be designed to deceive. Words can be apparently out of conformity with the facts and be true. *The other ground rule we follow is to recognize that Scripture alone must be our guide, and that cuts both ways.* If Scripture truly allows no exceptions, then we must allow none, no matter how poignant the circumstances. But if Scripture justifies exceptions to any law or principle, then we must not try to be "more spiritual" than Scripture.

My contention is that the Bible does justify deception in three categories: inconsequential social arrangements, war, and in opposing criminal activity. If these exceptions are valid biblically, then to deceive in these circumstances in any way, including verbally, is no evil to be confessed, but legitimate moral behavior.

- **Inconsequential Social Arrangements.** When Christ acted as if he would go on, but did not intend to (Luke 24:28 ff.), or when he instructed his disciples to use a little "makeup," so as not to appear as if they had been fasting (Matt. 6:17-18), he apparently did not consider these sinful deception.

Many of our greetings and social expressions are of this nature. Those who lay heavy burdens of explicit veracity on casual social exchange do not help the cause of truth.

If the biblical evidence for legitimate deception in inconsequential social arrangements is not abundant, either for or against (possibly for the very reason that it *is* inconsequential), this lack cannot be alleged against the case for deception in war.

- **Deception in War.** War by its very nature is waged with all available weapons, including psychology and deception. God himself wages war this way. He not only told Joshua to set an ambush (Joshua 8:2), a very deadly deception, he himself set an ambush on at least one occasion (2 Chron. 20:22). Elisha and God worked together on a project in which the prophet told the enemy troops, "This is not the way and this is not the city," when in fact it was the city.

Some have argued that Rahab was commended for her faith, not for her activity. Apart from the fact that all three of these passages say explicitly that it was *because* of what she did, how is it possible so to divorce faith and works? In fact, James, who emphasized not divorcing faith and works, said explicitly of Rahab that she was justified for what she did (as evidence of her faith) (James 2:25).

If war is legitimate, then ambushes, camouflage, spying, deceptive strategy, communicating in code, as integral parts of war, are also legitimate.

- **Deception in Opposing Criminals.** Deception is apparently one form of resistance that, like physical resistance, is ordinarily wrong, but not wrong in resisting a criminal or an enemy in war.

The Hebrew midwives resisted an ungodly and oppressive regime by disobedience and lying. For this "God dealt well with the midwives" (Exod. 1:15-21). How can it be said that their faith was good and their subversive activity bad? Or how can it be said that their disobedience was good and their lie bad? The Bible does not make such distinctions. It just says that God approved.

If a homeowner, away on a trip, leaves a timer on his light system to deceive potential robbers into believing a lie (that he is home), surely he does not sin. Deceptive police activity is a good thing when needed to apprehend a criminal.

One does not make exception to any biblical law on the basis of what may appear reasonable or loving. If exceptions are made, they are made on the basis of exceptions sanctioned by Scripture. In this way any exception is guaranteed by Scripture and cannot spill out and contaminate the rest of life with deception whenever it seems to the deceiver to be reasonable, loving, worthy, or necessary to achieve some good end.

I conclude, then, that it is a sin, a violation of the ninth commandment, to deliberately deceive someone whom Scripture gives no right to deceive. And though I am not under obligation to enlighten everyone on every subject on which I may have knowledge, I have no right deliberately to attempt to deceive in any manner anyone except in mutually agreed upon social arrangements, an enemy in war, and in resisting criminal activity.

We have dealt in some detail with possible exceptions to the law of truth because these matters are of such crucial importance to our daily lives and are so hotly debated among equally learned and committed believers.

God is the ultimate reality, and his reliability is what enables the world to hold together and make sense. If he were unstable and random, let alone deliberately deceptive and capricious, the world would be not simply an erratic rogue world—it would not cohere at all. It could not exist.

And so it is with our lives. To the extent we conform to reality, to that extent we live. To the extent we split from reality, especially when we consciously choose the untrue, to that extent we destroy and are destroyed. That is why God demands integrity and hates every form of dishonesty. To love the truth is to hate the lie. May we find our way out into the bright light and pure beauty of God, the trustworthy one, that we may be re-created by his Spirit into his own likeness, into people who are trustworthy.

February 20
How Must I Love?
Ephesians 4:29

"Do not let any unwholesome talk come out of your mouths, but only what is helpful for building others up according to their needs, that it may benefit those who listen." (Ephesians 4:29 NIV)

Most of us agree: "Do not murder" (Ex. 20:13). But we'll make a surprising discovery: we are all murderers! I hope no one doing this devotional will ever take someone's life, but there are many other ways to kill.

Each command in the Ten Commandments is like an onion, especially the one forbidding murder. Here's why. You can peel back layer after layer of that tear-inducing little vegetable, but all the way to the core, it's still an onion. It may not cause the same volume of tears, but it's the same vegetable.

So let's peel back the various layers of killing to discover what God had in mind in forbidding it. This commandment is so important for all of our relationships, let's take a look.

A direct attack on a person with criticism or depreciation, or sarcasm, or subtle insinuation can destroy something in that person. But just as deadly is the criticism or gossip spoken about a person to others. The law of love seals the lips. Any word that harms another is murder of character. Any rebuke must be spoken in love for the other person's well-being or edification (Eph. 4:29: *Let no corrupting talk come out of your mouths, but only such as is good for building up, as fits the occasion, that it may give grace to those who hear*) not simply to vent one's emotions. Speaking the truth in love will be constructive (Eph. 4:15, 29). Confronting someone who is wrong must be done discreetly and in a spirit of humility and grace, directed only to the believer in the wrong (Matt. 18:15-18; Gal. 6:1). Instead of engaging in a spirit of gossip, the absent person must be just as "safe" with the Spirit-directed child of God as when he is present with him.

Another way to harm is by doing and saying nothing when a word or an action would keep from harm. Failure to put a balustrade or parapet around a flat rooftop brought blood guiltiness if someone fell from the roof (Deut. 22:8). Failure to do good, when in one's power to do so, is sin (Prov. 3:27-28). So the poor, the helpless, and the starving are my responsibility to the extent I have ability to help. To be silent when another is falsely accused, whether in a court of law or in the presence of private gossip, is to participate in the harm. Neglect, then, is another form of murder (see also Exod. 21:29-31).

Incredibly, Christ's commentary on the sixth commandment includes a person's inner state. Contemptuous anger is subject to God's judgment (Matt. 5:22). This was not original with Jesus. Moses had already recorded God's will, "You shall not hate your brother in your heart…or bear any grudge against the sons of your own people, but you shall love your neighbor as yourself" (Lev. 19:17-18). Lack of love, as well as positive hatred, is a form of murder. How does this work with anger? First, this concrete action seeks to transforms the *angry person* from being trapped in the vicious cycle of anger into actively seeking to be a peacemaker with his enemy. Secondly, it transforms not only the angry person, but also the *relationship*—a relationship once marked by hatred, anger, and division and now transformed into one characterized by continued forgiveness and reconciliation. Finally, the goal is to transform the *enemy* himself into a friend. Which layer do you need to peel back? Anger? Criticism? Demeaning? Gossip? Or do you need to speak up about some harm to another? How can you pray today to love better?

February 21
The Lovers
1 Corinthians 13:13

"But the greatest of these is love." (1 Corinthians 13:13)

Today, let us consider lovers. This is the deepest longing of contemporaries, perhaps of any generation, is an intimate, enduring love relationship. Trust is often broken; hope is in short supply.

Several years ago I read about a New York Times reporter who wanted to report on street people, and he didn't want to report on something he hadn't experienced. So he went out one winter night, it was getting cold and dark and darker. So he went around behind one of the buildings to find a heat vent. And sure enough, there's a heat vent. But there was a street man on it. Well, the man moved over and invited him to share the heat vent with him. And then he said "a warm place on a winter night, that's the only thing." Then he paused and said. "Course, if you had somebody to care for you. That'll be even only-ier."

That's the longing of our human heart to love and be loved. Consider the purpose God had in creating you on his pattern. Wasn't it to enable a tight love relationship? Lovers, to be truly one must be compatible. So he created us God compatible. So he could enfold us in His love. He could hardly become one with a monkey. So he created us on his pattern. But that's not the only the goal of creation, it's the goal of redemption. A restored image to make possible that love relationship. That's what God is about. Always has been, always will be.

If the secret to a happy marriage is each living to fill up the other, my question for you this morning is this, How is your love relationship with God? You may be happy enough, but is He happy with your relationship? Is your marriage to God mostly one sided? Day and night he's filling you and you doing very little to fulfill him? Fulfill God? God is complete. What could you add to him?

The vulnerability of love is that God feels loss. God hurts. God feels happy. God feels sad. As the prophet Isaiah said. "In all their distress, He too was distressed. In his love and mercy he redeemed them, yet they rebelled and grieved his Holy Spirit." God feels your pain.

So how does the bride of Christ look to you? Divided, bickering, self-centered, dirty with the world values, unfaithful, disfigured, from self-inflicted wounds. And the Prince all glorious- what a deal? Oh, I know we should become like him when we see him as he is. We will be transformed without spot or blemish. That's true. But what about today? Do you bring him sadness today or joy? The good news is this, no matter how ugly and split up, the church as a whole may look to itself or to outsiders. No matter how misguided and impotent. We as individuals can come to that final celebration with gifts that bring him joy.

We don't pursue holiness and give our best for Kingdom advance to earn merit. It's a love gift to Jesus. That's why we do it. That's why we pursue holiness of life. But what about the how? Well, there are two false views that prevail on the how. God does it all. I must do it all or it's all of grace. It's all up to me. We're tempted to move toward one of these extremes or the other instead of settling on the biblical center. God does it, of course. It won't be done, but I participate with all my heart, with all my soul, with all my mind, or it won't happen. And why do I do it? Because I love him. We were created for that. We were redeemed for that. The ultimate goal of life is not power packed ministry. As exciting as that is, nor is the goal to become ever more godly in character. Because the holy life is a means toward the ultimate goal. For only as we are like him, God compatible, can we respond in the kind of loving intimacy He designed us for. Compatibility. That's the key to a happy marriage, isn't it? Sad the marriage where a husband and wife have no shared interests, no common values, no passionate commitment to the same goals, no special time or loving companionship. A miserable coexistence under one roof. Strangers or divorce. Incompatibility, the legal documents say. And thus it is with God and you. He wants you to be like him, God compatible, so you can be intimate .

What are you going say to God? Oh, we call it prayer. Let's start with Thanksgiving. Did you ever notice that children are not naturally thankful little guys? They just expect their parents to be there for them to buy it all they need and they certainly are not thankful for the spankings. So we have to grow up to a love relationship in which we tell our lover constantly of our gratitude.

But did you notice that Thanksgiving is me oriented? It is what God has done for me. Now that's a wonderful place to begin, but it's a dreadful place to end. So there's affirmation, praise, adoration.

And we learn that the heavy heart lifts on the wings of praise. Thanksgiving, praise, adoration- we call that kind of communication worship. But I think he intends something beyond worship. Something utterly astounding. Intimate companionship. He wants us to grow in knowing him, loving him, exulting in his companionship, delighting that every gift that he sends. Daily relishing his love letter to us. The goal of all that transforming grace is to be his intimate companion. Lovers. Today and every tomorrow.

February 22
Magnificent Gift Exchange
Isaiah 58:13 & 14

"If you turn back your foot from the Sabbath, from doing your pleasure on my holy day, and call the Sabbath a delight and the holy day of the LORD honorable; if you honor it, not going your own ways, or seeking your own pleasure, or talking idly; then you shall take delight in the LORD, and I will make you ride on the heights of the earth" (Isaiah 58:13-14a)

God gives his beloved children many wonderful gifts, few more wonderful than the one honored in Isaiah 58. And in the same passage we find an incredible gift we are invited to give him. God gives us the gift of rest and we give the gift of time to him, a magnificent gift exchange. It is a marvel that he would give us an audience with himself, let alone that he would desire our companionship. He tells us to set aside from ordinary, mundane use one-seventh of our time and thus honor him by honoring his special day. Just as we give a portion of our possessions to him on a regular basis as a token of the fact that all we have belongs to him, so we give him a portion of our time on a regular basis as a token of the fact that all our time is his.

Since he owns all our money and we recognize that in theory, we do not conclude that therefore we do not need to set aside anything at all to prove that ownership. We do not ask how little we can give to one we love, but how much. I don't try to figure how I can reduce time spent with my wife without losing her affection or our marriage. So it is with our loving father. And since the visible, mundane responsibilities and pleasures of life tend to crowd out the invisible, he has set aside a portion as "holy." A holy pot, for example, was set aside from ordinary use for ceremonial use in the temple. A holy person was set aside for special service. So the holy day was set aside from ordinary use to provide a time for rest and "joy in the Lord" (v 14), worship of him and companionship with him.

Such a wonderful gift--time set aside to rest and restore a troubled mind and tired body and time to renew and deepen our relationship with our beloved. But neither his gift to us nor our gift to him will ever be realized without certain conditions.

The gift of rest is packaged in a law and only in that package is it deliverable. If it were merely a helpful hint, a suggestion we would accept it and honor it so long as other pressures did not demand that same block of time. And it is precisely those other pressures, those demands upon me, that make the gift of rest so essential and so welcome. Only a law frees me to carefully safeguard that time. Otherwise, I would be pressured into using it to fulfill the many other obligations that pile up. But is it a law?

Bear in mind <u>when</u> the Rest Day began. What it was in the nature of God that caused him to stop his creative activity and rest, to turn inward, so to speak? Perhaps there was something in the relationships among the Father, the Son and the blessed Spirit that called for such. It began with God's own action at the end of his initial creative activity. <u>Therefore,</u> God blessed the Rest Day, set it apart, honored it, hallowed it.

God holds out a gift to us, and we turn away. God waits eagerly for our gift of a special time for him, and we squander it all on ourselves. Isn't it sad? Why do Christian people trash God's beautiful gift? Selfish--the theme of this passage. But it isn't even smart selfishness. In the end the one avoiding the Rest Day impoverishes himself above all.

But what of the one who accepts God's gift of a special time set aside meticulously for rest and refreshment of body and spirit and who carefully gives to God the gift of a special, regular time for fellowship with him? Oh, joy! God himself will <u>cause</u> you to ride high and to feast bountifully.

February 23
Love of God
Matthew 22:27

"Love the Lord your God with all your heart" (Matthew 22:37)

Christ tells us that this is the supreme objective: "Love the Lord your God with all your heart" (Matt. 22:37). This is the first command, first in importance, and the greatest, superseding all others as the controlling authority of life. Thus the Old Testament command (Deut. 6:5) identified by the teachers of Israel as the ultimate, comprehensive summary of God's will for man was affirmed by Jesus the Messiah as the most important commandment of all.

How does a mere human being love the infinite God? By the loving adoration of worship, by unceasing thanksgiving, by a life of steadfast obedience, by sharing his companionship and exulting in the endless profusion of his gifts. This is the goal of creation and redemption: to love God. Not so much to find my fulfillment, but to find his, to bring him joy, to seek his purposes, to do his will.

Indeed, to love God is the first and great commandment, but it is not the only commandment. The "law and the prophets" do not depend on this alone. There is another commandment. And, in truth, one cannot obey the first without obeying the second (Matt. 22:34-40; 1 John 3:11-18; 4:19–5:1 5:1). But how do we understand love?

"God is love," says John (1 John 4:8, 16). This is the basic difference between the biblical concept of love and our concept of love. The Bible defines love by the nature of God. We tend to define love by the nature of man.

To say that God is love does not mean that God *equals* love. Love does not describe God exhaustively. He has other qualities, such as wisdom and strength; but this does not mean that those characteristics in God's nature violate love. God always acts lovingly, even in judgment.

Again, "God is love" does not mean that *love equals God.* Love is not an entity, having existence as an object, let alone having personality. To say that love and God are equivalent would deify love and make it some absolute concept to which God himself is subject and by which he could be judged. Both situation ethics and Christian Science would tend to do this. Rather, love gains whatever stature it has because God is that way. He forms the concept by his nature. He is the source of all true love (1 John 4:7, 19). Since God himself defines love, true human love is godlikeness (1 John 4:16).

God was not obliged to love by some external "ought." Loving is the way he is. This is one of the greatest evidences for the Trinity. God the Father loves God the Son and God the Holy Spirit from all eternity. God the Son loves the Father and the Spirit, and the Spirit loves the Son and the Father. Thus, by love they are bound, and only out of love for others was that unity broken at the Cross when, by the power of the Spirit, the Son assumed our guilt, and the Father turned away in judicial rejection from part of his very being.

The loving nature of God is the basis for his creative and redeeming activity. He created man because he is love and desired a being designed on his own pattern so that he could love that creature and be freely loved in return. When man rejected this loving approach of God, breaking that relationship, God continued loving because God is love by nature. And so we have the story of redemption. Love became incarnate. Thus, all of life finds meaning in being loved by God and loving him.

By his life, Jesus demonstrated flawlessly how godlike love behaves, and in his death he demonstrated the ultimate proof of love. He was our model—we can now *see* how we are to "walk in love, as Christ loved us and gave himself up for us, a fragrant offering and sacrifice to God" (Eph. 5:1-2). We now can *see* what it means to have the kind of mind-set that was his who "being in very nature God, did not consider equality with God something to be grasped, but made himself nothing, taking the very nature of a servant, being made in human likeness. And being found in appearance as a man, he humbled himself and became obedient to death—even death on a cross!" (Phil. 2:6-8, NIV). "By this we know love, that he laid down his life for us; and we ought to lay down our lives for the brethren" (1 John 3:16). Throughout the New Testament Christ's love is given as our model: "This is my commandment, that you love one another as I have loved you" (John 15:12).

All of Christ's life puts on display God's loving character, but the Cross of Christ demonstrates the love of God more clearly than any other act of any other person in all history.

Christ himself is the perfect, living model of God's character; but God graciously re-creates that character in other people who, in turn, demonstrate true love. In fact, "By this all men will know that you are my disciples, if you have love for one another" (John 13:35). [6]

Do you know His love? Do you trust His love? Can you walk in and display His love?

---

[6] IBE (2014), 43.

February 24
God's Standard for Marriage
Exodus 20:12&14

Honor thy father and thy mother, that your days may be long in the land that the Lord your God is giving you. Thou shalt not commit adultery. (Exodus 20:12&14)

God's standards on human sexuality are treated in Scripture as the most important of all rules for relations among people. In the Old Testament, teaching against adultery is emphasized second only to teaching against idolatry. In the New Testament, both Christ and the apostles emphasized marital fidelity. Paul includes sexual sins in every one of his many lists of sins, and in most cases they head the list and receive the greatest emphasis. Why does the Bible view this relationship between the sexes as so important?

Sexual fidelity, more than most virtues, clearly demonstrates the purpose of law: man's welfare. Human sexuality is one of God's most delightful gifts. But the sordid record of human history and the anguish of personal experience highlight the basic reality that this joy is reserved for those who "follow the Manufacturer's instructions."

This outcome is not surprising because human nature was designed to reflect divine nature, and God's law is simply his expressed will that people conform to the moral nature of God. This reflection of the divine nature is many-faceted. "Image" includes the moral nature of God—and therefore fidelity and purity—but it also includes the ability to think rationally, to create, to love and be loved, and to communicate. Among these characteristics of God-similarity may be included human sexuality: "So God created man in his own image, in the image of God he created him; male and female he created them" (Gen. 1:27). The grammatical structure of this sentence does not demand a direct link between the two ideas. All that is certain is that God created human beings in some way similar to himself, and that he created humans in two different models: male and female.

Some have built an entire doctrine on the mistaken notion that this verse defines "image" as the male/female characteristic. Though Scripture does not present this as the only or even the paramount element of likeness to God, some contemporary interpreters seem to hold that this is the chief meaning of "image." "Image," in this view, means that man is a being-in-fellowship, as in the Trinity, and that male/female fellowship is the highest and best variety of fellowship. Even though this verse does not prove such a thesis, I think we are warranted in finding here and elsewhere in Scripture the idea that the maleness and the femaleness and their relationship, in some mysterious way, reflect God's own nature.

The truth is that Scripture nowhere defines "image" nor explains the concept. But certainly, since the Trinity is one, yet three, and the three are cemented in a relationship of loving commitment, we can see in the Godhead the ideal model for biblical marriage. Human marriage seems designed deliberately to reflect the eternal reality of the best of all relationships—that of the Father, the Son, and the Holy Spirit and of God's relationship with us.

If marriage laws reflect the very nature of God and were expressly designed for man's best interests, why are these standards the most often violated? Does anything demonstrate more clearly man's independent, arrogant, foolish, perverse, blind, and demonic fallenness?

We devote throughout the year, more attention to the topic of sex, marriage, and the home for several reasons. In the first place, we have combined the consideration of two of the Ten Commandments (the fifth and seventh). Furthermore, this is the area of life that seems to be most under assault by the powers of evil. We seem most vulnerable here, and we must do all within our power to mobilize the forces of our biblical understanding, of our combined

Christian commitment, and of the concerted action of right-thinking people to defend this basic building block of personal and social well-being. [7] What can you do to promote loving commitment in your own marriage or of those around you? How can you pray today for marriages you know and for those in your culture?

February 25
Male and Female
Genesis 1:27

So God created man in his own image, in the image of God he created him; male and female he created them. (Genesis 1:27)

The most obvious distinction between male and female is biological. Some say it is the only distinction and that other distinctions are made by society.

Certainly, distinctions are made by society; some are biblically valid, and some are not. Surely it is legitimate to have an all-male football team. Certainly, it is not fair to pay a woman less than a man for identical work. But are there innate psychological characteristics unique to each sex?

Traditionally, most societies have held that there are. Is it not reasonable to assume that physical characteristics that enable a woman to bear and nurture children should be accompanied in the design of the Creator by an inner disposition to reinforce those roles? The greater size and strength of the male may indicate something of the role intended by the Maker. But these assumptions have been strongly challenged. The new folk wisdom, following the behavioral scientists, holds that all psychological distinctions between the sexes have been socialized; they are acquired characteristics, not inherent. If the early environment conditioned all girls in a society to be dominant and aggressive and to assume leadership roles, that is exactly the way women would be. Though the Bible in places seems to assume the traditional viewpoint, it nowhere gives a clear-cut answer to this question. So we may safely classify the issue as nonmoral in nature. But what is the significance of the question?

The "unisex" view of human nature recognizes no inherent distinctives apart from the basic physical distinction that all must grant, however reluctantly. Most who advocate the unisex viewpoint are strongly in favor of eliminating all role distinctions. Roles based directly on the biological functions necessary to fathering and mothering (perhaps "inseminating" and "bearing" would be more accurate descriptions) are accepted, but all other role distinctions are negotiable, dispensable, and may, in fact, be pernicious, according to this view. If the Bible is silent on the question of innate characteristics, is it equally silent on the question of role differences?

Role Distinctions. There is no distinction between male and female as image-bearer: Each is equally designed on the divine pattern (Gen. 1:27). Each is equally a sinner, equally under judgment, equally redeemable, and equally a potential recipient of God's grace. Further, "in Christ Jesus" there is "neither male nor female" (Gal. 3:28). This verse is the cornerstone of the Christian feminist movement, and thus the meaning is greatly debated. Perhaps the expression

---

[7] IBE (20014), 219-220.

"in Christ Jesus" means simply, "as a Christian" or "before God" or is equivalent to "joint heirs" (1 Pet. 3:7). If so, the meaning is simply that God does not discriminate along sex lines in dispensing grace. This is the interpretation of most Bible scholars. But some hold that Paul here eliminates all role distinctions for the Christian. This interpretation, however, is too heavy a superstructure to build on a verse that also says, "In Christ there is no Jew or Greek, no bond or free." Paul could have added, no adult or child, no teacher or disciple, no elder or younger. But this does not keep Paul from elsewhere insisting on the distinct role responsibilities in one's position. In fact, he consistently insists on the unique responsibilities of servant and master, parent and child, teacher and disciple, elder and younger, husband and wife.

What role distinction, then, does Scripture make between the sexes? The hotly disputed question of roles in church governance does not fall within the scope of this book. But whatever role distinction Scripture may make in the home and in the church, it is unwarranted to extend these to society at large on the basis of biblical authority. One may see a paradigm of male/female relationships in the biblical model for marriage and apply this to civic or business relationships, but he may not do this on the basis of biblical authority, for the Bible is silent on the issue of female leadership in business, industry, or government. How much more distant from scriptural teaching is the ridiculous and altogether pernicious idea that every woman must be subordinate to any man with whom she is related.

God authorized certain women to be judges, prophets, and teachers, so there is nothing inherently sinful in such roles for women on some occasions: Miriam (Exod. 15:20), Deborah (Judg. 4:4), Huldah (2 Kings 22:14 ff.; 2 Chron. 34:22 ff.), Noadiah (Neh. 6:14), Isaiah's wife (Isa. 8:3), Anna (Luke 2:36-38), Philip's four daughters (Acts 21:9), Priscilla (Acts 18:24 ff.), and many other women (1 Cor. 11:5; Acts 2:17). The issue we must address here is the question: Is it a sin for a woman ever to be cast in a role of leadership over men? The question—at least outside the realm of the home and the church—cannot be argued from Scripture on moral grounds. Those who address the issue must do so from pragmatic or other grounds. The only possible way for Scripture to be introduced would be in drawing analogies from what the Bible teaches about husband/wife relationships, but such analogies must not be pressed as having scriptural authority. Let us not go outside Biblical grounds for placing women in subordinate roles. Oppression is not God's intent in establishing male and female.

February 26
Damages
Colossians 3:5

Put to death therefore what is earthly in you: sexual immorality, impurity, passion, evil desire, and covetousness, which is idolatry. (Colossians 3:5)

What are some ways coveting spiritually damages the coveter? Covetousness leads to all kinds of evil and is self-destructive. Here's the way it might work:

- To desire something that is not in the will of God for me is to put that object ahead of God, to make an idol of it. Paul called covetousness idolatry in Colossians 3:5: "Put to death therefore what is earthly in you: sexual immorality, impurity, passion, evil desire, and covetousness, which is idolatry."
- To covet is to profane God's name—giving a false image of Him by telling others His will for me is not adequate and He lacks wisdom, power, or love to provide what I need.
- Dishonoring parents begins with desiring for myself something that might benefit them.
- I kill with a gun, a word, or an attitude because someone stands in the way of what I covet.
- The tenth commandment says not to covet my neighbor's wife. What is adultery or lust but a synonym for sexual covetousness? In fact, the New Testament uses the same Greek term for both *lust* and *covet*.
- Stealing is the direct outcome of coveting.
- I lie to or deceive others to gain something I covet.

Why don't you ponder before God which commands covetousness has led you to violate in the past six months. This root sin stands opposite Jesus' commandments to love God and others (see Matt. 22:37-39). Covetousness is interested in getting; love is interested in giving. Covetousness is also a sin against the person who covets. Contentment is great gain (see 1 Tim. 6:6); discontent, great impoverishment.

Think of a time when you felt that you had to have a particular material object, but after a while the satisfaction faded. Why did the satisfaction go away?

Covetousness illustrates the basic principle that God's laws are for our good. A covetous person stays in inner turmoil. In fact, covetousness often leads to emotional illness. Materialism is a very frustrating way of life because you can never be satisfied. The more you get, the more you want. Of all foolish and frustrating activities, seeking to fill the void in one's spirit with material things must rank near the top. As followers of Christ, we must give priority to spiritual realities and combat the inner drive for material things. How far does God expect us to go in denying our desire for possessions?

But tangible objects aren't the only things we are tempted to covet. A covetous spirit is visible in those who steal, to be sure, but the Bible also identifies other violations of the tenth commandment. Examples are demeaning others, lusting sexually, fighting with a Christian brother to recover material losses, scheming and plotting to make unjust gain, pursuing recognition, being discontented, and giving sparingly or grudgingly. You can see why covetousness serves as the root to feed all other disobedience to God.

Perhaps envy is the most virulent form of covetousness found among believers. We may not covet our neighbor's wife, but how about those wonderful children who turned out so well? Maybe we don't covet his car or house, but what about his success in life? Envy is a deadly cancer of the spirit. That's why God carved in stone, "Do not covet" (Ex. 20:17). To help you apply this command, why don't you list the things you most envy. Then number them in order of the power they hold over you. Pray for God to free you from this destructive mindset.

February 27
Victim or Victor?
Ephesians 4:13

"...until we all reach unity in the faith and in the knowledge of the Son of God and become mature, attaining to the whole measure of the fullness of Christ." (Ephesians 4:13)

I was interviewing Jim, a counselor in a large church, as a prospective teacher. "A counselor friend tells me," I said, "that some people can't respond to God in obedience and faith because their chooser is broken. They can't choose God's way till a therapist helps restore their ability to make choices. What do you think of that idea?" (I didn't tell him my friend's judgment that perhaps five percent of Christians are in that situation). Jim agreed enthusiastically. So I asked him, "About what percent of the members of your church are in that category?" "Oh," he said, "perhaps 80-90 percent."

When I asked Drew, head of a large counseling staff in a megachurch, the same question, he replied: "We operate on the basis that everyone has the ability to make choices, unless a person has mental problems of an organic nature. The Bible assumes that people can, with divine assistance, respond to God's commands and are responsible to do so. We build our therapy on that biblical assumption." With whom do you agree?

The church is full of hurting people, some battered more than others. Most of us could use help toward healing, some by a skilled counselor. When a person is blind to his own sinful behavior, or her "chooser" is so damaged it can't function, or his "truster" is so violated he can't get through to God, a counselor may be able to help him see himself, others, and God in clearer perspective. Then that person can begin to trust God and choose God's alternative. However, when we begin to use human brokenness as an excuse to disobey God and remain in our patterns of sin, we do ourselves and others a severe disservice.

Jim and Drew have widely different expectations of the Christian life. A lowered expectation of what the Holy Spirit can do may come from treating people as victims like Jim did, rather than as responsible individuals as Drew did. We can easily see where lowered expectations of Holy Spirit-generated possibilities come from. Americans in general believe less and less in sin and guilt, more and more in a battered psyche that needs healing. We believe we are no longer guilty sinners needing salvation, but victims of someone else's hurtful behavior and need restoration of a healthy self-image.

If we buy into the pattern of viewing ourselves and others as victims, we may block ourselves and others from God. The view of self as a hurting person, damaged by wrongs inflicted by others, may lead persons away from taking responsibility for their feelings or actions. Gradually we descend into denial about our own guilt and personal responsibility to choose right. Lock-down in a black box of other's making. And no exits!

In contrast, Scripture bases its promise of salvation and power-filled Christian living on the assumption that we can respond to God in faith. We can choose His way. Some of us may need more help from the outside than others, and the mission or church should provide that help. But let us never underestimate the power of the Holy Spirit to give us the will and the way so that we can indeed "*work out our own salvation with fear and trembling*" (Phil. 2:12).

The failure syndrome and the victim syndrome are two major paths to expecting less of the Christian life. If I choose to believe that I cannot become an overcomer, that I cannot experience miracle intervention by the Spirit of God, surely my belief will prove self-fulfilling. Don't settle for too low an expectation of what your Christian life can be. Listen to Paul's great proclamation of victory: *Sin shall not have dominion over you*! (Rom. 6:14). He exults in the assurance that *we are more than conquerors* (Rom. 8:37). Incredibly, he promises a life filled by the Spirit to "*all the fullness of God*" (Eph. 3:19). In another passage he describes the Christian life as "*attaining to the whole measure of the fullness of Christ*" (Eph. 4:13)!

These are not isolated proof texts. They reflect the mood of the entire New Testament. Are you keeping a journal of your encounters with God? If so, why not write out your own prayer to him concerning any below-the-line expectations you have. Be very honest. If your expectations are quite low, tell Him so. But don't leave it there; ask for wisdom to understand what Scripture really teaches about what you ought to expect. Pray for the gift of faith to believe His promises. If you are excited about the possibilities, tell Him so. He's delighted to see His children liberated and fulfilled!

February 28
The Law's Purpose
1 Peter 1:14-16

"*As obedient children, do not be conformed to the passions of your former ignorance, but as he who called you is holy, you also be holy in all your conduct, since it is written, "You shall be holy, for I am holy."* (1 Peter 1:14-16)

Why is law to some a hobgoblin of incarnate evil to be exorcised from life, while to others it is the only hope of salvation? What is law's purpose, and how can it be known?

A law is any rule or injunction that must be obeyed. In religion, these rules normally make requirements of a ceremonial or ritual kind and of an ethical or moral kind. In fact, these laws are so prominent in most religions as to be considered the substance of those religions. This was true of the Jewish religious leaders in Christ's day, and it is true in much of Christendom today. Is this the biblical point of view? Certainly, there are many laws in the Bible—more than six hundred Mosaic commandments and more than six hundred direct commandments in the New Testament. Are they rules that must be obeyed? *Can* they be obeyed? If not, for what purpose were they given? Before these and other vital questions can be answered it is important to permit the Bible itself to define the term.

The Bible uses the term *law* in several ways, and often these meanings are not differentiated precisely. In some passages of the New Testament a more specific meaning is clearly seen. Some say there are as many as twelve distinct uses of the term. Here are some of them.

Is the law the expressed will of God that people be like Him morally? God created man in his own image morally. There are, no doubt, other elements in man's likeness to God, but *a morally right character is primary*. It is the basis of shared love and fellowship; it is indispensable to demonstrating in human life the glory (glorious character) of God. Mankind has ever neglected this aspect of God's image and worked to attain likeness to God in his attributes of knowledge and power. This was Satan's temptation to Eve: "*You will be like God*." How? She was already like God in his moral nature. She rejected this likeness in order to reach for God's infinities and from the outset lost both. All her descendants, save one, have followed in her steps. But God's purpose remained the same: He wanted people to be like himself.

This is the purpose of the sovereign Lord, commanded through Moses at the beginning of the Old Covenant and through Jesus Christ at the beginning of the New Covenant: *You must be holy as I am holy* (Lev. 19:2; 1 Pet. 1:16), you must be perfect *as your heavenly Father is perfect* (Matt. 5:48). It is not optional. Since it is a divine imperative, we properly call this will of God *law*.

It is wrong not to be like God morally. This wrong is not just a weakness or an unfortunate deviation from the norm. The Bible calls it sin. To be holy is to be separated from sin; to be right is to be in alignment with God's character. This is the holiness required of men. It is an obligation, not mere instruction or advice. Without it no one will see God (Heb. 12:14).

This most important use of the word *law* is often called the "moral law," God's expressed will concerning what constitutes likeness to God. Does the New Testament use the term in this way?

When Paul speaks of the work of the law being written in the hearts of those who do not have the written law (Rom. 2:14-15), he is speaking of God's moral law. When he says, "*Through the law comes knowledge of sin*" (Rom. 3:20), he is referring to the moral law, or the commandments of God that deal with human behavior. The author of the Letter to the Hebrews sometimes uses the term *law* in the same way: "*I will put my laws into their minds and write them on their hearts*" (Heb. 8:10ff.; 10:16). This is especially significant since the Letter to the Hebrews usually uses *law* to mean the ceremonial system. Of course, one would expect James to use *law* in reference to the right behavior God demands of his people, and he does (James 1:25; 4:11).

This, then, is a common use of the concept of law in the New Testament as well as the Old: God's expressed will that we be like him, commonly called the "moral law." How can you purpose today to conform your behavior to God's commandments? Not in an external adoption for approval rather in an alignment to God's character- our demonstration of what God is like, His character and His rightness.

March 1
Too Low or Too High?
Philippians 3:12

"Not that I have already obtained this or am already perfect, but I press on to make it my own, because Christ Jesus has made me his own." (Philippians 3:12)

"We confess, Lord," the man in the pulpit prayed, "that we your people turn our backs on you and shake our fists in your face every day of our lives." I didn't say the "amen." Would you? In a recent book, *Less Than Conquerors,* the author argues that the best we can expect in the Christian life is struggle and failure. He maintains that anyone who claims more is deluded or hypocritical.

For example, God is inviting me to come to Him just as I am. But if by saying, "He accepts me just the way I am," we mean, "He approves of me the way I am," or, "God accepts me, so what's with you? You've no right to expect me to change," we've missed the whole point of salvation. He accepts me as I am to transform me into what I'm not. He loves me too much to leave me just the way I am. That would be far too low an expectation.

Some people have expectations for the Christian life that are too low because they have been discouraged by their own lack of progress. Maybe they're frustrated with the level of spiritual immaturity they see in themselves and others. At any rate, they just don't believe God changes human beings all that much in this life. I sat under the fist-shaking pastor for a couple of years till it finally dawned on me he believed fervently in justification and glorification but not much in between! These are examples of some of the dangers of aiming too low in our Christian life. But the opposite can derail us, too. Some see the grand promises of Scripture and think they mean we can become sinlessly perfect in this life, perhaps even instantly, through a particular experience. Boris, missionary evangelist, enrolled in our graduate program and wanted me to experience what he had experienced years before when God had eliminated his sin nature. Since he was delivered of all sin, he had preached in mighty power all over the world. I'm not altogether sure why he enrolled in a school in which, he assured me, none of the teachers had experienced such a transforming encounter with God.

In contrast, another preacher who turned the world upside down testified that he had not yet attained perfection (Phil. 3:12). Paul struggled with temptation and weakness. He was sometimes filled with fear, for example, and had more than one squabble with his colleagues. How do we read the same Bible and come up with such different answers? By the way we define sin or perfect. The biblical standard is to be just like God morally (Matt. 5:48). Other attitudes and actions also fail to measure up, such as "sins of omission" (failing to think or do what I ought). Although to sin knowingly is indeed sin, it is nevertheless sinful to have attitudes or actions that are not Christlike, whether I am aware of them or not. We call them "sins of ignorance," but we are not innocent when we sin in ignorance. The biblical standard is to be just like God morally (Matt. 5:48). We would have no problem if people who teach the possibility of perfection in this life meant healthy (like the Smith's new baby) or mature (as in Eph. 4:13) or really good (like the ice cream).

Before pressing on to *"take hold of that for which Christ Jesus took hold of me"* (Phil. 3:12), we need to accept the biblical limitations on our expectations. In this life we'll never be absolutely perfect as God is, without sin, though when we see Jesus we shall be like Him (1 John 3:2). On the other hand, we must never settle for anything short of his promised victorious life in the Spirit. Why not pause and give thanks that the false expectations are false!

Thank you, blessed Spirit, for releasing me from the drivenness and disappointments of unrealistic expectations. Help me to accept my own limitations and those of others. And please, please don't let me swing to the other extreme and settle for less than You intend. I want to be all a redeemed human being can be. And that for Jesus' sake, not just mine!

March 2
The Ultimate Reality
Acts 17:28

"In Him we live and move and exist" (Acts 17:28)

Why does the American legal system fight so hard to prevent the display of the Ten Commandments on government property? Certainly not because these laws forbid killing, stealing, or lying. These are in the horizontal relationships of life. It's the first half of the Commandments that's offensive to secularists, the ones that address our vertical relationship with the Almighty. There the Sovereign of the universe sets forth His demands on His creatures. And that, to the modern mind, is unacceptable religious interference with human rights.

Yet God put the first half first. He did that because our relationship with Him is more important than our relationships with one another. In fact, a right relationship with Him is the only sure foundation on which to build right relationships with one another.

The first four of the Ten Commandments are prohibitions of sin against God because Scripture holds that sin against God is more serious than sin against others. In the first place, sin against God is a violation of our love relationship with the infinite, holy One; it hurts Him. But it not only hurts God; it also hurts us. God is the ultimate reality, the fundamental Being, the integrating factor of the universe. Therefore, to be rightly aligned with Him is the most important relationship in human existence. To be in alignment with God's reality and truth is life; to be out of alignment is destruction and death. Paul told the Athenians, *"In Him we live and move and exist"* (Acts 17:28). To leave God out of the equation of life or to diminish His role is utterly futile. God knows this, so His commandments simply reinforce the facts. He treats this relationship as the most important because it is the most important.

Yet it's not simply a matter of reality and truth. God cares about this relationship. That's why God's people are compared to His wife in the Old Testament and to the bride of Christ in the New Testament. Scripture repeatedly calls God a jealous God; He claimed that Himself in Exodus 20:5. The word for jealous in the Old Testament is the same word used when a husband is jealous for the affection of his wife. This jealousy isn't a petty envy of legitimate competition. It's a profound caring and total unwillingness to allow any other to replace the prior, ultimate love relationship. The term jealous indicates that it makes a difference to God whether we are rightly related to Him.

The first commandment, *"Do not have other gods besides Me"* (Ex. 20:3), has to do with our heart attitude, our thoughts, and our personal relationship with God. But God is also interested in our deeds, what we do about the way we feel. So the second command addresses the way we behave toward God. Furthermore, He is concerned about our words, how we use His name, and what we say about Him, so there's a third commandment. And the fourth sets aside special times in our lives that are devoted to cultivating our relationship with God and centering our lives in Him. These commandments make it clear that God is interested in deeds and words as well as in thoughts. What are some actions in your life indicating that God has first priority for you?

The manifestations of having other gods seem almost limitless. Pride, when I take or accept credit for what God has done. Unbelief—worrying that God can't handle a situation. Or trusting someone else, like myself. To trust my own wisdom or capabilities to accomplish God's will is to displace Him as the trustworthy one. A weak prayer life betrays what we really think about God. What or whom do you enjoy being with more than with God?

March 3
The Original Design
Ephesians 4:24

"*...put on the new self, the one created according to God's likeness in righteousness and purity of the truth*" (Eph. 4:24)

Today we consider three things God does to restore us to His original design. This is the first, when God forgave us of our sins, He declared us innocent, or righteous, because of the blood of Jesus. Scripture says we were justified. Justification is an act of God that pronounces us righteous because of Jesus' sacrifice on the cross. Paul explained that God "made the One who did not know sin to be sin for us, so that we might become the righteousness of God in Him" (2 Cor. 5:21). We were justified when we placed our faith in Jesus as Savior.

We can't make that claim when it comes to sin. The only analogy that would illustrate human justification in the biblical sense would be a man whose older brother persuaded the judge to let him take the just sentence of his younger brother, and the judge set the younger brother free. He could never be rearrested and serve time for the crime. It was paid for him, so he was justified. In the same way, believers are justified, judicially declared to be what we can't be experientially. Because we have a substitute who paid our penalty for sin, we are declared innocent. So God is just and at the same time the justifier of those who trust in Jesus: "God presented Him to demonstrate His righteousness at the present time, so that He would be righteous and declare righteous the one who has faith in Jesus" (Rom. 3:26). I see my sins and deeply grieve, but God, the righteous Judge, sees only Jesus. In God's eyes I'm not a stumbling, polluted sinner but as pure and holy and guiltless as Jesus! How does being justified through Jesus' righteousness give you hope in the Christian life?

The second thing God does to restore us to His original design is to make us a new creation. I was visiting a friend who was totally despondent. Louise asked me if I thought she had been born again. Jeda, a friend, had told her she wasn't. "I don't feel or think or talk like a Christian. What do you think?"

Louise reviewed the gospel with me and had no question about her faith in Jesus, her forgiveness, and her justification. But she was unsure of regeneration: "I wouldn't be this way if I'd been born again, would I?" Though miserable and probably mistaken, she's on to something. Scripture says, "*If anyone is in Christ, he is a new creation; old things have passed away, and look, new things have come*" (2 Cor. 5:17). I think Louise is a born-again believer, safe in Jesus, but she is right to ask the question because a new creation isn't supposed to think and behave in the same ways she used to. Maybe we should join Louise and ask what evidence of regeneration is present in our lives.

The third thing God does to restore us to his original design is that new things are born in your life. The change made by the Spirit in the core person is radical—so radical that you could liken it to a death. The beloved spouse who is strapped to the hospital gurney is the same person who, moments later, is free and fulfilled in the presence of the Lord. What new completeness, dimensions of being, glorious relationships, expansion of boundaries! And so with the one who has "*died with Christ*" (Rom. 6:8). The old sinful nature is dead. Paul taught in his letter to the Romans that just as death no longer ruled over Christ after He rose from the dead, "*you too consider yourselves dead to sin but alive to God in Christ Jesus*" (v. 11).

The change made by the Spirit in the core person is so radical that you could also liken it to a birth. That's why Jesus told Nicodemus he must be born again to enter the kingdom of God (see John 3:5). The nine-month-old fetus and the newborn are the same person but what radical new dimensions of being! New potentials, new relationships, new systems of nourishment, new expansion of boundaries! And so with the newborn in Christ. Paul said we "*put on the new self, the one created according to God's likeness in righteousness and purity of the truth*" (Eph. 4:24). Justified, regenerated and reborn! That is transformation! Why not celebrate today?

March 4
Why?
Psalm 139:16-17

"All the days ordained for me were written in your book before one of them came to be. How precious to me are your thoughts, God! How vast is the sum of them! " (Psalm 139:16-17)

So, why us, Lord? Perhaps you wonder why God allowed some adversity into your life. My beloved Muriel, at 55, twenty years too soon, with Alzheimer's. There are various theories. One alumnus said it was God's judgment on me for allowing contemporary Christian music on our radio station. I don't feel guilty about that, but I do know circumstances contrary to our desires are always intended to make us more like Jesus, and God has surely used these two decades of lingering grief to develop in me more Jesus-like attitudes and behavior where there are deficiencies. Of late I've begun to wonder if the Lord put me under "house arrest" so I'd do something my busy life didn't allow much of- writing books and articles. Of course, whatever other purposes God has in sending or permitting adversity, there is always the purpose of bringing God glory, either through his mighty deliverance from suffering or his mighty deliverance in suffering. And that he has done in wonderful ways I'll never fully understand. So it's obvious I have contemplated the "why?" question. Perhaps you have as well.

But I not fretted over the answer. Why have I not demanded healing from God or frantically pursued the many cures friends and strangers have suggested? The bottom line is this: we live in a fallen world--what else did one expect? Theology protects from destructive inner turmoil and allows me to accept reality.

Here's how. The whole of creation is under the curse of the fall and I'm not exempt, because of God's love for me, from the consequences of living in a world of vicious cancer and violent winds. Nor from a world of finite and fallen people who inflict harm on me, wittingly or unwittingly. I expect the worst and rejoice when, by God's grace, it usually doesn't happen! Sometimes when I wake in the morning I muse, *Lord, lots of folks died last night. Why not me?* At my stage of life so many of my dearest family and friends suffer painful, debilitating illness and agonizing death. Why not I? That's the only reasonable "why" question for one who lives in a fallen world.

I don't want to oversimplify the problem of evil; a whole complex of theological issues intertwine. For example, if God made his own people exempt from the human condition, who wouldn't become a believer? But what kind of believer would they become? Again, when does God heal and to what end? For what purpose does God protect or remove the protection? The theological questions seem endless, especially when faced with personal tragedy, but the bottom line for me is this: I'm fallen and so is my world. Not, "why me, Lord?" when trouble strikes, but "why not me, Lord?" when it so often misses.

But what kind of God? We discover three stories in the Bible that focus on the kind of God we don't have. The hired mourners knew the child was dead, so they ridiculed the God-man who said it would be all right. The distraught father, finding Jesus' disciples failing of the press releases, said to the all-powerful One: "If you can, please heal my son." The disciples, veteran sailors, despaired of life as the winds howled, and wakened the sleeping passenger, "Don't you care that we're dead men?" Some doubted his wisdom--they knew better. One doubted his power--"If you can," he said. And some doubted his love--"don't you care about us?" When this snaps into focus, we realize that when we worry about our impossible circumstances--death, illness, and storms—we are calling into question the character of God. Am I really smarter than God to know what is best? Is he truly impotent in the face of these impossible circumstances? Or maybe he just doesn't care that much about me? What blasphemy!

You may not know what God's purpose is in sending or permitting difficulty into your life, but that he has a purpose you can be confident. And a God with wisdom to know what is best for you, love to choose that best, and power to carry it through, you can trust. You do not have to be a victim, except a "victim" of God's love.

How often, when you try to untangle the reasons God seems to have abandoned you, have you returned finally to Calvary and whispered, "Dear Jesus, how could those hands pierced for me ever allow anything truly evil pass through to touch me? Help me trust you when I can't figure out the why."

March 5
I Believe
Romans 6:8

"... do not be anxious about anything, but in everything by prayer and supplication with thanksgiving let your requests be made known to God. 7 And the peace of God, which surpasses all understanding, will guard your hearts and your minds in Christ Jesus." (Philippians 4:6-7)

I believe in God

Muriel was a chain worrier. One stormy night she was totally stressed out about her three teenagers who were out in the fringes of the hurricane. She was just as distraught over the last 2 when the first arrived in good cheer, unscathed. And still immobilized by fear for the third after the second appeared. As she writhed in an agony of worry on her bed, harassing the Lord with her unbelief, he seemed to say to her, *Do you want to spend the rest of your life living like this?* Startled, she cried out, "Oh, no, Lord! I truly don't. Please deliver me!" And, as she never tired of testifying, he did. In an instant. For most of us it takes a bit of growing, but not for Muriel. She just quit once she got focused on who God really is. Later she wrote this couplet:

Anything, anytime, anywhere,
I leave the choice with you.
What e'er you say I'll do.

I may not know what God's purpose is in sending or permitting difficulty in my life, but that he has a purpose I am confident. Self-pity can't even get a hearing! Shake my puny fist in the face of God, as some testify? They must not fear the infinite, holy One. Or perhaps they've not watched the agony of the Father's face as his only Son hangs helpless, crying out, "why have you abandoned me?" Why indeed! For my sake it was! That's how much the Father and the Son love me. How often, when I've tried to untangle the reasons God seems to have abandoned me, have I returned finally to Calvary and whispered, "Dear Jesus, how could those hands pierced for me ever allow anything truly evil pass through to touch me? Help me trust you when I can't figure out the *why*."
Theology does indeed protect from the ravages of ungodly responses!

I believe in love

"How does God enable you to love Muriel when there's so little left to love?" I was being interviewed on camera, but I knew the young anchorwoman didn't make up that question. She'd been given it by the production manager who had asked me similar questions during the last 24 hours. I waved for the cameras to cut.
"I'm sorry, but I don't know how to answer that question," I said to the producer. "How would you feel if I said you were very difficult to like but that God was giving me supernatural ability to like you anyway? Not much of a compliment! I know that anything of merit in me comes as a gift from God, to be sure, but I love Muriel because she's altogether loveable. I can't *not* love her. She's my precious."

"OK," the producer responded, "that's fine. Just say that." And the cameras rolled.

She loved me passionately for 40 years and stored away countless memories that still flood me with joy. And in the morning when our eyes connect and she flashes that glorious smile for a fleeting moment, my heart leaps. She's so gentle and contented--oh, I can't explain love. But I believe in love.

Theology seems to have built up my spiritual and psychic immune system. But when that immune system fails, I've discovered theology also has the power to heal, to correct wrong thinking, to renew.

How is it with you? Building up your immune system? Are you healing? Correcting your wrong thinking by growing in your knowledge of God? Perhaps you are walking away from what you know. Recommit today to protect from the ravages of ungodly responses.

March 6
You Want What?
James 4:1-4

"What is the source of wars and fights among you? Don't they come from the cravings that are at war within you? You desire and do not have. You murder and covet and cannot obtain. You fight and war. You do not have because you do not ask. You ask and don't receive because you ask with wrong motives, so that you may spend it on your evil desires." (James 4:1-4)

God's last commandment of the Ten prohibits coveting: "Do not covet your neighbor's house. Do not covet your neighbor's wife, his male or female slave, his ox or donkey, or anything that belongs to your neighbor" (Ex. 20:17). This command prohibits desiring things that are not in God's will for me: my neighbor's house, wife, slave, ox, or donkey—anything that belongs to him. By specifying neighbor, God didn't mean it's OK to covet something that belongs to someone who isn't a neighbor. He just intended to focus on things that are nearby and thus accessible and enticing. For you it may be your neighbor's car, your coworker's watch, or an anonymous advertiser's product. I've often wondered why this one internal sin, a sin of the mind or spirit, was included in the Ten Commandments along with the action sins. Why not include pride or lust? We'll see that coveting is a fundamental command that, if kept, helps us remain faithful to all of the others.

Covetousness is a strange human characteristic. God views it as a terrible evil; humans view it as the route to all kinds of personal fulfillment. God put it in the Ten Commandments and listed it in the New Testament along with idolatry, adultery, homosexuality, and thievery; people consider it the least of human foibles. How evil is covetousness from God's viewpoint?

Covetousness is such a terrible sin that it separates a person from God, destroys community, breaks fellowship in the church, is the just object of church discipline, brings the wrath of God on humankind in this age, and brings the wrath of God in eternity. It is a form of idolatry, substituting things for the living God.

How could such an innocent feeling be so evil from God's viewpoint? We will find the answer by examining what covetousness is. To covet is to seek something, someone, a position, a recognition, or a pleasure that is not God's will for me. Notice that I used the word *seek* rather than *desire*. To covet is not merely wishing for more but going after it, lusting for it, working to hold on to it. Although the terms used in Scripture for a covetous attitude speak of strong desire for any of the things I mentioned, the chief use of the term, especially in Paul's letters, refers to longing for and going after material things. Although the slightest desire to get something or to hold on to something God doesn't intend is rightly called sin, the original word *covetous* is strong, meaning *greedy, avaricious, insatiable*. It seems the whole American culture is designed to cultivate covetousness. A consumer culture is fueled by the insatiable desires of the covetous.

The desire to have things is not evil in itself. It is the distortion of this God-given desire, a grasping for things that are not in God's will for someone, that is such a terrible and destructive sin; God deals ruthlessly with that. Yet we American Christians domesticate this sin like a house pet, feeding it with all of the enticements a materialistic society offers so seductively. Jesus often warned us not to accede to the world's offers of things and pleasure. In fact, He said more about our relationship to possessions than He did about heaven, hell, or prayer. Knowing covetousness stood in the way of a commitment to God, Jesus told the rich young man to sell his possessions in order to follow Him. But the young man could not let go of them and went away grieving (see Matt. 19:16-22). In contrast, Zacchaeus rejoiced to give half of his possessions to the poor and repaid fourfold the people he had cheated (see Luke 19:8). Many of Jesus' teachings on coveting are summarized in this succinct statement: *"Watch out and be on guard against all greed because one's life is not in the abundance of his possessions"* (Luke 12:15).

Why do you think God finds covetousness so objectionable? Like the other commandments, breaking this one interferes with our relationship with God and harms us. In fact, violating this final commandment can lead us to break the other commands. What do you really want today? What are you going after, lusting for, or working to hold on to? Join me in a prayer for freedom. "Lord I want to know the freedom and contentment you intend for your children. Help me to express gratitude and act with generosity this day and every day.

March 7
God's Love Life—and Mine
John 3:16

"For God so love the world, that he gave his only begotten Son, that whosoever believes shall not perish but have eternal life" (John 3:16)

Jesus did not say, "For God so loved Israel." That's what his disciples expected. Nor did he say, "God so loved America" or "God so loved Africa." God loved the ***world.***

But he only ***began*** His redemption plan with Jesus. He planned to finish the redemption of lost humanity by loving that world through you and me. And how has the church done in loving the world to Jesus? The commission was given 2,000 years ago.

Well, consider: 2 out of 3 people on earth have never yet heard the Good News. Even worse, half of that number—one of every three--CAN'T hear it because they live in an ethnic group where there are no Christians. If someone doesn't go in from the outside they CAN'T hear the gospel. Yet God loved the whole world of perishing people.

We're thinking about the God who loves the whole world. What is the church doing about that commission in our time? Praise God there is a new surge of sending streams from non-western nations. For example, Korea and southern India each send out tens of thousands of cross-cultural streams. Or consider Nagaland, a tribe in North-east India: With 1 million believers that church is sending 10,000 cross-cultural missionaries to other places that don't have Christians.

Praise God for what He is doing in and through you! Yet most of our sending is of short term ministry experiences. That's good. But to reach those who haven't heard, who can't hear because they're out of reach of present Gospel witness, short termers can't do it. What is needed are streams who are incarnational, like Jesus, and stay among a people long enough to learn their culture, to live out the life of Jesus so people can see it and be drawn to him.

So why did the Father send the Son to be incarnate among us and give his very life for us? That whoever hears and believes "will not perish but have everlasting life."

The OBJECT of God's love, then, is the whole world.
The GOAL of God's giving? That people not perish but have everlasting life.
Now consider the NATURE of God's love

"God SO loved…" we read. How much did God love? Enough to give His only Son. Indeed, love is proved by the sacrifice it makes. There may be genuine love without sacrifice, but it is unproved, untested. Yet the Father gives us the example for us to follow. Sacrifice for missions, sacrifice for the church, sacrifice for family. Love for the whole world, that people not perish but walk in loving oneness with God through the giving up of our own desires for His.

March 8
Feeling Forgiven
Romans 3:21-24

No one will be justified in His sight by the works of the law, because the knowledge of sin comes through the law. But now, apart from the law, God's righteousness has been revealed—attested by the Law and the Prophets— that is, God's righteousness through faith in Jesus Christ, to all who believe, since there is no distinction. For all have sinned and fall short of the glory of God. They are justified freely by His grace through the redemption that is in Christ Jesus. Justified! Never again can I be condemned, not " by man, not by myself, not by the master accuser, because God Himself has declared me righteous" (Romans 3:20-24)

When a believer sins, he doesn't forfeit his relationship with God. However, he has damaged that relationship by hurting and grieving his Beloved. If the person's conscience has been sensitized by the Word and by a close walk with the Spirit, he feels appropriate guilt—a conviction that he has done something wrong and a discomfort in his spirit. But his relationship with his Heavenly Father is still intact. He is still a Christian, and his salvation is still ensured. How can this be?

A judicial transaction has taken place between the holy God and His Son so that I walk free, not only forgiven but also declared righteous on the merits of Christ's atoning death. Hear the exulting voice of the apostle Paul by re-reading the verse for today.

What voices seek to condemn you as you walk with God? Is it Satan? Some authority figure? Perhaps a sibling? Sometimes it can be someone at school or work, even yourself!

Paul wrote, *"Who can bring an accusation against God's elect? God is the One who justifies. Who is the one who condemns? Christ Jesus is the One who died, but even more, has been raised; He also is at the right hand of God and intercedes for us"* (Rom. 8:33-34). Rejoice that the blood of Christ has fully justified you in the sight of God.

What about someone who claims to be a Christian but persists in continually unrepentant sin? John makes it clear such a person is not a Christian at all (see 1 John 3:6-15). Not forgiven, not made new, not justified. But if one is truly in Christ, the evidence of a transformed life will prove it. For the true believer there will be confession, repentance, and restoration when he sins. That's the one who proves he has been justified by the atoning death of the Savior. He is free indeed!

Trust is another step in living free of guilt. Though yielding and trusting are essential elements in biblical faith, most of us don't respond and grow at equal rates in yielding and trusting. For example, in gaining freedom from guilt, we may plead guilty—"Yes, Holy One, I'm the chief of sinners"—but we can't get free because down deep we're not so sure of the forgiveness or justification. We agree with God about our sin, intellectually assenting to our forgiveness, but we don't feel forgiven. Yielding to God's will in this matter can and should take place instantly and permanently, but trust must grow. The more we know Him, the more we trust Him. The secret to breaking out of bondage to guilt feelings is not more self-examination but a cultivated God-focus. When we truly know Him, we will trust Him to keep His promise to fully forgive. Run to His embrace and exult in the forgiveness and justification He provides for every failure. You are free from guilt through Jesus' all-sufficient sacrifice on the cross.

Think about God's forgiveness of a recent confession of sin, perhaps one you confessed recently. Do you feel forgiven, or do you still feel guilty? If you still feel guilty, spend some time in prayer. Remember that it is not your actions or feelings that bring forgiveness but His faithfulness and righteousness to forgive and cleanse (see 1 John 1:9). Place your trust in His power to forgive.

March 9
Freedom Through Trust
John 15:4-5

"Remain in me, as I also remain in you. No branch can bear fruit by itself; it must remain in the vine. Neither can you bear fruit unless you remain in me. I am the vine; you are the branches. If you remain in me and I in you, you will bear much fruit; apart from me you can do nothing." (John 15:4 & 5 NIV)

We start down the freedom trail—from confession to forgiveness and justification and finally to trust. That gets us started on the Spirit's reconstruction project. When we are forgiven and when we trust Him, He is free to do His transformational work in our lives, to reveal the life of Jesus, who lives within. Today let's consider two of the Spirit's activities that empower us for obedience and victory in the Christian life.

The first activity of the Spirit is regeneration: what the Spirit does to transform us into a new creation at the outset of our relationship with Him. Paul said we are saved "through the washing of regeneration and renewal by the Holy Spirit" (Titus 3:5).

We can agree that there is an external, visible part of us and an internal, invisible dimension—the irreducible, eternal self, the core person the Holy Spirit wants to transform. The old changes to the new in our choosing, our capacity to think, our values and our feelings.

Regeneration made you "a new creation; old things have passed away, and look, new things have come" (2 Cor. 5:17). The new you could clearly see for the first time that your failure was sinful because now you had 20/20 spiritual insight. And what's more, it mattered to you; that desirable thing became ugly. But it wasn't just your desires that changed. You found new empowerment in the Holy Spirit. You could reject that soul enemy you had always cuddled up to as a friend. You had the power to face down those sin-bullies that till now had always won out.

The second activity of the Spirit is indwelling: To become an altogether new person at the core with new capabilities and mighty transformations would seem to provide power enough to live successfully. But that's only part of the Spirit's work. He also empowers us for living, changing, loving, and growing. And the way He does this is very personal: He comes in person to live with us. The Bible teaches that Jesus and the Holy Spirit live within, or indwell, a believer. In fact, They are in us, and we are in Them.

I've come to exult in that; it's evidence of His glorious infinities. But because He created us on His pattern for an intimate love relationship, as we have seen, surely His indwelling has something to do with an altogether new relationship. Not only am I a new creation, but I also have a new relationship. Jesus taught about it: "Remain in Me, and I in you. Just as a branch is unable to produce fruit by itself unless it remains on the vine, so neither can you unless you remain in Me. I am the vine; you are the branches. The one who remains in Me and I in him produces much fruit, because you can do nothing without Me" (John 15:4-5). Notice that Jesus used the idea of "you in Me" and "I in you" interchangeably. Take a few minutes and ponder the implications for your life because of our intimacy and our relationship with the Trinity.

March 10
Connecting
John 13:34-35

"A new commandment I give to you, that you love one another: just as I have loved you, you also are to love one another. By this all people will know that you are my disciples, if you have love for one another." (John 13:34-35)

Surveys of missionaries consistently point to a major hazard to missionary health and effectiveness: loneliness. A sense of aloneness depends to some extent on temperament. Some people seem to thrive with or without other humans in close relationships, though the numbers may not be as large as might appear. Others can't survive without an abundance of human companionship—touchy-feely relationships are essential.

Most of us are probably somewhere in between. But God knows we need human companionship. "It isn't good for man to be alone" he concluded at the very beginning. Marriage. And church— we really do need one another even if some of us feel that more acutely than others. Some missionaries say, "For my emotional and spiritual needs I must have those of my own kind." There may be a legitimate cultural element in the equation, but let's be very sure there isn't a latent ethno-centrism feeding such feeling. And yet, even missionary Paul, surely as free of racism as a person could be, felt lonely on occasion because members of his team weren't there. The church and her members need to be on the alert to reach out to those who are silent in their loneliness. Special care for singles.

But as maturing Christians, we must also be proactive, taking the initiative to find and nurture friendships that are emotionally and spiritual satisfying to both parties. Not relying on individual technology or streaming. That's one major purpose of church! If you're strong and independent you may not feel the need so acutely, but beware! We really do need one another. Besides, others need you!

And if you're "people-addicted," in some measure of pain without plenty of close relationships, don't throw a pity party. Take the initiative to build mutually strengthening relationships.

If there are weak areas in your church life, it will likely impact your own spiritual well-being and your spiral up, because Church is one of the Spirit's major means for bringing the growth he desires. That is why it is so sad that a majority of American young people reared in the church no longer participate in the life of the church. Is one reason for this tragedy that the church is not fulfilling the purposes for which God designed it?

In fact, if connecting- with – people bonds are not being met in your life, why not pause now and reflect in prayer on any action steps you need to take to tighten church-bonds in your own life? How could the social distancing and disconnect created by the Covid pandemic be reversed in your church?

March 11
Spirit Evidence
Luke 10:21

"At that time, Jesus, full of joy through the Holy Spirit, . . ." (Luke 10:21)

Perhaps God intends spiritual fruit—the visible outworking of the Spirit's inner working—to be constant and the surges of feeling to be special gifts? Jesus was a man of sorrows and acquainted with grief. He agonized in the Garden, for example, but there were also times of surging joy—*"At that time,"* Luke tells us, *"Jesus, full of joy through the Holy Spirit, . . ."* (Luke 10:21). David, the joy-filled singer for the ages, often experienced dry times, times when God seemed distant, when he would cry out in alarm, *"Don't take your Holy Spirit from me!"* (Psalm 51:11). Even Paul had times of fear and called on friends to pray for the Spirit gift of boldness (2 Corinthians 7:5; Ephesians 6:19,20). It seems that the inner sense of fullness is not a constant, but a periodic gift. At least for the people I know that's the way it is.

In my own life I can count on having a truly exalted experience of God when I go away for my annual time of fasting and prayer. So much so, I can remember many of those occasions, even decades later. But only occasionally do I have that rushing sense of God's presence in my daily quiet time; even less often unexpectedly in the midst of a busy day. How I long, sometimes ache, to have those experiences often, yes, daily. But such has eluded me.

I'd say, "It's okay. No one does." But I'm not so sure. The mystics through the ages give testimony of such a walk with God. For myself, I'll keep exulting in the sporadic winds that blow and stay on the alert for a more constant walk on the highest plane—however God defines that for me.

Fullness, then, in the sense of an inner feeling, is not subject to analysis, but it can be a glorious experience and the Holy Spirit will give it to those who love and stay tight with Him. If my relationship with the Spirit, letting Him take charge, is clear enough to me, and my fruit and gifts—or the absence of them—are clear to others, the inner sense of fullness may not be so clear. It's difficult to analyze something that is beyond our understanding, yet God promises, in filling us with Himself, to give us love that is beyond comprehension (Ephesians 3:19). And we can't even fathom the kind of peace that stands guard at our mind's gate. But, says Paul, we can experience it (Philippians 4:7): *"And the peace of God, which surpasses all understanding, will guard your hearts and your minds in Christ Jesus."* How exciting to feel the surge of the Spirit!

March 12
Big Jim
1 Corinthians 6:19

"Don't you know that your body is a sanctuary of the Holy Spirit who is in you, whom you have from God" (1 Corinthians 6:19)

The old me could do good things. Bad people often do good. Cornelius did; Acts 10:2 calls him a devout man who feared God, did charitable deeds, and prayed. But he didn't have a new nature that comes with knowing Christ. An unconverted mother who dashes into a burning home to rescue her infant does a good thing. The problem is, she can't consistently choose good. Without Jesus she doesn't have the capability. Her jailer, sin, won't let her. In fact, she probably doesn't even know what good is- most of the time, and even if she does, she usually doesn't want it. Why? Because the old, unredeemed nature craves the things of the flesh, not the things of the spirit.

The new me can choose to do wrong, but I don't have to. Because of my new nature in Christ, I now know what's right, especially as my mind is informed by the Word and sensitized by the Spirit. Furthermore, my desires have been reprogrammed; I like the good, at least most of the time. But best of all, the new me has built-in capabilities to consistently choose good. All sorts of things have passed away; all kinds of things have become new! I'm a new creation, and that gives me hope. God has given me a new nature, transforming me into an altogether new kind of being.

As a fifth-grader, I was spending my recess at war—a water-gun battle with my best friend. As he ran from my barrage, Big Jim, the school bully, walked between us and caught the full force of a stream of water on the side of his head. Big Jim was about twice my size and could easily have bent me into a pretzel with his bare hands. Instead, he reached into his boot and pulled out a switchblade knife. I was reputed to be the fastest kid in school, and that day I proved it. Round and round the schoolyard we went. Finally the bell rang, and I shot through the door.

I knew that wasn't the end of it, so after school I didn't dash out the front door as was my custom but surveyed the prospects from a second-floor window. Sure enough, there stood Jim by the front gate. I eluded him by going out the back door and crossing neighborhood fences to reach the safety of home. But he caught on, so I had to plan new strategies. When I ran out of ideas, I resorted to staying at school until Jim had gone home.

Finally, after school one day as I forlornly wandered the darkened corridors, I glanced out to see my father walking down the sidewalk in the direction of home. Down the stairs and out the side door I shot, warmly greeting a bemused dad. Then, hand in hand, we walked past the waiting sentinel, who looked a bit nonplussed. I greeted him with studied nonchalance: "Hi, Jim!"

And so it is with us. The Big Jims of our lives are legion, the bully-sins that stalk us day and night. But Daddy is with us! No, not with us—in us! God doesn't just forgive our sins, declare us just, rearrange our thinking apparatus, reprogram our core being, and send us all kinds of blessings UPS, all the while keeping His distance. No, He comes in person to live inside us.

Does the Spirit literally reside inside your body? How about Christ—does He live in there too? And the Father? It's a mystery, isn't it? Nevertheless, Scripture teaches that God comes to reside in you, making you His intimate companion. Amazingly, the God of the universe, the God of the ages, the God of all infinities holds out to you a personal, one-to-one, intimate relationship. Jesus prayed for His followers, "May they all be one, as You, Father, are in Me and I am in You. May they also be one in Us. … May they be one as We are one" (John 17:21-22). Jesus was describing the intimate fellowship enjoyed by the Father and the Son. From the eternal love bonds that unite Father, Son, and Spirit, they invite you to join that relationship. It's so intimate that the only way to describe it is to say that God is in you and you are in Him. Think about it: uninterrupted companionship for eternity. Wow! Let's thank Him for that incredible gift!

March 13

What Does the Law Mean for Me Today?

Ephesians 4:13

"...until we all attain to the unity of the faith and of the knowledge of the Son of God, to mature manhood, to the measure of the stature of the fullness of Christ" (Ephesians 4:13)

There are distinct meanings of *law* in the New Testament, but the first three meanings are of primary importance, and not simply because they have been a theological battleground from biblical times. For anyone who wants to know and do God's will, it is of utmost importance to discover what that will is. Since both Jesus Christ and the apostles taught that some change had taken place in the relationship of God's people to "the law," we must be careful to discover exactly what that law is and what that change is.

All would agree that a change was long overdue from the damning idea that a person can gain acceptance with God through his own efforts. At least some elements of the Mosaic system of law were done away with in Christ's sacrificial death and the institution of the church. But here agreement ends. Some hold that Paul makes no distinctions among laws and that the Christian is not obligated to any of the Mosaic law, including the moral law.

At this point it is important to emphasize that the New Testament uses the term *law* to refer to (1) the moral requirements of God, (2) the Mosaic system of regulations, and (3) the figurative use of the *law* referring to obedience to it.

Yet how do we define the law in the Old Testament? Since Moses, the great lawgiver, recorded the law in his writings, the Pentateuch (the first five books of the Bible) was commonly called "the law" (Gal. 4:21). The Hebrew Bible was divided into three sections, commonly called the Law, the Prophets, and the Writings (or the first of that section, the Psalms). Thus Christ spoke of "my words which I spoke unto you, while I was still with you, that everything written about me in the law of Moses, and the prophets, and the psalms must be fulfilled" (Luke 24:44). Here the "law of Moses" clearly refers to the first division of the Hebrew Old Testament, the Pentateuch.

Sometimes the Old Testament was simply referred to by two divisions, the Law and the Prophets (ex. Matt. 11:13). Sometimes the term *law* actually refers to specific commandments such as the Ten Commandments. "We have a law" (John 19:7) is another example of a specific law in mind. When Paul speaks of fulfilling the law of Christ in Galatians 6:2 and when James speaks of the royal law (James 2:8), the reference is to the specific law of love. Again, when James speaks of keeping the whole law (James 2:10), he is speaking of specific laws, probably the Decalogue, or Ten Commandments.

Consider the law as an operating principle. Sometimes the New Testament uses the term *law* to mean a principle much as we would say the "law of gravity." "The law of my mind" and "the law of sin" (Rom. 7:23, 25), "the law of the Spirit of life" (Rom. 8:2), and "the principle of faith" (Rom. 3:27) are all examples of the term *law* being used as a synonym for "principle."

Because *law* is used in many different ways and often with several meanings overlapping, it is important to be sure from the context which meaning was intended by the author. Otherwise we shall be applying a teaching concerning the law that does not actually apply. For example, if we speak of being free from the law and use this to refer to the moral law of God when in fact Scripture is referring to the condemnation resulting from the law (Rom. 8:1-2) or the Old Testament system of sacrifices, we are making a great error. For the time being, we will use the term *law* in its primary meaning: law as the expressed will of God that people be like him morally.

This ultimate standard for the Christian is not merely a code of ethics or system of doctrine or a subjective feel for what is right. The standard for the Christian is God himself (Matt. 5:48). This is exciting. It means that the foundation of our moral standard is not man, his wisdom, his fallen nature, his desires, his values, his traditions, nor his culture. These may be the foundation of man-made law, but not of the Christian standard of life. Since God himself is our standard, our standard is not relative, changing with each age or society. God's law is *absolute,* perfect, unchanging, and eternal.

Since God himself is our standard, the standard is *universal.* The moral character of God as a standard applies to all men of all ages. This standard is *personal,* living, and visible rather than a dead code. It is not something that God imposes on us arbitrarily. It derives from his own nature.

This truth also means that God's character is not derived from the moral structure of the universe. Some would hold that God behaves rightly and lovingly because he is obliged to do so by ultimate "natural" law. Rather, we say that righteousness and love are good because that is the way God is. We see these standards flowing out of the nature of our infinite, ultimate, personal God. Thus, God's will for man is that we be like him. We were created in his moral likeness, reflecting the glory of his character. His purpose in redemption is to restore that image, which has been marred. How incredible!

March 14
The Insiders
Roman 8

"...there is now no condemnation for those who are in Christ Jesus!"--to be in him is to be safe in him (Romans 8:1).

What takes place the moment one moves from outside a relationship with God to inside? Is there a life filled so full of good things that it overflows? We discover God's own guarantee of a life overflowing with love and joy, of effective service to God and others (John 15). And the plan was not to provide this fulfillment for some special cadre of super saints, but for everyone who is "in Christ." Yet how that life may be experienced seems to elude most people.

Part of the problem is that many start at the wrong place in their search for fulfillment. One must begin, not with discovering something about God, but something about oneself. The Bible and the dominant counseling theories agree that fulfillment must begin with self-discovery. But there the agreement ends. The counseling theories start with good news about you, the Bible starts with bad. The counselor affirms you, assures you that you are OK, that someone has messed you up by denying that you are OK or even by putting you on a guilt trip. But the Bible starts with bad news about you. In fact, it says that apart from Christ you are "*like a branch that is thrown away and withers; such branches are picked up, thrown into the fire and burned*" (Jn 15.6).

The passage in John 15:2,6 has become a battleground for Arminian-Calvinist dispute: was this "branch" in Christ and then got cut off? Or was this person safe in Christ but was merely disciplined? Or was he never in Christ at all? Explanations abound, each seeking to come to terms with a broader theology. I suggest that the passage is figurative, an allegory, and thus should not be treated as a literal doctrinal statement. To fit the vine-and-branch analogy Jesus was simply saying that people who do not live an authentic Christian life should not consider themselves joined to him, that people who do belong to him will give evidence of it in attitudes and action. But even if one insists on bending this picture language to conform to a doctrine of eternal security or lack thereof, whatever the interpretation, it seems clear that those who are not "in Christ" are in bad trouble. And this is the consistent witness of Scripture. By nature, I am a sinner headed for eternal judgement.

But we don't like the bad news. We like it so little we have re-written our hymns. We used to sing with the ex-slave trader, John Newton, "Amazing grace how sweet the sound that saved a wretch like me." Now we sing of how it saved "someone like me." We can't even bring ourselves to identify with the self-pronounced wretched Paul! Isaac Watts wrote, "Alas and did my Savior bleed and did my sovereign die, would he devote that sacred head for such a worm as I?" He may have gotten that expression from what God called Jacob. But we have corrected the grandest of hymnists so that now it reads, "...for sinners such as I." There was a day when we sang, "Beneath the Cross of Jesus two wonders I confess, the wonders of his glorious love and my own worthlessness." No longer. It sounds better to sing, "..my unworthiness." But the Bible is clear that without Christ I am a worm, a worthless wretch. Indeed, a withered branch fit for burning. We don't like to hear it put that way. Oh, I am an image bearer of the glorious God, to be sure, spoiled and damaged though the likeness is. But the bad news I must confront first of all is that I am hell deserving.

James R. Graham heard of revival fires sweeping the interior of China. His renowned missionary career was just beginning, but evidence of it was visible already. Still, he longed for a fuller measure of God's blessing. Graham hesitated to travel the great distance into the interior to discover the secret of such spiritual power because the igniter of those revival fires was a woman, a diminutive Norwegian at that, and Graham did not believe in women preachers. Finally, to assuage his thirst for all there was of God, he humbled himself and went to sit at her feet. The first night of the public meetings she spoke on the Ten Commandments. Fair enough. But when she continued with messages on the law a second and third night, Graham began to lose patience. Following the service he confronted her. A giant of a man, James R. Graham towered over the little lady and demanded, "Why do you not leave the somber legalisms of the Old Testament to the ancient people to whom they were addressed and nourish us with the grace of Calvary?" "Dr. Graham," she responded with gentle firmness, "until the ears of the heart are opened with the thunders of Sinai one cannot even hear the sweet grace notes of Calvary."

The law always precedes the Gospel. Paul understood this. The most glorious description of our salvation, of what it means to be "in Christ" (Romans 3-8) follows hard after the very bad news of humankind's moral rottenness and total lostness apart from Christ (Romans 1-3). First the bad news, then the good.

The glorious implications of that relationship is the entire eighth chapter of Romans. It begins with the proclamation: "*...there is now no condemnation for those who are in Christ Jesus!*"--*to be in him is to be safe in him* (8:1). To be in Christ is to be free from the domineering authority of sin and resultant death (vs 2). To be in Christ is to have an infused power to think and live like him (vs 4-6). To be in Christ is to have peace with God (vs 6,7). To be in Christ is to have the Holy Spirit within (vs 9). It is to be alive--eternally alive (vs 10, 11). To be in Christ makes me a beloved child of God and, indeed, an heir (vs 15-17). To be in Christ means that God the Spirit, God the Son, and God the Father are active in my behalf, that they even work all the circumstances of life toward an assured destiny of likeness to him and that nothing--absolutely nothing--can ever separate me from God's love (vs 24-39). All of this -- and more -- comes the moment I am united with him by faith.

But that is just the beginning. To "abide in Christ" is something more. Much more. Have you experienced that initial entering into Christ but find yourself not so new after all? Perhaps you are very like the old you, not such wonderful new capabilities for coping with life, not truly fulfilled. Has the new relationship grown a bit stale and routine, not bringing much joy to Jesus or you? Perhaps you need to explore what Jesus meant when he said we must "abide." Take some time and decide are you united with him by faith? Do you regularly abide in Him? Do you have an infused power to think and live like him? What choices must you make?

March 15
The Big Connection
John 15

Abide in me, and I in you. As the branch cannot bear fruit by itself, unless it abides in the vine, neither can you, unless you abide in me. I am the vine; you are the branches. Whoever abides in me and I in him, he it is that bears much fruit, for apart from me you can do nothing. As the Father has loved me, so have I loved you. Abide in my love. If you keep my commandments, you will abide in my love, just as I have kept my Father's commandments and abide in his love. (John 15: 4,5,9,10)

An ikebana is a beautiful thing, often exquisite, always exotic to the western eye. But it is misnamed. Two words, "flower" and "living," are combined to name the Japanese way of arranging flowers. But ikebanas are made with cut flowers. More living than plastic or silk flowers, to be sure, but the connection with life is broken--hardly "living," at least not for more than a few days. Jesus says that's the way with our lives. They may be beautiful, even awe inspiring, but cut off from the source of life they can never be all they were meant to be nor last more than a few days. At least when measured by the calendar of eternity. The connection with real life and the secret to fulfilling life's potential is to connect with him, says Jesus in John 15. And that connection is a relationship so intimate you could describe it as being in him.

Getting into Christ involves two things: a new creation and a new relation. What "exceeding magnifical" new persons we have become! What an astonishing new relationship we have entered! Paul emphasizes this union with Christ as the key to successful Christian experience. But Jesus emphasizes an even deeper "in-ness"--if you abide in me, he says, a bumper crop of fruit will be yours (vs. 5): love, joy, peace, victorious Christian living and effective service. And that is what you were made for, true fulfillment.

We know the biblical terminology, but what it means literally and practically is not always clear. As a graduate student once wrote to me, "What, what, WHAT am I supposed to do, how, how, HOW can I actually experience this life he promises?" There are three abidings in John 15, not one, and each throws light on the others: abide in Christ (vs 4,5), let the words of Christ abide in you (vs. 7) and abide in love (vs 9,10).

The key word of John 15 is translated "abide" in earlier translations, "remain" in some more recent translations. Remain is indeed a basic meaning of the Greek term *meno*. For example, the promise in verse 16 is of fruit that will remain, using the same word. "*The Word of the Lord remains forever*," says Peter (I Pet 1.25). Paul said the sailors must remain in the ship (Acts 27.31). But the English word "remain" falls far short of the full meaning in John 15. *Meno* was used in secular Greek writing to indicate a holding out against all odds, of standing fast when others might waver or buckle.

Britisher Derek Redmond had this characteristic. Redmond provided the emotional high point of the Barcelona summer Olympics when he popped his right hamstring and fell to the cinders 160 meters into the 400-meter race. We watched in growing wonderment as he fought off the officials who came to escort him off the track. Redmond rose and began to hop on his one good leg to the cheers of the crowd. Soon his bad leg dropped to the ground and he dragged it behind him, face contorted in pain, hobbling toward the finish line. The applause reached a crescendo surpassing that for Lewis who had won the gold, riotous cheers for the slowest finish in the 1992 Olympics! Said Redmond, "There was no way I was going out on a stretcher, and there was no way I was going to let all those official people keep me from finishing." That's *meno*, staying in the race no matter what. And those who *meno* in Christ will not only win the cheers of the "cloud of witnesses," they will win the gold!

To abide in Christ is first of all, then, to hold steady, to stick with one's commitment to him. Fidelity, you might call it. Jesus repeatedly defines "abiding" as obedience: "if you keep my commandments, you will abide in my love, just as I have kept my father's commandments and abide in his love (10)." "You are my friends if you do whatever I command you (14)." To abide in Christ is to keep on obeying him no matter what. Fidelity.

March 16
I Believe in Victory
2 Corinthians 5:17

"Therefore, if anyone is in Christ, he is a new creation. The old has passed away; behold, the new has come." (2 Corinthians 5:17)

When I became a new person in Christ, I was given new potentialities. Whereas before I could do right but couldn't consistently choose the right, the new me can choose wrong but need not. Besides, the Holy Spirit took up residence and in that new relationship I'm empowered to win out in the battle against temptation. Oh, I'll not be sinless till I meet him in person, but in the meantime I have power to say "yes" to God and "no" to sin whenever I have the conscious choice. But then there are those involuntary sins and my uninterrupted falling short of God's glorious character. In those areas the Spirit promises to change me, to grow me up more and more into the likeness of Christ, if I only let him. I believe this because Scripture teaches it, but also I believe it because I've seen it in my life.

Take patience, for example. As a teen I'd shoot from the lip and occasionally settle things with my fists. But gradually I came to abhor this and by the age of 18 I began to ask God daily to deliver me and give me patience. I saw a remarkable spurt of growth and thought I'd been delivered. Until, following marriage, my wife and I disagreed on how our first child should be disciplined. I didn't say anything in anger, but I seethed inside for days. Three days, to be exact. When I could stand it no longer, I confessed my heart attitude to God and asked him to deliver me. This happened three times during the first decade of our marriage until finally I had a showdown. "Oh Lord," I said, "how can I give these Japanese people the hope of salvation when you haven't saved me from my own temper? If you don't deliver me, I'm out of here." God knew I meant it. He heard and delivered--never again did that evil spirit intrude into my relationship with Muriel. But God wasn't though with me. Our children became teens and I found that patience was not yet the natural fruit of my spirit. After that it was a board, then certain faculty. And now I'm in a graduate program in patience with a beloved wife who is in the advanced stages of Alzheimer's. God didn't give me the instant deliverance I longed for and begged for. But he did do what he promised and transformed me "*from one degree of glory to another by the Spirit of the Lord*" (Cor 3:18). I believe in victory. I'll never settle for lockdown into some intractable dysfunction of spirit.

I've shared a sampler from my life in an effort to demonstrate how theology works to help hurting people see themselves and their world more nearly from God's perspective. That viewpoint protects from wrong feelings and attitudes and heals when I fail. I call it "therapeutic theology." Are you empowered to win out against temptation? Indeed! Where is the victory? How do you see growth "*from one degree of glory to another*" in your life?

March 17
Falling Short is Sin
James 4:17

"*Whoever knows what is right to do and fails to do it, for him it is sin*" (James 4:17).

The primary word for sin in the Old Testament *(chata)* means to miss the point or to miss the mark. It was used of missing a target or losing one's way, as well as the moral meaning of missing God's standard of behavior or losing one's way spiritually. The translators of the Old Testament chose a word in Greek that had the same basic meaning *(hamartano)*. The final result of this process, across the years, was that New Testament writers transformed another form of the word *(hamartia)* into the idea of sin as the disposition of human nature. Sin in the singular, describing a mentality of alienation from God, came to predominate over the idea of sins, or specific violations of various laws. Sin against the law rather than sins against laws became the focus of attention.

This Christian idea of sin was in sharp contrast to the Greek idea of man as mortal, encumbered with a finite body, subject to error through ignorance. For the Greeks the problem was not moral; defects did not bring guilt; the gods were not offended. But the Bible taught that man is essentially morally flawed in his nature and that he is guilty before God as a result. The biblical concept of sin as an inner state for which a person is responsible is seen in three basic teachings about sin: sinful nature, sinful thoughts, sins of omission.

Sinful Nature. Most people believe one becomes a sinner if and when he commits sinful acts. The Bible puts it the other way around. The Bible teaches that man is a sinner by nature (Eph. 2:3) and that he sins because he is a sinner. According to Scripture, the root problem is not a poor environment, and it certainly is not the responsibility of another person such as a parent (Ezek. 18). The human heart is, from birth, inclined to evil. This does not mean that a person is incapable of doing anything good (Rom. 2:14). It does not mean that everything an unconverted person does is wrong (Acts 10:31). It simply means that people are fallen and do wrong things inevitably because it is their nature to do wrong. Thus before a person chooses deliberately to transgress a specific commandment, he has already "missed the mark," fallen short in his inner being. It is from this polluted spring that flow streams of contaminated behavior. It is lack of conformity to the holy character of God that is the ultimate sin.

The Bible speaks of an evil heart (Heb. 3:12) that is *deceitful above all things and desperately wicked* (Jer. 17:9). Paul, in the most thorough analysis of sin, its origin, results, and cure (Rom. 1–8) identifies the root problem as a wrong heart.

Sinful Thoughts. Many believe that a person sins only if he commits sinful acts, but the Bible teaches that the inner thoughts are sinful as well (Matt. 5:28ff.; 15:18-19). Hatred is not wrong merely because it may lead to acts of violence. Hatred itself is sin. The underlying contention is that every lack of conformity to God means we fall short and sin. This includes lack of conformity in action, in motive and in affection.

Sins of Omission. We sin also by failing to do what we ought. All have sinned, to be sure, but also all are continuously falling short of the glorious character of God (Rom. 3:23). "*Whoever knows what is right to do and fails to do it, for him it is sin*" (James 4:17). "*For whatever does not proceed from faith is sin*" (Rom. 14:23). Here Paul does not speak of a positive choice to think or do evil, but clearly teaches that failure to measure up to the right is sin. It is not only sinful to actively hate my neighbor; it is sinful to fail to love him as I ought. I am commanded to love as Christ loved; when I do not, I have not merely demonstrated a morally neutral personality weakness, I have sinned.

The sin offering for sins of ignorance (Lev. 5:14-15), the trespass offering for sins of omission (Lev. 5:5-6), and the burnt offering to expiate general sinfulness (Lev. 1:3; cf. Luke 2:22-24) all witness that sin is not confined to mere act. [7]

It is significant that the Westminster divines, in answering the catechism question "What is sin?" began with sins of omission, rather than sins of transgression: "Sin is any want of conformity unto or transgression of the law of God."

Biblical sin, then, is not just sin against men but sin against God; not just sinful behavior but a sinful nature; not just sinful activity but sinful thoughts; not just sins of violation but sins of omission, falling short of likeness to God.

Who can stand before such a standard? "Wretched man that I am!" we cry with Paul. His picture of the titanic struggle with sin (Rom. 7) was surely not the battle to refrain from theft and murder. No, it was the warfare within, his total inability to measure up to God's standard, to "*be perfect, as your heavenly Father is perfect*" (Matt. 5:48). He stood condemned and guilty, though he testified of keeping the law perfectly (Phil. 3:6).

Sin And Guilt. Sin in Scripture is almost indistinguishable from guilt. There was never a sharp distinction to the Hebrew between sin and guilt. One is guilty of violating God's standard when he may not even know of it. The plea of ignorance does not excuse. The involuntary, unconscious moral deficiency of one's disposition brings guilt.

There are two elements of guilt: blameworthiness and obligation to suffer punishment. Christ assumed our obligation to suffer punishment and thus cleansed our guilty record. But he was never worthy of blame. In fact, his innocence is what qualified him to stand in place of the guilty. As a result, those who have been redeemed will never have to pay the penalty for sin (are guiltless in the legal sense), but are nevertheless guilty in the sense of being blameworthy. It is the glory of God's grace that we who are blameworthy, guilty sinners have the just results of our sinfulness set aside. God today does not see us as weak, failing, guilty sinners, but as pure and innocent and holy as the one who took our place. But to understand the glory of grace, we must first understand the wicked depth of iniquity in that corrupt nature on which God's grace has fallen. We are more guilty today than ever—we have sinned and are blameworthy. But we are guiltless today, free from any obligation whatsoever to pay for our sin. Jesus paid it all.

March 18
What is Sin?
Ps. 81:11-12

"But my people did not listen to my voice; Israel would not submit to me. So I gave them over to their stubborn hearts, to follow their own counsels." (Psalm 71:11-12)

Sin is moral wrong. There is much wrong in the world that is not moral. Rust on my automobile fender is evil, and so is a bank failure, the weakness of old age, or an earthquake that destroys a city. Evil, indeed, but we do not hold anyone guilty for poor judgment, for the troubles and grief of our human condition, or for natural disasters. When the lion pounces on the antelope, the antelope, at least, considers it an evil. But we do not say the lion sinned. Why not? Because unlike "wrong," "evil," "badness," or even "crime," sin introduces the idea of *God.* Sin has to do with moral conditions and behavior relating to the righteous character of God and his will for creatures made in his moral likeness.

The Bible views sin as both active and a choice of the will and also as dispositional. Sin is transgression against the law. In fact, where there is no law, there is no sin (Rom. 7:7). It can be volitional, a deliberate choice—and usually it is. The rebel deliberately violates the law. The individual knows to do right but doesn't do it. That is sin (James 4:17).

But sin is not the violation of just any law—laws of reason, laws of parents, laws of state. Sin is against the law of *God.* In fact, to violate the law of God is to violate God. The great problem is vertical, and from a wrong vertical relationship flow all the horizontal wrongs (Gen. 39:9). When David said, *"Against thee, thee only, have I sinned,"* (Psalm 51:4) he did not mean that he had not sinned grievously against Uriah and Bathsheba and, indeed, the whole nation. What he meant was that these responsibilities to fellowmen pale into insignificance compared with the terrible sin of violating God and his law.

Some would say that deliberate violation of the known will of God is the only attitude or activity we may classify as "sin." Sin is the willful disobedience of God—the knowing transgression of his law, the conscious denial (in effect) of his absolute sovereignty in the universe.[8]

The condition of sinfulness some theologians called "total depravity." The Westminster Confession of Faith speaks of this original corruption as making all men "utterly indisposed, disabled, and made opposite to all good, and wholly inclined to all evil."

All people are equally wicked; not that any person is as thoroughly corrupt as it is possible for a person to be nor that we are destitute of all moral virtues. The Scriptures recognize the fact, which experience abundantly confirms, that people, to a greater or less degree, are honest in dealings, kind in their feelings, and beneficent in their conduct. Even the unsaved, the Apostle teaches us, do by nature the things of the law.[9]

Total depravity does mean that the downward trend is irreversible by human effort and that every person is infected in every dimension of their life—our thinking, our affections, our body, our relationships, and, above all, our will. We are incapable of consistently choosing the right.

God judges sin because of his own nature. Therefore, by nature he is incompatible with anything not morally right. The two cannot coexist. This is the meaning of holiness: God is separate from sin. Thus, the judgment of sin is the inevitable result of the nature of God and the nature of sin—separation. Adam and Eve experienced this judgment as the immediate result of that first, fatal choice to reject God's way. They were not only driven from the Garden; their

---

[8] John Calvin, *Institutes of the Christian Religion*, trans. John Allen, vol. 1 (London: James Clark, 1949), 310.
[9] "Nomos," in TDNT, 1069.

intimate companionship with God was ruptured. The independence for which they grasped was granted, which itself was the judgment—separation from God. Most people would not consider this a very terrible judgment, never having known union with God. But separation from God, the source of life, means separation from the gifts God would give, including, supremely, the gift of life. *"The wages of sin is death"* (Rom. 6:23).

This death works inexorably in every facet of a person's life. God in his grace gives us a probation period (one's lifetime) to reverse the choice of Eve and during that time gives gifts in abundance. The goodness of God is designed to lead to repentance (Rom. 2:4). But if the rejection of God's grace continues till physical death, the judgment—separation from God—is complete. This is the essential characteristic of hell. Sin by definition is violation of the law of God, rejection of the will of God, and thus the judgment for sin—separation—is actually chosen by the individual. He or she chooses to distance themselves from God, and God allows us to do so. This is the awful outcome of sin.

The psalmist shows how the judgment of separation is the choice of the individual: *"My people did not listen to my words and Israel would have none of me; so I sent them off, stubborn as they were, to follow their own devices"* (Ps. 81:11-12, NEB).

Paul reiterates the same truth in his terrible denunciations recorded in Romans 1: *"God gave them up . . . God gave them up . . . God gave them up."* What loss for anyone! Aren't we glad for grace?[10]

March 19
Gaining through Chance
Proverbs 18:18-19

"The lot puts an end to quarrels and decides between powerful contenders. A brother offended is more unyielding than a strong city, and quarreling is like the bars of a castle." (Proverbs 18:18-19*)*

Even though games of chance and other forms of gambling predate the writing of Scripture, the Bible is silent on the subject. Perhaps that is why the church has vacillated in its teaching. It is very difficult—if not impossible—to make a convincing case from Scripture against gambling or games of chance as inherently wrong, but it is no difficult task at all to marshal biblical evidence against gambling (as different from games of chance) as a social evil.

When the church has opposed gambling as inherently wrong, what has been the rationale? Although some have held it to be a form of stealing, this charge seems ill-founded, since stealing is taking by force that which one has no right to take. In the case of gambling, the loser has agreed in advance, and the risk of loss is freely undertaken in the hope of making a gain or having fun.

Gambling is said to violate the law against covetousness. This is certainly true for the serious gambler, but it can hardly be alleged against the person who gambles for recreation. Furthermore, though most gamblers may violate the law of love by seeking personal gain through another's loss, a motive of malice or lack of love can hardly be demonstrated as inherent in the act of gambling itself.

---
[10] IBE (2014), 494-495.

A definition that would apply to virtually any game at all, certainly games of chance implies an artificial risk, taken for personal gain at another's expense, having no social good as its goal. Games are inherently artificial, someone wins, someone loses, and there is no visibly constructive product, though there may be the social good of relaxation. I do not deny that the attitudes of covetousness and selfishness are present in most gambling and therefore that gambling of any kind may be inappropriate for the Christian. But are these poor attitudes inherent in the act?

The most common argument against gambling is the sovereignty of God—to deliberately take a risk on an uncertain outcome is to call in question God's sovereign control of our affairs or actually to invoke God's involvement in our attempt to gain at another's expense.

The same argument was used in earlier centuries against insurance. It will not do, this position holds, to say that all of life is a risk and that we constantly take chances—the farmer on the weather, the insurer on the insured's longevity, the businessman on the market. But these are not deliberately taking risk with the intent of avoiding exchange of value. These are people who make every attempt to reduce risk, who intend to pay an honest return on investment, and who have every right to humbly ask the Almighty to intervene should they err.

The argument against gambling based on God's sovereignty carries more weight than the others but is not compelling for two reasons. In the first place, it is really only applicable to the serious gambler. In the second place, even for the serious gambler, the argument could be turned the other way. In Scripture gambling was specifically used in making decisions because man is finite, and God alone knows and can intervene on behalf of one party or the other: "*The lot is cast into the lap, but the decision is wholly from the Lord*" (Proverbs16:33; see also 18:18). In fact, "casting the lot" was standard practice in settling disputes, dividing the Promised Land, choosing people for a position—all things that could well be of greater value than money. Even an apostle was so chosen (Acts 1:26). Contemporary gambling differs from the biblical examples of making decisions on the basis of a "chance" outcome in that two or more people were not offering something of value with the hope of gain and the risk of loss. Nevertheless, subjecting the outcome of a decision of great moment to the chance toss of the dice was seen as deliberately invoking the intervention of the Sovereign One, not flaunting his will or authority, much less making light of it. I suppose the same motive could be in the mind of the contemporary gambler, though. I grant it is not likely. The point is, if one deliberately trusts God with the outcome of a chance event—either planned ("artificially contrived") or unplanned—it can hardly be said that he is resisting God.

In summary, I find it difficult to make a strong case from Scripture to categorically affirm that all games of chance are inherently evil. A person could conceivably be generous, not covet, love his neighbor more than himself, and explicitly trust the sovereignty of God while betting a Coke on the outcome of a game. But that most gamblers violate one or more of these principles is beyond dispute.

Human experience indicates that even recreational gambling promotes covetousness and leads away from giving as a way of life. It often nurtures the fantasy that luck rather than hard work is a way to prosperity. All too often it sucks the gambler into a life of dishonesty. Even if one should escape the common evil results, is it right for the strong to validate gambling by personal example and help create an atmosphere in which others will fall? Seeing the practice in real life outcomes leads to the conclusion of the difficulty with gambling as a legitimate part of a God-pleasing way of life.

March 20
Love Chooses
John 15:13

Greater love has no one than this, that someone lay down his life for his friends. (John 15:13)

Most people choose and act from the motive of self-interest. The highest loyalty for unredeemed man is to self. In biblical love the ultimate, controlling love, the integrating factor of life, the pivotal relationship, is love for God. How can I tell if I love God supremely?

It is futile to try to decide whether we have as warm an affection for God as we do for a parent or child, a wife or husband, but there is a way to tell which love is paramount. The controlling love becomes quite evident when a confrontation comes. When the best interest of another or ourselves and the best interest of God come into conflict, love must make a choice.

Ordinary human love gives for another to a point. But when the cost of acting lovingly gets too high, loving behavior ends. God's kind of love is different. How can I tell if I truly love my neighbor as Christ would have me love? Ask the key question: Does my love for self-limit the expression of my love for the other person, or does my love for the other limit the expression of my love for myself? Love is measured, not by the intensity of its feeling, but by the sacrifice it stands ready to make.

Jesus indicated this when he said, "*Greater love has no man than this, that a man lay down his life for his friends*" (John 15:13). Often love is present without sacrifice, but so long as there is a return benefit, there is no *proof* that the love is truly other love rather than self-love. No matter what our emotional response, if we choose to sacrifice what we perceive to be our own interests for the welfare of another, we have loved as God loved. Sacrifice. That is God's way of loving. And the world finds it beyond comprehension.

Natural man does not ordinarily want to get involved for someone else's benefit. Above all, he does not want to suffer loss for someone else. When Kitty Genovese was brutally stabbed to death in front of her apartment in New York in March 1964, thirty-eight people watched from behind darkened windows. No one did anything to help her, though she cried for help for thirty minutes. Why? The police investigator said, "The word we kept hearing from the witnesses later was *involved.* People told us they just did not want to get involved. They do not want to be questioned or have to go to court." Her case was celebrated because of nationwide coverage, but the story is repeated daily. No one wants to be involved. But godlike love is precisely the opposite: It chooses to get involved, no matter what the cost. yet the sacrifices we shrink from are not usually life-threatening: the sacrifice of a parent to allow the child to be childish when he is young and to let him grow free when he is older, the sacrifice by a spouse of their right to be right—all the small irritations of the daily routine. For the conflict of interests to be resolved, someone must be sacrificed. Who will it be? Will I take up my cross or nail him to his? It depends on whom I love the more.

Shirai was a young Japanese wife whose husband was the traditional lord of the house. When she came to faith in Christ, he was furious. If she ever went to that Christian meeting again, he warned, she would be locked out. Sunday night Shirai came home to a darkened, locked home. She slept on the doorstep till morning, and when her husband opened the door, she smiled sweetly and hurried to prepare the best possible breakfast of bean soup, rice, and raw fish. Every Sunday and every Wednesday the story was the same. Winter came, and with it the rain and cold. Shirai huddled in the darkness as her wet cotton-padded jacket froze about her. Week after week for six months she forgave, freely and fully. No recriminations, no sulking. It was costly—she bore his sin. But her poor husband finally could stand it no longer. Love finally won out. When I met him, he was a pillar in the church, learning to walk the thorny path of sacrificial love. Shirai's example shatters my own complacency with a sharp, clear picture of what it means to deny oneself, take up one's cross daily, and follow Jesus.

Perhaps one of the most painful sacrifices that love makes is forgiveness. To forgive is costly, for someone must pay the price of wrong. If I choose to treat the person as if the wrong had never been done (forgive), then I may have to pay for it. It is not just the sacrifice of ego—that seems to be painful enough. But if I forgive—truly forgive—the smashed fender, then I pay for it. And I do not make the guilty party pay for it in installments through petty insinuations. Even when the relationship is such that discipline is necessary, as with a parent and child, forgiveness means full restoration without the haunting specter of subtle reminders.

Must I forgive if the other person does not repent, does not ask forgiveness? Jesus said, "If your brother sins, rebuke him, and if he repents, forgive him" (Luke 17:3). So we must forgive the one who indicates their sin against us. That is when God forgives. But Christ and Stephen both prayed that God would not hold accountable those who sinned against them, even though the murderers had not asked forgiveness. So it is all right to forgive anyway. And since we are not godlike in our knowledge of the other person's thoughts, it may be the best thing to forgive anyway. Usually the other person does not view the circumstances from my perspective and does not sense a need to repent or ask forgiveness. In any event, an attempt at reconciliation is always my responsibility, no matter who the chief wrongdoer was. Besides, unforgiveness is a cancer that eats away at the spirit of the one who fails to forgive, so there is great therapeutic value in forgiveness as a way of life, no matter how the offenders in one's life behave.[11]

How is your love life today? Will it be love for yourself or love for the other? Will it be forgiveness? How costly will it be? Are you willing to pay the price?

March 21
Changing my Hard Drive
1 Corinthians 2:14

The man without the Spirit does not accept the things that come from the Spirit of God, for they are foolishness to him, and he cannot understand them, because they are spiritually discerned. (1 Corinthians 2:14)

The 20th century could be called the century of the Holy Spirit. In 1901 the modern Pentecostal movement was born, and for the first time some identified speaking in tongues as the necessary evidence of being filled with the Spirit. The Pentecostal movement had phenomenal growth world-wide. Then in mid-century it broke out into mainstream denominations in what came to be called the charismatic movement. Finally, toward the end of the century, the missionary enterprise was inundated with an emphasis on power encounter, emphasizing the need for visible demonstrations of supernatural power to accomplish world evangelism. Many in that movement seemed to focus more on the enemy, the unholy spirits, than on the Holy Spirit. Still power encounter has grown directly out of the Pentecostal and charismatic context. In reaction to this, many Christians have rejected all demonstrations of the Spirit's activity

---

[11] IBE (2014), 23.

and have been afraid to emphasize the ministry of the Spirit at all. This attitude is a tragic loss since the Holy Spirit is the source of all spiritual blessing. We humans find it easier to take one side of biblical truth to one extreme or the other, neglecting the balancing truths of Scripture, rather than find the center of biblical balance.

Whatever your present knowledge or experience of the Holy Spirit, I hope you'll want to tap into His resources for living the Christian life. He has made full provision for you to do just that. Apart from Him there's no way you can experience a close friendship with God or become the person He intends you to be.

Since the mid-eighties I've been computer-dependent in my writing. I was satisfied with the way my old computer worked-after all, it used to be state-of-the-art. But increasingly I experienced difficulties. Gradually I found my computer could "talk" with fewer and fewer other computers. It couldn't read what other people sent me. I began to use electronic mail, but the Internet was designed for speedy new models, not for my Noah's ark. I upgraded, but it wasn't enough. I needed a new model altogether. Dressing up the old one wasn't good enough. Our experience with the Spirit resembles my situation with the computer. We humans were originally created God-compatible. We could communicate with Him. At least our first ancestor, Adam, could. But a breakdown occurred. I tried self-improvement-reprogramming my mind to think more like God so I could understand what He was saying in His Word-but it didn't work. I needed to be an altogether new model, a new creation (1 Corinthians 5:17). That's exactly what the Holy Spirit provides-a new creation. My body and brain is the same, but when He recreated me, He put a new spirit within me. The inner workings of the new me are different from the old me. The new me is made God-compatible. Theologians call this change regeneration. It represents so radical a transformation; the Bible calls it "a new birth" (1 Peter 1:3). Most of us, however, underestimate the potential in the new model. We don't tap into the resources the Holy Spirit has provided by making us new (2 Cor. 5:17).

Not only does the Spirit re-make us into new models, He begins a new personal relationship with us. His names hint at the personal aspect of our relationship. He is called Comforter and Counselor. Descriptions of His activity, such as convicting of sin and teaching us all things also point to His personal ministry in our lives.

When movies or fairy tales transform one creature into another, some secret formula or potion may work the magic. But God doesn't do it that way. When God reconstructs us in His likeness, He doesn't stay at a distance and send us a do-it-yourself kit. God's provision for changing us is very personal: He gives us Himself. The Holy Spirit comes and personally works the miracle. He makes new people out of us, and then comes inside as a constant companion. Better than that-He fills us up with Himself!

We've seen how God Himself, by the Spirit, has made full provision for us to spiral up into His very likeness and into intimate companionship with Him. But maybe that isn't happening. Maybe you're sort of plateaued out in your Christian life. Perhaps you are even starting to spiral down away from God. What's wrong? Why doesn't the Spirit-filled life seem to work?

There are three possible reasons Christians fail to grow; 1) we may be ignorant of God's provision or of my responsibility; 2) I may have unbelief, lack of confidence in God; 3) I may be practicing disobedience. If disobedience is the problem, it can occur in two different ways, conscious rejection of God's known will or unconscious drift out of a close relationship. What is going on in your life? Take some time and examine if you are growing in your likeness to Him and in your companionship with Him. If not, why not? Decide today to reconnect or if you never connected, ask Him to recreate you on the inside.

March 22
The Designer's Plan
1 John 4:7 & 16

"Dear friends, let us love one another, for love comes from God. Everyone who loves has been born of God and knows God. God is love. Whoever lives in love lives in God, and God in him." (1 John 4:7,16)

From all eternity God the Father, God the Son, and God the Holy Spirit were bound together in love, for God by nature is love (1 John 4:7,16). From the overflow of His loving nature, He wanted people to whom He could show His love and who would love Him back.

For communication and love to flow freely, the people God made would have to be like Him. The relationship couldn't be like you and your dog. Fido may be a great friend, but communication is limited, and a dog is not exactly a "suitable helper" to you, as God said of the mate He was creating for Adam (Genesis 2:20). Fido is a different species, but Adam and Eve, that's another story. They were made for each other.

Just as God created Adam and Eve compatible with each other, He created us to be God-compatible. If that compatibility weren't there, in-depth communication would not be possible, intimate companionship would be missing. That is why God the Holy Spirit created humankind on God's own patten. As a result, Adam and Eve walked with God in the garden of Eden, sharing His presence and love. They were created to love God and be loved by Him. They were created in His likeness so they could experience that love.

God's design determines genuine life purpose. What do you consider to be your supreme purpose in life? The ultimate goal of our lives is to love God. Even becoming Christlike in character falls short of that supreme goal. Becoming more like Jesus enables us to fellowship with God, but it is not the ultimate goal. The more like Christ we become, the more we will be able to love God and receive love from Him. Becoming like Christ is so important that the major emphasis of this devotional is how we become like Him; *transformed*. But keep in mind that becoming like Christ is not the final goal.

The goal is to develop our love relationship with God. He created us on His pattern and provided the salvation process as a way for His image in us to be restored . He did all these things with the ultimate goal of loving us and us loving Him. Before we close the study of God's purpose in making us like Him, let us reflect on ways we are becoming like Him and ways in which we are not. Take a few minutes and list five ways in which those who know you best would say you are growing in Christlikeness-ways in which He is making you more like Himself. Now list five ways in which you are least like Jesus, or ways in which people who know you best would say you least remind them of Jesus . If you fear someone may see this, you may want to list them on a separate sheet of paper, such as in your journal. But it will be very helpful to have them before you for reflection and prayer. I encourage you not to just read this but to do it and consider the implications.

Sometime during the next week ask someone close to you to answer those two questions about you. Ask someone who will tell you the truth. Write that person's answers in another color so you can see clearly and reflect on the differences between your own perceptions and those of the other person. Comparing ourselves to Jesus could lead to discouragement. We fall so far short. Actually becoming more like Him is the great desire of the true lover of God- to develop a character that is just like Him so that we can experience His purpose in making and redeeming us. We want to know an ever-deepening love relationship that will bring Him joy and bring us joy, too.

As you conclude your study today spend some time talking with God about the following areas :

- First, thank the Lord for what He has done to change you into Christ's likeness.
- Spend time confessing the ways you haven't changed but want Him to change you.
- Finally, thank the Lord that He loves you with an everlasting love, and tell Him how much you love Him. Like the surge of joy I feel when my wife responds with a smile, your Eternal Lover is waiting for your response.

March 23
The Transformation Connection
Habakkuk 2:4

"The righteous will live by his faith" (Habakkuk 2:4)

How do we connect to let His power flow? How do we move from an average to a normal Christian life? We connect with Him through faith. "'The righteous will live by his faith'" (Habakkuk 2:4) was the only message of an Old Testament prophet that was repeated, not once, but three times in the New Testament (Romans 1:17; Galatians 3:11; Hebrews 10:38).

Faith is the uplink with divine power, whether for salvation or for being restored into the original design. God provides the power for living through the activity of the Holy Spirit. We respond to God's provision through faith. Faith releases the power of the Holy Spirit to work in our lives. Faith means:

- Believing what God has said.
- Choosing to trust God by putting your life in His hands even when everything seems to be going wrong.
- Placing your confidence in His love and knowledge of you and His ability to order your life for your greatest blessing.

God is the standard for our lives-we were meant to reflect His image. God also restores and empowers us to become like Him; the Holy Spirit can build character and make us more like Christ. We connect with God through faith.

God is spirit. He created us on the same model-spiritual beings-so we could join His circle of love. We broke that relationship and damaged ourselves. But God pursues us with passionate love, intent on repairing us, remodeling us into His moral likeness so we can again be God-compatible.

In the normal Christian life, God has first place in our lives. We value the welfare of others above our selfish desires. The functioning Christian has power not only for godly living but also for effective service in the church. Above all, he or she has the joy of constant companionship with the Lord.

The average church member typically thinks and behaves very much like morally upright non-Christians. They are decent enough but with nothing supernatural about them. Their behavior is explainable in terms of heredity, early environment, and present circumstances. They often yield to temptation, lusting when their body craves it, coveting what they do not have, and taking credit for their accomplishments. The touchstone for their choices is self-interest. Though they have a love for God and others, strained or broken relationships with others prove that the Spirit does not control their lives. The average church member experiences little change for the better. In fact, many don't seem to expect much improvement and have little concern about the prospect for change. Scripture is not exciting, prayer is perfunctory, and service in the church demonstrates little touch of the supernatural. Above all, life seems to have an empty core, for it does not center around a constant, personal companionship with the Lord.

Each of us has areas of strength and weakness, some we are aware of, some perhaps not. But God knows, and when we acknowledge our need to Him, He will move in and begin restoring our broken-down models to function as He designed them to operate (1 John 1:5-2:2).

"How, HOW, HOW, HOW can I ever live that kind of life?" A troubled graduate student scribbled the question on a scrap of paper and passed it to me after class. She had heard me talk about a Spirit-empowered life. She desperately wanted an answer. Let me summarize the answer to that student's question briefly, in the words of Scripture:

- *For those God foreknew he also predestined to be conformed to the likeness of his Son (Rom. 8:29).*
- *We, who with unveiled faces all reject the Lord's glory, are being transformed into his likeness with ever-increasing glory, which comes from the Lord, who is the Spirit (2 Cor. 3:18).*
- *The new self... is being renewed in knowledge in the image of its Creator (Col. 3:10).*

Notice that in all these passages the restoration to our original design is not in a study lesson, not in a formula, but in a Person. The transforming presence and power of God the Holy Spirit will enable us to be what God designed us to be. I hope you will discover that the model you were built on, God's own pattern, when restored by the Master Repairman, can indeed run the program as designed. You can daily experience a beautiful life of spiritual effectiveness. You can begin to resemble Christ more and more. As you continue this study I pray that you will examine and experience those truths in all their exciting dimensions. Here is my suggested prayer:
Thank You, blessed Spirit, that You have not abandoned me. You have shown me a secure hope that You personally stand ready to show me the way, enable me to travel it, and companion with me to the end of it. Amen!

March 24
Gifts and Talents
1 Corinthians 12:4-7

"There are different kinds of gifts, but the same Spirit. There are different kinds of service, but the same Lord. There are different kinds of working, but the same God works all of them in all men. Now to each one the manifestation of the Spirit is given for the common good." (1 Corinthians 12:4-7)

First in our considerations for today, note that both natural ability and spiritual ability are gifts from God. We must use both natural and supernatural gifts for His glory, not our own. To use either natural or spiritual gifts for our own glory is sin. We are responsible to use all that we are to glorify Him. The second thing to note is that the Bible doesn't explain the relationship between natural and spiritual giftedness.

There are those that people might be successful at without Spirit-enabling if they had great natural ability in the following list of church activities: singing, ushering, preaching, teaching, counselling, leading a group, hospitality, and managing finances. Even witnessing can be faked if the person has enough personal charisma; but we're talking here of those who truly lead people to Christ. If my opinion is anywhere near correct, the conclusion is scary!

Most of the work of the church could be carried on by gifted people without the Spirit of God doing anything. Some people refer to ministry as either "in the flesh" or "in the Spirit." A difference does exist between the two, but the difference may not be between spiritual gifts and natural abilities. The difference is between depending on self or depending on the Spirit. Evidence of a supernatural touch is one indication that a ministry is accomplished in the Spirit. For example, Paul wasn't a world-class public speaker-he agreed with the Corinthians in that judgment (1 Cor. 2:1). But when he taught the Bible, lives were transformed. Whether the Spirit merely lifts a natural ability to a higher power we may not know; but if it's a Spirit-gift, there will be the Spirit's miracle touch.

Though the word "manifestation" in our verse for today means "visible evidence" and that is the ultimate proof, we need to exercise two cautions.

• some may have "visible evidence" resulting from strong natural ability, not really the work of the Spirit. For example, the magicians in Pharaoh's court managed to duplicate some of the signs Moses performed (Ex. 7:11), but they certainly did not do them through the power of the Spirit.

• a person may have been given a gift and still experience a lack of evidence because of adverse circumstances. For example, Ezekiel was God's own prophet, but the people were rebels and wouldn't listen (Ezekiel 3).

Paul was no doubt the greatest of evangelists, but in Lystra they stoned him out of town (Acts 14). In general, however, if no evidence shows the Spirit at work, if the ministry makes no spiritual impact, we need to ask if the ministry is God's.

When I fail to see evidence in my own ministry, I ask myself the following diagnostic questions:

1. *Am I harboring unconfessed sin?* When I've preached my heart out and lives aren't changed, I first examine myself to see if something in me blocked the flow of the Spirit. Do I have some unconfessed sin, a wrong motivation (wanting "success" for human praise), unbelief (not trusting God to do what only He can do), or lack of prayer preparation? I don't immediately conclude that I don't have the gift or that He hasn't called me after all.

2. *Do I need to be persistent?* When I felt called to do missionary work, I kept asking God for the gift of evangelism. People came to Christ through my ministry only sporadically, and I longed for the ability to consistently win people to Christ.

The principle is to keep asking until you see one of two things: "visible evidence" of the gift you long for, or the assurance that God doesn't intend that gift for you. Stop asking only when God shows you that the gift is not for you.

3. *Am I in the Right Place?* In Japan, we discovered that we were ministering in a very unresponsive area. We asked God if there should be a change of location to a place or people who would respond. This is what Paul did more than once (See Acts 13:46 for example).

4. *Is God vindicating Himself?* Perhaps, on the other hand, God intends a gifted person to stand firm when there is no "fruit" or outward result, as His vindication among an unresponsive people (as in Ezekiel's case).

You can see from the above examples that a legitimate gift may be without "visible evidence" in some situations. But in general, we distinguish between natural ability and supernatural ability by the outcome of the ministry. The most exciting thing about the gifts of the Spirit is that He has given some ability to serve God to every Christian. Where are you currently serving? Is there visible evidence of the Spirit at work? How might the four diagnostic questions provide direction for the next phase of your ministry?

March 25
Building Bridges
1 Corinthians 9:22

"To the weak I became weak, that I might win the weak. I have become all things to all people, that by all means I might save some." (1 Corinthians 9:22)

Once there was a fisherman out on the pier and he had his line in the water. I asked him what he was fishing with, and he said "Blackberries".

"Blackberries?" I asked, "that won't work.

"But I love blackberries!" he replied.

And so it is with sharing our faith. We use what we like and miss using what the other likes or can even comprehend. Perhaps we are still in an age where "what is true for you, may not be true for me." Certainly, truth continues to be relative to many. Absolutes are hard to find with morals rapidly disappearing. How can we fish in this contemporary era without using blackberries? What will connect with generations coming of age in the world today? Let me propose three directions for you to consider; elements of thinking to adopt, adapt and elements of thinking to oppose.

(1) **elements to adopt**

* *The spiritual trumps the material.* Well, hallelujah! Of course, we have to help define spiritual, but isn't it great we can champion the prevailing view that the unseen is the important part of our lives? From there it may not be so difficult to move on to the idea that the unseen is the real, the eternal.

* *Reality must be experienced.* True, my experience doesn't alter reality and there is objective reality that can be known, but when we offer vibrant, living experiential salvation and sanctification we're on solid biblical ground.

* *How I feel is more important than what I think. More* important? Well, actually you can't really have one without the other, can you? And which comes first? But we do a grave disservice to this generation if we don't speak to the heart, stimulate feelings, godly feelings. Today's thinking has recaptured the heart, opened us to our emotions, and for that we must be grateful, for it leads toward greater biblical reality than we knew as rational modernists.

* *Relationships are paramount.* What more could you ask? Not only human relationships which some preachers slight, but we must ever lead on to the ultimate relationship -created, as we were, God-compatible for the very purpose of loving companionship with him. Intimacy, you might call it, a favorite word to the younger generations. In fact it isn't too much to say that a person's chief end is to love God and be loved of him forever.

* *Hope is in short supply.* But desperately wanted. So we offer hope. But we mustn't offer mega-hope too soon. Better to offer modest hope, at least to begin with. The young person may not be able to change the course of history, but, we may assure them, You can make a difference!

(2) **Elements to adapt.**

* *Anti-intellectual.* It is the renewing of our **minds** God is after and transformational preaching certainly can't bypass the mind. But we can use the contemporary anti-intellectual mood to dethrone scientific naturalism and a materialistic mind-set. We may harness the mood to demolish a deadly enemy of spiritual reality.

* *Propositional truth is a fiction, the only reality is a fusion of what may be "out there" and my personal perception of it, post moderns contend.*

Yet the Bible is full of propositional truth, of course, and we can capture one element of this mood, since narrative, not propositional truth, is the preferred mode.

* *Tell me a story, they say.*

Story? That does have a familiar ring to it, doesn't it? Sounds like the Bible! The stories of ancient Israel, the stories of Jesus--in fact, it is written, he didn't speak at all except in stories! (Matthew 13:34)

**Radical individualism.*

If the only reality admitted is composed of what's out there with my perception of it, everyone's "reality" differs. And that's cool.

When I was researching on what made the X and Y generations tick I asked a powerful youth evangelist to give me some time and educate me. He said, "No need to spend time. I can tell you in one word." Then he shaped his two thumbs and forefingers in the shape of a W-- "Whatever," he said with a shrug. Now I tell young people that "whatever" is an ok feeling but point out the difference between an ungodly whatever that doesn't care and a godly whatever that lets God have his way.

* *Personal fulfillment is the goal of life.*

No, no. **God**'s fulfillment is the goal! But when we chart the way to God-centered living we do no wrong in pointing out that as the only path to personal self-fulfillment. Try to fill up on stuff, sex, and significance- on self, that is and you'll get ever more empty, taught Jesus. On the other hand, work at emptying out life into God's purposes and you'll discover yourself is filling up, fulfilled.

* *Personal freedom is the* sina qua non *of finding fulfillment.*

Why aren't we the chief champions of freedom? Of course, we point toward freedom as power to do what I ought rather than license to do what I please.

**Celebrate diversity. The only sin is intolerance.*

I can attack this error head-on. And lose my audience. Or I can celebrate unity in diversity among God's people, in God's creation, while flashing the caution light of biblical limitations to the concept. If I champion unity in diversity, it won't be quite so easy to dismiss me as a hard-nosed right-wing obscurantist.

(3) elements to oppose

**Absolute relativism.* Not only must we point out the absurdity of this ultimate oxymoron, we must show graphically how it is not a liberating concept as supposed, but how it leads inexorably to dreadful bondage.

* *Self-sacrifice is bad. It's dishonest, a betrayal of self, destructive.* The God-story, the story of Jesus is our ultimate weapon to destroy this perversion of the enemy. We must hammer away at the theme of love and the joyful fruit of love. We must demonstrate powerfully how self-orientation is in the end destructive; how self-denial is the affirmation of our true self, the ultimate healing power.

* *Commitment is stupid.* We should find it easy to demonstrate from marriage stories the end results of non-commitment vs. commitment. And we can demonstrate from all of life how commitment is the glue that holds together that ultimate desire of the younger generations: relationship, and bonding. With one's fellows, yes, but above all with God. You might even persuade them to hope for an ultimate love relationship.

Fishing with blackberries? Catching fish needs an attractive bait to the fish, not the fisherman!

March 26
Filled Full
Ephesians 3:19

(I pray that you may) know this love that surpasses knowledge - that you may be filled to the measure of all the fullness of God. (Ephesians 3:19)

Several of the fruits of the Spirit involve our emotions, but even the ones that seem mostly matters of feeling have practical results. To love, for example, is to act lovingly no matter how you feel. Maybe that's why God seems to expect us to have these qualities as a steady state in our lives-all the fruit, all the time. Their presence is evidence of the Spirit at work. But the emotions that accompany them may not be surging all the time. Perhaps God intends the fruit to be constant and the surges of feelings to be special outpourings?
- Jesus was a man of sorrows and acquainted with grief. He agonized in the garden of Gethsemane, but he also experienced times of surging joy-"*At that time Jesus, full of joy through the Holy Spirit*" (Luke 10:21).
- David, the joy-filled singer for the ages, experienced dry times. When God seemed distant, David cried out in alarm, "*Do not . . . take your Holy Spirit from me*" (Ps. 51:11).
- Paul had times of fear and called on friends to pray for the Spirit-gift of boldness (2 Cor. 7:5; Eph. 6:19-20). For these Bible characters, the inner sense of fullness seems not to be "steady state."

If full feelings are elusive, the other meanings of "full" are not. Most of the examples have to do with power in ministry, but some subjective evidences appear. We find joy, boldness, and faith. However, both the boldness and faith are related directly to ministry! So, in the biblical examples, the subjective element of feelings, which we so emphasize today, is not prominent. Our obedience to the Spirit or lack of it should be clear. If I have a full crop of faith and ministry effectiveness, that should be clear to others. But the inner sense of fullness may not be all that apparent-it may defy analysis. But that is OK. Think about it: in filling us with Himself God promises to give us a love beyond comprehension (Eph. 3:19) and He speaks of a peace that is unfathomable (Phil. 4:7). How exciting to feel the mysterious surge of the Spirit!

Ephesians 5:18- *And do not get drunk with wine, for that is debauchery, but be filled with the Spirit.* This verse in a subtle way ties together the three different aspects of being filled with the Spirit. The verb be filled is unusual in that it is a command something I must do-but it's in the passive form, something the Spirit does to me. "Be being filled" would be an awkward translation but gets at the meaning. So how do you obey if He is the one who does it? You take the initiative and deliberately yield control. Then you keep on praying and expecting Him to produce the fruit of godliness and power for ministry. If He chooses to surge through with a flood of some special emotion, how blessed! The command be filled is also a continuous action verb: "Keep on being filled with the Spirit." Being filled is a constant in that sense, an abiding relationship. Steady-state filled, you might call it. If the Holy Spirit has control of your life, He'll continuously fill you with power to live and serve.

In Ephesians 5:18-20, Paul also identifies some of the inner feelings associated with being filled: singing, praise, and prayer. Paul says to let the Spirit fill you always as a way of life. Then, from time to time out of His grace, He'll blow into your life with gale force and fan the embers into an all-consuming fire of His own making. When that happens simultaneously to a lot of people, we call the result revival. Take a few minutes and examine; are you steady state filled? Does He sometimes blow into your life? Are the fruit to be constant and the surges of feelings special?

If you can't remember anything out of the ordinary in your relationship with God and you are thirsty for a full surge of awareness of God's presence, why not pause right now and tell Him so? But don't leave it there. Tell Him how much you love Him, how grateful you are for Him, for His constant companionship, and for all the wonderful blessings

He floods into your life. Ask Him to fill you up with Himself. Pause now and write out in your journal either the description of your experience of fullness, the prayer for fullness, or both.

March 27
A Book and a Guide
2 Timothy 2:15

"Do your best to present yourself to God as one approved, a workman who does not need to be ashamed and who correctly handles the word of truth." (2 Timothy 2:15)

God didn't just make up rules. God's laws actually flow from His own character. They express His will that we be like Him. We might not understand if He just sent instructions and gave us examples of Bible characters. He Himself came to show us what the Father is like (John 14:7-11; Hebrews 1:1-3). The exciting thing is this: Jesus in person is our standard for life. He is the supreme revelation of God's will.

God's revelation is not merely truth about the unseen world, given to satisfy our curiosity. Revelation shows us what God wants us to be and do. The Holy Spirit enables us to become like Jesus; He is God's standard for the Christian. Seeing how far we fall short of reaching that standard can be discouraging, but if we don't first see our need, we'll never attempt to meet it!

Even with our map for living we will make wrong turns. But God always provides a way back! A serious disciple of Christ has at least two reasons to obey:

1. We want to know what will bring joy to the one we love. We want to please Him by doing what He wants. "You are my friends," Jesus said, "if you do what I command you" (John 15:14). Love makes obedience to God's rules a joy because the result is fellowship with Jesus.

2. Obedience is practical. I need direction for my life. Only on the tracks laid out by divine wisdom will I find the fulfillment of life's purpose. As the Psalmist said, " Oh, how I love your law!" (Ps. 119:97).

Interpretation-determining the meaning the author intended-is the next step in knowing the will of God. And that is crucial for living life in the Spirit. Has any truth become clear or especially important to you, perhaps demanding some response on your part? If so, you may wish to enter it in your journal for today.

To understand God's character and His will we need to understand and interpret the Bible. What do we mean when we say we need to interpret the Bible? How does depending on the Spirit affect interpretation? What about those passages that we find confusing or controversial? Interpretation must be the most abused word in discussing the Bible. Many people believe that everyone's "interpretation" is valid, no matter how outrageously it twists the meaning of the Scripture. Curiously, the popular view of "interpretation," as if no objective truth exists, is most often used of the Bible. Can you imagine two engineers debating whether or not 2 x 2 = 4? Interpretation always begins by determining what the author intended to communicate. Interpretation does not mean justifying my view of an issue by twisting the passage into a new shape. When we assume that the Bible communicates specific meanings, some people call our approach "literalistic." I want to ask them, "Do you mean literalistic like literalistic news, history, or law?" As we approach any written communication, we assume that the author intended to say something. The writer may have used literal or figurative language, but the task is to understand the intended meaning, not impose our own "interpretation" on the written material.

We all struggle with some issues in the Bible. Some passages in the Bible I still don't understand. When we read the Scriptures, our assumptions condition how we understand what we read. Our culture, life experiences, understandings of words and ideas come with us . Sometimes what we bring with us can lead us astray. We must always be willing to challenge our own thinking to allow the Spirit to lead us into His truth. Interpretation means working diligently to make sure exactly what the author intended to say. Bible scholars call the study of Scripture hermeneutics-the science of determining the meaning of a text and applying it authentically to life . Good interpretation follows principles to separate the message of the Bible from my own thoughts, opinions, and ideas.

If our goal in Bible study is to find out what the Holy Spirit wants to say to us, we must treat the Book as both human and divine, not going to one extreme or the other. As we study, we may become confused or discouraged, so I have good news for you. We have more than a Book, we have a Guide! The Holy Spirit comes alongside to guide us in understanding the Book.

Years ago, friends said I should get on the information super-highway so I could send and receive electronic mail. They said things like, "You could send letters to Zimbabwe free of charge! Instantly!" But I was intimidated. I'd used a computer for years but had never read one of the manuals on my shelf. They might as well have been written in a foreign language. If I hit a snag, instead of picking up a manual, I'd call an expert.

Some people approach Bible study the same way. The Bible sits on the shelf, so intimidating. How could I ever understand it? I'll just give the expert a call; I'll just wait to hear what the preacher says. But the Bible was given to us to use. It's so much more important than a computer manual. But like the manual, it takes effort to comprehend its message. How committed are you to understanding God's Word? It takes effort and time. Regular systematic reading and study. Can you commit to understanding God's Word and in it God's intention for your life? Why not stop and pray, committing anew to the Guide and the Book!

March 28
Law and Faith
James 2:22

"You see that faith was working with his works, and as a result of the works, faith was perfected" (James 2:22, NASB)

Does Paul bad-mouth the law when he says, *"The law is not of faith"*? (Gal. 3:12). "May it never be." Law and faith are different in character. Comparing them is like comparing apples and oranges. The law is a standard; faith is a disposition or an attitude. Paul was saying, "Don't ask the law to do only what faith can do." But that doesn't do away with the law. They fit together beautifully in God's design for the Christian life.

Faith is the only way to respond to grace. When God speaks to me in grace, he does not say "do for me," but rather, "I have done for you." I cannot earn grace. This is faith. The whole Christian life is characterized by faith.

"Whatever does not proceed from faith is sin" (Rom. 14:23). Faith is taking what God gives—but taking it on God's terms. God does not ask me simply to agree with him that his grace is true, effective, and glorious. He commands

me to live in the light of its radical implications. He calls me to be converted, exchanging my commitment to sin and self for commitment to God through Christ. Merely claiming to have faith is easy but ineffectual. Commitment to God through Christ in faith, however, is life itself. True faith, biblical faith, works (James 2:17-18). It is a persevering faith that does not pick and choose when to follow the Lord (a *de facto* denial that Christ is the Lord). Biblical faith presupposes obedient discipleship.

Before Paul said, "*The law does not rest on faith*" (Gal. 3:12), he said, "*No man is justified before God by the law*" (3:11). Old Testament and New Testament speak with one voice, "*The just shall live by faith*" (see Hab. 2:4). The law is a standard that, by itself, pronounces a curse. A law is given to be obeyed, not merely to be acknowledged (i.e., "believed"). We had broken the law and were guilty. No amount of belief in the law's perfection or accuracy of its evaluation could remove its curse. Likewise, no amount of obedience could alter previous disobedience. Here is where God's grace in Christ intervened. Paul continued, "*Christ redeemed us from the curse of the law, having become a curse for us*" (3:13). He perfectly obeyed the law so that he could be condemned by the law in my place. God gave Christ to us so that the law would not condemn us legally, not so that the law need not characterize us behaviorally. For Paul continued in the next verse to give the purpose for redeeming us from the law's curse—"*that in Christ Jesus the blessing of Abraham might come upon the Gentiles, that we might receive the promise of the Spirit through faith*" (3:14).

The Spirit is present in the life of the believer by faith, but to what end? We walk by the Spirit or are led by the Spirit to produce the fruit of the Spirit (Galatians 5:16, 18, 22-23). The Spirit's fruit, a cluster of nine godly character traits, is perfectly satisfying to God and us. Why? Paul said, "*against such there is no law*" (5:23). Paul did not say there is no law. He did not say that the law no longer functions. Paul's statement here would be meaningless unless the category of law was still applicable to the Christian. Paul was saying that the Spirit-led Christian fulfills the law as the goal of redemption in his or her new, Spirit-indwelt status. God masterfully neutralized the law's curse through Christ's sacrifice and now enables me to fulfill the demands of the law through the Spirit's indwelling.

So, though the law is not of faith (laws are to be observed and grace is to be believed), the believer believes (as believers should) what God has said about the law (that we are free from its curse to fulfill it in the Spirit). The Christian is thereby free in faith to obey the law. Obedience is a dimension of genuine biblical faith. Faith and the law are not opposed unless one is using the law legalistically. When converted, Abraham (Genesis 15:6), the father of the faithful, offered Isaac in obedience to God's command. Scripture says, "*You see that faith was working with his works, and as a result of the works, faith was perfected*" (James 2:22, NASB). Why not pray today that you are free in faith to obey the law and that you live in the radical implications of grace?

March 29
Is the Law Relevant?
1 John 1:5-7

God is light and in him is no darkness at all. If we say we have fellowship with him while we walk in darkness, we lie and do not live according to the truth; but if we walk in the light, as he is in the light, we have fellowship with one another, and the blood of Jesus his Son cleanses us from all sin. (1 John 1:5-7)

The law of God is often likened in Scripture to light (e.g., Psalm 119:105). Like the streetlight, God's law restrains evil (1 Timothy 1:9-10). God's law does not control evil men, but it is a retarding influence to the forces of evil in the world. Some call this the *political* use of the law. By moral standards a society is held together. When moral standards loosen, a community or nation begins to come apart.

Like the light in the washroom, God's law reveals man's moral defilement (Romans 3:20; 7:7). By the law comes the knowledge of sin. If I do not believe I am dirty, I will not seek cleansing. If I do not think I am lost, I will not welcome a rescuer. But if I know that I am polluted and incapable of doing that which I wish to do, I will seek a savior and welcome him. This is the "custodian" work of the law that brings us to Christ (Galatians 3:24). The law in Paul's sense here is not, strictly speaking, a teacher ("schoolmaster"). Rather, the law for the sinner is the school bus driver or even the truant officer to bring the lost to Christ. For the lawbreaker, the law makes sin very plain, "sinful beyond measure" (Romans 7:13). Thus the terrifying law condemns us and is designed to make people seek a way of escape. This is the *evangelistic* use of the law. If he does not flee to the Cross, the law becomes the basis for his judgment in the last day, and law will have failed in its evangelistic purpose (Romans 3:19).

For the Christian, the law has an entirely different function. Like the headlights on an automobile, the law for the Christian shows the way he must go if he is to reach the destination of being like Jesus.

The *spiritual* use of the law, or the *instructional* (didactic) use of the law is this standard which is the goal of our Christian life. Thus God's purpose in giving the law is for our good, for our fulfillment, whether we are unsaved or saved.

And now, Israel, what does the LORD your God require of you, but to fear the LORD your God, to walk in all his ways, to love him, to serve the LORD your God with all your heart and with all your soul, and to keep the commandments and statutes of the LORD, which I command you this day for your good? (Deuteronomy 10:12-13)

Legalists forever want to turn it around and re-create people for the sake of the law, whereas Jesus insisted that the law (of the Sabbath) was made for man and not man for the law (Mark 2:27). "He puts that law into practice and he wins true happiness" (James 1:25, Phillips).

Man's welfare, happiness, fulfillment is ever the purpose of a loving God. The more like him we become, the more we are fulfilled. This is the way of freedom, not restriction and bondage. James calls this the "*law of liberty*" (James 2:12). The tragedy of the lawless person is that he is forever diverted from the true and right trajectory. Righteousness is alignment with reality, and the one who is out of alignment with reality will finally destroy himself. But to be true and right, in alignment with ultimate reality, will make a person free, fulfill the purpose of his existence.

The person who abides by the rules of the game is the one who enjoys the game and the only one who is qualified to win. The owner who follows the instruction manual of the manufacturer is the one who finds satisfaction with the product. And so it is with traffic laws or criminal law—each is for our good. It is not simply that God rewards good behavior and punishes evil behavior, true as that may be. Sin brings its own punishment, righteousness its own reward: "The iniquities of the wicked ensnare him, and he is caught in the toils of his sin" (Proverbs 5:22).

This common theme of Scripture (Numbers 32:23; Psalm 7:15; 9:15; 40:12; Proverbs 1:31; 11:1-31) does not mean merely the obvious, that the drunkard may get hurt, will have a hangover, and often ruins his own life as well as others. It is even deeper than the truth that "the measure you give will be the measure you get" (Mark 4:24). The sin itself warps and ultimately destroys the person. Covetousness eats like cancer, taking away peace and joy, binding and demeaning the spirit—even if it does not lead to some other grosser behavior. In adultery a person sins against himself, depriving himself of the very things that make life worthwhile: love, security, belonging, fidelity, peace, integrity, the ecstasy of full oneness. Indeed, there is inherent punishment in sin (2 Peter 2:13).

On the other hand, *"Great peace have those who love thy law; nothing can make them stumble"* (Psalm 119:165). *"And I shall walk at liberty, for I have sought thy precepts"* (v. 45). The law is the birthright of all who are his. No wonder the longest chapter in the Bible is devoted to extolling the glorious wonders of the law of God (Psalm 119).

Note carefully that the purpose of God's law is different from the purpose of regulations and laws in other religions. The law was never intended to make us righteous. There are passages in the Old Testament that sound as if the law had this purpose, and a few in the New Testament as well. (See Leviticus 18:5; Matthew 19:17) But Paul repeatedly emphasizes that no one—under the Old Covenant or under the New—has ever been or ever will be justified by obedience to the law: *"For no human being will be justified in his sight by works of the law"* (Romans 3:20; Gal. 2:16). Paul insists that this theme was taught in the Old Testament, from the days of Abraham (Romans 4:1-3) through David (vv. 4-8) to the age of the prophets (Galatians 3:11). Jesus himself clearly taught that none was good (Matthew 19:17), that even the best of us must be born from above (John 3:1-7) and are saved by grace through faith (vv. 14-16). This truth of man's depravity does not mean, of course, that every person is as wicked as possible, that no one ever does anything good. The uniform testimony of Scripture is that God's image is marred, not totally effaced. God always recognizes and welcomes obedience, goodness. But all people sin and fall short of God's glorious character (Rom. 3:23). No man is good enough to merit acceptance with God. No one is pure enough to be united with God.

Like a bridge halfway across the chasm, the works of a good person are all the more poignant in their utter inability to save. The law never was intended to make us righteous. The law simply shows us what we ought to be. For the lost sinner this is good news, for it leads him to the Savior. For the saved sinner this is good news, for it describes clearly what he is growing toward, what he longs to be in order to satisfy his Savior: likeness to Jesus Christ. With such a glorious purpose, our minds and hearts are moved to run to this wonderful gift of grace, the law. Ponder how you view the law. Is it to crimp your lifestyle or to provide the very things for which you yearn, love, security, belonging, fidelity, peace, integrity, and the ecstasy of full oneness? In which direction are you headed? Redirect if need be, towards all God created you to become.

March 30
A Magnet Life
1 Corinthians 12:4-6

"Now there are varieties of gifts, but the same Spirit; and there are varieties of service, but the same Lord; and there are varieties of activities, but it is the same God who empowers them all in everyone." (1 Corinthians 12:4-6)

If you were to name several gifted evangelists you know or know about, who would that be? You might name Billy Graham. Two gifted evangelists include Iijima and Ruth. They are very different from Billy Graham and from one another. Iijima is old; Ruth, young; Iijima is very timid, Ruth is bold; Iijima doesn't say much, Ruth talks a lot. Iijima is a widow who has won several to faith in Christ just by being their friends. Ruth has won many to Christ also by deliberately becoming friends but also through explaining Bible truth to them. She writes them letters, gives them pamphlets and books, provides transportation, throws birthday parties and plans special times for them. Billy Graham, Iijima, Ruth-all with the ability to win people to faith in Christ. That's the Spirit-gift of evangelism. Not everyone is gifted in evangelism and even those who have greater and lesser effectiveness. Who can compare with Billy Graham, for example? But all of us are responsible to share our faith. Some call that witnessing. We witness by the way we live a magnet life-drawing others to Jesus by the quality of our life. We witness by our talk-explaining how we got where we are. However, even witnessing can be faked if the person has enough personal charisma; but we're talking here of those who truly lead people to Christ. Thus, every one of us is called to show and tell. If the church is witnessing, people will come to Christ. We could call it body-life reproduction.

"For God so loved the world." I'm so glad He does, aren't you? But we tend to love our own more than others. Why not write the names of people you believe need to know Jesus? Let me see if I can guess your order: family, friends, acquaintances, unknown people. That's natural and not necessarily wrong. But maybe you had few or none in the acquaintance-of-another-kind-of-people category or in the personally-unknown-but-prayer-request category. I think the more we have God's heart, the more we'll care about people at a distance, too, because God loves the whole world. As we try to feel God's heartbeat, we see the world with God's eyes, and discover how the Spirit will help us reach out to those who are presently out of reach.

Do we need to be persistent? Perhaps you feel called to evangelize. Keep asking God for the gift of evangelism. People may come to Christ through your ministry only sporadically, and most of us long for the ability to consistently win people to Christ. So we pray, we live Godly lives, we love people, we share our faith, and we trust God for the outcomes.

March 31
Doing the Twist
Proverbs 21:2

"Every way of a man is right in his own eyes, but the Lord weighs the heart." (Proverbs 21:2)

God Himself is both the standard for the Christian life and the provision for reaching that standard. Our responsibility to connect with that provision is faith, with its two parts-yield and trust. When we yield and trust what can we expect as a result? Here again, sadly, we're tempted to go to one extreme or the other, either expecting too little of our lives in the Spirit or having unbiblically high expectations.

Today let us consider some of the basic truths about our responsibility and God's provision for Christian living. One of the first steps toward living transformed is to understand God's provision. Then we must move from understanding to obeying. Failure to respond obediently to the Holy Spirit damages our relationship with Him because disobedience distorts our belief system. Our beliefs ought to determine our behavior, but unfortunately, the opposite is often the case. Unless we become people who live very purposefully, we will follow the pattern below.

1. We experience temptation.
2. Rather than examine our value system and choose right, we give in to temptation.
3. We feel guilty because we have violated our value system.
4. So we twist our beliefs and values to relieve our guilt.

When we live in disobedience, we automatically twist our understanding to rationalize our behavior. Thus, we blind ourselves to an accurate understanding of the Spirit and of the Christian life. Examine how this occurs in your life. In what situation have you twisted your values and beliefs to keep from being wrong and relieving your guilt? Now, challenge yourself often at the point of obedience. Make the decision to trust and yield yourself to God. Carry out that decision by committing each area of your life to Him. Have you linked up with the Spirit by yielding to His will and trusting in His power? The trust will grow, but the yield part you can settle right now. Tell Him you're not able on your own to live life as He intended but that you want to live a life of obedience. Commit yourself to God, through Jesus Christ, by the power of the Spirit. Ask Him to make you into Christ's likeness. Don't write conditional clauses in the contract, just respond to the Spirit with a simple, straightforward, complete, "Yes!" Perhaps you have already yielded completely to the Spirit of God. This would be a good time to reaffirm that and ask Him to increase your faith and spiral you up into ever greater likeness to the Son. Thank Him, too, for the intimate companionship He offers.

When we make the big turnaround, yielding to God's will and trusting Him to work, the Holy Spirit begins to change us. We become more like Jesus in our attitudes, in our view of things, in our goals and ambitions, in our responses and behavior. Consequently, we get closer and closer to Him in daily companionship (2 Corinthians 3:18). The more we know Him, the more we love Him; the more we love Him, the more we want to be with Him; the more we're with Him the more we want to be like Him; the more we change to be like Him, the better we know Him, the more we love Him-the spiral continues toward likeness to Christ and a greater love relationship with God.

The ultimate goal God has in mind for you isn't merely a change in character to resemble Jesus. God intends for you to be like Jesus in another way, in your intimate love relationship with the Father. That's not only the grand climax of your existence as a redeemed human being, but this is also what it means to be best friends here and now, and to experience that intimacy.

April 1
Five Smooth Stones
1 Samuel 17:40

"Then he took his staff in his hand and chose five smooth stones from the brook and put them in his shepherd's pouch. His sling was in his hand, and he approached the Philistine." (1 Samuel 17:40)

As you Davids descend into the dark valley of reality to face your looming Goliaths I want to make sure your pouch is filled with 5 smooth stones. If you lack even one of them, you risk going down in failure because for you, the battle looms.

Do we ask ourselves, "Does God care how I go about ministry? We search Scripture to see. Then we examine church history for the spiritually dynamic movements and conclude that indeed God does care how we do ministry. And that he went to great effort to reveal his mind to us. Not in a handful of proof-texts hidden away here and there, but in five major themes of Scripture. Theologians call them bibliology, ecclesiology, pneumatology, soteriology, and Christology.

Today let's name them in the hope that you will be stirred to start picking up your stones from the flow of the Spirit through the Word. You may have them in your pouch already. If so, today I charge you to use them faithfully in your ministry.

Every traditional method or new proposal rigorously brought under the functional authority of *Scripture*. Will we pause and identify the issue. Perhaps as in multiple areas, the issue is defined differently. Can you agree on what the issue is?

I will build my *church*, said Jesus, identifying his method for carrying out the purposes on earth. And what was that church to look like? Those who received his commission gave us a whole book of examples and then went on to explain the implications of what took place as recorded in the book of Acts. Which purpose comes to mind when you hear: Methodist? Baptist? Fundamentalist? Charismatic? Salvation Army? Presbyterian? Now—your own congregation?

God designed his purposes for the church to be fulfilled by people whom he gifts by the *Holy Spirit* to carry out those purposes. Didn't Paul assure us that the Spirit distributes his gifts to EACH ONE as he designs?. But what if some necessary Spirit enablement is missing? Desire earnestly. How about you? Do you have a dream, a passion of how you want to be used of God?

God consistently works through leaders to focus and mature a congregation. Whatever we value enough to invest our leadership energy and prayer and financial support in is what the congregation accomplishes. A good question to reflect on is, "Do we have a biblical balance that reflects the principle: God's plan of redemption is the mission of every disciple." *Evangelism* is one biblical purpose of the church, it is also the central mission of every believer's life.

By nature we don't really want him to be *Lord*. We want to be our own Lord, and the lord of the others in our lives. Indeed, lord of the church. Follow Jesus' model and where do you end? When every member, especially the leaders embrace the basin of servanthood, indeed the cross, there is a mighty resurrection. Unity, power. So how is it with YOU? Who is lord?

There you have it—the Five Smooth Stones. Be sure you have every one of them in your pouch. If you do, since they ae God's own blueprint for ministry, I can promise you a life-time of effective ministry.

April 2
Mixed Motives
Luke 22:39-46

"Whoever finds his life will lose it, and whoever loses his life for my sake will find it". (Matthew 10:39)

When president of Columbia International University I received a letter signed "Miss Sarah." I didn't know Miss Sarah but in the letter she said she prayed for us every day. Then she added, "many times a day." I knew immediately I needed to see this lady to thank her in person. Her return address was a local nursing facility and soon I found myself in the lobby of the nursing home.
"Could I see Miss Sarah?"
"You can try, but she may be in bed."
"At five in the afternoon?"
"Well, yes, she goes to bed early."
"Why so early?"
"She gets up very early."
I made my way down a hall where there were occasional unpleasant odors and one persistent cry of someone in distress, hopefully imagined distress. Finally I reached her room and sure enough she was in bed—a tiny angel perched against the pillow in her frilly nightgown.
"Oh, Mr. McQuilkin," she sings out, "Isn't God good?"
"Indeed he is. How has he been good to you?"
"My room," she said. I glanced around the tiny cubicle that had space for a bed, a table, and a dresser—and not much more. "So what's special about your room?" I asked.
"Why, the window. Look at my window." I looked and all I could see out her window was the cement block wall of the next building, twelve feet away. "Tell me about your window, " I said.
"Can't you see? It's facing east. Every morning I look out that window and say, 'Maybe my Jesus will come today!'"

For seventeen years alone and infirm, a retired missionary, spending her days in prayer for God's people and God's work around the world, filled with hope and joy. Why? Preparing for the coming of her Lover!

For people like Miss Sarah it's not what I enjoy most, how may I best build my kingdom, what sort of security is there in it, can I maintain my standard of living? Not: "what?" "where?" "how?" but:
WHY?

So how can I unmix my motives? How can I measure love? Let's see. . This past week, 35% of choices were from self-love, 50% because of love for others, 25% love for God, You say, that doesn't add up. No, it never will, so don't try. All motives are legitimate and you can't analyze your inner self like a chemical analysis. But you can measure love. Love is measured not by the intensity of feeling but by the sacrifice it stands ready to make. You can tell when the loves are in conflict. Which love wins out?

It might be a small thing like, who gets up at 3 A.M. with the crying baby. Who gets sacrificed? That might depend on whom I love the more. A little thing. Or it might be a major thing, like where I'm willing to serve God. Or like a cross.

Think of the battle of the loves in the Garden of Gethsemane (Luke 22:39-46) *"Please, Father, let me off..."* he cried in an agony. But in that battle of the loves Jesus' love for the Father won out. *"Nevertheless,"* he concluded,

"not my will but yours..."
Perhaps you're in a personal Gethsemane today. What battle of the loves faces you—a call to sacrifice self-interest for love of another or for all the others to whom God has sent you? A conflict with whether God's desires through you will be sacrificed for your own? Would it help to name the conflict of motives you experience today?

April 3
Show me Your Scars
John 20:27

"Then he said to Thomas, "Put your finger here, and see my hands; and put out your hand and place it in my side. Do not disbelieve but believe." (John 20:27)

What love!
Which love will win out? That depends on which is the controlling, the dominant motive of life. "Take up **your** cross daily. ." says the Master. Are you prepared to say "no" to self-interest in favor of their interest? Of God's interest? So the first question is not, *what are you doing?* or *how well are you doing it?* But *WHY*?
At a commencement, I told the graduating students just that. "I'm not overly concerned with what you do or how you get it done. I want to know one thing: why?" This message reached one of them who had recently talked with me about his conflicting responsibilities. He was disturbed because he felt God wanted him to serve on the mission field, but his father wanted him home in the family business.
"Does your father need you?"
"No, four of my brothers are with him already," Chet responded.
"How did you get through school? Who paid the bills?" "My father," he said.
"Then you're not a free man. You need to go home and work with him. But not necessarily forever. When you stand before God to give account for your life, your father isn't going to stand in for you. You'll give account for your own life investment."
He took my advice, returning home to work with his father. But three years later I met him in Dallas, far from his home in Pennsylvania. He was preparing for mission service in Latin America. Two years later, in language school in Costa Rica, preparing for service in Colombia, he noted in his diary that to reach Colombia someone might need to lay down his life. "...I find this recurring thought that perhaps God will call me to be martyred for Him in His service in Colombia. I am willing." Two years later, headlines across America told of the abduction of missionary Chet Bitterman, as a hostage of the guerillas. They played out his captivity with constant photographs of Chet, and news releases. They even let him talk and the Colombian newspapers carried the full text of his gospel witness. But Wycliffe wouldn't pay ransom and three months later they found Bitterman's body in an abandoned bus. In the battle of the loves—for his father with his filial demands, for his wife and two small daughters, for the people of the unreached tribes of Colombia, for his Commander-in-Chief—every motive was godly and powerful. But God won out, to the everlasting good of multitudes.
First to his own father. Upon Chet's capture, a father who had drifted far from God planned to raise a mercenary

123

force and go after the guerrillas, but on his son's death, returned to his first love and became a clear witness for God. Then to the many young people who learned of Chet and followed his example in giving life for reaching the unreached.

Most of us will never face such choices. But there are all the little battles, day by day. I sometimes think our love is best proved, not in the major crises of life, but in the daily choices.

The little conflicts can leave lasting scars. The pastor of a church in Atlanta took me out for Sunday dinner along with a couple from the church. While waiting for our order I asked the "what" question: "what do you do for a living?" He worked at the federal penitentiary as a guard. For how long? 25 years! I blurted out the first thought that popped into my head,

"Show me your scars!" I was joking, but he held up his arms, pulled back the sleeves and revealed a patchwork of scars he had gained in defending himself from contraband and homemade blades. I was astounded. But there was more. His wife chimed in, "Those aren't all the scars. He's got scars on his legs. Bite marks."

I sat there and thought to myself, Someday I'll sit down to the marriage banquet of Jesus and he'll show me his scars. "That's how much I love you," he'll say. Then, I thought, then maybe he'll turn to me and say, "Now show me your scars."

Will I have to weep and say, "I don't have any. I didn't take any risks, I didn't make any sacrifices." Or will I be able to say with joy, "Here they are, Lord. That's how much I love you."

April 4
How Does Trust Grow?
Psalm 28:7

"The LORD is my strength and my shield; in him my heart trusts, and I am helped; my heart exults, and with my song I give thanks to him." (Psalm 28:7)

"Crisis" is simply a decisive turning point. Sort of sounds like a u-turn, doesn't it? And that's exactly what the Christian needs who has gotten out of phase with the Spirit. To reconnect, for the power to surge, you must yield unconditionally to the will of God. No fine print in the contract, no reserve clauses—unconditional. To do that may be cataclysmic if you have resisted long and hard, pushing your resistance ever deeper into the sub-conscious, or if you are of a temperament to feel intensely. But it can be a matter-of-fact transaction of turning everything over to the Master: past, present, future, successes, failures, relationships—everything.

Are you stalled out, slipping back maybe, in your spiral with Jesus? Then you need to go back to the initial transaction, you need a crisis of turning. If that is your present condition and heart-longing, why not list in your spiritual journal all the things you need to yield up to your Sovereign Lord? Don't hesitate, don't delay. And be very honest and thorough—don't leave anything out or rationalize it away. There's no other way to connect with the Spirit's power or to experience intimacy with him.

That's the "yield" part of faith and it can be accomplished in an instant. It never has to be re-done. You can enter that contract—or re-enter it— and never have to do it again. Oh, of course there's the daily, even constant, reaffirmation of Jesus' Lordship, all the little "yesses" of life. But never again need there be the crisis of "who's boss?" What about obedience—don't we grow in that? True, we're in process of ever more perfect obedience, but growth in obedience is in understanding the will of God more perfectly, in growing stronger against temptation, becoming more Christlike. So there's growth in obedience, but not in yieldedness. It's either a "yes" or a "no" to God as the basic heart orientation. And don't forget, "maybe" or "later" or "why" qualify as a "no"!

So, in a basic sense we don't grow in "yield." The trust pole of faith, however, that's another matter. Of course we'd never yield in the first place if we didn't trust him, so the two can't be separated. But seen from another angle, trust must grow. And that means a process, a spiral.

I don't trust the panhandlers that come to my door. I don't know them. Oh, I may trust them with a dollar or two, or a sandwich. But John— that's a different story. I've walked with him for many years. We've agonized together, laughed together, worked together. I'd trust him with anything I have. I do, in fact. He's my power of attorney—he could liquidate my assets and move to Hawaii. I trust him. And so it is with the Spirit. The more I companion with him, the greater my trust. I can believe him for greater things today than I could ten years ago. Trust grows.

Sometimes I have a hard time believing that God will do what He says He will do. Can He get me out of the mess I've worked myself into, putting things together so this will really work out for any kind of good—mine or God's? "All things work together for good?" Really, now, all? Or giving me the victory over a weakness—I'm reluctant to call it what He probably does, "sin," something that has plagued me for years. *"Thanks be to God who always causes us to triumph in Christ?"* Really, now, always? Perhaps there's some sin-bully that has you on the run, some persistent temptation like a loose tongue or volatile temper or irresistible craving. Can God really give victory? Or perhaps you struggle with other promises like *"my God will supply all your needs"* or *"I will be with you always"* or *"my peace I give to you."* Maybe the promised fruit of the Spirit just doesn't ripen: Love for that particularly unlovable person in your life, or joy when things are truly miserable. You wish you could see the touch of Holy Spirit power on your witness or ministry—the way He promised. Sometimes it's hard to believe the promises.

If it's sometimes hard to believe absolute promises, what about trusting Him to do something He has not promised? Like healing arthritis? Showing you plainly which option you should take in a decision? Protecting a son or daughter who lives at the edge? Those are all unpleasant or scary parts of life. Oh, He has promised to heal in answer to prayer, to guide, to protect. But heal this illness, now? Guide you infallibly in this particular choice? Protect all believers from all harm? There are no guarantees. Sometimes it's hard to trust Him with the outcome when He doesn't let us in on what He has in mind. If it's sometimes hard to rely on God when He hasn't revealed His will, what if He has revealed His will and you trust Him not to do it? Now, that would be some kind of faith!

But to trust Him you must companion with Him. And in companioning with Him, thanksgiving, praise, adoration—worship, to sum it up—builds the trust bonds best of all. How about setting apart next Sunday afternoon, or a few hours on your next day off, and write out all the things you like about God and all the things you are grateful for that he's done for you?

April 5
Set Apart
John 3 & Romans 6

"Jesus answered him, "Truly, truly, I say to you, unless one is born again he cannot see the kingdom of God." (John 3:3)

To sanctify is, literally, to set apart, and in the biblical context it means set apart to God. In the Old Testament this setting apart was both moral and ritual. An object such a bowl was set apart from common use for exclusive use in the temple ritual. It was then considered holy (from the same root as *sanctify*). But of deeper and more enduring significance was, on the one hand, a personal separation from sin, and on the other hand, his or her consecration to God. One who is set apart from sin (sanctified) is rightly called a saint (from the same root as sanctify or holy).

This moral and theological sense of sanctification is the one I invite you to consider. To be sanctified is of utmost importance, because without it, one will not see God (Heb. 12:14). That is, until the sin problem is cared for, no one is qualified to associate with a holy God, who is Himself completely without sin and who, moreover, cannot countenance sin in any form.

God is not only holy, He is supremely a God of love, and therefore His ultimate desire for is for us to be restored to full loving fellowship with Himself. But there is a barrier: sin. For complete unity of heart, two persons must be compatible, in harmony of spirit. They must have the same purposes, outlook, and way of life. If one is sinful and the other holy, what oneness can there be? Their total mindset is in conflict. So in order to accomplish the ultimate purpose of our existence, namely to live in oneness with God, the sin barrier must be removed. The removal process is called sanctification. This is God's work of Grace.

There are three ways we are set apart from our wrongdoing. First the person is *forgiven* so that the result of sin, eternal punishment, is done away with. Second, a person is *justified*, so that his or her guilt is removed, the guilty record is expunged. God views the person no longer as a weak, stubborn, and failing sinner but now as an individual who is as clean and pure as His holy son, Jesus. These two aspects of positional sanctification are judicial, that is, a transaction between the Father and the Son that declares the sinner forgiven and made right with God. Third, the forgiven, justified person is *regenerated,* or set free from the controlling authority of a sinful disposition. Some make this step a part of experiential sanctification, since it is a condition experienced more than a legal standing granted, as in the case of forgiveness and justification. I include it under positional sanctification, since it is part of the initial salvation transaction and results in a position that is the condition of every true believer.

The change is so radical as to be comparable to the change that a person experiences at birth (John 3) *"Jesus answered him, "Truly, truly, I say to you, unless one is born again he cannot see the kingdom of God."* (ESV, v3) or death (Romans 6). Though there is continuity with the same human personality, as in the case of birth or death, in regeneration also there is passage into a totally different dimension of human life, with totally different characteristics of personal being. Sin is the prevailing characteristic of persons who live apart from God. They do not have the desire or power to choose consistently the right or to change their condition. Upon union with God the process is reversed, and right begins to prevail. A new life-force has been introduced. How is this freedom from the controlling authority of a sinful disposition demonstrated in you today?

April 6
"Father, Forgive Them..."
Luke 23:34

"Jesus said, *"I tell you, Peter, the rooster will not crow this day, until you deny three times that you know me."* (Luke 23:34)

There is a sin that totally destroys relationships, is a deadly cancer eating at one's own psyche, and--worst of all--shuts a person off from God's grace. And yet nowhere does the Bible define it. Scripture seems to assume that everyone knows in all circumstances what it means to forgive. A large assumption.

<u>Webster's Dictionary</u> lists three meanings, all related to the idea of pardon, remission of guilt, cancellation of debt. That's easy to understand, though it may not always be easy to do: treat the guilty party as if the offence had never occurred. But there sometimes seems to be something left over after canceling a debt, something that eats at my spirit. So Webster's comes through with another possible meaning: "to cease to feel resentment against." Ah, there's the rub! Don't make him pay for his offence against me, scrub out the debt. Fine. But how do I scrub out the feelings? Does God really expect me to forgive in <u>that</u> sense before he forgives me? So the first problem is to define what I will do and feel if I forgive. But that is far from the last of the problems.

For example, must I forgive even if the person doesn't ask for it? And what of responsibility for discipline on the part of parents, church officers, or civil authorities--can they treat the offender "as if it never happened"? Another thing: how can I untangle my feelings so as to distinguish between pain or fear on the one hand, which may be legitimate, and resentment or bitterness which are not? Simple forgiveness turns out to be not so simple.

The Bible may not define forgiveness, but it does point to a model. Of course, that may not be very helpful since the model seems so far out of reach. But God's own forgiveness is the central theme of Scripture. And what we are to do is follow his example: "Forgive one another <u>just as</u> God in Christ forgave you" (Eph 4.32; Col 3.13). The amazing concept, that an infinite, holy, all-powerful deity should make arrangements--at great personal loss--to expunge all the rotten filth of our lives and treat us as clean, is so overwhelming that Bible dictionaries deal almost exclusively with God's forgiveness. The other startling thing is that I am to do the same! If I fail to follow his example, if I don't forgive, Jesus repeatedly warns that God will not forgive me (Mt 6.14,15; 18.35; Mk 11.25,26; Lk 11.4).

How can that which seems so "natural" to God prove so unnatural to us? Because God is love. Forgiveness flows from an inner spring of love and our springs are fouled so often with self-love if not hatred. Sensing the connection between love and forgiveness, many have combined them, defining forgiveness in terms that the Bible assigns to love. Much confusion and guilt result from this failure to clearly distinguish between the demands of love and the demands of forgiveness. For example, God's love is unlimited, for everyone. And ours ought to be. But God's forgiveness is strictly limited to those who repent. Confusion and guilt overwhelm many of God's people who demand that we do what God does not do--forgive everyone of everything.

Perhaps the distinction would be clarified by returning to the two basic meanings of forgive: to remit the guilt and to relinquish resentment. In the sense of remitting guilt, pardoning, treating as if it never happened, God, in love, does this for a specified few and, in love, does not do this for the majority of humankind. But he never for a moment felt resentment or ill-will against anyone because, again, God is love and that is the way love relates to people, whether friend or enemy. To follow his example is not always easy, but this is what we are to do.

April 7
Love Seeks Reconciliation
Matthew 5:23-24

"So if you are offering your gift at the altar and there remember that your brother has something against you, leave your gift there before the altar and go. First be reconciled to your brother, and then come and offer your gift." (Matthew 5:23-24)

One of the chief points at which love and forgiveness converge is that love always seeks reconciliation, and the asking and receiving of forgiveness is the basis for reconciliation. Seeking reconciliation is not optional. Our first obligation when sinned against is go to the person--and not to anyone else--tell him about it (Mt 18.15,16), seek reconciliation. I assume Christ here speaks of sin heavy enough to merit heavy action, not the daily small offenses that love simply overlooks. How miserable the home in which this is not done a hundred times a day! But if the offence is grave enough to break fellowship, love seeks reconciliation and forgiveness makes it possible.

Of course, we need to keep reminding ourselves that it's a thin sheet of paper with only one side. Rare is the occasion when the offence is 100% on one side. As a result, the question of whether it is my responsibility to ask forgiveness or to extend it may not be clear, at least not clear to both parties in the same way. In seeking reconciliation, it doesn't matter who offended, whether I have offended someone (Matthew 5:23-24) or the other person has offended me, it is always <u>my</u> move! I am the one who must seek reconciliation.

But suppose even though I go to the offending person about the matter they still don't repent or accept my quest for reconciliation? If the offence was theirs and they don't recognize or accept that, am I obligated to forgive anyway? How many times do I go and seek reconciliation?

One answer is another question: how many times does God seek to reconcile us to himself? So love keeps reaching out. But in the Bible's key passage on forgiveness, note that the formal procedure is to exhaustively seek reconciliation by going first alone, then with others and finally to the officials. After that the offended one is to break relationships--treat the offender as an outsider (Mt 18.15-17). That is an outline of the responsibility of the offended party. But most situations are too complex for this to happen quickly and cleanly. In the meantime, to act in love for the eternal benefit of all concerned is the key to evaluating the complexity of ruptured relationships. Remember that God doesn't give up easily! And he is our model. Also remember that love, unlike forgiveness, sometimes holds guilty people accountable. When does love cease seeking reconciliation and begin to hold accountable? We shall examine accountability shortly, but in the meantime, in seeking reconciliation, another truth should be kept in mind.

Love always seeks reconciliation when fellowship is broken, but love cannot--and would not--force reconciliation. So there comes a time when even love may give up the quest, even though love always remains open to the "return of the prodigal." When forgiveness is requested, love always stands ready to cancel the debt. God graced us with full forgiveness. Then he turns to us and commands us to forgive in the same way, even if it means paying for the offence of the other person, just as he did for us.

The sincerity, the motivation is for God to judge, the canceling of any debt against me is my responsibility (Lk 17.3ff). That is impossible! So thought the disciples, too. But they didn't ask for more love, enough to keep on forgiving the person over and over. They asked for more <u>faith.</u> Faith to believe that God can handle this situation, overrule it for his glory, and protect me. Faith must be strong to wait for God to change the other person. Or me. And if the guilty party-- as God sees the guilt--does not change, faith waits for God to vindicate the cause of the innocent.

April 8
Guidebook
2 Timothy 3:16

"All Scripture is inspired by God and is profitable for teaching, for rebuking, for correcting, for training in righteousness, so that the man of God may be complete, equipped for every good work" (2 Tim 3:16, 17 HCHB)

Consider our theme verse for today. What does "all" mean? Maybe it means ***all--e***verything from Genesis to Revelation. Well, then, what does "inspired by God mean"? Actually, the word literally means "God-breathed-out." And what could that mean when God doesn't have a body, doesn't breathe? The word for breath is actually the same word in the original as "spirit." So we might say that the Bible—all of it—was given by the Spirit of God.

Then Paul tells us ***why*** God gave us the book: He provides in the Bible everything we need to believe ("teaching") and everything we are **not** to believe ("rebuking"); every behavior we're to reject ("correcting") and everything we're to do ("training in righteousness"). How to think and how to behave—that pretty much sums up God's expectancies, doesn't it? But to what end? So that through the Scripture he plans to complete me (the term literally means "perfect" or "mature"), and to equip me for every good work. That's what the Holy Spirit wants to do in you and me! The God-intended life, you might call it. And he gave us the Book to lead us in that direction.

Whether or not any word is to be believed depends on who said it. If I say, "there will be an earthquake in California tomorrow," you have every right to ask, "and who are you?" So, because God said it, you can count on it. It's *trustworthy*. Jesus trusted it! As you recall, that's why I began to believe it—I'm not smarter than Jesus! Not only the trustworthiness of any statement, but the *authority* of any word also depends on who said it. If I say, "come here" and I'm the King you'd better jump! And since this Book is "God-breathed-out" it's the final authority. So the Bible is trustworthy—you'd better believe it. And the Bible is authoritative—you'd better obey it! That fundamental fact about the Bible is what transformed my life and became the foundation on which I've been trying to build ever since my encounter with Jesus on the beach. What is the foundation you are building your life on? What do you expect when you read the Bible?

So the Book the Spirit gave is not purely human, full of good advice but also containing not a few errors, the way most people view it. That's why they pick and choose what to believe, what to obey. But **all** Scripture is God-breathed out, says Paul. Of course, that doesn't mean the Bible is purely divine in origin, either to be used like a ouji board to give some hidden meaning. Many use it that way. But, no, the book is both human **and** divine, as Peter told us: "Holy men of God spoke as they were moved by the Holy Spirit." (II Peter 1.21, NKJ)) And Paul teaches us, as we have seen, that such a book is to be used for our spiritual maturing and for our effective ministry.

Is God's purpose in giving us the Bible being fulfilled in your life—to trust it, to obey it? Why not pause right now and talk to him about it? Tell him how you feel about the Bible. Tell him what you intend to do about this Book in the future that might be different from what you've done in the past.

The surrendered heart wants to know what the Bible says, not what it can be made to mean. The acceptance of the possible meaning, rather than the certain, is often done to make a self-consistent scheme. But the system must not force the Bible into its logical mold. The Bible gives the system all it can legitimately have. If it needs more to complete it, it must wait for the fuller light of eternity. Charles Simeon of Cambridge said: "My endeavor is to make out of Scripture what is there, and not to thrust in what I think might be there. I have a great jealousy on this head [point] never to speak more or less than I believe to be the mind of the Spirit in the passage I am expounding. I would run after nothing and shun nothing."

We must be willing to obey. Surrender is not merely a passive openness of mind, but it is also a willingness to believe and to obey. It is seen in an active, positive attitude: a hungry heart that is eagerly seeking. When one comes to the Bible with a willingness to learn and obey only when cornered, or with fear and cringing lest it change his opinions and reprove his conduct, that one gives evidence of a stubborn, unyielded heart and cannot be sure he is discovering God's truth.

The aggressively seeking mind proposes new hypotheses, and then tests them mercilessly in the clear light of what the Bible actually says. It is constantly testing and re-examining, perfectly willing to discover the truth in conflict with the sanctions of tradition. It purposefully ousts opinion—even widely held opinion—and demands that it return only with the authorized credentials of solid Bible evidence. It fears the bog of semantic stagnation—traditional statements and terms that hide or obscure the pure biblical statements, or those that have lost their vitality and accuracy through common use or misuse.

The eager search for basic truth is evidence of an active surrender of heart, which is a parent indispensable in the birth of humility. This spirit of unconditional surrender coupled with an honest facing of the facts produces humility. The humble mind does not aspire to omniscience, nor to any measurable degree thereof. It has sought out the facts with an open, yielded mind, recognizing the difference between established fact and matters of conviction or opinion. It keeps them separate, content to leave outside the realm of certainty those things that are not clearly revealed. As the psalmist wisely declares: *"O Lord, my heart is not proud, nor my eyes haughty; nor do I involve myself in great matters, or in things too difficult for me. Surely I have composed and quieted my soul."* (Ps. 131:1-2)[12]

April 9
Therapeutic Theology
Matthew 28:20

And behold, I am with you always, to the end of the age." (Matthew 28:20)

I arrived just as Virginia was lifted from the ambulance, strapped to a metal stretcher. When she saw me, her greeting was simply, "God has abandoned me." Maybe you'd feel that way, too, if your husband had died an agonizing death of cancer less than a year before and this was the second accident since then, the one you knew intuitively had ended your driving forever. But her voice was flat--no wail of self-pity or angry accusation against God. It wasn't the first time my sister felt God had abandoned her. Actually, she's felt that way periodically over the past 20 years since Margie, the joy of her life and only daughter, was brutally killed. It didn't help that the killer had done it before and had just been released from prison on the advice of a court-appointed psychiatrist. It didn't make sense that a young woman who loved God and people so intensely should be snuffed out by a madman. Perhaps God abandoned her, too...

I thought to myself, *why do I never feel that way?* Some judge that I have cause enough, but I never had those

---
[12] Excerpts from *Understanding and Applying the Bible*, 229.

feelings. This started a train of thought about other things I've never felt: despondency, depression, anger with God, for example. Then I began to think of feelings I **have** had that I wish I hadn't: unforgiveness, impatience, numbness of spirit. Why the difference? Perhaps theology has something to do with it.

Theology? More likely heredity or environment. Except that Virginia and I sprang from the same gene pool, were raised by the same parents. In fact, we're much alike in personality. As I thought about my inner responses to external circumstances I was drawn irresistibly to the theology factor. What I truly believe seems to have set me up-- both for success and for failure.

When asked to share some of my life experience for an audience of professional counselors, I thought, *I'm no counselor. What could I contribute? I've spent my life at theological reflection, not psychological.* But then I realized my life story might point up some of the interface between the two, an interface theologians seldom consider and an interface a counselor might be tempted to by-pass. So without trying to explicate how that interface should work for either theologian or psychologist, let me tell the story.

Consider a few positive examples from my life, then a few negative examples which seem to support the idea that theology played a major role in who I have become and continues to play a major role in what I am yet to become. You see, theology provides protection.

More than therapy to heal the broken, perhaps, theology builds an immune system to keep a person from breaking in the first place. Here's how it worked for me.

I believe I'm finite. I didn't always believe that. Oh, I would have admitted to finitude if asked, but my youthful self-confidence led me to believe I had a corner on **the truth.** Then, in my early twenties I entered the dark tunnel of agnosticism--from knowing "everything" to knowing nothing for sure, especially about God and his Book. I wasn't arrogant, affirming that no god existed, just that I, at least, couldn't find him. When, by God's grace, I emerged from that dark tunnel I had great confidence in the basics: that God is, that the Savior actually saves, that God has purpose for my life. But I was shorn of any pretense of infallibility about the details. My expectancies--for myself and others-- were lowered to the realities of human finitude.

I exulted in the confidence of what God had revealed for sure--so sure that all believers of all time would affirm it. But I concluded that most things I'd never figure out no matter how long I investigated and contemplated--things about God's infinities, and things about my finitude. Like the meanings of my past, the hopes of my future, the reasons for my circumstances, the goings-on of my inner self. I'm comfortable with that ambiguity about life, now, though I recognize others may not be. Some seem to need to have everything settled for sure.

For an inquisitive thinker and an intense activist, the realization of one's finitude can be a marvelous relaxant and stabilizer. Besides, lowered expectancies of oneself is a doorway to making room for others. Maybe they're finite, too--and in a different configuration, yet! That realization could make a peace-maker out of a person. For example, when Mack set out to get rid of me as leader of the ministry, I didn't have to try to "be good" and not get angry, fight back, or hold a grudge against him. After all, he saw things differently than I. Besides, maybe he was right. I didn't think so, but neither did I conclude he was devilish. Our finitudes had clashed and we both thought we were doing God's own service. My theology had protected me in the crisis.

I believe I'm fallen. And so are others. So I expect them to behave that way and that helps make allowances for their failures, which doesn't come to me naturally. What comes naturally is to be easy on myself and hard on the other fellow. So it's a trick to be realistic about my fallenness without justifying my own ungodly behavior because I've been easing off on the other fellow. I haven't figured out all the ramifications of the doctrine of the fall for protecting me from wrong thinking about myself and others, but on the larger scale, that doctrine has been a powerful deliverer in my life.

Here's how. The whole of creation is under the curse of the fall and I'm not exempt, by being loved of God, from the consequences of living in a world of vicious cancer and violent winds. Nor from a world of finite and fallen people who inflict harm on me, wittingly or unwittingly. I expect the worst and rejoice when, by God's grace, it usually doesn't happen! Sometimes when I wake in the morning I muse, *Lord, lots of folks died last night. Why not me?* At my stage of life so many of my dearest family and friends suffer painful, debilitating illness and agonizing death. Why not I? That's the only reasonable "why" question for one who lives in a fallen world.

I don't want to oversimplify the problem of evil; a whole complex of theological issues intertwine. For example, if God made his own people exempt from the human condition, who wouldn't become a believer? But what kind of believer would they become? Again, when does God heal and to what end? For what purpose does God protect or remove the protection? The theological questions seem endless, especially when faced with personal tragedy, but the bottom line for me is this: I'm fallen and so is my world. Not, "why me, Lord?" when trouble strikes, but "why not me, Lord?" when it so often misses.

Muriel was blessed with eternal youth--looking forty when she was actually 55. But that's still far too young to fall before Alzheimer's, the disease of the old. "Early onset" they called it in clinically sterile terminology. Early onset of what? Of grief for me who must watch the vibrant, creative, sparkling person I knew dimming out. No grief for her, however, except for momentary frustrations quickly forgotten--she never knew what was happening.

So, why us, Lord? There are various theories. One alumnus said it was God's judgement on me for allowing contemporary Christian music on our radio station. I don't feel guilty about that but I do know circumstances contrary to our desires are always intended to make us more like Jesus, and God has surely used these two decades of lingering grief to develop in me several deficiencies in my model-of-Jesus' role in life. Perhaps God wanted new leadership at Columbia International University, though the Board and administrators didn't buy that theory. Of late I've begun to wonder if the Lord put me under "house arrest" so I'd do something my busy life didn't allow much of: writing books and articles. Of course, whatever other purposes God has in sending or permitting adversity, there is always the purpose of bringing God glory, either through his mighty deliverance from suffering or his mighty deliverance *in* suffering. And that he has done in wonderful ways I'll never fully understand. So, it's obvious I have contemplated the "why?" question.

But why have I not fretted over the answer? Why have I not demanded healing from God or frantically pursued the many cures friends and strangers have suggested? The bottom line is this: we live in a fallen world--what else did you expect? Theology protects from destructive inner turmoil. How about you? Wrestling with feeling abandoned? Or wondering why? We may know some of the answers, but *mystery* is God's glory. We are finite, He is not.

April 10
Final Destiny
Matthew 25:31-46

"And these will go away into eternal punishment, but the righteous into eternal life." Matthew 25:46

The crucial issue for missions and world evangelism in this decade is the question of final destiny. Never in the history of the church has the teaching of Jesus Christ on this subject been questioned so widely by those who profess allegiance to his authority. To the extent these views prevail, to that extent motivation for missions diminishes. I speak on this theme periodically, but it is so critical I feel I must address the issue again and build on that foundation.

What does Jesus say about the final destiny of human beings? Read Matthew 25:31-34, 41, 46. The historic view of the church is that all who have not trusted Jesus Christ for salvation will go into eternal, conscious punishment. There are problems with this concept. Is not eternal pain a disproportionate punishment for sin lasting no more than a few decades at most? Like giving life imprisonment for parking in a handicapped parking space. Is it fair, let alone loving, to send Socrates to hell when he never even heard of Christ? It's like giving the death penalty to a mother who gave her child the wrong medicine, in error.

In response to these basic questions about the justice and love of God, many proposals have been made contrary to the traditional view, but let us focus on the three major theories.

Universalism. There are verses in Scripture that sound like all will ultimately be saved: *"Therefore, as one trespass led to condemnation for all men, so one act of righteousness leads to justification and life for all men."* (Rom 5:18) There are a few others, but the vast majority of Scripture texts that speak of final destiny, assign some to life and some to death. So it is a hermeneutical problem--which set of texts do you explain in the light of the other?

The first principle is to look at the context. Context is king! Consider Romans 5:18. Now, look at verses 15, 19, and then at chapters 1,2,3. For example: Romans 1:32 after the "God gave them up's" and 2:12. There are not many texts that could be made to imply universal salvation and virtually all of them have contexts similar to this.

The second principle of interpretation that bears on this is to seek the unity of the Scripture, interpret any passage in the light of all Bible teaching on the subject, giving weight to the clear and pervasive. The teaching of both Old and New Testaments on the destiny of humankind is overwhelming and clear that there are two destinies. The small number of passages that seem to diverge from this should be understood in that light.

It is impossible to reconcile the vast majority of texts to the concept of universal salvation and it is quite easy to reconcile the handful of universalist-sounding texts to those which speak of judgment and final separation from God. In fact, the biblical case is so weak for universalism that very few--if any--who hold it also hold a high view of Scripture.

Limited Universalism. The idea is that salvation is universal and will be received by all unless a person opts out, deliberately rejects Jesus Christ.

The primary text for this position is John 3:36: "*Whoever believes in the Son has eternal life, but whoever rejects the Son will not see life, for God's wrath remains on him*" NIV. I'm not aware of other passages to which an appeal may be made, so the case for this is very weak. Even the same chapter repeatedly says that salvation comes only to those who have faith in Jesus Christ.

There is also a philosophical problem with this position--if people are lost only upon rejection of Jesus Christ, to proclaim him is not good news but bad news. As long as you don't know about him you're safe, but if you hear about him you will be lost if you reject him. Better to bury the gospel than to proclaim it.

Suppose a person responds sincerely with obedience to this universal light? This view holds that God will receive him because he is already redeemed and has not chosen to reject the light he has been given. A cluster of verses which suggest that salvation depends on one's own effort is used to support the position.

In Matthew 25 Jesus seems to divide the sheep and the goats on the basis of behavior. Peter, after meeting Cornelius, concluded, *"I now perceive that whoever fears God and has done good works is acceptable to God."* Thus, it is held that salvation is granted in response to sincere good behavior, a positive response to the light one has.

This position must be held against the overwhelming New Testament teaching that salvation is not attainable by good behavior, that it is granted only to those who have faith in Jesus Christ. Once again, the minority teaching of Scripture must be reconciled to the majority teaching, not the other way around, if Scripture is to be held as the final authority.

But what if a person does accept the light of creation and innate moral conviction? God's response is not salvation, but more light. Scripture is clear that rejection of light brings greater darkness and acceptance of light brings greater light. As in the case of Cornelius, when one responds positively to the light he has, God takes the initiative and gets greater light to him.

And whatever the ultimate, complete truth, should we not follow his example and not affirm what he did not? If we discover that some have been saved through some extraordinary means not revealed in Scripture we can rejoice then, but not hold out that hope now based on speculation. It would be criminal to do so.

God is brokenhearted over the lost, so must we be. I dread to speak on this subject. I hate even to think of it. If revelation were not so clear and the consequences so terrible I would banish it from my mind. Weep with Jesus and follow him to your own Calvary for a lost world.

April 11
Gifts and Fruit
1 Corinthians 12:28

"And God has appointed in the church first apostles, second prophets, third teachers, then miracles, then gifts of healing, helping, administrating, and various kinds of tongues." 1 Corinthians 12:28)

Spiritual gifts are important to God. Surely all the gifts are of equal importance to Him? Careful! The central purpose of 1 Corinthians 12-14 is to get the church to understand that gifts are not all of equal importance for accomplishing God's will. Some gifts are less important.

The church at Corinth was focusing on one of those less-important gifts (speaking in tongues). Furthermore, the church at Corinth should have focused on some very important gifts, but they didn't-gifts like apostle, prophet, teacher. Paul even numbered them 1, 2, and 3 (1 Cor. 12:28), so they wouldn't miss the point. He doesn't continue his numbering system beyond those three, so they may just be representative.

But these three give a hint as to what Paul considers more important- roles which seem to have the greatest impact for God's purposes in the church and in the world. My personal definition of his top three would be pioneer missionary evangelist (apostle), power-filled preaching (prophesy), and spirit-anointed teaching. These three represent important tasks indeed.

If you read chapters 12-14 of 1 Corinthians in a hurry, you may conclude that Paul is contrasting lower gifts with the highest gift, love. If you draw that conclusion, you will miss the point . Paul is teaching the people at Corinth about spiritual gifts, and having exhorted them to seek the higher ones, he pauses for a mid-course correction. "Don't get me wrong," he says. "These gifts, even the more important ones, aren't the most important thing. Love is most important." Love isn't a "gift" in the sense Paul is talking about; he calls it a "way." *"I'll show you an even better way"*- better than the best gift (see 1 Corinthians 12:31).

Elsewhere Paul describes love as the fruit of the Spirit. So let's not confuse fruit with gifts. Gifts are Spirit-given abilities; fruit represents Spirit-developed character. Paul's command in verse 31 is to desire Spirit-given abilities to serve God, but his teaching in all of chapter 13 is that love is more important than any gift. The importance of a gift does not imply that one gift is more spiritual than another. Spiritual likeness to Jesus, has to do with fruit of the Spirit, as Paul concludes in 1 Corinthians 13. Also, importance does not equal greater reward. Reward is based on faithfulness, not outward results.

To accomplish God's mission on earth, however, some gifts are of greater importance than others. For 12 years I was a pioneer missionary evangelist. My job was starting churches, a very high calling according to Paul. Today I'm primarily a homemaker, which calls more for fruit than for gifts. My Spirit-given gifts have a limited outlet through some writing and speaking. But I'm not claiming that my role in life is as important as anyone else's. My calling cannot compare with that of others in terms of eternal impact. God only expects that we be faithful to our own calling. Then the whole body can function smoothly. In turn, we will find personal fulfillment, and God will be pleased.

Although we've learned something about what the gifts are by examining the biblical lists of gifts, apparently the Holy Spirit didn't intend to give a clear-cut list of specific job descriptions. Perhaps He intended for us to see what needs doing and trust Him to provide people with the abilities needed to do it. Consider how you are using your spiritual gifts and manifesting spiritual fruit. Concentrate more on outward outcomes or inward character and behavior? Fruit or gifts? This is not either/or, it is both. Pray for the higher gifts. Ministry and life is most productive when accompanied by love, joy, peace, patience, kindness, goodness, gentleness, faithfulness, and self-control.

April 12
Gifts and Tasks
1 Corinthians 12:4-6

*"Now there are varieties of gifts, but the same Spirit; and there are varieties of service, but the same Lord; and there are varieties of activities, but it is the same God who empowers them all in everyone." (*1 Corinthians 12:4-6)

We had just finished a faculty workshop on helping students identify their gifts when Kenneth Kantzer, distinguished theologian, seminary leader, and former editor of Christianity Today, came to the microphone. "I've never known what my gift is," he said, to our astonishment. "All my life I've seen a need, been asked to fill it, and trusted the Holy Spirit to enable me to do it." Maybe Kenneth is on to something.

As you work through possible definitions of spiritual gifts you may be frustrated that they are not more precise, especially if I questioned your favorite gift definition. I felt that way for years. I read books filled with precise definitions and self-evaluating checklists, searching for my personal gift. Could I ever really know my specific gift for sure?

I finally understood that the Scripture did not define the gifts precisely, and that imprecision was not by accident. I suddenly felt truly liberated. I recognized that I should focus on the tasks that needed to be done rather than worrying about my gifts or lack of them. We should ask God for the abilities necessary to accomplish what He has clearly told us are His purposes for the church. We can leave the combination of abilities, natural and supernatural, to the Holy Spirit to decide-"*as he determines*" (1 Cor. 12:11).

We can tell when that custom-designed pattern of gifts is from Him: the outcome will demonstrate the supernatural power of God. I conclude that we should focus more on roles for another reason. Each of the biblical gift lists are different. No one particular gift appears in all of them. Teaching and prophesy appear in three, apostle shows up in two, and the others occur only once. None of the lists is exhaustive; they're just representative or suggestive. Perhaps other gifts are not listed. Tasks may need to be done in your church which Paul didn't include in any of his lists. Can you think of any?

You might list music, a major ministry of the church. If your church uses drama, you list that; you don't want your dramatic efforts to be purely human talent. You want the strong anointing of the Spirit to produce eternal outcomes. You may have listed other activities that don't clearly fit under any of Paul's categories, for example, children's work. Many other activities might either be listed as separate gifts or be combined as forms of "teaching" or "prophetic proclamation." Writing, for example, might fit under one of those. You may have listed counseling. I would consider that the activity of one gifted to "pastor," which literally means "shepherd." The Bible doesn't define "pastor." Today we use it as the over-arching identification of the chief church leader, and certainly the shepherd was called to lead the flock. But the original idea was more like what today we call discipling, counseling, or nurturing. "Encouragement" in the Romans list of gifts might fit here, too.

"All these are the work of one and the same Spirit, and he gives them to each one, just as he determines." (1 Corinthians 12:11) Many Christians are like Barnabas, good at "coming alongside" and helping others through the tough times. The ancients called counseling the "cure of souls." Professional counselors who have the gift of curing the whole soul, who see supernatural results in the counseling process, might be said to have the gift of pastoring. If the Spirit anoints the professional's natural talent and training, he or she can be especially effective in healing the soul. Other possibilities exist for linking contemporary tasks with biblical gifts. Leading, administration, wisdom,

discernment, or helps, for example, are capable of wide application. Just be sure not to be too dogmatic in claiming that your understanding of a gift name is the only meaning it could have . Always identify the touch of the Spirit by spiritual outcomes.

The 5 purposes of the church are united worship, fellowship, discipleship, ministry, and evangelism. Let's think about how these five purposes of the church can help you identify and use your spiritual giftedness. The Holy Spirit gives gifts or abilities so that the purposes of the church may be fulfilled. Think about how the spiritual gifts empower the church to fulfill its purposes.

Is God calling you to seek some gift to help fulfill the purposes of the church? There may be other roles in your church that don't easily fit into the above categories. If you have a gift or desire a gift that could be used in that way, be sure to add it to your lists above. If you have a strong desire to see some of the gifts used more in your church, this would be an excellent topic to discuss in your next group meeting. Do you have a strong desire to be used more than you have been? Paul says to "earnestly desire" the higher gifts. That's a command! So if you don't feel strongly about something you'd like to accomplish for God, now is the time to pause and ask God to give you such a holy desire. If you already have a longing for a particular gift, pause now and ask God for it! Write out your petition in your journal.[13]

---

[13] Rather than using the extensive lists as they appear in the Bible, unexplained, let me consolidate and describe some of the key gifts Scripture points toward-abilities clearly needed to fulfill the purposes of the church. My description of eight key spiritual gifts includes the abilities to: 1. teach the Bible in such a way that lives are changed 2. win people to faith 3. help the physical and social needs of the community in such a way that people are drawn to God 4. discern a person's spiritual need and give wise counsel in such a way that they grow spiritually 5. lead people to worship in spirit and in truth 6. proclaim (preach) God's truth with life-changing authority 7. understand the way God wants the church to go and get people to go that direction 8. help in practical ways like financial management, feeding people, seeing needs and meeting them.

April 13
Worship
Revelation 15:3-4

"Great and marvelous are your deeds, Lord God Almighty. Just and true are your ways, King of the ages. Who will not fear you, 0 Lord, and bring glory to your name? For you alone are holy. All nations will come and worship before you, for your righteous acts have been revealed." (Revelation 15:3-4)

Glorifying God doesn't have to be a "major production." Muriel was often an example to me of spontaneously giving God credit. In the grocery store check-out line, I've heard her exclaim to the clerk, "Wow! Isn't God good! Look what He helped me find!" Her heart full of love was forever bubbling over. Many genuine Christians don't experience much worship in a "worship service"; they don't feel much warm devotion in their "devotional" time. Yet God longs for those who will worship Him in spirit and in truth (John 4:23).

To get a running start on bringing to life your "worship service" next Sunday, let's worship Him now. We can do that in many ways-actually all of life should exalt His worth. Telling Him how greatly we value Him, exulting in His person, that is worship. Worship with Scripture. Do you have a favorite Psalm of praise? If none comes immediately to mind, try Psalm 8 or 19. To "tune your heart to sing His praise" slowly read aloud the Psalm you chose, consciously speaking those words to God.

Worship in Song. Look at the topical index of your hymnal under "Worship," "Praise," and "Thanksgiving" and choose some of your favorite hymns of praise. Don't choose testimony songs that focus on your personal experiences. Choose those that speak to God and worship Him. If you don't have a hymnal, perhaps you can recall a favorite hymn or song of adoration or search the internet.

Sing your heart out to the all glorious One!

"Holy, Holy, Holy" Hoy, holy, holy! Lord God almighty! Early in the morning our song shall rise to thee; Holy, holy, holy, merciful and mighty! God in three Persons, blessed Trinity!

Holy, holy, holy! tho the darkness hide thee, Tho the eye of sinful man thy glory may not see; Only Thou art holy; there is none beside thee, Perfect in power, in love, and purity.

Holy, holy, holy! Lord God Almighty! All thy works shall praise thy name, in earth, and sky, and sea ; Holy, holy, holy; merciful and mighty! God in three Persons, blessed Trinity! -Reginald Heber[14]

Worship in Your own Words. Now that others have inspired you with their expressions of worship, we're ready to worship Him in our own words. Write out in your journal a prayer of worship. If you're courageous try putting it into verse a hymn of worship! Write 3 stanzas: 1. First, tell God everything about His person you admire, His marvelous characteristics. That's worship. 2. Next, review the major activities of God since the start of time, His works of creation and redemption. Praise Him for each of those activities you admire or for which you are especially grateful. That's praise. 3. Finally, thank God for everything He has done for you personally. Be sure to include earthly blessings as well as the spiritual. That's thanksgiving.

Worship Him Forever. If I asked you to name the hymnbook of the Bible I'm sure you'd name the Book of Psalms. You'd be right-it's the hymnbook of God's people of all the ages. But a close second is found in the New Testament. Do you have any idea which book would qualify? John was overwhelmed with dreadful visions of future

---
[14] Public Domain (1826).

doom, but he constantly bursts into praise. He records some of the worship that will one day be offered to God on high in the last book of the Bible, Revelation. As he lets us in on that celestial worship, I think he's inviting us to join him in adoration. He gives us a preview of the glorious worship in which we will one day participate. Let's join him in that worship now . . . "*Holy, holy, holy is the Lord God Almighty, who was, and is, and is to come. You are worthy, our Lord and God, to receive glory and honor and power, for you created all things, and by your will they were created and have their being.* " -Revelation 4:8,11 If you know a contemporary song that sets music to those words, don't hesitate to sing it now! Amen! *Praise and glory and wisdom and thanks and honor and power and strength be to our God for ever and ever Amen!"* -Revelation 7:12

Remember, the heavy heart lifts on the wings of praise. To love God is to worship and adore Him and to tell others incessantly about His greatness. May your worship today be part of a life filled more and more with worship of the God who is worthy of all glory, honor, and praise.

April 14
Repentance
Hebrews 6:1

"Therefore let us leave the elementary doctrine of Christ and go on to maturity, not laying again a foundation of repentance from dead works and of faith toward God…" (Hebrews 6:1)

Jacob wrestled all night with the angel, holding out for God's full blessing (Genesis 32: 22-32). I guess he thought he could force God's hand, which was futile; but he knew what he was after. Because he was so sincere, so determined in his quest for spiritual blessing, he finally won out. God gave Jacob the blessing he sought. Of course, Jacob took a heavy hit-the angel gave him a permanent limp to remind him that God is in charge after all, and He alone is the source of all good. When we get so desperate in our wrestlings with God that we are prepared to obey no matter the cost, the promised power will flow. The turning point for the sinner is called repentance. In the life of a wayward saint it's sometimes called reconsecration or recommitment. How would you define or describe repentance?

Christians through the ages have described this turning point in a number of ways. Like Jacob, some say they wrestled with God. Some say the love of Jesus overwhelmed them. They realized that rebellion against God is an affront to His love. Others have seen their own arrogance and been humbled by the example of Jesus as the suffering servant. Other words for repentance include yield, surrender, commit, abandon self, change management, get off the throne of my life and let God take His rightful place, or acknowledge Christ's lordship. No matter how the Spirit breaks through to us, we must finally come to the place where we give in unconditionally. We say, "I quit, you win!" That's the turning point. Have you had such a turning point since your initial turning to God, your salvation repentance? If you have, write out your story in a paragraph, either here or in your journal.

Here's a simple summary of how disobedience worked in my life. At first I knew I was. I had started a relationship with Christ and I thought that was enough. I didn't worry much about what salvation was supposed to produce in my life. Both the goal and the way to the goal were blurry in my thinking, but I sensed something was lacking. Surely Christianity was more than a fire-insurance policy! The Holy Spirit convicted me of my selfishness and wrongdoing. As a result, I turned my life over to Him unconditionally. Unfortunately, I was still in the passive mode. My motto was: "God, You shove and I'll move." I wasn't eager to find out how to make Him happy. I wasn't trusting Him for any miracle change in my life, but a longing for a more genuine Christian experience began to grow in me. Finally, I had a moment of enlightenment. I realized that He has made full provision to do in me what I can't do on my own, and He will do it if I only trust Him. I accepted that moment of enlightenment as God's word to me. I began to trust Him to keep the promises in His Word. I began to grow. I began to understand more about God's ways and experience the Spirit in my life.

Trust is central to our Christian experience. Trusting comes before yielding. We won't surrender to God until we trust Him. But trust follows commitment as well. Sometimes "simply trusting" turns out to be not so simple! Since faith is a combination of yielding and trusting, we'll also consider what we can do to increase our faith. Trust, whether in human beings or in God, must grow. We know that an electric appliance must be plugged in to operate. The plug-in that got me moving had two prongs: trust and yield. Of course, we cannot trust someone we do not know. Faith implies knowledge. To have faith you have to know the Holy Spirit. You must know how He acts, whether or not He is dependable, and how to connect with Him. Ignorance can keep you disconnected. Thus, the three elements of knowing, yielding, and trusting go together. They build upon each other. Stated negatively, three roots can result in failure in the Christian life: ignorance, unbelief, and unyieldedness. What keeps you from trusting God for all He has for you?

April 15
Designer Plan
1 John 4:7 & 16

"Dear friends, let us love one another, for love comes from God. Everyone who loves has been born of God and knows God. God is love. Whoever lives in love lives in God, and God in him." (1 John 4:7,16)

Muriel was pretty, vivacious, talented, fun, a great lover of God-and a lover of me! Finally, she agreed to be mine and everything in life was aimed toward the wedding day, August 24 . I was so intoxicated with love for Muriel that I constantly did irrational things like subsisting on one meal a day so I could save money for the great day; and reading her love letters the minute they arrived, in spite of the fact that they consistently pre-empted my history class.

Shortly before the big day, I gathered some of my family in South Carolina, borrowed my father's car, and headed for Nebraska. In a long, sweeping curve through the wheat fields of Kansas, a tractor had backed up traffic for what seemed like miles. The creeping traffic blocked our way. Finally, my chance came. I could see around the curve, ahead of dozens of creeping cars, and no one was coming toward us. I whipped out into the left lane of that two-lane highway and put the accelerator to the floor-not very smart. But I was crazy in love. I had one objective: to get to the one I loved.

Half-way through that curve, a speeding car appeared from nowhere, aimed right at us. I headed for the shoulder. "Oh, no! Why did they put that telephone pole there?" The thought barely had time to flash through my mind. I closed my eyes and aimed at the narrow gap between the approaching car and the telephone pole. We left one of my father's fenders on that pole, but we limped on to Beaver City where Muriel and I began a lifetime odyssey together. And now?

Now Muriel lies in bed, unable to stand, walk, or feed herself. Knowing nothing, really, a victim of Alzheimer's disease. But her contented smile sometimes breaks through the dimness and brightens my day. People speak of my care of Muriel as if it were something heroic-far from it. I love her more now than I ever did on that mad dash to Nebraska.

When I'm away on a speaking engagement, I miss her more. I long to be with her, to feel the squeeze of her hand. But there is a big difference. Now the love flows mostly one way. The connecting point is gone. We used to share our dreams, our work, our play, our children, our laughter, and our tears. We drew ever closer to one another. We became more and more like one another, actually. But we're not much alike now. The mutuality is almost gone. Is that the way with God and you? He created you to be like Him so you could share His life and His love. He had a mutually satisfying love affair in mind. The relationship started out so gloriously, didn't it? But for many Christians, something has happened. Oh, He still loves them and lavishes that love on them daily. But how do they respond? Communication is sporadic; love has lost its passion. Perhaps they can't even identify with Him, because they are so unlike Him now. Sad, isn't it? But that was never the Designer's plan.

From all eternity God the Father, God the Son, and God the Holy Spirit were bound together in love, for God by nature is love (1 John 4:7,16). From the overflow of His loving nature, He wanted people to whom He could show His love and who would love Him back.

For communication and love to flow freely, the people God made would have to be like Him. The relationship couldn't be like you and your dog. Fido may be a great friend, but communication is limited, and a dog is not exactly a "suitable helper" to you, as God said of the mate He was creating for Adam (Genesis 2:20). Fido is a different species, but Adam and Eve, that's another story. They were made for each other. Just as God created Adam and Eve compatible with each other, He created us to be God-compatible. If that compatibility weren't there, in-depth communication would not be possible, intimate companionship would be missing. That is why God the Holy Spirit created humankind on God's own pattern. As a result, Adam and Eve walked with God in the garden of Eden, sharing His presence and love. They were created to love God and be loved by Him. They were created in His likeness so they could experience that love. God's design determines genuine life purpose. What do you consider to be your supreme purpose in life?

What about Christlikeness? Becoming more like Jesus enables us to fellowship with God, but it is not the ultimate goal. The more like Christ we become, the more we will be able to love God and receive love from Him. Becoming like Christ is so important that the major emphasis of this devotional is how we become like Him, but keep in mind that becoming like Christ is not the final goal. The goal is to develop our love relationship with God. He created us on His pattern and provided the salvation process as a way for His image in us to be restored. He did all these things with the ultimate goal of loving us and us loving Him. Before we close our time considering God's purpose in making us like Him, let us reflect on ways we are becoming like Him and ways in which we are not.

April 16
Confirming the Word
1 Corinthians 2:14

"People who aren't Christians can't understand these truths from God's Spirit. It all sounds foolish to them because only those who have the Spirit can understand what the Spirit means." (1 Corinthians 2:14, NLT)

My struggle with disbelief led to a lonely period of my life with no dependable truth. Finally, I prayed an arrogant but honest prayer. I asked God to prove to me that He exists. I was surprised to find that God had answered my prayer before I was even born. My search took me back to the Bible.

I had come to believe that the Bible was riddled with errors, yet the Holy Spirit began to use the Bible itself to build a foundation for my faith. For example, I realized that the Old Testament predicted many details about the Messiah:
- When and where He would be born.
- What He would do.
- How He would die.
- That He would live forever.

These were predictions made hundreds of years before Christ's birth. I was discovering revelation, supernatural revelation-the Bible, a miracle in my hand. I began, ever so tentatively, to embrace God with my mind. I was experiencing personally what God did through history- God revealed Himself. I call it the great unveiling.

If God had not chosen to reveal Himself, He would remain forever a mystery to us. I have no doubt that the Holy Spirit was leading me into truth. That's His job. Jesus said, "When he, the Spirit of truth, comes, he will guide you into all truth" (John 16:13). Many believers go through periods of questioning or doubting. If you have, recall one or more of your concerns. How would you describe how you dealt with them? God provided a written record of everything we need to know about Him, so we can enter into relationship with Him. The Spirit of God led the writers of Scripture to communicate what we need to know to experience fellowship with God. But you may ask legitimate questions about the Bible:
- How do we know the words of the Bible are from God?
- How did the Holy Spirit inspire Scripture?
- Can we understand Scripture so that we know God's will?

Understanding the Bible and relating to God through His Holy Spirit go together. We cannot know God apart from Scripture, and we cannot understand the Bible apart from the Spirit. Reread 1 Corinthians 2:14 above. How could you explain why any person without the Holy Spirit is unable to understand spiritual things?

Several terms describe the relationship between the Bible and the Spirit. Some of these terms are: revelation, authority, inspiration, interpretation, and illumination. God has chosen to disclose truth about the universe, about humanity, and about Himself- truth that we would not otherwise know.

I call this self-disclosure The Great Unveiling. The Bible is our authority because it is the only completely dependable means through which God has revealed Himself to us. The Holy Spirit gave revelation through a process we call inspiration. We have the privilege and the responsibility to determine what each passage means through interpretation. For the task of interpretation, we have the assistance of the Holy Spirit guiding us into all truth through the process of illumination.

About the Bible Herschel Hobbs wrote: "Revelation is God's unveiling of truth. Inspiration is receiving and transmitting truth. Illumination is understanding truth (cf. John 16 :13). In the biblical sense revelation and inspiration were completed with the close of the New Testament. But illumination is a continuing activity of the Holy Spirit." [15]

What is your attitude toward the authority of Scripture? Which of the following descriptions best fits?
- I can't believe some things in the Bible are true.
- The Bible is good literature, but it doesn't have divine authority.
- I believe the Bible is true, but I still want to choose my own values.
- The Bible is true in all its parts, and thus is the final authority for what I believe and how I behave.
- Other?

Now would be a good time to thank the Lord for His authority in your life. Thank Him for the Bible. Ask Him to empower you to understand more clearly the role His Word should play in your life. Would it help to write out your response to God for today?

April 17
The Battleground
Romans 12:2

"Do not be conformed to this world,[a] but be transformed by the renewal of your mind, that by testing you may discern what is the will of God, what is good and acceptable and perfect." (Romans 12:2)

The mind is the battleground where spiritual battles are won or lost. I use the term 'mind' as a comprehensive category-it includes all of you, what you think, how you feel, what you choose. You need all the activities of your mind renewed. Notice several things about Paul's command. First, the word for renew in Greek is metamorphosis. Consider how we use that term. The little earth-bound fuzzy worm metamorphosed into a gorgeous creature of the skies! That's what Paul says we're to work at-"be totally renovated in your entire outlook and response."

Second, the form of the Greek verb is passive- meaning to have this done to you by the Holy Spirit. But that passive verb is contained in a positive command. The command calls for some initiative on your part. You must participate with the Spirit. Third, though the grand presentation (v . 1) is a "point action" verb-speaking of a decisive turning point, the transformation (v . 2) is a "continuous action" verb, speaking of a process. You have to keep working at it. The mind is the battlefield where a deadly war is in progress. You either win or lose the battle in your mind. In the war against the conforming influences of your environment you must take the initiative to have your entire mind-set transformed. To do that we use the Bible, prayer, and the church as offensive weapons of the Spirit at the time of confrontation.

---

[15] Herschel Hobbs, *What Baptists Believe.* Broadman Press, 1964, 12. (available at: https://www.google.com/books/edition/What_Baptists_Believe/EBu5AwAAQBAJ?hl=en&gbpv=1)

How does it work for the Bible to be an offensive weapon? Last night I felt an excitement about today-I was looking forward to writing this lesson on winning the victory over temptation! About 4:00 a .m. I woke to the persistent ringing of the phone. My heart jumped- I immediately thought, which of my children is in an emergency? The voice said, "Is this Mr. McQuilkin?" "Yes," I responded. A dread settled in as I realized it was a police officer on the phone. Oh, no, not again, I thought. Three months ago, my car had been stolen from my backyard. While the police officer talked, I looked out the back window and, sure enough, my car was gone again. And once again, the police had found it, torn up as before. I was angry. "I'd like to put a booby trap on that car. Guess what would happen to the next person who touches it!" I said to myself. And I was afraid. Was it the same people? Will our house be next? Maybe we should move out of this inner-city neighborhood we deliberately chose to live in.

Very early the next morning as I reviewed my responses the night before, I knew which were unacceptable to God. The booby-trap strategy is vengeful, and I would be disobedient if I left my calling to live for God in this neighborhood. Anger and fear are not necessarily sinful; it depends on who they're directed at and why. I lapse into unbelief if I conclude God won't care for me.

There was no use to go back to bed-I was too agitated. So I turned to Scripture for an earlier-than-usual devotional time. I was reading Hebrews 10, but I couldn't concentrate. This chapter seemed irrelevant to my crisis, so I decided to quit halfway through. I'll pick it up here tomorrow, I told myself. Then, listlessly, I decided to read on. The next words hit me like a bolt from heaven: *"You cheerfully accepted the seizure of your possessions, knowing that you possessed something better and more lasting"* (Heb . 10:34, NEB). The Word of God was a sword to annihilate those evil temptations that had been winning out in my mind.

That morning as I reviewed; Was I cheerful? Hardly. Better and more lasting? Definitely. A couple of chapters later the Spirit gave me more reassurance about my situation: *"Be content with what you have; for God himself has said, "I will never leave you or desert you" and so we can take courage and say, "The Lord is my helper, I will not fear; what can man do to me?"* (Heb. 13:5-6, NEB).

God is my better and lasting possession! Notice that the Spirit used the Scripture in a way that was legitimate and in context. Once I tried to find guidance from Deuteronomy 1:6 *"You have stayed long enough at this mountain"*? At that time I was making the verse speak to me in a way different than its original meaning. In the case of Hebrews 10 :34 God showed me Christians who were faithful when they faced a trial worse than my own. Their response challenged me to be faithful.

The Bible is not only our defensive weapon as we stockpile its truth against the hour of temptation, it's our offensive weapon at the moment of temptation. Like Jesus in the wilderness, we wield the sword of the Spirit against temptation and rout the enemy. My agitated mind settled down in a miraculous calm, and cheerfulness actually began to bubble up as I focused on the positive things God is doing in my life.

- Though it was all the transportation I had, it wasn't much.
- They broke into my car, not my house.
- They took my car, not my life .
- They were the thieves, not I.
- They can take my possessions, but they can't take my God.

I was tempted, but the Spirit delivered me-through the Word. Hallelujah! What mighty firepower we have right in our hands! Let's wield the sword of the Spirit against temptation and rout the enemy!

April 18
Discipleship
Proverbs 27:17

"Iron sharpens iron, and one man sharpens another." (Proverbs 27:17)

The vast majority of congregations in the world don't need to structure small groups-they *are* a small group. For them the challenge is to transform that great asset into a disciple-making relationship! Also, it seems that the way to actually fulfill Christ's command is to intentionally multiply small congregations. Consider what is happening around the world in the burgeoning church multiplying movements.

The churches in Church Planting Movements begin as small fellowships of believers meeting in natural settings such as homes or their equivalent... Meeting in small groups certainly has economic implications. Liberating the fledgling movement from the burden of financing a building and professional clergy is no small obstacle to overcome.

Although these movements may be the most exciting development in the evangelization of the world today, the paradigm may not be established easily in traditional church contexts. But the benefits of the small group in any church context could hardly be more powerfully articulated.

Not only is discipleship best done "small," but the New Testament model would indicate it is normally best done in gender-specific groups, men-to-men (usually, but not always older to younger) and the same by implication for women. There are exceptions, of course. For example, there can be value in a mixed gender setting for couples just starting a Christian life; the support of the spouse can be very important. But in many cultures men hide their true feelings in mixed gender settings. They don't want to appear weak to the women. And women may tend to focus on topics they feel safe discussing. Furthermore, many topics essential for discipleship, such as dealing with sexual temptation should occur only in same-sex interaction. I believe there is a strong need for single gender small groups, since that allows a transparency and depth seldom found in mixed gender settings.

Both (1) teaching the congregation gathered and (2) small group intensive discipleship, were modeled by Jesus in his earthly ministry. But, there is a further method of making disciples that neither he nor Paul are depicted as using: one-on-one. Just because they didn't seem to have used this method of disciple-making, doesn't mean it is not a worthy approach, only that it might not be essential. Yet, in today's church context it does seem to be of great benefit.

A personal mentor is often considered the fast track to spiritual growth. In recent decades, borrowing from the Roman tradition, one type of mentor has been increasingly called a "spiritual director," considered essential to "spiritual formation." Though the more recent articulation of that role has become quite specific, the more commonly used paradigm is the "counselor." If the professional counselor actually aims at spiritual development, then he or she would be participating in disciple making. Whatever the approach, clearly the concept of having someone gifted and called to the role of personally instructing and holding accountable could indeed be a major source of spiritual development, of becoming ever more like Jesus, of having the lost image restored, of living out life in the presence and power of the Spirit. In short, of becoming a true disciple of Jesus Christ.

It is said that relationships occur at five levels, beginning with talking about inconsequential matters, moving to offering an opinion, then expressing a belief, listening to them share their dreams, fears, and emotions, and finally, sharing these things with others. A personal relationship that results in spiritual growth may need time to develop. That may not be the case, however, when mentoring is intentional on the part of both mentor and disciple.

To really grow spiritually it takes more than a teacher teaching and a hearer listening. Ideally, for mind renovation and behavioral change to take place, accountability to another person or persons is essential. The small group and personal mentoring (above) are sub-authentic if they end in teaching/learning, let alone if they end in no more than warm fellowship and encouragement. Accountability within the group or in the mentoring relationship should be a part of the relationship if true growth and discipleship are to take place.

It won't do merely to proclaim the truths of holiness from the pulpit. In some structured relationship-small group or one-on-one- all of us, including leaders, need to have accountability partners. That's what "small group", "mentoring", "pastoring" are all about! When we are to take action and how it is to be done have everything to do with success in the making of disciples. What is happening in your spiritual life? Do you attend church regularly? Or have you let that drop? Participate in a small group? Perhaps mentoring is better for you, one-on-one. We can't live the Christian life alone. We are not made that way. It is not effective for life transformation. For true growth in discipleship ALL that Jesus taught is included. And for that we really do need one another.

April 19
Worship
John 4:23

"But the hour is coming, and is now here, when the true worshipers will worship the Father in spirit and truth, for the Father is seeking such people to worship him." (John 4:23)

The year was 1636 and Black Death or bubonic plague was sweeping Europe once again. Pastor Martin Rinker that year buried 5,000 parishioners, an average of 15 a day. As he heard the cries of the bereaved and dying outside his window, he penned these words:

Now thank we all our God with heart and hands and voices,
Who wondrous things hath done, in whom his world rejoices;
Who, from our mother's arms, hath blessed us on our way
With countless gifts of love, and still is ours today.

O may this bounteous God through all our life be near us,
With ever joyful hearts and blessed peace to cheer us;
And keep us in his grace and guide us when perplexed,
And free us from all ills in this world and the next.

All praise and thanks to God....

Now *that's* worship. It's the kind of worshiper God seeks "one who worships" in spirit. Focus is wholly on God, not on the "flesh" or visible world which was for Rinker full of dread beyond comprehension. And it was "in truth," genuine, no fakery. As leaders in the congregation, it's our responsibility to see that God finds among us that kind of worshiper.

But what is worship, after all? After all the centuries of tradition and re-inventing, after all the definitions and re-definitions, what is it we are supposed to help our people do? In Hebrew and Greek the word meant to prostrate one's self before someone or something: a god, for example, or an important person. In ancient days it often meant to kiss the feet of the person worshiped. It still does in some places. Far out in the desert of Tanzania I was waiting at a lonely telephone outpost when a young man approached. He bowed and began to kiss my feet. Embarrassed, I tried to prevent this "worship," but the missionary, culturally attuned, told me not to resist, that he was simply showing respect. When the Israelites used the term, gradually the kissing part disappeared because their God was invisible.

What do you think of when you see a picture of Muslims at prayer? Maybe they're onto something we may be missing. The chief word in the Old Testament for a right relationship to God is not love or faith, but fear--you prostrate yourself before deity with humble awe. We like to think of the the lover, the friend. We seem to have lost the majesty, the grandeur, the holiness -the wholly otherness of our God. Most of us never prostrate ourselves before his majesty.

Since to prostrate one's self was a way of showing honor and the highest honor was reserved to their God, Jewish people gradually began to include in the idea of prostration, the inner spirit of it, the fealty, the adoration. So when the English translators looked for the right word to translate the Bible term of prostration, they came up with "worth-ship," because bowing down to express fealty is what you did before people of worth.

Gradually the term "worship" came to mean not only the praise and adoration of one's heart, but all the outward evidences in religious symbols and rituals. A "worship service" we called it. One of those worship activities is music, so gradually, in 20th Century America, "worship" came to mean praise and adoration in song. So we no longer speak of a song leader but of a worship leader and we mean music.

But not just any kind of music. We invited Phil, a graduate who had returned to faith through the Jesus movement in California, to lead our "worship" in a conference on the campus of Columbia International University. After a day or two of contemporary praise songs, one of the faculty members approached me. "Would it be possible to sing just one grand old hymn of the church?" I passed this request on to our worship leader and he exploded. "I thought you wanted *worship!*" Thus in the last quarter of the 20th century "worship" came to mean not just music, but a certain kind of music. This newer definition of worship fits well the contemporary psyche since music, more universally than anything else, defines contemporary youth.

When a Bible scholar asked Jesus what was the most important thing, the ultimate, he replied, borrowing from Moses, "You shall love the Lord your God with all your heart, with all your soul, with all your mind, with all your strength. This is the BIG ONE, this is the great commandment." Then he added, the whole teaching of our Scriptures hangs on this. Sounds like you might say, "A person's chief end is to love God and be loved of him forever." It's so beautiful if you truly love a person you will glorify them, keep the spotlight ceaselessly on the true worth of the beloved. If you truly love a person and he is God, you will honor and glorify him so highly you will worship him, you will bow down in humble adoration, you will sing to high heaven. So to glorify and worship God doesn't automatically lead to love, but love, to truly love, will always bring praise and worship.

So to worship him "in spirit" is to love him with all your heart. To pursue a lifetime of loving intimacy with him. But it's not just a worship in spirit, it is a tight connection spirit-to-spirit. Why not worship Him today?

April 20
Prayer Connection
Ephesians 6:18

"...praying always with all prayer and supplication in the Spirit, being watchful to this end with all perseverance and supplication for all the saints." (Ephesians 6:18)

While they were worshipping the Lord and fasting, the Holy Spirit said...So after they had fasted and prayed, they placed their hands on them and sent them off. (Acts 13:2,3)

The Holy Spirit is indispensable in accomplishing all of God's work, not the least his work in and through the church. The reason for this is evident. We cannot accomplish God's work without the Holy Spirit because he alone has the knowledge of all the factors involved in any situation, he alone has the wisdom to make the right decision, and he alone has the power to carry through the decision.

We are extremely limited in our knowledge, even after long study and careful investigation of all facets of any situation. We know only indistinctly the spiritual dimension, particularly what is going on inside other people involved in the issue at hand. We know only partially the historic context that led to the current circumstances, and we certainly do not know any of the future. In fact, we know only a fraction of all the infinite number of factors which bear on any decision that must be made. God the Holy Spirit alone has this knowledge and so he alone is adequate for evaluating the situation.

If we were infinite in knowledge and had access to all the information impinging on any decision, we would still lack the wisdom necessary to make the right decision. We are not only finite; our judgment is warped by sin. God the Spirit is the only one with wisdom sufficient to make the choices.

Finally, even were we to make the right choice, our power is totally inadequate to accomplish God's purposes. So God the Holy Spirit must empower us to do the work.

The good news is that all the resources necessary have been provided in the person of the Holy Spirit, and in him alone. Indeed he is *Indispensable*.

* The Spirit is indispensable for salvation--*convicting* (John 16:8) and *regenerating* (John 3:3-8).
* The Spirit is indispensable for *sanctification*-- we are changed ... into the same image by the Spirit of the Lord (2 Corinthians 3:18).
* The Spirit is indispensable for *renewal*-can these dry bones live? I will put my Spirit in you and you will live (Ezekiel 37:14).
* The Spirit is indispensable for *guidance*-the Spirit ...will guide you into all truth (John 16:13).
* The Spirit is indispensable for *provision*-my God shall supply all your needs (Philippians 4:19).
* The Spirit is indispensable for spiritual power-The Spirit works...*distributing* to each one (I Corinthians 12:11).

If the Spirit's power is not freely flowing, there must be a disconnect. If salvation, sanctification, renewal, guidance, provision, spiritual power doesn't seem to be flowing full force in your congregation or ministry, it could be the lack of prayer. The infinite knowledge, wisdom, power of the Spirit does not flow through the people in the congregation without activity on our part. But not just any kind of prayer will do. The pray-er must be connected. All Christians, but particularly the leaders in the congregation, must have an attitude of faith and obedience. If there is an unwillingness to do the will of God or a doubting that it can be accomplished, the Spirit is not free to do what he desires.

Note, however, that is not enough to have the right attitude; this attitude must be expressed, and the channel of expression is prayer. The prayer of faith is the connection with the Spirit that lets the wisdom and power flow. Believing prayer by believing Christians, however, is not sufficient. This conscious dependence on the Spirit in believing prayer must also be in prayer *together*. This is the way God's people may discern his plan.[16] It is the way they will be empowered.[17] There are special promises for the church at prayer: *"where two or three are gathered in my name"* and *"when two agree on earth as touching anything"* (Matthew 18:18-20).

The Spirit works in response to the united prayer of faith by an obedient people.

John 13-17 is often called the Upper Room Discourse and is the last block of teaching Jesus gave his disciples before going to the cross. The purpose of the teaching time around the table was to prepare them to live the Christian life without Christ being physically with them. So, how do *we* live the Christian life without Jesus being physically with us? Jesus told them what he intended to give them --and us—the gift of his presence in the person of the Holy Spirit, the Spirit who had been with them and would soon be IN them. But he is not a silent, impersonal force within, he is as personal as was Jesus to the disciples. So we can converse with him—prayer is the connection.

A few weeks later, Jesus left them. The disciples had experienced three years under the personal mentoring of the very Son of God. They had witnessed his death and resurrection up-front. They had received his commission four or five times, but still they weren't ready. They had the wrong goals because they misunderstood Scripture. They were trapped by traditions and misled by their own ambitions. So, he told them to wait and pray. And they did-united prayer of faith by an obedient people. Then the Spirit fell (Acts 1) and Spirit-power surged.

When God's people pray, the Spirit gifts the church, guides the church, empowers the church, and provides fully for all its needs.

April 21
Sensitive to my Audience
2 Corinthians 1:12-13

"For our boast is this, the testimony of our conscience, that we behaved in the world with simplicity and godly sincerity, not by earthly wisdom but by the grace of God, and supremely so toward you. For we are not writing to you anything other than what you read and understand and I hope you will fully understand..." (2 Corinthians 1:12-13)

Much of my preaching is for missions conferences. This spring I was in a small-town Mississippi church that was weak from its untimely birth. Circulating among the early arrivers before the first service, I met a bouncy little lady who announced that she was church organist. "Oh," I responded, "and how long have you been organist?" "50 years!" she said with a bit of well-earned pride.

---
[16] Acts 13:1-3; 16:6-10
[17] Acts 1:21; 4:23, 24, 29, 31

"50 years! That's been a time of great change in music. It must have been quite challenging."

"I do not change," she stated, jaw firmly set. Then she continued, "if they want Bach and Mendelssohn, well and good. If not, they can get themselves another organist."

In an instant I changed the metaphor about my ministry from frustrated typewriter salesman in the computer age. Here I am, constantly crisscrossing the country offering Bach pipe organ recitals to an audience dancing to the music of electronic praise bands. I preach commitment, sacrifice, and incarnational investment of life to reach people living and dying out of reach of gospel witness. It's like I'm from another galaxy! They're interested in sending their members on 2-week junkets to exotic places, sending their money for nationals to do the job, and staying put in their pews, praising God. And not with a pipe organ!

I have hesitated to be specific about possible responses to postmodern thinking because, in the nature of the case, so complex a set of issues can't even be accurately named in so short a space, let alone adequately explored. Besides, I myself am on pilgrimage in these matters--developing a whole new generation of messages and revising old faithfuls in my personal attempt to connect more effectively with the postmodern generations I have opportunity to address. So I'm reluctant, but I overcame my reluctance with the thought I might be able to set a few markers toward harnessing the all-pervasive postmodern engine to drive spiritual formation.

Let's address the pragmatic question of what a preacher should preach if he is to bring the content of his message under the authority of Scripture. But in addressing the entire scope of ministry and in seeking to do it all under the authority of Scripture, the problem becomes broader and deeper.

Do we use the historic approach in Bible interpretation, or the emerging postmodern hermeneutic as our control? For example, is there objective truth? Increasing numbers of evangelicals would hold there is enduring truth only in the major doctrines of Christianity, that beyond that we arrogantly go astray when we seek to establish "biblical authority."

Again, does God even have a will for us in matters of ministry or do we simply use Scripture as a source of historic reference, sort of a case book of stories for reference? God's stories, to be sure, but intended by him to make normative demands on those at another point in time, living in another culture.

Does "meaning" exist objectively? And if so, does it reside in the text or in the mind of the interpreter, bound as she or he is by their culture? And is the Reformation dogma valid that holds the perspicuity of Scripture and the priesthood of each believer, capable and responsible to understand and obey Scripture? Or are the doctrines and practice of the church created from our own cultural understandings combined with the historic interpretations of the universal church?

The historic response to these questions among evangelicals until the 1980's would have been: The Scripture and the Scripture alone is the final authority for faith and practice. Words do convey meaning, and in Scripture, it is God's meaning, objective and unchanging across time and culture. Further, it is fully adequate to teach us what we must believe and not believe, how we are not to behave and how we are to behave. The text is the bearer of objective truth and the meaning intended by the original author is accessible to the diligent student. Our responsibility is to understand and obey that truth. That is the foundational presupposition, so we must begin with an honest confrontation of the insidious inroads of postmodern thinking.

It is the renewing of our *minds* God is after and transformational preaching certainly can't bypass the mind. But we can use the contemporary anti-intellectual mood to dethrone scientific naturalism and a materialistic mind-set. We may harness the mood to demolish a deadly enemy of spiritual reality. Is it my way or the highway? Do we never change or do we use rational yet biblical thinking to transform our minds and the minds of those with whom we minister?

April 22
Trending
John 17:18

"As you sent me into the world, so I have sent them into the world." (John 17:18)

Two new ways of approaching the "uttermost ends of the earth" evangelistic mission of the church have become dominant in recent decades. They have become so pervasive among American churches, I have no illusions of changing them significantly. But since both seem to violate some of the biblical paradigm, I feel compelled to highlight some of the hazards as I see them. I will attempt to, bring all aspects of ministry under the functional authority of Scripture. I do this in the hope that a rising generation may make enough course correction in these approaches to capture them for a new era of biblical mission advance in finishing the task Christ gave.

I was invited to address a large group of pastors from the Calvary Chapel network. The "father" of the Jesus People movement, Chuck Smith, is also the founder of the Calvary Chapel movement which at the time of my first visit numbered about a million strong across the nation. I was invited to talk to the pastors about missions. On the way from the airport to the conference center I asked about the movement's missions involvement. "Very strong," I was told, "we send tens of thousands of missionaries." That puzzled me, for the entire Protestant church of the United States sends fewer than 50,000 of what I call "missionary." A week later I had begun to wonder about the significance of that conversation so, on the way back to the airport, I asked a more discriminating question, "How many career missionaries have Calvary Chapels sent?"

"We don't do numbers, of course, but I would estimate about 200." What I didn't know was that my speaking had been something of a set-up. Some of the younger men wanted to introduce the novel idea of sending career missionaries.

Calvary was the first major wave of the tsunami that has swept missions-interested churches in America: send all the people you can on short term ministry. But as far as career missionaries is concerned, at 200, I figured they were sending about .002% of their membership into career missionary service. The reason I was so startled was that up until then I had been preaching in churches that were sending 2%, 10%, up to 20% of their membership into apostolic missionary service!

Another thing I learned that week, they also spearheaded the other phenomenon in late-twentieth century North American missions: support the nationals. At the time they were supporting 3,000 pastors in India, for example.

I have returned for a number of their pastors' conferences by which some of the leaders hoped to move toward a more Pauline-type ministry, intentional targeting of the last half of the world, seeking to reach those who live out of reach of both national pastors and short-term witnesses. Many Calvary chapels have begun to send long-term missionaries to reach the yet unreached peoples of the world.

In other words, how do we make sure mission is done under the functional authority of Scripture? Consider, "*let-the-nationals-do-it*" phenomenon.

The first problem, and a fatal one, is that in the lost half of the world by definition, there are not churches to partner with. If those now out of reach are to be reached, some churches somewhere are going to have to reach across borders without the luxury of a receiving brotherhood.

But there are other problems. Even for those the plan would seem best positioned to help, it can prove more damaging than helpful. Around the world this paradigm has created a spiritual welfare state, with poorer churches becoming dependent on American dollars. The need to trust God and sacrifice for him gives way to dollar searching and the church becomes spiritually anemic since God-dependency is the foundation of spiritual vitality. So great care must be given to accepting the invitation to send us your dollars, not your people

Short term missionaries. Everyone is called to go to "the uttermost parts of the earth," we're told. Don't worry about formal preparation. What Christ called for was witnesses and everyone is called to that role. Actually, some would say, to prepare or train a witness undermines his authenticity, so don't pause for any kind of formal training. And don't worry about long-term commitment. Just go! If everyone goes, even for a few weeks—we'll get the job done quickly

But there are some problems with the new paradigm. Biblical problems for starters. The Commander-in-Chief has not only designated all his troops as witnesses to the resurrected Christ, he is commissioned his church to ***disciple*** the nations. "Teaching them to ***observe*** all that I commanded," he proclaimed as the job description. Discipling takes more than a few weeks witness through an interpreter. Besides, we can't escape the model "as the Father sent me..." He became one with us, lived among us, absorbed our culture, spoke our language. In fact, he emptied himself of all his heavenly prerogatives and became a servant among us (Philippians 2:6-8). Ultimately, he gave his life for us. Now, says Jesus "as the Father sent me so send I you." That's his plan and we by-pass it only to short-circuit his purpose of building his Church all over the world.

But it's not only Scripture, it's the reality of today's world. Half the people on earth live today out of reach of gospel witness. They don't have access to the good news. Short-term witnesses aren't going to reach that final half. First, the "sent one" must stay long enough among a people to understand them sufficiently to communicate clearly and winsomely the good news and, secondly, long enough to win the trust of the people.

On the other hand, is there no role for the short-term witness? Since fewer are willing to become incarnational and the questions of preparation and gifting are by-passed, our task is to figure out how the short-termer can fit into the New Testament paradigm. Why not spend a few minutes praying over these questions: Is short-term ministry carefully planned and deliberately harnessed to maximize Kingdom effectiveness? Are there effective policies in place to make sure money sent overseas is not causing collateral damage either for donors or recipients?

April 23
An Unassuageable Grief
John 10:28

"I give them eternal life, and they will never perish, and no one will snatch them out of my hand." (John 10:28)

"That's a pain so deep no one can touch it," Em said. A half century ago she spoke to me of her son. Not all our children fully adopt our faith. For one young man, Jim, there were questions about the faith, a faith he had embraced at his mother's knee. Just a little guy then, yet his profession of faith seemed real and, with occasional teenage time-outs, he tried to live it. But now there were questions. Still, no hint of what was soon to come.

After college graduation Jim confided in his older brother, "It worked for you guys, but it never worked for me. For my Dad's sake, I've tried and tried, but it's no use. I'm opting for atheism." And so it has been. A splendid husband and father; a loving, generous son and brother. But no God. What went wrong? And, more important than affixing blame, what is his final destiny? Unassuageable grief.

The haunting question: where did the parent fail? Or, seeking another cause, was it the college professor he so admired, the one who took exception to much of what the school stood for? One day I heard a famous radio preacher say, "All my children follow the Lord, and if you do what I tell you in the next ten minutes, so will yours." Yeah. Right. *Too bad he didn't clue God in on the secret,* I thought. God had two children with a perfect heredity and Paradise for an environment and they both blew it. Big time. So was God the ultimate parental failure? No, with my mind at least, I couldn't buy into environmental determinism. Each person is responsible for his or her own choices, as the prophet reminds us again and again (Ezekiel 33). At the final Judgment no one will be able to plead, "Go after my parents. They're to blame." But doesn't the Bible say what the preacher quoted, *"Train up a child in the way he should go and when he is old he will not depart from it"*? Indeed it does, right there in the book of promises, right? No, it's in the Book of Proverbs. Just like, "The man of diligence will stand before kings." Yes, it often happens, that's the way things normally work, but it's no promise, no guarantee. I knew all that, but still the guilt.

I know I failed as a parent in many ways, and how I have grieved. But I'm forgiven, and in that I rest. No, my pain is not my guilt, but apprehension over the final outcome. Do I run for comfort to the promise, *"I give them eternal life, and they shall never perish; neither shall anyone snatch them out of My hand"*? (John 10.28); or do I agonize over the assurance that "No one who lives in him keeps on sinning. No one who continues to sin has either seen him or known him." (I Jn 4.6). I've given up on solving the theological mystery. God knows; and *"shall not the judge of all the earth do right?"* (Gen 18.25).

I'm responsible *to* my children, no longer *for* them. Once they're grown, my responsibility is to love them and pray for them. Period. So how do I pray? I can't ask God to force one of my children into the Kingdom--he's clearly said he won't do that. But I pray almost daily that the Holy Spirit will not give up on them. He does give up on people, we read. So I pray that he who was sent to convict of sin and righteousness and judgment to come will not give up yet but do his work. Or that the kindness of God will lead them to repentance. Just <u>one more</u> day.

April 24
Cancer in the Body
2 Timothy 3:16

All Scripture is God-breathed and is useful for teaching, rebuking, correcting and training in righteousness, so that the servant of God may be thoroughly equipped for every good work. (II Timothy 3.16-17)

We have a great medical manual telling us what a healthy body is and how you get and maintain that health. Not only for our body but for every member of the body. In fact, that is the purpose of the manual, to enable us to have healthy attitudes and behavior.

Any manual has as much reliability as its author, so when we say this ultimate manual is from God we are recognizing its absolute authority. Thus, the degree of our health is directly proportioned to our faithfulness in following the medical manual. It is a wonderful provision, but the tragedy is that the people who swear allegiance to this book are shot through with malignancies of all kinds. Some of the malignancies move through the body more rapidly than others, some are curable, but all are deadly if not treated. Today I want to call your attention to three varieties of cancer that eat away at the authority of this book, and thus undermine the health of members and of the entire body.

I've called these malignancies leukemia, tumors, and skin cancer, but you may discover better names, more appropriate analogies. The first malignancy is the leukemia of affirming error in Scripture.

I call it leukemia because, though it starts with a few innocent-looking cells in the bloodstream of the body it inevitably grows and spreads, contaminating and destroying. Only rarely has this cancer been arrested, and then usually only for a brief period of remission.

The manual says ALL Scripture has God as its source. Nowhere does the Bible affirm error. If Christ ever thought there were error, he never let on! Rather he said not the dot of an "i", the cross-stroke of a "t" would fail. Scripture cannot be broken, he said, though present-day evangelicals increasingly break off pieces here and there. Maybe they're smarter than Jesus? The authority has shifted from the author to the picker and chooser.

The second malignancy is the tumor of misinterpretation. If a person affirms the full trustworthiness of Scripture, he can still go astray through assigning a meaning to the words that the original author did not intend. I call this a tumor because it can be an isolated instance and if you catch it in time and cut it out, it need not spread. But it is a destructive malignancy and if let run its course it could spread the infection to other passages. The text says that it is Scripture that is God-breathed, not my interpretation.

Since it is important, in hearing the authentic voice of God, to allow Scripture to say what it intends. Understanding the single meaning intended by the author is of utmost importance. There should be in your hermeneutical medical bag enough surgical instruments to cleanly cut out any significant tumor of misinterpretation.

Thirdly there is the skin cancer of misapplication. If a person genuinely accepts the full authority of Scripture and carefully works to expose the meaning intended by the author it is highly unlikely that he will fall victim to a fatal malignancy. But he can get some troublesome surface blemishes that can destroy if not cared for. He can get the right meaning but misapply it. Not the question "what did the author mean?" but what response does God desire today? So we isolate the destructive cells, we clean out the malignancy, we keep it from spreading. How about you? Had a cancer check recently? That troublesome symptom that doesn't go away? Catching the malignancy early prevents a host of damage. To that end we re-commit in understanding the scriptures- without error, interpreted appropriately and applied as intended.

April 25
Those Elusive Feelings
Ephesians 6:19-20

"Pray also for me, that whenever I open my mouth, words may be given me so that I will fearlessly make known the mystery of the gospel, for which I am an ambassador in chains. Pray that I may declare it fearlessly, as I should." (Ephesians 6:19,20)

The picture word "full" (of the Spirit) seems to have three different emphases. A person is full when, in his or her relationship with the Spirit, the Spirit is in full control. Second, a person is full when plenty of evidence shows the Spirit at work-a miracle quality of life (fruit) or a miracle impact in ministry (gifts). People can see it. The third emphasis is more elusive, as feelings always are. Do I feel full?

Feeling full is a mystery, like a good marriage. Full can also speak of a personal relationship-the kind of thing that defies scientific analysis. How do you analyze a relationship? Like a good marriage, the outward evidence, such as a home and children, may be obvious, but the feelings are more mysterious. A relationship includes moments of shared ecstasy and shared agony, a deep and constant sense of well-being and surges of passionate love. So it is living in a deep relationship with the Spirit. If we're filled with the Spirit we'll have joy, confidence, or peace when there's no earthly reason to have any peace at all. Our affection for God will be filled with passion-an excited sense of anticipation when we worship Him, a rush of pleasure when we think about His love for us. We may not sustain an emotional high; but we will have moments of uninhibited ecstasy, especially in devotional times alone with Him. But also, unexpectedly in the midst of a busy day the wind of the Spirit may blow in gale strength. I can't explain it, but we can feel it.

Have you recently had such a surge of affection or some other emotional response to God's presence? If you can't remember anything out of the ordinary in your relationship with God and you are thirsty for a full surge of awareness of God's presence, why not pause right now and tell Him so? But don't leave it there. Tell Him how much you love Him, how grateful you are for Him, for His constant companionship, and for all the wonderful blessings He floods into your life. Ask Him to fill you up with Himself. Pause now and write out in your journal either the description of your experience of fullness, your prayer for fullness, or both.

Which of the fruit of the Spirit in Galatians 5:22 are emotional words? You may choose some or all. Several of the fruits involve our emotions, but even the ones that seem mostly matters of feeling have practical results. To love, for example, is to act lovingly no matter how you feel. Maybe that's why God seems to expect us to have these qualities as a steady state in our lives-all the fruit, all the time. Their presence is evidence of the Spirit at work. But the emotions that accompany them may not be surging all the time.

Perhaps God intends the fruit to be constant and the surges of feelings to be special outpourings?

• Jesus was a man of sorrows and acquainted with grief. He agonized in the garden of Gethsemane, but he also experienced times of surging joy- "*At that time Jesus, full of joy through the Holy Spirit*" (Luke 10:21.
• David, the joy-filled singer for the ages, experienced dry times. When God seemed distant, David cried out in alarm, "*Do not . . . take your Holy Spirit from me*" (Ps. 51:11).
• Paul had times of fear and called on friends to pray for the Spirit-gift of boldness (2 Corinthians 7:5; Ephesians 6:19-20).

For these Bible characters, the inner sense of fullness seems not to be "steady state." In my own life, I can count on having a truly exalted experience of God when I go away for my annual time of fasting and prayer. So much so, I can remember most of those occasions, even decades later. But only occasionally do I have that rushing sense of God's presence in my daily quiet time; even less often do I have it unexpectedly in the midst of a busy day.

The following are most of the examples in the New Testament where the context indicates the meaning of being filled with the Spirit. Each example gives the evidence of the Spirit's fullness and indicates which seems to be subjective awareness or feeling. What feelings do you find in the following?"

- All of them were filled with the Holy Spirit and began to speak in other tongues" (Acts 2:4).
- "The disciples were filled with joy and with the Holy Spirit" (Acts 13:52).
- "Then Peter, filled with the Holy Spirit, said, . . . 'Enable your servants to speak your word with great boldness.' And they were all filled with the Holy Spirit and spoke the word of God boldly." (Acts 4:8,29,31).
- "Choose seven men from among you who are known to be full of the Spirit and wisdom" (Acts 6:3).
- "He was a good man, full of the Holy Spirit and faith, and a great number of people were brought to the Lord." (Acts 11:24).
- "Then . . . Paul, filled with the Holy Spirit, looked straight at Elymas and said…" (Acts 13:9).

Most of the examples have to do with power in ministry, but some subjective evidences appear. We find joy, boldness, and faith. However, both the boldness and faith are related directly to ministry! So, in the biblical examples, the subjective element of feelings, which we so emphasize today, is not prominent. Your obedience to the Spirit or lack of it should be clear to you. If you have a full crop of faith and ministry effectiveness, that should be clear to others. But the inner sense of fullness may not be all that apparent-it may defy analysis. But that is OK. Think about it: in filling us with Himself God promises to give us a love beyond comprehension (Ephesians 3:19) and He speaks of a peace that is unfathomable (Philippians 4:7). How exciting to feel the mysterious surge of the Spirit!

So let's keep praising God for the sporadic winds that blow and stay on the alert for a more constant walk on the highest plane-however God defines that for you. Fullness, then, in the sense of an inner feeling is not subject to analysis; but it can be a glorious experience. The Holy Spirit will give it to those who love and stay close to Him.

April 26
God's Word
Galatians 2:16

"....yet we know that a person is not justified by works of the law but through faith in Jesus Christ, so we also have believed in Christ Jesus, in order to be justified by faith in Christ and not by works of the law, because by works of the law no one will be justified." (Galatians 2:16)

Scripture is our final authority for knowing God's standards for our lives, but it's quite possible to abuse Scripture. One way is through legalism. We see legalism in the following: judging others, depending on the Old Testament law for salvation, obeying the Old Testament law, and imposing rules on others.

Who wants to be a legalistic Pharisee? How would you know if you were one? Yet the term legalism is without doubt one of the most abused words in the English language. In Scripture legalism literally means worship of the law, that is, depending on obedience to the law to bring salvation. That's what the Book of Galatians is all about: the Pharisees demanded obedience to the laws of the Old Testament as a condition of acceptance by God. To Paul that was a wicked heresy because it minimized God's work of grace in providing salvation through Jesus' sacrifice on the cross. Paul wrote, "No one is justified by the works of the law but by faith in Jesus Christ" (Galatians 2:16).

However, making up rules, even lots of picky rules, is not in itself legalistic. A rule may be misguided or even unbiblical, but that's a different problem, not rightly called legalism. People who shout legalism the loudest may actually be against law itself, not merely against the abuse of it. But Paul assures us, "The law is holy, and the commandment is holy and just and good" (Rom. 7:12). The law is not something God created to test us, much less to bring us down. It is the expression of His character, the way He thinks, and the way He behaves, and it shows the things He values. God is altogether holy; just; pure; and above all, loving. His design from the beginning was for us also to be like Him. Godly or Godlike, we call it. It's because He loves us that He wants us to be like Him; it's for our eternal good to be like Him.

Laws which governed human relationships, were designed not only to produce a peaceful society but also to highlight God's character. Because He loves and respects life, He doesn't want us to murder. Because He is pure and holy, He doesn't want us to commit adultery. Because He is Truth, He doesn't want us to steal and lie. Because He is sovereign, He wants us to be satisfied in Him, not to covet things. God's laws instruct us in how to be like Him.

God's law was given for our benefit and blessing as we relate to God and other people. So we don't fear God's law, much less subvert it. We embrace it. We call it law because it's not optional, like a series of helpful suggestions. It's God's requirement of His subjects. Yet God's law isn't burdensome. It's something the psalmist embraced with gratitude. *"Your word is a lamp for my feet and a light on my path."* (Psalm 119:105)

God doesn't want Christians to view His law as a spotlight that reveals how filthy we truly are, bringing condemnation, but as a light to illumine the path ahead, leading to holiness. The Old Testament law was a vital part of God's revelation to His people, and the moral part of that law is just as binding on us today. We can depend on the Bible to show us God's will for our lives. The Bible reveals God's will for us.

April 27
Law and Works
1 John 2:4-5

"Whoever says "I know him" but does not keep his commandments is a liar, and the truth is not in him, 5 but whoever keeps his word, in him truly the love of God is perfected." (1 John 2:4-5)

The apostles consistently appealed to the life and teaching of Jesus as having the highest authority. No wonder the apostles made this teaching the touchstone of truth. For example, Paul exhorts Timothy, *"If anyone teaches otherwise and does not agree with the sound words of our Lord Jesus Christ . . . he is puffed up with conceit, he knows nothing."* (1 Tim. 6:3-4) Then with apostolic authority they added teaching they themselves received from God. This was in the form of commandments—hundreds of them—and in descriptions and explanations of the way Christians should think and live. For example, the description of love in 1 Corinthians 13 or of the fruit of the Spirit in Galatians 5 presents a standard of thrilling grandeur for Christian behavior. Negative descriptions also abound, as in Paul's description of the works of the flesh—*fornication, uncleanness, lasciviousness, idolatry, sorcery, enmities, strife, jealousies, wraths, factions, divisions, parties, envyings, drunkenness, reveling, and such. Does he intend this as benevolent counsel or as law? He leaves no doubt: "I warn you . . . that those who do such things shall not inherit the kingdom of God!"* (Gal. 5:19-21). Happily, all shades of theological opinion affirm that the teaching of the apostles in the Epistles is fully authoritative as a standard for Christian living.

But what about the law revealed in the Old Testament? Do the apostles join Jesus in affirming this law as authoritative for the era of the church? The apostolic answer, as in the case of Jesus Christ, seems to be a yes and a no (see 1 Corinthians 9:19-23). Are we under the law? Yes, say the apostles: (Romans 13:8-10). Are we under the law? No, say the apostles, especially Paul: (Romans 6:14).[18]

The words the apostles use seem clear enough: "He who says, '*I know him'* but disobeys his commandments is a liar, and the truth is not in him" (1 John 2:4-5). "*So the law is holy, and the commandment is holy and just and good*" (Rom. 7:12). "*You are not under law but under grace*" (Rom. 6:14). "*But now we are discharged from the law*" (Rom. 7:6).

How may these teachings be reconciled? Only a very small minority of Bible scholars have ever denied that the Old Testament law and the teachings of Christ prior to the upper room discourse (John 13–17 17) are addressed to Christians. Rather, the majority of theologians throughout church history have sought a resolution of this apparent conflict by making a clear distinction among the various uses of the term *law* and, on the basis of this, holding that the moral law is enduring, and the ceremonial law has been done away with. But this is not easy to do. Neither Moses nor the prophets made this distinction, and it is not always apparent what is moral and what is merely ceremonial. Furthermore, though Jesus seemed to distinguish the two by his behavior and what he stressed, neither did he make this distinction explicitly. But the gravest problem with this interpretation is that Paul himself did not seem to make this distinction. He seemed often to lump together everything in the Mosaic economy as "the law" and to teach that in Christ we have done away with it. In Paul there is no distinction between the Decalogue and the rest of the law. The law is one, the revealed will of God.

But what of "moral" law? In solving this dilemma of strategic importance, perhaps the common wisdom will

---

[18] See *Introduction to Biblical Ethics* (IBE) for a fuller explanation.

lead us to the best solution. Throughout church history the Ten Commandments have been taken as the epitome of moral truth, a summary of what God expects of man. The Ten Commandments seem to summarize what the descendants of the Patriarchs already understood. Did they understand solely because the laws were imprinted in their moral consciousness, or were those laws communicated by God in other ways unknown to us?

Does the law produce "legalism?" The law is good (Romans 7:12), the law is spiritual (v. 14), the law is continuing in effect (Matthew 5:17-19), but it is only good if it is used lawfully, as it was intended (1 Timothy 1:8). How is it possible to misuse the law? How can the law be used illegally or unlawfully?

The Bible opposes legalism. It has ever been man's method of attempted salvation. This is the primary meaning of legalism—relying on obedience to law for acceptance with God.

It is quite possible to teach salvation by grace through faith alone and yet to be legalistic, misusing the law by seeking to "save" oneself through obedience to the law. can be seen when a Christian measures his own acceptability with God or the acceptability of other Christians with himself on the basis of performance. Closely related to the motive of obedience for self-glory is obedience through one's own strength. When we try to obey the law without relying on the enabling of the Holy Spirit, we, though saved by grace, are "saving" ourselves by works. Yet the highest motive is love. Obedience out of gratitude for all the gifts of grace is the best antidote to the virus of legalism.

April 28
Choosing How to Behave
Romans 14:7-8

"For none of us lives to himself, and none of us dies to himself. For if we live, we live to the Lord, and if we die, we die to the Lord. So then, whether we live or whether we die, we are the Lord's." (Romans 14:7-8)

The goal of the Christian is not to please himself but to please his Lord. He does not wish to settle for that which is least harmful, but to reach for that which is highest and best. He is not seeking to avoid punishment but to bring joy to his heavenly Father. He is not testing himself to see how much darkness he can stand but striving to see how near he can get to the Light.

His is not a negative obedience demanded of him but a positive eagerness to please God in every possible way. If this is his orientation, he will not choose between two interpreters on the basis of personal preference. Rather, he will soon recognize that not all learned people are godly, and not all godly people are learned. One of the greatest sources of confusion in Christian matters is that so few of those highly acclaimed as theologians are equally highly acclaimed as devout, and few of those who are noted for personal godliness seem to be masters of Biblical interpretation. Each Christian must assume responsibility to work at both thorough understanding of the Bible and making godlikeness the goal of life. Only one who has high achievement in both areas simultaneously is a reliable guide concerning questions on what you should do in which Christians differ.

Once a person's attitude on the disputed issue is settled, and he eagerly desires God's will alone, the next step is to discover whether it is truly a moral issue. When Scripture does not speak plainly on a question of conduct, the Christian must seek for biblical principle to guide him. Scripture is much more a book of principles than of precepts; any issue will have biblical principles bearing on it—either to direct the Christian or to free him to do as he pleases.

Often these will be specific principles. For example, the biblical principle of purity applies to a whole range of activity not directly dealt with in biblical precept, such as publishing or selling pornography. "Freedom of the press" may make it legal in some societies, but the biblical principle of purity makes it wrong before God.

Below are thirteen questions you can ask about questionable matters which seem especially helpful in making choices concerning disputed or uncertain practices.

1. Is it for the Lord? Does it bring praise to him? "So, whether you eat or drink, or whatever you do, do all to the glory of God" (1 Corinthians 10:31).
2. Can I do it in his name (on his authority, implicating him)? Can I thank him for it? "And whatever you do, in word or deed, do everything in the name of the Lord Jesus, giving thanks to God the Father through him" (Colossians 3:17).
3. Can I take Jesus with me? Would Jesus do it? "Where shall I go from your Spirit? Or where shall I flee from your presence?" (Psalm 139:7). "Christ . . . lives in me" (Galatians 2:20). "Christ . . . leaving us an example that you should follow his steps" (1 Peter 2:21).
4. Does it belong in the home of the Holy Spirit? "Do you not know that your body is a temple of the Holy Spirit within you, which you have from God? You are not your own; you were bought with a price. So glorify God in your body" (1 Cor. 6:19-20).

5. Is it of faith? Do I have misgivings? "But he who has doubts is condemned, if he eats, because he does not act from faith; for whatever does not proceed from faith is sin" (Rom. 14:23). "Beloved, if our hearts do not condemn us, we have confidence before God" (1 John 3:21).
6. Does it positively benefit, build up (not simply, "Is it harmless?")? "Let us then pursue what makes for peace and for mutual upbuilding" (Romans 14:19). "Let all things be done for edification" (1 Corinthians 14:26).
7. Does it spring from, or lead to, love of this world and its value system? "Do not love the world or the things in the world. If anyone loves the world, love for the Father is not in him" (1 John 2:15).
8. Does it involve union with an unbeliever? "Do not be mismated with unbelievers. For what partnership have righteousness and iniquity? Or what fellowship has light with darkness?" (2 Corinthians 6:14).
9. Does it come from or have the potential of leading to bondage? "All things are lawful,' but not all things are helpful. 'All things are lawful,' but not all things build up" (1 Corinthians 10:23).
10. Is the motive pride or love? "We know that 'all of us possess knowledge.' 'Knowledge' puffs up, but love builds up. If anyone imagines that he knows something, he does not yet know as he ought to know" (1 Corinthians 8:1-2).
11. Is a godly mind-set the context of my decision on the matter? "Finally, brethren, whatever is true, whatever is honorable, whatever is just, whatever is pure, whatever is lovely, whatever is gracious; if there is any excellence, if there is anything worthy of praise, think about these things" (Phil. 4:8).
12. What does the church say about it? "He who thus serves Christ is acceptable to God and approved of men" (Rom. 14:18).
13. Would I like to be doing this when Jesus comes? "And now, little children, abide in him, so that when he appears we may have confidence and not shrink from him in shame at his coming. . . . We know that when he appears we shall be like him, for we shall see him as he is. And everyone who thus hopes in him purifies himself as he is pure" (1 John 2:28; 3:2-3).

This is not a list to memorize, but a few examples of general principles that help decide disputed issues.

Furthermore, many have found it a useful checklist to consult when making a decision or choosing behavior. What is questionable in your life? How can these questions guide your behavior?

April 29
Protection
Psalm 139:16

"…..in your book were written, every one of them, the days that were formed for me, when as yet there was none of them" (Psalm 139:16)

As I once thought about my inner responses to adverse circumstances I was drawn irresistibly to the theology factor. What we truly believe seems to have set us up--both for success and for failure.

Consider a few positive examples from my life, then a few negative examples which seem to support the idea that theology played a major role in who we have become and continues to play a major role in what we are yet to become.

<u>Theology Provides Protection.</u> More than therapy to heal the broken, perhaps, theology builds an immune system to keep a person from breaking in the first place. Here's how it worked for me.

I believe I'm finite. I exulted in the confidence of what God had revealed for sure--so sure that all believers of all time would affirm it. But I concluded that most things I'd never figure out no matter how long I investigated and contemplated--things about God's infinities, and things about my finitude. Like the meanings of my past, the hopes for my future, the reasons for my circumstances, the goings-on of my inner self. I'm comfortable with that ambiguity about life, now, though I recognize others may not be. Some seem to need to have everything settled for sure.

For an inquisitive thinker and an intense activist, the realization of one's finitude can be a marvelous relaxant and stabilizer. Besides, lowered expectancies of oneself is a doorway to making room for others. Maybe they're finite, too--and in a different configuration, yet! That realization could make a peacemaker out of a person.

I believe I'm fallen. And so are others. So I expect them to behave that way and that helps make allowances for their failures, which doesn't come to me naturally. I haven't figured out all the ramifications of the doctrine of the fall for protecting me from wrong thinking about myself and others, but on the larger scale, that doctrine has been a powerful deliverer in my life.

Yet I believe I'm of value. I live with the acute realization of my own finitude and fallenness, but the contemporary assures me I cannot be truly free and fulfilled if I put a low value on self. If I measure my worth by what I own, how much fun I'm having, and how successful people recognize me to be, I've given in to the world's value system and have doomed myself to bondage and unfulfillment because those things--no matter how abundant--cannot liberate me nor fill me up. Yet the truth is that I'm worth a lot!

* I'm a designer brand. I'm valuable not because of what I own or have done but because of how God designed me. He created me on his pattern. I have his insignia stamped on me. I'm an image bearer of the Infinite One and that's impressive, no matter what others may think of me.

*I have a very high sticker price. God himself valued me so highly he paid an outrageous price to buy me back from my slave-holder, my bondage to stuff, fun, and an inflated self-image. I'm of infinite worth to God, not for my achievements or possessions, but because he invested in me the life of his own Son.

*Those values are shared by all believers, but I have a value no one else shares. I have a unique destiny. God not only created me to bear his family likeness, he not only purchased me with the life of his only Son, but he did so on purpose. He has a purpose for me, something he wants to accomplish on earth through me. No matter how the world or the church may evaluate my contribution, the grand Designer valued me enough to plan my unique role to bring him the greatest possible honor. That's why I'm proud to be a home maker. I try to be the best cook, housekeeper, gardener, and nurse I know how. I'm not the best at any of those, to be sure, but I give it my best because it's my assignment, God's purpose for me. And I greatly enjoy it, never fret about what I'd rather be doing, about what might have been. Much less compare my "value" to others with higher callings and greater gifts.

* And there's something more. Worth is often judged by the company a person keeps--royalty, skid row-- whatever. And I'm a member of high society--the highest! Incredible as it may seem, God has planned my life around him, uninterrupted companionship with the greatest Lover who ever lived. Living a life planned by the master Designer of the planets, the suns, and every atom, constant companion of the King of Kings . Indeed, theology can liberate and fill a person full.

April 30
Care for Creation
Genesis 1:28, 2:15

"And God blessed them, and God said to them, "Be fruitful and multiply, and fill the earth and subdue it; and have dominion over the fish of the sea and over the birds of the air and over every living thing that moves upon the earth" (Gen. 1:28). *"Then the LORD God took the man and put him in the garden of Eden to till it and keep it"* (Gen. 2:15)

Starting in the early 1970s a national furor developed over ecological concerns. The general public became aware of the fact that environmental pollution and the depletion of natural resources were more than nuisances, more than a menace to quality of life. Scientists with one voice rose up to testify that they were a menace to life itself.

The most serious depredation is air pollution; the second, water pollution. Scientists say that both resources are in imminent danger. A further concern is the rapid depletion of unrenewable resources like oil and coal. Although no apparent immediate threat to human life, a particularly poignant loss is the gradual extinction of many species of animals.

Are science and technology to blame? Man himself is the ultimate polluter and disturber of the delicate balance of nature's varied elements. The cause of the crisis is clearly human sinfulness, though not always deliberate. Sometimes there is deliberate ethical misbehavior for personal or corporate gain, but more often the cause is blind pursuit of affluence. Growth in consumption is the deliberate governmental policy and corporate practice of America, a nation composing 6 percent of earth's population but consuming 40 percent of earth's resources.

Increasing interest in environmental issues by society at large have provoked Christians to reexamine the biblical teaching about ecology. Two texts of Scripture have guided the discussion: *"And God blessed them [Adam and Eve], and God said to them,* **"Be fruitful and multiply, and fill** *the earth and* **subdue it**; *and* **have dominion** *over the fish of the sea and over the birds of the air and over every living thing that moves upon the earth"* (Gen. 1:28, emphasis mine). *"Then the LORD God took the man and put him in the garden of Eden to till it and keep it"* (Gen. 2:15, emphasis mine).

First, these texts indicate that humans do not have merely a responsibility to creation. We are a part of creation. God created us out of the *"dust from the ground"* (Gen. 2:7). This means that all theologies based upon a spirit vs.

nature dualism are fundamentally flawed. God created nature "good" and us "very good." Rather than indicating a higher level of spiritual growth, avoiding or ignoring issues of ecology are signs of imbalance and ignorance. Because we are a part of creation, we cannot live apart from it.

Second, the Genesis passages seem at first glance to send a mixed message. Should the Christian be guided by the dominion (fill, subdue, and have dominion) motif of Genesis 1:28 or the nurturing (till and keep) motif of 2:15? But the Christian does not need to choose between the two. Both are divine mandates. God called human beings to be creative in the oversight of nature. God is pleased when we use his creation to create instruments to praise him, irrigation systems to feed people, and technology to disseminate worthwhile information.

God also calls human beings to be faithful stewards of nature. He *owns* it (Ps. 24:1). It is *his*. We are just tenants. Just as we are stewards of our bodies, which are his, and thus must care for them; just as we are the stewards of our finances, which are his and must be used responsibly for the advancement of his kingdom; so it is with our physical environment. We can be good stewards, caring well for his world, using it for human welfare and the glory of God, or we can wantonly abuse and destroy it as the Israelites did (Exod. 23:10-11; Lev. 25:1-7). We also may be evicted! So we have a heavy responsibility for personal stewardship.

Good stewardship of nature requires action. To the three R's of "reduce, reuse, and recycle," Christians are called to *resist* the values and allure of a consumer society. Instead, Christians should *rejoice* at the wonder and promises of creation.

Creation's fallenness does not render it valueless or useless. The second great command, to love one's neighbor as oneself, prohibits the Christian from depriving others of the benefits of creation for the sake of his own gain. Since the current "rape" of nature is clearly depriving succeeding generations of benefit, if not of life, and is often built on the exploitation of the natural resources of poverty-bound people today, we have no choice but to work for a restoration of ecological balance and a halt to environmental pollution and resource depletion.

Some observers are not convinced that the future of the environment is grim. Data used to support predictions of the rise in global temperatures, commonly referred to as the "greenhouse effect," are inconclusive. Some say it is real and will cause flooding, produce severe weather, and put wildlife and crop growth at risk.[19] Others say that much evidence disputing the dire warnings of environmentalists has been ignored and suppressed.[20] Still others suggest that even if the earth is warming, it will be negligible, it has happened naturally before, and it will most likely have a beneficial effect on the environment.[21]

In the face of conflicting claims, what course of action should we take? We should continue to gather evidence in order to make informed decisions in our political and personal life. It is prudent to err on the side of caution, especially since it is our relatively lavish lifestyle that strains the environment. Moreover, we have the resources to "clean up after ourselves." A word of caution is in order. Some environmental groups espouse a quasi-religious, pantheistic worldview in promoting their agenda. Discernment is required.

What course of action will you take? How will you steward the earth? To whom will you listen? How can we stop wasting?

---

[19] Wallace S. Broecker, "Global Warming on Trial," *Natural History,* April 1992, 6f.
[20] Serwood Idso (physicist with the U.S. Department of Agriculture), *Carbon Dioxide and Global Change: Earth in Transition* (Tempe, Ariz.: IBR Press, 1989).
[21] Warren T. Brookes, "The Global Warming Panic," *Forbes* (144) 25 December 1989, 96f.

May 1
Be Real
Leviticus 19:11

"You shall not steal; you shall not deal falsely; you shall not lie to one another. " (Leviticus 19:11)

What is a lie? "To say words that do not conform to reality" is not a useful definition, for although we constantly say things that do not conform to reality, we don't necessarily lie. We may err. Does lying mean deliberately saying words that don't conform to reality? This is also inadequate, for it's quite possible to deceive someone without using false words. So we must broaden the definition to include the conscious purpose to deceive. To lie, then, is deliberately attempting to deceive, using words or other means.

There is no more sure method to destroy our own character than to deceive. Any other sin can be recognized and dealt with, but deception leads away from reality, so that ultimately, truth is not even recognized. As a result, repentance and restoration are very difficult to pursue. As an old Chinese pastor said, "I can save anyone but a liar." Falsehood is a basic fault line in the foundation of the soul, putting the whole superstructure in jeopardy. All the believability a person has, his very integrity, totters on the shifting sand of a single lie. Deceit holds hostage all virtues.

Deceit not only erodes the character but also fails to solve problems. Instead, it complicates them. Deceit fouls all relationships. Once a person has deceived another and is known to have done so, it is difficult ever to restore full confidence. He may try to counterbalance his lies with a greater number of truths, but it doesn't work that way. No amount of truth can quickly erase the indelible imprint of a lie, for the person who has been deceived may rightly wonder, *When will it happen again?* Deceit is the ultimate destroyer of good relationships, because good human relationships are built on mutual confidence and trust.

Here are some other ways we can lie. Exaggeration. Are you as tempted to exaggerate as I am? If you are tempted to exaggerate, the occasions or situations when you do so might include to give a lesser or greater assessment of time or distance than is true to get my way, excuse myself, or make a point. Exaggeration is to embellish a report to protect my image, boost my ego, or justify my actions, to add to a story some elements I have imagined or created to make it more fun or acceptable. Or to make a point stronger, to round a number up or down. When telling a story, the details of which are fuzzy in my memory, I find it easy to fill in the blanks with some embellishment.. If we're caught exaggerating, we may laugh nervously and make light of it. But it's lying.

Hypocrisy is pretending to be something we are not. Christ condemned the Pharisees for hypocrisy more than anything else, comparing them to *"whitewashed tombs, which appear beautiful on the outside, but inside are full of dead men's bones and every impurity. In the same way, on the outside you seem righteous to people, but inside you are full of hypocrisy and lawlessness"* (Matt. 23:27-28). In fact, His name for them, play actors (the meaning of *hupocrites* in Greek), changed the meaning of *Pharisee* forever. People called them "the holy ones," but Jesus exposed them as phonies. By trying to project an admirable but false image, they were not only lying but also misrepresenting what it means to live a holy life.

Jesus taught, *"Be careful not to practice your righteousness in front of people, to be seen by them"* (Matt. 6:1). However, He also instructed us, *"Let your light shine before men, so that they may see your good works and give glory to your Father in heaven"* (Matt. 5:16). The difference between letting your light shine and practicing righteousness in front of others would be motive.

It isn't always easy to find the biblical balance of honesty about our failings while making sure our light shines brightly to spotlight God's excellencies and inspire hope in those who follow.

May 2
Five Reasons to Hope
Lamentations 3

"Remember my affliction and my wanderings, the wormwood and the gall! My soul continually remembers it and is bowed down within me. But this I call to mind, and therefore I have hope…" (Lamentations 3:19-21)

We may not remember hearing so many people lament: is there any hope for peace? In the Middle East? In Africa? In Asia? Is there any hope for my personal situation? Where is the economy headed? When and where will the next terrorist strike be? Is world evangelism a viable enterprise? Perhaps you've been writing your own book of lamentations...

"Yet this I call to mind and therefore I have hope" (Lamentations 3: 21). Here are 9 reasons for hope in the darkest hour. And remember, we're talking about biblical hope. Not the usual sort of a wish, "I hope it doesn't rain on our picnic," but confident expectation.

Warning: the first reason is a little downbeat...

1. **It could be so much worse.** Lamentations 3:22a. We are not consumed. Count the evils you don't have! I sometimes wake up and exclaim: I'm still alive. Wow! So many died last night, why not me? Look at that friend eaten alive of cancer. Why not me? It's been more than a decade, now, since my son died and still an emptiness lingers on, an unassuageable grief. But then I think of those who have rebellious sons and I say, "why not me?" My son Bob is safe at home with Jesus. You've heard the saying, "I complained I had no shoes till I met a man who had no feet."

2. **God's blessings abound.** Lamentations 3:22b Count your blessings--his compassions never fail--new every morning. Count, name over, focus on your blessings. Often. Can you, *In the course of the day do more 'thank-you's' cross your mind than complaints?*

When my wife died, I wondered. How does hope happen? I remembered a heavy heart lifts on the wings of praise! But does praise work in the really heavy stuff? When my beloved slipped away from me after 25 years of fading away with Alzheimer's disease, there was a wrenching, a deep sense of loss–deeper they tell me, not less, for her being wholly dependent on me for a decade. Grief. No dancing, no celebration in my heart. At the same time, as I wrote family and friends, there is gratitude. Grief and gratitude. God's blessings abound.– count 'em! Focus on ***them.***

3. **God is faithful**. Lamentations 3:23b God holds steady though nothing else does. You can rely on him. In our society who is reliable? Politicians? Media? Advertisers? Educators? Judges? Business tycoons? Husbands? Mothers? But you can always count on God. He's faithful and that gives hope!

4. **God is good** . Lamentations 3:25,26. Notice the promise of God's deliverance is for those who hope in HIM, seek him, and wait quietly, patiently for him to act. It's not for those who trust in their stock portfolio or retirement plan, who seek human deliverance. Certainly not for those who are impatient, resist, resent their lot in life. Faith. I was riding in the limousine with Mark Shepherd's father, back from the grave site to the funeral home. We'd participated in a funeral and somehow that brought to my mind his dying son. Mark lived the difficult life of a hemophiliac, crippled, in unrelieved pain, in constant danger of bleeding to death. In the end he contracted AIDs from a blood transfusion and from that he died at age 40. I never heard Mark complain. In that ride from the grave, shortly before his death, I asked his father if he actually never did complain. Well, yes, he said, he did once. When he was about 6 years old, one day he said, "Daddy, why did God make me this way?" Faith in the faithful one--then you'll have hope!

5. **Suffering is not forever.** Lamentations 3:31,32. "Tough times never last, tough people do." We do hope for a better day. It was Easter, 1992, and I received a letter from a lady I'd never met. It was about Muriel. She wrote, "Isn't it wonderful that the next face your beloved will recognize is Jesus?" Saturday can seem long. How long since your personal bad Friday? Will Easter Sunday ever come? How long till resurrection dawns? Our long goodbye was 25 years. But Sunday's coming! For my beloved, it already has. Suffering is not forever.

May 3
Four More Reasons to Hope
Lamentations 3

"...and hope does not put us to shame, because God's love has been poured into our hearts through the Holy Spirit who has been given to us." (Romans 5:5)

When a new trouble strikes or an old one obsesses our mind we need to think, *how can this particular trial of mine focus people's attention on God, his glorious character?* It really depends on how I respond, doesn't it? Faith is the alchemy that turns dread into praise to God. Praise to God when people see our faith response. And growth in us, too. Instead of spiritual deterioration that comes of un-faith, through trusting him in that adversity, the adversity itself becomes a fast track to becoming more like Jesus, the one who learned obedience through the things he suffered. And the greater the victory, the more glory to God. Here are four more reasons to hope:

1. **God isn't gleeful about your pain.** Jeremiah 3:33. God is the reluctant pain dispenser. He weeps with us. During the Iraq war I watched on TV a young wife weep over the terror her husband was facing in the gulf and heard her testify of how she was praying for his success, that he would "wipe 'em out" and then she thought--"those Iraqi boys, their mothers, their wives are people, too. God have mercy on us all!" That young wife had caught God's heartbeat. God takes no pleasure in the death of the sinner or the chastisement of the saint. He weeps with us. He understands, he feels our pain.

2. **Expect trouble.** Lamentations 3:38 "Expect the worst, rejoice when it doesn't happen." We live in a fallen world. There is going to be sin. Against you. There's going to be disease. In your family. There's going to be failure, war, death. We're not exempt. We should never be surprised that trouble strikes but should try to discern what God has in it for good. And what good can come of MY trouble? Many possibilities, but always 2. And when we work with God to bring about those 2 purposes, the pain is transformed into blessing: our growth, God's glory. Don't complain--you deserve it! Lamentations 3: 39,40. Pain in my body causes me to investigate, to take action. Without pain we'd deteriorate and die. Many do. How many cancer victims die because they didn't have the blessing of pain? And with pain of spirit–it's the same. But we don't treat it as a blessing nowadays. In the old days when tragedy struck people immediately said, "For which of my many sins is God judging me?" Nowadays we say, "What's wrong with God? Why me? I who deserve so much better?" Our society has become the fellowship of the victims.

There is a highway sign on I-77 advertising a new upscale development called "The Summit." "Get what you deserve." Hallelujah I don't! If I did I wouldn't take up residence at the Summit, I'd take up residence in hell. When trouble strikes, reflect on whether it's God's discipline to turn me from some wrong way.

Do all the wicked of earth deserve to be punished? What about Saddam Hussein? We think so. But remember the ruthlessness and power of his predecessor, Nebuchadnezzar. In evil, he makes Saddam look like peewee league. Yet how does God describe Nebuchadnezzar through Jeremiah the prophet? "I will hand all your countries over to <u>my servant</u> Nebuchadnezzar, king of Babylon" (27.6) Who is God's rod today? If we conceive America to be God's rod to punish the wicked despots of the world, does that mean we deserve no punishment for our own idolatry of material things, sex, prestige, for our anti-god behavior, like the murder of the unborn innocents? Or perhaps the rising confrontation between Islam and the West is God's rod to punish his church. Let's examine ourselves and repent. Then there can be hope!

    3. **God is with you.** Lamentations 3:55-57. He comes near, so don't be afraid. God will go with you through it, all the way. Indeed, he is with you in your suffering today. you don't have much that could be called hard-core pain. Just wait! And when it hits, don't forget–no matter how alone you feel, you've got a close companion.

    4. **Ultimate redemption.** Lamentations 3:58. In Jeremiah's case he may be thinking of his salvation from the mud of that deep cistern into which his enemies had pitched him. Like Jeremiah, our redemption is not always the way we would wish, in the time frame we would hope. It certainly wasn't for those four missionaries killed in Iraq. But even if not in this life--we've read the final chapter of the story. That's our ultimate hope! Rejoice that your name is written in the Lamb's Book of Life. "*My soul is downcast within me,*" laments Jeremiah, *"Yet this I call to mind and therefore I have hope."*

May 4
Global Powerline
Colossians 4:2-4

"Continue steadfastly in prayer, being watchful in it with thanksgiving. At the same time, pray also for us, that God may open to us a door for the word, to declare the mystery of Christ, on account of which I am in prison— that I may make it clear, which is how I ought to speak." (Colossians 4:2-4)

    One night during a thunderstorm I was watching the magnificent display of cosmic fireworks when all of a sudden there was a mighty explosion right in our own back yard, an extravaganza of sight and sound. Lightning had struck the transformer. In a moment we lost all light and power. For days. Interesting, because giant towers trooped through the fields a half mile away, bearing unlimited supplies of light and power. But here we were without refrigeration, without light, without hot water, without capacity to cook.

    Like many Christians. The power flows all around them, but they aren't connected with the source. The connecting line, of course, is prayer. Through prayer, the resources of heaven flow to us in light and power and through us to a dark world under siege. As E M Bounds said, "much prayer, much power; little prayer, little power, no prayer, no power."

    Pray for what? What do you pray for? Healing? Yes. Our loved ones? Yes, of course. In fact, he invites us to ask whatever we wish. But if you're in love with someone what do you seek after most? What will please her, what will fulfill him, right? So are you in love with Jesus? Then what does he want, what is his #1 desire? John 3.16: *"for*

God so loved the world that he gave his only begotten son that whoever believes should not perish but have eternal life."

So, for a lost world, the first and most important activity is to link up through prayer with the omnipotent and let the light and power flow through. Improbable as it may seem, scary as it may seem, **we** are the power line, the conduit for world evangelism. How do we connect and let it flow? And when we do connect, what should flow? Consider, then, the How and What of prayer for missions as found in Colossians 4:2-4: *Continue steadfastly in prayer, being watchful in it with thanksgiving. At the same time, pray also for us, that God may open to us a door for the word, to declare the mystery of Christ, on account of which I am in prison— that I may make it clear, which is how I ought to speak.* First the "how". **Continue**—regular and don't quit.

Consider the Korean church. How can we explain the incredible growth and missionary sending power? Peter Wagner said that no Korean pastor spends less than 1 hour a day in prayer and 47% spend 2 hours or more. At a Missions rally in early 80's there was perhaps the largest gathering in history. One million, seven hundred thousand! At the last night 600,000 prayed all night. What was the result? Thousands stood to commit to missionary service. Result of such praying? A church of power. 30,000 missionaries committed to going!

How to pray? Continue in regular, daily, persistent prayer. This is more than mentioning a name. Pray ***Earnestly.*** A morning sleepy salute toward heaven won't do. It is spiritual warfare: see Colossians 2.1: *know how great a struggle I have for you ....and for all those who have not seen me face to face.* Also 4:12: *Epaphras....always struggling on your behalf in his prayers.* Paul says, "Continue ***earnestly".*** Warfare!

Be ***vigilant.*** This is a military term which means to keep your watch, be on battle alert. Pray, not only in the regular, daily spiritual combat, but on guard for the in-between times, too. I was on a trip to Tanzania, Thanksgiving, 1988 and was detained in the airport. For hours, alone and unsure what would happen. But in New Jersey there was a soldier on battle alert. In a nursing home, 90 years old, Mrs. Eisenrach prayed. In the middle of her night for me. A few hours later, the pilot returned unexpectedly to take me to safety.

With ***thanksgiving.*** What does that mean? Intercession and thanksgiving, too. Yes, but more: prayer that can give thanks in advance. In other words, faith! Expectancy of faith.

How can we be sure we are heard and that the answer is on the way? When, like Daniel, we pray according to the promises of God. For these you can pray with thanksgiving that he will answer, because he's told us in advance what he wills to happen.

In other words, ***frequent, fervent, faith - filled.*** That's HOW to pray.

May 5
To Everything There is a Season
Ecclesiastes 3:1

"For everything there is a season, and a time for every matter under heaven." (Ecclesiastes 3:1)

For many of us, feeling like there is not enough time is the most persistent temptation to violate the commandment to not covet. The demands, opportunities, dreams, and needs all around us are so far beyond our time resources, how could we not desire more time? But to be constantly discontented with our time allotment is destructive and demoralizing.

Consider two presuppositions basic to successfully handling the problem of time.

1. God has a custom-designed plan for your life. He spoke through the prophet Jeremiah, "'*I know the plans I have for you*'—this is the LORD's declaration—'*plans for your welfare, not for disaster, to give you a future and a hope*'" (Jer. 29:11).
2. God has provided all the time resources necessary to carry out His plan. So if the 168 hours each week seem inadequate, either I've missed God's will in doing something He never intended, or I'm doing it inefficiently. David wrote a beautiful passage about this basic presupposition. "*All my days were written in Your book and planned before a single one of them began.*" (Psalm 139:6)

When Jesus said, "*My time has not yet arrived*" (John 7:6) or "*My time has not yet fully come*" (John 7:8), we might say in contemporary language, "The time isn't right" or "It's not time yet." The Teacher in Ecclesiastes 3:1 referred to this principle. "*To everything there is a season, A time for every purpose under heaven.*"

This poetic passage closes with a wonderful word: "He has made everything beautiful in its time" (Eccl. 3:11, NKJV). God has planned everything, and when it comes according to God's plan, it's indeed beautiful. But a problem is presented: "*Also He has put eternity in their hearts*" (v. 11, NKJV). This is the core of the problem. It's a beautiful thing to fulfill God's purpose moment by moment, day by day. But we have eternity in our hearts. We want to do so much more— an infinity of things.

What are some things you want to do that you don't seem to have time for? Rate your general level of anxiety about not having enough time in your life.

We were created for eternity, so our aspirations drive us to take on more. Too often we get caught up in a whirlwind of frenetic activity that causes us more stress than satisfaction. Yet Jesus taught us not to be anxious even about tomorrow. To paraphrase Jesus, which of us, by frenetic endeavor, by worry and concern, can add 1 hour to the 168 we've been allotted this week (see Matt. 6:27)?

What's the solution? These practical steps may help.

1. Set priorities. To set priorities, you first have to figure out how you are currently spending your time. On a sheet of paper, list in order of priority what you are currently doing in a typical week.

2. Examine for inefficiencies. Examine your time log to determine whether you could manage your time more efficiently. For example, could you combine responsibilities into a single activity? Don't think *eliminate*. Think *evaluate and prioritize*. In examining our priority list for inefficiencies, we need to be brutally honest.

3. Start at the bottom and cut. This may be the time to learn to say no to others (in a gracious way) and to your own wants (graciousness not necessary) to make room for your yes to God.

If your list of activities still overruns your time allotment, you must get serious about your prioritizing. Start at the bottom of your log, negotiable or optional items, and start eliminating activities until the remainder fit in 168 hours.

This may be painful, and it certainly should be done prayerfully. But if we fail to make the hard decisions, we condemn ourselves to coveting the time God doesn't give. And that is a very destructive way to live.

May 6
Filled Full
Acts 4:31

"And when they had prayed, the place in which they were gathered together was shaken, and they were all filled with the Holy Spirit and continued to speak the word of God with boldness." (Acts 4:31)

One evidence of being filled with the Spirit is some result in our work for God we can't account for by a person's natural abilities or training. The Bible doesn't tell us how to distinguish spiritual gifts from natural gifts. But it's fairly easy to tell. Is the outcome supernatural? The Corinthians said that Paul was an unpolished pulpiteer, in fact a sorry communicator (II Cor. 10:10). And he didn't dispute their judgment (II Cor. 11:6). But when Paul taught the Bible, lives were transformed. There's the touch of the Spirit! Others may seem gifted, but is there a spiritual impact? Are lives changed? That's the touch of the Spirit.

As you reflect on the effectiveness of your role or ministry, remember that "effectiveness" means some Holy Spirit effect, some outcome that can't be fully explained in terms of your natural abilities, training, or experience. If God so empowered you that whatever gift you had was greatly used so that everyone could plainly tell the origin of your success, maybe that could be called "full."

Actually, that's the way the Bible seems to use the term most often. The Apostles were filled with the Spirit on the day of Pentecost and 3,000 people were converted (Acts 2:41), not just "someone" which would have been evidence enough of the Spirit's presence. I'd call 3,000 responses really full. Yet a few weeks later they had a special need—their leaders had been arrested. So they did the only thing they knew to do, they called a prayer meeting. Once again they were filled with the Spirit (Acts 4:31) and as a result proclaimed the word with boldness. *"And when they had prayed, the place in which they were gathered together was shaken, and they were all filled with the Holy Spirit and continued to speak the word of God with boldness."* Amazing! Spirit-filled men were filled! It's common throughout Acts—Spirit-filled people are said to be filled. How can that be?

Remember, it's a picture word. We get the picture of a great schooner plowing through the Atlantic with sails full of wind when suddenly a gust of wind sweeps down and the schooner surges ahead under really full sail. So it is with the wind of the Spirit (the Hebrew and Greek words for "spirit" are "breath" or "wind"). Sort of an overdrive surge of power, as when a car appears from nowhere, heading toward you, and you put the pedal to the floor to get out of there. Perhaps you've had such an experience: Your language is still halting and you find it difficult to give a clear explanation of the gospel to your neighbor, you plead with God for help, and you're astounded to hear yourself give a winsome, clear presentation; or as you taught your Bible study class, suddenly a hush fell over the group and several told you later their lives had changed.

Did you notice? You may be steady-state "filled," but sometimes there's a surge of Spirit energy and you're over the top. Any need to fill up on the Spirit? Every day. And sometimes, when things are particularly frustrating we cry out for fresh power and he never fails to hear that prayer. Like us, he likes to be needed!

I do some preaching and writing. Before I preach I always remind the Lord that though I've been at it a long time and can explain Scripture and tell stories and people will listen and say nice things, if He doesn't act, nothing of eternal value will happen. Then I watch in wonder as God transforms lives. Sometimes there's a mighty "wind" of God and many are moved. Other times, I watch in vain for some small sign of the Spirit at work and my heart is wounded, sometimes broken. I need to be filled up once again.

How we long to be ever filled up with the Spirit so that people will know for sure it is God and give Him the credit. Do you have some gift at a minimal level, but it's not full-throttle, other people can't tell for sure whether it's God or just you? Now's the time to ask Him to fill you up. Open your heart to the wind of the Spirit and trust Him to do His thing. And begin the habit of asking Him, at the time of special opportunity or challenge, to put it on overdrive and fill you really full!

To be full of the Spirit, then, is so to live a miracle quality of life that others can see the "fruit" and the "gift." There'll be a bumper crop of fruit, attitudes and actions that are produced by God-power. The Holy Spirit will be seen clearly in the ministry God gives. That's a small glimpse of what "full" looks like.

May 7
The Masquerade
1 John 2:16

"For all that is in the world—the desires of the flesh and the desires of the eyes and pride of life is not from the Father but is from the world." (1 John 2:16)

In Romans 12:1 (*Do, not conformed to this world but be transformed*) Paul emphasizes the pressure of *the world*—other people, things, circumstances, perhaps. People can cause us to stumble (Matthew 18:6,7), making us angry, seducing us, or making sin look attractive. Also, things and circumstances like poverty or riches (Proverbs 30:8,9) can put pressure on us. External sources.

Paul also identifies minds that need renovation—our inner desires and impulses. Ultimately it isn't the people or circumstances, it's our response to them that's the source of our temptation. We've given ground already in our minds—"Every man is tempted when he is drawn away of his own lust and enticed" (James 1:14).

Of course, Satan is the original source of all temptation, and he still is on the prowl, ever ready to pounce on the unwary (1 Peter 5:8). We should be ever on guard (Ephesians 6:1), never give ground (Ephesians 4:27), always fight back (James 4:7), stay alert to his stratagems (2 Corinthians 2:11).

All those above can be sources of temptation except one: God. God tempts no one (James 1:13). How then does the Bible sometimes finger the same tempting circumstances as coming from both Satan and God? It's the motive. Satan uses people or circumstances to bring us down whereas God uses those same circumstances to bring us up, or to test and prove our allegiance.

Have you ever stopped to analyze just what temptation is? It doesn't look bad, it looks good; otherwise, it wouldn't tempt. And actually God is the one who designed our desires in the first place. Enticement to sin is actually the temptation to abuse a God-given desire. God created us to enjoy our bodies, to possess things, to amount to something. But we are forever trying to fulfill those desires in wrong ways. And that's sin. So the next step is to identify the enemy, discriminate between what is temptation and what isn't.

Some hold that all sin is found in one or another of these categories— lust (abuse of our desire to enjoy food or sex), covetousness (desire to possess something not mine or not in God's will for me), and pride (taking credit for some achievement of God). But I think there is a further variety of sin that may not be any of those: unbelief. Some say it's the source of all the rest! Eve certainly fell before temptations to lust, covet, and act arrogantly because she doubted God's word, so maybe unbelief is the taproot sin. In any event, it helps to identify the enemy precisely so I can fight it successfully.

Eve fell to the temptation to enjoy the tasty fruit which God had forbidden; Christ resisted the temptation to use his power to create bread from stones. What temptation do you have currently to enjoy what God doesn't intend or to enjoy it in wrong ways? Eve fell to the temptation to get something very pleasant to see and Jesus resisted the temptation to get in a wrongful way the world which was rightfully his. Your temptation to covet? Eve reached for that which the Liar said would give her the very wisdom of God and lost everything. If the crowds in the temple courtyard saw angels intercept Jesus' free fall, the applause would have thundered to the heavens. He chose rather to hang on a tree in humiliation. What is your temptation to gain recognition?

Temptation always masquerades—it looks so appealing, promises so much good. That's why it's a temptation. If it wore it's own face it would be so ugly we'd run! So the first task is to unmask the temptation, identify it for exactly what it is: lust, covetousness, pride, or unbelief. Such enemies—they could destroy you! And they certainly make the Spirit sad.

May 8
Overcoming Temptation
Romans 12:1-2

"I appeal to you therefore, brothers, by the mercies of God, to present your bodies as a living sacrifice, holy and acceptable to God, which is your spiritual worship. Do not be conformed to this world, but be transformed by the renewal of your mind, that by testing you may discern what is the will of God, what is good and acceptable and perfect." (Romans 12:1&2)

Diane had been a Christian for two years, open and eager for all the Spirit was teaching, spiraling up. Then she made a discovery. She took a class I taught on the Christian life where the assignment was to write a paper on developing a battle plan for overcoming temptation. The paper wasn't to be theoretical, overcoming just any temptation. The assignment was very personal: a strategy for overcoming their own strongest temptation. Diane should have known about temptation—even Jesus had to slug it out with the devil! But in the exuberance of her newfound faith, she missed it.

Students really got into this project, some writing almost book-length theses, many testifying that the project was life transforming. "My life has been radically changed. For the first time I'm beginning to see progress toward victory." Once in a while I get a letter from a former student, "Remember the assignment on developing a strategy to overcome temptation? That was the turning point in my Christian experience." Each of these students discovered that being filled with the Spirit doesn't lift one beyond temptation. In fact, the battle may be hotter! Too many sincere, growing Christians are caught off guard by this, falling before they know what hit them. And others know full well they are being tempted, but don't know how to defend themselves and so go down in defeat.

Perhaps you, too, need to develop a personal battle strategy for partnering with the Spirit in winning the victory over those temptations that assault us daily. Here's the Bible passage we can use to develop such a plan.

"I appeal to you therefore, brothers, by the mercies of God, to present your bodies as a living sacrifice, holy and acceptable to God, which is your spiritual worship. Do not be conformed to this world, but be transformed by the renewal of your mind, that by testing you may discern what is the will of God, what is good and acceptable and perfect." Romans 12:1&2.

People need a battle strategy to conquer their temptations, a strategy that will work. On the other hand, I'd hear a response that was one sentence long: "I have no strategy; the Holy Spirit lives in me and that's all the strategy I need." Which will it be? Do I get out of the way and let God do His thing in my life or do I personally fight it out with the enemy? We may be tempted to go to one extreme or the other, to opt for a spectator role and leave it up to God or, on the other hand, to go with most Christians and develop a do-it-yourself mind set.

The Bible teaches both a faith that rests and a faith that wrestles. We trust the Spirit to do the work of re-making us or it won't be done. But we must also use the weapons He provides and fight the evil in our lives. If we concentrate solely on what He does, we may slip into complacency or presumption and get ambushed by the enemy. If we concentrate exclusively on our responsibility to fight the good fight, we may become battle weary and discouraged. May even give up the battle toward which end have you found yourself—concentrating on the Spirit's enabling so much you've tended to forget your own responsibility or concentrating so much on your own efforts you've tended to forget the resources of the Spirit?

Strange, isn't it? When faced with temptation, the only way to win out is to give up! Not to the enemy, the temptation, but to the Victor. "I plead with you," says Paul, "to make a grand presentation of yourself to God." That's where victory begins.

So the first step in winning the spiritual war is the Big Surrender, the Grand Presentation, the Living Sacrifice. That can be painful, of course— that's what sacrifice meant. But the grand presentation He demands is more than little particulars—it's all of you, a living sacrifice. That's where victory begins. That alone sets you on the way to holiness and that alone is acceptable to God, says Paul. But it's only reasonable in the light of all God has done for you. So the first step to victory is to give yourself over unconditionally to God. But that's only the beginning. Where do you stand today?

May 9
Show and Tell
Proverbs 23:26

"My son, give me your heart, and let your eyes observe my ways." (Proverbs 23:26)

Which is more important in relating to your children—to act lovingly or to talk lovingly? That's a trick question, of course. One without the other is counterfeit. Constantly show and tell. If you're the strong and silent type, you need to get over it! Your children need to hear of your love, or they might not see it clearly, especially when it's time to discipline.

The writer of Proverbs captured the essence of modeling God's ways for our children. By watching you, your children should be able to open their hearts to Jesus as you express His character and teach His ways to them. By following your example, your children will be following Jesus. What greater gift could you give them?

Of course, most parents provide for their children's physical needs. Let's look at some ways Mary and Joseph provided for Jesus. Read Luke 2:52 and we see that Jesus increased in wisdom and stature, and in favor with God and with people. Jesus' parents helped Him grow spiritually, physically, socially, and intellectually.

Parents today need to facilitate multidimensional growth in their children's lives as well. If there is an area of greatest neglect in the home, it is in spiritual training. Paul admonished parents to bring up their children *"in the training and instruction of the Lord"* (Eph. 6:4). That means parents must take responsibility for spiritual instruction and be intentional about it. Deuteronomy 11:18-20 says: *"Imprint these words of mine on your hearts and minds, bind them as a sign on your hands, and let them be a symbol on your foreheads. Teach them to your children, talking about them when you sit in your house and when you walk along the road, when you lie down and when you get up. Write them on the doorposts of your house and on your gates."* Imprint them on your heart and mind. Bind them on your hands. Teach them. Talk about them. These are deliberate, concrete actions designed to convey God's Word to the next generation.

In general, Christian parents want to accept and discharge their responsibility to rear their children "in the training and instruction of the Lord" (Eph. 6:4). Yet environmental determinism has so influenced our thinking that many parents become burdened by the assumption that it's all up to them. Some are afraid to have children and are nervous about them when they come.

Many who want to be parents are plagued by questions like these: If it's possible to determine the outcome of a person's life by creating the perfect environment, what parents are smart enough or good enough to create such an environment? If the children don't turn out as hoped, how can the parents bear such a burden of guilt? If early environment determines what someone will be forever, what hope is there to become something else, to be free from the results of parental failure? Or, If the children turn out according to parental hopes, who gets the credit?

Though many preachers and counselors teach that it all depends on the parents, the doctrine is thoroughly humanistic. If it were true, God Himself would be the greatest failure; He had two children with unflawed genes and placed them in the perfect environment, paradise, and both failed miserably. So other factors besides environment must play a role in successful parenting. Take a few moments to name a number of ways you express love to your children. What indications do you have that your children are confident of your love for them?

May 10
Loving Parents
Ephesians 6:4

"Fathers, don't stir up anger in your children, but bring them up in the training and instruction of the Lord." Ephesians 6:4

We are parents or we have parents, so how should parents love? Ephesians 6:4 provides a good starting point for understanding our responsibilities to our children: *"Fathers, don't stir up anger in your children, but bring them up in the training and instruction of the Lord."* Let's look at some ways we can obey the biblical mandate to rear our children to be godly followers of Christ.

As in all other relationships, responsibility for our children requires loving well. My parents were strict disciplinarians of the old school. They'd probably be put in jail today! Thrashings with bamboo canes came often (from my mother) and, when I was too much for her to handle, with the belt (from my father). Mother would wash out my mouth with soap when sass came out of it. One day she discovered me in the bathroom nibbling on the Ivory soap. I liked it! So she switched to Octagon soap. That'll cure any foul mouth!

Furthermore, my parents didn't believe in complimenting their children. They held it would give us "the big head". I never remember any affirmations mixed in with the regular—and well-deserved—rebukes. They broke all the contemporary rules, and yet no one who knows me would ever accuse me of suffering any of the dire results that are supposed to follow a strict upbringing. Why? Because somehow I knew I was well-loved and my parents were proud of me and believed in me. Never a doubt.

What is the middle way between child abuse and domestic anarchy? Consider three guidelines.

Maintain consistency. When discipline is erratic and unpredictable—whether on the part of one parent or when one parent seems to specialize in love and the other in justice—the child will become discouraged. We agreed early on that any disagreements we had would be in private. No disunity before the children, especially regarding their discipline.

Exercise balance. The results of undisciplined permissiveness on the one hand or unloving discipline on the other are equally damaging. Many earnest young Christian parents try too hard, determined that this firstborn will bring glory to God, not to mention credit to his parents. Therefore, the tendency is to drive children to perfection beyond their years and capacity. At any rate, it is humanly easier to go to one extreme or the other—to become permissive or severe—than to stay at the center of biblical tension, balancing a loving, affirming atmosphere with instruction and guidance in the ways of God. Are you creating a hammock or a safety net for your child? There is a difference. Knowing which is

Use discipline only when a moral principle is at stake. An example is deliberate, repeated lying. Of course, any issue can become moral if the parent issues a direct command. Some parents seek such confrontations, but constant showdowns on nonmoral issues cause a child to become discouraged or rebellious. Rules should be appropriate, clear, and as few as possible. Why not invite participation, counsel? Discipline may become virtually unnecessary in a partner relationship custom designed for each little person. As my friend and colleague Buck Hatch would say, "remember that they are but dust". How is your love life today?

May 11
Principles and Specifics
Isaiah 35:8-10

"There will be a highway there, called "The Road of Holiness." No sinner will ever travel that road; no fools will mislead those who follow it . . . Those whom the Lord has rescued will travel home by that road. . . . They will be happy forever, forever free from sorrow and grief...." (Isaiah 35:8-10, GNB)

The Holy Spirit uses Scripture to guide us, but we often want specific and simple answers to our questions. The Bible does give "do's" and "don'ts," but it is much more a book of principles than a list of rules. I'm glad the Bible gives both. I need specific instructions, but I especially need principles. Unlike rules, principles are comprehensive-covering all possibilities, but how the principle applies to life may elude me. So specific examples are also in the Scripture. "Love your neighbor as yourself," is a principle that covers all relationships, but the Bible also describes specifics of how love will behave. For example, when someone sins against me, if I truly love him or her, I will go to the person alone and confront him or her (Matt. 18:15-17). That's specific, but by giving the underlying principle of love, the Bible covers all potential attitudes, actions, and relationships. When the Bible gives a general principle, we have the responsibility to apply the principle to specific situations. To make that application, we have help from the Holy Spirit.

First Corinthians 13 describes loving behaviors without tying them to specific situations. For the following descriptions of love, give a specific illustration from your life of a loving behavior that you could do today that would demonstrate this quality:

1. Love is patient (v. 4)
2. Love is kind (v. 4)
3. Love does not keep a record of wrongs (v. 5).

How long would the Bible be if it gave specific examples or precise commands covering every possible attitude and activity for all people of all time? Even if God put all that detail on some mega-computer, how could we possibly access our specific directive at the moment of decision? No, the Spirit has given us something far better- principles to guide in the decisions of life. In the exercise above, I listed these examples of love: I can be patient while waiting on a child to get ready in the mornings. I can be kind in my choice of language when I am expressing hurt feelings to my spouse. I can choose to forgive and not hold a grudge against a fellow employee. We also encounter non-moral questions like: Should I take this job? What school should I attend? Should we stay here or move to another place? Even in those dilemmas of life, the Bible provides principles for guidance. God deals with us as individuals. His plan for your life will not be just like any other person's. Abraham's experience was unlike Moses', and Moses' experience did not resemble Jonah's. But Abraham, Moses, and Jonah lived by the principles of God's Word. Their example is given to help us understand God's will for us.

The Scripture teaches both by precept and example. It states truth, and it demonstrates the truth at work in the lives of people. We could compare the Bible to a road map. It shows us the route from our beginning point as sinners without hope (Ephesians 2:12). From our beginning we move to our point of conversion where we accepted Christ as the "way" (John 14:6). It leads us through the triumphs and pitfalls of everyday living to our ultimate destination (John 14:1-3).

Like any road map, the Bible has specific directions. What good would a map do if it only gave general directions for your journey through life? I recall a trip Muriel and I took to London . Muriel always wanted to go there. An artist, my wife never tired of visiting art museums; and London was, in her opinion, the art capital of the world.

But with six children at home, we only traveled when necessary. However, a window of opportunity opened when I had a speaking engagement in England. We knew where we wanted to go. We talked with people who had been there, we accumulated videos, travel books, and maps. We learned, for example, that the Tate Museum contained the largest collection of paintings by our favorite artist. But examples, descriptions, and principles would never have gotten us to the Tate Museum. We needed specific directions.

The principles and commands of Scripture are never in conflict. You cannot justify violating a direct command by appealing to some broader principle. The specific commands are God's official application of some principle and must be obeyed. My application of the principle doesn't have God's authority, so I must not set my interpretation in opposition to a clear directive from God. Furthermore, the fact that no command covers a specific situation doesn't set us free to do as we please. We are still bound by the principles of Scripture. Thus we need both the principles and the commands to know God's will.

What do you struggle with in deciding God's will? Are you choosing your wants over his commands? Perhaps you want to be happy, so you step outside God's direct commands. Just remember: You cannot justify violating a direct command by appealing to some broader principle.

May 12
Spotting The Enemy's Diversions
Acts 13:2-3

"While they were worshiping the Lord and fasting, the Holy Spirit said, 'Set apart for me Barnabas and Saul for the work to which I have called them.' Then after fasting and praying they laid their hands on them and sent them off." (Acts 13:2-3)

In the Gulf war, should Iraq launch an air attack, we would counter-attack with guided missiles, smart missiles. But the enemy may have sophisticated electronic diversions that can mislead and make ineffective even the smart missiles. One is called chaff. A cloud of millions of tiny foil strips is fired off and creates a dummy target within a second. The missile gets confused and may hone-in on the chaff. A second diversion is electronic. When the anti-aircraft missile is guided by radio from the ground, the aircraft emits similar radio signals that are just enough different to mislead. A third method is for heat-seeking missiles. The aircraft drops flares that are hotter than its own emissions and deceives the heat-seeking missile into going after the wrong heat.

Our arch Enemy has diversions, too. We are in war-college, so to speak, preparing to bring down the Prince of the Power of the Air; yet if we aren't smart, he'll deceive us. Of his many diversions, I want to identify three important diversions that we will identify as chaff so we won't be deceived and miss our trajectory, miss the target God designed us for- world evangelization.

Chaff in dealing with our enemy are decoy definitions of "missionary". These are not the real thing.

* Chaff: "Everyone is a missionary or a mission field." To assign a vocational name to a universal responsibility

is chaff that deflects from the churches' objective. While understanding the intent is to raise the level of commitment on the part of all; the effect is to lower the level of commitment to the specialized task, the missionary vocation.

* Chaff: A missionary is one who goes away from home to minister and is paid by his home constituency. We can consume all the church's resources in doing many good things and never hit the target of world evangelism.

* Chaff: To expect of a short-term experience what it can't provide. For example: using a short-term experience to test out your gifts or calling. Short term missionary is a little like trial marriage--you try out something, but it isn't marriage. Plan youth group's short-term experience carefully to provide what it can provide: education and inspiration. Part of preparation is to be sure they don't have unrealistic expectations or false motivations --that they don't go after chaff. Use the experience to recruit for career missionary service through thorough preparation, working with the field supervisors to assure a positive experience, de-briefing and long-term follow-up. Use the program to spread the vision to others.

What is the target? Understanding that a missionary is an apostle, sent by the home church to evangelize and start the church where it does not exist. To concentrate on location rather than vocation can confuse and draw us out of trajectory. We want to clearly identify the basic New Testament calling of apostolic church founding, recruit for it, prepare the task force needed, and support them. This is our responsibility as God's people. How accurate are you in reaching the target- in avoiding diversionary chaff? Has God called you to start a church where it does not exist? So we take risks to fly in unchartered skies. If we don't, if our next generation doesn't do things differently from the last 60 generations, the job will not be done!

Would you pray today for laborers for the harvest? For culturally appropriate, Spirit energized ministry? For new believers from all nations to walk close with Jesus? For us to recognize chaff and not get diverted from the trajectory of world evangelization? *"For God so loved the world that he gave his only begotten Son that whoever believes will not perish but have eternal life."* John 3:16

May 13
Tools for Growth
Philippians 3:12-14

"Not that I have already obtained all this, or have already been made perfect, but I press on to take hold of that for which Christ Jesus took hold of me. Brothers, I do not consider myself yet to have taken hold of it. But one thing I do: Forgetting what is behind and straining toward what is ahead, I press on toward the goal to win the prize." (Philippians 3:12-14)

God is primarily in the business of remodeling our thought processes–our values, attitudes, ways of viewing things. This inner mind is the primary arena for growth. A normal Christian loves more and more like God loves; grows in self-control, contentment, humility, and courage; grows in understanding of God's ways; and is increasingly other-oriented and less self-oriented in the choices of life.

The inner transformation is visible in outward conduct. One's character changes, and even those personality traits that reflect sinful thought patterns are changed. Note that this growth into more Christlike behavior is in areas of unconscious sin or sins of omission, falling short of Godlike qualities. In deliberate sin there is no pattern of gradual growth. What tools does God use to make us more like Him?

Through *prayer* our companionship with God reaches its highest intensity. Not only do we grow more like Him through this companionship, but we find that prayer is the great means of victory at the moment of temptation.

The Bible is God's means of revealing His character and thus His will for our thoughts and actions. Therefore, the more we know His Word, the higher potential we have for conforming to His will. It is the milk and bread and meat of the soul. Furthermore, Jesus demonstrated in His hour of temptation that Scripture is a great weapon in spiritual warfare. As we study it diligently to understand it and as we meditate on it constantly to apply it to life, we will be prepared to use it effectively to overcome temptation.

The congregation of *God's family* is indispensable for spiritual growth. United worship and observance of the ordinances, teaching, fellowship, discipline, service, and witness within the responsible structure of the church are God's ordained means for the growth of each member.

Suffering may be God's great shortcut to spiritual growth. Our response to suffering determines its benefit to us, of course, for the same adversity may be destructive or life building. The response of faith, that is, confidence that God has permitted the trial for His glory and our own good, transforms a potentially evil circumstance into a means of making us more like the Suffering Servant Himself.

These four "tools of the Spirit" are indispensable to Christian growth. But though they are equally available to all, not all Christians seem to mature at the same pace.

Some Christians use the means of grace more diligently than others. Although in a passive sense all believers may be equally "yielded" to the will of God, the Christian life is nevertheless a war, and some are more aggressive and seem to have more of a will to fight. Though faith must rest, relying on God to do what we cannot do, it also must wrestle, struggling in warfare. Christians live in a world that is opposed to all they yearn to be. Some seem more aware of these adversaries and more persistent in opposing them.

We are fools if we compare ourselves among ourselves (2 Cor. 10:12), for we can never have God's full perspective. If we must make a comparison, we should compare ourselves with our model, the Lord Jesus. On the other hand, it is proper to compare ourselves either with what we once were or with what we would be, apart from the grace of God. Comparisons along these lines give God the credit and bring us closer to His perspective. May we recognize how far the Spirit has brought us in our Christian growth and where we have yet to go in becoming what He intends for us! What hope! What joy! What glory! To this end we pray.

May 14
Finite and Fallen
Romans 9:20

"But who are you, a human being, to talk back to God? "Shall what is formed say to the one who formed it, 'Why did you make me like this?' (Romans 9:20)

    We may not always believe that we are finite. Oh, we would have admit to finitude if asked, but our self-confidence can lead us to believe we have a corner on ***the truth.*** In my early twenties I entered the dark tunnel of agnosticism--from knowing "everything" to knowing nothing for sure, especially about God and his Book. I wasn't arrogant, affirming that no god existed, just that I, at least, couldn't find him. When by God's grace, I emerged from that dark tunnel, I had great confidence in the basics, you can have that confidence as well; that God is, that the Savior actually saves, that God has purpose for our life. We are shorn of any pretense of infallibility about the details. Our expectancies--for ourselves and others--are lowered to the realities of human finitude.
    We exult in the confidence of what God has revealed for sure--so sure that all believers of all time would affirm it. But most things we'd never figure out no matter how long we investigated and contemplated--things about God's infinities, and things about our finitude. Like the meanings of the past, the hopes for the future, the reasons for our circumstances, the goings-on of our inner self. We can be comfortable with that ambiguity about life, now, though others may not be. Some seem to need to have everything settled for sure.
    For an inquisitive thinker and an intense activist, the realization of one's finitude can be a marvelous relaxant and stabilizer. Besides, lowered expectancies of oneself is a doorway to making room for others. Maybe they're finite, too--and in a different configuration, yet! That realization could make a peacemaker out of a person. For example, when Mack set out to get rid of me as leader of the ministry, I didn't have to try to "be good" and not get angry, fight back, or hold a grudge against him. After all, he saw things differently than I saw them. Besides, maybe he was right. I didn't think so, but neither did I conclude he was devilish. Our finitudes had clashed, and we both thought we were doing God's own service. My theology had protected me in the crisis.
    We believe we are fallen and so are others. So we expect them to behave as fallen people and that helps make allowances for their failures, which doesn't come to us naturally. What comes naturally is to be easy on myself and hard on the other fellow. So it's a trick to be realistic about my own fallenness without justifying my own ungodly behavior because I've been easing off on the other fellow. I haven't figured out all the ramifications of the doctrine of the fall for protecting me from wrong thinking about myself and others, but on the larger scale, that doctrine has been a powerful deliverer in my life.
    Here's how. The whole of creation is under the curse of the fall and I'm not exempt, because of God's love for me, from the consequences of living in a world of vicious cancer and violent winds. Nor from a world of finite and fallen people who inflict harm on me, wittingly or unwittingly. I expect the worst and rejoice when, by God's grace, it usually doesn't happen! Sometimes when I wake in the morning I muse, *Lord, lots of folks died last night. Why not me?* At my stage of life so many of my dearest family and friends suffer painful, debilitating illness and agonizing death. Why not me? That's the only reasonable "why" question for one who lives in a fallen world.
    I don't want to oversimplify the problem of evil; a whole complex of theological issues intertwine. For example, if God made his own people exempt from the human condition, who wouldn't become a believer? But what kind of believer would they become? Again, when does God heal and to what end? For what purpose does God protect or

remove the protection? The theological questions seem endless, especially when faced with personal tragedy, but the bottom line for me is this: I'm fallen and so is my world. Not, "why me, Lord?" when trouble strikes, but "why not me, Lord?" when it so often misses.

May 15
Parenting
Luke 2:52

" And Jesus increased in wisdom and in stature and in favor with God and man." (Luke 2:52)

Parents are responsible to provide materially, physically, socially, spiritually, and mentally (education in contemporary American society) for dependent children. In this way children will grow in wisdom and stature, in favor with God and man (Luke 2:52).

Providing for the family in our society takes money, and earning money almost always takes time away from home. The Christian parent thus faces one of the most critical factors in the current crisis in family stability. At a deeper level, the care for children requires time spent with them. How can this double demand on parental time be reconciled? Though the feminist drive for equal pay is understandable, the end result may well be a leveling down rather than the hoped-for leveling up, and increasingly both parents will have to work to maintain financial viability. In most societies of the past, mothers worked outside the home, just as the ideal mother of Proverbs 31 . But until the Industrial Revolution (a terrible time for mothers and children), that work was in the field or forest, with the whole family participating so that the caring and nurturing continued unabated. How do we solve the dilemma?

The attitude of parents toward one another and toward the children and the quality of time spent together have more to do with the creation of a health-giving atmosphere than does the amount of time together. Nevertheless, the amount of time is part of the equation.

To begin with, children need both parents as a vital part of life. True, the mother seems to have been assigned by nature and Scripture the primary role in nurturing, at least the younger children. But both parents are essential. The solution may be connected with motive: Why does the father work such long hours? Why does the mother seek outside employment?

The father may work long hours because of unbiblical values or a misperception of how love is best expressed. Many a sincere father is genuinely surprised to find children alienated when he has "proved his love" so unstintingly by such tireless work for many years, never dreaming that his son or daughter really wanted him all along, not his lavish gifts. Others are simply materialistic and put the acquisition of things above the development of quality relationship. Still others are proud and driven to prove their worth through outdistancing others in achievement or wealth. Still others are selfish and enjoy work or hobbies or recreation or fun with "the boys" more than time with the family. All these motives are wholly inadequate and if followed may well lead to the crippling or destruction of the family or of some member of the family.

Christian workers sometimes neglect family responsibility for a higher motive—advancing the kingdom of God. There are times when such a motive is legitimate. Motives must be clear, however. Many a traveling minister travels because he enjoys it. He may even be afraid to face the reality of failure at home and thus seek to escape. If a man is truly called to an itinerant ministry, he may well be called to a life of celibacy, like Paul. If he is already married, he has part of his ministry call already settled—his home—and he will neglect that responsibility only at the risk of everything, for church ministry is reserved for those who succeed in the responsibilities of the home (1 Tim. 3:2-5; Titus 1:6-9).

And why does the mother seek outside employment during the hours a child is at home—or ought to be? If economic survival is the question, the choice is right, but "economic survival" and a better standard of living are not synonymous. Instead of glorying in what must surely be the highest of all callings—making a home—they are deceived into thinking that success in the marketplace is the only way to prove their value. Others work as an escape from the drudgery of diapers and dishes, only to find the drudgery of a nine-to-five routine. And in our society at least, 95 percent return home to play catch-up and do the housework anyway. If material goals or self-image or competing on "an even footing" with men are more important than nurturing children, perhaps the choice not to have children is more reasonable—a choice increasing numbers of "liberated" women make. But that choice, though honest, does not redeem a distorted system of values.

Scripture places a premium on teaching one's children. Fix these words of mine in your hearts and minds. . . . Teach them to your children, talking about them when you sit at home and when you walk along the road, when you lie down and when you get up. Write them on the doorframes of your houses and on your gates, so that your days and the days of your children may be many in the land that the LORD swore to give your forefathers. (Deut. 11:18-21, NIV)

Train up a child in the way he should go, and when he is old he will not depart from it. (Prov. 22:6) Instruction in the ways of God is the responsibility of both parents, but the father is responsible to be sure it takes place. This includes full participation in the life of a Bible-teaching church, but it is also to be on a daily basis as part of the family life. A daily time when the family gathers to hear and discuss a portion of Scripture, pray, and sing together should be the cornerstone of family life. So how is it in your family? How can we promote the welfare of each person in the family? How do you function together as parents? How can you support those you know who are parents?

May 16
Friendship
James 2:23

"And the Scripture was fulfilled which says, 'Abraham believed God, and it was accounted to him for righteousness.' And he was called the friend of God." (James 2:23)

I'm sure every one of the disciples would have said, "Jesus is my best friend." They walked the village streets and dusty country roads together and listened intently as He talked. But they didn't just listen-they talked, too, and without inhibition. Such an intimate companionship! Do you ever wish you could have been there? Jesus anticipated our loneliness. He promised to send another Comforter who would not just walk with us but who would actually be in us (John 14 :15-21). He was telling us, "I love you with an everlasting love. I won't leave you orphaned."

The God kind of love is more than my love for Him expressed in worship and praise. Much more. It's His love for me! As in marriage, love is the bridge that must reach out from both sides if ever there is to be a union .

Levels of intimacy. Consider the following six levels of intimacy in a human relationship:

1. Muriel and I met and liked one another. We'd get together occasionally and talk about things of mutual interest.

2. Then love began to fill the relationship, so each of us began to move out of our comfort zones. Muriel tried to figure out football, and I dragged myself to art museums. But still we didn't touch certain topics.

3. Eventually we reached the stage of mutual trust and agreed that nothing is off-limits-we'll fully share our hearts, no secrets.

4. Then we were married and intimacy was complete, or was it? We hadn't been together long enough to have pain. But we did enjoy one another's companionship and moments of delight.

5. We hit the difficult times and ran to embrace one another in shared agony.

6. Finally, my life came to the place where fun wasn't all that fun if Muriel wasn't with me; heartache was almost unbearable if she didn't share it. It was as if the other was there even when she/he wasn't; and when we were apart, the desire to be together became a gnawing hunger. Outsiders couldn't disturb the freedom and comfort between us.

Reflect on your relationship to God and, in the list above, consider the level of human relationship that parallels most closely your present experience of God . Actually, there's a seventh level, a closer intimacy than Muriel and I could ever experience, because we're finite humans. Such intimacy can be experienced only with God, as we shall see.

Let's explore three levels of union with God. *Basic Friendship*. Josh was furious about his Christmas gift. It wouldn't work right. Suddenly, he threw it across the room where it crashed through a valued lamp shade. In the following months, Josh tried-with varying degrees of success-to bridle his temper. Ours was an unlikely friendship. He was only three, and our conversations didn't rise to great heights. Josh taught me something about God and me-another unlikely friendship. I certainly can't converse on God's level. Sometimes I get angry with a gift God gives me. I sometimes say a bad thing, do a foolish thing, or enjoy a wrong thing. Through it all God continues to love me. Against the backdrop of this lopsided love affair, Jesus calls us friends (John 15 :15). He doesn't call us slaves or even children, both of which we are, but friends! Josh has been my friend now for several years. He's especially hard to resist when a smile breaks across that pixie face as he offers a gift of atonement (usually some well-loved toy), hugs me tight, and says, "Sorry, Pawpaw." Josh moved to a distant city and entered first grade. A few weeks later I received a letter, the first from my buddy: "I Luv Yoo Yoo Are The Bes Fred I everhad." It's so good to be best friends with God! But there's a level of intimacy above basic friendship.

Daily Companionship. Walking daily with Him. Companioning. Have you thought about how God-intoxicated you are? Since beginning your quiet times, has your daily time with God increased? Has your sense of God's companionship in that daily time grown closer and more real?

Constant Awareness of His Presence. At age 20 I discovered the motto of Frederic Franson, the pioneer who founded 5 Scandinavian mission agencies at the close of the 19th century. Franson's life theme was CCCC-Constant Conscious Communion with Christ. The moment I heard it my heart leaped. "That's what I want, Lord!" I cried out. And God heard my prayer. For about 2 months that summer I was not only always conscious of the Lord's presence, I seemed to be constantly, consciously conversing with God. But then the feeling of closeness slipped away. I pled for the return of that experience, but it never came back. I'm not sure why He gave me that foretaste of heaven nor why He withdrew it. Was it something like Paul's brief visit to "the third heaven," not intended to be permanent, not designed for daily human experience? Yet the mystics down the ages testify of a life pattern of constant conscious communion with Christ. Perhaps God would give you that high level of intimacy if you sought it. Don't let my experience discourage you. In the meantime, until that day when we all have such a life-filling experience in His presence, I can promise something very special: a constant relationship of intimacy, an uninterrupted awareness of the Spirit's presence.

May 17
The Healthy Life
1 John 1:9

"If we confess our sin He is faithful and just to forgive our sins and cleanse us from all unrighteousness." (1 John 1:9)

The more complicated the product you purchase, the longer and more detailed the manufacturer's instructions that come with it. And what could be more complex than a human being? The Manufacturer didn't produce us and then abandon us to figure out how best to operate the product. No, He provided a manual for the way we work best, how we can fulfill and enjoy the purpose of the Manufacturer's design.

That revealed will of God is His law. We call it law because it isn't optional if we want to find God's highest and best purpose in creating and redeeming us. And God didn't make laws because He is a bully or a capricious potentate. It was because He loves us and wants the best for us. That's what every law in God's Word was designed for—our best.

As we have seen, God communicates His will in a number of ways through His Word. I would list direct commands—more than one thousand; scriptural principles; biblical examples—good examples to follow, bad ones to avoid; and our paramount model, Jesus. Would you list conscience? A Spirit-sensitized and Scripture-informed moral judgment is a prime source of guidance. But it isn't infallible, so we must make sure our conscience is renewed and transformed by exposure to God's Word. So there are many ways to find God's will in His manual.

Like our first parents, we have decided to ignore or water down God's laws and write our own rules. Today the only universally accepted law seems to be the evil of intolerance. But believers are responsible to accept God's laws as commands, not suggestions or guidelines, and to obey them. Do they seem to you a dreadful litany of Christian failure?

God's law is not full of dread for us, because Jesus took the blow of the law and cleared us of guilt. Marvelous grace! The law is no longer a bright light in the interrogation room to amass evidence that condemns me. It's a bright light in the surgery room to reveal the malignancy that hinders spiritual healing and health.

When the law spotlights a malignancy, what will we do about it? We can cover it, or we can expose it to the light. We can cover our failures with denial, calling them mistakes instead of sins. We can cover them with rationalization, inventing an acceptable reason to explain our failure. Or we can cover them with faulty doctrines of cheap grace. And what will result? *"The one who conceals his sins will not prosper."* (Proverbs 28:13)

A cover-up artist says, "The commandments? Those are Old Testament legalism." Hold on! The consequences of sin in the New Testament are fairly severe as well; believers who sinned sometimes experienced illness and even death (see Acts 5:1-10; 1 Cor. 11:29-30). Covering our sin will shut us off from all the glorious promises of Holy Spirit empowerment. That's why we begin the pursuit of an obedient relationship with God by examining the law, allowing the Spirit to shine the bright light of His revealed will into the inmost recesses of our hearts. Then we are eager to open the door to His treasure house of spiritual guidance and blessing.

How do we open the door? *"If we confess our sins, He is faithful and righteous to forgive our sins and to cleanse us from all unrighteousness"* (1 John 1:9). Confessing our sins means agreeing with God about them, uncovering them, exposing them to the light of His Word. Remember, no excuses, no rationalizing—full disclosure. And no generalizations either. We need to be specific.

Think about your shortcomings in keeping the commands. Pause and pray. Thank God for a law you have studied that will help you realign your thinking or behavior. Confess and repent of any offense against God's law of which you have been convicted, if you have not already done so. Thank God for His promise of overcoming power through His Holy Spirit. Commit to trust Him for that.

May 18

Adoration

Psalm 9:1-2

"I will give thanks to the LORD with my whole heart; I will recount all of your wonderful deeds. I will be glad and exult in you; I will sing praise to your name, O Most High." (Psalm 9:1-2)

An older understanding is nearer the truth about worship: it should be all that takes place during the "worship service," not just the music. That view must govern our thinking and planning if we are to worship in spirit and in truth. For example, to give generously in the offering should be to worship God most authentically. And the sermon, above all elements of worship, should point people Godward, put his glories on display, enable people to live out their lives in the coming week as true worshipers. So every element of the time of God's people gathered should be worship.

Having said that, however, the directly spoken worship of God (prayers and singing) is essential to true corporate worship. And it needs to be monitored carefully to see that it incorporates all biblical elements of verbal worship: thanksgiving, praise, and adoration. These certainly may blend, but if care is not taken to insure that each element is fully expressed in corporate worship, we will come up short in bringing pleasure to our God.

Thanksgiving-thank him specifically for what he has done for you.

Praise-praise him for who he is. Tell him what you like about him, each glorious characteristic.

Adoration-tell him how you feel about him. Love talk.

Here's a sample from my own experience. When on my annual retreat alone with the Lord, the following worship overflowed. It's not immortal prose, to be sure, but gives an indication of what these essential elements of worship might mean.

Thank you, Father, for your marvelous gifts: salvation and hope, the Savior's loving presence within and about, the blessed Spirit who transforms and empowers, your friendship, incredible as that is. Thank you, thank you, for the wonderful Book. And thank you for the gift of such a magnificent world: the flowers, the grass and trees, the lovely birds and wondrous beasts, mountains and seas, streams and mighty rivers, rocks and sands and all things beautiful. And food-what a delightful way to survive and thrive! And what a glorious idea marriage was! And family. Friends so loyal and loving and bountiful. And humankind, displaying your image-imprint, creating magnificent art and literature and music. I love fine architecture and astounding technologies. You've given me work to do that counts for eternity: _____, _____, _____ The gifts of health and abilities and, especially, my wife. Thank you.

I praise you, Father, for what you have done, your mighty acts: You saved me and save me and will save me, and a world of men and women besides. Creation that seems almost as infinite as you; the invincible Church, made of impossible building material. Your incredibly complex and wondrously beautiful planning and your meticulous execution of every intricate part; your sustaining power for all the worlds and for each sparrow. What a wonder you are! Hallelujah!

My adoration, Father, above all is for who you are. Every characteristic speaks your majestic godhood. But from among them all, in splendid array, I focus often on your wisdom, power and love. Wisdom to know all things, power to do all you will, and love to count me in. What more could I ask? I could ask for holiness, for what kind of god would we have if he could figure everything out, accomplish anything and felt affectionately toward us, but were crooked, no model of right and dispenser of justice? And what if you were unpredictable and given to change? How insecure we would be! And what if you had a beginning or worse an end? That would be the ultimate insecurity. But no, you are all there is of perfection, beyond all imagination. And today I bow in humble gratitude.

Note that the thanksgiving, praise and adoration interplay throughout. It isn't necessary to make each part of worship a discrete element, but only to be sure all elements are present when we worship. We can't express our love for him too extravagantly, just as two young lovers find praise and adoration exploding beyond containment. Take a few minutes now to express your adoration!

May 19
Seek the Better
1 Corinthians 12

"To one there is given through the Spirit . . . to another . . . to another . . . and to still another. . . . Are all apostles? Are all prophets? Are all teachers?" (I Corinthians 12:8-11 & 29)

I asked a group of high school students, "Are all occupations of equal importance?" They unanimously agreed that all are equal.

"That's an interesting concept," I said, and told them the story of my flight to Norfolk. " On the way here, I sat by a man who wanted to sell me stock in his company . He said it was the fastest growing industry in the country."

"What's the industry?" I asked him.

"Cosmetics," he answered.

"In your industry is there some segment that is growing faster than others?"

"Oh, yes . Male cosmetics."

"Like-what? Deodorant? After-shave lotion?"

"Oh, no," he said. "Last year we sold a quarter million dollars worth of false eyelashes for men ."

"There's an occupation," I told the students, "selling false eyelashes for men. Here's another one. My nephew is a skilled surgeon who could make a bundle of money in the United States. Instead, he chose to care for a forgotten people in the heart of Africa. He barely escaped one country as the communist insurgents swept to power. Now, in Kenya, he tells me he does more surgery in a week than he used to do in a year at a renowned hospital in Pennsylvania. Then he adds with a wry smile, `and none of it is cosmetic!' " "There you have it," I said, "selling false eyelashes for men or healing the bodies and souls of thousands for whom you're the only hope? Let's vote again: Are all vocations of equal importance?"

That split the crowd and about half wavered. On the front row sat a 16-year-old girl who didn't vote either way. "Not going to vote?" I asked her. "No. It's a bad question." "What's bad about it?" "You didn't say important for what." She caught me! Which is more important: a knife, a fork, or a spoon? The answer might depend on whether you had a bowl of bullion or a steak. Vocations need to be considered likewise- important to whom? For what?

So it is with spiritual gifts. A spiritual gift is a Spirit-given ability to serve God. So much confusion reigns in the church over the subject of spiritual gifts that many give up and avoid the whole subject. That's a big mistake. The only way the church will be effective, and the only way we'll spiral up into likeness to Jesus, is through each believer using the abilities the Spirit gives. We won't try to settle all the controversy about spiritual gifts. Instead, we'll focus on the basic teaching on which we all can agree. Some Christians believe the gifts-or at least some of them-are no longer given. However, even they must agree that unless the Holy Spirit empowers us we can never accomplish the tasks He gives us to do. Other Christians distinguish "sign" gifts and "ministry" gifts, but a little reflection will make clear that the sign gifts were also for ministry, to build up the body of Christ. So we will concentrate on the common ground, the all-important ways the Spirit enables His people to accomplish His work. Today we'll look at three things the Spirit's gifts are not. They are not fruit, talents, or offices.

Now we need to ask another question: "How do the fruit and gifts relate?" In the most thorough discussion of gifts in the Bible, I Corinthians 12-14, fruit is said to be more important than gifts. Right in the middle of Paul's discussion of gifts, immediately following our memory verse, he says, "Now I'm going to describe something far more important than all these gifts combined" (my paraphrase). Then he gives the magnificent love chapter, 1 Corinthians 13. Love is a fruit. In fact, some say it is the summation of all the fruit of the Spirit.

God intends for all His children to be like Him-to bear all the fruit of the Spirit. Yet, I Corinthians 12-14 demonstrates clearly that the Spirit does not give all the gifts to any one person. In the list of gifts and fruit, love, patience, goodness, peace, joy, and humility are fruit. It's just as well He doesn't give all the gifts to one person. God wants everyone to be completely like Him in character, but not like Him in His abilities.

He never intended anyone have infinite wisdom or power. However, He does want His church to have wisdom and power, so He distributed abilities (gifts) among the members to enable the church to accomplish His purposes. No one member can be Godlike in power lest he or she be tempted to use the gifts in accumulating personal authority and prestige.

In summary, fruit is for everyone, always; gifts, some to one, some to another. The exciting fact is that every member is given at least one ability to serve God. That includes you! How the gifts and fruit relate is a mystery. The Bible does not spell it out for us. God sometimes mightily uses a person who is egotistical or quick-tempered. We see another who is very godly in character but is not gifted to serve in any conspicuous way. How is it with you? Which do you pursue? Gifts or fruit? Which is more important?

May 20
Harvesters
Matthew 9:36

"When he saw the crowds, he had compassion for them, because they were harassed and helpless, like sheep without a shepherd." (Matthew 9:36)

Pray to the Lord of the harvest but don't get caught up in an error. Some people say that's all you can do. You can't recruit, that's God's business. I wonder what they think about evangelism. Regeneration is God's business, wouldn't you say? But how does He do it? Through you and me, through human instrumentality. How does He thrust them out? Through you and me, through human instrumentality.

For example, Barnabas didn't just wait around for Paul to volunteer. He spotted Paul, and he kept his eye on Paul, and then at the right time, he recruited him. He didn't say, "Now, Paul, if the Spirit moves you." He said, "Paul, we need you down here, will you come?" So they put him to work. Then the church got together prayed, then thrust out Paul and Barnabas as the first pioneer missionary church-starting evangelists.

So you have the responsibility, not only to go but to spot others, to enlist them, to put them to work, and then to give them some training. We need a new kind of training for this new breed. Do you know how many people are in training in all the seminaries, in all the Bible colleges of the United States? About 100,000. Do you know how many of them will go to the mission field? Of the half who graduate, 3.7% will go to the mission field if past proportions continue. And that 3.7% includes all kinds of missionaries, not just evangelists. We're going to have to recruit and train an army to get the task done.

How are they going to be sent? God's going to send them, but He's going to use you and me. He's going to use the Church to provide the laborers.

Why, if the harvest is so great, are the laborers so few? I think the secret is found right here in the same passage. When Christ saw the crowds, He had *"compassion on them because they were harassed and helpless, like sheep without a shepherd"* (Matthew 9:36). Do you know why we aren't getting the job done? It is because God's people don't care. They are not moved as Christ was. They shut their eyes to the harvest, to the need. And when someone pries them open to show them the need, they are moved with DISINTEREST. That is the problem -- we don't have the compassion of Christ.

On the northern island of Hokkaido in Japan, four young brothers were swimming in the Pacific when one of them let out a scream. "It's a shark, it's a shark." The three younger brothers clambered up on a shelf in the shallow water, and watched their 14-year old brother in his race with death. That black dorsal fin sliced closer and closer. All of a sudden, the three of them let out a yell. The fin disappeared as the shark dived to strike from beneath. When they yelled, their brother, sea-wise, knew what it meant, flailed back in the water as the shark struck. It missed him, but as it was going past, he reached out and grabbed it around the belly. The three brothers on shore were safe enough. What do you think they did? Just like one, they hit the water. One of them scooped a stone off the ocean floor, grabbed the shark and began to pound him on the nose. Another grabbed him around the tail and began to beat him in the belly. That poor shark didn't know what hit him. He made a lunge but got confused and went in the wrong direction.

The parents down the beach heard all the noise and came running. When they got there, they found a 9-foot shark on the beach, flipping out its last, and four proud shark killers circling it. The 7-year-old, trembling, looked up at his father and said, "I was scared!"

That brother dove in, not knowing if he would ever come back. He only knew that he was going out. Why? Because his brother was in trouble, and he knew it. And he loved him. That's the motive. It's compassion. The Bible says that "*when Jesus saw the people. . .He was moved with compassion.*" Literally, it says His stomach was tied in knots. What does your stomach get tied in knots over? But when Jesus saw the lost of the world, His stomach was tied in knots, and He moved out to shepherd those lost sheep. How do you feel about it? What will you do about it? [22]

May 21
Good, Acceptable and Perfect
Romans 12:1-2

".....be transformed by the renewing of your mind, that you may prove what is that good and acceptable and perfect will of God. " (Romans 12:1-2, NKJ)

In life, when you make godly choices, you put on display-or prove-for all to see how good, acceptable, and perfect the will of God is by exhibiting God's character. Let's take a look at those three words Paul uses to describe what you'll look like: good, acceptable, perfect.

The purpose of suffering is always growth and glory and: our growth, God's glory. Would He have those same purposes for allowing temptation to assault us? Yes and no. Yes, both suffering and temptation are tests (often intertwined) and His purpose in allowing either kind of test is always our growth and His glory. But a big difference exists between suffering and temptation. Sometimes we are to accept suffering as God's will for us, but we can never accept temptation we fight it! God's good will is to overcome temptation. If we don't, we neither bring credit to Him nor growth to ourselves.

When we yield to temptation, we grow weaker, less like Jesus, and that's not God's good will. We demonstrate God's *good* will when we do His will. Victory is His good will; defeat is certainly not His will. Dennis and Brad came to me with a theory they found liberating. They were forever defeated by lustful temptations. "We've decided lust is the cross Jesus is calling us to bear," they said. .

I explained that God's good will is to nail our evil desires to the cross, not excuse them. God purposes to give victory over temptation, not that we give up in defeat. When continuing in lust, Dennis and Brad were demonstrating what the will of God is not. They brought dishonor to the Lord and more rapid descent down the spiral for themselves.

On the other hand, Cubby saw a positive demonstration of God's good will. His business partner, Det, found Christ and was radically changed. Cubby said he'd never seen anything like this. Det was a big-time political operator and hard-driving businessman, but Cubby watched in amazement as a transformation took place. One day in a particularly difficult confrontation with competitors, Det responded calmly and graciously, not like the old Det. Cubby returned to his office, shut the door, fell to his knees and prayed, "Lord, whatever Det has, I want it!" Cubby had seen

---

[22] Taken from (Seeds of Promise: World Consultation on Frontier Missions, Edinburgh '80 edited by Allan Starling. Copyright 1981. Used by permission of William Carey Library, P. O. Box 128-C, Pasadena, California, 91104.)

God's good will on display in Det, and as a result something very good happened. Cubby became a Christian and transformation began.

Another word Paul uses to describe God's will is *acceptable,* or as some translations have it, pleasing. Success in overcoming temptation is pleasing all right, but to whom? Bible scholars may debate which of those Paul had in mind, but I would say, all the above! To overcome temptation brings joy all around. It's a victory celebration! To fail and not do the good will of God is pleasing only to unholy men and unholy spirits. To you, God, and all good people, surrender to temptation is distressing.

Paul's meaning for *perfect* in describing God's will worked out in your life would include, flawless, without defect mature, adult, full-grown. It includes loyal, sincere, whole-hearted obedience to the known will of God. Perfect is the ability and readiness to meet all demands, outfitted. Those are indeed our ultimate goal, that we will one day be flawless, just like Jesus. His will is that we demonstrate maturity and obedience . When we demonstrate that, what a celebration of the glorious will of God! It's perfect! And that's very pleasing and very good!

Every plan to overcome temptation needs to be custom designed for the individual . It may change for each stage of life, whether the temptations and uncertainties of youth, the frustrations and failed dreams of middle years, or the regrets and anxieties of age. Where are you today in your spiral up toward likeness to Jesus? It's time now for the big assignment: write out your own plan for overcoming the failure that most grieves the Holy Spirit and embarrasses you. This is for real, not just an idea to be pondered. Create your own strategic plan to overcome temptation. We will get into the specifics of a plan for overcoming temptation tomorrow. First pray and decide the temptation you need to develop a plan to overcome. Now pray, do you really want to overcome this temptation?

Your strategy will need revision as you put it into action. Let it be a developing plan. No matter how satisfied you are with your strategy, remember: success in the Christian life does not ultimately depend on a technique, a strategy, or your own activity. Ultimately, the Holy Spirit within is the overcomer. But the indwelling powerful One does not displace your personality with His. Rather, He is a personal companion. He prays for us when we don't know how to pray (Romans 8:26-27) ; and as we rely on Him, He enables us to pray effectively. God the Spirit gave us His Word and enables us to understand and appropriate that Word in the face of testing. He enables us to live in the kind of relationship with other Christians that will make us overcomers together. What a great God we serve!

May 22
The Plan
Luke 11:5-10

"Then he said to them, "Suppose one of you has a friend, and he goes to him at midnight and says, `Friend, lend me three loaves of bread, because a friend of mine on a journey has come to me, and I have nothing to set before him.' "Then the one inside answers, `Don't bother me. The door is already locked, and my children are with me in bed. I can't get up and give you anything.' I tell you, though he will not get up and give him the bread because he is his friend, yet because of the man's boldness he will get up and give him as much as he needs. So I say to you: Ask and it will be given to you; seek and you will find, knock and the door will be opened to you. For everyone who asks receives; he who seeks finds; and to him who knocks, the door will be opened" (Luke 11:5-10).

Let's begin to develop a plan to overcome temptation. Yesterday you asked yourself what is the temptation you need to develop a plan to overcome? Then ask yourself, "do you really want to overcome this temptation? ? Are you yielded unconditionally to the Spirit about it?" This may feel overwhelming or too complicated.

When you can say yes from your heart, Holy Spirit power is released and you're on your way to victory. Go ahead with your plan! But if you couldn't answer yes to those questions, no need to proceed. First you must become willing to obey. How do you become willing to obey? Find assurance in the words from Luke 11 that *"everyone who asks receives; he who seeks finds; and to him who knocks, the door will be opened.* Jesus was speaking specifically about persisting in prayer.

To begin developing your plan to overcome temptation, pause and ask the Holy Spirit for wisdom. Ask Him to enlighten your mind and bring to mind both Scriptures and principles you have been studying. Ask God to make you willing to obey. Ask Him to give you a desire to overcome. Don't ask and give up. Keep asking, knocking, and seeking until God gives you the desire to obey Him. Using those points you've chosen, plus others you may have heard about, discovered in Scripture, or learned through experience, make a broad outline of your own personal strategy for overcoming temptation. The following is an outline of how you might proceed:

1. Who or what most often causes this temptation?

2. What are the camouflages this enemy uses-how do I tend to rationalize the attitude or behavior?

3. Among lust, covetousness, pride, and unbelief, which is most likely the root cause(s) of my temptation?

4. What is my defensive strategy-how do I plan to use the Bible, prayer, and the church to build up strength to face this particular temptation when it comes?

5. What is my offensive strategy-how do I intend to use the Bible, prayer, and the church at the time of temptation?

How did it go? Are you pleased with the outcome? Time and space may not have permitted you to finish your plan to your own satisfaction. Remember your strategy will need revision as you put it into action. No matter how satisfied you are with your strategy, success in the Christian life does not ultimately depend on a technique, a strategy, or your own activity. Ultimately, the Holy Spirit within is the overcomer. But the indwelling powerful One does not displace your personality with His. Rather, He is a personal companion, living in you to:

- strengthen you when you falter
- remind you of truth from His Word when your focus is blurred
- point out the enemy when you're under attack
- comfort you
- lift you up when you fall
- forgive you when you fail
- guide you when you're confused
- sensitize your moral judgment
- strengthen your will when you waver.

Glorious as those activities of the Spirit are, it's not all He does. He prays for us when we don't know how to pray (Romans 8:26-27) ; and as we rely on Him, He enables us to pray effectively. We do not have to go down in defeat!

May 23
Champions
Philippians 3:12-14

"Not that I have already obtained this or am already perfect, but I press on to make it my own, because Christ Jesus has made me his own. Brothers, I do not consider that I have made it my own. But one thing I do: forgetting what lies behind and straining forward to what lies ahead, I press on toward the goal for the prize of the upward call of God in Christ Jesus." (Philippians 3:12-14)

Today, we celebrate champions. How can YOU...and I become champions? I think we follow a great pace-setter in the race, Paul the marathon champion. Where was Paul when he was running so hard? Well, he was in his own rented condo where he could have guests and house his friends. But he was chained to 2 Roman soldiers! Have you ever been in jail, trapped so you can't run free? What do you do when trapped? Give up? Kick back and watch TV? Fret and lie awake all night? Hit the bottle? Not Paul!

"One thing!" Paul was chained between two Roman soldiers, he's dictating a letter to his beloved friends in Philippi and reflects that he hasn't finished his race, hasn't won the prize, hasn't got hold of what Christ got hold of him for. He stops and shouts to his secretary, Timothy (Or was it Luke?) across the room as he wrote down with a brush on parchment what Paul dictated–"one thing!"

If I were in lockdown I'd be thinking of ONE thing, too. How do I get out of here? When can I get out of here and get on with life, get in the race again? But not Paul. He was in hot pursuit of the purpose God had in mind when he saved Paul. One thing! If you get focused on the one thing God has in mind for you, you'll have to avoid all distractions. No looking back. That's when the runner stumbles. No looking around to see how others are doing. He didn't keep reviewing and savoring past successes. Nor did he spend a lot of time grieving past failures. One thing! I don't look back, says Paul. I'm stretching with all my strength toward the goal Christ set for me. One thing!

What did Christ lay hold of him for? Remember when he first met Christ on the road to Damascus? He told Paul what he wanted him for–to be his agent to reach the Gentiles. How could he do that in his present circumstances–chained? Chained to whom? A couple of Gentiles! So he wins them! 4:22!! And he does more–in chains he has time to write a major part of Scripture, something he could hardly do when running so hard all over the world as a pioneer missionary. God said to Paul: hold on. I'll re-direct you with some chains. But, trapped and house-bound, he keeps pressing on to fulfill what Christ created him for.

How about you? Do you know why he laid hold of you for his Kingdom? If you don't, why not ask him? Are you giving it all you've got? Even if you seem locked up in some heartache, pinned down by some problem, chained by adverse circumstances. One thing!

But there's more Paul had in mind. He told us in verses 8-10. To know Christ. One thing! But Paul, you've known him ever since the Damascus Road encounter. No, no, says Paul, I haven't reached the goal yet. To know him in intimate companionship. We were created and redeemed for this.

How does that happen? Do verse 10 in reverse. (1) death: Jesus said over and over. Take up YOUR cross. Gethsemane– **But if not.** (2) fellowship of his suffering–what was that? Win our redemption. We're call to fill up that which was lacking. What could be lacking? But I'm not capable of doing that! Right! So (3) the power of his resurrection! End result–knowing him in Scriptural sense. Is that how you know Christ today? One thing!

Will you be a champion? Getting a handle on the ministry God has in mind for you, becoming daily more like Jesus, tighter in your relationship to him. A true champion. Maybe you say, that's for people like Paul. No, no, says

Paul–it's for YOU. See verses 15-17. If you do become a champion, give it all you've got, what can you look forward to? Paul looked forward to the "Upward call"– grandstand in the stadium.

But he's not there yet! Neither am I. Neither are you! Scholars agree that after two years Paul was released and what did he do? Retire? He'd reached retirement age and who wants to risk winding up in jail again? Or in the arena fighting lions again? Or nailed to a cross? ONE THING! He started out again and ran hard, pressed on, according to tradition, all over the Roman world, including perhaps maybe even to Spain. If you feel trapped, hindered, chained by your circumstances today, maybe God will release you for a new lap of the race. But maybe he'll keep you locked down. In the end, that's what he did with Paul. Mamertine dungeon. Under Capitoline Hill across from the famed Roman Colosseum where tradition says he died. But still, One Thing! Timothy wasn't with him–Paul is writing his partner who serves in a distant place. In fact, Paul was abandoned by all his friends, he tells us. Lonely. What was his response? II Tim 4.6-8. He could see his beloved Savior there in the celestial grandstands calling him up to receive the reward.

But wherever you are, will you be a champion?

If you get focused on the one thing God has in mind for you, you'll have to avoid all distractions. No looking back. That's when the runner stumbles. No looking around to see how others are doing. He didn't keep reviewing and savoring past successes. Nor did he spend a lot of time grieving past failures. One thing! I don't look back, says Paul. I'm stretching with all my strength toward the goal Christ set for me. One thing!

What did Christ lay hold of him for? Remember when he first met Christ on the road to Damascus? He told Paul what he wanted him for–to be his agent to reach the Gentiles. How could he do that in his present circumstances–chained? Chained to whom? A couple of Gentiles! So he wins them! 4:22!! And he does more–in chains he has time to write a major part of Scripture, something he could hardly do when running so hard all over the world as a pioneer missionary. God said to Paul: hold on. I'll re-direct you with some chains. But, trapped and house-bound, he keeps pressing on to fulfill what Christ created him for.

How about you? Do you know why he laid hold of you for his Kingdom? If you don't, why not ask him? Are you giving it all you've got? Even if you seem locked up in some heartache, pinned down by some problem, chained by adverse circumstances. One thing!

But there's more Paul had in mind. He told us in verses 8-10. To know Christ. One thing! But Paul, you've known him ever since the Damascus road encounter. No, no, says Paul, I haven't reached the goal yet. To know him in intimate companionship. We were created and redeemed for this.

How does that happen? Do verse 10 in reverse. (1) death: Jesus said over and over. Take up YOUR cross. Gethsemene–*But if not.* (2) fellowship of his suffering–what was that? Win our redemption. We're call to fill up that which was lacking. What could be lacking? But I'm not capable of doing that! Right! So (3) the power of his resurrection! End result–knowing him in Scriptural sense. Is that how you know Christ today? One thing!

Will you be a champion? Getting a handle on the ministry God has in mind for you, becoming daily more like Jesus, tighter in your relationship to him. A true champion. Maybe you say, that's for people like Paul. No, no, says Paul–it's for YOU. See verses 15-17. If you do become a champion, give it all you've got, what can you look forward to? Paul looked forward to the "Upward call"– grandstand in the stadium.

But he's not there yet! Neither am I. Neither are you! Scholars agree that after two years Paul was released and what did he do? Retire? He'd reached retirement age and who wants to risk winding up in jail again? Or in the arena fighting lions again? Or nailed to a cross? ONE THING! He started out again and ran hard, pressed on, according to tradition, all over the Roman world, including perhaps maybe even to Spain. If you feel trapped, hindered, chained by your circumstances today, maybe God will release you for a new lap of the race.

But maybe he'll keep you locked down. In the end, that's what he did with Paul. Mamertine dungeon. Under

194

Capitoline Hill across from the famed Roman Colosseum where tradition says he died. But still, One Thing! Timothy wasn't with him–Paul is writing his partner who serves in a distant place. In fact, Paul was abandoned by all his friends, he tells us. Lonely. What was his response? II Tim 4.6-8. He could see his beloved Savior there in the celestial grandstands calling him up to receive the reward.

But wherever you are, will you be a champion?

May 24
The Newspaper
1 Corinthians 3:11-13

"Now if anyone builds on the foundation with gold, silver, precious stones, wood, hay, straw—each one's work will become manifest...." (1 Corinthians 3:11-13)

On what will our eternal rewards be based? For years I had the Pauline role—missionary church planter among an unreached people. To me, that's the top vocation. From there I stepped down to head an educational institution in a country where there are hundreds of seminaries and Bible colleges. Still, we were sending out hundreds of missionaries as well as pastors and teachers. So finally, from there I stepped down again, to the role of homemaker— cooking, cleaning house, changing diapers. Which work of mine do you feel will receive the greater reward at the final assize.

You're correct— reward will not be based on gift or calling. After all, the people to whom Paul wrote the assurance of reward were menial, household slaves! So don't be arrogant about your gifts and calling, nor envious of others. Rewards are for those whose work is steadfast, unmovable, always abounding and for Jesus' sake. That spells "faithful" and reward is based on faithfulness, not giftedness nor prominence.

I met with missionaries gathered from across Tanzania on the shore of Lake Victoria for their annual conference. On the last night there was a presentation for Doris Shafer who had finished her missionary career— 35 years delivering thousands of babies in the hot, dusty, lonely backside of the desert. There was a brief speech of appreciation, and they presented her with a notebook of letters from her colleagues. I was angry. Is this *it? All* of it? 35 years of heroic effort to save a forgotten people and she quietly slips away?

I sat there reflecting on my own country where a 250-pound hunk of muscle grabs a pig skin, smashes down the field and headlines scream his glory across the land. I remembered the year before when an entertainer noted for blaspheming God and man got $50,000,000 for his efforts. I was angry. But then I remembered—I've been reading the wrong newspapers. In the Celestial Times Doris is the one in the headlines, not the football star. I've been tracking the wrong Emmy Awards. Doris is the one who will receive *the* reward.

On that glad day when you offer him the gift of a lifetime of hard work, he will be pleased. You worked to fulfill him, not you, and that will be the joy! I stayed close to home base when evangelizing in Japan, but occasionally I'd take a trip to speak to some missionaries' conference. When I returned home it was always to a jubilant celebration. On one such occasion when I entered the front gate, 3-year-old Kent was the first to spot me. He had flooded the back yard and made an immense black mud pie. He shouted the alarum and dashed to greet me. Here I am in my one preacher-suit and there he is, a little glob of gooey mud. What do I do? Why, I lift him up and embrace him, of course.

By then there was a flurry of activity as each of his five brothers and sisters prepared their own welcome—one brought a chair to put on the veranda, another plugged in the electric fan, a third brought hand-fans and began to churn the turgid air to provide for my comfort. Kent just stood there, dripping mud, watching his older brothers and sisters. Suddenly he disappeared. He had thought of something for my comfort they had not. In the kitchen, he pushed a chair over to the cabinet where the powdered drink mix was stored, then over to the sink to get a glass of water. He knew about a delicious drink made from powder and water, he just didn't know about stirring it. Powder and water now combined he dismounted his chair and reached up chubby fingers to get the gift for his Daddy. He might spill it, so better anchor the glass with a couple of fingers over the rim.

As I sat there on the veranda, treated like royalty, suddenly Kent reappeared and proudly offered me his gift, a tall glass of brownish water. "Did you make this yourself, Kenbo?" I asked. Standing there with his muddy midriff protruding between shirt and pants, he jerked his dirty little head in affirmation. What to do? Distract his attention and pitch it into the garden? He watched me like a hawk. So I took a swallow. Immediately Kent said, "Did you like it?"

You think I lied, don't you? But I didn't. I told the solemn truth: "Kenbo, I love it!" Oh, I didn't care for the gritty brown drink, of course, but I loved his love. And so it is with you. On that last Day, the most godly and gifted among us will offer a gift with a muddy finger or two in it. But he'll love it! Your offering of love, of a lifetime of steadfast, immovable, abounding hard work will bring him great joy.

May 25
Functional Authority of Scripture
2 Timothy 3:16-17

"All Scripture is breathed out by God and profitable for teaching, for reproof, for correction, and for training in righteousness, that the man of God may be complete, equipped for every good work." (2 Timothy 3:16-17)

Perhaps your church is deciding how to be seeker friendly as a church. Perhaps there is division as to whether to have a Saturday evening service or gather only via Zoom. Short term missions vs long term missions? Pastor search procedures, and perhaps leadership strategy, even divorce, arranged marriages, care for parents, or women in leadership policies are activities of the church in which we differ.

When struggling to ascertain God's revealed will for any concept or activity of ministry or to make sure one has no preference in the matter, certain steps must be followed.

These are offered in simplicity. We will not try in one day's reading to fully analyze, much less establish conclusions, but today we will simply demonstrate how to use this approach to knowing God's revealed will for ministry.

1) ***Identify the issue so precisely that both advocates and opponents agree with the identification***

Begin at the right place-defining the issue. Precisely what is being advocated? Until that is settled, there is no need to proceed. In fact, you can't proceed. At least, not very far.

2) ***Identify all Scripture that might bear on the issue, both pro and con***

If there isn't exhaustive Bible knowledge in the group, begin with a concordance or topical reference volume, or a Bible computer program! When it comes to a theological issue, good sources are systematic theology texts. Then of course, in many cases at least, there are many books both for and against. The local church may not have time to read all of them, but it is important to check out an authoritative treatment that holds a position opposing the one advocated. That tends to keep everyone honest and pinpoints Scripture that might correct or balance the position advocated.

<u>What then, should we look for in approaching this subject?</u>

a) <u>Are there any direct commands that demand this change?</u>

Caution, no direct command can be invalidated by some principle we derive. But we must obey the principles, too, and what could be of higher priority than God's own example in the Incarnation, and Paul's example in doing evangelism?" Failing to find a direct command doesn't end the matter. Principles are merely pushed to the next level of inquiry.

<u>b. Are there any principles that demand this approach?</u>

Leaders need to give attention to how they establish a principle from Scripture. Of course, principles may be directly stated in Scripture, such as, "It isn't good for man to be alone." If the principle is directly stated, the principle is just as binding as a specific command, and it is our responsibility to aggressively seek out how God intends us to apply the principle. Principles, unlike specific commands, have a universal application and are thus very powerful. But principles can also be ***derived*** from direct commands. Nowhere does Scripture condemn pornography or voyeurism but forbidding them on the basis of the command, "You shall not lust," is not only acceptable. It is a principle demanded by the command.

And then there is historical precedent. But as a source of deriving authoritative principles that's tricky. But just because Paul did something or even because God did something doesn't necessarily mean that we are bound to do the same thing. History is recorded in Scripture on purpose, and we do well to attempt to identify that purpose. But if Scripture itself does not identify the action or event as an example to follow (or avoid), we may not use it to derive an authoritative principle. Sometimes the historical context commends or condemns an action that is reported. Then we have a clue as to God's intent for his people. Sometimes another passage will point out the good or bad in what was done, as in the case of the deception of the Egyptian midwives. If they are commended for their lies, we are pressed to search for the reason. But if we are not told in Scripture *why* an action is commended or condemned, we are still left with the dilemma of figuring out from other commands or principles whether or not the action illustrates an abiding principle. Pastor Bookman made this point.

Yes, if Christ or God does something, it can't be wrong. At least for God! But that doesn't mean *every*thing Christ did is an example we must follow. For example, his remaining in Israel for his entire ministry-is that the example we should all follow? Christ commanded his disciples to do the opposite. So debate rages over how his atoning death can be an example without undermining his unique role in our salvation. Historic precedent, then, must be handled with care. Look for confirmation in direct teaching, principle or command before seeking to establish principle from history. Even with biblical confirmation of a principle, the history is better used as illustration than prescription.

Worst of all is the notorious argument from silence on which so much debate over ministry is based. If the argument from silence were valid, how do we justify church buildings, denominations, praise bands, children's work, and youth ministry? None appear in the New Testament church. Silence alone can't decide an issue.

Thus there are acceptable ways for establishing what a biblical teaching is, whether direct command or derived principle. The church leadership should do their best to ferret out all the Bible has to say about adapting the message of the gospel to specific audiences. But there's more...

3) ***Determine if any given passage cited is addressed to the contemporary church***

Once the search for God's will in a matter moves to specific passages of Scripture, the first thing that must be ascertained is whether the teaching was intended for all people or just for some. How do you go about deciding? The context itself may indicate a limited audience: "Blessed are you poor," said Jesus. Are all poor of all time blessed? He addressed a particular audience. The context may not clearly limit the audience, but other Scripture may, as in the case of Old Testament ceremonial law, set aside by Jesus or the Apostles (Hebrews 9, 10).

4) ***Exegete the passage carefully to determine the meaning intended by the original author***

We shall risk going far astray if we impose meaning on the text. Most often this has happened historically by imposing a pre-determined doctrinal structure on a given passage. The only way "God so loved the world" can be interpreted as "God so loved the elect" is to have already decided from other Scripture a doctrine of the atonement that requires setting aside the plain meaning of the text. More recently, cultural norms have been given greater authority than the text. But our goal is to determine what the author of any given text had in mind when he wrote it. Establishing those principles of interpretation lies far beyond the scope of today, yet this step may be the most important of all.

5) ***Test for biblical emphasis and balance with other teaching***

On which side does Bible emphasis lie? Since all Scripture is our authority, how can two apparently diverse teachings be reconciled without discounting either? This step requires that we bring into harmony, as best we can, ***all*** Scripture teaches on the subject. Only then are we ready to launch, modify or dismantle the approach--launch the new program or ministry, or dismantle the old. We may need to adjust the approach to bring it under the functional authority of all the teaching of Scripture.

6) ***Implement if demanded by Scripture. Free to implement if not in violation of Scripture and it is judged desirable.***

How do you think a proposal will fare if the entire group in humility (each recognizing their own finitude and fallenness), give faithful diligence to search the Scripture (2 Timothy 2:14-16), and love one another, each preferring the other better than themselves (Philippians 2:1-4)? My guess is that they will decide on the side of biblical emphasis, that the proposal is not prohibited by Scripture and that they could move forward, being careful to safeguard their implementation from violating any basic biblical principle. Making changes is never easy and must be pursued with great care, especially if the initial investigation yields a "free to implement" conclusion. In that case the debate shifts to pragmatic concerns. That shift must be carefully noted and observed, with neither side claiming to be on "God's side!"

In this brief outline of the steps needed to bring proposals under the authority of Scripture, rather than examining the issue to a conclusion, we have mined for illustrations of how the steps could be implemented. [23]

---

[23] For an in-depth analysis of this algorithm, the reader is encouraged to read Robertson McQuilkin's texts, *Five Smooth Stones* and *Understanding and Applying the Bible*.

May 26
Two weapons: Prayer and the Church
Matthew 26:41

"Watch and pray so that you will not fall into temptation." (Matthew 26:41)

Today let's cover two weapons available to us for overcoming temptation: prayer and the church. Perhaps you remember the story of how I put in my prayer notebook "T & T"? Every day I pinpointed the enemies of a renegade tongue and an explosive temper. I didn't wait until the enemy loomed on the horizon and started his barrage of temptations. I started every day with a plea for the Holy Spirit to send in His troops and knock out the enemy in my life. The Spirit knew in advance what I'd face that day. I asked Him to prepare me, to give me strength to win, to alert me to ambushes I wouldn't even see. I didn't pray : "Lord, help me be good today" or, "Lord, make me victorious today ." I prayed about the specific sins that were winning in my life. I targeted my big enemies, and I prayed daily for victory over them. From your own list of personal temptations choose the one that brings you down most and write a model prayer you might use on a daily basis until God gives consistent victory.

The defensive use of the local congregation is primarily to build a support network of people who grow strong together in studying the Word, uniting in prayer, exhorting one another, and setting the example for one another. Together we build spiritual muscle in preparation for our battle over temptation in a way we never could on our own. A high-ranking Air Force officer sat by me on the plane. He had been a pilot during the Vietnam war. Though American planes over North Vietnam took an average of one hit every 12 missions, he came through more than 300 flights unscathed . "What a great pilot!" I exclaimed. "No," he responded, "what a great partner! You always go in pairs and you're responsible to watch the tail of your partner. Your job is to warn him when a missile is coming. If you fail, there's no hope for your partner."

So it is in spiritual warfare-you need a faithful partner to watch out for you! An accountability partner is someone you can share with openly about your temptations, your victories, and your defeats. A word of caution: to share with a partner who is vulnerable to the same temptation you are fighting is usually unwise. A drowning man doesn't need another drowning man to come to the rescue! But one of the greatest defences against temptation is a buddy in the battle, an accountability partner to pray with you about your besetting temptation. If you have a prayer buddy or accountability partner and haven't shared your struggle with temptation, why not do it this week? Consider why you haven't shared your struggle with your prayer buddy. Perhaps you are not serious about overcoming temptation and you want to continue in defeat.

If you don't have an accountability partner, have you prayed about who to enlist? Take time to pray now. Ask God to show you who you can join forces with to help each other overcome temptation. As you go about your activities this week, keep asking God for the person and the courage to enlist such an accountability partner.

We've considered a defensive strategy that uses the weapons of the Spirit to prepare for battle. Only this way can we build a defensive wall around our minds to block out the ideas of the world and counter the onslaughts of the enemy. "Reject and keep on resisting the conforming influences of your environment," says Paul. This we will do with God's Word, with prayer, and with our fellow soldiers.

How might you use these questions to bring consciously and constantly to the bar of Scripture evaluation of the validity of church-based counseling and preaching/teach?

May 27
Is War Just?
Matthew 5:9

"Blessed are the peacemakers, for they shall be called son[1] of God." (Matthew 5:9)

We have in the New Testament the combined affirmation of government force and the lack of condemnation of those exercising that authority, supporting the overall biblical distinction between government and the private individual and the legitimate response of each to evil. Government has a responsibility for restraining evil, protecting its citizens, and maintaining their welfare. If it has a responsibility to protect its citizens from criminals, does it not also have the responsibility to protect them from criminal nations? Christ's teaching of nonresistance, if it is to be harmonized with the rest of biblical teaching on human authority, was not given to nations, police, or parents in their official capacities.

Though the data of the New Testament on the issue of the Christian's participation in war is not direct nor abundant, the basic principles are clear: To be godlike is to make a sacrificial, loving response to maintain a non-vindictive, nonresistant attitude in all personal relationships when one's own rights are at stake; and human government is responsible, with accountability to God, to use force when necessary to assure righteous behavior for its citizenry.

Based on this foundation, what theology of war and peace can be deduced from other biblical principles? Consider three areas of concern: values, God's sovereignty, and man's responsibility.

Values: *War vs. Peace.* Peace is preferable to war, ordinarily. God is on the side of peace, ordinarily. We know this because peace will be the final state of those who have made peace with God. So, "blessed are the peacemakers." Always. But sometimes war is to be preferred to peace and may be the only route to righteous peace. When people speak of war as the lesser of two evils, as when war is said to be preferable to bondage, it cannot mean that God-initiated, God-approved, or God-executed war is a lesser moral evil. If war is ever waged in the will of God, it is a moral good. It may, of course, be a lesser (or greater) human grief than some other value. But peace is not the ultimate value to which all other values should be sacrificed.

Justice vs. Love. The dichotomy is often made in favor of justice or love, but never is it made biblically; true love is tough, and true justice is tempered with mercy. Sometimes punishment is the truest expression of love for the person receiving it as well as for others who need protection from him. God holds both as ultimate values.

Physical vs. Spiritual. Though the claim is often made that even a single human (physical) life has infinite worth, this is not the biblical view. Continued physical life is not the supreme value. Many things are of greater value, such as loving relationships, loyalty, truth, justice. Perhaps even freedom, though only the lonely hero has ever acted on such a premise. He who inordinately clings to earthbound life, Jesus told us, will lose it in the end. Spiritual life is infinitely more important than the physical. Furthermore, spiritual warfare is more significant and more deadly than physical war ever could be.

Time vs. Eternity. The human life span is brief enough, whether cut short by illness, accident, or violence, or lived out to the painful weakness of old age. It is nothing compared to the eternal existence that lies before each human being. To pay too high a price for time is foolish in the light of eternity.

Individual vs. Group. If one individual means so much to God and to the person himself, surely the more people, the greater the value. And so war escalates the cost of human loss immeasurably.

Church vs. State. Church and state both are of value, though neither is of supreme value. Christ and the martyrs laid down their lives for the church, and soldiers lay down their lives for the state. But the modern nation-state is an artificial contrivance at best and certainly has no biblical basis to claim ultimate allegiance. It cannot legitimately control the church, nor demand sinful behavior of the Christian. On the other hand, the church, though speaking prophetically to the state, should not use the force of the state to accomplish its spiritual goals. Furthermore, the church is a brotherhood that knows no national boundary, and citizens of heaven have stronger ties with Christians of other lands than with non-Christians in their transient citizenship here on earth. The church is eternal and God's own, so its value must be far greater.

Human Rights and Freedom vs. Order. Rights and freedom are valuable, but none are of absolute value. Every person's rights are limited, if by nothing else, by the freedom of others. Order, then, adjudicates among the rights and freedoms of those whose lives are associated. Tyranny is order gone mad, and anarchy is freedom gone mad. And yet, Scripture has very little to say about civil rights and freedoms and a great deal to say about order. To overthrow order for the sake of rights and freedoms may be too high a price to pay.

Note that a biblical resolution of the tension in each value seems to lean more toward a "just war" position but note also that the issue of values is very complex.

God's Sovereignty. Though human beings are responsible for their behavior, individual and corporate, God is in sovereign control and will bring his purposes to a successful conclusion, whether through human instrumentality, just or unjust, or through divine intervention. He will not shuffle off the stage of time in red-faced defeat. Justice and righteousness will triumph at last, and in this confidence his people can rest, whether oppressed or free.

Man's Responsibility for War. Humankind may not lay the blame for war on God or Satan, for man is responsible for war, one of the most grievous results of his sinfulness. Because of this sinful, selfish disposition, conflict is inevitable, and for this sinful behavior he is accountable to God.

A second aspect of man's responsibility is that humans have been chosen as instruments both of God's judgment and grace. God has chosen civil governments as the primary agents of his judgment, and the church as the primary agent of his grace. If he waited for perfectly good and wise people to mediate his purposes on earth, his purposes would go unaccomplished. So human government—whether family or state or employer—is hobbled by its own finitude and fallenness. Nevertheless, it is God's own instrument. Yet always our hope is in God.

May 28
Considerations in Counseling
Psalm 1:1-2

"Blessed is the man who walks not in the counsel of the wicked, nor stands in the way of sinners, nor sits in the seat of scoffers; but his delight is in the law of the LORD, and on his law he meditates day and night. He is like a tree planted by streams of water that yields its fruit in its season, and its leaf does not wither. In all that he does, he prospers." (Psalm 1:1-2)

One time I spoke to the Evangelical Theological Society on the theme "The Behavioral Sciences Under the Authority of Scripture." I told the delegates that while we sat and debated the finer points of theology, the pastors and missionaries had left us for the psychologists and anthropologists. To illustrate I told them of two recent classes at our school, Columbia Biblical Seminary. A small upstairs class of twelve students met with the dean of Evangelical theologians, Carl F. H. Henry, while downstairs in the auditorium 120 students met with a newly minted psychologist, Larry Crabb. That was a paradigm for the future, I told them. And so it proved to be.

A quarter century later I was in a conference of several hundred pastors where I shared the platform with a world-renowned psychotherapist. In the breakout sessions he would deal with psychological issues for several hundred pastors and I would, by request, introduce the study course, *Life in the Spirit,* to a handful of pastors. As I taught, my mind wandered. I contemplated what psychology could do and what the Holy Spirit could do.

We accept with gratitude every advance of medical science and celebrate the ways in which our bodies feel better and last longer. But we don't expect the doctor to give us eternal life. We have to go to the evangelist for that! But when it comes to counseling, somehow we tend to forget that deep and permanent healing and health of our inner person ultimately awaits the work of the Holy Spirit. For the most part, we aren't doing our behavioral sciences under the authority of Scripture.

At one point at Columbia Biblical Seminary we needed to find professors of counseling/psychology who were actually doing their work under the authority of Scripture. The search was not easy. I developed a check list of key questions to test the extent to which a prospective teacher did his work under the authority of Scripture. When the reader needs to choose a counselor, perhaps these questions will guide the choice.

1. *Who needs professional counseling?* When the response is that the majority of people have their "trusters" or "choosers" broken so they *cannot* obey the injunctions of Scripture until the professional "fixes" them, I think, "It's too bad the Holy Spirit didn't know that and make provision in Scripture." When the candidate responds that they do their work on the assumption that, with the Holy Spirit's enabling, anyone can understand, trust, and obey Scripture, unless there are organic reasons for the dysfunction, I know we have a candidate who attempts to do counseling under the authority of Scripture.

2. *What are the major causes of dysfunctional attitudes and behavior?* If the answers are limited to early environment and present circumstances, and sin as the root cause is left out of the equation, I know we have a therapist who doesn't do his work under the authority of Scripture.

3. *What are the major factors in what a person becomes?* Here I'm fishing for the four basic factors Scripture teaches, not the single factor of environment, especially not environmental determinism. True, early environment is recognized in Scripture as a factor, as is the impact of inherited factors such as a sinful disposition. But far more than heredity and environment, Scripture emphasizes from start to finish two factors: human responsibility for choices made and the intervening grace of God. If these two factors do not dominate therapy, how can it be said to be under the authority of Scripture?

4. *Are feelings morally neutral?* Of course, the therapist should not go to the other extreme and promote false guilt, when the subject is fighting off temptation, not sinning; and he should certainly promote honesty about one's feelings. But to make all feelings morally neutral is to undercut a major emphasis of Scripture. The Bible holds the basic problem to be of "the heart" and the victory promised is not just for bad actions but a bad heart, yes, for wrong feelings.

5. *What is the goal of therapy?* If the goal is diagnosis and developing coping strategies to modify behavior, and no hope is offered of supernatural transformation by the power of the Holy Spirit to ever greater likeness to Jesus, to a restored image, how can the therapy be of deep and lasting value? Naturalistically-based psychology can help in diagnosing the problem and helping develop strategies for more healthful attitudes and behavior, but is impotent to transform the essence of human nature. Restoration of God's image isn't in the objectives of most practitioners, yet that is the core message of Scripture.

7. Is a person responsible when unable to change behavior? The Bible holds us responsible for our choices and what we become, but it does much more: it offers differing degrees of supernatural change.

8. *Are any common counseling or therapeutic techniques unacceptable for a Christian therapist?* Many hold that none are off-limits if they work. Express your anger, it's unhealthy to hold it in, use pornography, if necessary, to improve your marriage, lie if it's the loving thing to do. But Scripture makes no such allowance for breaking ethical standards.

9. *How important is self-love to wholeness?* This usually lies at the core of therapy, but to be under the authority of Scripture one must delve into two other loves- love for God, and love for others. My wife and I were reading a devotional book that insisted we are commanded to love ourselves. I asked for the references, and she read them off. All were repeats of the command to love *others*—"love your neighbors as you love yourselves."

How might you use these questions to bring consciously and constantly to the bar of Scripture evaluation of the validity of church-based counseling and preaching/teaching?

May 29
Desire
Romans 12:2

"Do not be conformed to this world, but be transformed by the renewal of your mind, that by testing you may discern what is the will of God, what is good and acceptable and perfect." (Romans 12:2)

Temptation always masquerades-it looks so appealing, promises so much good . That's why it's a temptation . If it wore its own face, it would be so ugly we'd run! The first task, then, is to unmask the temptation-identify it for exactly what it is: lust, covetousness, pride, unbelief, or just plain self-love. These enemies take away the power or filling of the Holy Spirit in our lives, and they grieve Him. Our sins of unbelief and self-love reveal themselves in the temptations of lust, covetousness, and pride. In developing your plan to overcome temptation, you begin with unconditional surrender to the will of God. That propels you out of a dangerous no man's land or out from behind enemy lines and solidly on God's side. Thus you became ready for the next step-to identify the enemy. The underlying source of your temptation may not be that easy to spot, so you may have bypassed that step and identified the temptation itself. That isn't always easy either since temptation fights dirty; but you can spot any disguised temptation by focusing Scripture on your situation. Finally, make your choice about that temptation. Choose right and grow stronger, choose wrong and grow weaker.

Sometimes distinguishing between legitimate desire and sinful desire is difficult. Is this new TV a legitimate need or coveting what God doesn't intend? Is my reaction to this situation righteous indignation or sinful anger? Is the pain I feel justifiable, or am I so unhappy because my ego took a heavy hit?

We must not run to the extreme and assume that the Holy Spirit within is all we need. He deliberately provided other means of knowing His will, so we are sure to go down in defeat if we neglect any of them. The Spirit is no substitute for the other means of understanding; He's their energizer. What about depending on our conscience? "Let your conscience be your guide," we say. But natural conscience is a very unreliable guide since it is no more than our judgment in the realm of right versus wrong. That judgment has been programmed by home, school, and society, not to mention our own sinful inclinations. As a result, we seem to have infinite capacity to con ourselves into believing what we want to believe. For conscience to be a reliable guide we must constantly

- be transformed into a new creation by the Holy Spirit.
- use Scripture as a guide for the decision-making process.
- keep in tune with the Spirit.
- develop judgment by consistent, obedient practice.

I had just returned from a 12-year TV famine. In Japan we rarely watched TV and understood little of what we did see. Besides, Japanese TV was very tame by American standards. I was astounded to hear friends guffawing over sexual innuendos in a popular show. "They put garbage like that on television?" I remonstrated. Twenty years passed. I hadn't watched TV much, but enough to get a feel for the programming. Suddenly I woke up to an astonishing change in me. For a year or more I had been periodically watching reruns of the same show I had criticized previously and feeling grateful for an oasis of good family fare in the moral Badlands of network television. What had happened? I had been molded by my world into its way of thinking. And Paul says, "Stop!" Today's verse might be literally translated: "Resist the conforming influences of your environment and keep on resisting." Who will deny that popular media is hell-bent (literally) on cultivating lust, covetousness, and pride? And I was letting it happen to me. In fact, I recently made a covenant with myself to stop surfing the channels. When I finally got honest with myself and God, I had to admit what I was actually looking for-and it wasn't purity, contentment, and humility!

Sometimes I watched TV just to relax and unwind after a difficult day but doing so ate up priceless time. Even worse, it was subtly molding me into a different kind of person. Paul says to resist and keep resisting-eternal vigilance is the price of spiritual freedom. To take this proactive stance we must do four things : a) be involved with a warfare mentality, b) decide firmly on whose side we belong, c) identify our major enemies, and d) take hold of or use our weapons. In the fight for our spiritual freedom the Bible, prayer, and the church are our frontline weapons. The Spirit uses them in combination to create an effective defensive strategy. Let's examine one of these weapons.

Scan the war stories recorded in Genesis 3:1-6 and Matthew 4:1-11. Here we have deadly battles. First is the battle between Satan and Eve, then between Satan and Jesus-the welfare of billions depending on the outcome of each battle. Eve met the enemy with a background of perfect heredity and a perfect environment while Jesus' heritage on His mother's side was a fallen humanity and His environment was a sin-cursed world. But Eve lost, Jesus won.

Eve quoted God's Word, but she wasn't all that committed to its authority. She quickly abandoned her only defense and accepted the enemy's word over God's. Satan cynically used Scripture to push his ungodly ends. Only Jesus used the Word of God as His weapon. He won! You will, too. But you must stockpile your ammunition, or you won't have it available at the time of testing. Will you today commit today to the authority of God's word? Yielded and Obedient? Stockpiling ammunition?

May 30
Spiritual Formation
Colossians 3:10

" put on the new self, which is being renewed in knowledge after the image of its creator." (Colossians 3:10)

When it comes to promoting spiritual formation, three grand themes of Scripture will control my content: God's standard for the Christian life--what he expects of me; God's provision for me to reach that standard; and my responsibility in accessing that provision. These themes are pervasive in Scripture, but they're more than pervasive. Actually, they are the point of revelation. Consider them briefly:

God's standard. God's standard is no less than God himself. From Genesis where we are created in his likeness to Revelation where the image is fully restored, from Jesus' command that we are to be perfect as the Father is perfect (Matthew 5:58) to Paul's assurance that the new self is being renewed after the likeness of him in whose image it was originally created (Colossians 3:9,10), our goal is God. We must ever hold in pragmatic detail and specific application God's standard for the Christian life. That could be dreadfully distressing but for God's provision, so the second great theme of Scripture is God's provision for our salvation in it's full splendor from initial forgiveness through the final denouement when we shall be like him for we shall see him as he is (I John 3:2). The standard must be coupled always with the provision.

God's provision. Enter the Holy Spirit, the one who created us on God's pattern in the first place (Genesis 1:27), who convicts us of our hopelessness and helplessness (John 16:8), who breathes new life into us (John 3:6), changing us into altogether new creations with vastly new potentialities (2 Corinthians 5:17), who takes up residence as our inside companion (John 14:17), the one who gave us the Book in the first place (2 Timothy 3:16, 17) and who daily illumines it's meaning, the one who transforms us from one degree of Jesus' glorious character to another (2 Corinthians 3:18). The person of the Holy Spirit is the provision of the triune God for living godly in an ungodly world.

In the church I attended for two years I loved the profound expository preaching. Gradually, however, I began to realize something was missing. He obviously believed strongly in human sinfulness. He also believed in justification and glorification. But, I gradually came to understand, he didn't believe in much in between. By selecting only those passages that advanced his "doctrines of grace," as he termed them, we were left with little hope for the interim between initial and final salvation. But God has made full provision in the person of the Holy Spirit, empowerment to be transformed from one degree of his glorious character to another.

Just as the standard is God himself, so the provision. But, you will ask, how do I connect? How does it happen? So we must be faithful to the implications of our personal responsibility for accessing that provision.

My responsibility. The access code is so simple. And the glorious truth is, it's available to all! Faith. Faith for initial salvation, faith for transformation, faith for growth toward our goal. "*...let us rid ourselves of all that weighs us down, of the sinful habit that clings so closely, and run, with all endurance, the race for which we are entered, our eyes fixed on Jesus, on whom faith depends from start to finish*" (Hebrews 12: 1,2 Knox, NEB). Why do so many church members seem to be spiritually on hold? Of course, a spiritual plateau isn't really possible--we're either spiraling up toward every greater likeness to Jesus and ever greater intimacy with him or we're spiraling downward, away from that tight connection, ever less like him. So what must we do when the spiral up falters, what's gone wrong? We say faith is the key, but why doesn't it seem to work? Why doesn't the connection seem to produce the promised results?

Perhaps there's a disconnect after all, perhaps we only plugged into the positive pole of faith, neglecting the negative pole. Bible faith--whether for salvation or sanctification--is bi-polar. Repentance toward God and faith toward our Lord Jesus Christ (Acts 20:21). If the "faith" is just intellectual assent to certain essential truths, a person is no more saved than the devils who also believe (James 2:19). And sanctification? Yield and trust, the same two poles of biblical faith. Neglect one or the other and growth stops because there's a disconnect.

These if we are serious about nurturing spiritual formation: God's standard--himself; God's provision-- the Spirit; and our responsibility--faith. How do you line up with these three themes in spiritual formation? Which of the three are you strong? Which needs further growth? How will you address growing in spiritual formation?

May 31
Fidelity
Ephesians 5:22-23

"Wives, submit to your own husbands, as to the Lord. For the husband is the head of the wife even as Christ is the head of the church, his body, and is himself its Savior." (Ephesians 5:22-23)

The marriage relationship is used throughout Scripture to instruct us concerning God's desired relationship with people. God is love and from the overflow of this love among Father, Son, and Spirit came the creation of a being on the same pattern, designed to love and to be loved as in the divine model. Which is the ultimate reality, which the reflection? In a good reflection it is sometimes difficult to distinguish. However, in one sense both the divine/human and the husband/wife relationships are real and interrelated. The male-female is transient and imperfect because human beings are finite and sin-damaged. The divine-human is eternal. But the more we learn of one relationship, the more we are able to understand the other.

Stress and conflict in marriage are said to damage seriously 60 to 90 percent of Christian marriages. Seminars, books, and counselors devoted to treating this epidemic increase geometrically, but the infection seems to spread and deepen. The vast majority of these "combat zones" do not really need sexual or psychological adjustment. Often the cures advocated simply apply Band-Aids to cancers and drive the true illness deeper inside. The root problem in most cases is old-fashioned sinful selfishness. Unity is impossible without self-giving as a way of life on the part of both mates. If one or both insist on personal rights and personal fulfillment rather than personal self-sacrifice in love for the other, true and lasting unity is impossible.

The most serious violation of marriage is adultery, excoriated in the Old Testament second only to idolatry, and in the New Testament, second to none. Infidelity, though commonplace in most societies, has had few advocates in Western society until recently. But now adultery is promoted by popular media and many behavioral scientists.

Yet laws of purity, built around God's wonderful gift of sexuality, are, like all his laws, designed for our good (Deut. 10:12-13). Violation means loss, not just because God promises punishment, though that would be reason enough for careful obedience. But God has established these standards to protect us from the loss that is inherent in one kind of behavior, and to direct us to the rewards that are the natural result of another. Violation of God's law of purity, just as violation of God's law of gravity, brings destruction. Keeping God's laws promotes one's own welfare. Fidelity in marriage is good because it maximizes the potential relationship between mates; it maximizes sex itself; it protects the more vulnerable wife; it provides the atmosphere needed for children to grow up as whole people; and it safeguards a person's relationship with God.

Marriage is too good to risk diminishing its potential. People were made for a loving, permanent, exclusive, secure, intimate relationship. Sex is a delightful part of this. It enhances and brings to a periodic exquisite climax the enduring unity of spirit. But when physical intimacy is pulled out of the various elements of a marriage relationship and used separately, it fouls the whole relationship. Trust can never be quite the same again; a third party often intrudes on the intimacy, in the mind of one partner or both. True unity is fractured. In fact, so serious is the rupture that Christ indicated it could legitimately be affirmed as total and permanent (Matt. 5:32), though this is not a recommended or required response to infidelity.

Fidelity in marriage maximizes sex itself. The discipline of focusing one's mental fantasies on the marriage partner alone has the great benefit of intensifying sexual fulfillment. Furthermore, the pure in heart are safeguarded from the deception of an unreal world created by skillful photographers and makeup artists. The illusion created constantly in our society is that the world is filled with young, beautiful, available, eager, perfect bodies awaiting the conquest of the smart playboy or playgirl. One is easily seduced into thinking he is missing out on something, and by feeding his imagination on this fare he sets himself up for failure in a marriage that cannot compete with the mirage. If he had never indulged his mind in such a dream world, he might have discovered more quickly and more fully that sexual fulfillment itself is most intense, most enduring, and constantly growing only in the commitment of two who have become one flesh exclusively and permanently. The insecurity of a tentative relationship or of a defiled marriage cuts the heart out of the sexual activity itself. When one is not sure he or she is worthy of an ultimate, permanent love commitment or whether she or he is simply a desirable or available sex object, the sex-fun itself has a hollow ring, a bitter aftertaste, decreasing satisfaction.

Some have held that variety intensifies sexual pleasure. Perhaps so. Therefore the loving partner uses imagination in sex play, suspense, surprise. But variety in partners loses all the other ingredients that go to make the sex experience the climactic ecstasy it was designed to be.

Fidelity is also a prerequisite for the kind of home atmosphere that grows children in wholeness to maturity. The love, the faithfulness, the integrity, the loyalty are all essential elements. Infidelity tells a child, "Your mother is not worth much, and your father is a liar and a cheat. Furthermore, honor is not nearly as important as pleasure. In fact, my son, my own satisfaction is more important than you." Such a home is about the worst atmosphere in which a child could be raised. The greatest gift parents can give their children is the demonstration of faithful, loving commitment to each other.

Finally, fidelity in marriage is necessary if a person would be accepted by God. Sin separates from God, and impurity in mind and body is one way to break fellowship with God. More important, it is one way to hurt him grievously. Not only does the cheating partner harm himself, his mate, and his children, he is "crucifying the Son of God" (Hebrews 6:6, NEB). Violations of one another are ultimately violations of God himself as Joseph testified (Genesis 39:9), David experienced (Psalm 51:4), and the prophet proclaimed (Amos 2:7). Want tightness with God? Choose fidelity. For yourself, your children, your church and your God.

June 1
Knowing God's Will in Matters Not Revealed in Scripture
Psalm 23:3

"He restores my soul. He leads me in paths of righteousness for his name's sake." (Psalm 23:3)

How can you know God's will? Through the Bible, as the most explicit way. But suppose you need to know His will about something that isn't revealed in Scripture—nonmoral choices that we often face in life. You may be puzzling over what career path He wants you to take. Does He want your wife to be healed or for you to care for her full-time? Does He want you to save this money for retirement or give it away? Does He want you to rebuke an erring church member or keep silent? The decisions are never-ending, and a serious disciple wants to please God in the choices made.
Name something about which you need the Lord's guidance that does not seem to be addressed in Scripture.

With most biblical truth we humans seem to find it much easier to go to an extreme than to stay at the center of biblical tension. So it is with guidance. Some people use Scripture in a sort of magical way, looking for words that seem to speak directly to their current dilemma or, on the other hand, denying that God has any particular will for nonmoral choices.

How comforting it would have been, when we were trying to decide whether to leave our educational work in the mountains of North Carolina, to find a Scripture that spoke directly to our situation: "You've been traveling around this hill country long enough" (Deut. 2:3). Comforting? Wrongheaded! It is wrong to use Scripture to say something the Holy Spirit never intended to communicate when He inspired the author to write it. The Bible is given to communicate a specific meaning, and our task is to determine the meaning the author had in mind, not to use words totally out of context because we see a correlation between those words and our present circumstances.

But there's the possibility of running to the opposite extreme. A once popular book captured the imaginations of thousands of believers by insisting that, counter to historical understandings of divine guidance, God does not have an individual will or plan for each believer. Go to Scripture to find moral guidance, he argued, and beyond that, anything an obedient disciple chooses is OK. I admit that the chief focus of God's will and God's guidance in Scripture is moral guidance; He promises to *lead us in right paths for His name's sake* (see Psalm 23:3). But God also guides us in the nonmoral choices of life—where to go, what to do, how to do it. One of God's great gifts is guidance; He leads His sheep each step of the way.

God indeed has a plan for each life. He is even more interested than we are in our discovering and fulfilling that plan. But how does He guide us toward His purposes? I heard a speaker once say that he looks for four "running lights" to line up on the runway before he takes off. When they're in line, he said, he moves. Then he added, "Often, however, I'm not 100 percent sure till I'm in flight!"

The running lights are: the Bible: the commands or principles of Scripture that address the choice; the voice of the church or those to whom I am responsible: individual counsel by wise and godly individuals as well as official corporate decisions; circumstances; and fourthly, inner conviction. Remember, all four lights have to be in line. It's not wise to base a decision only on inner conviction or the counsel of a friend who might have a vested interest in the outcome. What does each running light indicate about the decision you identified earlier for which you need the Lord's guidance?

June 2
Wings of Praise
Exodus 15:2

"He restores my soul. He leads me in paths of righteousness for his name's sake." Exodus 15:2

It was a dry time in my pilgrimage. My life had gone stale and times of prayer had become a dull routine, so I went away on one of those retreats. "What's wrong?" I pled with God to renew me, to revive my spirit, to restore a robust faith. After several hours, I sort of wore out on that approach and, a little listlessly, turned to praise. Once again I re-learned the lesson: a heavy spirit lifts on the wings of praise. Here's what I wrote in my journal, the prayer that set my spirit free, renewed intimacy in the relationship with my Lover, induced a surge of faith:

Father, thank you for your marvelous gifts: salvation and hope, the Savior's loving presence within and about, the blessed Spirit who transforms and empowers, your friendship, incredible as that is. Thank you, thank you, for the wonderful Book. And thank you for the gift of such a magnificent world: the flowers, the grass and trees, the lovely birds and wondrous beasts, mountains and seas, streams and mighty rivers, rocks and sands and all things beautiful. What a glorious idea marriage was! And family. Friends so loyal and loving. And humankind, displaying your image-imprint, creating magnificent art and literature and music. I love fine architecture and astounding technologies. You've given me work to do that counts for eternity. The gifts of health and abilities and, especially, my wife. Thank you for your gifts.

But best of all, Father, I'm forever grateful for who you are. Every characteristic speaks your majestic God-hood. But from among them all, in splendid array, I focus often on your wisdom, power, and love. Wisdom to know all things, power to do all you will, and love to count me in. What more could I ask? I could ask for holiness, for what kind of god would we have if he could figure everything out, accomplish anything and felt affectionately toward us, but was crooked, no model of right and dispenser of injustice? And what if you were unpredictable and given to change? How insecure we would be! And what if you had a beginning or—worse—an end? That would be the ultimate insecurity. But no, you are all there is of perfection, beyond all imagination. And today I bow in humble gratitude.

Not immortal literature, you say? But when those words burst from deep within me at three a.m. in a borrowed mountain hideaway, my hobbled, heavy spirit took flight. I was free again! Praise will do that. Moses, on a grander level, experienced a surge of incredible faith as he rehearsed to God all His excellencies. Exodus 15:2: *"The LORD is my strength and my song, and he has become my salvation; this is my God, and I will praise him, my father's God, and I will exalt him."* Moses' prayer focused on God, worshiping Him, praising Him. He constantly reminded God of His mighty acts and magnificent promises (eg. see Exodus 32:11-13). Praise, fixing our attention on God, is a powerful builder of confidence in Him.

There are other ways Moses shows the way to build trust. First of all, to trust Him we must companion with Him. And in companioning with Him, thanksgiving, praise, adoration—worship, to sum it up—builds the trust bonds best of all. How about setting apart next Sunday afternoon, or a few hours on your next day off, and write out all the things you like about God and all the things you're grateful for that he's done for you?

June 3
Expectations
2 Corinthians 13:9-11

"For we are glad when we are weak and you are strong. Your restoration is what we pray for. .... Aim for restoration, comfort one another, agree with one another, live in peace; and the God of love and peace will be with you." (2 Cor. 13:9,11)

Paul prays for the perfection of the Christians in Corinth and tells them to aim for it! Before going on, brainstorm for a moment. What might result from a person seeking to live with unrealistic expectations?

For many, however, the danger is discouragement in not being able to achieve or maintain what they expect. Many become so discouraged they drop out altogether. Unrealistic expectations lead to self-deception through rationalization, especially by redefining sin or a particular sin so we no longer acknowledge the attitude or act as sin or hypocrisy from knowing we fall short but professing otherwise. Unrealistic expectations can also lead to discouragement from expecting perfection and failing to achieve it.

We've spoken of expectations that are too low and too high, but a strange combination of the two exists. This odd hybrid can't be found in any church's formal teaching, but it is common in Christian practice. People say, "I'm not half as sinful as most people" and think that's good enough (see 2 Cor. 10:12). Another variety of the same syndrome is the Christian who prays, "forgive us of our many sins," but doesn't pause to think of any specific wrong he needs to right. Both may be jealous of another person or critical in spirit, but quite satisfied with their own level of achievement. Their expectations are too low by biblical standards, but their evaluation of themselves is way too high! They, too, qualify as misguided in expectations; and they, too, may be self-deceived or hypocritical.

We've looked at some of the results of holding unrealistic expectations about our potential for life. Before pressing on to *"take hold of that for which Christ Jesus took hold of me"* (Phil. 3:12), we need to accept the biblical limitations on our expectations. In this life we'll never be absolutely perfect as God is, without sin, though when we see Jesus we shall be like Him (1 John 3:2). On the other hand, we must never settle for anything short of his promised triumphant life in the Spirit. Before examining that theme, let's pause and give thanks that the false expectations are false!

We might ask, "Can we be perfect even as God is perfect?" Never for a moment do I love as Christ loved. I never— and never shall in this life—have his level of courage, of purity, of contentment, of faith. Yet that's my goal. I intend to move in that direction. But notice, I said that I don't get up in the morning and say, 'today I'm going to get irritated 4 times, lust six times, covet my friend's new house, worry for 10 minutes, and grouse about certain things that keep bugging me.' I don't intend to do those things; I don't choose to do them. And when I find myself thinking that way, when my falling short of Christlikeness rises to the conscious level, I immediately cry for help and by God's grace quit.

That deliberate kind of sin that calls for total success—the new believer doesn't cut down his bank robberies from 10 to 2 a year, he doesn't try to seduce fewer women than he used to, she doesn't quit cheating on state income tax while still fudging a little on the feds, quarrel only with those colleagues who're totally unreasonable, talk about people hurtfully only when it's true. They just quit! And hallelujah! the new "me" with the new inside Partner has that capability.

June 4
Oneness in Marriage
Ephesians 5:31

"Therefore a man shall leave his father and mother and hold fast to his wife, and the two shall become one flesh." (Ephesians 5:31)

The first purpose of marriage is loving companionship—the unity of two in a relationship mirroring the nature of God himself (see Eph. 5:22-23). One way to violate this unity from the outset is to marry an unbeliever. Marriage to an unbeliever reveals a very low view of marriage, of one's relationship to God, or of both. For unity to be complete, oneness in spirit is the prime requisite. If the most important relationship in life is with God, how can a couple have unity at any real depth when one is with God and the other is not?

Not only does marriage to an unbeliever diminish the potential for fulfilling the first purpose in marriage, it also puts in great jeopardy the second purpose—having children in a God-fearing home environment. Finally, it completely rules out the third purpose of demonstrating the relationship God desires with his people. If the believing partner gives up his relationship with the Lord, some measure of unity can be built on a godless foundation as if both were unbelievers. But unless the unbeliever comes to Christ, no Christian marriage can be achieved, and no oneness at the deepest levels can be experienced.

At any rate, the Bible expressly prohibits such a union (Deut. 7:3-4; Neh. 13:23-27; 1 Cor. 7:39; 2 Cor. 6:14-18). Of course, one who is married to an unbeliever should remain married (1 Cor. 7:12-13). Though union will be limited, it is better than divorce, according to Paul.

How should others relate to a Christian who is planning marriage to an unbeliever, besides prayer against the consummation of the plan, and biblical counsel? Any minister of the gospel who officiates at a marriage between a believer and an unbeliever participates in the sin. Having said this, however, it should be emphasized that Christian people and pastors need so to relate to the Christian who is bent on unbiblical marriage that a trusting relationship is maintained even if the advice is rejected. Because the continuance of the marriage becomes the will of God once it has been consummated, it is important for Christian people to help the Christian partner come to repentance for disobeying God, and to assist in building as true a unity as possible in the mixed marriage.

"What is the root cause of disunity?" you might ask. Stress and conflict in marriage are said to damage seriously 60 to 90 percent of Christian marriages. Seminars, books, and counselors devoted to treating this epidemic increase geometrically, but the infection seems to spread and deepen. The vast majority of these "combat zones" do not really need sexual or psychological adjustment. Often the cures advocated simply apply Band-Aids to cancers and drive the true illness deeper inside. The root problem in most cases is old-fashioned sinful selfishness. "Lack of maturity is at the bottom of 90 percent of all marital problems," said widely read counselor Norman Vincent Peale.[9i] Unity is impossible without self-giving as a way of life on the part of both mates. If one or both insist on personal rights and personal fulfillment rather than personal self-sacrifice in love for the other, true and lasting unity is impossible.[24]

Whether married or not, we can pray for marriages around us. For love for the other that if needed, one sacrifices personal rights for the well-being of the family. We pray for ourselves that self-giving marks our relationships. Pray there is companionship and unity, demonstrating the relationship God desires with his people. Love…..Unity….Sacrifice….Pleasure….Oneness with God and with one another.

---

[24] IBE (2014), 234-235.

June 5
Created God-Compatible
John 14:23

"If anyone loves Me, he will keep My word. My Father will love him, and We will come to him and make Our home with him" (John 14:23)

In 1957 a group of monks was relocating a clay Buddha from their temple to make way for a new highway. When the crane lifted the idol, it cracked. Seeing a bright glint in the crack, the head monk ran for hammer and chisel, and soon a solid-gold Buddha was revealed, today worth perhaps three hundred million dollars. It seems several hundred years ago the Burmese army was poised to strike Siam, now Thailand, so the monks disguised their precious treasure with clay. The monks were slaughtered and with them their secret, a golden treasure hidden in a clay masquerade.[1]

And so with many Christians: a golden treasure covered in layers of common clay, our fallen, cracked humanity hiding the reality within. Through believers God wants to put His glorious character on display, but we are hiding our true character beneath all-too-human attitudes and actions. It doesn't have to be this way. The Master Sculptor intends to chisel away the clay and let the golden treasure stand revealed.

We've been studying God's law to learn His standard for the way we are supposed to live. As damaged vessels, we aren't capable of living up to God's standard. Our quest today will be to discover God's resources for living in obedience to His standard.

God's plan for cracking off the clay to leave Jesus on display is His provision of the Holy Spirit, but it seems most Christians are disinterested in, afraid of, or ignorant of the Spirit's role I hope you can understand that the living Spirit of God is your inside companion who wants to remake you in the image of Jesus.

When you accepted Jesus as your Savior and Lord, He sent the Holy Spirit to live inside you. *"He is the Spirit of truth. ... He remains with you and will be in you,"* Jesus promised in John 14:17. In some mysterious way all three members of the Trinity live within. Jesus explained, *"If anyone loves Me, he will keep My word. My Father will love him, and We will come to him and make Our home with him"* (v. 23). But the Spirit is the point person of the Trinity, the executive who carries out God's purposes. It is the Spirit who works in us to transform our mind and character into the image of Christ. It is He who teaches us God's ways and enables us to live in obedience to the standards He set forth in His Word.

To be transformed for deeper relationship with God, we were created to be God-compatible. The Holy Spirit played a role in creation, hovering over the formless waste (see Gen. 1:2). And the Spirit created each of us. Job professed: *"The Spirit of God has made me, and the breath of the Almighty gives me life."* (Job 33:4) He created us in God's image (see Gen. 1:27).

Porpoises, pandas, monkeys, and ants are marvelous creatures. Porpoises communicate with signals, maybe even a language. But no dictionaries yet! Pandas are toolmakers, breaking off sticks to probe for food. But no automobiles yet! Monkeys are smart and mischievous; they do bad things. But none have been seen to blush! Ants build complex cities, but no one has ever discovered a temple or a church in one of them.

Other characteristics come closer to what Scripture means by being created in God's image. Unlike the animals, we are born with a moral consciousness and a spirit, so we are designed to be God-compatible. We were made to fit in a relationship with the Almighty. Love doesn't grow much between two who are incompatible, so God made us in some respects like Him so that we would be able to share in the love relationship of Father, Son, and Spirit.

Our God-compatibility is the bedrock of all hope for anything more than animal contentedness: we are specifically designed for intimate companionship with the infinite One. So there's hope that we can have a meaningful relationship with Him. Wow, what a privilege! What might being God-compatible mean to you and your life today?

June 6
The Loving Husband
Ephesians 5:23-28

"Husbands, love your wives, as Christ loved the church and gave himself up for her"(Ephesians 5:25)

The first and predominant responsibility for the husband is to *love* his wife, and the standard in that relationship is the way Christ loved the church (Eph. 5:22-23). He loved the church through total sacrifice. Although no mere mortal can attain this goal fully, this is the standard by which a man must ever evaluate his performance as a husband.

How does Christ love the church? There are many ways to consider this, but think of what Paul alludes to, the dark hours on the cross when he gave his life. Five of the seven sayings were on behalf of others.

"Father, forgive them." Forgiveness is the standard—and he forgave even when they did not ask for it. Long-suffering, forbearance. Even when she usurps my role? Yes, even when she crucifies you—that is God's kind of loving.

"Today you will be with me in Paradise." He accepted the sinner as he was, the ultimate failure, hanging on a cross. So with one's wife, fastidious or sloppy, disorganized or computer-perfect, young and beautiful or aging and overweight—acceptance. By grace, introduce her to paradise.

"Mother, here is your son; Son, here is your mother." Incredibly selfless, kind, and gentle. He makes provision for all her needs, all her weaknesses, even while he himself is in mortal agony.

"Why have you forsaken me?" The ultimate sacrifice—his most precious right, union with his Father. But what of my right to time for my own fun or my important ministry? God's kind of love is to forsake all rights necessary to love her well, to choose and act in her best interests as a way of life.

"It is finished." Faithful to the end. To the end of the argument, to the end of the day, to the end of life.

The husband's first provision is for the wife's spiritual welfare, which is encouraged by means of daily Bible study and prayer together. Closely associated with this is provision for full development of a wife's intellectual potential. For the husband to live on the sacrifice of his young wife while he goes to school and then to shut her up at home with no opportunity for growth is to fail in loving provision. Her emotional health is his responsibility as well. Provision physically means protection, but increasingly the greatest need for protection is from the husband himself. Physical abuse should be unthinkable, and the standard must be never to touch her in anger.

Ever.

Of course there are other, more deadly, ways of harming—verbal abuse, psychological wounds—and from all these his responsibility is to protect her. If any home is caught up in un-Christlike behavior, outside help should be sought by the wife if the husband is not man enough and Christian enough to seek it.

Finally, provision includes social relationships. A husband's desire in relationships with those outside the home may not dictate the extent of social involvement.

Limits of Responsibility. Although loyalty to one's wife takes precedence over loyalty to parents, to children, or to anyone else, loyalty to God takes highest precedence. When and how is one to "hate his wife" (Luke 14:26) or behave as if he were unmarried (1 Cor. 7:29)?

A new idolatry has crept into evangelical thinking, the idolatry of family. All resources of time and money are reserved for family above church, family above service to God, family above work, family above national security. This attitude has come as a reaction to earlier attitudes that put wife and children last. Correction was desperately needed. But there are times when the interests of the kingdom of God demand that a husband "hate" his wife and children—that is, that he choose to sacrifice some potential benefit of theirs for the sake of fulfilling God's purposes in the world. Thus the husband (and/or wife) has chosen for a particular time in a particular way to behave "as if he were not married." The order of Scripture is clear: self-sacrifice as needed for the welfare of wife and children, family sacrifice as needed for the welfare of the kingdom of God. [25] That balance is found in an intimate walk with Christ.

June 7
The Bride
Ephesians 5:25-27

"Christ loved the Church and gave Himself up for her, to make her holy, cleansing her with the washing of water by the word. He did this to present the church to Himself in splendor, without spot or wrinkle or anything like that, but holy and blameless." (Ephesians 5:25-27)

For lovers to be truly one, for the love to reach the deepest levels of affection, the highest flights of ecstasy, the lovers must be compatible. So the Spirit created us God-compatible and seeks to restore that compatibility. But it isn't only the intimacy of a fond embrace, the emotions of it. True love acts. Such a lover lives for the welfare of the other. What greater joy in heaven than when we bring new sons and daughters into the circle of love? But not just our witnessing activity; the most powerful ministry of any kind flows from that love relationship. Furthermore, Christlikeness and ministry reinforce one another in many ways. For example, an unholy witness is bad news, not good news. The interrelatedness of image/love/ministry is so intertwined you may have needed an additional page to answer that question!

The secret to a happy marriage is each living to fill up the other. Is your marriage to God a happy one or is it one-sided, day and night he filling you and you doing little to fulfill him? Fulfill **God**? God is complete—what could you add to **him**? Of course, but remember, to love is to be vulnerable. That's one of the glorious mysteries of our God. Unlike Allah or Buddha, for example, he makes himself vulnerable, the vulnerability of love. God feels loss, God hurts, God feels happy, God feels sad.

---

[25] IBE (2014), 320.

Once upon a time the heir to the throne of a magnificent kingdom, a handsome and wise prince, traveled to a distant realm to find a bride. When word came back that the prince had found her, the palace came alive with anticipation and began to celebrate. But soon the joy began to fade. The bride-to-be bombarded the palace administration with phone-calls and faxes demanding to know the financial state of the kingdom, the laws concerning the rights of immigrants such as the division of an estate upon divorce. Then rumors began to spread among the citizenry that the chosen one had an unsavory reputation. In fact, it was said, since her divorce she has had more than one affair. Finally, the local newspaper ran an investigative report that said the lady had been under psychiatric treatment for multiple personality disorder. Still, the King went ahead with plans for the wedding, the most glorious the Kingdom had ever known. He had confidence in the judgment of his son.

Imagine the anticipation of the people as they jammed the cathedral for the great occasion. All eyes were on the doorway as the wedding march began. When the bride appeared, a groan spread like a tidal wave across the congregation. Her wedding gown was torn and mud-spattered, her hair disheveled. She looked more like a derelict than a bride. Though mesmerized by the spectacle, some forced their gaze to the front and the waiting prince. To their astonishment, there he stood in regal splendor at the altar, beaming broadly as if he were about to marry the most lovely woman of the land.

How does the Bride of Christ look to you? Divided and bickering, self-centered, dirtied with the world's values, unfaithful, and disfigured from self-inflicted wounds? And the Prince all-glorious—what a deal! Oh, I know—we shall become like him when we see him as he is, the bride will be transformed—without spot or blemish, true. And that glorious day will mark the consummation of the Spirit's plan for us, bringing us to the marriage supper of the Lamb.

But the godliness, the intimacy was never planned to begin then. The Spirit designs it for now. So what about today? Do you bring him sadness today? Or joy? The good news is that no matter how ugly and split-up the church as a whole may look to itself or to outsiders, no matter how misguided and impotent, we as individuals can come to that final celebration with joy.

June 8
Our Wedding
Revelation 19:6-8 & 1 Corinthians 3:10-15

"Then I heard what seemed to be the voice of a great multitude, like the roar of many waters and like the sound of mighty peals of thunder, crying out, "Hallelujah! For the Lord our God the Almighty reigns. Let us rejoice and exult and give him the glory, for the marriage of the Lamb has come, and his Bride has made herself ready; it was granted her to clothe herself with fine linen, bright and pure for the fine linen is the righteous deeds of the saints." (Revelation 19:6-8)

Today, let us consider our engagement time, our time on earth when we are preparing for our wedding to our Beloved by growing in His image. What will the wedding itself look like? Let's consider 2 videos of our wedding day.

How do you see yourself in that video, how are you dressed? Is the glorious apparel that clothes you the imputed righteousness of Christ? Or is it something else? Of course you'll be clothed in his righteousness, or you'd never get into the banquet hall at all! But that's not the picture here. John explains that this wedding gown is your own right acts!

Consider this second video. 1 Corinthians 3:10-15: *"According to the grace of God given to me, like a skilled master builder I laid a foundation, and someone else is building upon it. Let each one take care how he builds upon it. For no one can lay a foundation other than that which is laid, which is Jesus Christ. Now if anyone builds on the foundation with gold, silver, precious stones, wood, hay, straw— each one's work will become manifest, for the Day will disclose it, because it will be revealed by fire, and the fire will test what sort of work each one has done. If the work that anyone has built on the foundation survives, he will receive a reward. If anyone's work is burned up, he will suffer loss, though he himself will be saved, but only as through fire."*

The specifics may not be altogether clear. The context focuses on unity/ disunity in the body. But the picture as a whole is of building the church. Not our godly or not-so-godly behavior or attitudes but what we have done in life to build his Church. We'd better be very careful for there's coming a day when our life-investment will bring honor or dishonor to the one we profess to love. I think we could summarize the scene by concluding that those whose work was faithful, focused, and Spirit energized will *"shine like the stars forever!"* (Daniel 12: 2&3)

But, as we have seen, the ultimate goal of life is not power-packed ministry, exciting as that is. Nor is the Spirit's goal merely to make us godly in character. The holy life is a means toward the ultimate goal, for only as we are like him, God-compatible, can we respond in the kind of loving intimacy he designed us for. Compatibility is the key to a happy marriage. Isn't it so? Sad the marriage where husband and wife have no shared interests, no common values, no passionate commitment to the same goals in life. A miserable co-existence as strangers under one roof. Or divorce. "Incompatibility," the legal documents say.

And so with God and you. He wants you to be like him, God-compatible, so you can be intimate companions. And he empowers for ministry so you can partner with him in bringing about his purposes in the world, bringing others into the family. But above all, the celebration on that Great Day will focus on the climax of a lifetime of intimate companionship, uninhibited union with your forever Lover.

So in your relationship with God, how would your Lover like you to express your affection to him? Oh, surely with a life that points people his direction and surely with Spirit-energized ministry. But it's much more than being good and doing good. True lovers not only act out love, they say it. Often. On the run, to be sure, but planning unhurried times as well. Let me ask, what all will you say to God?

June 9
The Mindset of War
Romans 12:1

"I appeal to you therefore, brothers, by the mercies of God, to present your bodies as a living sacrifice, holy and acceptable to God, which is your spiritual worship." (Romans 12:1)

Sometimes it is not easy to distinguish between legitimate desires and the bad stuff. Is this new TV a legitimate need or coveting what God doesn't intend? Is this jerk squeezing righteous indignation out of me or is this sinful anger? Is the pain I feel justifiable or am I so unhappy because my ego took a heavy hit?

How do I distinguish between legitimate desires and the bad stuff? I trust the Holy Spirit to show me what's right. But we mustn't run to the other extreme and assume that the Holy Spirit within is all we need. He deliberately provided the other means of knowing His will, so we'll surely go down in defeat if we neglect any of them. He's no substitute for the others, He's their energizer.

Then there's conscience. "Let your conscience be your guide," we say. But native conscience is a very unreliable guide since "it" is no more than our judgment in the realm of right versus wrong. That judgment has been programmed by home, school, and society, not to mention one's own sinful inclinations. As a result, we seem to have infinite capacity to con ourselves into believing what we want to believe. But the person who has been transformed into a new creation by the Spirit, has regularly disciplined his or her judgment by Scripture, who keeps tuned in to the Spirit, and who has developed judgment by long, careful use and can be trusted more and more to make godly decisions. In developing a battle plan against sin, you begin with unconditional surrender to the will of God, the Grand Presentation. You've made your beachhead! That gets you out of a dangerous no-man's land or out from behind enemy lines and solidly on God's side. Now you're ready. The next step is to take aim, identify the enemy. The source may not be that easy to spot for sure, so you may by-pass that step and identify the temptation itself. That isn't always easy, either, since temptation fights dirty, always slips up incognito. But you can spot any disguised temptation by focusing Scripture on your situation especially the clear-cut laws of Scripture, allowing the Holy Spirit to illuminate your mind. Then, finally, to release his fire-power, you make your choice about that temptation. Choose right and grow stronger, choose wrong and grow weaker.

Being honest with yourself, accurately identifying the enemy, and yielding control to the Spirit puts you in a winning position. So the battle itself should be fun war games? Not! It's hot, hand-to-hand, mind-to-mind deadly combat. To the death—of the temptation or of your spiritual vitality.

Every battle plan needs defensive strategies and offensive strategies. How do we defend, ward off temptation even before it strikes?

Romans 12:1 might be literally translated: *resist the conforming influences of your environment and keep on resisting.* Who will deny that popular media is hell-bent (literally) on cultivating lust, covetousness, and pride? In fact, I recently made a covenant with myself to stop surfing TV channels because when I finally got honest with myself and God, I had to admit what I was actually looking for—and it wasn't purity, contentment, and humility! Sometimes it was just humor just to relax and unwind after a hard day, but it ate up priceless time and—worse—was subtly molding me into a different kind of person. Paul says to resist and keep it up—eternal vigilance is the price of spiritual freedom.

To take this proactive stance, having gotten into the warfare mentality, decided firmly on whose side I really am, and having identified my major enemies, I take hold of my weapons and go for it. The Bible, prayer, and the church are means of grace, and we consider them our front-line defensive strategy again debilitating sin.

June 10
Faith-builders
Romans 10:17 & Matthew 16:18

"Faith comes by...the Word of God" (Romans 10:17)

One resource for building up our faith is the Bible, but Moses didn't have that resource! He wrote the very first part of the Bible, so could hardly learn to know God through a written revelation. But he did have the stories of God's interventions in the life of his people and he knew God's covenant promises well. In fact, he referred to those in all his dealing with God (eg. Exodus 32:13). To remind God of what He Himself has said gives power to prayer, reinforces confidence. The Bible is a faith builder. In fact, *"Faith comes by...the Word of God"* (Romans 10:17). Oh, there are times when doubts nibble at the fringes of consciousness even now and faith falters before some immovable mountain of difficulty, but it is the Word of God that restores.

An intimate companionship with God means a daily encounter with Him in His Word. How else can we get to know God? And knowing Him is the only way to strengthen those trust bonds. That's why the Holy Spirit gave us the Book. A careful listening for the voice of the Spirit, talking over with him the truth he reveals each day is the pathway of strengthening trust bonds.

Prayer and Bible meditation can be private, but there's one faith-builder that is very public: the church. Moses, mighty in faith, seemed capable of operating successfully on his own—a team with God and Moses should be unbeatable. But he didn't try to solo. When God suggested destroying the rebellious people and starting over with Moses' descendants, Moses pleaded with God to change His mind. Later, when Moses tried to do his work single-handedly, his father-in-law, Jethro, told him he needed to delegate his authority to others and Moses, called by God the meekest man on earth, agreed. In the grandest solidarity of all, Moses did an incredible thing. The people stood under judgment for their vile sins and Moses pleaded again for their forgiveness. Then, sensing that a holy God might not be able to forgive, he offered himself as a sacrifice in their behalf (Exodus 32:30-32).

We don't think of Israel as a church, though Stephen called it that in Acts 7:38. But the solidarity of God's people was central in Moses' thinking and behavior. And so it will be with us if we are to advance in faith. I'm sure there are those heroic figures throughout church history who have stayed true to God while utterly alone, as, for example, when imprisoned for their faith. Or a missionary on initial pioneering assignment. But I have never personally known a professed believer who has made it without the church. I've known many who tried and I've watched, grieving, as they drifted further and further from a living relationship with Jesus. He gave a promise, *"I will build my church and the very Pentagon of hell will not overcome it or even be able to hold out against it"* (Matthew 16:18, paraphrase). The book of Acts follows and shows what the Holy Spirit actually built: a string of local congregations across the Roman world. He said, "I will build my own invincible church."

These "means of grace" are accessed by faith—that's the indispensable access key. Yet, paradoxically, one of the first things the Spirit uses them to do in us is to build our faith. So the spiral upward is not only in becoming more like Jesus in character and thus eligible for ever greater intimacy, the access key itself—faith—spirals upward too! We discover a glorious interplay of graces that transform us from what we are by nature to what the Spirit intends us to become by grace. But remember, faith is two-pronged: yield and trust. There's the crisis of unconditional yielding, whether to start or to re-start the process, and there's trust in him to do what he promised in transforming our core nature. What a glorious spiral upward toward God himself! Today we exult in God's provision for the life of promise.

June 11
Power Potential
Proverbs 4:23

Power. Let me read a description of that power potential as found in in the words of Scripture's most famous lover, Shulamite: *"Your left hand is under my head/and your right hand caresses me. Love is powerful as death; passion is as strong as the grave. It bursts into flame and burns like a raging fire/water cannot put it out; no flood can drown it. Her beloved says: Let me hear your voice from the garden, my love; my companions are waiting to hear you sing. Shulamite sings in response: Come to me, my lover, play like a gazelle upon my scented slopes!"* (Song of Songs, 8)

That's powerful stuff! Sex is so potent it seems to be the lifeforce that drives society. At least the advertisers think so. One of those marvelous psychological studies of man's interior tells us that the American male has thoughts of sex on an average of once every 27 seconds!

But it isn't just the drive that leads to various delights and the continuance of the human race, when sublimated into other channels, we are told it is the dynamo of life that powers all varieties of creative activity. In fact, Unwin in his famous study of hundreds of civilizations concluded that attitudes on sex determine the course of a civilization.

Channelled. But the incomparable power of sex does not produce a power marriage, powerful human relationships, the highest levels of creativity, powerful ministry when left to run its own course. The secret is found in the same passage: Song of Solomon in chapter 8: Shulamite's family gives us the secret: *We have a young sister/and she has no breasts yet; but what shall we do with our sister when wooers come? If she holds out like a wall, we will adorn her with silver for dowry; If she gives way to lovers like a door, then we will plank her up!* She responds to this challenge by her brothers by saying that she has been a wall, a garden fully kept for her husband alone. And as a result, both of them are fully satisfied.

To have a power marriage and a power life and ministry, sexual drives must be channelled. If there are not strict boundaries, high walls, the power potential will leak away, in fact it may break loose and meander in a vast swampland in which you get lost and bogged down, immobilized. But if it is channelled it becomes the driving force, a dynamo, the power turbine to drive the engines of life.

The Bible leaves us in no doubt as to what those embankments are: Command #7: thou shalt not commit adultery. And in case you want to get legalistic and restrict this wall to married people and sexual intercourse, Jesus comes along and builds the wall even higher, really planks it up: Whoever looks on a woman to desire her has already committed adultery, has already breached the dike, has already messed up. The Proverbs uses a similar analogy. It speaks of sexual potentials as a cistern which is to be carefully kept; *"drink water from your own well, why should the streams of your lifeforce be dissipated, spread abroad through the marketplace?"* (Proverbs 5:15-19). The tragedy of cracked cisterns, broken dikes, purity breached, integrity compromised.

Erosion. We read almost daily of some pastor or leader who has broken loose. Not only has his sexual activity, which seemed so desirable, turned to mucky unfulfillment, but his marriage jeopardized or wrecked, his children forever shamed, his ministry fouled, the cause of Christ damaged.

How does it happen? Not suddenly. Before the break, there has been an erosion of the high walls of purity and integrity. You can't blame the floods of sexual stimulation our society condones. The greater the flow of a river, the greater its power potential if it is channelled. No, there has been an erosion. The TV evangelist, featured, I'm told, in the Playboy magazine, says he has had a problem with pornography from his youth. The leading pastor has a brother and father who breached the dike before he did. The Christian college VP who ran away with the art teacher, leaving two families of young children, had messed up earlier in the Christian college he served before.

Scripture describes exactly how the erosion begins and grows. [26] The first breach is in the mind: fantasy, imagination of satisfying sexual appetite with someone who is not yours. For a married person: emotional infidelity. Flirty talk can seem innocent but may come from or promote emotional infidelity. Perhaps there is talk in counselling sessions, talk can breach the walls.

The first breach is made in the mind, widens with the eye and gains irresistible force with intentional touch. If accompanied by feelings that would not be present in same-sex contact, it is romantic or sexual in nature and is a major erosion of integrity and usually of purity as well. Holding hands? How silly can you get? Well, how long would I remain president if I were seen walking across campus holding your girlfriend's hand? The intent of the touch is the key.

Building the walls. Some people act like God is damming up the river of life. Never! He knows how beautiful, how powerful it can be so he tells us how to make it that way: channel it. If you're like a door, plank yourself up! Get others to help you build your embankments of purity and integrity. Don't tear down the banks with your own hands. Or eyes. Or imaginings.

But how do you build, or rebuild? *"Keep your heart with all diligence, for out of it are the issues of life."* (Proverbs 4:23) Sex is primarily a mental activity. The walls that you have breached can be rebuilt and your power potential channelled once again. Have a disciplined mind. Erosion starts at the top layer of the bank, the mind, and quickly accelerates. *"I made a covenant with my eyes, said Job, not to look on a virgin. "*(Job 31:1). Covenant.

Flee fornication. Every other sin a person commits is outside the body, but the sexually immoral person sins against his own body. Or do you not know that your body is a temple of the Holy Spirit within you, whom you have from God? You are not your own, for you were bought with a price. So glorify God in your body. (I Corinthians 6:18 - 20).

Treat every member of the opposite sex as your sister (or mother) or as your brother. Another way is to view the other person as engaged unless you and the other person are both single and both serious about the possibility of marriage. For whether or not he or she is presently engaged, if God intends marriage, He has committed that person to another. If He does not intend marriage, it is even heavier. According to Paul he is keeping that person for himself.

Build the walls of purity and integrity high and keep them strong, channel the life force of that beautiful gift of sex God has given you. Then you can build a power marriage, a power life, a power ministry.

---

[26] Proverbs 6:24,25,29,32,33;7.15:24-27; 9:17,18

June 12
Simple Lifestyle
Luke 12:33-34

"Sell your possessions, and give alms; provide yourselves with purses that do not grow old, with a treasure in the heavens that does not fail, where no thief approaches and no moth destroys. For where your treasure is, there will your heart be also." (Luke 12:33-34)

As the wealthy are growing more wealthy and the poor more poor, the response of many Christians around the world has been to assume some form of a simple lifestyle. Several thousand church leaders committed themselves to this at the great Lausanne Congress on Evangelism:

We cannot hope to attain this goal without sacrifice. All of us are shocked by the poverty of millions and disturbed by the injustices which cause it. Those of us who live in affluent circumstances accept our duty to develop a simple lifestyle in order to contribute more generously to both relief and evangelism.[27]

But what is a simple lifestyle? The debate is never-ending. For practical purposes, let us make an attempt. If "absolute poverty" is defined as existence below subsistence level, and "poverty" is defined as subsistence-level living without things others in the society consider necessities, perhaps a "simple lifestyle" would be all the basic necessities.

If this comes anywhere near indicating a biblical view, every believer who lives above a simple lifestyle should sacrifice to the limits of his faith and love in an effort to bring those who live below that level up to the provision of basic necessities. Whatever, he can hardly rest at ease so long as there are those who lack basic necessities.

And what are necessities? At least it is safe to say that the salespeople of our consumer-driven economy should not decide. How does one define need in a society where standards of living are constantly rising? . . . How do the generals of the sales army in their carpeted offices on Madison Avenue plot their strategy for meeting our "needs"? What angles do they play on besides our greed? Our anxieties? (Is your family protected?) Our sexual preoccupations? (Does your breath rob you of kisses?) Our guilt? Our snobbery? (You deserve the best).[28]

Perhaps we could make room for savings toward a specific objective (to give a gift, to buy a house to live in) or in businesses that have a very irregular income, such as farming. We may also say that the judgment of unbelief applies equally to those who do not have enough to save, when they are enslaved to worry about the future. Surely we must come to terms with the underlying principle of faith.

A moderate position is advocated by Larry Burkett, who holds that savings for protection against possible future adversity is acting in unbelief, but that saving as a provision for future known needs is acceptable. Savings or insurance for what might prove crippling loss through common accidents or fire can be made in faith, but any attempt to protect against all potential hazards in life is futile as well as unbelieving. He sees the greatest failure in this regard to be in inheritances.

If I had to identify the area of Christian finances that is least understood, I would have to vote for inheritance. Not only do many people wreck their lives by hoarding, but they also wreck the lives of their children and children's children with an abundant inheritance. . . . Large amounts of money given to children will usually be squandered to their disservice, and large amounts of money stored up for children in trust can be used to buffer them from God's will. . . . Allow your children the joy of earning their own way.[29]

---

[27] The Lausanne Covenant, in *Let the Earth Hear His Voice,* ed. J. D. Douglas (Minneapolis: Worldwide, 1975), 6.
[28] John White, *The Golden Cow: Materialism in the Twentieth-Century Church* (Downers Grove, Ill.: InterVarsity Press, 1979), 73.
[29] Larry Burkett, Your Finances in Changing Times: God's Principles for Managing Money (Glendale, Calif.: Campus Crusade for Christ, 1975), 130-131.

My conclusion after evaluating the competing viewpoints in the light of Scripture comes down to a revision of John Wesley's dictum: "Get all you can, save all you can, give all you can." Perhaps it will serve as a summary statement of the individual's responsibility if we qualify this carefully: Earn all you can with integrity, save all you can toward meeting known future obligations, give all you can in sacrificial love and faith in the God who provides.

June 13
Battle Plan
Romans 12:1-2

"I beseech you therefore, brethren, by the mercies of God, that you present your bodies a living sacrifice, holy, acceptable to God, which is your reasonable service. And do not be conformed to this world, but be transformed by the renewing of your mind, that you may prove what is that good and acceptable and perfect will of God." (Romans 12:1-2, NKJV)

Diane had been a Christian for two years, spiraling upward, open and eager for all the Spirit was teaching. Then she made a discovery. She took a class I taught on the Christian life. The assignment was to write a paper on developing a battle plan for overcoming temptation. The paper wasn't just about how to overcome temptation. The assignment was very personal: "A Strategy for overcoming My own Strongest Temptation." Diane should have known about temptation-even Jesus had to slug it out with the devil! But in the exuberance of her newfound faith, she missed the issue of dealing with temptation. She added a note to her paper: As a "toddler" Christian, I had had very little knowledge about Satan and his tactics. I never felt plagued by temptation. Consequently, when you gave the assignment, I did not feel a need to devise a plan to overcome temptation. After researching this paper, life isn't as comfortable. I now realize the devil is working in my life, and I see the temptations that beset me. This discovery is both terrible and wonderful. I've already defeated Satan in one way, because I'm no longer ignorant of and oblivious to his attacks in my life.

Students really got into the project, some writing almost book-length theses, many testifying that the project was life-transforming. "My life has been radically changed. For the first time I'm beginning to see progress toward victory." Once in a while I get a letter from a former student, "Remember the assignment on developing a strategy to overcome temptation? That was the turning point in my Christian experience." Each of these students discovered that being filled with the Spirit doesn't lift one beyond temptation. In fact, the battle will escalate! Unfortunately, this battle catches too many sincere, growing Christians off guard-faltering before they know what hit them. Others know they are being tempted; but they don't know how to defend themselves, so they go down in defeat.

Each of the papers I received from students was unique. Each student offered a different approach to overcoming temptation, but the temptations were similar. Men most often wrote of sexual temptation. "How can I control my lustful thoughts and even my eyes?" Often the women spoke of emotional struggles. Sandra is 38, single, and worried she'll never get married. An unsaved guy keeps asking her out and she knows she can't marry an unbeliever, but . . . Maribelle has lots going for her and she knows it. It's hard not to feel a little smug when she sees someone else who isn't as well-dressed, attractive, or intelligent. Even weak Christians are fair game for her condescension. She hates herself when these attitudes erupt.

Everyone needs a workable battle strategy to conquer temptations. Apparently some seek to deal with temptation in a different way. Once or twice in every batch of papers I found a "paper" that was one-sentence long: "I have no strategy; the Holy Spirit lives in me and that's all the strategy I need." Which will it be? Do I get out of the way and let God do it all, or do I personally slug it out with the enemy? We may be tempted to go to one extreme or the other-to opt for a spectator role and leave it up to God or develop a do-it-yourself mind-set.

The Bible teaches both a faith that rests and a faith that wrestles. We trust the Spirit to do the work of remaking us. But we must also use the weapons He provides to fight the evil in our lives. If we concentrate solely on what He does, we may slip into complacency or presumption and get ambushed by the enemy. If we concentrate exclusively on our responsibility to fight the good fight, we may become battle weary and discouraged-even give up the battle. The spiritual war differs from all other battles . In this battle, surrender is victory . The first step in winning spiritual war is surrendering ourselves to the Lord. Surrender seems a strange way to win a victory, doesn't it? When faced with temptation, the only way to win is to give up! "I plead with you," says Paul, "to make a grand presentation of yourself to God . Present yourself as if you were a carefully prepared sacrifice at the temple. Surrender yourself, your rights, even your life. That's where victory begins."

Are you battle weary? Or perhaps you got so far out of God's way you can't recognize temptation when it comes. Why not examine your battle and ask God to give you strength for the battle and wisdom to know when to get out of His way when He want to accomplish victory?

June 14
Overcoming
James 1:13-15

"Let no one say when he is tempted, "I am being tempted by God," for God cannot be tempted with evil, and he himself tempts no one. 14 But each person is tempted when he is lured and enticed by his own desire. 15 Then desire when it has conceived gives birth to sin, and sin when it is fully grown brings forth death." (James 1:13-15)

Surrender seems a strange way to win a victory, doesn't it? When faced with temptation, the only way to win is to give up! However, we do not surrender to the enemy or temptation but to the Victor. "I plead with you," says Paul, "to make a grand presentation of yourself to God . Present yourself as if you were a carefully prepared sacrifice at the temple . Surrender yourself, your rights, even your life . That's where victory begins" [my paraphrase] . Sacrifice can be painful . Sometimes you must give up
- a friend who deflects you from God's highest and best.
- the ambition that is really an ego trip.
- that fun thing that eats up time you should be spending on God's business.
- a purchase so that the hungry of the world may eat.

Those sacrifices can hurt. But the grand presentation God demands is more than those little particulars. God wants all of you-a living sacrifice. That alone starts you on the way to holiness and is acceptable to God, but in the light of all God has done for you this living sacrifice is only reasonable. Presenting yourself unconditionally to God is only the beginning. The next step is to identify the source of temptation.

Paul also identifies minds that need renovation-our inner desires and impulses. Ultimately our source of temptation isn't the people or circumstances, it's our response to them. We've given ground already in our minds-*"Each one is tempted when, by his own evil desire, he is dragged away and enticed"* (James 1:14) . Satan is the original source of all temptation; and he still is on the prowl, ready to pounce on the unwary (1 Pet . 5 :8). We should be on guard at all times (Ephesians 6 :11), never give ground (Ephesians 4 :27), always fight back (James 4:7), and stay alert to his tricks and deceptions (2 Corinthians 2 :11).
From where do your greatest temptations come? Which are your most frequent temptations . Number them in order of their strength: Satan, inner desires, impulses, other people, things, circumstances, or God.

All the sources of temptation you numbered can be sources of temptation except one-God. James 1:13-14 clearly states that God tempts no one. How then does the Bible sometimes credit the same tempting circumstances as coming from both Satan and God? (See 2 Samuel 24 :1 and I Chronicles 21:1). The motive is the key. Satan uses people or circumstances to bring us down. God uses those same circumstances to test or prove our allegiance and make us stronger.

Have you ever stopped to analyse just what temptation is? It doesn't look bad, it looks good; otherwise, it wouldn't tempt. Actually, God designed our desires in the first place. He purposely gave us the ability to experience desire. Enticement to sin is the temptation to abuse a God-given desire. God created us to enjoy our bodies, acquire possessions, and accomplish worthwhile goals. But when we try to fulfill those desires in the wrong way, we sin. The next step in our strategy is to discriminate between God-given drives and our destructive responses to those desires. God has given us the ability to enjoy many things, but we can easily twist the ability to enjoy into sinful responses that become destructive life patterns. When we recognize the legitimate desires, we can identify the root sin behind our temptations.
Some people believe that all sin can be placed under one of these categories:
- lust (abuse of our desire to enjoy food or sex).
- covetousness (desire to possess something that is not mine or not in God's will for me).
- pride (taking credit for something God has achieved).

If I give in to any impulse long enough, I will become that type of person. Lust yielded to creates a sensual person. Covetousness too often indulged ends in a materialistic outlook. Pride may so often prevail that I become egotistical. To win the battle against temptation, we sometimes need to recognize the root sin, not just the outward result. We especially need such understanding when a sinful attitude becomes entrenched as a disposition. For example, outbursts of anger may actually be rooted in some unresolved bitterness. From where did the bitterness come? What caused it? To root out the basic problem, we must identify both the problem and the source.

So far in this lesson we have looked at three root temptations. We might picture temptation as a tree with three roots : lust, pride, and covetousness. However, some scholars point to an underlying taproot-unbelief. Some say unbelief is the source of the other three! Eve fell before temptations to lust, covet, and act arrogantly because she doubted God's word. The taproot is the single root that grows deepest into the ground.

Other scholars say the fundamental flaw in human nature is self-love. A problem exists with that idea. Self-love is more like the innocent drives God built into us-the desires to enjoy, possess, and exist. However, like those innocent drives, rightful concern about one's own interests can run out of control. When you act in your self-interest at the expense of God or someone else, You have sinned. Perhaps you have committed the most fundamental sin of all, since the first and great commandment is to love God supremely. If self-love is the source of your sin, you are not going to win the battle till you obey God's first commandment. We must identify, as best we can, the roots of the temptations we face. Unbelief and love skewed toward self-interest seem almost always to be present, but they are so general that it may be more helpful in our battle strategy to look at the root sins more easily identified: lust, covetousness, and pride.

Temptation always masquerades-it looks so appealing, promises so much good. That's why it's a temptation. If it wore its own face, it would be so ugly we'd run! Temptation fights dirty; but you can spot any disguised temptation by focusing Scripture on your situation. Make your choice about that temptation. Choose right and grow stronger, choose wrong and grow weaker. Which will it be?

June 15
Salt and Light
Matthew 5:13-16

"You are like salt for all mankind. But if salt loses its taste, there is no way to make it salty again. It has become worthless, so it is thrown away and people walk on it". (Matthew 5:13, TEV)

Let us work for the good of all (Gal 6.10 NEB)

Does your congregation have programs and involvement in ministries to effectively promote the welfare of the community at home and abroad? The church by its nature as the body of Christ is the visible embodiment of His presence on planet earth. Therefore, the local congregation needs to fulfill the purpose of being salt and light in the world (Matthew 5:13-16). Jesus spelled out his interpretation of "light" -that men may see your good works and glorify God. There could be an evangelistic purpose in that. But what is salt? Did he have in mind flavor for an insipid society that insistently stays flat in godless living? Or did he have in mind the preservative influence of believers in a decaying society? At least the concept of influence, of permeating one's environment with good, must be present.

The church is designed to be God's visible evidence of His design and desire for each person. The world is to see in the church God's own love and holiness. The people of God and the Spirit of God are in partnership to give the world truth (accurate definitions of sin, love and righteousness) so that people can know of the freedom and life that is so opposite of Satan's kingdom.[30]

In that responsibility, two things come to mind: ministering mercy and seeking justice. The religious leaders of Christ's day were strong on justice, as they interpreted it, but weak on mercy. Jesus emphasizes a major theme in the good news of the Kingdom of heaven. He desires mercy to govern our relationships (Matthew 9:9-13 and Matthew 12:1-8). This difference in their understanding of God's priorities separated most of the religious leaders from Jesus. But God's plan is for his people to pursue both justice and mercy for the welfare of its community. It is true that the record of Jesus' ministry gives more space to reporting his healing ministry than his teaching ministry. His acts of mercy were intended as "signs" validating who he was, but, unlike Moses' miracles, they were not merely signs pointing to God's power; they were very focused- healing a broken humanity. It would seem the biblical way is to

---

[30] John 8:34-37; John 10:10; John 16:7-11

emphasize evangelism and then, through transformed lives, transform the community. "Redemption and lift," Donald McGavran called the common phenomenon of societal reformation when large numbers become Christian.

Promoting community welfare should not be amputated from the purposes of the church. Throughout history the church has indeed fulfilled this purpose, taking the lead in providing health care and education, for example. In the Western world for centuries the only hospitals and schools were Christian. The same was true in pioneer missionary penetration of non-Western societies. In fact, often the church became so involved in seeking the earthly welfare of the community that the evangelistic mission was eclipsed. Nevertheless, the church, if true to the example of its Master will reach out in mercy to the surrounding community. The church presents the loving heart of Christ who came to seek and save by being a loving presence in the community. We are called to do this as a church, that is, and not merely through those members who do so privately from personal compassion. Nevertheless, it is much easier to go to a consistent extreme than to stay at the center of biblical tension and most of the evangelical church tends toward neglect of the social dimension of church responsibility. The question for us is to which extreme do we tend? Towards evangelism only or to only administering justice and mercy to the neglect of evangelism? Perhaps to neither, needing us to refocus on God's priorities. Pray today that you might better love what God loves within the balance that He desires.

June 16
The Onion
Exodus 20:13

"Do not murder" (Ex. 20:13)

Each command in the second half of the Ten Commandments is like an onion, especially the one forbidding murder. Here's why. You can peel back layer after layer of that tear-inducing little vegetable, but all the way to the core, it's still an onion. It may not cause the same volume of tears, but it's the same vegetable.

So let's peel back the various layers of killing to discover what God had in mind in forbidding it. This commandment is so important for all of our relationships that we explore its implications for a Christian walk.

The Sixth Commandment is brief and to the point: *"Do not murder"* (Ex. 20:13). But don't let its simplicity fool you. This is a command with multidimensional meanings for an obedient walk with God. Most of us aren't tempted to murder someone physically, although too many in our society wouldn't hesitate to do so. But there are several dimensions to this command that might hit closer to home, even for Bible-believing Christians.

There are multiple categories of unlawful killing. Examples of categories would be murder and suicide. You would probably add euthanasia, abortion, and infanticide. Depending on your theology, you may have included capital punishment and war. It's difficult to list most of the ways to kill unless you peel back the full-grown "onion" of literally taking someone's life to the next layer of deliberately causing physical harm, the next layer of verbal abuse, and so on.

The Bible clearly teaches the sanctity of human life, and this command reflects that fundamental value. God created each of us, forming us in the womb according to His plan (see Ps. 139:13-16). He made us in His own image, and He loved us so much that He bought our redemption with the priceless sacrifice of His Son. The Sixth

Commandment sets forth the foundational human responsibility to care for and preserve human life, including the unborn, the aged, the poor, and the sick.

Murder is considered the worst of all crimes more universally than any other but, at the same time, is the sin most universally practiced. It is the most practiced because Christ would not let us get away with restricting the law to those who slit throats or blow off heads. Jesus said, "You have heard that it was said to our ancestors, 'Do not murder,' and whoever murders will be subject to judgment. But I tell you, everyone who is angry with his brother will be subject to judgment" (Matt. 5:21-22). Even anger violates the Sixth Commandment. That's peeling the onion back pretty far, right? But not all the way to the core. If the ultimate command is to love, then a lack of love is surely the hard little onion core that, when planted, will surely grow to negligence; dislike; hatred; anger; verbal harm; if unchecked, physical harm; and finally, when full grown, murder. Are you beginning to see more complexity in the simple command not to murder?

Notice that Christ lumped together all of these behaviors and attitudes in the same category of sin. Nevertheless, He wasn't equating verbal abuse with murder. Throughout Scripture and even in this passage, God recognizes levels of sin and guilt, as well as levels of punishment. Not all categories of killing are equally sinful, then, but all are the same variety of sin. All of these ways of harming others violate the sixth commandment. Although genuine Christians may not often let that onion grow to full maturity, how much foul-smelling, tear-inducing evil lurks beneath the surface of that killing "onion"!

June 17
Conflict!
James 3:13-18

Who is wise and has understanding among you? He should show his works by good conduct with wisdom's gentleness. But if you have bitter envy and selfish ambition in your heart, don't brag and deny the truth. Such wisdom does not come from above but is earthly, unspiritual, demonic. For where envy and selfish ambition exist, there is disorder and every kind of evil. But the wisdom from above is first pure, then peace-loving, gentle, compliant, full of mercy and good fruits, without favoritism and hypocrisy. And the fruit of righteousness is sown in peace by those who cultivate peace. (James 3:13-18)

We see that we can kill others through physical abuse, verbal abuse, anger, hatred, and a lack of love. When we fail to love as we ought, what results? Conflict! We see conflict everywhere in our world, from arguments among family members to wars among nations. Yet God's ideal is for His people to live in peace. Jesus is the Prince of peace (see Isa. 9:6), and peace is a fruit of the Spirit (see Gal. 5:22). Therefore, believers are to be characterized by peace as we live out the traits of Christ, who resides in us. Paul taught, *Do not murder"* (Ex. 20:13) and "*Be at peace among yourselves*" (1 Thess. 5:13).

Several key attitudes help us avoid conflict. The first is a Godward orientation: yield and trust. The only place to start in avoiding conflict in family or church relationships is to unconditionally yield our will to God; and trust Him with the outcome.

If someone in the home or a faction in the church doesn't yield and trust, conflict is inevitable. But when both parties yield and trust, conflict can usually be avoided or resolved.

The following verses and identify worldly or evil attitudes. God highlights attitudes that come from Him.

Who is wise and has understanding among you? He should show his works by good conduct with wisdom's gentleness. But if you have bitter envy and selfish ambition in your heart, don't brag and deny the truth. Such wisdom does not come from above but is earthly, unspiritual, demonic. For where envy and selfish ambition exist, there is disorder and every kind of evil. But the wisdom from above is first pure, then peace-loving, gentle, compliant, full of mercy and good fruits, without favoritism and hypocrisy. And the fruit of righteousness is sown in peace by those who cultivate peace. (James 3:13-18)

Did you notice the word selfish? The opposite of a Godward orientation is self-love. James said selfish ambition leads to disorder—conflict. Yielding to God brings His wisdom to the situation, and His wisdom is "peace-loving, gentle, compliant, full of mercy and good fruits" (v. 17).

Let's peel back a few layers and examine our own hearts, allowing the Holy Spirit to destroy these behaviors that occur when there is a lack of love: first physical violence; then verbal violence; anger; hatred; and finally, a lack of love.

Hidden behind the closed doors of many Christian homes lurks a violent temper that sometimes erupts. But if you, husband / dad or wife/mom, have ever touched your family in anger and have not repented and asked forgiveness, now is the time to do it. Otherwise, your study of God's commands will be of little value since your sin inhibits a walk of obedience to the Spirit's direction in your life.

Perhaps you have repented and asked forgiveness, only to fail again. You just can't stop. Now is the time to seek professional help. Get help immediately. Physical violence can escalate, with deadly consequences.

The same warning should flash for child abuse, of course, and perhaps even more urgently. A mother of a 5-year-old once called, pleading with me to pray for her temper problem. She loved the little guy so much, she said, but when she became stressed with work and mothering, she raged against her own son. She needed help before it was too late. And "too late" can come all too soon in the psyche of a little person.

If you have a problem with physical abuse, start by praying for forgiveness and strength and by apologizing to the victim. Get help. End this cycle of hate today.

June 18
Colorblind
Proverbs 15:18

*"A hot-tempered man stirs up strife, but he who is slow to anger quiets contention." (*Proverbs 15:18)

We read Jesus' warning about anger: "Everyone who is angry with his brother will be subject to judgment" (Matt. 5:22). Jesus spoke these words in the context of teaching about murder. He was peeling back the layer of the "onion," beyond physical murder to an emotion so out of control that it can be linked to the act of murder itself.

Is It OK to get angry? Anger isn't always wrong. God gets angry. God isn't angry just over sin; He's also angry with wicked people. His wrath is seen throughout the Old and New Testaments, the inevitable result of the collision between a holy God and unholy humans' attitudes and actions. While on earth, Jesus was angry on more than one occasion (see Mark 3:5; 11:17).

Is it possible for a sinful mortal to be Godlike in his anger? It must not be easy, for the Bible is filled with warnings about anger. (Start with Romans 12:19, Galatians 5:19-20, Ephesians 4:31, James 1:20)

In addition, the Book of Proverbs is full of flashing red lights about anger. For example: *"A hot-tempered man stirs up conflict, but a man slow to anger calms strife.* "(Proverbs 15:18) and "A fool gives full vent to his anger, but a wise man holds it in check." (Proverbs 29:11)

I'm sort of color-blind when it comes to anger. I find it difficult to distinguish between the green light and the red light. But it must be possible, for the Bible instructs us in our anger to refrain from sinning (see Ps. 4:4; Eph. 4:26). Jesus, by the power of the Spirit, was successful in making the distinction. He refrained from getting angry when He seemed to have every right to. *"When He was reviled, He did not revile in return; when He was suffering, He did not threaten but entrusted Himself to the One who judges justly."* (1 Peter 2:23)

Jesus' example seems to point the way. What ignites the wrath? Is it an offense against me? Then follow Jesus and be like a lamb before its shearers—silent (see Isaiah 53:7). Is it an offense against God or someone else? Then anger can be a good thing in expressing God's justice on earth (see 2 Cor. 7:11).

The difficulty is that our motives are mixed. Am I distressed over a sin that offends God and harms people, or am I angry over the way I am affected? Because motives are impure, the safe thing may be to eschew anger altogether when the sin of another person directly affects me, as when my child does wrong but the wrong embarrasses me. Wait until the anger subsides to make sure the resulting action doesn't come from a mixture of righteous and unrighteous indignation.

To keep anger from igniting for the wrong reason or from burning out of control, Scripture gives two ways to douse the flames: Cool the anger. Don't get angry suddenly. James wrote, *"Everyone must be quick to hear, slow to speak, and slow to anger"* (Jas. 1:19). Don't let the anger keep burning. Don't let it last until the next day. Paul advised, *"Don't let the sun go down on your anger"* (Eph. 4:26).

Both a low flash point—a quick response without reflection—and a slow burn seem to risk causing even righteous indignation to go astray. Practice discriminating between righteous and unrighteous indignation- don't be colorblind.

June 19
Steady-State Fullness
Ephesians 5:18

.....be filled with the Spirit.... (Ephesians 5:18)

Today's verse in a subtle way ties together the three different aspects of being filled with the Spirit . The verb be filled is unusual in that it is a command, something I must do-but it's in the passive form, something the Spirit does to me. "Be being filled" would be an awkward translation but gets at the meaning . So how do I obey if He is the one who does it? I take the initiative and deliberately yield control. Then I keep on praying and expecting Him to produce the fruit of godliness and power for ministry. If He chooses to surge through with a flood of some special emotion, how blessed! The command be filled is also a continuous action verb: "Keep on being filled with the Spirit." Being filled is a constant in that sense, an abiding relationship. Steady - state filled, you might call it. If the Holy Spirit has control of my life, He'll continuously fill me with power to live and serve. In Ephesians 5 :18-20, Paul also identifies some of the inner feelings associated with being filled: singing, praise, and prayer. Paul says to let the Spirit fill you always as a way of life. Then, from time to time out of His grace, He'll blow into your life with gale force and fan the embers into an all-consuming fire of His own making. When that happens simultaneously to a lot of people, we call the result revival.

Until now we've talked of being filled with the Spirit on a very personal level, but we do not live as individuals only. We are part of a larger community of believers. Can you imagine the power unleashed when a group of Christians simultaneously surrender to the Spirit? What would a worship service be like with such a group? How would their prayer meetings be? What kind of impact would they make on unbelievers? Do you ever long to be part of such a Holy Spirit outpouring? We call it revival. Since the Bible doesn't use the term "revival," why have Christian people always used the term? The Bible repeatedly describes great movings of the Spirit; and the church has experienced such movings periodically through its history. We've called those times revival- "re" means again and "vival" means life. So when I speak of revival I mean a renewal of life that once was, or ought to have been. Even with the examples from the Bible and church history coupled with the plain meaning of the term itself, however, revival doesn't seem to mean the same thing to everyone. People use the term to describe a great variety of different events and experiences.

The Bible doesn't use the term revival but does report movements of spiritual renewal of various kinds. Perhaps we are safest not to prescribe the details of what must happen to qualify as true revival. We can, however, discern some common features:

1 . Revival is the work of the Holy Spirit.

2 . He revitalizes or renews those He has already given life.

3 . Others see the renewed vitality, resulting in change in them also. Revival spreads among believers and unbelievers turn to Christ.

This last characteristic would seem to rule out the idea of a "personal revival," which some use to describe a fresh encounter with God. Anyone can experience personal renewal at any time he or she is prepared to acknowledge a need, yield to God's control, and trust Him to give renewed life. Personal renewal may best be referred to by terms like being filled with the Spirit. I can experience the fullness of God's blessing whether or not others participate.

Do you easily identify spiritual needs in your church? Are evidences of spiritual vitality hard to find? Are you satisfied with the way things are, or do you hope for revival in your church? Vern Strom was a wheat farmer in Western Canada who tells of the "dirty thirties" when they planted 1,000 bushels of precious seed and reaped barely 1,000 bushels in return. On 1,000 acres, that's a bushel an acre! Like many a church hard, hard work for a "survival" harvest. But in 1942 the rains came, and they averaged a crop of 55 bushels an acre on 1,500 acres! The silos, barns, and garages wouldn't hold it all; so they stored it in piles outside, 12,000 bushels to a pile. That's the kind of harvest when God sends rain. Wouldn't such an abundant spiritual harvest be great for your church? If you are experiencing a drought, you can do two things:

1. Be sure that you personally are experiencing the fullness of the Spirit as a continuing pattern of life; and

2. Pray diligently for revival, recruiting others to join you in prayer.

G. Campbell Morgan said, "We cannot legislate spiritual awakening, but we can set our sails to catch the wind." My son Bob and I were trying to cross a large lake on the boundary between the United States and Canada, but the wind kept driving us toward the shore long before we reached the end of the lake. We paddled our canoe with all the energy we could muster, like the poor remnant in a church that stays faithful and tries to move things forward. Also, like that remnant, we wore out, went with the wind and beached our canoe. After a rest we started out again but made little progress. Then Bob, the veteran canoer, told me to tie his poncho between two paddles, sit in the prow and hoist my "sail" to the wind while he relaxed in the stern and navigated. Amazing! We began to skim across the lake under full sail, much to the astonishment of other canoeists struggling vainly to make progress. So it is when the mighty Wind of God blows through His people with renewing power. So let us set our sails, covenant to pray, and keep on praying till revival comes. In the meantime, until God chooses to unleash a widespread renewal, you can make very sure that you personally are eligible for revival and thus no barrier to what God would do. That's the first meaning of being filled with the Spirit-unconditional yieldedness to His will, making sure each day that He is in charge. We've seen that by keeping a close connection with the Spirit we can be sure of a full harvest of godly characteristics and powerful service, and at least a periodic inner sense of God-intoxication. We can do what Paul says in Ephesians 5:15 and keep on being filled with the Spirit! As He "pours in," we will be truly filled full, or we could say fulfilled. On top of that-as if that were not exciting enough-by daily obeying the command to keep on being filled, we open the door for the Holy Spirit to do His work. We do our part to set up the whole church for joining in that filling. We pray that the entire church will experience a "chain revival," leaping on from one degree of glory to another.

June 20
Metamorphosis
Romans 6:6

*"We know that our old self was crucified with him in order that the body of sin might be brought to nothing, so that we would no longer be enslaved to sin." (*Romans 6:6)

The man in the pulpit said something so simple I wondered how I, a grown man of 20 years, could have missed it so long. "The key to the successful Christian life," he said, "is surrender and faith." I hadn't been at all sure I could make it spiritually or that God would enable me. But, sitting there on the plank bench in that tabernacle, the confidence began to surge that God would make me into a different person. And that's the meaning of the word in II Corinthians 3:18—metamorphosis, a transformation of nature. I began to believe it really could happen in me, I tightened the trust connection.

Once those inhibitors of growth are identified and removed—ignorance, unyieldedness, unbelief—the Spirit is free to move in transforming power. But He doesn't do it to a passive individual. Romans 6:6 tells us; *"We know that our old self was crucified with him in order that the body of sin might be brought to nothing, so that we would no longer be enslaved to sin."* He expects us to participate in the process through using the "tools" He provides: prayer, Scripture, church, adversity. Let me illustrate how each of these worked in changing me from a short-fused, shoot-from-the-lip person into something more like Jesus.

I was praying, reading my Bible, and attending church faithfully—had been doing those things all my life. But they weren't focused on growth, especially growth out of my occasional outbursts of bad temper. Now that the turnaround was complete and I was "going for it," those "tools" began to work.

➢ The Word enlightened me and gave me confidence of what could be.

➢ My daily prayer focused on a desperate cry for deliverance from my personal quagmire of spiritual failure. I didn't say, "God, help me be good today;" I said," Lord, I've got a big patience deficit. Help me win out today over my short fuse and loose tongue."

➢ The church? The worship service enlightened and got me started, but at that point I didn't know about small group accountability, and I didn't have a spiritual "buddy." My father, however, was "church" to me. I wouldn't have made it on my own. He instructed me, was always gently available, and, above all, lived the life I longed for. That kind of close-up view will give a person assurance about the reality and possibility of a life of "victory"!

Those three tools became an indispensable part of my upward spiral, but to answer my prayer for mouth-control and a patient spirit, God used the circumstances of life, adversity.Fifty years and counting! They were God's severe mercies, designed to make me like Jesus. Paul calls suffering a grace (Phil 1:29)—the same word used of salvation—an unearned gift for our welfare, a "means of grace."

What is the Spirit of God up to? He will, if we let Him, make us into working models of Jesus to attract people to himself. How has he been doing that in your life? Look back at your own life. How have you changed from impatience toward inner tranquility, from lust toward purity, from gluttony toward self-control, from materialism toward contentment and generosity, from ego-centric thinking toward preoccupation with the concerns of others, from doubt toward confidence in God's promises? Or maybe it's been something else God has been working on. . .

Have you experienced a step forward in knowledge, yieldedness, or trust? Note how the Bible, prayer, the church or adversity participated in the change; the metamorphosis, a transformation of your nature!

June 21
Ignorance
2 Peter 1

"For this very reason, make every effort to supplement your faith with virtue, and virtue with knowledge, and knowledge with self-control, and self-control with steadfastness, and steadfastness with godliness, and godliness with brotherly affection, and brotherly affection with love. For if these qualities are yours and are increasing, they keep you from being ineffective or unfruitful in the knowledge of our Lord Jesus Christ. For whoever lacks these qualities is so nearsighted that he is blind, having forgotten that he was cleansed from his former sins." 2 Peter 1:5-9

Paul remonstrates, "Don't you know?" (Rom. 6:16). His readers ought to know what happened when they came to Christ, and they ought to know how to live godly lives today–but maybe they do not. So Paul explains. In fact, the abundance of biblical teaching on the subject of sanctification implies that it is possible to be ignorant, that a person needs to learn what is right and wrong and how to do right.

But there is little direct teaching about the problem of ignorance, especially as a reason for one's failure to live like a normal Christian. Perhaps the lack is because there is a moral responsibility for ignorance. A new believer may be excused for ignorance and spiritually infantile behavior (Heb. 5:11-6:3), but to continue in that condition is not only unnecessary but also wrong (2 Peter 1:5-9, 12-13, 15, 3:1-2). In other words, to some degree a person is responsible for their ignorance about their own sub-Christian condition, about God's provision for successful Christian living, and about their own responsibility to appropriate that provision. If they were responding to the light they had, God would be providing all the information they need to keep progressing in a normal Christian life.

Having said this, however, I recognize that many Christians have never been exposed to teaching concerning the possibility and necessity of a life that overcomes our own inclination to wrong choices. They need to be enlightened. At the point of enlightenment, the root cause of failure becomes clear. If the root cause is primarily ignorance, there will be an immediate response to the new information. Accepting it and living by it. If, on the other hand, the true reason all along has been disobedience or unbelief, masquerading under the guise of ignorance, there will be resistance to any exhortation to repent or to trust God for a radically different quality of life. Because a common cause of failed expectations in the Christian life is ignorance of the possibilities and resources, God's people need constant instruction. The more common and more basic the reason for failure, however, is unbelief.

Which is it for you? *Ignorance* about God's standard and God's provision? Pursue knowledge of God's word and ways that you might respond in faith and live differently. Perhaps it is *unbelief*, you are not quite convinced God can really change your life. Or *active rebellion*. This cause for failure in the Christian life is easiest to identify. God is still available; He has not changed and He is capable of winning the conflict. No one who is deliberately rejecting the known will of God in one area of life can expect to receive His enabling to live supernaturally in other areas, a truth that most Christians who are actively rebellious know. Why not settle the issue now? What keeps you from becoming all God wants for you?

June 22
Unbelief
Galatians 3:3

"Are you so foolish? Having begun by the Spirit, are you now being perfected by the flesh?" (Galatians 3:3)

By *unbelief* I refer to a lack of the only response acceptable to God. Biblical faith is two-sided, including the more passive aspect of reliance and trust and the more active aspect of obedience. In the Old Testament, *faith* might be more accurately rendered *faithful* in most instances, for the objective aspect of an obedient response to God was intended. The more common word was *fear*, or reverent awe–the unconditional amen of the soul to God, the expression of the same basic requirement for any acceptable relationship between creature and Creator. In the New Testament, the subjective aspect of *reliance* predominated the writings of John and Paul, but the original concept of *obedience* was never lost. James explored fully the relationship between obedience and trust as aspects of saving faith. It is, therefore, often helpful, in searching for the root cause of subnormal Christian attitudes and conduct, to distinguish between disobedience and lack of trust.

Active rebellion. This cause for failure in the Christian life is easiest to identify. God is still available; He has not changed and He is capable of winning the conflict. But *"your wickedness has separated you from your God, and your sins have hidden His face from you so that He does not hear."* (Isaiah 59:2 Amp) No one who is deliberately rejecting the known will of God in one area of life can expect to receive His enabling to live supernaturally in other areas, a truth that most Christians who are actively rebellious know.

Passive drift. This second way of disobedience is far more common and not as easily identified. Through failure to pursue actively God's highest standards, through neglect of Bible meditation, prayer, or active church involvement, or through the accumulation of small, hardly conscious disobediences into a callous pattern of spiritual insensitivity, a person may leave his or her "first love" (Revelations 2:4) and become lukewarm and actually obnoxious to God (Revelations 3:15-16). Passive drift will distance a person from God just as surely as active rebellion, though it may take longer and prove more difficult to identify. Because the relationship is not easily recognized, especially by the person experiencing it, this condition is more dangerous than that of conscious rebellion. The original covenant relation with God has been violated, and the person can no longer experience the normal, Spirit-empowered life God promises. I believe that this passive drift into a condition of disobedience is the most common reason for failure in the Christian life.

Some earnest, fearful souls may be guilty of unbelief in a second way. They seem to long for holiness of life, to be unconditionally yielded to God's will, to strive and struggle, but yet they fall short. Such failure may partly be due to unbiblical expectations, but often the root problem is lack of trust in God that He will do what He promised.

We have identified disobedience and lack of trust as the reasons most Christians subsist in a condition of defeat and spiritual poverty. These reasons reflect the common malady of unbelief, for which the cure of faith is necessary. How is it for you? Do either of these reasons cause you to live in a condition you do not desire? Choose faith today, choose obedience believing God will do all He says He will do!

June 23
Cure for Spiritual Failure: Faith
Romans 6:11

"Now unto him that is able to keep you from falling, and to present you faultless before the presence of his glory with exceeding joy, to the only wise God our Savior, be glory and majesty, dominion and power, both now and ever. Amen." (Jude 24-25).

First, let us reaffirm that there is a cure. There is indeed freedom from the wretched condition of bondage to sin and failure: it comes through Jesus Christ our Lord (Rom. 7:24-25). It is possible to live in the Spirit and not fulfill the desires of our sinful disposition, to be more than conquerors in Christ, indeed, to participate in "all the fullness of God" (Eph. 3:19).

When Scripture faces the problem of failing Christians and offers a better way, it consistently points back to what happened when we first experienced saving grace. *"Even so reckon yourself to be dead indeed unto sin, but alive unto God in Christ Jesus"* (Romans 6:11). In fact, the central biblical passage on the subject, Romans 6, repeatedly points back to the initial transaction, the original event in which we were freed from sin. Recognize and rely on what has already happened to you, says Paul.

The problem of Christians who behave like decent non-Christians is addressed in 1 Corinthians 3. What is the solution? Paul points us back to the time of their "planting," to the original laying of the foundation: *"Do you not know that you are God's temple and that God's Spirit dwells in you?"* (v. 16). Paul calls into question their salvation: *"Examine yourselves to see whether you are in the faith; test yourselves. Do you not realize that Christ Jesus is in you–unless, of course, you fail the test?"* (2 Cor. 13:5).

Peter exults in the fact that God has given us, with Christ, all the resources needed for life and godliness. After describing the incredibly beautiful life that the Christian has, he admits that not all Christians experience such a life. What are they to do? *"But if anyone does not have them (these glorious characteristics of a fruit-filled life], he is nearsighted and blind, and has forgotten that he has been cleansed from his past sins"* (2 Peter 1:9).

Scripture treats failure in this way because success in continuing the Christian life, like success in beginning it, depends upon a relationship with a Person. Simple faith is the secret, whether for initial salvation or for experiencing success in the Christian life today. Faith is the answer to the sin question–both for the unredeemed person and for the redeemed individual

The key to the problem of subnormal Christian experience is found in a personal relationship. Is Jesus Christ Lord of your life? Then He has assumed the responsibility for making you successful. The original commitment must be reaffirmed if that initial faith-contract has been violated. Then, just as repenting, believing people received life by God's grace, so now the yielded, trusting person will receive abundance of life by God's grace.

Faith is thus the key to appropriating God's provision for successful Christian living. We cannot live the Christian life until we have that provision; by faith we are justified and receive the life of the Spirit. So may we now, this day, live the God-intended life!

June 24
Provision
Ephesians 5:25-29

"Husbands, love your wives, as Christ loved the church and gave himself up for her, that he might sanctify her, having cleansed her by the washing of water with the word, so that he might present the church to himself in splendor, without spot or wrinkle or any such thing, that she might be holy and without blemish. In the same way husbands should love their wives as their own bodies. He who loves his wife loves himself. For no one ever hated his own flesh, but nourishes and cherishes it, just as Christ does the church" (Ephesians 5:25-29)

The biblical view of God-ordained relationships between a husband and a wife could more accurately be called complementary rather than egalitarian. As each fills a complementary role to the other, the husband and the wife form a complete union. Today we will consider the biblical role of a husband.

Scripture indicates the husband is to provide for the health and well-being of the wife and family. If you are a husband, evaluate your care for your wife in the areas discussed below. If you are a wife or want to be a wife, I suggest you pray that your husband take on his God given responsibilities. But be careful that you don't take it away again! So how does a husband provide for the family?

Material. The most obvious need is material. Paul wrote, *"If anyone does not provide for his own, that is his own household, he has denied the faith and is worse than an unbeliever"* (1 Tim. 5:8). The husband is responsible to see that bread is on the table. That doesn't mean the wife can't earn money too, even more than he. But his is the final responsibility to guarantee family livelihood.

Spiritual. The husband is responsible to do all in his power to provide for a spiritually healthy family. Many husbands abdicate spiritual leadership of the home to their wives, not realizing they are forfeiting the benefits of solidarity in God. A marriage that isn't founded on God and His Word is spiritually impotent. When problems arise, how sound can the solutions be if the couple doesn't seek the Lord's guidance? And what kind of message is the husband communicating to his children about the priority of a walk with God?

Intellectual. A husband is also to provide for his wife's full intellectual development. It is selfish for a husband to go through school on the sacrificial labors of a loyal wife and then make no provision for her to maximize her potential, pursuing advanced education if she wishes.

Protection. Protect her in the demands on her time, safety in her life, finances and even in unhealthy relationships. Increasingly, the greatest need for protection is from the husband himself. Physical abuse should be unthinkable, and the standard must be never to touch the wife in anger.

Emotional. A husband is also responsible to protect his wife from other means of harm, such as verbal abuse and psychological wounds. Her emotional health is intertwined with her spiritual and intellectual well-being. If any marital relationship is being poisoned by emotional abuse, the husband should seek counseling. If he won't seek help, the wife must. If she is intimidated or has a false view of loyalty that discourages her from taking action, church leaders must step in to prevent disaster.

Sexual. Another physical provision is for sexual fulfillment, Paul explains in 1 Cor. 7:3-4. A husband who is consistently gratified sexually but doesn't take the time and care to provide fulfillment for his wife grievously wrongs her. After all, she owns his body. In the admonitions for the husband in this passage, we see the picture of a loving, sacrificial servant leader who takes responsibility for leading the home but is never domineering. Why? Because his leadership is to resemble that of Jesus, whose leadership of the church is sacrificial and caring (Ephesians 5:25,29). And remember that love colors everything about the husband's leadership role (Ephesians 5:25,28).

June 25
Partnering in Growth
Hebrews 10:25

"...not neglecting to meet together, as is the habit of some, but encouraging one another, and all the more as you see the Day drawing near." (Hebrews 10:25)

One of the purposes of the local congregation is to build a support network of people who grow strong together in studying the Word, uniting in prayer, exhorting one another and setting the example for one another. Together we build spiritual muscle in preparation for our spiritual battle in a way we never could on our own.

But there's more. A high-ranking Air Force officer sat by me on the plane. Though American planes over North Vietnam took an average of one hit every 12 sorties, he came through more than 300 flights unscathed. "What a great pilot!" I exclaimed. "No," he responded, "What a great partner! You always go in pairs and you're responsible to watch the tail of your partner. Your job is to warn him when the missile is coming. If you fail, there's no hope for your partner." So it is in spiritual warfare—you need a faithful partner to watch your tail!

That's where an accountability partner comes in, someone you can share with openly about your temptations, your victories, your defeats and with whom you can stand heart to heart in prayer for victory. A word of caution: it's not usually wise to share with a partner who is vulnerable to the same temptation you are fighting. A drowning man doesn't need another drowning man to come to the rescue! But one of the greatest defenses against temptation is a buddy in the battle, an accountability partner to pray with you about that besetting temptation. As Hebrews 10:25 reminds us: *"do not neglect to meet together, as is the habit of some, but encourage one another."* If you have a prayer buddy or accountability partner and haven't shared your struggle with temptation, why not do it this week?

Thus we have a defensive strategy that uses the weapons of the Spirit to prepare for battle. Only now can we build a defensive wall around our minds to block out the ideas of the world and counter the onslaughts of the enemy. *Reject and keep on resisting the conforming influences of your environment,* says Paul in 1 Corinthians 12:1- 2 and this we will do with the Word, with prayer, and with our fellow soldiers.

Scan the war stories recorded in Genesis 3:1-6 and Matthew 4:1-11. Here we have deadly battles, first between Satan and Eve, then between Satan and Jesus—the welfare of billions depending on the outcome of each battle. Eve met the enemy with a background of a perfect heredity and a perfect environment; Jesus had a dreadful heredity and environment. But Eve lost, Jesus won.

Eve wasn't all that committed to the authority of God's word and quickly abandoned her only defense, accepting the enemy's word over God's. Satan cynically used Bible quotes to push his ungodly ends. Only Jesus used the Word of God as His weapon. And He won! You will, too. But you must stockpile your ammunition, or you won't have it available at the time of testing.

There are two ways we can stockpile ammunition: regular reading and selective study. For example, I may be blind to the discontent in my life that is choking out the growth of joy and peace. As I read the Word, day by day, I see how great He is, how greatly He cares about me. Then I begin to realize how sinful my discontent really is, how stupid it is in the light of his greatness. The Word has spotlighted a temptation I didn't even know existed, has alerted me to a hidden enemy. Selective study, on the other hand, is to search out all the Bible teaches about some personal temptation. Those passages can then be used as a weapon in the moment of temptation, like Jesus did.

You do well to start the day in devotional reading. This sets your heart in the right direction. Do you add a purposeful stockpiling of regular reading and study of God's word? Are you growing in knowledge of God's heart for you and your life by knowing His word? If so, well done!

June 26
Birth Rate
Acts 1:8

But you will receive power when the Holy Spirit has come upon you, and you will be my witnesses in Jerusalem and in all Judea and Samaria, and to the end of the earth." (Acts 1:8)

When God commissioned the church to reach the world, He told them to start at home-in Jerusalem. He's concerned about the lost people in your world: where you live, work, and play. If God's passion is the salvation of people and His method for reaching them is other people, surely the Spirit-given ability to win people to Christ is very important. But what does the gift of evangelism look like? My ambition was to be a pioneer church-starting missionary among those who had never heard the gospel, but I was a schoolteacher. So I prayed earnestly for the gift of evangelism. And I went to work, preaching on weekends and during vacation. Sometimes many would come to Christ, sometimes no one would respond. I pled with God, sometimes with tears, to give me the gift of evangelism. After all, the Spirit had told me through Paul to do that: "*Eagerly desire the greater gifts*" (1 Cor. 12:31).

My problem was, I had the wrong idea of what the gift looked like. I thought of "evangelism" as a public meeting in which the gospel is proclaimed, an invitation given, and people respond. That is one type of evangelism, but it isn't the only form.

A witness is someone who has a personal experience and talks about it. Think of the term witness as used in a court of law. If I've only heard about the crime but haven't seen it, I'm no witness. If I've seen it, but won't talk, I'm no witness.

In the last of the great commissions (Acts 1:8), all disciples are commissioned as witnesses. Disciples have experienced God and are to tell others the good news. But not all are given the gift of evangelism (1 Corinthians 12:29-30). All believers are part of a "team" that brings people to faith. In that way the church grows. And God does expect His church to grow-"*I will build my church,*" said Jesus (Matthew 16:18). The Book of Acts records how He did it: the Spirit won large numbers to Christ and started local congregations all over the Roman Empire through many witnessing Christians and a handful of pioneer evangelists. Every church should be baptizing new believers unless there are special circumstances.

When I agonized over not having the gift of evangelism, my definition of "evangelism" was too limited. Perhaps God heard my prayer, was giving me the gift, and I just wasn't smart enough to recognize it. When we got to Japan, we found we could live in a community and love people in Jesus' name and many would come to faith. In a land where the average church has 25 members, even after decades of existence, we were baptizing 20 new converts a year. God had answered my prayer for the gift! Or had He? I rarely prayed with someone to receive Christ, and we never gave a public invitation. Then how did they come?

I call it body-life reproduction. We discovered that the Spirit-led or Spirit-filled church as a body can bring new believers to God's family. If church members are living authentic, Spirit-filled lives, and talking about it, people will come to faith. Ordinarily, every church should be baptizing new believers. Church-growth experts say that in the typical American community a church should be growing at 5 percent a year. This 5 percent should not be through baptizing its own children or from believers coming from other churches. New converts should account for a 5 percent increase. If a church isn't reaching new believers, something is wrong. Here are some possible reasons:

• The church may be spiritually ill, incapable of reproducing, in need of revival. Members may not be modeling an authentic Christian lifestyle that's attractive to unbelievers. The passion for lost people may have died out, or united prayer for the lost may be weak.

• Not many members may be sharing the gospel-too few faithful witnesses.

• Too few members have the gift of evangelism. Analysts say that in most churches that are growing through new believers coming to faith, about 10 percent of the members have the gift of evangelism.

• In some cases, the people to be evangelized may be especially unresponsive. For example, a missionary working among Muslims in New York City would not likely get this kind of growth.

The problem is that we often use unresponsive people as an excuse. Wherever I am, if people are not being saved, I'm tempted to proclaim it to be "hard soil." Assuming that we aren't rationalizing, unusual hardness in a given community can be a cause of little fruit.

How is the "birth rate" in your church? Do you think God is pleased? We don't want to be judgmental, but as spiritual "fruit inspectors" it wouldn't hurt to make a general estimate. In fact, I think it's important to be honest in evaluating our own church life as best we can.

June 27
Non-Property Robbery
Exodus 20:15

"You shall not steal" (Exodus 20:15)

There are varieties of theft. "Thou shalt not steal" applies not only to property; many other things can be stolen— reputation, for example. This is a form of stealing as well, often depriving the owner of a most precious possession, his name. Talk is constantly used to steal a person's position, his job, a friendship, or even a marriage. All of these thefts are far more serious in effect than the theft of property, yet rarely can be prosecuted and never compensated.

Idea Theft. Idea theft is often combined with deception to cover the theft, thus violating the ninth commandment as well. Researchers claim that a majority of American students cheat, and an increasing number of teachers accept the practice. At least one judge has ruled in favor of the cheater and against the "honor system" that requires students to report cheating. Plagiarism, "the appropriation or imitation of the language, ideas, and thoughts of another author, and representation of them as one's original work,"[31] is commonly practiced by students, but also by teachers who sometimes steal not only the grand ideas of other scholars, but also the work of their own students!

It may be difficult at times to know when the ideas of others have been so assimilated as to be one's own, but the use of quotations from others, giving the impression that they are one's own words, or the use of a concept that is unique to its originator clearly violates the commandments against lying and stealing.

Idea theft is not confined to schools, however, since the practice is rife in industry as well. How many technicians or junior executives have been hired away from their company in order to get at its secrets? So the theft is no longer merely private, but corporate.

A related way of stealing is to preempt the benefit due someone else. Copyright law is supposed to protect authors and artists from this kind of robbery, but all too often it is the church that steals the benefit due an author by

---

[31] The Random House Dictionary of the English Language, 1968.

duplicating musical scores for the choir or a "Peanuts" cartoon for the church bulletin.

There is no clear-cut principle to establish when an idea or piece of literature or art, published for the general public, becomes public domain. The limits of how long an author or artist deserves protection for additional benefit he or his descendants might get is a matter of judgment as to what is a fair return. In civilized society this judgment is corporate and established by law, though legitimately subject to change.

Laws do change, but the Christian is obligated to abide by the law as it stands, and copyright law is an honest effort to protect people from violations of the eighth commandment, "Thou shalt not steal."

Time Theft. Finally, it is possible, at least in the Western world, to steal time. The employee who comes late or fritters away time on the job is not, technically, stealing time, but the benefit contracted for and due his employer. This becomes more difficult as work returns to the home office and time becomes more fluid. Are we hired for time or task? But to carelessly or deliberately keep a person waiting for an appointment is felt by most people in Protestant nations to be a form of stealing. "Time is money," we say, and to steal my time is to steal my money. This would apply equally to the teacher who is careless about the time of students or the physician the time of his clients, just as much as to the guest who holds up a dinner party.

But people in other cultures do not always share this view. In Latin and Eastern lands, for example, people are said to be event-oriented rather than time-oriented. People are not expected to be "on time" in starting or closing a meeting or engagement, nor even in getting the bus to the terminal on schedule. In such a culture, is tardiness an ethical matter? Or, instructed by others who are more casual about life, should Americans stop being so "hyper" about promptness?

For us the question becomes what will you and I do about these considerations? Are we careful to attribute ideas to their source? Or do we freely use others' work thinking. "Well, it advances Kingdom ministry" so it doesn't really matter? Do we honor copyright law? Do we steal time? Are we perpetually late, leaving others waiting? Are we taking time from our employers? How can you not be a thief in these areas?

June 28
Culturally Defined Ownership
Exodus 20:15

"*Do not steal*" (Exodus 20:15)

If we accept that stealing is taking from another that which one has no biblical grounds for taking, the precise boundaries of what is "private property" and what is "one's right to take" may be somewhat conditioned by the views of a particular society. In ancient Israel it was ethical to glean the leftovers of harvest and illegal for the owner to harvest the entire crop, but in many societies this "gleaning" would be viewed as stealing. In America one certainly does not "glean" in Sears after a major sale! In Joseph's Egypt it may have been all right to expropriate people's land in exchange for a welfare handout, but the mayor of New York City had better not try that! In some tribes any property left outside one's hut is available for anyone to take, but don't try that with your neighbor's lawn mower. When people groups following two different definitions of ownership meet, there can be a clash. To the Native American who did not recognize private land ownership, the white man, coming with a different set of rules, was the ultimate thief.

These differences do not necessarily undermine the commandment not to steal, for all societies recognize the right of personal ownership and consider robbery a crime. This understanding does not relativize biblical standards because the difference is not in the definition of stealing, but in the definition of ownership, and when taking what by whom is considered legitimate. Along the borders of definition of personal ownership there is some latitude for a society to establish its own norms, and it is wrong for the Christian in that society, even if he is the citizen of another society, to violate those norms. Whether the violation is inherently sinful or simply sinful by being declared illegal or unacceptable, the Christian should prove blameless.

Perhaps the question of stealing time falls in this category. If the person who loses time is offended, that is, considers it an unwarranted personal loss, then the sensitive Christian should not carelessly or deliberately "take that which is another's," for the Scripture gives him no right to do so.

Stealing and lying are often intertwined and feed one another. Furthermore, they have a single underlying principle: They violate integrity. Personal integrity demands honesty, complete freedom from any form of cheating, stealing, or taking advantage of others. Divine guidance, according to the traditional view, is one of the Christian's deepest needs and highest privileges. Scripture is replete with reports of God's guidance in nonmoral matters. The Bible gives the unbiased observer the strong impression that the examples are chosen, not only (or even always) for their special significance in the plan of redemption, but also as windows on God's way of doing things. though Scripture nowhere speaks of human "free will," it is full of admonitions concerning full responsibility for the choices humans make.

Perhaps the strong biblical teaching on God's sovereign purpose is the key to understanding guidance. He knows exactly where he is going, and he is going to get there. Furthermore, we are called to participate with him in the accomplishment of his purposes.

Some say that God is interested in or has a "will" only in important matters; the insignificant matters are of no concern to him. But this can be a loose cannon on deck. While I grant that there is a legitimate and important distinction, often what appears the least significant can prove in the end to have been the most significant. How less consequential can a decision be than when and where to take a bath? Yet the whole career of the greatest human leader of all time was decided by that choice of Pharaoh's daughter. For an Eastern potentate to take a slave girl for a night (and with a good purpose in mind, yet, and in response to his wife's urging) was not considered a moral issue and would not have seemed a very significant event. But, in point of fact, Abraham's liaison with Hagar resulted in a conflict that rages four thousand years later with greater intensity than ever in the confrontation between Arabs and all others, especially the descendants of Sarah. "Little" choices have a way of becoming "big"!

In any event, biblical teaching on God's sovereignty is clear that he does have a plan for human affairs and that our primary link with that plan is prayer.

June 29
Right to Wealth or Care for the Poor?
Luke 16:13-14

"No servant can serve two masters. . . . You cannot serve God and mammon." The Pharisees, who were lovers of money, heard all this, and they scoffed at him. (Luke 16:13-14)

True, "freedom" is important in Scripture, but the freedom advocated, especially in the New Testament, is primarily spiritual and only minimally political. Economic freedom to make unlimited amounts of money is not presented in Scripture at all; the only *economic* freedom addressed is freedom from poverty and oppression. Legislation can make citizens free to accumulate, but freedom to do so does not make it happen. "Economic freedom" can mean freedom to get (capitalism) or freedom to subsist (socialism). Since freedom to get always works to the advantage of the smart, ruthless, or economically powerful, it is only proper that the biblical emphasis should be on protecting the weak and less fortunate.

Whose freedom is more violated, a wealthy person prohibited from becoming more wealthy (or compelled to become less wealthy) or a poor person who is trapped in poverty? Who is in greater bondage, the one who has and is prohibited from getting more, or the one who has not and is prohibited by his circumstances from getting at all? On which kind of freedom does the Bible lay emphasis?

Since Scripture is strong on setting free those oppressed economically, the crucial question becomes whether the right of private property in Scripture is the right to unlimited accumulation and possession. The law of Jubilee (Leviticus 25) clearly presents strict limitations to permanent accumulation on the part of the strong at the expense of the weak or unfortunate. The concept of taxation also clearly sets limits. So it would seem impossible, on biblical grounds, to make the right of private property an unlimited right.

Though it is difficult to prove from Scripture that civil government must guarantee the right to accumulate unlimited wealth, it is replete with strong teaching on the obligation of a society to protect and provide for the poor. Give justice to the weak and the fatherless; maintain the right of the afflicted and the destitute. Rescue the weak and the needy; deliver them from the hand of the wicked. (Psalm 82:3-4)

Is not this the fast that I choose: to loose the bonds of wickedness, to undo the thongs of the yoke, to let the oppressed go free, and to break every yoke? Is it not to share your bread with the hungry, and bring the homeless poor into your house; when you see the naked, to cover him? . . . If you take away from the midst of you the yoke, . . . pour yourself out for the hungry and satisfy the desire of the afflicted, then shall your light rise in the darkness. (Isaiah 58:6-10)

For three sins of Israel, even for four, I will not turn back my wrath. They sell the righteous for silver, and the needy for a pair of sandals. They trample on the heads of the poor as upon the dust of the ground and deny justice to the oppressed. (Amos 2:6-7, NIV)

Depart from me, you cursed, into the eternal fire prepared for the devil and his angels; for I was hungry and you gave me no food, I was thirsty and you gave me no drink, I was a stranger and you did not welcome me, naked and you did not clothe me, sick and in prison and you did not visit me. (Matthew 25:41-43)

The Bible has a great deal more to say to the capitalist about how his behavior must be modified than it does to the socialist. But since an economic *system* cannot be imposed without political sanctions, and since human beings are radically self-oriented, thus subverting any economic system, I conclude that neither system has a biblical mandate for imposition. Either will founder on the shoals of human nature.

Therefore, the Christian in either system should work toward change to bring it increasingly into conformity with the great biblical principles of justice and mercy. If freedom can be combined with these far more basic concepts, all the better. Perhaps, in a fallen society, the freedom won through the painful balancing of the rights of one group against those of another is the only hope for some measure of justice. Regardless, let us remember personal integrity in any economic system demands honesty, complete freedom from any form of cheating, stealing, or taking advantage of others.

June 30
Default Setting
Romans 2:14-15

"…when the Gentiles instinctively do what the law demands, ... they show that the work of the law is written on their hearts. Their consciences confirm this. Their competing thoughts will either accuse or excuse them" (Rom. 2:14-15).

Even though we have been designed in God's image, forgiven, declared innocent, justified, given a new nature, and indwelled by the Holy Spirit, we continue to sin. But "Christ has liberated us to be free" (Gal. 5:1)! Today we will look at God's provision to liberate His children from the bondage of guilt, setting us on the freedom trail. Identify a particular sin that holds you in bondage and brings relentless feelings of guilt.

The first step on the freedom trail is to confess sin. First John 1:9 tells us, *"If we confess our sins, He is faithful and righteous to forgive us our sins and to cleanse us from all unrighteousness."* Confessing means agreeing with God about our sins, stopping the rationalization and the other ineffective methods we studied yesterday, and facing up to our guilt. Of course, that means confessing with a view to change—repent, we might say. The result? He will set us free! Instant sin, instant confession, instant forgiveness.

But there's a problem. We're so adept at covering our trail that we may not even recognize the sin. So what happened to our conscience? Isn't it supposed to alert us to guilt?

Paul wrote that when Gentiles *"instinctively do what the law demands, ... they show that the work of the law is written on their hearts. Their consciences confirm this. Their competing thoughts will either accuse or excuse them"* (Rom. 2:14-15). Did Paul have in mind a function of the soul or maybe a separate entity designed to monitor human behavior? I think not. Notice that he connected conscience with heart and thoughts. Conscience is simply human judgment in moral matters. Conscience is to the health of the soul what nerve endings are to the health of the body. A deadened conscience is a death-dealing malady; a quickened conscience, a precious gift to be nurtured. So to have a reliable conscience—judgment in moral matters—we need to reprogram our thinking by the Word and by sensitivity to the voice of the Holy Spirit. Romans 12:2 tells us how to reprogram our thinking through the Word. *"Do not be conformed to this age, but be transformed by the renewing of your mind, so that you may discern what is the good, pleasing, and perfect will of God."*

It's very important to work constantly at renewing our minds so that our moral judgment becomes ever more reliable. A malfunctioning conscience or deafness to the Spirit is deadly. Eternal vigilance is the price of freedom from misleading moral judgment.

Taiho, a beautiful collie, was the most marvelous pet we ever had. But Taiho wasn't a reliable watchdog. A stranger was greeted with excited tail wagging and dog kisses to the extent permitted. But when one of us returned home, the barking was deafening. Some Christians seem to have a Taiho conscience—friendly embrace of the deadliest enemies and wild alarms at the most innocent conduct. Is your judgment in moral matters reliable?

How do I distinguish among the various voices I hear? Is my conviction of sin the voice of the Spirit or the yapping of my own malfunctioning moral judgment? Perhaps it's neither. Maybe those impulses are from the Enemy, the Accuser, the Liar. How can I tell?

Learn what the Word of God says on the subject. Is this desire a temptation to sin as defined by Scripture, or is it something I've picked up from tradition or from a hyperactive, guilt-ridden conscience?

The conviction of the Spirit is specific, not a general sense of unease or guilt. He puts His finger on the spot with scriptural truth, either directly or through someone else. Another difference from Satan's promptings is that the gentle Spirit doesn't harass me. He's persistent, but His is a gentle, perhaps intermittent pressure, not constant, indiscriminate, accusing agitation. I accept the accusation, treat it as a sin, confess it, and forsake it.

July 1
What do I Love?
1 John 2:16

"For all that is in the world—the desires of the flesh and the desires of the eyes and pride of life—is not from the Father but is from the world." (1 John 2:16)

Many cultures are saturated with idolatrous practices, and in fact, anyone who worships a god other than the God of Scripture is worshiping an idol. We Christians in the United States may not experience those exact temptations, but there are still other idols that tempt us today.

One day as I walked past my father's bedroom door, he called out to me: "Robertson, come here. I want to tell you something very important about ministry." I went to his bedside, wondering why he would tell me about ministry when that was the furthest thing from my teenage mind. "The three great temptations of the ministry," he continued, "are girls, gold, and glory." I was literally dumbfounded. I had always assumed everyone in ministry was like my father, and those sins were as far from him as fire from ice. Nevertheless, I tucked away the idea for future reference.

In Japan I never heard of a single pastor who fell to adultery. Across the years I knew hundreds of pastors, some of them leaders who knew other hundreds. One national church leader, in answer to my query, said he knew of one moral lapse. One! So I was ill prepared for an experience during my second term of service.

At a meeting of hundreds of pastors, the church leader announced his sermon topic, "The Three Sins of the Ministry." I remembered my father's comment years earlier and carefully listened to see how different things were in Japan. Imagine my astonishment to hear him list the same three temptations.

Is sex, money, or fame a special temptation for you? If so, why not confess it before the Lord and covenant with Him to launch a major idol-smashing campaign until the power is broken? Ask Him to give you discernment and courage to identify and take the actions needed to rid your life of these idols.

1 John 2:16: For all that is in the world—the desires of the flesh and the desires of the eyes and pride of life—is not from the Father but is from the world.

Let's look more closely at one of our most common idols. We don't bow before carved images, to be sure, but Paul referred to covetousness as idolatry (see Col. 3:5). In addition, he classified covetous people with fornicators, idolaters, and thieves, saying they will never even see the kingdom of God (see 1 Cor. 6:10). Coveting material possessions is a form of idolatry.

It's possible to idolize something you already own. Imagine your house burns down tonight and consumes everything you own. List in order of priority the losses that would crush you, things you would grieve over.

I sometimes go through these exercises to be sure I hold things of this earth lightly. I don't want to have even the faint scent of materialism about me. If I discover a sticking point—something I'm beginning to crave, something I hold too tightly—I immediately confess it and ask deliverance. I recognize it as idolatry creeping in, and God insists that I deal ruthlessly with it because idolatry is the ultimate disloyalty. To focus on material things is a sure sign I haven't found Him and His gracious will sufficient. God's command is clear: *"you shall not bow down to idols or serve them."*

July 2
Guilty
Matthew 5:48

"Be perfect, just as your Father in heaven is perfect" (Matt. 5:48, NKJV)

Baffled and distressed though still functioning as a valued teacher in our Christian high school, Taylor asked whether I would talk with his wife. Betsy, the school nurse, was virtually immobilized, increasingly depressed. It was Christian-life week at school, and she sent word that she needed to see me. Gradually, it came out. Betsy had given the wrong medicine to a student. In a hurry, overlooking the label, she chose the wrong medicine. No permanent bad outcomes, but Betsy was coming apart. Forgiven? Perhaps, but she could never forgive herself.

Therapists would say, "Of course. Guilt feelings are the most destructive force in a person's life, even in Christian lives, maybe especially in Christian lives." Then they would set about freeing all the Betsys in their care from those damaging feelings. But there are effective and ineffective ways to get free. I'll share with you some responses to guilt that I think are counterproductive or destructive. Are any impacting your life?

Denial. This is the problem with much therapy. Even Christian therapists can lead guilty people to dead ends by delivering them from guilt feelings without dealing with the guilt. But seeking deliverance from the feelings without being delivered from the guilt itself causes a greater problem. When therapy delivers us from the feelings alone, the deliverance won't last if the real guilt remains.

Rationalization. We can almost always find a good explanation for our bad behavior, especially if it isn't too egregious. When we speak hurtfully, we may say, "It's just a misunderstanding." But if we had been honest about it, we were just insensitive. "Well, yeah, I didn't handle that just right, but I meant well." Good motives justify bad behavior, right?

Transference. If there's failure, surely there's someone else to share the blame with, maybe to shift it to them altogether. That's easy—and perhaps justified—No sin of mine to repent of, except maybe stubbornness. But who's to say my transfer of blame to another person isn't an attempt to cover up something deeper and darker? Like a desire for power, ego satisfaction, or pride? But it's a dead-end maze.

Impotence. The pervasive conviction today is that a person isn't responsible for what he can't help. Fornication? He had been drinking. Drinking? Alcoholic parents. Alcoholic parents? Unjust society. Or how about my short fuse? Blame your father! What else do you expect? The bottom line is, I'm not really responsible. It's something I can't help, or I'm a victim of someone else's bad behavior.

Diminution. A great way to relieve guilt feelings is to redefine sin. Indeed, *"sin is the breaking of law"* (1 John 3:4), but that was not intended as a comprehensive definition. Stating a more comprehensive definition like deliberate transgression of the known will of God is to diminish God's high standard of being *"perfect, just as your Father in heaven is perfect"* (Matt. 5:48, NKJV). To be true to Scripture, ignorance is not a legitimate excuse (see Rom. 1:20), so unintentional offenses are sinful too. So is failing to be or do what I ought (see Jas. 4:17). To diminish the biblical definition of sin may give temporary relief from guilt feelings, but it's a dead-end tactic.

Not only are we unable to pay off our own debt—including the debt of continually falling short of God's glorious character—but by our attempts to do so, we also denigrate the work Jesus did on the cross to pay the debt for us. I'm saying God doesn't keep His promise of full and free atonement or He can't forgive this particularly grievous sin and still stay true to His holy and righteous character. But if I can't rely on Jesus' death to take away my guilt, I've reached another dead end. That was never His intent! God keeps his promise of full and free atonement! Today, pray that you rely on His abundant forgiveness!

July 3
The Reconnect
Romans 6:1

"What shall we say then? Are we to continue in sin that grace may abound?" (Romans 6:1)

There are two major streams of thought on the question of the warfare of a believer overcoming sin and those saying it all depends on God. One holds that there is an encounter with God at a time subsequent to salvation that lifts a person beyond all struggle and failure, sort of an instant rocket shot to the summit of perfection. So people spend a lifetime seeking to be in the right place at the right time to experience the launching. or to cling to the illusory summit! An alternative view is what I call the spectator role. A special encounter with God doesn't lift a person beyond all possibility of failure, but rather to the grandstands to watch the Spirit (or, more likely, the indwelling Christ) live out his life through you. "Let go and let God," we're instructed. You can never do anything good anyway, so get out of the way and trust Jesus to speak, to act, yes, even to think in your stead. Those are two very different views, but they have this in common: God does it all.

As we might expect, Scripture refuses to be pushed to one extreme or the other, something we're forever trying to do to it! According to Paul and other Bible authors, God must do the transforming, or it won't be done. At the same time we must participate or it won't be done. But let's be reminded that the goal is likeness to Jesus, by little and by little, and the means, as in our initial salvation, is the activity of the Spirit. But we must participate fully with his activity.

But not all Christians are spiraling up; in fact not all seem to be running a race at all. Paul asks this question. *"What shall we say then? Are we to continue in sin that grace may abound?"* (Romans 6:1)

What's the problem? What can be done about it? The New Testament often addresses the problem of substandard performance, but nowhere does it point failed Christians to some new, advanced experience, the Bible consistently points the failing Christian back to the original transaction—don't you know who you are? Don't you know who lives in you? Don't you know to whom you belong? And notice another thing—I mentioned plateauing as a self-description of many stalled Christians, but the truth is that's impossible. Either we're spiraling up, even if ever so slowly, or we're spiraling down, further and further from our goal. Oh, we will never spiral down to final destruction, but we'll certainly spiral down, further and further from intimate companionship with God, less and less like him. And that's very destructive. *"He who is not with me is against me"* (Mt. 12:30), said Jesus and so it is.

Let's go back to the re-connect. What was that "original contract" the Bible points back to? Well, salvation on God's part. He promised to save us from the penalty of sin, the power of sin, and, one day, the very presence of sin. It's the "power" we're concerned about today. And our part of the transaction? The same as in the salvation contract: faith! Does that mean the failing Christian, the one who isn't surging forward on the upward spiral, lacks faith? Indeed, it's as simple as that. But remember, there are two poles to faith, whether for salvation or sanctification. To connect with God we must repent (negative pole of faith) and believe (positive pole of faith). And so for the re-connection when there's a power outage. Yield (negative pole) and trust (positive pole). In fact, you might say it's "by faith from start to finish!"

To reconnect, for the power to surge, we must yield unconditionally to the will of God. No fine print in the contract, no reserve clauses—unconditional yield. To do that may be cataclysmic if a person has resisted long and hard, it can be a matter-of-fact transaction of turning everything over to the Master: past, present, future, successes, failures, relationships—everything. Are you stalled out, slipping back maybe, in your spiral with Jesus? Then you need to go back to the initial transaction, you need a crisis of turning. If that is your present condition and heart-longing, why not identify all the things you need to and yield these up to your Sovereign Lord? Don't hesitate, don't delay. But never again need there be the crisis of "who's boss?"

July 4
True Freedom
Hebrews 12:14

"Strive for peace with everyone, and for the holiness without which no one will see the Lord." (Hebrews 12:14)

How do we live in true freedom? That is our question for today. How can we live holy lives fully for Christ?

To *sanctify* is, literally, to set apart, and in the biblical context it means set apart to God. In the Old Testament this setting apart was both moral and ritual. An object such as a bowl could be set apart from common use for exclusive use in the temple ritual. It was then considered *holy* (from the same root as *sanctify*). But of deeper and more enduring significance was, on the one hand, a personal separation from sin, and on the other hand, his or her consecration to God. One who is set apart from sin (sanctified) is rightly called a *saint* (from the same root as *sanctify* or *holy*). This moral and theological sense of sanctification is the one I invite you to consider.

To be sanctified is of utmost importance, because *"without holiness, no one will see God"* (Hebrews 12:14). That is, until the sin problem is cared for, no one is qualified to associate with a holy God, one who is Himself completely without sin and who, moreover, cannot countenance sin in any form.

God is not only holy, however; He is supremely a God of love, and therefore His ultimate desire for human beings is for them to be restored to full, loving fellowship with Himself. But there is a barrier: sin. For complete unity of heart, two persons must be compatible, in harmony of spirit. They must have the same purposes, outlook, and way of life. If one is sinful and the other holy, what oneness can there be? Their total mind-set is in conflict. So in order to accomplish the ultimate purpose of our existence, namely, to live in loving oneness with God, the sin barrier must be removed.

Today we consider the way in which we are set apart from our sin for the purpose of becoming God's own possession. We are set apart from sin in three ways.

First, we are forgiven, so that the result of sin, eternal punishment, is cancelled.

Second, we are justified, so that our guilt is removed, our guilty record is expunged- cleared. God sees us no longer as weak, stubborn, and failing but now as one who is as clean and pure as His holy son, Jesus. These declare us forgiven and made right with God.

Third, we are set free from the control of a sinful disposition. The change is so radical as to be comparable to the change that a person experiences at birth (John 3) or death (Romans 6). Though there is continuity with the same human personality, as in the case of birth or death, in regeneration also there is passage into a totally different dimension of human life, with totally different characteristics of personal being. Sin is the prevailing characteristic of persons who live apart from God. They do not have the desire or power to choose consistently the right or to change their condition. Once we become a believer, a new life-force has been introduced that has power to prevail against our disposition that chooses wrong. Some of us may not behave this way, but this is our potential.

In these three ways, every believer has been sanctified through the atoning death of Christ (Heb. 10:10), we have been made holy (Eph. 4:24), and is thus legitimately called a saint (I Cor. 1:2, 6:11). Not all believers are saintly, as we shall see, but all true believers are saints, officially released from the condemnation due their sins, the guilty record, and the tyranny of a sinful disposition. Take a few minutes today and consider, " Do I know I am released from condemnation? Am I living free or do I live under the oppression of habitual sin? We can live consistently choosing right. May we do so!

July 5
The Spiral
1 Corinthians 3:18

"And we all, with unveiled face, beholding the glory of the Lord are being transformed into the same image from one degree of glory to another. For this comes from the Lord who is the Spirit." (1 Corinthians 3:18)

We're all born on the spiral, separated from God in a downward descent, ever more estranged from him, ever less like him, descending into ever greater destruction. Some, to be sure, are on a faster track than others, more rebellious, even defiant. And greater destruction, too, increasing dysfunction in the realm of the spirit. Then comes the big U turn— repentance and faith—and the Holy Spirit intervenes, halts the downward spiral and reverses our course so that from that time onward we've been spiraling upward. Or so it was intended.

love...obey...know...yield...trust...intimate companioning...oneness of heart...likeness to Jesus.... Is there an order to some of the responses of a believer toward the Lord as he spirals upward? Each reinforces the other, flows from and into the other. Catch the wonder of it, here's the way I listed them, at least for today:

The more I know him, the more I love him; the more I love him, the more readily I yield to him; as I yield to him and obey him, the more like him I become; the more like him I become, the greater capacity I have for love; the more I love him, the more intimately I companion with him; the more I companion with him, the better I know him.... Upward and upward toward ever greater oneness with him! What a grand spiral of ever greater likeness to Jesus and greater intimacy with him!

That is the essence of 1 Corinthians 3:18: *"And we all, with unveiled face, beholding the glory of the Lord are being transformed into the same image from one degree of glory to another. For this comes from the Lord who is the Spirit."*

Does it always happen that way? Is every true Christian on an automatic escalator, spiraling up, no matter how slowly? Or have some, as they say, stalled out? Notice that Paul doesn't say, "We all are being transformed." He gives two qualifications: (1) unveiled-face people and (2) focused-on-Jesus people are the one's who experience a steady transformation at the core of their being. By the way, that's what the word means—a change in nature, not just in appearance. In the preceding verses Paul explained how Jewish believers read Scripture but can't understand it because there's a barrier—a curtain has covered their "heart," "mind," "face" (Paul uses the three interchangeably). When they turn to the Lord, however, make the big U-turn, the Spirit sets them free from the sin bond and starts them on the upward spiral, says Paul. That first condition is clear—the sin-veil must be removed. The other condition, though clear throughout the New Testament, is not so clear in this passage. "Beholding" could also be translated, "reflecting," as most modern translators seem to favor. Both are possible translations and both are biblical truths—"beholding" people "reflect" Jesus!

What a grand spiral of ever greater likeness to Jesus and greater intimacy with him! Which are you? Going up or going down? Why not stop and settle this question with God right now? Be free from the sin-bond, on the upward spiral, intimate companionship with Jesus!

249

July 6
Immovable
1 Corinthians 15:58

"Therefore, my beloved brothers, be steadfast, immovable, always abounding in the work of the Lord, knowing that in the Lord your labor is not in vain." (1 Corinthians 15:58)

Some people are immovable, all right. We spent more time in annual conference debating mission policy on flush toilets than on evangelistic methodology! Some people think no music written after the death of Bach should be permitted in church. Actually, that kind of immovability is the temptation of the veteran—hardening of the categories! Change is threatening. But that's not what Paul is speaking of. He means we must never be shaken by the enemy's assault, by looming difficulties, by failure. I met an immovable missionary once.

The annual Pakistan-wide missionary convention was held at Murree on a ridge of a mountain in the foothills of the Himalayas. At 8,000 feet, it was a mere foothill in that company of giants! We stayed at the MK school and each morning traveled in the school van the length of the ridge to the church where the missionaries gathered. On that van was Earlene who, though a graduate of our seminary, didn't say much to me, or to anyone for that matter. She looked the stereotype of the veteran missionary, as anyone might after 25 years in the hinterland of Pakistan. Someone asked if I had talked with Earlene Voss and I said I had, but not more than passing greetings. "You'd better talk with her," he said. So I did.

"Earlene, tell me about your work. I hear you work among Muslims. Do you believe Muslims can become Christians?"

There was a reason for the question. I'd just spent a week at a pastors' conference and they didn't believe Muslims could be converted. They worked exclusively in the tiny subculture of "Christians" descended from a tribal movement Christ-ward generations earlier. Then I spent several days in a seminar on church growth and the missionaries in attendance didn't believe Muslims could be converted, at least not enough to have what you could call "church growth."

"Certainly they can," asserted Earlene with greater force than I had anticipated.

"How so?"

"Because I've seen them converted," said Earlene.

"How many have come to Christ in your community," I asked.

"About 400 at the last count," she said.

"Four hundred Muslim converts! I should think that would cause a riot."

"Well, now that you mention it, I guess we haven't had a riot in two years."

She told me how she handled the last riot. An angry mob approached her refuge for abused women. Earlene stepped outside and shut the door behind her. As the lead thug approached she gave him a swift kick in the shins and told him he should be ashamed of himself and to get out of there. Obediently, he complied!

An MK school teacher would spend vacations with Earlene. She told me that on one occasion she heard her name and Earlene's over the public address system on which the mullah provided the town "newspaper" as well as the calls to prayer.

"What did he say about us?" the young missionary asked, apprehensively. Earlene laughed.

"He just told everyone to gather at our place to kill us!"

For a quarter century, most of the time alone, Earlene labored among a hard-core Muslim people, loving 400 of them to Christ. Unmovable.

July 7
The Unholy Christian
Matthew 7:16-23

"You will recognize them by their fruits. Are grapes gathered from thornbushes, or figs from thistles? So, every healthy tree bears good fruit, but the diseased tree bears bad fruit. A healthy tree cannot bear bad fruit, nor can a diseased tree bear good fruit. Every tree that does not bear good fruit is cut down and thrown into the fire. Thus you will recognize them by their fruits. "Not everyone who says to me, 'Lord, Lord,' will enter the kingdom of heaven, but the one who does the will of my Father who is in heaven. On that day many will say to me, 'Lord, Lord, did we not prophesy in your name, and cast out demons in your name, and do many mighty works in your name?' And then will I declare to them, 'I never knew you; depart from me, you workers of lawlessness.'" (Matthew 7:16-23)

In God's project of making unholy people holy, we might ask, how may the believer experience freedom from sinful thoughts and actions? Why is it that the average Christian is not very saintly, does not reflect the character of Christ very clearly, lives much like any morally upright but unbelieving neighbor, and also relies on basically the same resources as those neighbors?

Scripture recognizes a basic difference among Christians. It distinguishes between carnal ("of the flesh") Christians, who behave like unconverted people, and spiritual Christians, whose life is dominated by the Spirit of God (I Cor. 3:1-3). All Christians are indwelt by the Holy Spirit (Rom. 8:9), but some Christians are "filled with the Spirit." The Bible speaks both of immature Christians and of mature Christians (Heb 5:11-6:3). More than exhibiting simply a difference in degree of growth, Christians' lives manifest qualitative differences: some Christians have a life pattern of defeat, whereas others have a life pattern of spiritual success.

A student once asked me, "How can you be 'carnal'?" An interesting question! Did he mean, "How long can you live in sin without losing your salvation?" Or did he mean, "How long can you live in sin before you prove that you never were really in the family of God?" Or was he hoping that one could choose the low road and follow it all the way safely home? The question perplexes sincere believers, fascinates theologians, and divides Christendom. But Scripture does not favor us with a consideration of that question. Though the issue of eternal security is important, I am emboldened by the biblical approach to the problem of the sinning Christian to suggest that for pastoral (or evangelistic) purposes, in seeking to rescue the helpless person mired in the bog of subnormal Christian experience, it may be legitimate to by-pass the question, at least for the time being.

The Bible consistently deals with people where they are and only rarely answers the theoretical problems that plague us. For example, to fearful saints who desperately want to please God, Scripture gives an abundance of reassurance. No power can ever separate them from God (John 10:28-29; Rom. 8:31-39), and they will surely complete their course successfully by His grace (Phil. 1:6). But to those who continually and deliberately reject the known will of God, Scripture gives, not reassurance but fearful warnings.

Read Matthew 7:16-23 and 1 John 3:6, 8, 10, 14… *"By their fruit you will recognize them…..No one who lives in him keeps on sinning…..* These passages and many others (e.g., Matt. 23; 25:31-46; John 15:2, 6; Heb. 3:6-19; 6:1-8; 10:26-31) show clearly the position that Scripture takes in addressing the sinner: repentance is the only option.

But how does one reconcile the two lines of teaching? Are church members living in sin saved, or are they lost? Have they been saved? Will they prove to have been saved? Have they lost their salvation? I have opinions – even convictions – about the theological answers to some of those questions, but since the Holy Spirit did not feel it necessary to answer them directly in Scripture, I feel under no compulsion to do so in the context of addressing professing Christians who are living in sin. Rather than attempting to play God and answer the question they raise, I can with confidence answer the basic question that ought to be asked: what must I do to be saved? Whatever standing people may have before God (which is unknown to me), if they are not now in a right relationship with God, they need to be. If they continue to reject the known will of God and are comfortable in that condition, I can assure them on the authority of God's Word that they have no biblical basis for any assurance of salvation. Their only option is repentance. Just as a lost person can do right (Acts 10:4, 35) but cannot consistently choose to do right (Rom. 8:7-8), so a saved person can do wrong (James 3:2, I John 1:8) but cannot consistently choose to do wrong (I John 3). Which is true of you? What will you do?

July 8
Differences
2 Corinthians 10:12

"Not that we dare to classify or compare ourselves with some of those who are commending themselves. But when they measure themselves by one another and compare themselves with one another, they are without understanding." (2 Corinthians 10:12)

We find the difference among Christians may simply be a sign of different levels of maturity. One should, in the matters of differences among Christians, deal stringently with oneself and generously in judgment of the other person–both of which responses are the opposite of our natural inclinations!

In the first place, I am not responsible to judge my brother (Romans 14:3-12); furthermore, I cannot do so accurately for myself, let alone for others (1 Corinthians 4:4). Another reason for caution in making such judgments is that the differences may be more apparent than real. What is an appropriate standard of comparison?

One must have God's perspective in order to make a proper evaluation, and who among us has that? Therefore, we are fools if we compare ourselves among ourselves (2 Cor. 10:12), for we can never have God's full perspective. Certainly we all seek to bring honor to our God by putting His glorious character on display in mortal flesh. To be sanctified is of utmost importance, because without it, no one will see God (Heb. 12:14). That is, until the sin problem is cared for, no one is qualified to associate with a holy God, one who is Himself completely without sin and who, moreover, cannot countenance sin in any form.

And the good news is, we can put His glorious character on display in mortal flesh! Every believer has been sanctified through the atoning death of Christ (Heb. 10:10), has been made holy (Eph. 4:24), and is thus legitimately called a saint (I Cor. 1:2, 6:11). Not all believers are saintly, as we shall see, but all true believers are saints, officially released from the condemnation due their sins, the guilty record, and the tyranny of a sinful disposition.

The problem of Christians who behave like decent non-Christians is dealt with in 1 Corinthians 3. What is the solution? Paul points his readers back to the time of their "planting," to the original laying of the foundation: "Know ye not that ye are the temple of God, and that the Spirit of God dwelleth in you?" (v. 16 KJV). Paul excoriates the sinning Christians of Corinth, but he does not exhort them to seek some as yet untasted experience. Rather, he calls into question their salvation: "Examine yourselves to see whether you are in the faith; test yourselves. Do you not realize that Christ Jesus is in you–unless, of course, you fail the test?" (2 Cor. 13:5).

What glorious good news when we are in the faith! No matter what may or may not have occurred in the past and no matter how inadequate my understanding, if my relationship to God is one of unconditional surrender and confident expectation that He will keep His word, I can experience a life of consistent success over temptation and growth toward His own likeness, I can see His purpose for my ministry supernaturally fulfilled, and above all, I can daily experience loving companionship with my Savior.[32]

July 9
Centerpoint
Psalm 117

Praise the LORD, all you nations; extol him, all you peoples. For great is his love toward us, and the faithfulness of the LORD endures forever. Praise the LORD." Psalm 117

What is the centerpoint of your life? Is it the same as the centerpoint of your Bible? The centerpoint is important. Consider two children on the teetertotter, change the centerpoint and the entire dynamic of balance changes.

And yet, as it is difficult for theologians to balance the justice and mercy of God, and as it is difficult for parents to balance firm discipline and loving acceptance, so it is very difficult for the Church to maintain unity and purity at the same time. It is much easier to go to a consistent extreme than to stay at the center of biblical tension. Whether in the local congregation or in the Church at large, the Church of Jesus Christ seems incapable of living out both godlike oneness and godlike purity simultaneously. The result is that the reflection of God's image is distorted, the evangelistic thrust of the church is blunted, and Christians are stunted in spiritual growth.

Consider the balance of justice/mercy, or grace/holiness, oneness/purity, missions/growth. Where is the Centerpoint? The peril becomes that most of us think that we are in the center of biblical tension and others are at the extreme. For example, two things come to mind: ministering mercy and seeking justice. The religious leaders of Christ's day were strong on justice, as they interpreted it, but weak on mercy. Jesus emphasizes a major theme in the good news of the Kingdom of heaven. He desires mercy to govern our relationships (Matthew 9:9-13 and Matthew 12:1-8). God's plan is for his people to pursue both justice and mercy for the welfare of its community.

Centerpoint- where did Jesus find the centerpoint? The first thing he did was to sit them down and give them the sermon on the mount (Luke 6). Who is happy and who is unhappy, who is fulfilled and who is unfulfilled, who is blessed and who is cursed. A great place to begin. He sets all our values on end. Where else would a person get straightened out if he didn't companion with Jesus?

---

[32] Taken from Five Views of Sanctification by Melvin E. Dieter, Anthony A. Hoekema, Stanley M. Horton, J. Robertson McQuilkin, and John F. Walvoord. Copyright © 1987 by Zondervan. Used by permission of HarperCollins Christian Publishing. www.harpercollinschristian.com . For a more complete examination by the author of biblical teaching on living the life God intended, see *Life in The Spirit,* Nashville: Broadman, 2000.

Imbalance does not come from an over-emphasis. It is impossible to have too much love or too much faithfulness. However, it is quite possible to have *unfaithfulness* masquerading as love.

I do not ask the ecumenist to be less loving. I urge him to be more faithful. I do not ask the separatist to be less faithful. I urge him to be more loving. *Depart from evil and do good; seek peace and pursue it* (Psalms 34:14). This is God's balance.

The centerpoint of the Bible is Psalm 117, short and balanced: *"Praise the LORD, all you nations; extol him, all you peoples. For great is his love toward us, and the faithfulness of the LORD endures forever. Praise the LORD."* Praise puts Him in focus. First and last words of this central chapter of the Bible- *Praise the Lord.*

God is the centerpoint of the Bible. Praise puts him centerpoint in our lives. Romans 2 is the picture of humankind off-center, skewed, destroyed. *"There will be trouble and distress for every human being who does evil"* (verse 9).

When we chart the way to God-centered living we do no wrong in pointing out that as the only path to personal self-fulfillment. Try to fill up on stuff, sex, and significance, on self, that is, and you'll get ever more empty, taught Jesus. On the other hand, work at emptying out life into God's purposes and you'll discover your "self" is filling up, fulfilled.

Why should we praise him? For two reasons: His steadfast, unfailing love and His steady, long-term, permanent faithfulness. Balanced: love and faithfulness as John says, full, simultaneously full, of grace and truth! We are so unbalanced: either all "truth" or all "grace". What is the goal of this relationship and resulting character? The goal is that ALL nations, all peoples. Not just Jerusalem, Zion, Israel not just your people or your family know Him. We find the balance-To Know Him, To Make Him Known.

July 10
Justice and Mercy
Psalm 82:3-4

"Give justice to the weak and the fatherless; maintain the right of the afflicted and the destitute. Rescue the weak and the needy; deliver them from the hand of the wicked." (Psalm 82:3-4)

Nationalized healthcare? College debt forgiveness? Fair housing? Increasing the minimum wage? Inflation? Interest rate subsidies? Tax shelter for corporations and the wealthy? The honest Christian considers the Biblical balance in life, involvement in the community, politics, policy, and giving, so let us do so over the next few days.

Some propose a biblical mandate for capitalism, while others view Scripture as on the side of socialism. Capitalism is an economic system in which investment in and ownership of the means of production, distribution, and exchange of wealth is made and maintained by private individuals or corporations, and socialism is an economic system in which the ownership and control is by the community as a whole. Advocates of capitalism seem to dominate American evangelical thought; advocates of socialism dominate evangelical thought in most of the rest of the world. Yet there are those in America also who advocate a socialistic approach to economics.

The system which creates and sustains much of the hunger, under-development, unemployment, and other social ills in the world today is capitalism. Capitalism is by its very nature a system which promotes individualism, competition, and profit-making with little or no regard for social costs. It puts profits and private gain before social services and human needs. As such, it is an unjust system which should be replaced.[33]

The Bible has a great deal more to say to the capitalist about how his behavior must be modified than it does to the socialist. But since an economic *system* cannot be imposed without political sanctions, and since human beings are radically self-oriented, thus subverting any economic system, I conclude that neither system has a biblical mandate for imposition. Either will founder on the shoals of human nature.

Therefore, the Christian in either system should work toward change to bring it increasingly into conformity with the great biblical principles of justice and mercy. If freedom can be combined with these far more basic concepts, all the better. Perhaps, in a fallen society, the freedom won through the painful balancing of the rights of one group against those of another is the only hope for some measure of justice.

"In fact, neither theology nor Scripture gives us any criteria for evaluating one system against another. Since no economic mechanism corresponds to Christian truth, if we wish to choose we will have to do so for purely natural reasons, knowing that our choice will in no way express our Christian faith."[34]

The advocate of a free market economic system emphasizes freedom and the right to private property, while those who promote a controlled market economy for the welfare of all citizens emphasize justice, fairness, and equality. Capitalism is for freedom, socialism is for equality; neither economic freedom nor equality is very pronounced in Scripture. True, "freedom" is important in Scripture, but the freedom advocated, especially in the New Testament, is primarily spiritual and only minimally political. Economic freedom to make unlimited amounts of money is not presented in Scripture at all; the only economic freedom addressed is freedom from poverty and oppression. Legislation can make citizens free to accumulate, but freedom to do so does not make it happen. "Economic freedom" can mean freedom to get (capitalism) or freedom to subsist (socialism). Since freedom to get always works to the advantage of the smart, ruthless, or economically powerful, it is only proper that the biblical emphasis should be on protecting the weak and less fortunate.

Whose freedom is more violated, a wealthy person prohibited from becoming more wealthy (or compelled to become less wealthy) or a poor person who is trapped in poverty? Who is in greater bondage, the one who has and is prohibited from getting more, or the one who has not and is prohibited by his circumstances from getting at all? On which kind of freedom does the Bible lay emphasis?

Since Scripture is strong on setting free those oppressed economically, the crucial question becomes whether the right of private property in Scripture is the right to unlimited accumulation and possession. The law of Jubilee (Lev. 25) clearly presents strict limitations to permanent accumulation on the part of the strong at the expense of the weak or unfortunate. The concept of taxation also clearly sets limits. So it would seem impossible, on biblical grounds, to make the right of private property an unlimited right.

Though it is difficult to prove from Scripture that civil government must guarantee the right to accumulate unlimited wealth, it is replete with strong teaching on the obligation of a society to protect and provide for the poor.[35] We cannot ignore this question. How do you provide for the poor? When is enough enough for the wealthy? Therefore, the Christian in either system should work toward change to bring it increasingly into conformity with the great biblical principles of justice and mercy. If freedom can be combined with these far more basic concepts, all the better. Perhaps, in a fallen society, the freedom won through the painful balancing of the rights of one group against those of another is the only hope for some measure of justice.

---

[33] Quarterly of the Christian Legal Society, spring 1981, 6–7.
[34] Jacques Ellul, *The Ethics of Freedom,* trans. Geoffrey W. Bromiley (Grand Rapids: Eerdmans, 1976), 371ff.
[35] IBE (2014), 466.

July 11
Relationship of Church and State
John 18:36

"My kingdom is not of this world..." (John 18:36)

Throughout the history of the church, people have debated the question of whether it is legitimate to work toward Christianizing society. In the Reagan era the debate heated up again. Some decried "politicizing religion" or "religionizing politics." Others wedded church and state with enthusiasm.

Contrary to what some protagonists say, no one position is the exclusive domain of a given theological persuasion. Liberals and conservatives alike range through all positions, and most disconcerting, an individual may demand separation of "religion and politics" on some issues while demanding they mix in others. In other words, it is the agenda that seems to divide.

If the issue is race, equitable distribution of wealth, a guaranteed livelihood, feminism, or armament control, you can usually count on liberal involvement and fundamentalist uninvolvement; but if the issues are abortion, law and order, pornography, the traditional family, a large defense budget, or human rights, the roles are reversed. It is not exactly that one is for big government and the other wants government to shrink to minimal roles; each wants lots of government involvement to achieve what it thinks important to the public welfare and no government presence at all in what it considers its own private business. Just a different agenda. But in seeking to win, the cry is raised, "Politics and religion must not be mixed!" What we fail to add is, "by our opponents." This (unconscious, we hope) hypocrisy adds a great deal of confusion to the already complex controversy. But the church never has agreed on these issues.

Nevertheless, the dominant Reformation-Protestant teaching was not for separation of *influence,* but for separation of the *powers* of each so that neither controlled the other. Church and state were viewed as partners in separate but overlapping spheres of responsibility for achieving God's purposes in the world. This view prevailed in northern, Protestant Europe, while the legacy of Roman Catholic church-state intermingling dominated southern Europe. The New World fell heir to the Protestant approach in the northern hemisphere and the Roman Catholic approach in the southern, where these approaches continue to this day.

The professed fears of liberals that some conservative Christians intend to impose a rightist totalitarian regime with coercive moral requirements is not even a remote possibility. No person or group of people in a modern pluralistic democracy can impose its will on an unwilling majority—or even on an unwilling minority, for that matter. Every interest group executes whatever pressure it can to have laws made and interpreted in the way that best furthers its own interests, but this can hardly be called "imposing."

It is just that many long-silent conservative people have discovered their voices, and the liberal establishment finds it hard to accept. At first the roar to the right was dismissed as an illusion created by media hype; next, curiously, it was decried as unfair and then frantically opposed as an attempt at a takeover by mindless, un-American, rightist moralists who will soon impose all the worst kinds of Puritan and Victorian private moralities on freedom-loving, benevolent, intelligent, and morally relativistic true Americans. What can be said of the emotional reaction of the erstwhile sober *New York Times* to charge that "there are certain similarities in the theses advanced by the Red Guards who rampaged through China, the Ayatollah Khomeini's wild-eyed Islamic principles . . . and the Americans who call themselves the Moral Majority"?[5]

The government is made up of human beings whose values (or sense of "ought" and "ought not") determine the laws of that people. This sense of "what ought to be" comes from the entire cultural milieu, but most of all from the religious convictions of the people. Therefore, on the face of it, though the church and the state can be completely separated organizationally so that the church is prohibited from doing anything officially in the public domain, the so-called private religious or irreligious convictions of the people will still determine the final outcome of the rules people live by.

In the end, our experiment seems to be proving that public policy and private moral convictions cannot be split. They can't be split because each inevitably affects the other—whether the composite religious convictions of the people influencing lawmaking, or the structure of government in turn influencing the private behavior of citizens. Since an integral relationship exists between public and private, what arrangements best make that relationship productive of common good?

Church and state have distinct spheres of responsibility but will best discharge those responsibilities with mutual respect and negotiated authority and influence. Therefore, we conclude that the best arrangement is a benevolent cooperation between church and state in which the state is frankly open to religiously inspired moral influences and the church does not seek special privileges, confining its moral pronouncements to moral issues.[36]

July 12
Reflection
2 Corinthians 3:18

"We are transfigured by the Spirit of the Lord in ever-increasing splendour into his own image." (2 Corinthians 3:18)

What is the normal Christian life? Let us study 2 Corinthians 3:18. This verse seems to sum up all the teaching concerning our Christian life. In the verses that precede verse 18, Paul tells of how Moses had a veil on his face and then he says that the people who are reading the Bible, somehow their minds have a veil on them. Therefore, although they read it or they hear it, they can't really understand it. So to this day, whenever Scripture is read, a veil lies on their hearts, but when one turns to the Lord, the veil is taken away.

But we all with unveiled face, beholding as in a mirror the glory of the Lord, are transformed into the same image from glory to glory, even as from the Lord the Spirit. This passage, this verse, tells us what our ultimate goal is, and it's incredible. Perhaps you have been a Christian for some time, and so this is theological verbiage. You've heard it. It doesn't mean anything to you but consider that our goal is to be like God; the glory of the Lord, his glorious person, his character, and not a hidden character at all, but a revealed character, the out-shining of his glory. And we have as our goal to be transformed into the same image as it says here so clearly. Power to live a successful life. a triumphant life. Power to serve God effectively.

But the secret is found in this verse. Glory means different things in different contexts. Usually when we think of the glory of the Lord we're talking about His character, illuminating His character shining out. And that's what you are designed for. You were designed as a showcase for the glorious character of God, the beauty of Jesus, and this is the normal Christian life. Now you know the difference between the average and the normal. You know that distinction.

---

[36] IBE (2014), 517.

The average Christian experience is not the normal Christian life. and you take the spiritual temperature of the average Christian, and it's subnormal. It's not what it ought to be.

Perhaps you are a Christian worried when your circumstances are worrisome. Who's short fused when your circumstances are provocative. Who is impure. Who is self-centered. You are very much concerned about your self-image. You are very much concerned about whether things are going in a way to build your reputation and to make you comfortable.

And this is the average experience of the world, and it's the typical experience of many Christians. But only a minority of Christians are normal. The majority have the average experience very much like the world. But we were designed to let our light shine before men, that men may see our behavior, our good work, and give glory to God, who's in heaven. And then they praise God for what has been done.

What answers are given to this problem of weak faltering, failing Christians, the distortion of the image of God. Paul says in Galatians. "Are you so foolish?" No, he says. "If we live by the Spirit, if we've come to life by the Spirit. That is so exciting. because it is God, the Holy Spirit that will do it." The Christian life is not a self-initiated struggle towards some distant and unreachable peak or perfection. And the Christian life is not an instant magical sainthood in which God does it and we're not involved.

Cooperating with the Spirit is like a ski rope. A kind of a cable, and with a pulley at the top and a pulley at the bottom and a motor. Skiers do not get to sit comfortably, but they go over and grab hold front and back and there is some external power that was pulling them up on the way. That really is what the Christian life is like. You can't make it on your own. There is external power there and there's an internal power here. And God's going to take you, but you have a responsibility. You have a response. Actually it's a two-fold response. So it's God who does it. God, the Holy Spirit.

But of course he dwells within. God the Holy Spirit does not work in your heart, sort of in a vacuum, and just sort of chisel away at your wrong thinking, and work away and try to mold you into right thinking. He doesn't do that. Basically, when he wants to make you over to look like Jesus, he uses what the theologians call the means of grace, also called the tools of the Spirit. These various means of grace that God the Holy Spirit uses to change you around to be a very beautiful replica or likeness to the Lord Jesus himself. Will you hold on with both hands to the source of power to live the normal Christian life?

July 13
The Role of Government
Romans 13:1

"Let every person be subject to the governing authorities. For there is no authority except from God, and those that exist have been instituted by God." (Romans 13:1)

The strongest evidence for human government being an institution ordained of God is found in the New Testament rather than in the Old. To be sure, Israel was established as a human government, and the prophets certainly hold all human governments accountable to God's law, but it takes some strong imagination to make Genesis 9:1-6, for example, evidence of God's establishing human government in the abstract or in some particular form, as some have attempted. But human government as a divine ordinance is clearly affirmed in Scripture:

"Let every person be subject to the governing authorities. For there is no authority except from God, and those that exist have been instituted by God." What are the purposes of government?

Restraining Evil. According to the most extensive passage on government (Rom. 13), the purpose of human government is to restrain evil, especially in protecting the citizens. Human sin created the acute need for coercive civil government.

Most people have preferred human government to none, but since rulers have seldom been content with the minimum authority necessary to protect the rights of the citizenry, government has tended to expand to increasingly control the lives of citizens. For this reason some have held that no government was preferable. Those who oppose the idea of human government on ideological grounds are concerned with liberty. But desirable as total liberty may seem to be, in a society made up of sin-prone, selfish people, coercion seems the only way to keep some people from harming others.

Promoting Human Welfare. A minimal amount of government could conceivably achieve that protection, but when the purpose of "promoting the welfare" is introduced, the potential for expanding government seems limitless. For this reason some hold that the only legitimate role of government is to protect citizens from injustice, especially since this is the only role ascribed to government in the classic passages, Romans 13 and 1 Peter 2. But the only government superintended directly by God—ancient Israel—certainly established law for the promotion of the welfare of the citizens.

Furthermore, the biblical principle of neighbor-love would seem to demand such activity, especially in the twentieth century with states too large and complex for private charity to adequately meet human need. Nevertheless, the primary purpose remains the role of guaranteeing justice, protecting people from malicious harm. Most contemporaries value freedom of personal choice so highly that any governmental restrictions beyond the minimal needed for protection of human rights is resisted in situations where resistance is a viable option.

When government expands, either to control evil or to promote human welfare, it does so at the expense of human freedom.

Providing Freedom. The Bible has much to say about freedom, but not about *political* freedom. It speaks of freedom from sin (Rom. 6:14-23); from the power of darkness (Col. 1:13); from bondage to Satan (John 12:30-33); from the Mosaic law (Rom. 7:6; Gal. 2:4; 4:5, 21; 5:1); and from bondage to death (Rom. 8:21-23). There is a glorious freedom in Christ (John 8:32, 36); for where the Spirit of the Lord is, there is freedom (2 Cor. 3:17). Biblical freedom is spiritual, not a general, absolute, abstract, philosophical concept, but freedom from something very specific: freedom from sin.

No one is free in any ultimate sense, then. He may be free, for the time being, from the authority of God's law, but this means he is a slave of sin. On the other hand, if Christ has set him free from the penalty and authority of sin, this is only because he has chosen to put himself completely under the authority of Christ. Every person's freedom to do what he pleases is drastically limited by his finitude, his sin, and the circumstances of life that are beyond his control. So freedom is relative. When we speak of freedom or liberty, we should always define it, qualify it: What sort of freedom? Freedom from what?

Spiritual freedom, for example, is not license to do what I please, but ability to do what I ought. In the political realm, also, liberty is not an absolute, God-ordained right. Freedom cannot be absolute, for my freedom to do as I please will sooner or later run into your freedom to do as you please. No two people could possibly have absolute freedom simultaneously unless they perfectly willed the other's good, and that, in a fallen world, is not a possibility. If by "freedom of choice" we mean that people should be allowed to use their free will to make either an ethical or an unethical decision, without suffering for choosing unethically, we are engaged in an absurdity that, if carried to its logical conclusion, would put an end to public law.[37]

Nevertheless, we advocate personal freedom of choice to the extent possible in a just society. Though the Bible is not strong in emphasizing it, when God himself intervenes in human affairs, it is to set the captives free from Egyptian bondage and, indeed, through the Messiah to break the bonds of all injustice and set the captives free (Isa. 61:1; Luke 4:18).

If the case for political freedom is not strong in explicit biblical teaching, it certainly can be strongly advocated on the basis of the principles of Scripture. For example, the Bible teaches clearly that a person's first responsibility is to God; yet in feudalistic or totalitarian society one's freedom is often restricted to such an extent that he cannot follow his conscience in fulfilling that responsibility. Furthermore, God created each individual on purpose, and a measure of freedom is necessary to fulfill that purpose. Political freedom enables a citizen to discharge his primary responsibility in life, which is to God, not the state.

Perhaps the strongest reason for advocating maximum political freedom is the nature of man. Man is a sinner, and this includes all human authorities. In such a sin-filled society a check is needed so that human authorities do not misuse that authority for personal or partisan benefit or begin to arrogate to themselves godlike prerogatives of unbounded authority. Therefore, governmental authority must have limits.[38]

What does this mean for us? We advocate personal freedom of choice to the extent possible in a just society. Ponder who gets to decide. Who decides about life? Work? Safety? Provision? Conscience? Purpose? Well-being? Do my desires override another's? Freedom cannot be absolute, for my freedom to do as I please will sooner or later run into your freedom to do as you please. May we be wise! May we participate in government to the extent possible. May we yield to the governing authorities…..

July 14
The Church and Society
Matthew 5:13

*"You are the salt of the earth. But if the salt loses its saltiness, how can it be made salty again? It is no longer good for anything, except to be thrown out and trampled underfoot." (*Matthew 5:13)

All would agree that the church as the church must clearly proclaim the principles of justice and mercy. Furthermore, most would agree that it is imperative for the church either directly or through its representatives to organize medical care, social care, financial care, involvement in education, correcting poverty, and all other "works of mercy." Thus the church influences society. But what of political action?

Primary Spiritual Role. The church must ever keep its primary responsibility toward the world as one of evangelism, bringing people out of the kingdom of darkness into the kingdom of light. Furthermore, its primary

---
[37] Harold O. J. Brown, "The Passivity of American Christians," Christianity Today, 16 January 1976, 8.
[38] IBE (2014), 55-557.

responsibility toward its own is building new people. For this reason, social action must be secondary. If the church does not evangelize and disciple, no amount of political activity will improve society very much, and, more important, the basic business of populating heaven for eternity will go undone.

In seeking justice and mercy, the primary responsibility of the church is creating a climate, making new citizens and new leaders. To do this, the church must speak to its own. It must build Christians who are *committed, courageous, filled by the Spirit, and informed,* both of biblical truth and of the issues that harass the sinful, troubled community in which they live.

If the church does not follow Christ's example, concentrating on saving men, spiritual nurture, teaching eternal principles, and directly alleviating the suffering of men, it will run the risk of missing its basic purpose for existence. Furthermore, it will undermine its authority for proclaiming the eternal message, especially if it gives social or political answers that prove wrong. A credibility gap develops, and the lack of confidence in the church shifts back to lack of confidence in the Bible and ultimately to God. As C. S. Lewis has said,

This raises the question of theology in politics. The nearest I can get to a settlement of the frontier problem between them is this: that theology teaches us what ends are desirable and what means are lawful, while politics teaches what means are effective. Thus theology tells us that every man ought to have a decent wage. Politics tells us by what means this is likely to be obtained. Theology tells us which of these means are consistent with justice and charity. On the political question, guidance comes not from revelation, but from natural prudence, knowledge of complicated facts, and ripe experience. If we have these qualifications we may, of course, state our opinions: but then we must make it quite clear that we are giving our personal judgment and have no command from the Lord. Not many priests have these qualifications. Most political sermons teach the congregation nothing except what newspapers are taken at the Rectory.[39]

Not only does the church lack biblical authority and thus special competence to speak to the pragmatics of implementation, it is not certain that the church will advocate the right cause when questions of justice and morality are camouflaged in the complexities of political realities.

The German church of the 1930s is sometimes cited as an example of the dire results of political inaction. "If only the German church had opposed Hitler instead of remaining quiet," the argument runs, "how much better the world would have been." It is a compelling argument, but it has two flaws. First, it assumes that if the German church had been politically active, it would have opposed the Nazi movement. That is an enormous assumption. Churches have often in good conscience supported evil political movements. The czars were supported by a church. Their Communist successors receive the same support from the successors to that church.[23]

In the light of these many serious and abiding ambiguities I conclude that the church should concentrate on its primary mission modeled by Jesus and the apostles and clearly taught in the New Testament. But, the church does have an obligation to its community as "salt" and "light." How can you be salt and light and have political influence? How do you know your political persuasions are actually biblical?

---

[39] C. S. Lewis, *God in the Dock*, ed. Walter Hooper (Grand Rapids: Eerdmans, 1970), 94.

July 15
Christian Engagement in Society
Micah 6:8

"He has told you, O man, what is good; and what does the LORD require of you, but to do justice, and to love kindness, and to walk humbly with your God?" (Micah 6:8)

Legislated Morals. Can morals be legislated? The idea that morals cannot be legislated is usually based on a cultural or ethical relativism that teaches that moral behavior depends entirely on the culture and that nothing is right or wrong for all cultures at all times. This is a difficult position to follow consistently because the culture of the Mafia must be granted legitimacy just as much as the Supreme Court.

The truth is that most legislation is based on morality. If morality cannot be legislated, nothing can be. Most sensible people would agree with this in general, though there would be sharp disagreement as to which are private morals and which are public. Homosexual conduct is held by most Americans to be wholly private. But is it? Who pays the bills for gay AIDS patients? What impact will the beleaguered family sustain as children are indoctrinated in the notion that homosexual relationships are normal and beautiful? What sort of military defense will America have when gays "come out"? These are not exactly private issues. The same might be said of any moral issue.

If the government is representative or democratic, it cannot but reflect the judgment of the society as to what moral standards should be required of all its citizens. If such a society legislates morals that are not acceptable to the majority, or even to a large minority of its citizens, the law becomes unenforceable. It is a bad law because it promotes lawlessness. Therefore, if a Christian is interested in having morals legislated, he must not only ask what is right and what is good for society, he must also ask, What will this society accept? Of course, he may fight for a losing cause on principle. But if he actually intends to impose a minority standard on the majority, he should understand that the legal fabric would be weakened and in the end much more than the specific moral issue would be lost.

Order of Priorities in Social Responsibilities. Following the example of Christ, the Christian should order his priorities with primary concern for the reconciling of people with God and the eternal dimensions of life while at the same time maintaining a deep concern and involvement in relationships among people and their physical and material needs.

Responsibility for Self. As a foundation for social good, the Christian is responsible to provide for himself (1 Thess. 4:11-12; 2 Thess. 3:10).

Responsibility for Family. Furthermore, he has a primary responsibility for his own family (1 Tim. 5:8). The entire fifth chapter of 1 Timothy deals with one's responsibility to provide for his family. In connection with this the Bible clearly outlines the responsibility of parents in the training of their children (Deut. 4:9-10; 11:18-19; Prov. 13:24; 22:15; 23:13-14; Eph. 6:1-4). Here is the foundation for a society under the reign of God.

Responsibility for Fellow Christians. The believer's next responsibility is for fellow believers. "As we have opportunity, let us do good to all men, and especially to those who are of the household of faith" (Gal. 6:10). Large portions of 1 John emphasize the loving responsibility a Christian has for his fellow believers' physical welfare.

Responsibility for Neighbors. Finally, the Christian has responsibility for his neighbor—all those outside the immediate responsibility of human and divine family who, in some way, bring responsibility through relationship as "neighbor."

Responsibility toward Society. The Christian's responsibilities for his society are especially clear in a democratic society in which the Christian citizen is part of the governing body—the people.

The Christian is responsible to honor those in authority and to pray for them (Rom. 13; 1 Tim. 2:2).

The Christian is responsible to obey the civil laws and authority (Rom. 13:1-10).

The Christian is responsible to pay taxes (Rom. 13:6).

The Christian is responsible to practice justice and mercy, dealing justly with employees, working to relieve the poor, the minorities (aliens), the oppressed, the weak (widows, orphans). Perhaps the strongest passage of all is Matthew 25:31-46, where we are told in advance the basis of judgment on the Last Day: We shall be judged on the basis of whether we have fed the hungry, given drink to the thirsty, lodged the homeless, clothed the naked, and cared for the sick and imprisoned. There are other guidelines that seem consonant with the principles of Scripture, though they cannot be held to be the clearly revealed will of God:

In order to fulfill our responsibility in seeking justice and mercy, the Christian should study the Scriptures to determine God's view on any specific issue that arises. The Word of God must be our controlling authority.

Vote. The Christian in a democracy abdicates his responsibility for seeking a just and merciful society when he deliberately fails to vote. But does a single vote make any difference? Whether or not it makes a difference, a Christian ought to be involved. However, the truth is that it does make a difference. What difference will you make? To which specific areas of need would God be pleased for you to give your attention?

July 16
Law and Works
1 John 2:4-5

"Whoever says "I know him" but does not keep his commandments is a liar, and the truth is not in him, but whoever keeps his word, in him truly the love of God is perfected." (1 John 2:4-5)

The apostles consistently appealed to the life and teaching of Jesus as having the highest authority. No wonder the apostles made this teaching the touchstone of truth. For example, Paul exhorts Timothy, *"If anyone teaches otherwise and does not agree with the sound words of our Lord Jesus Christ . . . he is puffed up with conceit, he knows nothing."* (1 Tim. 6:3-4) Then with apostolic authority they added teaching they themselves received from God. This was in the form of commandments—hundreds of them—and in descriptions and explanations of the way Christians should think and live. For example, the description of love in 1 Corinthians 13 or of the fruit of the Spirit in Galatians 5 presents a standard of thrilling grandeur for Christian behavior. Negative descriptions also abound, as in Paul's description of the works of the flesh—*fornication, uncleanness, lasciviousness, idolatry, sorcery, enmities, strife, jealousies, wraths, factions, divisions, parties, envyings, drunkenness, reveling, and such. Does he intend this as benevolent counsel or as law? He leaves no doubt: "I warn you . . . that those who do such things shall not inherit the kingdom of God!"* (Gal. 5:19-21). Happily, all shades of theological opinion affirm that the teaching of the apostles in the Epistles is fully authoritative as a standard for Christian living.

But what about the law revealed in the Old Testament? Do the apostles join Jesus in affirming this law as authoritative for the era of the church? The apostolic answer, as in the case of Jesus Christ, seems to be a yes and a no (see 1 Corinthians 9:19-23). Are we under the law? Yes, say the apostles: (Romans 13:8-10). Are we under the law? No, say the apostles, especially Paul: (Romans 6:14).[40]

The words the apostles use seem clear enough: "He who says, *'I know him' but disobeys his commandments is a liar, and the truth is not in him"* (1 John 2:4-5). *"So the law is holy, and the commandment is holy and just and good"* (Rom. 7:12). *"You are not under law but under grace"* (Rom. 6:14). *"But now we are discharged from the law"* (Rom. 7:6).

How may these teachings be reconciled? Only a very small minority of Bible scholars have ever denied that the Old Testament law and the teachings of Christ prior to the upper room discourse (John 13–17 17) are addressed to Christians. Rather, the majority of theologians throughout church history have sought a resolution of this apparent conflict by making a clear distinction among the various uses of the term *law* and, on the basis of this, holding that the moral law is enduring, and the ceremonial law has been done away with. But this is not easy to do. Neither Moses nor the prophets made this distinction, and it is not always apparent what is moral and what is merely ceremonial. Furthermore, though Jesus seemed to distinguish the two by his behavior and what he stressed, neither did he make this distinction explicitly. But the gravest problem with this interpretation is that Paul himself did not seem to make this distinction. He seemed often to lump together everything in the Mosaic economy as "the law" and to teach that in Christ we have done away with it. In Paul there is no distinction between the Decalogue and the rest of the law. The law is one, the revealed will of God.

But what of "moral" law? In solving this dilemma of strategic importance, perhaps the common wisdom will lead us to the best solution. Throughout church history the Ten Commandments have been taken as the epitome of moral truth, a summary of what God expects of man. The Ten Commandments seem to summarize what the descendants of the Patriarchs already understood. Did they understand solely because the laws were imprinted in their moral consciousness, or were those laws communicated by God in other ways unknown to us?

Does the law produce "legalism?" The law is good (Romans 7:12), the law is spiritual (v. 14), the law is continuing in effect (Matthew 5:17-19), but it is only good if it is used lawfully, as it was intended (1 Timothy 1:8). How is it possible to misuse the law? How can the law be used illegally or unlawfully?

The Bible opposes legalism. It has ever been man's method of attempted salvation. This is the primary meaning of legalism—relying on obedience to law for acceptance with God.

It is quite possible to teach salvation by grace through faith alone and yet to be legalistic, misusing the law by seeking to "save" oneself through obedience to the law. can be seen when a Christian measures his own acceptability with God or the acceptability of other Christians with himself on the basis of performance. Closely related to the motive of obedience for self-glory is obedience through one's own strength. When we try to obey the law without relying on the enabling of the Holy Spirit, we, though saved by grace, are "saving" ourselves by works.

Yet the highest motive is love. Obedience out of gratitude for all the gifts of grace is the best antidote to the virus of legalism.

---

[40] See *Introduction to Biblical Ethics* (IBE) for a fuller explanation.

July 17
Prayer Support
Colossians 4:2-4

"Devote yourselves to prayer, being watchful and thankful. And pray for us, too, that God may open a door for our message...Pray that I may proclaim it clearly, as I should..." (Colossians 4.2-4)

Just as a military operation requires far more support troops than front-line combatants, so the missionaries in "far evangelism" require a strong home base or they will soon become casualties. Although there are other elements in a strong support system, the two main supports are prayer and finance. First, the most important: prayer.

A magnificent southern thunderstorm was entertaining me one evening. As I watched the display of cosmic fireworks from my side porch, suddenly there was a mighty explosion right in our own back yard, an extravaganza of sight and sound. Lightning had struck the transformer and in a moment we lost all light and power. For days. Interesting, because giant towers trooped through the fields just a half mile away, bearing unlimited supplies of light and power. How like many Christians--the power flows all around them, but they aren't connected.

The power connect is an attitude: yield and trust. Until we have an obedient and believing mindset or heart orientation, the deal is off because the Holy Spirit doesn't force his way on us. But if we meet that simple condition--the same faith response that connected us to him in the first place--we are poised to let the power flow.

Yet the power flow is more than an attitude; it's an activity. Its 'through prayer, the human conduit of divine energy, that Holy Spirit power and light flow. When it comes to world evangelism, since the Spirit acts in response to the believing prayer of an obedient people, prayer is the most important part of the missionary enterprise.

Paul gives straight-forward instruction on prayer for missions in his letter to the Colossians.

I want you to know how much I am struggling for you and for those at Laodicea, and for all who have not met me personally (2:1)

Continue earnestly in prayer, being vigilant in it with thanksgiving; meanwhile praying also for us, that God would open to us a door for the word, to speak the mystery of Christ, for which I am also in chains, that I may make it manifest, as I ought to speak. (4:2-4 NKJV).

Epaphras...always laboring fervently for you in prayers, that you may stand perfect and complete in all the will of God (4:12 KJV).

If we pray for our missionaries at all, it may be a routine mentioning to God of some brief request we've read or been given. But the kind of prayer Paul describes is so different--"struggling," "earnestly," "always laboring fervently." It sounds like a spiritual battle in prayer against unseen enemies that fight to hold captive those we aim to release. And notice that our prayer isn't to be occasional but continuing, regular--daily, at least. Furthermore, our fervent labor in prayer is not only the regular set times for prayer but in between times. The term "vigilant" is a military term, meaning "on battle alert." We are to be sensitive to the Spirit's intimations of special need for special prayer. To summarize what prayer was meant to be, in Paul's parallel passage in Ephesians (6:18) he instructs us to pray "in the Spirit." Spirit-guided, Spirit energized prayer is the secret to world evangelism. And when our prayers fall short, the Spirit, who knows the mind of the Father, goes to him for us with strong pleading (Romans 8.26,27) . That is the ultimate guarantee in this spiritual warfare.

I was under arrest in central Africa, detained at the border town "airport" because my papers weren't in order. When we had landed at the dusty outpost, the officials admitted the other handful of passengers, but said the pilot would have to take me with him. He refused, saying he was going on to Uganda and if he took me there I'd be in really big trouble. I would stay there at the airport, the officials seemed to have decided, till someone flew me out of the country. But what was the chance of that? The future looked bleak, especially if they ever transferred me to the local jail.

As I sat in that small room with my guard, without food or drink, I thought, "today is Thanksgiving Day at home!" I told the guard what we did on that day in the hope that when next he went for his own food he'd remember me. No such luck! What would the outcome be?

Thousands of miles away in a New Jersey nursing home, a 90-year old lady I had never met was strangely moved to pray earnestly for me at that very time. She was "on battle alert," she was "in the Spirit!" The British pilot who had put me down in that tiny outpost was concerned about me, changed his plans, and late in the day returned from Uganda to whisk me away, not on the wings of a Cessna so much as on wings of prayer.

Most of us are quite self-centered in our prayers, using prayer to capture some of God's power, if possible, to propel our personal interests. How sad, for all along the Spirit intended to use the channel of prayer for funneling blessing to others, especially to a world yet in darkness. Spirit-filled Christians are world Christians on their knees. As we companion with the Spirit throughout each day, we begin to see the world with His eyes and He catches us up into Himself till our hearts beat with His.

July 18
Faith-Filled
Ephesians 6:18-20

"...praying at all times in the Spirit, with all prayer and supplication. To that end, keep alert with all perseverance, making supplication for all the saints, and also for me, that words may be given to me in opening my mouth boldly to proclaim the mystery of the gospel, for which I am an ambassador in chains, that I may declare it boldly, as I ought to speak." (Ephesians 6:18-20)

What instructions does the Bible give about how we are to pray for missionaries? When Paul says, "with thanksgiving", he doesn't mean merely saying thank you when God answers, important as that is, but rather thanking God for the answer even as we ask. In other words, faith-filled prayer. That's the powerful kind. In fact, that's the only kind that prevails in heaven.

Paul gives instruction not only on how we're to pray, but also on what we're to pray about. Paul told the Colossians to pray that doors of opportunity would open up and that the missionary team would have the ability to make the mysterious gospel understandable. That's Spirit-energized ministry, because without the Spirit's intervention, heart doors will remain closed and the gospel will sound like gibberish to those who hear.

But your missionary needs not only the gifts to accomplish ministry, he or she must have the fruit of the Spirit or nothing of eternal significance will be done.

Pray for the missionary's spiritual life

You can see this in Paul's instruction to believers in that same passage:

Walk in wisdom toward those who are outside, redeeming the time. Let your speech always be with grace, seasoned with salt, that you may know how you ought to answer each one (4:5, 6).

Why, we could hardly do better than pray those very words for our missionary!

Furthermore, Paul tells the Ephesians in a similar passage (Ephesians 6:19, 20) to plead with God that he might have courage. Paul, the warrior who faced down lions in the arena, asked prayer for courage? Indeed! He wrote of "fightings without and fears within." The most intrepid missionary needs prayer for faith, for courage, for all the fruit of the Spirit, because, though he may have the most glorious good news, if his life doesn't demonstrate the beauty and strength of Christ, his proclamation will be bad news, not good news.

These, then, are the themes of missionary prayer warfare: the ministry and the life. Another way to put it, pray daily for the gifts of the Spirit and the fruit of the Spirit in the life of your missionary.

There's one more thing, however. We need to make it our business to find out the specific needs of the missionary.

On returning from service overseas, I had just completed my report on Japan and stood at the door of the meeting place to greet the people when I felt a tug on my jacket. Looking around I saw a tiny retired school teacher who said, "Robertson, I know you're busy, but please don't leave till I have a chance to talk with you for a minute."

"Why, Miss Ethelyn," I responded, "I'm not busy; let's talk *right now*." She was one I knew prayed for me continually and fervently, one who was combat-ready and fighting my spiritual wars with me. She had first claim on my attention! We went over to a nearby stone wall and no sooner had we sat than she began to pepper me with questions about my work. I soon realized she knew more about my work than my fellow missionaries. When she began to ask about the conference I had left in Japan just 48 hours earlier, I said, "Miss Ethelyn, how do you know all this stuff?"

"Why, Robertson," she remonstrated, "you're *my* missionary! I've been praying for you for 12 years. I ought to know *something*, shouldn't I?"

Are there missionaries about whom you could say, "He's *my* missionary, she's *my* responsibility for daily prayer warfare"? If you don't have such a prayer partnership already, perhaps it's time to link up with someone out on the frontiers, someone who faces daily hot spiritual combat. Not only do you provide "cover" for your missionary, you become a full partner in the war--what a high privilege!

If you're not already a co-combatant, how could you get linked up? Many ways, but primarily through your church. When missionaries visit the church, invite them home for dinner. And don't spend the time re-working the Super Bowl! Pull their story out of them, learn what their prayer needs are. Then pray! Most missionaries send out regular reports with prayer requests. Ask the missionary you choose to put you on their mailing or email list. If you don't have a missionary you could call "my missionary," why not make a telephone call to the church office or write a letter right now? Get started! Because the most important part of the missionary enterprise is prayer.

July 19
Unity
Ephesians 4:3-6

"...keep the unity of the Spirit in the bond of peace. There is one body and one Spirit...one faith...one God and Father of all, who is above all, and through all, and in you all." (Ephesians 4:3-6)

God designed the Church on the pattern of his own character. But today that pattern is twisted and distorted, sometimes beyond recognition. What is the character of God? *Hear, 0 Israel: The Lord our God is one Lord* (Deut. 6:4). God is one, and he intended his church to be one. *...keep the unity of the Spirit in the bond of peace. There is one body and one Spirit...one faith...one God and Father of all, who is above all, and through all, and in you all (Ephesians 4:3-6). Holy, holy, holy, Lord God Almighty* (Rev. 4:8). What is the character of God? He is holy, and he intended his Church to be pure, undefiled in faith and in life. *Put away from among yourselves that wicked person* (1 Corinthians 5:13).

How important is it for the Church to be united and pure? The answer is apparent in another question. How important are these characteristics of God? How important is it that God be holy, separated from all defilement? How important is the righteousness of God to his nature? Again, how important is the unity of the Trinity? How important is love as a characteristic of God? The Church was designed to be both holy and united in love. When it is unholy or disunited, it denies the character of God.

To the extent the Church loses this basic character of God it loses its power. When either the unity or the purity is lost, the Body of Christ no longer has a right to expect its ministry to be fruitful. A fighting, bickering, divided church projects an image of God that can be expected to turn people away. It is when people see the love that disciples have for one another that they believe (John 13:35). When the church compromises and becomes hypocritical either in doctrine or in life, the power is drained off.

But this is not all. A disunited church or a compromising church not only denies the character of God and loses its testimony to the world but cannot adequately fulfill God's purpose for its own members. For each member to grow into the likeness of Christ, the relationships among the members ought to be right. Consider the worship experience of the church, for example Paul (Romans 15:5-7) connects unity with the capacity to worship. Can a disunited body bring true worship to the triune One?

And yet, as it is difficult for theologians to balance the justice and mercy of God, and as it is difficult for parents to balance firm discipline and loving acceptance, so it is very difficult for the Church to maintain unity and purity at the same time. It is much easier to go to a consistent extreme than to stay at the center of biblical tension. Whether in the local congregation or in the Church at large, the Church of Jesus Christ seems incapable of living out both godlike oneness and godlike purity simultaneously. The result is that the reflection of God's image is distorted, the evangelistic thrust of the church is blunted, and Christians are stunted in spiritual growth.

On a larger scale, within the Church universal, there is a great polarization between the professional unifiers on the one hand and the professional purifiers on the other. It seems that a person must work at uniting all churches no matter how delinquent in doctrine or life or that he must give himself wholly to separating all the wheat from the tares. Now!

Do not misunderstand. Separation is good- this is the very meaning of the word "holy" or "sanctify." But there is an unholy separation that begins in the neglect of the complementary characteristic of love, then descends quickly into an unlawful judgmental role, and ends in the terrible sin of schism.

Unity is good- it is the ultimate character of God and is his revealed will for the church. But there is an unholy unity that begins by failing in faithfulness, quickly descends to unbiblical compromise and ends in the terrible sin of impurity- defilement of faith or life.

Is there no solution to this great dilemma? Can we have success in one characteristic only at the expense of the other? I believe God intended that we be successful in both at once. Furthermore, I believe he has given clear and rather simple instructions for achieving success in both.

It is significant that the New Testament emphasis on both unity and purity has to do with the local congregation. There the presence or absence of unity or purity is most visible to the world. And that is where the battle for unity or purity will be won or lost. The local congregation is also where unity and purity are most difficult to achieve and maintain.

As you finish today's reading, ask yourself, "Is unity in your congregation seen not only in the absence of conflict, but also by caring relationships that provide a safe haven for all and a sense of family solidarity?"

July 20
Lordship
John 13:13-15

"You call me Teacher and Lord, and you are right, for so I am. If I then, your Lord and Teacher, have washed your feet, you also ought to wash one another's feet. For I have given you an example, that you also should do just as I have done to you." (John 13:13-15)

It is true that Christ alone is absolute Lord of his church, but the amazing thing is that the Lord God Almighty has chosen to mediate his lordship through human beings. Consider...
* *Wives be in subjection unto your own husbands as unto the Lord.* (Ephesians 5:22)
* *Children obey your parents in the Lord.* (Ephesians 6:1)
* *Let every soul be in subjection to the higher powers; for the powers that be are ordained of God...for he is a minister of God to thee.* (Romans 13:1,4)
* *Servants be obedient unto them that according to the flesh are your masters...as unto Christ.* (Ephesians 6:5)
* *Obey them that have the rule over you and submit; for they watch in behalf of your souls, as they that shall give account.* (Hebrews 13:17)
* *Be subject for the Lord's sake to every human institution.* (I Peter 2:13-RSV)

We are uncomfortable with words like these. And the depth of our discomfort may be a measure of the depth of the crisis in authority which marks these last 2 centuries in the Western world. A driving value of the past 100 years has been that personal autonomy is a given right and anything that infringes on that is illegitimate. Of course, this spirit did not originate in the Western world of the twentieth century. From the days of Eve and Adam, humans have followed the example of Lucifer and sought to usurp the throne. At a minimum, each, to rule her or his own life.

If a measure of personal autonomy is achieved, we seek to use that power to control others. These efforts reflect basic rebellion against the Lordship of Christ. The rejection of human authority and the abuse of that authority ultimately stem from a quarrel with the Almighty, for He has chosen to mediate His authority--under strict limitations, to be sure-- through sub-authorities. Our acceptance of His Lordship in our lives, then, is tested and proved by our acceptance of the mediated authority on the one hand, and, for the sub-authority, by it's subjection to the ultimate Authority.

If we don't follow the Guidebook, we reap the harvest of this abuse and rebellion. The damage and destruction because of rebellious use of personal power applies to all spheres of mediated authority, but here we examine only relationships within the congregation, where Christ is named absolute Lord of the church. We seem to have developed an infinite variety of ways to subvert that authority, to our own great loss.

Church health, and consequently, church member spiritual health, begins with acknowledging Christ as absolute Lord. Unconditional allegiance of the human heart to the one true King is proved at the point of willing acceptance of the congregation's leaders. Obedience to human authority, of course, is not absolute, since human leaders sin and err. So ultimate allegiance is only to the Lord of the church. But willingness to accept human leadership is often the testing ground of one's allegiance to the Lord who instituted that authority. And there is a further significance in faithful "followership"-- no one qualifies to become a leader until he or she has learned to follow (John 13:14-17; Luke 22:24-30).

A congregation of autonomous members, each setting her or his own agenda and pursuing their own goals, is a sure recipe for failure of all the purposes God intends for his church. Having identified the basic foundation for church health in all members' relationship to the Lord of the church and having indicated the vital role of inter-personal relationships, with non-leaders willing to follow appointed leaders, we must move on to address the key issue, leadership in the congregation.

We won't try to synthesize the various views of what leadership is about, but rather go with a simple definition: A leader is one whom people follow.

The term, "servant leadership," has gained wide currency, but I wonder about its usefulness. The reason for my doubt is not in the term itself, but in the elasticity of its interpretation. In a denominational convention of thousands, I was the keynote speaker on servant leadership. The one who had invited me also spoke and took violent exception to the idea of leadership. Though he once wrote a booklet on leadership, he now told the congregation that leadership is nowhere taught in Scripture, only servanthood. What is the problem with that? This life-time friend of mine is as authoritarian a leader as you can imagine. This is not an isolated experience. So what does the term, "servant" mean? Many of those who speak most vigorously of "servant leadership" are domineering autocrats in their own ministry. How can this be? Perhaps they are thinking of themselves as servants, but servants of the Lord, not so much servants of his people. But that won't do. To truly serve the Lord is evidenced in one's attitude and relationship to those for whom one is responsible (2 Corinthians 4:5). The problem is that there is an in-built drive in each of us to control outcomes and to do that we must control the people within our influence. On the way to achieve commendable goals, therefore, we usurp the role of the Lord of the church.

This tendency is not confined to a particular form of church government nor to a particular culture, though some forms of government and some cultures may promote human lordship. Of the three basic forms of government– episcopal, representative, and congregational-- the episcopal would seem most likely to produce lordly behavior on the part of its bishops. But in many Presbyterian churches (representative form) the "ruling elders" do not rule; rather, the "teaching elder" is in full control. Again, if a Baptist (congregational form) pastor survives the first two years in a new tenure, he can easily become pope-like to his congregation. The human heart is effective at discovering how to get its way within any structured governance. How are you with unconditional allegiance of your heart to the one true King? If it is proved at the point of willing acceptance of the congregation's leaders, how are you with following? What attitude towards authority do you experience? What should you do about it?

July 21
The Task
Isaiah 49:6

"I will also make you a light for the Gentiles, that you may bring my salvation to the ends of the earth." (Isaiah 49:6).

Increasing numbers of Bible scholars and missiologists who consider themselves evangelical are calling into question the traditional ideas about hell and the way of salvation. The first question to ask, a question often skipped, is, "what are we talking about?" In other words, definition must come first. Are you advocating universalism, that all will ultimately be saved? Or are you advocating that many may be saved without the knowledge of Christ? Or do you merely mean that salvation by grace through faith alone is no longer a biblical non-negotiable?

After determining what the issue actually is, that concept must be rigorously examined in the light of Scripture. Have we identified all passages which deal with the issue and have we examined all teachings of Scripture which correlate with this teaching? Having identified all the passages, not a select few, have we done the rigorous work of applying all principles of interpretation to determine the meaning intended by the author of each passage and correlating all those passages and all those doctrines? For example, have we given decisive weight to the clear teaching over the obscure text, to the abundant teaching over the occasional, to the New Testament over the Old? Only with such rigorous, honest work can we claim to be doing missions under the functional authority of Scripture.

Increasingly, the way of salvation is being redefined and the lostness of those out of Christ is being called into question. For example, when salvation is treated as a direction, not an event, so that Muslims are acceptable to God when headed in the right direction, godward, culture has imposed its authority over Scripture in the most critical of affirmations. Again, increasing numbers of those who consider themselves evangelical no longer believe in hell. And that is in process of cutting the nerve of the Church's enterprise. Scripture is not in functional control of reasoning when such conclusions emerge.

Since Scripture does not describe what the evangelistic task will look like when it is finished, we can get on with the task of being sure that every person on earth has the opportunity to hear the Gospel and that a congregation of God's people is established in every community. Until that goal is accomplished, the church cannot say, "It is finished. The task you gave us to do we have accomplished." God may choose to say, "It is finished" before we do, but obedience to the command means that the church must pursue the goal of evangelization and church planting until then. To have more restricted, targeted goals is legitimate for tactical purposes as part of the over-all task, but it is not biblical to make a limited goal and market it as the biblically required task of the church.

And God's promises, from Genesis to Revelation assure a successful conclusion to his plan of world evangelization. *I will make you into a great nation and I will bless you; I will make your name great, and you will be a blessing...and all peoples on earth will be blessed through you* (Genesis 12:2, 3).

That's the reason God blessed Abraham--to make him a conduit of God's blessings to the nations. And why does He prosper us?

May God be gracious to us and bless us and make his face shine upon us that your ways may be known on earth, your salvation among all nations...God will bless us and all the ends of the earth will fear him (Psalm 67:1,2,7).

Remarkable! Abraham's blessings and ours are for the same purpose: that God's salvation may reach all people. And it **will** happen. God promises both Abraham and us. Yet, in spite of this revelation of God's redemptive purposes, Jews, including Jesus' own disciples, expected Messiah to deliver them from Roman bondage and set up a Jewish state.

In these two ancient promises of a coming Messiah, note how mistaken they were.

The Father promises the Son: *Ask of me, and I will make the nations your inheritance, the ends of the earth your possession* (Psalms 2:8).

The Father promises the Son*: It is too small a thing for you to be my servant to restore the tribes of Jacob...I will also make you a light for the Gentiles, that you may bring my salvation* **to the ends of the earth** (Isaiah 49:6).

Repeatedly in Old Testament prophesies the coming of Messiah was predicted, but he was not just for Israel. He was coming for all peoples. That's Old Testament. What does the New Testament predict about Christ's second coming?

Jesus Himself said: *And this gospel of the kingdom will be preached* **in the whole world** *as a testimony to all nations, and then the end will come (Matthew 24:14).*

John draws the curtain on the final act of earth's drama: *After this I looked and there before me was a great multitude that no one could count,* ***from every nation, tribe, people and language,*** *standing before the throne and in front of the Lamb" (Revelation 7:9).*

From Genesis to Revelation, the Bible is full of promises about God's plan of gathering from among all peoples his people. The Spirit has a global plan, and He is bringing it to pass in our day as never before.

God's promises assure that his salvation purpose will be accomplished. Surely this major theme of Bible promises demands that in my prayer life, in my conversations about heaven and hell, in my lifestyle of obedience, I reach beyond those glorious promises of personal peace, protection, and provision, constantly reaching out to embrace the world God loves.

July 22
What Has God Done?
Genesis 12:1-3

"Now the LORD had said to Abraham; "Get out of your country, from your family and from your father's house, to a land that I will show you. I will make you a great nation; I will bless you and make your name great; and you shall be a blessing. I will bless those who bless you, and I will curse him who curses you; and in you all the families of the earth shall be blessed." (Genesis 12:1-3)

Folk wisdom has it that actions thunder so loudly about one's character and true intent that feeble words of explanation cannot be heard. What do God's activities demonstrate of His loving character and purpose of world redemption? It is not too much to affirm that every major act of God since creation has been a missionary act.

Even creation does not focus on the intricacies of the atom nor climax with the infinite galaxies. The crescendo builds to a climax in the creation of a being in the likeness of God Himself. This was the overflow of a love which bound the Three in a unity from all eternity. God's desire was to create a being who would have the capacity to fully receive His love and, in turn, to love Him freely and fully. This very likeness to God, the freedom from coerced or programmed choices, set the stage for man's rebellion and alienation.

Man changed but God did not. And thus His purpose shifted from loving companionship with humankind to recreating the broken pattern of God-likeness so that the loving identity of life could be restored. Thus the sacrificial system, the calling of a special people, the redemption from Egypt, and the giving of the Law all centered in redeeming and restoring.

When God chose to communicate with man in written form, His purpose was the same. The Bible is not a revelation of all of God's activities or purposes from eternity. It is not a record of all antiquity. It is the story of redemption, climaxing in the greatest event in human history, the Incarnation. This invasion of human life by God Himself was deliberately designed from all eternity, we are told, to provide redemption through the death and resurrection of Jesus Christ. These events, more than anything else Scripture tells us, reveal the purpose and character of God: love reaching out to save hopelessly lost people. What has God done? "*God so loved ... that he gave his one and only Son ...* " This act of love goes beyond all human comprehension. What could reveal with greater clarity God's character and purpose? What could demonstrate more forceably the center and circumference of His attention?

The next major event, Pentecost, was the descent of the Holy Spirit to establish the church, to be sure. But the purpose was clear. The entire record of the early church reveals how the church viewed the primary purpose of the church toward the world. It was to be God's instrument for world evangelization.

Indeed, it is not too much to say that every major activity of God among men since the Fall has been a saving missionary act. This, then, is the biblical basis for missions: World evangelization is the expressed will of God. Spiritual redemption is the demonstrated activity of God. Evangelism and redemptive activity are expressed as the will of God and the demonstrated activity of God because it is the nature of God so to will and so to act. Love is the revealed nature of God. The salvation of lost men is that human event which brings greatest glory to God. Because God is such a God and has given the church such a command, our mandate for action is to make known the good news of life in Christ to every person and to establish a congregation of believers in every place. Until every person has heard with understanding and every community has a witnessing congregation of God's people we may not say to the Father, "It is finished ... the task which you have given, we have accomplished." Why is it that we are so far from fulfilling God's design in the world? One reason is that we have not opened ourselves to the full force of the missionary message of Scripture, and His will for us.

How come? Because we don't see well. God gives us so clear a revelation of His character, His purpose, His activity, but it seems that we deliberately wear dark glasses with blinders, focusing in Scripture on our own small self-oriented world. Meanwhile the world God loves is lost. May God open our eyes to see the world in focus as He sees it.[41]

---

[41] *The Great Omission*, Robertson McQuilkin, 1984, Gabriel Publishing, 31-38.

July 23
Fruit of Life
John 15:13

"Greater love has no one than this, that someone lay down his life for his friends." (John 15:13)

Young married couples were gathered in our living room to talk about how to build strong marriages. "I think I could handle my husband's death," my wife, Muriel announced. Her audience seemed a bit startled, but her comment didn't surprise me because she had periodically asked God to let me die first. Muriel maintained that she could handle life without me better than I could handle it without her. In the end, I didn't "die" first, but that night no one suspected that Alzheimer's Disease was lurking in the shadows.

She continued, "It's the little things that are hard to handle." I sensed it was one of those rare moments of grand enlightenment, but did I want the whole crowd enlightened? Reluctantly, I asked, "Like what?"

"Like when you don't agree with me!" she said with an infectious burst of laughter. Indeed, the daily dying to one's rights and desires may be more difficult than some major crisis. And though laying down one's life for another is the ultimate gift of love, laying it down in small pieces is just as certainly proof of love. And if we refuse to lay it down?

Muriel's way of life was to "lay down her life" for me. No wonder, when the time came for me to resign in order to care for her, I would tell the students at Columbia Bible College and Seminary, "She cared for me so selflessly for forty years, if I should care for her another forty, I would never be out of her debt." Indeed, I wonder if Muriel knew how to respond anyway other than in self-giving love. But her "revelation" to the young couples that night taught me it wasn't always easy for her. I wouldn't have guessed it, though. She was outrageously joyful. Always.

And that is the "fruit" Christ identifies. Joy is so important that Jesus says our joy is the reason he is giving this teaching! (John 15:11). In other words, the end product of abiding is joy--like some vine bursting exuberantly over the garden wall. Another source of joy may be indicated. The flow of thought in the immediate context could mean that joy is the product, not directly of abiding, but of love (vs 9, 10). Any engaged couple can testify that love has produced a special kind of ecstasy, a joy that won't stop, that overflows into all of life. And that kind of joy is the natural overflow of our ultimate love affair--his love for us and ours for him.

The text may also indicate that joy results from obedience. For the Christian, joy flows naturally from obedience. And no joy without it, that is certain. Whatever the immediate or ultimate source of the joy, Jesus promises an overflowing kind of joy that cannot be explained by the most brilliant psychiatrist with an analysis of one's early environment or present circumstances. It is supernatural, the fruit of life flowing from Jesus.

These same verses identify a cluster of fruit that includes all varieties of Jesus' beautiful character: everything he heard from the Father (John 15:15). Love summarizes the will of God that we be like Him (vs 11,12) but note that He describes in detail the specifics of how love will think and behave: "if you obey my commands, you will remain in my love" (vs 10).

God does not leave love undefined, some warm feeling that produces whatever one feels good about. No, the way love thinks and acts is spelled out in detail in "all that He commands." Furthermore, it is not a remote and unattainable ideal nor mere advice on how to find adjustment and fulfillment. He <u>commands</u> us to <u>obey</u>. No option to do otherwise. And to the extent we do what He says, by the enabling life-force of the Holy Spirit, we will prove to be His disciples (vs 8) and put on display the glorious product of full-orbed likeness to Jesus. This is the fruit He promises. But there is more. The expression, "all that He commands," prepares us for yet another expectation. His commands include, in addition to

Christlike attitudes and behavior, His plan for us to produce a crop of effective service.

A tomato vine is fulfilled only through bearing tomatoes. And it is really "filled full" when the vine is loaded with fruit. Jesus holds before us, in John 15, a beautiful portrait of ultimate fulfillment: Himself! And He describes in detail how we can have it: Himself! As you stay tight with Him, His life feeds into yours and the inevitable outcome is greater and greater likeness to Him. Not "falling in love," but growing in love, from one degree of His beautiful character to another. May He ever be satisfied with a bumper crop through us!

July 24
What is the Point?
2 Timothy 3:16-17

"All Scripture is breathed out by God and profitable for teaching, for reproof, for correction, and for training in righteousness, that the man of God may be complete, equipped for every good work." (2 Timothy 3:16-17)

Early in adulthood, I became consumed with a desire to determine which facts I *knew* would stand the light of eternal day, facts which would never be abandoned or altered. So it was that I reexamined every point of doctrine, endeavoring to sift opinion from certain fact.

For me this was no barren academic search for ultimate truth. I was driven to the search not only by a newly applied intellectual honesty–not to say spiritual integrity–but at the same time by an increasing conviction that God is not nearly so interested in what I *know* as He is in what I *am* and in how I *behave*. My whole life had been revolutionized by the dawning realization as Andrew Murray once put it, "Scripture was not given to increase our knowledge but to change our conduct." The Bible was not only given to teach us what to believe and what not to believe, it was also given to show us how to behave and how not to behave (2 Timothy 3:16). All of my rigorous Bible study should have been for the purpose of making the application to life, transferring the truth into day by day living.

For example, take the Bible doctrine prophecy. I had gone about delving into the future and attempting to write history ahead of time in great detail, like any good prophetic student or teacher. Yet the Bible tells us why prophecy is given–clearly not for the use commonly made of it. " (John 13:19). *"And now I have told you before it comes to pass, that when it is come to pass, ye may believe."* (John 14:29). This is clearly the *I tell you before it comes to pass, that when it is come to pass, ye may believe that I am He"* purpose of prediction after it has been fulfilled. But what about the great mass of unfulfilled prophecy, does it have any purpose for *today*?

The common definition of Bible prophecy, "Prophecy is primarily forthtelling God's message, not foretelling the future," is usually ignored by Bible students of prophecy. So I investigated and discovered that of some 164 prophetic passages in the New Testament,[42] 141 are directly related to conduct and apparently given to affect conduct–not to increase knowledge. "This hope *purifies.*" "*Comfort* one another with these words." "*Watch* for the Lord is coming." Only 23 passages seem to be given primarily to give information-as-such concerning the future. The study of Bible prophecy should be, then, primarily for two purposes: the study of fulfilled prophecy to confirm our faith, the study of unfulfilled prophecy to influence our conduct.

---

[42] Excluding the book of Revelation which is devoted exclusively to the subject.

What a release from mental gymnastics, peace among the brethren, and godly profit would exist if prophecy were so studied and Bible students refused to study for the sake of satisfying curiosity, refused to detail future events beyond the clear basic teaching of the Bible, and certainly refused to base fellowship on adherence to certain strongly held prophetic minutiae. If God had purposed to satisfy our curiosity concerning the future it surely would have been no more difficult to do than it was to give the great basic teachings on which His people agree. And for His primary purpose in giving prophecy–to influence our conduct–the clear teaching of the Bible is more than sufficient. *"It is not for you to know times and seasons, which the Father hath set within his own authority. But ye shall receive power . . . and ye shall be witnesses"* (Acts 1:7, 8). Prophecy is only one example, of course.

I began to realize that omniscience is not required of us. But faithfulness is. And this included faithfulness with what we know. In the realm of Bible study, at least, a lot of knowledge is a dangerous thing. For we are responsible in a special way to live what we know (Luke 12:47, 48).

As my life began to be radically realigned by the living Word through the light and power of the Spirit, and my knowledge, though far less inclusive than formerly, became much more certain and life-controlling, another conviction began to dawn. Though the doctrines of the one Body of Christ and Christian unity were sometimes discussed, I became increasingly aware that there was precious little reality to it, especially among ministers and church leaders. The divisions among Christians were real and deep.

What was the cause? In local situations, as in Philippi, division is often caused by personal sin, wrong attitudes and conduct. But in the great, deep-running divisions the basic cause is almost always in the realm of knowledge: difference in doctrine. Agreement in teaching concerning life and conduct is all but universal. Disagreement in matters of doctrine cuts sharply and deeply.

Is this inevitable? I have finally concluded, without much satisfaction, that perhaps it is, because we are all still human. But I continue to *hope* that it is not inevitable, because I do know one thing: such division is not the will of God. It grieves His Spirit. It mutilates the very hallmark of Christianity: "Behold how they love one another." It denies God's design in creation and redemption: oneness with the Father and with His sons, our brothers in Christ. It brings us squabbling, mob-like to the very portals of the Home He prepares for us, a home where perfect unity will be forever unmarred. It shadows the very nature of God for those outside the family.

The pattern is so simple. Knowledge puffs up and divides. Christ enters, infinite in all things, and we are deflated, humbled, shorn of all pretended knowledge, of all personal ambition, and of all denominational or organizational pride, jealousy, and exclusivism. Then love – not as sentiment, but as an all-consuming way of life – can operate for the building up of the one Body moves forward.

July 25
Turning Point
1 John 3:6

"No one who abides in him keeps on sinning; no one who keeps on sinning has either seen him or known him." (1 John 3:6)

For Christians who are experiencing a subnormal life, reentry into normal, supernatural Christian living is through the gate of surrender. They may concentrate their energies on gaining a more accurate understanding or on experiencing some emotional sense of release or well-being, but such efforts will all prove fruitless until they make the choice to yield.

Depending on the intensity of conflict, the length of time out of fellowship, and one's personality, this decision may be a major emotional crisis. But even without any emotion, in the sense of a turning point or a decisive event, this decision is rightly called a crisis. For such a person, a normal, successful Christian experience is not the product of a gradual process of spiritual development, let alone automatic progress. A decisive turning point is needed.

Is such a crisis event necessary in the life of every believer? As we have seen, Scripture points the failing Christian back to his or her original covenant relationship with God. Ideally, then, a person who enters that saving relationship can and should maintain it; there is no theological necessity for a second spiritual crisis. But in practical experience most believers do violate their covenant responsibilities, either through open rebellion or through spiritual drift, and therefore need to make a decision to turn from what they have become to what they can and should be in Christ.

God Himself is the key to successful Christian living, and both He and His resources are available only to the person of faith. By faith alone we enter and maintain a personal relationship that releases an unending flow of grace. This biblical faith is both choice and attitude. The choice is to obey; and obedience begins with repentance, continues in a yielded spirit, and proves itself in aggressive participation in using the means of grace and in eager affirmative action to be all that God intends. The attitude is childlike trust, relying with loving confidence on Him alone.

Faith results in salvation by the grace of God, but how do we define this salvation? Some hold that "full salvation" means a morally perfect life. As we have seen, the only way to describe any mortal as morally perfect is to define sin as the deliberate violation of the known will of God and perfection as a condition in which one consistently chooses to act obediently.

The distinction between deliberate and unintentional sin helps solve the problem of the teaching about sin in I John, for example, where the apostle tells us in the same short letter that (1) those who say they have no sin are lying (1:8-10) and (2) those who sin are not Christians at all (3:6, 8-10)! The apparent contradiction is at least partially alleviated when we note that the verb tense (in 3:6, 8-10) may easily be understood as referring to a continuing activity of sin, which by definition is at least conscious, if not certainly deliberate. This continuing sinful activity, says John, is the sure sign of an unconverted state. At the same time, when a person claims to have no sin whatsoever, he includes, by definition, all varieties of sin, including unintentional, even involuntary and dispositional sin. No one can claim freedom from all sin, says John, so no one is sinlessly perfect on biblical grounds, for at least he or she is constantly guilty of falling short of God's perfection, even when unconscious of the shortfall. On the other hand, to continue on deliberately in the practice of sin is to evidence alienation from God.

Though the distinction between deliberate and unintentional sin maybe a helpful key to unlocking some of the mysteries of our salvation, in everyday life the borderline between these two cannot always be easily or precisely identified. For example, when one becomes angry, is this attitude deliberate and conscious or is it involuntary? Perhaps it was involuntary to begin with, but if one continues in a state of anger, it surely becomes voluntary. But at what precise point does sin begin and perfection become forfeit (for one who believes in perfection)? No one wants to lose such a preferred condition, so it is much easier simply to baptize the response and call it "righteous indignation." The greatest hazard in distinguishing between presumptuous sin and unwitting sin is the infinite human capacity to rationalize. Furthermore, should we classify habitual sins like drunkenness or gluttony as voluntary or involuntary?

Having recognized the difficulties of distinguishing between sins, we must admit that for most behavior the distinction is clear and readily identified: people deliberately choose to do what they know is wrong or, on the other hand, they are genuinely unaware of their failure to measure up to God's perfection. But the problem here is much more basic: I believe that neither the definition of sin (as limited to deliberate choice) nor that of perfection (as the absence of volitional sin) is biblical.

As we have pointed out, sin according to the Bible, is any falling short of the glorious perfection of God Himself (e.g., Romans 3:23). The Bible does speak of Christian perfection (e.g., Matthew 5:48; Philippians 3:15; James 1:4), but the Greek word is often used of *maturity*, a term that fits the biblical teaching on sanctification much better than does the idea of being flawless. Let us take a few minutes and consider the following: "Do I rationalize my sin?" "Am I fully choosing God's will?" and "Will I pursue full maturity as a Christian?"

July 26
Care for one another
John 13:34-35

"A new command I give you: Love one another. As I have loved you, so you must love one another. By this all men will know that you are my disciples, if you love one another." (John 13:34-35)

Family solidarity is the least experienced of the five God-designed purposes for his church, at least in American congregations. Of the six or seven churches I have belonged to in all parts of America, not one had a program to monitor, let alone proactively care for members' spiritual, emotional, physical, and material welfare. And that's sad because what's a family for? And family was God's design- the blood ties of Calvary binding us closer than human blood ties.[43]

One exciting way to get an overview of what he had in mind is to review this chart for reciprocal commands of the New Testament. Reciprocal living refers to the mutual obligations and relationships which believers have as a result of their common relationship to Christ as members of His body. It may be defined as the outward manifestation of fellowship, in which each believer puts all that they are and all that they have, at the disposal of all other believers

---

[43] See: John 13:34,35; 15:12-13; Romans 14;17-19; 1 Corinthians 1:10; 13:4-8; Galatians 5:13-15, 5:25-6:10; Ephesians 4:1-3; Philippians 2:1-4; Colossians 3:12-15

and that others do the same for them in order to enable one another in Christian living.

TREASURING
Be humble with one another (Romans 12:16)
Accept one another (Romans 15:7)
Be at peace with one another (Mark 9:50)
Be devoted to one another (Romans 12:10)
Be kind to one another (Ephesians 4:32)
Belong to one another (Romans 12:5)
Encourage one another (1 Thessalonians 5:11)
Fellowship with one another (1 John 1:7)
Have equal concern for one another (1 Corinthians 12:25)
Honor one another (Romans 12:10)
Love one another (John 13:34)
RISKING
Confess sins and pray for one another (James 5:16)
Forbear one another (Ephesians 4:2)
Forgive one another (Ephesians 4:32)
Greet one another (Romans 16:16)
Live in harmony with one another (Romans 12:16)
Wait for one another (1Corinthians 11:33)
Wash one another's feet (John 13:14)
INITIATING
Admonish one another (Colossians 3:16)
Carry burdens for one another (Galatians 6:2)
Instruct one another (Romans 15:14)
Offer hospitality to one another (1 Peter 4:9)
Serve one another (Galatians 5:13)
Speak truthfully to one another (Ephesians 4:25)
DESTROYING
Do not slander one another (James 4:11)
Stop grumbling with one another (John 6:43)
Stop passing judgment on one another (Romans14:13)

"Spur one another toward love" (Hebrews 10:24) When something is edified, it is built up, strengthened or fortified. The New Testament uses this term of building up and strengthening of believers in their faith so that they live lives that are pleasing to God in every way. One of the ways that God has chosen to edify His people is through the ministry of believers themselves. Christians are to edify one another. Mutual relationships of love form the basis for this ministry of edification. In fact, Paul tells us that love edifies (1 Corinthians 8:2). The Christian life is more than relationships. It is obedience to all of God's will which He has revealed in His Word. This mutual edification begins, but does not stop, with love. To edify one another in the biblical sense of the term, believers must also help one another to learn and apply the Word of God in their daily lives. And this task is not meant only for pastors and teachers. All Christians are to be involved. Mutual edification commands tell Christians how they can help one

another, out of love for one another, learn and apply the Word of God in daily living.[44]

The thought of being a servant is not appealing to most people. Serving is a hard and sometimes thankless job. And servants must continually put the needs and interests of others before their own. But this is just what Christians are supposed to be; servants to one another, not grudgingly, but out of love for one another. Because Christ loved us He made Himself a servant to us throughout His life and finally in His atoning death on the cross. Because we love Him and His people, we are to make ourselves servants to Him, but also to one another.

Just as Christians who truly love one another will seek to edify one another, they will also seek to serve one another. These mutual service commands deal with ways that Christians can express their love to one another in practical and down-to-earth service.

The reciprocal commands form a biblical foundation for the whole life responsibility of the congregation for each of its members: spiritual, emotional, physical, and material/financial.

So, in the flow of God's grace-filled provision in the body of Christ, He provides the giver (and the gifts), the receiver, and the "asker". For us to mature, God may give the congregation opportunity to practice multiple ministries. Admitting need and receiving help can be the very classroom where God equips you with deep understanding of what people in need really feel and the level of humility it often requires to graciously receive. Furthermore, it won't do simply to leave the financial needs to the haphazard provision of benevolent members of the congregation. A structured program such as the "roll" for widows in the early church should be provided. Crisis intervention, job placement, retraining for employment-whatever the need, if family should provide, so with God's family.

Now ask yourself, "Does my care for my brothers and sisters reach beyond spiritual care to full-service emotional, physical, and material responsibility for all members? What do you do well? How can you love better and meet someone's needs?

July 27
Measuring One Another
2 Corinthians 10:12

"Not that we dare to classify or compare ourselves with some of those who are commending themselves. But when they measure themselves by one another and compare themselves with one another, they are without understanding." (2 Corinthians 10:12)

Some Christians use the means of grace more diligently than others and we have a tendency to evaluate each other. Although in a passive sense all believers may be equally "yielded" to the will of God, the Christian life is nevertheless a war, and some are more aggressive and seem to have more of a will to fight. Though faith must rest, relying on God to do what we cannot do, it also must wrestle, struggling in warfare. Satan is the great adversary and

---

[44] Romans 14:19; 1 Thessalonians 5:11; Colossians 3:16; Hebrews 3:12,13; Romans 15:14; Ephesians 5:18-20

destroyer, constantly seeking to immobilize, if he cannot destroy, God's people. Furthermore, Christians live in a world that is opposed to all they yearn to be. Some seem more aware of these adversaries and more persistent in opposing them.

In a sense, failure to do battle aggressively could be considered a spiritual flaw needing correction. At the same time this difference among Christians may simply be another sign of different levels of maturity. One should, in these matters, deal stringently with oneself and generously in judgment of the other person–both of which responses are the opposite of our natural inclinations!

. In the first place, I am not responsible to judge my brother (Rom. 14:3-12); furthermore, I cannot do so very accurately, even for myself, let alone for others (1 Cor. 4:4). I don't know my own motives; how can I know someone else's? Another reason for caution in making such judgments is that the differences may be more apparent than real. What is the standard of comparison?

One must have God's perspective in order to make a proper evaluation, and who among us has that? Therefore, we are fools if we compare ourselves among ourselves (2 Cor. 10:12), for we can never have God's full perspective. If we must make a comparison, we should compare ourselves with our model, the Lord Jesus. On the other hand, it is proper to compare ourselves either with what we once were or with what we would be, apart from the grace of God. Comparisons along these lines give God the credit and bring us closer to His perspective.

To compare ourselves with others is foolish for several others reasons. In the first place, each begins his or her growth from a different level of unlikeness to God. For this reason a non-Christian gentleman with a good early environment may be a much nicer person to be around than some veteran Christian who is actually Spirit-filled. The question is, however, what that veteran Christian would be if God had not been at work and the non-Christian gentleman could have been had God been in control. In the second place, each normal Christian is at a different stage of growth, though all are in a covenant relationship of full acceptance of the authority of the Spirit in their lives. To compare one another is to have the wrong basis of comparison. In the third place, the data for making an accurate judgment are available only to God. We are therefore wise to leave these judgments to Him, especially when we do not have a responsibility for the spiritual development of the other person.

Certainly we all seek to bring honor to our God by putting His glorious character on display in mortal flesh. And the good news is, we can! What glorious good news! No matter what may or may not have occurred in the past and no matter how inadequate my understanding, if my relationship to God is one of unconditional surrender and confident expectation that He will keep His word, I can experience a life of consistent victory over temptation and growth toward His own likeness, I can see His purpose for my ministry supernaturally fulfilled, and above all, I can daily experience loving companionship with my Savior.[45]

---

[45] Taken from Five Views of Sanctification by Melvin E. Dieter, Anthony A. Hoekema, Stanley M. Horton, J. Robertson McQuilkin, and John F. Walvoord. Copyright © 1987 by Zondervan. Used by permission of HarperCollins Christian Publishing. www.harpercollinschristian.com

July 28
Maintaining Balance
Psalm 34:14

"Depart from evil and do good; seek peace and pursue it." (Psalm 34:14)

Imbalance does not come from an over-emphasis. It is impossible to have too much love or too much faithfulness. However, it is quite possible to have *unfaithfulness* masquerading as love. When God's people compromise through sentimentality or self-love or for some other reason, they are unfaithful though they speak much of love. Again, it is quite possible to have *unlove* masquerading as faithfulness. When God's people create schism by disciplining the wrong person, or with the wrong motive, speak much of faithfulness, they are unfaithful to the very first commandment, to love as one loves one's self.

Righteousness and peace, usually estranged, are embraced at Calvary. May they embrace again in our congregations lest the King return and find us compromised and polluted or dismembered, grotesque and impotent. And yet, since there was no way for righteousness and peace to meet except on the cross, no doubt they will meet in our day only where there are those willing to be crucified. When God's people fill up that which is lacking in the suffering of Christ (Colossians 1:24) through choosing the way of personal sacrifice, God's own character will shine through again as it did at Calvary. The way of the cross is to exercise discipline faithfully, and with love that chooses to act for the welfare of another even at personal sacrifice. And the cross is always painful. The innocent always pay for the sins of the guilty.

Church discipline can be useful in protecting the reputation of Christ and of the Church. It is also useful in protecting other believers from defilement. However, it is quite significant that when the New Testament deals with the problem of church discipline it does not use protection as a motive. 1 John 1:19, 20, 1 Corinthians 5:6-8, and 2 John 11 may include this concept, but this is obviously not the central thrust of the teaching of the passages. Jude, who uses stronger words to denounce heretical teaching than any other biblical author, does not end with an injunction to begin disciplinary procedure or to separate from such people but instead exhorts the Christians who were faithful to keep on being faithful (20,21). He then concludes the passage with these words: *And on some have mercy, who are in doubt; and some save, snatching them out of the fire; and on some have mercy with fear; hating even the garment spotted by the flesh (22,23, ASV)*. Following this, Jude again turns to the faithful ones, assuring them that God is able to guard *them* from stumbling and to keep *them* till that day when they will stand in the presence of his glory *without blemish* in exceeding joy (24).

One could reasonably expect the protection of the reputation of Christ and the protection of the Church to have been the primary motives given for church discipline. But the Bible seems to take a rather nonchalant attitude at this point. Why? Perhaps because the name of Christ and the Church of Christ are strong and quite able to care for themselves. Or is it because if these were the primary motives rather than that of love for the sinner, discipline could quickly degenerate into inquisition? Christ also seemed to be less than careful- *He that is not against us is for us* (Luke 9:50). Paul also rejoices that the Gospel is preached whether in pretense or in truth (Philippians 1:18). He excoriates the heretic but doesn't give protection as the reason for church discipline.

Note that one motive is excluded as a motive for discipline or separation. Church discipline is not to be punitive, retributive. God clearly reserves this motivation to himself- *Vengeance is mine; I will repay, says the Lord* (Romans 12:19). This is different from God's pattern for relations with governmental authority and in the home where punitive intention may be legitimate. In the Church, only God can be the ultimate judge- *Who art thou that judges the servant of another?* (Romans 14:4). We are all in the fellowship of mercy-receivers.

From this brief outline of biblical teaching on motivation for disciplining an errant brother or sister, when Christians discipline or separate from motives of legalism, vindictiveness, fear, or pride rather than with the basic motivation of saving the brother, they are guilty of the sin of schism. We must ask ourselves whether in thought or practice could any of these motives impact our judgement of another?

July 29
The Fear of Hell or the Glory of God?
Matthew 28:19

"Go therefore and make disciples of all nations, baptizing them in[a] the name of the Father and of the Son and of the Holy Spirit..." (Matthew 28:19)

"The...core motivations for missions are changing. Once people preached and responded to the gospel out of fear of hell or because of the lostness of humanity. These motivations have waned in recent context. Motivation for missions is frequently defined recently by Christians as "giving glory to God" or "an overflowing of thankfulness."[46]

This quotation from *The Changing Face of World Missions* should not be construed as incipient universalism, for the author would repudiate such. Rather, he advocates going along with the contemporary change in motivation from "the fear of hell" to the "glory of God." My contention is that neither hell nor God's glory are, properly speaking, motivations. They are outcomes of the basic motivations of love for God and love for people. To make our appeal for involvement in missions to our love for God expressed in glorifying him is all to the good. But the deliberate down-play of the motive of other-love will prove fatal, I fear. Other-love in terms of "holistic" concern for health, education, and justice is ok, we're told by advocates, but other-love in terms of a rescue mission from a bad ending--well, that's so offensive to some, we mustn't even mention it, let alone emphasize it.

The way I read Scripture, however, is that God so loved people he gave his one and only Son to--do what? Save them from perishing (hell), we read. I believe the increasing shift among evangelicals to de-emphasize hell could prove the demise of Pauline-style mission. And thus the death of multitudes who would, as a consequence, never hear the good news of redemption.

If that should happen, of course, it would be *deja vu*, for that is precisely what took place in the early part of the last century. As we have seen, the mainline denominations moved away from saving people from hell to saving them in the here and now. With every move in that direction, the missions enterprise shriveled. And no wonder–why make such great sacrifice to reach the unreached if there is no eternal-destiny danger?

We may love others in many ways: seeking their health, promoting justice, advancing education. And we should. Furthermore, the missions movement always has. But above all, we should love them into eternal life, away from eternal death. May our churches never fail to love as God loves, to extend his provision of eternal salvation to the non-

---

[46] *The Changing Face of World Missions,* Pocock, Van Rheenen, McConnell, Grand Rapids: Baker Academic, 2005, p. 161.

Christian half of the world. God was motivated by people-love, so that must be our motivation as well, if we are to be God-like.

But we also are motivated by the *first* command, to love God. And one way to do that is to keep the spotlight on him, to glorify him. The move, however, to make "the glory of God" the primary "motive" so far has not increased missions passion in the churches. God's people seem to find other ways of glorifying God. At least if we gauge passion by the numbers of pioneer missionary evangelistic church starters we send, the talk of glorifying God has not increased the level of passion.

Love for God can be expressed in many ways–glorify him by singing his praises, testifying of his accomplishments, living a godly life. But the proof of love, said Jesus, is that we obey his commandments. And the great commandment that he returned to over and over following his resurrection? Go and proclaim the good news of redemption (Mark 16:15), go and preach repentance and remission of sin (Luke 24:47), go and disciple the nations (Matthew 28:19). Those who heard it, got it. And that's how they glorified God–proved their love, that is–as seen in the book of Acts.

Thus there are two issues surrounding "the glory of God"– (1) why does the church not glorify God by obeying his last command? And (2) dare we neglect God's own motive of people-love in terms of a rescue mission from hell?

I believe this third contemporary paradigm shift in approach to missions has the potential of far more damage to the Cause than the other major paradigm shifts, problematical though they may be. Increasing numbers of those who consider themselves evangelical have come to believe people who have never heard the gospel may be acceptable to God through some other way. Not only the historic view of the way of salvation is increasingly questioned, but alternatives to the historic church view of hell are offered by more and more theologians. This paradigm shift has the potential of cutting the artery of missionary passion. Indeed, for many it has already done so.[47]

We gave more attention to the evangelistic purpose because it seems to be the focal point of the New Testament church as viewed through the eyes of Luke and Paul in the book of Acts. And among the facets of evangelism those near and those far we have given attention to those "far" and the plan God has for reaching "the far." But to do that requires more than finding, recruiting, sending, going. The home base for those sent is of critical importance to their success. The home base has two major elements in that support system: prayer and giving.

Why not take an inventory on your missions commitment? What is your motive? Can that motivation endure? What do you really think about hell? Do people really go to hell? Are you concerned for those around the world? Perhaps prayer and giving mark your missions motivation. The task of reaching every tribe and nation cannot be accomplished without your involvement. What change will you make today?

---

[47] This most important topic and the defense of the biblical positions on the way of salvation and the reality of hell lie outside the scope of these readings. I have made a brief defense of the biblical doctrine elsewhere (*Perspectives on the World Christian Movement*, Ralph D. Winter and Steven C Hawthorne, Pasadena: William Carey Library, revised 1999, chapter 26), but a thorough examination may be found in *The Supremacy of Christ*, Ajith Fernando, Wheaton: Crossway, 1995.

July 30
Truth and Goodness
Acts 24:16

"So I always take pains to have a clear conscience toward both God and man." (Acts 24:16)

God reveals his will in many ways: through conscience, instruction, commandments, principles, and living demonstration. Truth and goodness are defined by, and flow from, the nature of God. There is not some ultimate "way things are" that would seem to sit in judgment on God. There is no "nature of things" to which God must conform if he is to be good. No, he defines truth and goodness by being good and truthful. It is true that God reveals his existence and his power through creation (Rom. 1:18-20), but the only sure guide for truth and goodness is the supernatural revelation of the written Word of God through prophets and apostles.

The Roman Catholic church, following the theology of Thomas Aquinas (1224–1274), has relied more on "natural law" than have Protestants. Both recognize, however, that some knowledge of right and wrong, however dim and distorted, apart from the Bible, is stamped somehow in the consciousness of human beings. This Paul teaches clearly (Rom. 2:14-15).

Innate moral judgment. Although the Old Testament does not use the term conscience, the idea is there (1 Sam. 24:5; 2 Sam. 24:10; Jer. 31:33), and it is explicitly taught in the New Testament (Acts 24:16; Rom. 2:14-15; 2 Cor. 1:12; 1 Tim. 1:5; 2 Tim. 1:3; Heb. 10:2, 22).

Conscience is no more and no less than one's judgment in the moral realm. Naturally, this judgment is strongly conditioned, like all our judgments, by what we have learned from parents and society. Nevertheless, the Bible teaches that moral awareness is innate—everyone knows that there is right and wrong, though not all agree on precisely what. Our moral judgment is distorted by our cultural environment and therefore is not an adequate moral light to follow.

Not only does environment condition our judgment, man's moral judgment is fallible, dimmed by his severe limitations of knowledge and wisdom. He doesn't have all the data needed to make the right judgment, and he doesn't have sufficient wisdom to evaluate the data he does have. Furthermore, his moral judgment is obscured by his separation from God, the source of moral light. His mind is inclined by sin to suppress the knowledge of the right, to distort the moral light he does have.

The human mind is like a computer of inadequate capacity, programmed with misinformation and short-circuited. Consequently, "Let your conscience be your guide" can be a dangerous maxim. Having said this, however, there is "the true light that enlightens every man . . . coming into the world" (John 1:9). And what a hell this world would be if God had not imprinted in man that moral likeness, however limited and blurred by sin.

A person's moral judgment is untrustworthy, but it can be renewed and become increasingly reliable. This mind renewal about which the apostles speak so insistently is intimately bound up in the idea of conscience or moral judgment. The regenerated mind, molded by study of the Word of God, obedient and sensitive to the Holy Spirit, and constantly asking for enlightenment, will become increasingly reliable.

The thought process of the Christian is the means by which God transforms him into the likeness of his Son. Often in the writings of Paul, when we might have used *heart* he used *mind,* and when we might have used *affections* he used *knowledge.* Of course, this is knowledge in the Hebrew sense, so it is not merely intellectual apprehension of truth, but personal experience and commitment. Nevertheless, it is the *mind* that God is after, the mind that bears the imprint of his likeness, the mind that must be renewed so that its moral judgments are increasingly reliable. Even that great experience of the heart and ultimate achievement of the moral good, love, has to do with the mind. Christ, in quoting the Old Testament law of love for God, deliberately added what was not said by Moses (Deut. 6:5), that we should love him with all the *mind* (Matt. 22:37). God's great mind-renewal program reprograms our moral judgment so that it becomes increasingly reliable.

Nevertheless, apart from the written, revealed will of God, even the renewed and Spirit-sensitized conscience is not wholly reliable. Revelation is essential.

In Scripture God reveals his will through instruction in right thinking and right behavior, through direct commandments, through principles, and through the example of good and bad behavior. Instruction seemed to be the primary mode before the time of Moses and in the New Testament, whereas commandments seemed the prominent mode during the era of "the law." Examples of right and wrong conduct abound in the Old Testament, but the supreme model is found in Jesus Christ. Principles, for living, whether stated as such or derived from example and instruction, permeate the whole of Scripture.

How can you build confidence in knowing God's will? What are you desiring to understand as God's will? How can you use these principles to discern how to live and choose?

July 31
How Might I Murder?
Proverbs 3:27

"Do not withhold good from those to whom it is due, when it is in your power to do it." (Proverbs 3:27)

By including anger and verbal abuse in the category of murder, Jesus did not say nor mean that they were as evil as murder. But they are the same variety of sin and may not be excused as mere human weakness. In fact, all sin, including murder, is rather like an onion. Beneath the final act are lesser acts, and beneath all the acts is a corrupt heart. Murder is highly visible, the full-grown sin, but when the outer layer is peeled away, various levels of violence are seen as part of the same "onion," and beneath the physical and verbal abuse is the heart of anger, hatred, or failing to love. If the core of inadequate love is planted and allowed to grow, the hateful activity will follow. And all of it falls under the judgment of God. Murder is not just physical. While there are multiple ways to murder today. Let's consider a few ways a normal Christian might not have in the forefront of their thinking.

One way to harm is by doing and saying nothing when a word or an action would keep from harm. Failure to put a balustrade around a flat rooftop brought blood guiltiness if someone fell from the roof (Deut. 22:8). Failure to do good, when in one's power to do so, is sin (Prov. 3:27-28). So the poor, the helpless, and the starving are my responsibility to the extent I have ability to help. To be silent when another is falsely accused, whether in a court of law or in the presence of private gossip, is to participate in the harm. Neglect, then, is one form of murder (see also Exod. 21:29-31).

Violence in the home has been the underreported and largely ignored crime of a society preoccupied with appearances. The murder of O. J. Simpson's wife has alerted many for the first time to the alarming extent of wife beating in America. The district attorney's office in Los Angeles reported that in his city domestic violence was responsible for an average of one homicide every nine days.

Christ's commentary on the sixth commandment emphasized verbal abuse. James (1:26; 3:1-12) and Solomon (Prov. 13:3; 15:1, 4, 23; 17:28; 18:8, 13; 21:23; 29:20) had a great deal to say about sins of the tongue, but the rest of Scripture is strong on the subject as well. James says that the tongue is like wildfire and poison. It not only poisons relationships and burns up the lives of others; it consumes the one himself whose tongue is not disciplined by the Spirit (James 3).

A direct attack on a person with carping criticism or biting depreciation, sarcastic humor, or subtle insinuation can destroy something in that person. But just as deadly is the criticism spoken about a person to others. The law of love seals the lips. Any word that harms another is murder, unless spoken in love to that person or spoken only to another who is responsible to correct the wrong (Matt. 18:15-18). The absent person is just as safe with the Spirit-directed child of God as the one who is present with him.

Racism technically refers to the idea that certain nonracial characteristics, especially cultural patterns, are the result of race. An example would be to generalize from the behavior of some people of a given race, assigning that kind of behavior to all belonging to the same race. The result is often hatred, intolerance, or unjust discrimination. Since this attitude is often expressed more freely and forcefully by the majority race in a given community, the label "racist" is often assigned to those who consider their own race superior and oppress others. But racist attitudes and actions are quite possible among an oppressed minority, even when the assumption of their own inferiority is accepted. No people group is immune to the virus of racism, ungodly attitudes based on racial differences. Of course, the same kind of sinful attitudes and behavior can be based on differences of culture, language, tribe, socially defined class or caste, as well as on race.

Christ's commentary on the sixth commandment emphasized verbal abuse. James (1:26; 3:1-12) and Solomon (Prov. 13:3; 15:1, 4, 23; 17:28; 18:8, 13; 21:23; 29:20) had a great deal to say about sins of the tongue, but the rest of Scripture is strong on the subject as well. James says that the tongue is like wildfire and poison. It not only poisons relationships and burns up the lives of others; it consumes the one himself whose tongue is not disciplined by the Spirit (James 3).

The law of love seals the lips. Any word that harms another is murder, unless spoken in love to that person or spoken only to another who is responsible to correct the wrong (Matt. 18:15-18). The absent person is just as safe with the Spirit-directed child of God as the one who is present with him.

Murder is highly visible, the full-grown sin, but when the outer layer is peeled away, various levels of violence are seen as part of the same "onion," and beneath the physical and verbal abuse is the heart of anger, hatred, or failing to love. If the core of inadequate love is planted and allowed to grow, the hateful activity will follow. And all of it falls under the judgment of God.[48]

---

[48] IBE (2014), 351.

August 1
For Who's Sake?
John 14:31

"...but I do as the Father has commanded me, so that the world may know that I love the Father. Rise, let us go from here." (John 14:31)

Why did that hardy band stick it out through three tough years in Jesus' discipleship school? Why hang in there to the very end—take the tests, determine to invest their lives in this risky enterprise? Let's accompany them for a few days...

The disciples were following along at some distance behind Jesus, having a heated discussion. When they arrived in their headquarters town of Capernaum, he asked what they had been disputing about (Lk. 9:46). They were embarrassed and didn't want to tell him. But he knew they had been disputing which among them would be the greatest. He drew a child to his side and explained that he who is least is the one who is great in His Kingdom. The same is true in a church or ministry.

Now we follow with them on their way up to Jerusalem where Christ was to make the supreme sacrifice. He had told them repeatedly he must die, but they rejected the idea of a suffering servant so weren't hearing Him. The mother of James and John, with her two sons in tow, asked for top rank for each of them (Mt. 20.20; Mk 10.35 ff.). How did the others respond to that idea? Especially after Jesus had rejected the request. Were they understanding and spiritual about it? After all, the mother and her sons were relatives of Jesus and the disciples understood near-eastern culture and family obligations. But no, they were angry! Jesus took the occasion to explain that if they were to be in His company, they must all be servants.

They reached Jerusalem and were gathered for the last meal together. Someone should have volunteered to wash the dusty feet so that the next person reclining would not to eat in uncomfortable circumstances. It was traditionally the youngest, the lowest in rank who should have volunteered. No one did. The lesson on the child and the servant somehow had never gotten through. The meal began with dirty feet and then they got into the same old dispute. This time it was not over who would rule, but who would serve (Lk. 22.24-27). Finally Jesus Himself took the servant's basin and towel and demonstrated the way rank was to work in His Church.

Why were they in this enterprise? For what they would get out of it. Their motive was love for self. Didn't they have any compassion for others? They wanted to call down fire on those who rejected them or were inhospitable. They wanted to bar from preaching those who had been to the wrong seminary. They had no time for women and children, the weak and oppressed. Oh, they loved God and His glory, His Name and Kingdom. Especially, they loved Jesus. But above all they loved themselves and were in it for what they would get out of it.

A disciple can give generously, witness faithfully, work up an ulcer serving God, even lay down life on a distant mission field from love of self. I should know. There is the story of my mid-life encounter with me in Izumicho. I was in financial trouble, one of my children was in rebellion, our church start was sputtering, the only couple in our new little church was on the brink of divorce. In desperation I cried to the Lord for deliverance. And what did he say? It was the "Why?" question. "Why do you want deliverance?" And I blurted out, "Who wants to fail?" In an instant the true me stood naked before God. All these years I'd been praying, "For Jesus' sake, amen" when all along I should have been honest and closed my prayer with, "For my sake, amen." Maybe you've seen Christians you suspected may have made choices primarily from love of self?

Jesus, Paul, and John concur: the dominating motive in the Father's sending was love for lost and hopeless people. Is that why you minister?

Before leaving the camaraderie of the upper room for the lonely cross, Jesus didn't say, "That the world may know how much I love them..." but rather, *"That the world may know that I love the Father, and as the Father gave me commandment, even so I do. Arise, let us go hence."* (John 14:31). And he got up and went straight to the cross! His all-controlling motive was love of the Father. Who lives with love for God as the all-controlling motive? Do you?

August 2
Marriage
Malachi 2:16

"'I hate divorce,' says the Lord God of Israel. ... So guard yourself in your spirit, and do not break faith" (Malachi 2:16, NIV).

The whole of the Bible teaches marriage as a lifelong union between a man and a woman (see Genesis 2:21-24). You probably pledged, "... till death do us part" at the altar, and God expects every married couple to live up to that vow. The prophet Malachi stated that divorce breaks a covenant between the husband and wife and is therefore an affront to God: *"'I hate divorce,' says the Lord God of Israel. ... So guard yourself in your spirit, and do not break faith"* (Malachi 2:16, NIV). God loves a promise keeper—the one *"who keeps his word whatever the cost"* (Psalm 15:4)—and hates promise breakers: *"When you make a vow to God, don't delay fulfilling it, because He does not delight in fools. Fulfill what you vow"* (Ecclesiastes 5:4).

When the Pharisees questioned Jesus about divorce, He responded that God didn't originally plan for divorce to occur (see Matthew 19:8). He continued, *"Whoever divorces his wife, except for sexual immorality, and marries another, commits adultery"* (v. 9). Paul said in 1 Corinthians 7:15, *"If the unbeliever [an unbelieving spouse] leaves, let him leave. A brother or a sister is not bound in such cases."* The position most commonly held throughout church history is that divorce is not permitted except in cases of infidelity or permanent desertion. With those two exceptions divorce is legitimate but not required, only permitted.

The number of divorces among committed Christians is still far below national averages, but it ought to be zero. For example, in our mission organization when we were on the mission field, there was not a single divorce for more than one hundred years among thousands of missionaries. So I know believers can live up to God's ideal for marriage. Why isn't it always that way?

What unworthy attitudes or actions may contribute to a marriage breakup? Here's my list: infidelity, desertion, illness, boredom, selfishness, commitment to personal fulfillment above other values or relationships, personal autonomy, addiction to pornography, "greener grass" illusions, unguarded relationships with opposite sex, abuse, neglect, finances, child discipline, and spiritual malnutrition. The list goes on.

Have you ever contemplated divorce? Go back to your list and highlight any factors that contributed to the alienation that was creeping into your relationship. If any of those issues still lurk in the shadows of your consciousness, flush them out and pray about them. Ask God to help you remain faithful to your spouse.

God gave us an incredible gift in marriage. Pledge to God and to your spouse to guard it with your very life.

August 3
Unity and Purity
Ephesians 4:11-16

"To equip the saints for the work of ministry, for building up the body of Christ, until we all attain to the unity of the faith and of the knowledge of the Son of God, to mature manhood, to the measure of the stature of the fullness of Christ .... each part is working properly, makes the body grow so that it builds itself up in love."(Ephesians 4:11-16)

How important is it for the Church to be united and pure? The answer is apparent in another question: How important are the following characteristics of God? How important is it that God be holy, separated from all defilement? How important is the righteousness of God to His nature? Again, how important is the unity of the Trinity? How important is love as a characteristic of God? The Church was designed to be both holy and united in love. When it is unholy or divided, it denies the character of God.

To the extent the Church loses this basic character of God, it loses its power. When either the unity or the purity is lost, the Body of Christ no longer has a right to expect its ministry to be fruitful. A fighting, bickering, divided church projects an image of God that can be expected to turn people away. It is when people see the love that disciples have for one another that they believe (John 13:35). When the church compromises and becomes hypocritical either in doctrine or in life, the power is drained off.

But this is not all. A disunited church or a compromising church not only denies the character of God and loses its testimony to the world but cannot adequately fulfill God's purpose for its own members. For each member to grow into the likeness of Christ, the relations among the members ought to be right. Consider the worship experience of the church. For example, Paul (Romans 15:5-7) connects unity with the capacity to worship. Can a disunited body bring true worship to the triune One?

God designed the Church to be a true family; the eternal blood ties of Calvary are even stronger than human blood ties. It is in the context of this *koinonia* or loving mingling of life that God does His work of building Christians into the likeness of Christ (Ephesians 4:11-16). This is no superficial Sunday-club relationship. God intended an intimate sharing of life on the pattern of the character of God. Furthermore, to have such family solidarity, there must be discipline. Fellowship without purity of faith and life is flawed at its core. Unity and purity are interdependent elements of a single relationship. Just as in the family so it is in the church that where either love or discipline is missing, the children will be greatly handicapped. "Love without criticism brings stagnation, criticism without love brings destruction."[49]

And yet, as it is difficult for theologians to balance the justice and mercy of God, and as it is difficult for parents to balance firm discipline and loving acceptance, so it is very difficult for the Church to maintain unity and purity at the same time. It is much easier to go to a consistent extreme than to stay at the center of biblical tension. Whether in the local congregation or in the Church at large, the Church of Jesus Christ seems incapable of living out both godlike oneness and godlike purity simultaneously. The result is that the reflection of God's image is distorted, the evangelistic thrust of the church is blunted, and Christians are stunted in spiritual growth.

On a larger scale, the Church universal, there is a great polarization between the professional unifiers on the

---
[49]John W. Gardner, *Journal of Educational Research,* "Uncritical Lovers, Unloving Critics" 5.5, 1969.

one hand and the professional purifiers on the other. It seems that a person must work at uniting all churches no matter how delinquent in doctrine or life or that he must give himself wholly to separating all the wheat from the tares. Now!

Do not misunderstand. Separation is good. This is the very meaning of the word "holy" or "sanctify." But there is an unholy separation that begins in the neglect of the complementary characteristic of love, descends quickly into an unlawful judgmental role, and ends in the terrible sin of schism.

Unity is good, it is the ultimate character of God and is His revealed will for the church. But there is an unholy unity that begins by failing in faithfulness, quickly descends to unbiblical compromise and ends in the terrible sin of impurity, defilement of faith or life.

Is there no solution to this great dilemma? Can we have success in one characteristic only at the expense of the other? I believe God intended that we be successful in both at once. Furthermore, I believe He has given clear and rather simple instructions for achieving success in both. How do we work this out in our lives?

Consider the area in which you live out being the church. How can you balance unity and purity in your ministry? Pray for uncommon wisdom in building this intimate sharing of life together on the pattern of the character of God.

August 4
God First!
Exodus 20:1-11

"And God spoke all these words: I am the LORD your God, who brought you out of Egypt, out of the land of slavery. "You shall have no other gods before[1] me. You shall not make for yourself an image in the form of anything in heaven above or on the earth beneath or in the waters below. You shall not bow down to them or worship them; for I, the LORD your God, am a jealous God, punishing the children for the sin of the parents to the third and fourth generation of those who hate me, but showing love to a thousand generations of those who love me and keep my commandments. You shall not misuse the name of the LORD your God, for the LORD will not hold anyone guiltless who misuses his name. Remember the Sabbath day by keeping it holy. Six days you shall labor and do all your work, but the seventh day is a sabbath to the LORD your God. On it you shall not do any work, neither you, nor your son or daughter, nor your male or female servant, nor your animals, nor any foreigner residing in your towns. For in six days the LORD made the heavens and the earth, the sea, and all that is in them, but he rested on the seventh day. Therefore the LORD blessed the Sabbath day and made it holy". (Exodus 20:1-11)

We find that a rest day is a good thing, one of God's good gifts for the welfare of mankind. It is a law rather than a recommendation because a recommendation would be no blessing at all. It is the binding aspect of the rest day that releases one for rest and worship. If the rest day is merely recommended, we are not free to rest from the pressures of life and turn without hindrance to joyful fellowship with God and His people. We must still face the pressures and frustrations of mundane obligations. But a required rest day sets us free.

If the teaching of Paul does not certainly bind the Christian to observe a special rest day, even less certainly does it annul the strong teaching of the balance of Scripture in setting a special day for rest and worship. Therefore, we positively choose that which certainly would please the Lord. To turn away from our daily occupation to spend a day in fellowship with Him and service for Him must certainly please Him even more than offering to Him a portion of all our possessions in token of the fact that all belongs to Him. The only way the careful observance of the rest day commandment could displease our Lord would be if a person looked to that obedience as a means of earning merit or as a way of salvation.

In light of God's action in resting after work, His setting aside at that time a day of rest sacred to Himself, the subsequent commands of Scripture concerning a day of rest, the example and teaching of Jesus Christ in affirming and interpreting the Old Testament standard, and the observance of the first day of the week by the New Testament church as a special day of worship, we must recognize Sunday as a special day of rest, worship, and service to the Lord.

In a thoroughly humanistic age in which man is the center, "God first!" thunders from Sinai. The first table of the Decalogue proclaims this ultimate message: "Above all else, O man, guard your relationship to your God. If this relationship is right, you will live. If this relationship is wrong, you will die."

Notice how every topic we study centers ultimately in God. We shall see as our reading continues that every standard for life is the same. Note also the outcome when God is not given first place in any standard, how quickly it disintegrates into meaningless and powerless, even destructive half-truth.

True love begins and ends with God. He defines it by His own character, and all other loves reach their potential only when yielding to love for God as supreme. Law is based on God's character—His expressed will that we be like Him. Thus, to violate His law is to violate His person. Even human authority derives its authority from God and must give an account to Him for how that responsibility has been discharged. Those under human authority owe ultimate allegiance only to God. All sin is, in the final analysis, against God. This is seen in the fact that sin is falling short of God's glorious righteousness, that sins of the mind and heart are crucial, and that sin is, above all, breaking the first four commandments. Lust is God-given appetite gone berserk, and covetousness is, at root, idolatry. Pride is the essence of sin against God, for in it man attempts to usurp the credit due God and establish His own autonomy. Of all failures, the most fatal is leaving God out in a horizontal-only personalism.

Thus, "God first" is far more than a theoretical, appropriately courteous starting point. It is intensely practical and, in fact, the only way to integrate all the other horizontal relationships. God in person is the beginning and ending point of all. Is your passion God first? Is your allegiance only to God? Do you leave God out? Let's settle these questions today.

August 5
Constant Conscious Communion with Christ
John 7:37-38

"Jesus stood up and cried out, "If anyone thirsts, let him come to me and drink. Whoever believes in me, as the Scripture has said, 'Out of his heart will flow rivers of living water.'"

Frederick Franson, founder of The Scandinavian Alliance Mission and four other Scandinavian mission sending agencies at the close of the last century, had a life motto: *Constant Conscious Communion with Christ* or "CCCC." Nothing new about that—the mystics through the ages have held that kind of closeness as the highest level of spiritual oneness with God. But I wasn't acquainted with the mystics and Franson's motto entranced me. *That's what I want,* I told the Lord. As a missionary volunteer I was out for all the fullness of God and His purposes in the world! No halfway stuff would do. He startled me with His response—the experience of constant, conscious communion was mine! I was euphoric— for about three months. And then it slipped away. I grasped to hold on to the experience, but to no avail. It was gone, never to return, except, perhaps, during some of those special fasting-and-prayer times.

What's wrong with me? If it's sin, it's surely unconscious—and that's hard to deal with! If it's spiritual immaturity, how many more decades of growth are needed? Besides, that first taste was surely vouchsafed to a neophyte, not a veteran! Maybe it's my finitude—perhaps my spirit just can't sustain such a high level of spiritual intensity, or my mind can't consciously engage in two activities simultaneously. Or perhaps it was like Paul's one-time exalted experience, something just to let me know what's in store for me one day? You can tell I've wrestled with this issue. I wouldn't be so honest with you about it if I felt it would hinder you from pressing on with the mystics to lay hold of that for which Christ laid hold of you. Maybe He'll gift you with such a relationship before the rest of us experience it on the great wedding Day.

But surely there's some relationship beyond the long silences we subject our Companion to. The mystics thought so. They describe an "intermediary" stage between the typical Christian worker's experience of periodic prayer and the ideal of constant conscious communion. They call it "intermittent." Sort of like a toddler playing happily in a room where her mother is sitting. She's aware of her mother's presence always. The evidence is that she goes after her with cries of protest when mother leaves the room! But as long as mother is there, she's content, occupied with her own interests, but occasionally conversing with her constant companion. Intermittent communion you might call it.

We, too, as well-loved children have our own agendas that keep us busy, but we can be aware of His loving presence at all times, entering freely into conversation throughout the day. He may whisper a caution when I start to stray, He may encourage when things don't go right, warm me with love-talk when I'm lonely. And if I'm tight with Him, I'll hear. There can be a constant sharing of joys and sorrows. When things go right, it's no longer just a sense of wellbeing or an ejaculation of "What luck!" Rather we'll feel loved and empowered once again and whisper—or shout—"Thank you, Jesus, you did it again."

You can tell I'm just probing at the fringes of intimacy, but whatever, I'm not going to settle for anything less than the intermediate stage, the constant awareness of God's presence and the intermittent communication that goes with that kind of intimate companionship. And remember, intimacy must be intentional. It doesn't just happen.

August 6
Overcoming
Colossians 3:10

"....and have put on the new self, which is being renewed in knowledge after the image of its creator." Colossians 3:10

How does Christ enable us to overcome, to grow, to succeed? How does He enable us to have a pattern of success in place of the old pattern of failure? Does He displace our personalities with His? The beauty and glory of God's victory in our humanity is that He does not by-pass or replace us. Rather, He renews our new person after the likeness of God Himself *("and have put on the new self, which is being renewed in knowledge after the image of its creator."* Colossians 3:10). As we shall see, this renewing work is primarily accomplished through the various means of grace that God provides, while we cooperate with Him.

But because God in us is not an impersonal resident force or influence in our lives but a person, the new life is one of delightful personal companionship. Like a good friend, His presence does wonderful things for us. He comforts us when we are discouraged. His very presence galvanizes our will when we are weak; His counsel clarifies issues when we are confused. He works within us to change our thought patterns and outside us to control our circumstances for our long-term good.

Scripture speaks of each member of the Trinity living in us, but because the agent for effecting God's purposes in this world is the Holy Spirit, most of the teaching in the New Testament on normal Christian living focuses on the work of the Holy Spirit. The person who is in covenant relationship with God is said to have been baptized by the Spirit into the body of Christ, to have been born of the Spirit, to be indwelt by the Spirit, to walk in the Spirit, to bear the fruit of the Spirit, and to have been sealed by the Spirit. Of all these analogies, the most common is the idea of being filled with the Spirit. What does this picture language mean literally?

A tank may be empty, half-full, or full, and some Bible teachers refer to the filling of the Holy Spirit almost in such material terms. But we speak of a person, not a force, much less a liquid. We are left in the realm of the figurative and still do not know what the expression means literally.

Nevertheless, Scripture does promise us a life of awareness of God's presence. Thus, one who is filled with the Spirit may have a continuous sense of the divine presence. The expression "filled with the Spirit" would mean that the person was characterized by Godlikeness, by God's being the predominant person or the pervasive influence in one's life. This must have been the meaning when people in Scripture were said to be Spirit-filled (e.g., Acts 6:3). Others could watch them and tell that their lives were characterized above all else by their association with God and by the results of that association.

An automobile running under full power may nevertheless use a passing gear for an emergency. The sail of a vessel is normally full of wind, enough to get it to its destination, perhaps, but then there are times when a welcome breeze comes up and the sails billow in even greater fullness. So the normal life of the Christian may indeed be Spirit-filled, but there are times when a special power is needed for a difficult problem or opportunity. Spirit-filled believers can trust God for a fresh "filling," a passing-gear thrust to carry them through triumphantly.

Let us return to the simple, beautiful assurance that the most wonderful Person in all the universe offers us more than doctrinal truth, more than exciting experiences; He offers us Himself in an intimate relationship that can be described adequately only as *full*. And when we respond to Him in uncomplicated – and unreserved – faith, the blessed Holy Spirit gives us, with Himself, truth that we may know all He intends us to know, fruit that we may be all He designed us to be, and gifts that we may do all He purposed for us to do. Simply stated, the new potential is for victory and growth. As we have seen, the new person in Christ has the ability to choose the right and to do so consistently. What hope! What assurance!

August 7
Measuring Missions
Acts 1:8

"But you will receive power when the Holy Spirit has come upon you, and you will be my witnesses in Jerusalem and in all Judea and Samaria, and to the end of the earth." (Acts 1:8)

    I spoke in two church missions conferences in the same state, the same month. The churches shared many similarities. Both were widely recognized for their missions interest; in fact, one was the anchor church for the eastern end of the state, the other for the west. Both were large, vibrant, growing churches. Both had very large budgets for missions, perhaps half their total giving. "East" had 1,800 members and gave enough money to missions to support 180 missionaries. "West" was half the size and gave enough money to support. They were their own sons and daughters. "West" was 150 years old, but only one of their own had ever gone to the mission field. She was now retired and present in the conference. "West" paid for the sons and daughters of others to go. Where would your church fit on a continuum between "West" and "East" so far as sending your own members into missionary service?

    Whenever we begin to talk about the needs of the world, someone always chimes in with: "But the need at home is so great." The need at home is great. Our first responsibility is for those nearby. The question is not either/or but both/and. Jesus' command was Jerusalem, Judea, Samaria, and the ends of the earth.

    In America 1 out of 5 people with whom you do business or associate will be Bible-believing Christians, in Calcutta 1 of 10,000. How many Bibles are in Columbia, South Carolina? A million? Calcutta may have a few hundred Bibles, while many of the languages in that great city have none at all. I use Calcutta merely as an example of the spiritually lost half of the world where people don't have access to the gospel. If someone doesn't go in from the outside-if an apostolic missionary doesn't come-they cannot even hear the gospel. Yes, our first responsibility is for "Jerusalem," but God loves the world.

    A large church contributed financial support toward 75 missionaries, including us. In fact, it was the second largest missions donor church in the nation, of any denomination. One day I walked down the long hallway in which photographs of the missionaries were displayed, studying the biographies of each. To my astonishment, not one of their missionaries was from that church! They gave lots of money to support other people's sons and daughters. A young businessman noticed the same phenomenon and decided to do something about it. Calling himself "God's scout," he volunteered to teach the college-and-career Sunday School class. Within 5 years 11 members of that church were on the mission field-all from that class! God hadn't called him to go as a missionary, but Frank heard the call to send. Could you become a "scout" used of God to encourage a potential missionary? Check off any strategy you think God wants you to use to help others find God's purpose for their lives.

    Do you know any boy, girl, or young adult about whom you think, "That youngster would make a great missionary? They are spiritually alive, gifted, and active in service to God." Think over the young people in church you know and list any such possible candidates. In the past, only young people who had not yet launched into some other vocation were considered potential candidates for missionary service. Today many missionaries have joined the task force in mid-life, leaving other vocations. Most Americans change careers several times.

Perhaps God would give you the high privilege of being His ambassador to a people who have had no chance to hear the gospel. Why not begin today to ask the Holy Spirit to give you that gift? When I was 18, I began to ask God for the gift of apostleship. I wanted my life to count to the maximum for God's purpose in this world. I found the same ambition Paul spoke of burning in my spirit-to proclaim Christ where He had never been named (Rom. 15 :20). We encountered many obstacles: I didn't think I had the gift of evangelism; I had an illness the doctors said was incurable; others said we shouldn't go because "God is blessing you where you are" (a strange logic); we had four children (several mission boards didn't like that); and finally, after we boarded ship for Japan, my daughter was injured and we had to disembark . But we kept on obeying the command to "desire earnestly"; we kept asking God to send us and use us. I'm so glad we did. Surely no joy is quite like living among people who have never heard the gospel and watching the Holy Spirit work in giving hope to the hopeless, healing broken lives, and forming a church where there was no witness before. Perhaps God would give you that high privilege. Why not write out in your journal how you feel about the idea, or how you feel about being a sender. Then talk to Him about it. Why might short term missions fail to reach the world for the gospel?

August 8
Factoring Unity
Isaiah 55:9

"For as the heavens are higher than the earth, so are my ways higher than your ways and my thoughts than your thoughts." (Isaiah 55:9)

If Christ is actually functioning as Lord of the congregation, unity is more likely, if He is not Lord, division is inevitable; unless it is the unity of the grave! Let us, however, name a few of the factors essential to unity.

1. Regeneration. In both letters to the Corinthians, Paul makes it clear that a major cause of disunity is the presence of unregenerate people in the fellowship. Or people who behave that way. An essential for unity of spirit is the presence of the Spirit in each participant.

2. Faith in the Book. Making the Scripture the true functional authority is the only sure basis for unity in the congregation. If some members are not committed to the authority of the book, schism is almost inevitable. This faith is **biblical** faith-- commitment to obey. And that can't be merely passive obedience. It includes pro-actively searching Scripture on the part of the whole body whenever an issue that divides arises. A pronouncement by the leader won't suffice. Faith in Scripture means not only determination to obey, no matter if it means painful change, it means openness and ruthless honesty. The believers in Berea were commended because they received the Word with all readiness and because they searched the Scriptures daily to find out whether the teaching of the esteemed visitor were so.

On the solid rock of Biblical truth alone can a church find true unity. It may be important for practical reasons to unite on some teaching that the Church through the ages has not always agreed on. But such peripheries should not become part of the foundation of faith demanded of the members or it may well become divisive. As Augustine said, "In essentials, unity; in non-essentials, liberty; in all things charity." Deciding among those three categories may not be easy but should always be attempted when divisive issues arise.

3. Prayer. Only a praying people will ever be truly united and often it is only on its knees that the church will find unity. Since it is the Enemy himself who attacks the church through fostering division, there is spiritual warfare and that can be waged only in prayer.

4. Humility. This fruit of the Spirit may not come easily for one who is in leadership, especially successful leaders. Power-holders (or aspirers) usually stress the virtue of unity! So for the church to experience unity at the deepest level, leaders must give special care to produce an abundant crop of this fruit.

Why should the leader be humble? Because he is finite and fallen. We are finite so we know ultimate truth only partially. That's because God's ways and his thoughts are infinitely above us. Humility becomes a finite person. Furthermore, we are fallen. What we do know is distorted. And though our minds are in the process of being straightened out, being brought ever more into alignment with Christ's mind, still we are fallen, reality is still obscured by sinful understandings and predispositions.[50]

When the leader's demeanor is one of humility, willingness to accept correction, to change, to be united is much more possible in the body.

Therefore if there is any ... fellowship of the Spirit, if any affection and mercy, fulfill my joy by being like-minded, having the same love, being of one accord, of one mind.

And how does that happen?

Let nothing be done through selfish ambition or conceit, but in lowliness of mind let each esteem others better than himself.

Even when they obviously are not? Yes..

Let each of you look out not only for his own interests, but also for the interests of others.

Why?

Let this mind be in you which was also in Christ Jesus... (Philippians 2:1-5)

If the Lord of creation is humble, how can I not be? And that is a prerequisite for unity in the congregation. Here's how it works:

I...beseech you to have a walk worthy of the calling with which you were called, with all lowliness and gentleness, with longsuffering, bearing with one another in love, endeavoring to keep the unity of the Spirit in the bond of peace. There is one body and one Spirit, just as you were called in one hope of your calling; one Lord, one faith, one baptism; one God and Father of all who is above all, and through all, and in you all.

But to each one of us grace was given according to the measure of Christ's gift...And He Himself gave some to be ... pastors and teachers, for the equipping of the saints for the work of ministry, for the building up of the body of Christ, till we all come to the unity of the faith and the knowledge of the Son of God, to a perfect man, to the measure of the stature of the fullness of Christ...speaking the truth in love, may grow up in all things into Him who is the head-Christ-from whom the whole body, joined and knit together by what every joint supplies, according to the effective working by which every part does its share, causes growth of the body for the building up of itself in love (Ephesians 4:1-16).

Such is the magnificent vision of Paul as to what God designs the church to be and how he intends to accomplish it.

---

[50] 1 Corinthians 2:6-16; 2 Corinthians 3:14-18, 1 Corinthians 13:12, Isaiah 55:9, 2 Corinthians 3:14-18, Romans 12:2

August 9
The Blockade
Luke 11:42

"Woe to you Pharisees, because you give God a tenth of your mint, rue and all other kinds of garden herbs, but you neglect justice and the love of God" (Luke 11:42).

One of the greatest blockades on the road to victory for King Jesus is something very practical, quite earthy, really--money. And the lack of it for the missionary enterprise is a major roadblock to world evangelism. We seem to have plenty for our own needs and for the needs of our local churches, but when it comes to sending out American missionaries, it dries up. In fact, only four cents on each dollar given by evangelicals in the USA is used for world missions. Ninety-six percent of giving is spent at home, on ourselves. Many are fully prepared and ready to go, but the money isn't there. What's the problem?

Part of the problem of funding the enterprise may spring from misguided priorities. There often seems to be funding enough for building church edifices and even for sending more than a million short-termers annually at a cost of several billion dollars. And many churches give largely to support the ministries of poorer churches overseas.

Actually, the wealth of American churches is unprecedented in church history. But put in the context of (1) the need and (2) the proportion Christian people keep for themselves, giving is far from sacrificial. Even far from generous when compared with what the Church in other places and other times has done. So the basic problem may be one of spiritual maturity.

Maybe it would help to remember that Paul teaches that the willingness and ability to give is a grace, a gift from God. Paul viewed every disciple as living in the flow of the grace of God, into a life and then through that life. This is not just in terms of spiritual blessing. The grace of physical financial resources are provided as an act of God's grace and then flow through the Christians to others (2 Corinthians 8:7). I may not be able to graduate to a new level of giving but God is quite able to grace me up a step. Trust Him!

We've listened to Jesus teaching about giving because lack of giving is a major obstacle to world evangelism. So money is a key factor in both the missionary enterprise and simultaneously in the life of participants. Anyone can evaluate your spiritual maturity if you'll let them see your check-stubs, Jesus seems to say. In this way, giving ties together the *fruit* of the Spirit with the greatest of all *gifts* of the Spirit, evangelism. And because the key to our response about money is love, the chief of the fruits the Spirit gives, this very earthy part of our lives becomes of critical importance simultaneously both to personal spiritual health and to world evangelism.

We've emphasized the role of the individual in missions finance, but the church has a critical role:
* to teach and encourage all members toward biblical giving, nurturing spiritual maturity and
* to manage what has been given with biblical priorities in control of the budgeting process.

We know the painful, then liberating, move to make from tithing to managership. And we know very well, as we see the abject poverty of the world, almost none of us live a sacrificial lifestyle. Spurts of sacrifice, maybe, but far from Jesus' model of giving. How about you? Honesty about our finances may be the hardest honesty of all. As you review your giving for the past year, checking your records if you aren't sure, at what level of giving have you been? Are you pleased with that level? Is God pleased? What kind of lover does that show you to be? What kind of truster?

God's standard for giving is one He Himself models. He created you, so He is owner. We stole His property-

-took possession of ourselves. But in love He purchased you at terrible cost, just as if He had no claim on you, making you twice His. If you will only respond with love in obedient giving He guarantees your livelihood (Luke 12:31); rewards you lavishly in this life as if you were giving what is your own property; and in heaven He rewards you all over again! (Luke 18:28-30). That's God's level of giving, love giving.

In response to such love, are you ready to move up one step? If you've never been a faithful tither, isn't it time to promise Him that 10%? Trust Him! He'll take care of you. Perhaps you've been a tither for years but you did pretty much what you pleased with the other ninety percent. Isn't it time to stop that foolishness and become an honest manager of the property of Another? Whatever level of maturity you've achieved in your walk with God, don't you want to step up? If you are unwilling to move up from your present level of maturity it may be because you don't trust God to meet your needs, or a lack of faith. Or love. If because of your love for Jesus, you're ready to take that leap of faith to the next level, tell Him so. Now.

August 10
The Big Connection
John 15:4

"Abide in Me, and I in you. As the branch cannot bear fruit of itself, unless it abides in the vine, neither can you, unless you abide in Me". (John 15:4)

An <u>ikebana</u> is a beautiful thing, often exquisite, always exotic to the western eye. But it is misnamed. Two words, "flower" and "living," combine to name the Japanese way of arranging flowers. But <u>ikebanas</u> are made with cut flowers. More living than plastic or silk flowers, to be sure, but the connection with life is broken--hardly "living," at least not for more than a few days. Jesus says that's the way with our lives. They may be beautiful, even awe inspiring, but cut off from the source of life they can never be all they were meant to be nor last more than a few days. At least when measured by the calendar of eternity. The connection with real life and the secret to fulfilling life's potential is to connect with Him, says Jesus in John 15. And that connection is a relationship so intimate you could describe it as being <u>in</u> Him.

Getting into or "being in" Christ involves two things: a new creation and a new relation. What "exceeding magnifical" new persons we have become! What an astonishing new relationship we have entered! Paul emphasizes this union with Christ as the key to successful Christian experience. But Jesus emphasizes an even deeper "in-ness"--if you <u>abide</u> in Me, He says, a bumper crop of fruit will be yours (vs. 5): love, joy, peace, victorious Christian living and effective service. And that is what you were made for, true fulfillment.

We know the biblical terminology, but what it means literally and practically is not always clear. As a graduate student once wrote to me, "What, <u>what, WHAT</u> am I supposed to <u>do</u>, how, <u>how, HOW</u> can I actually experience this life He promises?" There are three abidings in this chapter, not one, and each throws light on the others: *abide in Christ* (vs 4, 5), *let the words of Christ abide in you* (vs. 7) and *abide in love* (vs 9, 10). Today let's consider our "abiding in Christ"

The key word of John 15 is translated "abide" in earlier translations, "remain" in some more recent translations. Remain is indeed a basic meaning of the Greek term <u>meno</u>. For example, the promise in verse 16 is of fruit that will <u>remain</u>, using the same word. Meno was used in secular Greek writing to indicate a holding out against all odds, of standing fast when others might waver or buckle.

Britisher Derek Redmond had this characteristic. Redmond provided the emotional high point of the Barcelona summer Olympics when he popped his right hamstring and fell to the cinders 160 meters into the 400 meter race. We watched in growing wonderment as he fought off the officials who came to escort him off the track. Redmond rose and began to hop on his one good leg to the cheers of the crowd. Soon his bad leg dropped to the ground and he dragged it behind him, face contorted in pain, hobbling toward the finish line. Said Redmond, "There was no way I was going out on a stretcher, and there was no way I was going to let all those official people keep me from finishing." That's meno, staying in the race no matter what. And those who meno in Christ will not only win the cheers of the "cloud of witnesses," they will win the gold!

To abide in Christ is first of all, then, to hold steady, to stick with one's commitment to Him. Fidelity, you might call it. Jesus repeatedly defines "abiding" as obedience: "*if you keep my commandments, you will abide in my love, just as I have kept my father's commandments and abide in his love* (10)." "*You are my friends if you do whatever I command you* (14)." To abide in Christ is to keep on obeying Him no matter what. Fidelity.

We are responsible to make the choices, to keep on "abiding" in our relationship, but we do not do so unaided. Not only do we have a new capability to choose the right, an ability infused at our re-creation, we also have the intimate relationship of one who comes alongside and enables, who will not let us go. Derek Redmond had someone who came along side, as the Associated Press reported:

> Redmond's father, Jim, jumped from the stands, brushed past the officials who tried to stop him and ran to his son's side. The two walked together for a few yards, father consoling son, and then Redmond stopped, covered tear-filled eyes with his hands and buried his head in his dad's shoulder. Then he lifted up and pointed with one finger to the finish line, too close to stop now.
>
> Jim Redmond drew Derek's arm around his shoulder, and the pair slowly made their way up the track as the applause grew louder. Finally, tears of disappointment and pain streaming down his face, Redmond staggered across the line, still leaning on his father's shoulder.

There's the secret: "still leaning on his father's shoulder." And that is the key to success in the Christian life--"*He who abides in me, and I in him, bears much fruit; for without me you can do nothing*" (vs 5). His responsibility is to hold us up, to see us through to the finish line. But ours is the responsibility to maintain the connection with tough endurance. It is our responsibility to make the right choices, to obey. No basis here for saying we can't, for blaming our dysfunctional family background or our present impossible circumstances. "*If you obey my commands, you will abide...*" (vs 10).

That is to abide--to keep faith, to hold steady, to bounce back, to endure. The first element of abiding, then, is fidelity. Tomorrow we will consider two additional abidings: "let the words of Christ abide in you" and "abide in love," so that we can gain an even fuller sense of what Jesus commands.

August 11
The Great Connection- Part 2
John 15:7

"If you abide in Me, and My words abide in you, you will ask what you desire, and it shall be done for you." (John 15:7)

Yesterday we examined how to abide in Christ: to hold steady, to stick with one's commitment to Him- fidelity. Today we consider two additional abidings: *"let the words of Christ abide in you"* and *"abide in love."* Actually, Jesus spoke of His words abiding in us (vs 7) rather than our abiding in his word. But, as in the case of abiding in Jesus and He abiding in us, the concept is a reciprocal "in" relationship, mutual interpenetration, if you will.

As we shall see shortly, "to abide" includes the very deepest level of inner emotional responses, but it doesn't usually start with the emotions, and it certainly doesn't end there. Nor is it anchored there. Yet the dominant approaches among evangelicals to solving life's problems are inward directed. They do their business in the arena of the subjective. There are problems with this. In the first place, our feelings or subjective experiences are subject to change, notoriously unreliable and unpredictable--the opposite of steadfast meno. A second problem occurs if the insights of the therapist or fellowship group leader--or the group as a whole, for that matter--are treated as final in authority. Sometimes they are treated as revelational as well--the authority is viewed as God's own.

To abide in Christ, on the other hand, is to stick with His Word. *"You are clean through the word..."* (vs 3) *"If you abide in me, and my words abide in you, ask what you desire and it will be done..."* (vs 7) *"...all things that I heard from my Father I have made known to you"* (vs 15). Our faith, though subjective, is based on objective, unchanging revelation. The Word alone is our final authority, and we are instructed to live in it and make sure it lives in us.

Many believers hold tenaciously to faith in Scripture, but the Bible for them is a constitutional monarch, reigning splendidly in theory while the choices of life are based on something else--tradition, subjective desires or impressions, cultural values. The task of bringing all of life under the functional authority of Scripture is hard work. To abide in Christ is to abide in His words--to study diligently, searching for the meaning intended by the author, and reflecting carefully on that meaning. For Christ to abide in us is to make sure His words abide in us--courageously applying those words to life in faithful obedience. To live with fidelity to Christ is to live with fidelity to His Word.

But many who study the Bible diligently and seek to obey it are not abiding in Christ in the deepest sense because the study itself has become their preoccupation or because the obedience has become legalistic. They are diligently accumulating knowledge and are faithful in choices, but the emotions are dormant. They have missed the third "abiding" of John 15--"*abide in love.*"

The faith of most believers, Kierkegaard said, could more accurately be described as resignation. Resignation can be a form of faith, but it is not complete, robust faith. I experienced this recently when the bludgeoning of life's circumstances had numbed my spirit. My wife was slipping toward oblivion under the ravages of Alzheimer's Disease and my eldest son was taken in a tragic diving accident. I had resigned from leadership roles to care for my beloved just at a time when most men would feel they were reaching the peak of usefulness. I loved God so far as basic commitment was concerned, but the passion was gone. I wasn't what lovers would call, "in love." Yet Jesus said that to be in Him was to be in love (vs.9-17).

The model for love is the way the Father loves the Son (vs 9). We must do more than maintain our commitment and stick with the Word. If we love Him with the same kind of passion that unites the Father and Son, we will be abiding in His love.

The result of this loving relationship is joy. In fact, that we should experience full-bodied joy was at least one purpose He had in teaching us about abiding (vs 11). I had lost the joy. Was it because I had lost the love?

The evidence of "in-love-ness" is interesting. It is not measured by the temperature of the emotion but by two very external, objective measurements: obedience to his commands and our relationship to others. *"If you obey my commands, you will abide in my love, just as I have obeyed my Father's commands and abide in his love"* (vs 10). *"My command is this: Love each other as I have loved you"* (vs 12, 17). So the critical element in love is volition--what do I choose to do? No need to speak of loving Him if I am unwilling to obey Him.

What a beautiful interplay of the three abidings: abiding in Christ, obeying His word, and loving Him are viewed as almost identical, each defining the other, each reinforcing the others in a marvelous interaction, each essential to experiencing the others.

To obey may be evidence of genuine love, but sheer obedience will not produce the intoxicating joy of a loving relationship. Love as a passionate affection will bring the joy, however, and that kind of emotion is inherent in meno. But for now, a word for any who, have lost the joy of a passionate love. When your spirit is numb by the Novocain of bitter experiences, keep learning that heaviness of spirit lifts on the wings of praise. As you focus on the beauties of the Lord, as we contemplate in great detail all that God is, all that he has done, all the gifts He has given, a passionate love for Him can flood your spirit. Begin again to abide in love. And the joy returns! So this is the big connection, the meno, the abiding: commitment in permanent fidelity to a wonderful person and to His words in a love-suffused oneness of life.

August 12
Steady On!
Philippians 2:12-13

"Therefore, my beloved, as you have always obeyed, so now, not only as in my presence but much more in my absence, work out your own salvation with fear and trembling, for it is God who works in you, both to will and to work for his good pleasure." (Philippians 2:12-13)

God is primarily in the business of remodeling our thought processes—our values, attitudes, ways of viewing things. This inner mind is the primary arena for growth. A normal Christian loves more and more like God loves; grows in self-control, contentment, humility, and courage; grows in understanding of God's ways; and is increasingly other-oriented and less self-oriented in the choices of life.

The inner transformation is visible in outward conduct. One's character changes, and even those personality traits that reflect sinful thought patterns are changed. Note that this growth into more Christlike behavior is in areas of unconscious sin or sins of omission, falling short of Godlike qualities. In deliberate sin there is no pattern of gradual growth. People do not reduce their bank robberies annually as they "grow in grace." They do not lie less frequently or cheat in fewer matters. In the Old Testament there was no redemption for presumptuous sins (e.g., Exod. 21:14; Num. 15:30-31), and in the New Testament that type of deliberately chosen sin occurs consistently in lists that identify those who are unredeemed and under judgment (e.g., 1 Cor. 6:9-10; Gal. 5:19-21; Rev. 21:8).

In matters where a person makes a deliberate choice, the normal Christian will choose God's way. But much of our behavior falls short of Christlikeness involuntarily and even unconsciously. It is in this area that the normal Christian grows steadily to reflect more and more accurately the likeness of Christ.

God does influence our minds directly, but His primary method of bringing about growth is through what are commonly called "means of grace," or conduits of divine energy. In these means we are not passive but must participate actively. Even though God indeed works in us both the willing and the doing of His good pleasure, we are to work out our own salvation with fear and trembling (Phil. 2:12-13).

Prayer. Through prayer our companionship with God reaches its highest intensity. Not only do we grow more like Him through this companionship, but we find that prayer is the great means of victory at the moment of temptation.

Scripture. The Bible is God's means of revealing His character and thus His will for our thoughts and actions. Therefore, the more we know His Word, the higher potential we have for conforming to His will. It is the milk and bread and meat of the soul. Furthermore, Jesus demonstrated in His hour of temptation that Scripture is a great weapon in spiritual warfare. As we study it diligently to understand it and as we meditate on it constantly to apply it to life, we will be prepared to use it effectively to overcome temptation.

Church. The congregation of God's family is indispensable for spiritual growth. United worship and observance of the ordinances, teaching, fellowship, discipline, service, and witness within the responsible structure of the church are God's ordained means for the growth of each member.

Suffering. Suffering may be God's great shortcut to spiritual growth. Our response to suffering determines its benefit to us, of course, for the same adversity may be destructive or life building. The response of faith, that is, confidence that God has permitted the trial for His glory and our own good, transforms a potentially evil circumstance into a means of making us more like the Suffering Servant Himself.

These four "tools of the Spirit" are indispensable to Christian growth. But though they are equally available to all, not all Christians seem to mature at the same pace.

Some Christians use the means of grace more diligently than others. Although in a passive sense all believers may be equally "yielded" to the will of God, the Christian life is nevertheless a war, and some are more aggressive and seem to have more of a will to fight. Though faith must rest, relying on God to do what we cannot do, it also must wrestle, struggling in warfare. Satan is the great adversary and destroyer, constantly seeking to immobilize, if he cannot destroy, God's people. Furthermore, Christians live in a world that is opposed to all they yearn to be. Some seem more aware of these adversaries and more persistent in opposing them.

In a sense, failure to do battle aggressively could be considered a spiritual flaw needing correction. At the same time this difference among Christians may simply be another sign of different levels of maturity. One should, in these matters, deal stringently with oneself and generously in judgment of the other person–both of which responses are the opposite of our natural inclinations!

August 13
Avoid-Flee-Escape
2 Timothy 2:21

"Therefore, if anyone cleanses himself from what is dishonorable, he will be a vessel for honorable use, set apart as holy, useful to the master of the house, ready for every good work. " (2 Timothy 2:21)

A couple came to visit my home, he was a good brother in the faith and had a lovely teenage daughter. They were visiting the university to choose a college for next year. But when I heard their story, I was astounded! If I had experienced what he did, I would be taking my daughter to the ends of the earth- anywhere else. He visited three friends who were in the seminary. One was working on his degree; another was my teaching assistant for ethics- my course on the Christian life. He was the most gifted TA I ever had. The third was studying to be a pastor. The three came to have something in common. Within two decades, all three had fallen to the sex goddess. Their ministry destroyed; their marriages dissolved.

For the missionary it was internet pornography. He abandoned his wife and left her to provide for six small children. The second was the church secretary. He terminated his ministry, badly damaged his church and his family. The third was also a pastor.

Paul gave some advice to Timothy. In 2 Timothy 2:19 Paul says *Avoid*. And then in verse 20 he says *Flee*. Thirdly in verse 26 he says *Escape*. That was the word. Avoid. Flee. Steer clear. Depart, avoid. Paul says in verse 19, "Let everyone who names the name of Christ depart from iniquity."

Avoid all iniquity. Are you a Christian? Then affirm your vows of purity today. Remain what he calls clean, set apart, useful, ready for service. We're not only vessels of gold or silver, but also wood and clay, some for honor and some for dishonor. "Therefore, if anyone cleanses himself from what is dishonorable, he will be a vessel for honorable use, set apart as holy, useful to the master of the house, ready for every good work" ready for service."

Consider this escalator. I call it the emotion or the affectional escalator: thrown together with an attractive person> time alone together> talk of personal matters>of prayer together> deliberately plan time together> preoccupation with thoughts about the person>signals that attraction is mutual> fantasy of intimate conversation> verbal expression of affection> embraces> finally sexual intercourse.

God made it. We all go on this escalator. But let us keep ourselves pure for Him. Just get off the escalator. The proper time is now. Billy Graham does not go beyond the first step. In fact, he doesn't even get to the first step. He has a rule that he'll never be alone with anyone of the opposite sex other than his wife, that's pretty safe. That's pretty serious.

So where is your line? Covenant with God to flee at anything even approaching that line, determined to avoid it. Avoid the temptation situation as Solomon instructed us. Remove your way, far from her, the seductress, and do not go near the door of her house across the street and hurry on. But he had. Don't visit her neighborhood. Get off the escalator. Too bad Solomon didn't follow his own advice; *"Keep your way far from her, and do not go near the door of her house, lest you give your honor to others"* (Proverbs 5:8).

Now, there are three ways to avoid in Scripture. Your thoughts, your eyes and your touch. Thoughts? Avoid even that first imagination, the first emotion. Did you know that the stronger sex organ in your body is between your ears?

Well, how do you decide where you're going to draw the line? Well, if it's sexually stimulating, avoid it. Here

304

is a practical test: if you saw some other guy doing that with your girlfriend or wife, how would you feel about it? So until you're pledged to live your life together, in God's eyes, she belongs to someone else. Don't go near. Avoid the temptation. And then in verse 22 he says flee-flee youthful lusts, but pursue righteousness, faith, love, peace with those who call on the Lord out of a pure heart. Flee.

The bird with a broken wing may fly again. But never may fly so high again. You say, but David was rehabilitated. Yeah. But don't forget his miserable ending, a bitter old man with a radically dysfunctional family. One son was out to kill him. And the one son who stuck by his father accumulated 300 wives and 700 concubines.

Solomon made at least 999 unwise choices. I reflect on David and Solomon and recall God's principle that the sins of the father are visited on the son.

There you have it. Avoid. Flee. Escape. Will you pledge to follow this instruction? For a lifetime. But there's another message for men and women. I am my brother's keeper. Back to the escalator. You have a responsibility to each other, not to deliberately draw another up the escalator by your dress or behavior.

Where are you? Is there something you need to avoid? Tell Him so. Has it already started? Is there something you need to flee? Get out of there. Have you already been trapped? Agree with God about it. Turn around and he'll spring the trap. Clean vessels honoring the master with useful service. Go for it!

August 14
How's your Aim? Too High or Too Low?
Matthew 5:48

"Be perfect, therefore, as your heavenly Father is perfect." (Matthew 5:48)

"We confess, Lord," the man in the pulpit prayed, "that we, your people turn our backs on you, shake our fist in your face every day of our lives." Would you say the Amen to that pastoral prayer, or do you think he's aiming too low? A recent book entitled *Less Than Conquerors* expresses the author's point that the best we can expect in the Christian life is struggle and failure, and anyone who claims more is delude or hypocritical.

Here are a couple of statements that are true, but dangerous. They're often used by those who settle for too little of the Christian life:
- "Nobody's perfect, and God understands that. I, too, am weak and flawed."
- "God loves me unconditionally and accepts me just the way I am."

I'm a little uneasy about these common statements, and maybe you are too. Perhaps it's because the thought is incomplete, and we worry about what conclusion the person draws from the statement. Perhaps we hear, "no one is perfect," but what is left unsaid? Is "so don't bug me about changing for the better. "

To be biblical, a person would need to say, "Nobody's perfect, but I want to be on the upward spiral toward that goal." It's true that I'm invited to come to God "just as I am without one plea." But if by saying, "He accepts me just as I am," we mean, "He approves of me the way I am," or "God accepts me, so don't you be a judgmental hypocrite." We have missed the whole point of salvation.

He accepts me as I am to transform me into what he designed me to be. He loves me too much to leave me just the way I am. That would be far too low an expectation. It is God who saved us and chose us to live a holy life. (2 Timothy 1:9 NLT). We are God's masterpiece. He has created us anew in Christ Jesus, so that we can do the good things that he planned for us long ago (Ephesians 2:10). The purpose of our salvation, from the beginning, was to make us what we what we are not. Holy!

Some people have two low expectations for theological reasons. As we have seen, they just don't believe God will change human beings that much. But there are others who have low expectations for psychological reasons. They believe too few people have the ability to choose God's way-most have been disabled by circumstance. I met someone who based his ministry on that assumption. Who's right??

The truth is that the church is full of hurting people, some battered more than others. And when people are blind to their own sinful behavior, or their "chooser" is so bummed up that it can't function, or their "truster" is so violated they can't get through to God, A trained counselor, using some of the tools of the profession, may be able to help them see themselves, others, and God in clearer perspective. Then they can begin to trust God and choose God's alternatives.

A lowered expectation of what the Holy Spirit can do without professional intervention, may come from making the therapy model the rule rather than the exception. It's easy to see where lowered expectations of Holy Spirit generated possibilities come from. Americans in general, believe less and less in sin and guilt, and more and more in a battered psyche that needs healing. We are no longer guilty sinners needing salvation; we are victims of someone else's hurtful behavior and we need to have a healthy self-image restored, by therapy if necessary.

We've seen some of the dangers of aiming too low in our Christian life. But the opposite can derail us, as we'll soon see. Some see the grand promises we've just discovered and think they mean we can become sinlessly perfect in this life, perhaps even instantaneously, through a full post conversion experience.

How do we read the same Bible and come up with such different answers? By the way you define quote "sin," or "perfect." Sin has been defined in various ways:

Sin is an action that violates God's laws- feelings don't count. Christ carefully designated wrong attitudes as sin as well as outward acts.

Sin is a transgression of the law. We have to agree with that definition because it's a biblical statement! (1 John 3:4). But it was not intended as an exhaustive definition of sin- There are other attitudes and actions which don't actively transgress the law but which fall short, such as sins of omission or failing to think or do as I ought.

Sin is any transgression, any falling short of the moral character of God. Here's one that is thoroughly biblical because God standard is to be just like him morally. (Matthew 5: 48) and yet, "all have sinned and are falling short of the glorious character of God." Who is as good as God? As contented, courageous, clean as Jesus? Who acts always in love towards others? We're all falling short. If we lower the standard, then it's easier to reach it. If I'm guilty of sin only when I deliberately violate the known will of God, maybe it's possible to live a life relatively free of sin. Of course, it's no doubt better to aim too high and fall short than to aim too low and hit the target! In fact, Paul prays for the perfection of the Christians in Corinth and tells them to aim for it! (2 Corinthians 13:9, 11).

August 15
What has God Said?
1 Chronicles 16:8

"....make known among the nations what He has done." (1 Chronicles 16:8)

Folk wisdom has it that actions thunder so loudly about one's character and true intent that feeble words of explanation cannot be heard. What do God's activities demonstrate of His loving character and purpose of world redemption? It is not too much to affirm that every major act of God since creation has been a missionary act.

Even creation does not focus on the intricacies of the atom nor climax with the infinite galaxies. The crescendo builds to a climax in the creation of a being in the likeness of God Himself. This was the overflow of a love which bound the Three in a unity from all eternity. God's desire was to create a being who would have the capacity to fully receive His love and, in turn, to love Him freely and fully. This very likeness to God, the freedom from coerced or programmed choices, set the stage for man's rebellion and alienation.

Man changed but God did not. And thus His purpose shifted from loving companionship with humankind to recreating the broken pattern of God-likeness so that the loving identity of life could be restored. As a result, the sacrificial system, the calling of a special people, the redemption from Egypt, and the giving of the Law all centered in redeeming and restoring.

When God chose to communicate with men in written form, His purpose was the same. The Bible is not a revelation of all of God's activities or purposes from eternity. It is not a record of all human antiquity. It is the story of redemption, climaxing in the greatest even in human history, the Incarnation. This invasion of human life by God Himself was deliberately designed from all eternity, we are told, to provide redemption through the death and resurrection of Jesus Christ. These events, more than anything else Scripture tells us, reveal the purpose and character of God: love reaching out to save hopelessly lost people. What has God done? "God so loved ... that he gave his one and only Son ... " This act of love goes beyond all human comprehension. What could reveal with greater clarity God's character and purpose? What could demonstrate more forcibly the center and circumference of His attention?

The next major event, Pentecost was the descent of the Holy Spirit to establish the church, to be sure. But the purpose was clear. The entire record of the early church revealed how the apostles viewed the primary purpose of the church toward the world. It was to be God's instrument for world evangelization. Indeed, it is not too much to say that every major activity of God among men since the Fall has been a saving missionary act.

Surely David, like all the chosen people, clearly remembered God's promises to Abraham and the patriarchs. Often they forgot God's worldwide purpose through them. But not David:

"Give thanks to the LORD, call on his name; make known among the nations what he has done. Sing to the LORD, all the earth; proclaim his salvation day after day. Declare his glory among the nations, his marvelous deeds among all peoples. Ascribe to the LORD, 0 families of nations, ascribe to the LORD glory and strength, Tremble before him, all the earth! The world is firmly established; it cannot be moved. Let the heavens rejoice, let the earth be glad; let them say among the nations, "The LORD reigns!" (1 Chron. 16:8, 23-24, 28, 30-31).

The psalmist leads us in what must surely be our daily prayer: "May God be gracious to us and bless us" (Psalm 67:1). How hopeless we would be if we received what we justly deserve, so we plead for mercy. We pray, "God bless my work, God bless my health, God bless my family, God bless my church."

The psalmist adds, *"and make his face shine upon us."* If God mercifully forgave us, received us, and graciously prospered us but did not smile on us, assuring us of His favor, what a bleak life we would have. So we rightly ask for God to forgive our sins, bless our affairs, and lovingly companion with us. But why? The psalmist continues: *"that thy way be known upon the earth, thy saving power among all nations."* (RSV). How could the ancient songwriter of Israel declare more clearly his own missionary purpose in total alignment with the purpose of his missionary God?

All this revelation of God's purpose of world redemption was gathered up in the magnificent declarations of the prophet Isaiah:

"Turn to me and be saved, all you ends of the earth; for I am God, and there is no other" (Isa. 45:22).

"It is too small a thing for you to be my servant to restore the tribes of Jacob and bring back those of Israel I have kept. I will also make you a light for the Gentiles, that you may bring my salvation to the ends of the earth" (Isa. 49:6).

August 16
Benefits
2 Corinthians 11:23

"I have worked much harder, been in prison more frequently, been flogged more severely, and been exposed to death again and again." (2 Corinthians 11:23)

I was asked concerning the young people from the United States. They said " What's with them? They're so different." And I said, "What kind of thing are you concerned about?" And they said, "Well, it seems that young people are concerned with the hours of work, what they can charge to the mission, how much they will get out of it when they can retire, how long do they vacation? These questions seem to be paramount, right up front in their questions."

What is paramount in their concern? Let us ask, "How did compensation for pastors in the Apostolic era compare with other professionals at the time?" We don't really know, do we? But make an educated guess. "How many vacations did Jesus take during his three years of public ministry?" Well, he did plan to go off for a prayer retreat. We wouldn't call that a vacation because vacation means play. But at any rate, he started to go off and then 5,000 people descended on him and that was sort of aborted. Now let's see, "How many hours was the average work week for slaves in the Roman era?" What did slaves have to do with apostles? The majority of Christians in the early church were slaves. You remember Paul always called himself a slave of Jesus Christ, and by implication we are as well. "At what age did the apostles retire and what were their retirement benefits?" I only know of one who retired, and that was after the age of 90. It was an involuntary retirement, and his benefits was an island all to himself. That was John on Patmos.

Which did Paul emphasize more? Rights or responsibilities? These questions aren't to get an answer. We are just seeking to focus in on what the contemporary high priority concerns are, and I'm suggesting that we will never have excellence if we measure it by contemporary community standards, no matter what the community and no matter what the contemporary.

Tony Campolo tells a story of a pastor friend in downtown Philadelphia. The pastor had been listening to the introductions of a number of his young people who were attending prestigious universities, working toward prestigious degrees, with a prestigious vocation in mind. So the preacher got up and said, " When you were born, you cried. But everybody else was happy. When you die, they will all be crying. Will you be happy?"

And then he went on to say, "The answer to that question depended on whether you lived for titles or testimonies. When you die, he said, your titles won't bring you much joy. But if the same people standing around your grave give testimony of the impact of your life in their lives. Then you'll have joy."

Olympic athletes were asked if there were a pill available which would guarantee a gold medal but also would guarantee that in five years they would be dead. Would they take the pill? 61% said yes. We have our heroes, too. Let me tell you about John Wesley. At the close of his long life estimated he had traveled 250,000 miles on horseback, which would be an average of 20 miles a day for 40 years. He preached 40,000 times, which is an average of three messages a day. He produced hundreds of books and pamphlets. He knew 10 languages. At 83, he was greatly annoyed because he could not write more than 15 hours a day without hurting his eyes. At 86, he was ashamed he could not preach more than twice a day. He complained in his journal he had an increasing tendency to lie in bed until 5:30 in the morning.

When CT Studd cleaned up on China, then he moved to Africa and after long years he was an old man. His friends and family in England wrote and urged him to come back. And he replied that he would not come back. He was going to stay and gain more ground for the King. And then he wrote this to them, "May the victors when they come, when these forts of folly fall, find my body near the wall.. Somebody has to scale the wall, or the fortress will never fall."

How do you interpret the passage where Jesus said the gates of hell will not prevail against the church? One interpretation is that the church is under siege, but it's going to be victorious. It's going to be able to hold out against the powers of the enemy. But I'm with the other interpreters who hold that the gates of hell or the powers of hell will not be able to withstand the attack of the Church of Jesus Christ. That is a whole different mentality, a crash the gates mentality.

Jesus has given a promise to us. Not some tiny little mountain wilderness in the Near East bit of real estate, but the whole world and its people. The Father promised the Son, "I will give you the nations for your inheritance," all the nations as a gift from the Father to Son. But we have to take it for Him. We have to take it nation by nation, people by people, stronghold by stronghold. Now. What are you going to choose? Are you going to choose a place where Hell's resistance is great? Are you going to quit? Are you going to claim the promise of the Father to the Son? Stake out your possession.

Young man, get a clear vision. Go for it. Young woman, can't settle for mediocrity? Go for it. Be a hero, take territory for God. Don't give up. Don't quit. You know there may be other people smarter than you are, more gifted, but who will never turn in an excellent performance because they're fuzzy in their vision. Or they don't really go for it. Afraid to pay the price? Excellence always costs.

August 17
Chosen on Purpose
Romans 15:20-21

"...thus I make it my ambition to preach the gospel, not where Christ has already been named, lest I build on someone else's foundation, but as it is written, "Those who have never been told of him will see, and those who have never heard will understand." (Romans 15:20-21)

When I lived in Japan, every Japanese school boy knew the expression, "Boys, be ambitious." Often they could repeat it in English. The great American pioneer of higher education in Japan, William Smith Clark, as he left Japan, gave a farewell that somehow captured the spirit of Japan and it has become universally quoted, "Boys, be ambitious." And those first students were ambitious. They became leaders in the modernization of Japan in the 19th Century.

"Be ambitious!" Are you? If you are ambitious, what is your ambition? If you have no great, burning ambition, is it because you think there's something unworthy about ambition, a little arrogant, or presumptuous? Paul was ambitious. He said so. Or perhaps you think it's OK for others to be ambitious, but you'll just rock along through life without driving hard to fulfill some goal or dream?

I was ambitious. When I was five years old I wanted to be a fireman or garbage man, at 11 years old a civil engineer. Once grown, my ambition moved in the direction of Paul's ambition. "I have made it my ambition to preach the gospel, not where Christ was named...but as it is written, 'To whom He was not announced, they shall see; and those who have not heard shall understand.'" (Romans 15: 20, 21) Paul's ambition was to proclaim Christ where he was unknown. I began to make that my ambition. Decades before the expression was coined, I began to become a world Christian. Though I still didn't know what God had in mind for me to do, I had a growing passion to make my life count to the maximum for what he was up to in this world. How could I best advance the Kingdom? And that is what Clark originally said as he left Japan, something NO Japanese school boy knows. They don't know it because the full quotation is never given. What Clark actually said was, "Boys, be ambitious for Christ!"

Is there any place Christ has not been proclaimed? In about half the nations of the world if they wanted to find out they could. They have access to the gospel message. But the thing that must break God's heart is that half the people on planet earth cannot hear the gospel because no one has ever gone to their people, their tribe, their place to tell them. It's not just that they haven't heard the good news of life in Christ, it's that they *can't* hear until someone gets Paul's ambition to go there to tell them.

We had hoped to go to China as missionaries, but that door was closed, so the mission suggested we go to Japan. But Japan was not a ripe harvest field. The best of evangelists–native or foreign-- did not have a great harvest. And there was an even greater problem: the attrition rate was higher than anywhere else. So we needed a special assurance from God. God gave us John 15:16. This is one of the most thrilling truths in my life. God chose me on purpose, set me apart for a specific task and invested me with his authority to accomplish it. What a promise!

The force of the word is "to send". That reminds us of what Jesus told the disciples a few days later, the first night following his resurrection, right in this same upper room: "As the Father sent me so send I you." (John 20:21). Not only are we chosen and appointed to a divine destiny, it is on the model of what the Father and Son did, the Father who so loved the world that he sent the Son on purpose to save. Now the Son sends us! With the same motive--love for the lost; with the same goal--the world. You did not choose me, but I chose you and commissioned you to go and produce a bumper crop of fruit, fruit that will remain.

"*You did not choose me,*" Jesus said. "*I chose you.*" So don't give up, don't be discouraged. God chose you. And he chose you on purpose. Fruit, lots of fruit. Fruit that remains. He keeps his promises!

Maybe you don't know what God put you here on earth to do. But whatever it is, figure out how what you are doing can best advance his program of world evangelism. And maybe he would give some of you the high privilege of serving as Paul did, pioneering the gospel among people who are not only unevangelized today, but have no chance of hearing unless someone goes to them. What does God want you to do about them?

You may not know the role he wants you to play, you may not know the location to which he will send, but you can be sure that the One who called you did so on purpose. And you can be sure the role he designs for you will have a key part in world evangelization. Why not begin today to make that your life's ambition?

My challenge to you is to commit your life to the cause of making Christ known to everyone on planet earth, to live for it, to die for it, if need be. And if you will, I have a wonderful gift for you, a promise that the great Promise Keeper gives, "You did not call me, I called you. And I appointed you as my personal representative to go and serve me effectively, to produce results that will last to eternity." Boys–girls, men, women--, be ambitious. For Christ!

August 18
Muriel
Psalm 15:4

"*...honor those who fear the Lord; who stand by their oath even to their hurt*" (Psalm 15:4)

Robertson once said to his second wife, Deb, "How would you like to be famous for having quit?' Quit? Hardly, but his story of the decision to step down from Columbia International University as president might help you to sort your thoughts and feelings about commitments, and about God. His story goes:

Muriel's love for me was not just a noun describing her feelings, but a verb describing her activity. Oh, she had the feelings--take my word for it--plenty of passion. But it was so much more--she lived out her life for me. No wonder it was a happy partnership.

But then. . .

But then the brightest light in my galaxy began to flicker. And she was only 55, looked no more than 35. In the summer of 1978 on a trip to Florida, as we visited with friends, Muriel began a story she had told only moments before. When I pointed that out, she just laughed and continued the story. I thought, "That's funny. Never happened before." But it happened again. And again. A college president's wife does a lot of entertaining, and Muriel was a gifted hostess. But now those special occasions for people important to the institution began to become hazardous. What sort of menu might we expect? What sort of food preparation and when?

In 1983 we visited a neurologist friend to see exactly what was happening. After she'd consulted with Dr Taber, he asked me to come in while she sat outside in the waiting room. When I returned, Muriel cheerfully greeted me, "Well?" Stalling for time, I responded, "'Well' what?"

"Well, am I batty?"

"I guess, just as we suspected, we may have a problem," I responded rather lamely.

I told the Board of Trustees what was happening and suggested they develop contingency plans because, I assured them, when my sweetheart needed me full time, she would have me.

No two patients are the same, I discovered as people told me their stories, not in the losses suffered (apart from memory loss), not in the order of loss, not in the pace of loss. But it was to be 15 years before the obvious dawned on me. This is a disease of the elderly. If you're 85 at onset you're likely to die of something within seven years. So much for averages. But Muriel was not even 60 when diagnosed. "Early onset" they call it. Sometimes the "long goodbye" is very long indeed.

There was one thing she did do with unrelenting determination: escape the prison guarded by that pesky caregiver and dash for her husband's office a half-mile from home. More often than not the effort would prove futile, for Sherry, my secretary, would bar the entrance. "There's someone in his office, Mrs. McQuilkin. You can't go in just now." She would speed-walk home, only to return a few minutes later. As many as 10 times a day--10 miles of walking, walking, walking.

When would the time come when I could no longer fulfill my obligations adequately both to the schools and to my beloved? I wrestled with the question. It wasn't, as some have said, a battle of the loves because I loved Muriel above all, whereas the work--well, it was exciting enough to dream great dreams and see them come to pass, but I never considered myself indispensable. I wasn't married to an institution.

I said I loved Muriel above all. And that's true of all human loves, but there's Another I want to love with all my heart, will, mind, and strength. And that was the root of the problem. The battle centered on what love for God would choose when his instructions don't seem to point in a common direction. "He who does not care for his own is worse than an unbeliever." "Husbands, love your wives as Christ loved the church and gave himself up for it." Fair enough, let's go for it! But then again, what of the many verses on which I've never heard a sermon, verses like, "If anyone comes to me and does not hate his father and mother, his wife and children, his brothers and sisters--yes, even his own life--he cannot be my disciple"? Or the promise: "...no one who has left home or wife or brothers or parents or children for the sake of the kingdom of God will not fail to receive many times as much in this age and, in the age to come, eternal life." What would love do? Love for God, that is.

The Board meeting was in early February, so I didn't have much time to think about my personal situation, but the night before that meeting I could put it on hold no longer. I lay awake beside my beloved. How she needed me. There were many people, no doubt, who could lead Columbia Bible College and Seminary (now Columbia International University), perhaps better than I, but no one could care for Muriel as I could. At three AM the decision was made. Now at peace, I drifted off into a deep sleep.

The next morning, after telling the Board of my decision, I went to the chapel to tell the faculty, staff and students. Next it was time to share with the whole constituency:

Twenty-two years is a long time. But then again, it can be shorter than one anticipates. And how do you say good-bye to friends you do not wish to leave? The decision to come to Columbia was the most difficult I have had to make; the decision to leave 22 years later, though painful, was one of the easiest. It was almost as if God engineered the circumstances so that I had no alternatives. Let me explain.

My dear wife, Muriel, has been in failing mental health for about 12 years. So far I have been able to carry both her ever-growing needs and my leadership responsibility at Columbia. But recently it has become apparent that Muriel is contented most of the time she is with me and almost none of the time I am away from her. It is not just "discontent." She is filled with fear--even terror--that she has lost me and always goes in search of me when I leave home. So it is clear to me that she needs me now, full-time.

Perhaps it would help you understand if I shared with you what I shared in chapel at the time I announced my resignation. "The decision was made, in a way, 42 years ago when I promised to care for Muriel 'in sickness and in health. . . till death do us part.'" So, as I told the students and faculty, "as a man of my word, integrity has something to do with it. But so does fairness. She has cared for me fully and sacrificially all these years; if I cared for her tor the next 40 years I would not be out of her debt. Duty, however, can be grim and stoic. But there is more: I love Muriel. She is a delight to me--her childlike dependence and confidence in me, her warm love, occasional flashes of that wit I used to relish so, her happy spirit and tough resilience in the face of her continual distressing frustration. I don't have to care for her, I get to! It is a high honor to care for so wonderful a person."

I've heard that 72% of marriages break up when one partner contracts a terminal illness. I've never been tempted, but if I were I'd remember that God loves promise keepers, gives no audience to promise breakers. [51]

August 19
The Successful Life
2 Corinthians 2:14

"But thanks be to God, who in Christ always leads us in triumphal procession, and through us spreads the fragrance of the knowledge of him everywhere." (2 Corinthians 2:14)

The approach to defining sin, clearly enunciated in the Old Testament, seems to provide the key to unlock the mystifying teaching of I John. John assures us that to claim sinless perfection is gross self-deception. And it makes God a liar, too! (I John 1:8-10) How then can the same author a few verses later assure us that anyone who sins does not even know God? In fact, belongs to the Devil! (I John 3:6-10). I'm convinced that the solution lies in the fact that John's thinking was from the context of his Scripture, the Old Testament. Based on the Old Testament distinction among sins, he assures us that anyone who claims to be free of any and all sin is badly deceived, because even if we have not chosen to violate some command, still we fall far short of God's moral likeness (I John, chapter 1). But, if I take that awareness of sinful failure as license to choose sin, again I am badly deceived. My choices have proved I don't belong to God at all. That this is the teaching of John in chapter 3 seems clear from the verb tense he chose, a tense which is not clear in most English translations. "If anyone is sinning..." says John, if anyone continues in deliberately choosing to violate God's known will, that person does not know God. At least any assurance of belonging to God does not come from Bible affirmation. Nowhere does the Bible assure the person who persists in deliberately sinning that he or she is acceptable to God. The Bible tells such a person, rather: Repent! Quit that sinning!

Though this distinction between two categories of sin is not taught by all advocates of successful Christian living, it may well help define our hope of victory. Do we speak of sin as deliberately choosing to violate the known will of God? Then the Bible promises full deliverance, consistent victory. No need to ever fail. Do we speak of involuntary failure to measure up to God's likeness? Then the Bible promises us steady growth toward that goal, though we will not be fully delivered from sinful attitudes and behavior until we "become like him" when we "see him as he is" at the end of our life.

---

[51] Note: for a more complete story, there's a book: A Promise Kept, Chicago, Moody Press (2005).

I call this the mediating view of sanctification because it stands midway between those who hold out hope for absolute perfection on one hand and those who hold out no hope for a victorious life on the other. It is much easier to go to a consistent extreme than to stay at the center of biblical tension!

In reaction to perfectionist teaching, some have concluded that there is no hope beyond the common Christian experience of struggle and defeat. Their preaching and writing about the inevitability of living in constant, deliberate sin does not sound exactly like Paul's great proclamation of emancipation: sin shall not have dominion over you! (Romans 6:14). He gives thanks to God who always causes us to triumph (2 Corinthians 2:14) and exults in the assurance that we are more than conquerors (Romans 8:37). These are not isolated proof texts but rather reflect the mood of the entire New Testament. These texts extend from the promise of abundant life (John 10:10) and a bumper crop of Christlike characteristics (John 15) by Jesus himself to the promises of Peter that we can escape from the world's corruption and experience abounding godliness (2 Peter 1). These texts continue on to John's assurance that we must (and can) live out life in the moral light (I John 1). If we don't live life in the light, we should question if we even belong to God at all (I John 3). The gospel is good news not merely for life beyond the grave, but good news for victory in daily life today.

This does not mean, however, that living the God intended life is easy. Ours is no spectator religion in which we relax and let Christ live out His life in our bodies. There is indeed the rest of faith, but there is also the wrestle. Nevertheless, it is warfare with victory assured, not defeat. And those who settle for a life of defeat are "shortsighted, even to blindness, and have forgotten that they were purged from the old sinful ways" (1 Peter 1:9). In fact, Paul calls such people "carnal" because they behave like the unconverted (1 Corinthians 3:3).

Not all Christians, then, experience the God intended life. The difference among Christians is not merely one of degree, all on a growth track with some growing more rapidly than others. Who are the defeated, the "carnal," the "shortsighted"? There are three varieties: 1) some are ignorant of God's plan for victorious living or the way to experience it; 2) some may know basic principles but have drifted out of a tight relationship with God, perhaps through neglecting the means of grace; and 3) some are in flat-out rebellion, deliberately saying "no" to God in some matter.

What do people need when they find themselves in habitual sin? They need a fresh encounter with God, a return to the original contract of faith they signed when they received salvation. They need to yield and trust. No person is more than two steps away from a life of victory in Christ: surrender and faith, consciously yielding to God unconditionally and trusting Him to keep His word. Such is the relationship that releases Holy Spirit power for living. It does not provide instantaneous perfection, but it does start the process of transformation from one degree of His glorious character to another till we are finally made complete in Christ when we see Him as He is. That is our glorious hope!

August 20
Relevant
Matthew 10:16

"Behold, I am sending you out as sheep in the midst of wolves, so be wise as serpents and harmless as doves." (Matthew 10:16, NKJV)

We live in a global society, movement of peoples around the globe is common. How to we relate to these diverse peoples? How do we communicate with our neighbor? When speaking of cross-cultural communication, we may think of a culture foreign to our own, but in truth all communication of spiritual truth is cross-cultural. The more distant the fundamental cultural elements of a given culture are to our own, the more aware we are of the un-biblical elements, perhaps, but the closer to our culture, more subtle and difficult the distance is to discern. But the necessity to try is essential. We seek to wed theology with ministry to bring all ministry under the functional authority of Scripture. But to communicate God's truth, we also need to study the recipient of our communication carefully. That study has been called "cultural anthropology."

Let's provide an example: When I was a missionary in Japan, I sensed that anthropology must be focused on getting the task done, so I began the serious study of the Japanese value system. I wanted to know what Japanese valued, not what I valued. For pre-evangelism I wanted to connect with some motivational point for which our faith offered help. I was astounded to discover that many things important to me were of little or no importance to Japanese: eternal life, propositional truth, individual freedom, forgiveness of sin, a personal God, history. These were things I had been trying to "market." At the same time I found things important to the Japanese that were not priorities for most westerners, but, I discovered, things to which Scripture speaks: approval and sense of belonging, security, relationships, feelings, honor of parents, here-and-now "salvation," obligation, loyalty, beauty, love of nature, and the value of suffering.

Hirota was soundly converted and grew like an amaryllis. About six months after his conversion he came to me. "Sensei, you always talk about heaven and I've said to myself, 'Who wants that? One life is enough!' But now that I've gotten acquainted with Jesus I really want to go there to be with him forever."

I had been trying to entice with visions of heaven a people whose idea of paradise is cessation of existence, to get off the wheel of reincarnation altogether. I was using bad bait. Cultural anthropology is a great tool to discover the values and non-values of a people so that the would-be communicator can start with good news about what is valued, not with what is valueless.

Do I spend time seeking to bring the serious seeker under conviction of sin (which, in a shame culture, he may not even recognize as existing) by stressing what he is so constantly guilty of--lying? It's a big one for me. Why can't he see it? Because, as his proverb instructs him, "A lie also is a useful thing." My attempts to convict him of the heinousness of such a sin will no doubt prove futile. If I switch to sins he is acutely aware of, like relationships he has broken or his failure to meet his eternal obligations to his parents, however, I might make some progress in bringing conviction of sin, which my theology and good psychology teach me a person must have before they become interested in a savior. I might even switch to shame instead of sin as an entering wedge if shame is what his tightly knit culture recognizes. After all it is a shameful thing to fail in our obligations to God and forgiveness of that shameful offence might prove desirable.

Another example of cultural handicaps in evangelism. We value individualism, rugged individualism. The problem is we try to convert people into our image in order for them to qualify for receiving our message. The person who won't stand out against family and friends is not worthy. Yet, the African or Asian may not think such a trait desirable at all. He may value contrasting virtues to which we give slight attention, even though they may be major biblical themes. Community and loyalty, for example, honor of parents and human relationships, acceptance and affirmation are biblical attitudes which don't mix easily with individualism.

Individual responsibility is a major strand of biblical teaching, but it is not the only strand, and if not held in tension with balancing characteristics can become demonic. In a society in which a person's all-important security is provided by those who guarantee his life, his family and employer, the offer of freedom and independence may not sound like good news. This may be the Achilles heel of all Western efforts to democratize Islamic peoples. Cultural anthropology might help politicians, too! We must include in our message values which we may have overlooked in our ethnocentric astigmatism if we are to be true to the whole revelation of God's will for us humans and if we are to convince people that we bring truly good news. Thus, church growth anthropology--anthropological insights for more effective evangelism--will assist.

My conviction is that only a spiritually mature indigenous church can make a full integration of biblical truth with the local culture, true to that culture and true to Scripture. The foreigner should always be modest about his insights. Of course, the indigenous church leadership may have been so acculturated to western concepts that they, too, could benefit from the insights of anthropology, but the foreigner's basic stance should be one of learning.

Anthropology is a wonderful bridesmaid to help the Bride ask the Bible questions that have not been asked and find solutions that are at once biblically authentic and culturally attuned. We all engage with peoples different from us - in our communities, ministries and work. Can and will we use informed cross-cultural communication to effectively and biblically engage with those with whom we work and minister? Appropriate engagement is for the sake of the Kingdom and the glory of God!

August 21
Betrayal
Luke 23:34

"And Jesus said, "Father, forgive them, for they know not what they do." (Luke 23:34)

Have you ever been deserted by everyone–all your friends? Alone, lonely. Perhaps something worse– have you ever been betrayed by a friend? How did you respond? Self-pity? Bitterness? That's saying "Yes" to self, affirming your own self. How did Jesus respond? "Follow me," he said, "do it the way I do it." On the cross, in a physical, spiritual agony, what were his thoughts of himself? Most of what he said was in compassion for others. For the soldiers, he sought clemency. For his mother, provision and care. For the thief– he sought paradise, what he least deserved. But when you've been deserted, betrayed, left alone where do your thoughts focus?

Have you ever been misunderstood, accused falsely? Unjustly punished? Unfairly treated? Passed over? Perhaps on the job? How did you respond? Were you offended, offering unending explanations, defensive? Did you fight back or retaliate?

How did Jesus respond to betrayal and false accusation? With quiet dignity. *"Father, forgive them*, they're clueless." He understood ***them.*** Not so preoccupied with their misunderstanding of him. And how they did misunderstand! Greatest blunder of the ages, trying to kill God! Actually they had no sense of guilt. They were just obeying orders. And the Jews–they were defending their God. That's why religious wars are so intractable. Each is on God's side, defending the truth. Or church division, not like the world where the power struggle is overt, acknowledged. We fight for the truth, we're on God's side. We can't back down. It's very hard to hear the quiet voice, *"Take up **your** cross and follow me."*

Have you ever been mocked, ridiculed, put down? Have your rights been violated? Didn't get what you deserved? Perhaps from your wife or your own children? How did you respond? Burn with resentment? Affirm your selfhood? Marshall your troops? Gather your resources to set things right? That's saying "yes" to self.

How did Jesus respond? "This day you will be with me in Paradise"–saving the very one who moments earlier had taunted him. And he stayed on his cross. He said "no" to his own rights.

One of the greatest pains in life is betrayal. To discover a trusted friend scheming to bring you down can unleash all kinds of ungodly responses. But I who had experienced forgiveness was ready to make allowances and forgive--not holding against him what I considered evil and he considered good. But it took years to face the fact that though I wanted to forgive and forget, I didn't want God to! *Father, forgive them...* I found no echo in my soul for the gracious response of Jesus on the cross or Stephen under assault. I might not seek retaliation nor even rejoice in some trouble in the life of my nemesis, but God surely will bring justice. *Don't let him off the hook, God!* I realized that I wasn't so Christlike after all and asked God to cut out the cancer that was eating away at my soul. The healing began when I noticed what the disciples asked for when Jesus told them to forgive the same offense 490 times. They didn't ask for more love; they asked for more faith. I was doubting God's ability to handle the situation properly. When I turned it all over to him, asking him to let my "friend" off the hook, healing began. But I hadn't yet gotten the theology of forgiveness worked out.

Years later when a ministry for which I had great hopes was deliberately snatched from me by nefarious scheming, I was consumed with the inner struggle to forgive. I discovered my "rehabilitation" wasn't complete. So I returned to the Book and made a thorough study of forgiveness in Scripture. Once again I found that theology does indeed rehabilitate. It taught me of grace. God's grace, yes. But also how I also must grace my brother.

Have you ever seen evil and injustice triumph, felt that God had forsaken you in your suffering? How did you respond? Despondent, despairing? How did Jesus respond? He did cry out–"why"? " Why, Father, have you forsaken me?" But then he concluded triumphantly, "Into your hands I commend my spirit" and "It is finished!" Father, I trust you in the darkest moment of the ages with desertion, betrayal, unfairness and misunderstandings. For lovers to be truly one, for the love to reach the deepest levels of affection, the highest flights of ecstasy, the lovers must be compatible. So the Spirit created us God-compatible and seeks to restore that compatibility. But it isn't only the intimacy of a fond embrace, the emotions of it. True love acts. Such a lover lives for the welfare of the other. What greater joy in heaven than when we bring new sons and daughters into the circle of love? But not just our witnessing activity; the most powerful ministry of any kind flows from that love relationship. Furthermore, Christ-likeness and ministry reinforce one another in many ways. For example, an unholy witness is bad news, not good news. The interrelatedness of image/love/ministry is so intertwined you may have needed an additional page to answer that question!

The secret to a happy marriage is each living to fill up the other. Is your marriage to God a happy one or is it one-sided, day and night he filling you and you doing little to fulfill him?

August 22
Five Smooth Stones
1 Samuel 17:40

"Then he took his staff in his hand and chose five smooth stones from the brook and put them in his shepherd's pouch. His sling was in his hand, and he approached the Philistine." (1 Samuel 17:40)

Here you have it-the "five smooth stones" for your David, whether church or other ministry, to slay Goliath and all his brothers! As you move into a new autumn schedule and ministry, upon what will your ministry be based? Here I suggest a firm foundation.
* The BIBLE only and the whole Bible our only final authority for life and ministry
* The CHURCH, central to all God's plans for redeeming a world
* The HOLY SPIRIT, his energizing power indispensable to all life and ministry
* The PLAN OF REDEMPTION, the calling of every disciple full participation
* The LORD Jesus Christ, sovereign in every believer and in his church

THE BIBLE. To get anywhere with God's purposes through his church, the leaders and congregation must take seriously the responsibility to bring every aspect of the ministry under the functional authority of Scripture, every new idea, every old tradition, every activity, every plan. Otherwise it will fail to be what God intends. It won't be easy. Diligent, objective, thorough Bible research combined with determined full compliance and eternal vigilance are the essentials.

THE CONGREGATION. Don't forget that a congregation weak in even one of the purposes of the church is crippled by so much, falls short of full obedience. Remember, too, that for a para-church ministry, concentrating on some specific purpose of the church, to be biblically authentic, must flow into and/or out of the local congregation.

THE HOLY SPIRIT. His energizing power in a congregation is seen primarily in the supernatural ability(s) he gives each member. The church is responsible to make sure every member fully uses his or her gifting - discovering, developing, deploying and, when a purpose of the church is weak, united in desiring earnestly the gift needed to lead the church in fulfilling that purpose. But the Spirit does so much more - guiding, providing. All this activity of the Spirit, however, is released only as we connect with him in prayer. A praying church is a growing, victorious church, fulfilling all the God-designed purposes. A prayerless church or other ministry is limited to what can be achieved by purely human wisdom and power.

THE PLAN OF REDEMPTION, every member's calling. Beyond the varied callings and enablings of the Spirit is the first and paramount calling of ***all--*** to complete what Christ began, to fulfill Christ's last mandate, to participate fully in redeeming a lost humanity. Near-evangelism for all as witnesses and far-evangelism, specialists sent by the church to enable it to reach it's goal. That goal? Every person on earth hearing with understanding the way to life and a congregation of God's people established in every place. Until that task is complete, the primary assignment of the Church remains unfulfilled. And for that every member must accept the Spirit's call.

THE LORDSHIP OF CHRIST. For any of this to happen, of course, Jesus Christ alone must be absolute Lord of his church. First he must be Lord of each member, but for him to actually function as Lord of the congregation or ministry, the leaders must embody the leadership model of God Himself. To the extent he is Lord in their lives and ministry to that extent will the church be united and pure, bringing about the fulfillment of all the purposes God has for the congregation.

Thank you for journeying together in searching for the key to success in ministry. Perhaps for you, too, it will be found in the wedding of theology and ministry in some combination that pleases God.

August 23
The Escalator
Mark 9:35

*"And he sat down and called the twelve. And he said to them, "If anyone would be first, he must be last of all and servant of all." * (Mark 9:35)

During our first term of service in Japan, in establishing a new congregation we sought to implement the principal of Christ's lordship. We trained new believers in leadership, including teaching and preaching as the ability developed. I did not do all the baptizing, marrying, burying, presiding, or preaching. I wanted to follow the New Testament pattern of a plural eldership in the church. But it was totally counter-cultural.

The first Japanese pastor to whom the work was entrusted, took as his first objective getting rid of those threatening non-professional church leaders. He himself had to be present for every meeting of members, even the women's meetings. Each member must be tied to his authority and dependent on him for all vital spiritual services. He closed all the daughter churches, insisting that those in outlying districts fold their lives into the mother church. He could not control those four or five congregations-at-a-distance. No matter that he lost most of those outlying members, he was a strong leader and the church thrived. Depending on the strength of the leader, that is what may well happen anywhere.

I learned my lesson. On the second term we started a church more in line with Japanese patterns of relating. Years later, I learned that the pastor of the first church also learned his lesson and grieved for what he had done to the flock. Surely there is a biblical way of leading that is both culturally appropriate and biblically sound.

In my experience, many leaders do not move up the escalator to usurpation of God's prerogatives, but no leader and no church is immune. Why is that? Perhaps it has to do with the source of our fallenness. Immediately following Peter's classic description of godly leadership (1 Peter 5:1-6) he gives a warning: *"Be self-controlled and alert. Your enemy the devil prowls around like a roaring lion looking for someone to devour. Resist him, standing firm..." (vs. 8)*.

Whether or not Isaiah quoted only the spirit of the king of Babylon when he referred to Lucifer or whether he had in mind the evil power behind that king, he certainly captured the spirit of Satan when he said: *"I will ascend into heaven, I will exalt my throne above the stars of God... I will be like the Most High"* (Isaiah 14.13, 14).

Without doubt, Satan, like all the creatures of God, was created in the moral image of God. But he was not satisfied with that. He aspired to God's divine authority, his incommunicable attributes–his sovereignty, his power, his knowledge, his glory. And thus he became God's adversary.

Prowling like a lion, says the first senior pastor, Peter. I always considered the lion to be very bold and all-powerful, but on reflection he may be something of a coward. He does not often attack the strong, only the weak, the ill, the young, the small. So it is with Satan.

There are signs to recognize in a leader when the enemy is gaining ground in a church, devil-like characteristics that may begin small but gradually lead on to more and more usurpation of God's role as ultimate lord of the church.

* If the pastor is not functionally accountable to anyone but himself in the day-to-day management of the "corporation," have care. The enemy is on the prowl.

* An early indication is for the leader to become less and less approachable. The "little people," do not find a warm welcome, especially when they don't agree with what the leader has said or done.

* Then there is more and more isolation–isolation from criticism, isolation from a close personal relationship

with ordinary members as the "yes men" are gathered round in protective formation.

    * This leads soon to infallibility–the "pope" cannot be controverted. A tell-tale sign is when the pulpit often resounds with phrases such as, "God told me." If God told him, there is nowhere to turn; that settles the matter. Infallible direction, vision and even building plans are all baptized under God's name and beyond challenge.

    * Finally such a leader reaches the pinnacle–immutability, incapable of change. He has taken on the prerogatives of Deity.

    The stages of his ascent to the throne are, then, less and less accountable, then less and less accessible, then less and less pliable and finally less and less fallible.

    In reality, of course, those heights are impossible to attain. When a leader tries to project an image of infallible wisdom, fully adequate strength, and unfailing success, it is actually a false image and no leader should feel embarrassed when the truth of his humanity becomes known. A Christ-dominated leader will be mature enough and transparent enough not to attempt to cover his own ignorance, weakness, and failure.

    This fact of life needs balance, however. It doesn't mean he should go with the contemporary in "honestly" making himself "vulnerable" by flaunting his "humanity," or, as some seem to do, celebrating his sinfulness. If he is truly spiritual, the lordship of Christ in his life will be a constant reminder to the people that it is possible to maintain an attitude of irrevocable and unfailing commitment to Christ as Lord, never failing through consciously rejecting the known will of God. This is true servanthood, bowing to the Lord of life in every aspect of life. Thus there is an appropriate "open heart" of vulnerability and transparency of leaders while consistently modeling the life of spiritual maturity, a balance of grace with truth (2 Corinthians 6:11-13).

    Man-dependency, if not man-worship, tends to develop. One final result of human lordship is the potential division or loss of membership when the pastor leaves or dies–the central authority figure is no longer there, but loyalty to him lingers on. Where are you on the leadership escalator? Are others afraid to address concerns with the leader? To whom do you teach others to submit? Why? Is this man worship or God worship?

August 24
Pursue the Welfare of Your Community
Matthew 5:13, Galatians 6:10

"You are like salt for all mankind. But if salt loses its taste, there is no way to make it salty again. It has become worthless, so it is thrown away and people walk on it." (Matthew 5:13, TEV)
"Let us work for the good of all" (Galatians 6:10 NEB)

The Church by its nature as the body of Christ is the visible embodiment of His presence on planet earth. Therefore the local congregation needs to fulfill the purpose of being salt and light in the world (Matthew 5:13-16). Jesus spelled out his interpretation of "light" *"that men may see your good works and glorify God."* There could be an evangelistic purpose in that. But what is salt? Did he have in mind flavor for an insipid society that insistently stays flat in godless living? Or did he have in mind the preservative influence of believers in a decaying society? At least the concept of influence, of permeating one's environment with good, must be present.

The Church is designed to be God's visible evidence of His design and desire for each person. The world is to see in the Church God's own love and holiness. The people of God and the Spirit of God are in partnership to give the world truth (accurate definitions of sin, love and righteousness) so that people can know of the freedom and life that is so opposite of Satan's kingdom.[52]

In that responsibility, two things come to mind: ministering mercy and seeking justice. The religious leaders of Christ's day were strong on justice, as they interpreted it, but weak on mercy. Jesus emphasizes a major theme in the good news of the Kingdom of heaven. He desires mercy to govern our relationships [53] This difference in their understanding of God's priorities separated most of the religious leaders from Jesus. But God's plan is for his people to pursue both justice and mercy for the welfare of its community. It is true that the record of Jesus' ministry gives more space to reporting his healing ministry than his teaching ministry. His acts of mercy were intended as "signs" validating who he was, But unlike Moses' miracles, they were not merely signs pointing to God's power. They were very focused- healing a broken humanity. Yet his final instructions for what he wanted his disciples to do in *"building his church"* make slight mention of this purpose, and, in fact, the record of Apostolic activity in the New Testament (especially Acts) emphasizes the purpose to win people to faith, disciple them and build his church. To be sure, there was healing ministry, but it wasn't featured as the chief purpose of the church toward the world outside.

Yet the balance between these purposes "evangelistic and healing, helping" is a perennial source of conflict, especially among missiologists. The so-called "incarnational" approach cites Jesus' words in Nazareth (Luke 4:18-19) where he quotes from Isaiah 61:1-2:

The Spirit of the Lord is upon Me,
Because He has anointed Me to preach the gospel to the poor.
He has sent Me to heal the broken hearted,
To preach deliverance to the captives
And recovery of sight to the blind,
To set at liberty those who are oppressed,

---
[52] John 8:34-37; John 10:10; John 16:7-11
[53] Matthew 9:9-13 and Matthew 12:1-8

To preach the acceptable year of the Lord.

This statement of Jesus' calling is taken as the model for church today so that healing and seeking justice in society are on a par with "preaching the gospel." Indeed, since the Prophet specifies the audience, "to the poor," even that hint of evangelistic activity actually tends toward the mercy/justice end of the spectrum. In spite of this, we stand by the Great Commission as the mandate for the church and see the Apostles in agreement with that understanding, acting out what Jesus intended- the evangelization of the world, making disciples, building his church. Nevertheless, it's much easier to go to a consistent extreme than to stay at the center of biblical tension; and most of the evangelical church tends toward neglect of the social dimension of church responsibility.

So, when congregations neglect reaching out in an organized way to the community, dispensing mercy and seeking justice, they seem to have biblical precedent of a sort. It would seem the biblical way is to emphasize evangelism and then, through transformed lives, transform the community. "Redemption and lift," Donald McGavran called the common phenomenon of societal reformation when large numbers become Christian.

But the purpose of promoting community welfare should not be amputated. And throughout history the church has indeed fulfilled this purpose, taking the lead in providing health care and education, for example. In the Western world for centuries the only hospitals and schools were Christian. The same was true in pioneer missionary penetration of non-Western societies. In fact, often the church became so involved in seeking the earthly welfare of the community that the evangelistic mission was eclipsed. Nevertheless, the church, if true to the example of its Master will reach out in mercy to the surrounding community. The Church presents the loving heart of Christ who came to seek and save by being a loving presence in the community. We are called to do this as a church, that is, and not merely through those members who do so privately from personal compassion.

August 25
Failure
Philippians 2:3-8

*"Do nothing from selfish ambition or conceit, but in humility count others more significant than yourselves. Let each of you look not only to his own interests, but also to the interests of others. Have this mind among yourselves, which is yours in Christ Jesus, who, though he was in the form of God, did not count equality with God a thing to be grasped, but emptied himself, by taking the form of a servant, being born in the likeness of men. And being found in human form, he humbled himself by becoming obedient to the point of death, even death on a cross." (*Philippians 2:3-8*)*

The ego is very delicate, so it erects barriers to protect itself from damage, little knowing that if reality were only allowed to crash through, the truth about self could lead to freedom. A proud person is easily humiliated (offended, hurt) but not easily humbled. To prevent that, he mounts a skillful defense.

Rationalization. When I have failed, it is painful to admit it even to myself, so I seek for an explanation that makes the failure appear inevitable, if not actually good: I fell again before the temptation to lust, but with a sex-saturated society engulfing me, I can hardly be expected to do otherwise. I do have a short temper, but then my father did, too, and the repression I suffered under my parents you wouldn't believe! The boss didn't seem pleased with my performance, but that's just the kind of guy he is.

And so we survive the failure with self-image intact, but we thereby forfeit the success that might come from acknowledging the truth and being pressed to trust One who *is* capable of coping. Our use of language is the clearest evidence of rationalization. We "goof" or "make a mistake" or "hurt" or "have an illness"—anything but "sin."

Projection. If the excuse is too weak to provide an adequate defense, we may try to find relief by ascribing to someone else our own unworthy attitudes or thoughts. Somehow it lessens the guilt of selfish behavior if we can discern that motive in the actions of others, especially in good and great people. It is said, with some measure of evidence, that we tend to see in others our own weaknesses. Those who declaim against corrupt politics most loudly have sometimes proved to be the most corrupt. The liar trusts no one, the immoral person convinces himself that "everyone is that way."

Repression. When the two more direct defenses prove inadequate, it helps to forget about it, to refuse to admit the failure. It is quite possible, they tell us, to reject from consciousness painful or disagreeable ideas, memories, feelings, or impulses. They also tell us that this is psychologically damaging. But it is also spiritually damaging, for one can hardly seek forgiveness or strength from another to overcome a weakness he doesn't admit exists. Thus in our depravity, we are not only set up for a fatal fall by a distorted view of reality, we invest enormous energies in keeping ourselves and others deceived. What results?

Pride brings tension with others (Prov. 13:10) and the opposition of God himself (James 4:6). Pride brings many a fall (1 Cor. 10:12) and finally leads to destruction (Prov. 16:18). These are built-in results, for a break with reality always tends to brokenness in every other area. But humility—honest appraisal of one's own inadequacies and God's full adequacy—leads to benefits unending.

Pride may lead to a fall, but humility has the opposite effect, a lifting up the opposite direction one might expect in both cases! Humility brings God's approval and honor indeed his very presence God's salvation and mercy are reserved for the humble. Along with himself and his salvation God bestows many other graces on the humble: peace (Ps. 131:1-2) and rest (Matt. 11:29), guidance (Ps. 27:11), wisdom (Prov. 11:2), and joy (Isa. 29:19).

What is the antidote for pride? In all other virtues, in all righteousness and holiness, God himself is our perfect example. But can God be humble? Does he not refuse to give his glory to another? Is it appropriate to speak of God's humility? Strange as the words may ring, it must be appropriate, for we are clearly told to model our own thinking after Christ's way of thinking when he deliberately humbled himself (Phil. 2:1-8). In Jesus, humility exists with the most exalted claims for the reason that the claims were not exaggerated nor were they the expression of an aspiring ambitious spirit. Pride is an exalted, inflated opinion of self—in other words, a lie. So the truth about oneself, whether good or bad, cannot be sinful pride. Indeed, God himself, as seen in his Son, is the model of true humility. How do we follow his example?

Recognize and Publicly Acknowledge the Truth. As we have seen, the task is to have a true evaluation of self. This includes the reality of my sin and inadequacy as well as the wonder of all God's great grace revealed in this human "showcase" of his own glorious excellencies. But how can a person inclined by nature in the opposite direction resist the lie of pride?

Gratitude and Praise are the Greatest Antidotes to Pride. It is very difficult, while giving God the credit for some great success in my life, to take any credit to myself—if I am genuinely giving him the credit and not mouthing hypocritical spiritual passwords.

Faith comes along with praise and is, in a sense, more the opposite of pride than humility. To trust God is possible only to the one who distrusts himself. Faith, fostered by a continual spirit of thanksgiving and praise, is a great antidote to pride. Central to the teachings of Jesus was the assertion that there is no way to God apart from becoming as a child, trusting him for everything, and self for nothing.

Assume the Servant Role. We are called on to stop seeking great things for ourselves lest we become incapable of believing God because we are preoccupied with courting the praise of men (John 5:44). We must actively humble ourselves (1 Pet. 5:6), even put on the clothes of humility (Col. 3:12, NIV). Assume the role of a servant, and humility will come as a by-product. The apostles, like us, were busily trying to decide who was Somebody, the Very Important Person, jockeying for position, when Christ taught them through startling example what it means to take the servant role. The task that was needed at the beginning of the meal had gone undone, refused by everyone present, no doubt because of inflated evaluations of personal importance. Finally, Jesus took the towel and basin himself, deliberately modeling the servant role for all true disciples (Luke 22:24 ff.; John 13:1-17). How about you? Will you be a servant? Are you grateful and giving the credit to God? Seems hard, pride wants to win out. May we have a true evaluation of ourselves this day.

August 26
Competing Loves
John 13:15

"For I have given you an example, that you also should do just as I have done to you." (John 13:15)

When you meet someone for the first time and want to get acquainted you may ask, "What do you do?" You may wrestle with the *"what"* question for yourself from time to time: "What should I do? Am I in the right role? Should I make a change?"

But more often the question you put to yourself is "How? How can I be successful in my work, my ministry, my Christian life?" But, however, there is a much more important question than what you do and how you do it. And until you find the answer you will not really know a person, not even yourself. And the answer to that question will have a lot more to do with the outcome of your life than what you may do or how you may get it done.

WHY? Why do you do what you do? This question is more important because it is the motive question. More than vocation or location, your know-how, skills, and motivation will determine the outcome of your life. Why work so hard or not work so hard? Why buy what you just bought, why save, give, witness, keep silent, behave, misbehave? Reflect for a moment on the motives of your own life. When you peel back all the surface impulses, what is the driving force? Or what are the driving forces, the root motivations of your soul? To get at the possibilities, let's look briefly at that mysterious, overwhelming word of Christ on the night of His resurrection, for there we find people who are moved by all three of the basic motives that cause people to do what they do, choose what they choose. Three motives.

The disciples were following along at some distance behind Jesus, having a heated discussion. When they arrived in their headquarters town of Capernaum he asked what they had been disputing about (Luke 9:46). They were embarrassed and didn't want to tell him. But he knew they had been disputing which among them would be the greatest. He drew a child to his side and explained that he who is least is the one who is great in his Kingdom. In a church, too. Or mission team. Now we follow with them on their way up to Jerusalem where Christ was to make the supreme sacrifice. He had told them repeatedly he must die, but they rejected the idea of a suffering servant so weren't hearing him. The mother of James and John, with her two sons in tow, asked for top cabinet rank for each of them (Matthew. 20:20; Mark 10:35 ff.).

How did the others respond to that idea? Especially after Jesus had rejected the request? Were they understanding and spiritual about it? After all, the mother and her sons were relatives of Jesus and the disciples understood near eastern culture and family obligations. But no, they were angry! Why? Perhaps each of them wanted the top rank and were offended that these two were muscling in ahead of them?

Jesus took the occasion to explain that if they were to be in his company, they must all be servants. They reached Jerusalem and were gathered for the last meal together. Someone should have volunteered to wash the dusty feet so that the person reclining next would not have to eat in uncomfortable circumstances. It was traditionally the youngest, the lowest in rank who should have volunteered. No one did. The lesson on the child and the servant somehow had never gotten through. The meal began with dirty feet and then they got into the same old dispute. This time it was not over who would rule, but who would serve (Lk. 22.24-27). Finally Jesus himself took the servant's basin and towel and demonstrated the way rank was to work in his Church.

Why were they in this enterprise? For what they would get out of it. Their motive was love for self. Didn't they have any compassion for others? They wanted to call down fire on those who rejected them or were inhospitable. They wanted to bar from preaching those who had been to the wrong seminary. They had no time for women and children, the weak and oppressed. Oh, they loved God and His glory, his Name and Kingdom. Especially, they loved Jesus. But above all they loved themselves and were in it for what they would get out of it. A disciple can give generously, witness faithfully, work up an ulcer serving God, even lay down life on a distant mission field from love of self. In desperation we cry to the Lord for deliverance. Remember what he said? It was the "Why?" question. "Why do you want deliverance?" We might say, "Who wants to fail?" In an instant the true us stands naked before God. We pray, "For Jesus' sake, amen" when all along we should have been honest and closed our prayers with, "For my own sake, amen."

Most of us operate at the level of self-interest most of the time, according to the researchers. The "duty to self-ethic," they call it. But there's a higher motive; the commission Christ gave to us. Who did he set as our model?

"As the Father sent me..." said Jesus. And what was the Father's motive? *"For God so loved the world..."*

August 27
God's Will Revealed in Jesus Christ
Ephesians 2:10

"For we are his workmanship, created in Christ Jesus for good works, which God prepared beforehand, that we should walk in them."(Ephesians 2:10)

The question of what Jesus thought of the law is not easily answered, for he seemed to say both yes and no to it. "Think not that I have come to abolish the law and the prophets," he said, "I have not come to abolish them, but to fulfill them" (Matthew 5:17). On the other hand, "You have heard that it was said, 'An eye for an eye and a tooth for a tooth.' But I say unto you . . ." (v. 38). Indeed, they had heard it said, over and over: in Exodus (21:24), Leviticus (24:20), and in Deuteronomy (19:21)! And this was not a ceremonial or merely a civic law. This was moral.

In what sense, then, did he fulfill the law, and in what sense did he set it aside? *Fulfill* translates a rich word, used of fulfilling predictions, of completing or bringing to maturity or perfection, and of obeying.

1. *Jesus fulfilled the moral law by obeying it.* He obeyed the moral requirements of the law without fail. (Luke 23:41; 2 Corinthians 5:21) Thus he became the basic working model for Christian behavior.

God's will for man has ever been likeness to himself. But what is he like? For centuries God sent prophets to tell us. But in the end, he himself came to show us by living example. "He who has seen me has seen the Father" (John 14:9ff.). How blessed we are in the age of grace—we can see God in Jesus Christ. This does not mean that we can be right with God by imitating his Son. No, salvation is a free gift of his rightness to replace my wrongness. We are justified only by faith in Christ. But we were "created in Christ Jesus for good works" (Ephesians 2:10), and he has clearly demonstrated that life since he came to do the will of the Father (John 4:34; 14:31; 15:10). In his faithful reproduction of the character of the Father, he is our sure and certain example.

2. *Jesus fulfilled the law by fulfilling the prophecies contained in the law.* His birth, life, and ministry had been predicted in great detail, and these prophecies he fulfilled. Among them all, the great central event in history was his death, by which he simultaneously brought the law to completion and abolished it. He brought it to completion by becoming *the* sacrificial lamb to satisfy the demands of the law once for all. He "abolished" it by destroying the power of the law to condemn. By enacting the reality foreshadowed in the symbolism of the ceremonial laws, he brought them to an end (Hebrews 7:26-28; 9:1, 9-10, 23-27).

Jesus Christ fulfilled the entire system of ceremonial laws and thus set them aside. This explanation of the meaning of Christ's death after he accomplished it fits perfectly with the pattern of his life and teaching. He consistently affirmed the authority of the "law," but his teaching was ever centered in the moral law. He never affirmed the ceremonial elements of the law. In fact, he rather did the opposite on occasion. For example, he "declared all foods clean" (Mark 7:19) even before the Cross, thus setting aside all the dietary regulations.

But his death was more than the fulfillment of the law in the sense of paying the penalty demanded by the law. It is also our example of supreme godlikeness. In fact, he put on display the highest form of love—complete sacrifice of self, even for one's enemy (Romans 5:8). Never had the world even imagined such love. And it became the foundation for Christian behavior as well as the source of Christian life.

3. *Jesus fulfilled the law by affirming and explaining it.* He fulfilled the law by "completing it" in the sense of bringing out its perfect, ultimate meaning: Murder is wrong, to be sure, but so is hatred (Matthew 5:21 ff.). Adultery

is sinful, but so is lust (v. 27). He gave the essence, the inner meaning of the law; he radicalized it, raising it to the highest. He gave the positive stimulus of love as well as the negative prohibitions. Throughout his ministry, he consistently affirmed the Old Testament as the authoritative Word of God (e.g., Matthew 5:17-19; 23:23. Jesus, then, catches up all the enduring truth about the character of God and his will for man revealed in the Old Testament and clarifies it, extends it, deepens it.

4. *He fulfilled the law by being the real substance of which the law was only a shadow.* He accomplished what the law promised; he became the sacrifice that did what the law of animal sacrifice could never accomplish. In this he established the validity of the ceremonial law, becoming what it pointed toward, but he also established the validity of the moral law. He demonstrated just how holy God really is, just how terrible sin really is in the sight of God.

The Cross of Christ is indeed the supreme fulfilling of the demands of the law. And by this he simultaneously proved the righteousness of God, who long forgave sin before the sacrifice had been made (Romans 3:21-31). Indeed, Jesus the Messiah came to fulfill the law!

What does this mean for us? He is our example. How to love. What sacrifice is needed. What the moral law requires. He became the basic working model for our Christian behavior. What will you follow today?

August 28
Shrivelling Fruit
Psalm 16:5-8,11

"You, Lord, ... give me all I need; my future is in your hands. How wonderful are your gifts to me; how good they are! I praise the Lord because he guides me; I am always aware of the Lord's presence: he is near, and nothing can shake me...You will show me the path that leads to life, your presence fills me with joy and brings me pleasure forever." (Psalm 16:5-8,11)

Sometimes we face unexpected pain. One might be loneliness; the Bible has two resources for this great hurt. *"If anyone does not provide for his relatives, and especially for his immediate family, he has denied the faith and is worse than an unbeliever."* (I Tim 5.8) This instruction is given in a teaching about widows, aging parents. To neglect caring for one's own parents is a terrible sin and no Christian should ever be guilty of it. The 5th of the 10 commandments is that we must honor our father and mother, and Scripture tells us to love and care for them as part of that honor. Parents care for children during their younger years. Children then have the honor of caring for parents, if need be, in their older years.

But suppose one's children fail or suppose one has no children? Perhaps they are far away, like mine. Be a friend, reach out. Friendship cures the sense of loneliness. Be a friend. But there's an even better resource, one that will never fail: *"You, Lord, ... give me all I need; my future is in your hands. How wonderful are your gifts to me; how good they are! I praise the Lord because he guides me; I am always aware of the Lord's presence: he is near, and nothing can shake me...You will show me the path that leads to life, your presence fills me with joy and brings me pleasure forever."* (Psalm 16:5-8,11)

To have such a companion all the time! He loves me so much he gave his life for me. He has forgiven all my sins and promised me a home in heaven with him. But even now he walks beside me, talks with me. And nothing can separate me from his loving companionship. (Romans 8:31-39).

Another temptation of unexpected pain is bitterness. If a person feels useless or lonely, even misused, she or he may become bitter. Bitter because God hasn't given me health and strength to do what I want to do, bitter because my children neglect me, bitter because someone wronged me long ago, bitter because I fell short of my life ambition. Bitterness makes a person very ugly and hard to live with. So one becomes even more lonely as people tend to leave them alone.

What does Jesus say to this? *"Let not your heart be troubled. You believe in God, believe also in me"* (John 14:1). If we truly trust him we know he will take care of us and one day make all the wrongs right. Read John 14:2-6. Bitterness is a sin that's especially foolish. It harms no one but the person who holds it. And it is a useless sin since it can make nothing right, but only contributes to making everything in life worse. And it is an unnecessary sin because if we trust God, that very trust cures our bitterness.

Do not let bitterness sprout. It will poison everyone in your life and you, yourself, will be the first casualty. Yet some cultivate the noxious weed. Root it out! *"Pursue peace with all...looking diligently ... lest any root of bitterness springing up cause trouble, and by this many become defiled..."* (Hebrews 12:14,15)

Insecurity is a third painful fruit. Will I become ill? Will my financial resources fail? I feel so vulnerable--what will become of me? Margaret who had her entire estate wiped out, her son-in-law was out of work for 2 years, granddaughter killed in accident and soon after her missionary son in Taiwan was almost killed and permanently damaged. What will become of her? And yet I wonder if I don't worry about her more than she does for herself. Such cheerful faith. What a model!

God promises: "*I have cared for you from the time you were born. I am your God and will take care of you until you are old and your hair is grey. I made you and will care for you, I will give you help and rescue you."* (Isaiah 46:3,4)

August 29
Our Toil
Colossians 1:28-29

*"Him we proclaim, warning everyone and teaching everyone with all wisdom, that we may present everyone mature in Christ. For this I toil, struggling with all his energy that he powerfully works within me." (*Colossians 1:28-29)

Wherever I go, there are some people who are getting things accomplished for God. They seem to have boundless energy, incredible output. The hardest working people I've known are missionaries. Of course, we've all met some of the laziest, too. But missionaries as a class work hard. In the Philippines a missionary heard God had blessed our efforts at church starting evangelism in Japan and wanted to know what methods we used.

"Did you do mass evangelism or personal? Did you go door-to-door or do street evangelism?" He never paused for an answer. "Inside the church or outside? Home Bible studies? Newspaper evangelism, radio evangelism? Friendship evangelism?" He paused to take a breath and I said, "Yes!" Then, before he had recovered from that I continued.

"We did more. We did *chingdonya.*" He wanted to know what that new method was so I explained about the ancient Japanese custom of advertising the opening of a new business or a sale. A group of men dressed in outrageous costume would snake through the community with trumpets, drums, and paper lanterns, producing a distinctive sound that would draw a crowd to follow them to the desired destination. Muriel's chalk art is drawing people to our nightly tent meeting, I thought, but maybe we could do more. So I borrowed a drum, bought a trumpet at the pawn shop, lit a couple of lanterns and paraded a bunch of blond little *chingdonya* through the streets of Tsuchiura, drawing a crowd to the desired destination.

I didn't tell my Philippine missionary friend that we only did that the first term. The second term we cut back to those methods that had worked well. But I wanted to make a point: Church planting takes unremitting hard work.

I tried to make the same point at a missionary conference in Japan where missionaries from various missions gathered each summer. We were back to that favorite theme, how to make the church grow in very difficult soil. Experts from the US joined veterans from our own field on the distinguished panel. It was the end of our first term and, as was my custom in those youthful days, I sat in the back and held my peace. Finally someone stood and said, "Why don't we ask McQuilkin how he does it?" A clamor began until I reluctantly conceded.

"Well," I began, groping for some useful idea, "I figure that in Japan if you want to have one person continue on in the faith you have to baptize 5. To baptize 5, you must have 20 professions of faith, to have 20 professions of faith you need 100 serious seekers; to have 100 seekers you need solid contact with 1,000 people, and to have contact with a thousand, 5,000 need to know you're there." Then I sat down.

Fifteen years passed and I had returned to Japan for the annual conference as the devotional speaker. Then the church growth experts from the US were introduced and we got back to our favorite subject. In the interaction time following the presentations a man stood and said, "Some years ago there was a scientific survey made in Japan and it was determined that to have 1 person continue on in the faith it was necessary to baptize 5, to baptize 5, 20 must make profession of faith . . ." I was astonished at the accuracy of his memory, but even more astonished that my off-the-cuff response had become a "scientific survey." All I was trying to say, fifteen years earlier, was that it takes hard work, unremitting hard work.

Paul tells us in Colossians 1:28-29; *"Him we proclaim, warning everyone and teaching everyone with all wisdom, that we may present everyone mature in Christ. For this I toil, struggling with all his energy that he powerfully works within me."*

And so it is. If your labor is half-hearted or low energy it may be in vain. But if it's hard work it will not be in vain. So how is it with you?

August 30
Conflicting Principles
1 Corinthians 10:13

"No temptation has overtaken you that is not common to man. God is faithful, and he will not let you be tempted beyond your ability, but with the temptation he will also provide the way of escape, that you may be able to endure it." (1 Corinthians 10:13)

Practically speaking, how does a Christian, committed to the absolute nature of the whole law of God, face a situation in which laws seem to conflict? Ethics asks the question "What *should* I do?" We ask this multiple times a day. When Christ tells us to preach the gospel and the government tells us to be quiet, what do we do? When authorities close a nursing home to families during Covid, do I go anyway? When the same God who commands, "Thou shalt not kill" also commands to destroy a whole people, what does the soldier do?

Christ himself gives a classic example of "biblical situationism" when he tells us that David did *well*—not a bad but forgivable act—in violating the law by eating the showbread in an emergency (Matt. 12:3 ff.). When the priests profane the Sabbath, he does not say they are forgiven, but rather that they are *blameless*. If the Pharisees only understood these things, they would not have condemned the *guiltless* disciples who did on the Sabbath a *lawful* thing that otherwise would have been unlawful.

How does one decide when to keep the law and when to violate it?

Define the law carefully. The first step in solving this dilemma is to define the particular activity precisely. Is it truly a sin on *biblical* terms? For example, many people feel that all deception is a form of sinful lying; all killing is a form of sinful murder; all civil disobedience is a form of sinful lawlessness; all work on Sunday violates the Sabbath law. However, these definitions are not only naive, but they are also not biblical. When a soldier kills, he is not necessarily committing murder. When the government taxes, taking some of my possessions by force, it is not stealing. It is important to insist that the Bible itself define what kind of deception, if any, is legitimate; what kind of killing is legitimate; what kind of taking by force is legitimate; what kind of civil disobedience is legitimate. We are not free to decide; the Bible itself, giving the command, must be allowed to define the limits of that command.

The faith way of escape. Normally there is a third alternative when we face a moral dilemma. Scripture promises that God will provide a way of escape (1 Cor. 10:13). Often, this is the way of faith.

Situation ethics not only misunderstands love, in which it specializes, and law, which it opposes. Situation ethics misunderstands human nature. The New Morality places a burden on people that is too heavy to bear.

If humans were not finite and sinful, perhaps they could make the judgment in each situation, but human beings are finite and very sinful. A person can't make the right decisions because he doesn't have enough information, and he wouldn't make the right decisions even if he had the information because his motivation is never pure. That is why God never laid the heavy, frustrating, and impossible burden on him that the new moralist would.

Here is a load too heavy for finite man to bear adequately. The situation rarely allows enough time to figure things out in order to make the proper decision. A person is asked an embarrassing question in the presence of others. In the split second before he answers he must evaluate seven or more questions about that situation, including the question as to the immediate and long-range results of telling the truth, telling a lie, or finding some other way out. Even if a computer were nearby, only a fraction of the necessary data is available to program the computer, and even if it were available, will his questioner wait?

Where is the wisdom of this? Where is the time for this? The Bible takes man's finitude seriously and gives more than complicated advice concerning a multitude of conflicting principles; it gives commands.

People are not only finite, they are very complicated. Not only does finite man find it almost impossible to judge exactly what constitutes his neighbor's highest good, he will find even greater difficulty in deciding which neighbor's good! The loving "surrogate husband" may decide to provide for the sexual needs of an unmarried and lonely fellow church member, but what effect may that have on other "neighbors"—his wife, his children, the church, God himself?

Life is complex. How can one judge the outcome of a single act toward a single person, let alone what a series of acts involving many people might become in the future? Abraham taking Hagar could hardly imagine the impact four thousand years later as the Arab sons of Ishmael fiercely pursue their destiny.

Situationists not only underestimate the significance of human limitations; they seem to deliberately downplay an even greater handicap people must overcome to succeed at situational ethics: sin. Even if a person could consistently figure out what was the ultimate good of each person in his life, would he choose to act in accordance with that knowledge if the cost to himself were very great? Neither experience, history, nor revelation leave us much hope that he will consistently make this choice. Man is sinful and consistently chooses to sacrifice his neighbor's welfare for his own. Thus, the ideal of the situationist—to act always for the highest good of all involved in a given situation—is possible only for God. Humans are too finite to know even the fringes of such a vast and complicated situation, and they are too fallen to choose consistently what they do know to be best.

But the most important and basic truth about ethics in Scripture is that it is theistic or God-based, not personalistic or man-based. By his own nature God defines what is good and loving. He went to a great deal of effort to reveal this. To build an ethic on love divorced from the unchanging character of God and the clear and absolute requirements revealed by that God is to distort the concept of love and law from the outset. This godlessness is the ultimate flaw in situation ethics. How does God define your actions and choices?

August 31
The Value of Life
Psalm 139:13-14

"For you formed my inward parts; you knitted me together in my mother's womb. I praise you for I am fearfully and wonderfully made." (Psalm 139:13-14)

Suicide and euthanasia, like abortion and infanticide, have generated intense controversy because of changing attitudes in Western civilization. As with abortion and infanticide, Scripture does not address the issues directly. Until recently, the major church bodies have always condemned all four activities as violations of the sixth commandment, "Thou shalt not kill."

Not all societies have condemned suicide and euthanasia. In Japan, for example, suicide to expiate one's lost or threatened honor is heroic. Even as an escape from intolerable circumstances, suicide is quite acceptable. Japanese Christians have told me of the ecstatic feeling of freedom they experienced in their pre-Christian days as they journeyed to some special scenic spot, hallowed as the trysting place with death by countless suicides, and of their disappointment when their plan for suicide was thwarted.

Now, increasing numbers in the West espouse similar views. Societies that endorse suicide produce detailed handbooks on how it may best be committed. Scholars in heavy tomes and pragmatic lobbyists in state legislatures promote new ways for family and others to find a "good death" for the sufferer.

Why the new, more lenient attitudes? Do they well up from long-suppressed reservoirs of compassion, or do they come from an overall depreciation of the value of life? If a person is no more than a time-bound animal with no responsibility to Deity and no hope beyond the grave, why should human life be viewed as "sacred"?

The Christian view of physical life is both higher and lower than the view of the secularist. It is higher because man is created in the image of God, indwelt by God, belongs to God, and will exist forever; the secularist views man as an animal facing extinction. On the other hand, to the Christian, physical life is temporary and not the ultimate value; it is the supreme value of the nonbeliever since it is all he has.

Thus, in the paradox, to the believer life and death are simultaneously more significant and less significant than to the unbeliever. The true believer does not cling to life because he cannot lose it and because it does not belong to him anyway. In fact, by losing it, as Christ taught us, by treating it as expendable, we find it in its full, true meaning. On the other hand, because life is a gift of God, reflects his own likeness in some mysterious way, and belongs ultimately to him, we hold it in sacred trust as one of the highest values. One's own life is not higher in value than truth, honor, justice, and love, for example. But certainly the life of another is a far higher value than one's own higher comfort, ease, material prosperity, or a host of other self-oriented rights and privileges. Indeed, Scripture treats human life as so sacred that a society's view of the value of human life is a sure test of its moral integrity and social durability.[54]

So how is it with you? Struggling with your health? Ready for a better home? Perhaps shame from the past marks your insides in damaging ways. Perhaps you or someone you love had an abortion. What pain is faced in any of these! Life is a gift of God, perhaps the following principles will help as you consider this difficulty issue of the value of life:

- God's love for people extends to their bodies, which he made. An aspect of God's desire for all to be saved (2 Pet. 3:9) is God's desire that all be well physically.
- God's purpose in Christ is to end all sickness and suffering. He will do this through the bodily resurrection of believers and the restoration of creation.
- Sickness and suffering are a result of the Fall, the effects of which will be felt by all until Christ's return. It is both a judgment upon sin (1 Cor. 11:30) and a prod to deal with eternal matters before death.
- We are all dying. Divine intervention alone can rescue human beings from death's consequences, not human ingenuity.
- As Christ ministered to those who suffered because of sickness through understanding and direct intervention, so should the followers of Christ. (Matt. 25:31-46).
- It is always right to care for the sick and suffering with empathy and grace. Sickness and suffering will not always be overcome.
- Though some are specifically gifted and called into a vocational medical ministry, all believers are responsible before God to care for sick (physically and mentally) believers and unbelievers alike.

Advances in medical science (as in all other branches of science), far from being unwarranted meddling in the affairs of God, can actually be to the glory of God. God calls us who bear his image to participate with him in creativity. Christians should always pray for the sick, but never merely pray for the sick, provide care and support. These are essential. As you consider these issues, where can you step in and relieve suffering? Perhaps the chronically ill? Or those in chronic pain? The unplanned pregnancy? The hopeless individual? Perhaps you are that person facing daily pain or a crisis for which there seems no answer. There is care and support. Somewhere. Can you find it?

---

[54] IBE (2014), 394-395, 383-384.

September 1
Self-love
1 Corinthians 10:24

"Let no one seek his own good, but the good of his neighbor." (1 Corinthians 10:24)

Paul identified love as a fruit of the Spirit (Galatians 5:22), and in the sublime love chapter, 1 Corinthians 13, he extolled love as the greatest quality a believer can possess, far superior to knowledge and gifts. The love described here and in other New Testament passages is *agape* love, a self-giving, Christlike love that we are humanly incapable of. Only through the constant filling of the Holy Spirit can we love others the way Christ intended.

Read Matthew 20:20-28 then consider the results of putting self-love first.
- We seek privilege.
- We want to exalt ourselves over others.
- We seek power.
- We fall short of Christ's example.

These are results of self-love. When we put ourselves first, the last thing we want to do is serve others. Christlike love, on the other hand, is selfless, putting the needs of others first. The potential fruit of this root sin—putting ourselves first—is virtually limitless, manifesting itself in selfish behavior and conflict that look very much like the world instead of followers of Christ. When these behaviors appear in the church, they can damage Jesus' reputation in the world. That's exactly what was happening in the Corinthian church when Paul wrote to address the issues of sexual immorality, conflict, and selfishness within the body. Paul reminded the spiritually immature congregation, *"No one should seek his own good, but the good of the other person"* (1 Corinthians 10:24).

The book of James reminds us that love is something we do, not just a quality we possess by virtue of being in Christ. James wrote, *"Be doers of the word and not hearers only"* (1:22), and he even defined religion this way: *"to look after orphans and widows in their distress and to keep oneself unstained by the world"* (1:27). Many of us do a better job of keeping ourselves unstained by the world than becoming involved in meeting the needs of the world. Jesus taught that when the curtain is drawn aside at the final judgment, the most severe judgment will be meted out to those who failed to feed the hungry, clothe the naked, and care for the oppressed (see Matt. 25:31-46). To ignore human problems that we could help is moral negligence. Christians are called on to be sensitive, compassionate, generous people who willingly and lovingly meet the physical, emotional, and spiritual needs of others.

How does self-love manifest itself in your life? Consider the following ways: a judgmental attitude, preoccupation with my own agenda, thereby giving inadequate attention to people in my life; impatience with unwanted delays or with irresponsible behavior, stinginess in giving to God's work, prejudice against those who disagree with me or are different from me, perhaps a reluctance to spend time in ministry. What can you choose to address now?

September 2
Believability
Matthew 5:16

"In the same way, let your light shine before others, so that they may see your good works and give glory to your Father who is in heaven." (Matthew 5:16)

"To say words that do not conform to reality" is not a useful definition for the verb "to lie," for although we constantly say things that do not conform to reality, we don't necessarily lie. We may err. Does lying mean deliberately saying words that don't conform to reality? This is also inadequate, for it's quite possible to deceive someone without using false words. So we must broaden the definition to include the conscious purpose to deceive. To lie, then, is deliberately attempting to deceive, using words or other means.

There is no more sure method to destroy our own character than to deceive. Any other sin can be recognized and dealt with, but deception leads away from reality, so that ultimately, truth is not even recognized. As a result, repentance and restoration are very difficult to pursue. As an old Chinese pastor said, "I can save anyone but a liar." Falsehood is a basic fault line in the foundation of the soul, putting the whole superstructure in jeopardy. All the believability a person has—his very integrity—totters on the shifting sand of a single lie. Deceit holds hostage all virtues.

Deceit not only erodes the character but also fails to solve problems. Instead, it complicates them. Deceit fouls all relationships. Once a person has deceived another and is known to have done so, it is difficult ever to restore full confidence. He may try to counterbalance his lies with a greater number of truths, but it doesn't work that way. No amount of truth can quickly erase the indelible imprint of a lie, for the person who has been deceived may rightly wonder, *When will it happen again?* Deceit is the ultimate destroyer of good relationships, because good human relationships are built on mutual confidence and trust.

Here are some other ways we can lie; e*xaggeration and hypocrisy*. If you are tempted to exaggerate, identify occasions or situations when you do so. *Exaggeration* might include: giving a lesser or greater assessment of time or distance than is true to get my way, excuse myself, or make a point; embellish a report to protect my image, boost my ego, or justify my actions, or add to the story elements I have imagined or created to make it more fun or acceptable.

Hypocrisy is pretending to be something we are not. Christ condemned the Pharisees for hypocrisy more than anything else, comparing them to "*whitewashed tombs, which appear beautiful on the outside, but inside are full of dead men's bones and every impurity. In the same way, on the outside you seem righteous to people, but inside you are full of hypocrisy and lawlessness*" (Matt. 23:27-28). In fact, His name for them, play actors (the meaning of *hupocrites* in Greek), changed the meaning of *Pharisee* forever. People called them "the holy ones," but Jesus exposed them as phonies. By trying to project an admirable but false image, they were not only lying but also misrepresenting what it means to live a holy life.

Jesus taught, "Be careful not to practice your righteousness in front of people, to be seen by them" (Matt. 6:1). However, he also instructed us, "*Let your light shine before men, so that they may see your good works and give glory to your Father in heaven*" (Matt. 5:16).

What do you think is the difference between letting your light shine and practicing righteousness in front of others? It would seem that motive is the demarcation between play acting, thus dishonoring God with a lie, and letting your light shine. Are you doing it to be seen by others or to give glory to God? Never fake it. Always be honest, especially where your relationship with God and your witness to others are concerned.

It isn't always easy to find the biblical balance of honesty about our failings while making sure our light shines brightly to spotlight God's excellencies and inspire hope in those who follow.

September 3
Trusting God
Exodus 33:11

"Thus the LORD used to speak to Moses face to face, as a man speaks to his friend. When Moses turned again into the camp, his assistant Joshua the son of Nun, a young man, would not depart from the tent." (Exodus 33:11)

Sometimes we have a hard time believing that God will do what he says he will do. Can he get me out of the mess I've worked myself into, putting things together so this will really work out for any kind of good—mine or God's? "All things work together for good?" Really now, all? Or giving us the victory over a weakness—I'm reluctant to call it what He probably does, "sin," something that has plagued me for years. "Thanks be to God who always causes us to triumph in Christ?" Really now, always? Perhaps there's some persistent temptation like a loose tongue or volatile temper or irresistible lust. Can God really give victory? Or perhaps you struggle with other promises like "my God will supply all your needs" or "I will be with you always" or "my peace I give to you." Maybe the promised fruit of the Spirit just doesn't ripen: love for that particularly unlovable person in your life, or joy when things are truly miserable. You wish you could see the touch of Holy Spirit power on your witness or ministry—the way he promised. Sometimes it's hard to believe the promises.

If it's sometimes hard to believe absolute promises, what about trusting him to do something he has not promised? Like healing my arthritis? Showing me plainly which option I should take in a decision I must make? Protecting my son as he risks his life? Those are all unpleasant or scary parts of life right now. Oh, he has promised to heal in answer to prayer, to guide, to protect. But heal this illness, now? Guide me infallibly in this particular choice? Protect all believers from all harm? There are no guarantees. Sometimes it's hard to trust him with the outcome when he doesn't let us in on what he has in mind.

If it's sometimes hard to rely on God when he hasn't revealed His will, what if he has revealed His will and you trust him not to do it? Now, that would be some kind of faith! And that's exactly the kind of faith Moses had. Not just on one heroic occasion, either; it seemed to be part of Moses' friendship with God.

God was furious. "Out of my way, Moses," he said, "I'm going to wipe out the Israelites and start over with your descendants." In a few short weeks they had forgotten God's mighty deliverance from Egypt and gone to worshiping a gold-plated bull. What did Moses say? What would you say? Moses begged God to change His mind! he prayed against the clearly stated purpose of God (Ex. 32:11-14). What faith! How we would love to have that kind of faith! How did Moses get it? Was he born with it? Did it come of his early environment? Hardly. His early environment was in a foster home, the palace of a pagan Pharaoh! And his first attempt to serve God and his people was disastrous.

In fact, he failed so badly he apparently developed a stutter and he certainly went on the lam for 40 years. That was how much courage and faith he had. Sounds like we feel, sometimes. How, then, did Moses develop such mighty faith, such a tight relationship with God? If we found out, it might give us a clue on how we can grow in faith. The story is found in Exodus, chapters 32 and 33. Pause now and scan those two exciting chapters, looking for clues to Moses' incredible faith.

First of all, Moses spent time with God. To trust a person, we have to know them, and to know them, we need to spend time with them. It's risky to trust a stranger too much. Moses spent time with God, lots of time. So much time, in fact, that when he left one encounter with God, people could see God's own glory lingering about him (Ex. 34:28 ff). Notice several things about Moses' prayer life.

His times alone with God were part of his daily life. He set up a special place to meet with God, called the "tent of meeting" (33:7). There God talked with him, "face to face." Exodus 33:11: *"Thus the LORD used to speak to Moses face to face, as a man speaks to his friend."* That's the kind of close friendship Moses had with God. Intimate. God knew him by name, not account number. God accepted him, favored him, and companioned with him, we're told. A survey in the 80's showed that American evangelical pastors, on average, spend 7 minutes a day in prayer. Is this enough time with God to get to be friends, to grow in faith? If you want your faith to grow like Moses' did, are you prepared to spend regular, daily, extended time alone with God?

September 4
Looking Towards Home
2 Corinthians 4:16-5:5

"So we do not lose heart. Though our outer self is wasting away, our inner self is being renewed day by day. For this light momentary affliction is preparing for us an eternal weight of glory beyond all comparison, as we look not to the things that are seen but to the things that are unseen. For the things that are seen are transient, but the things that are unseen are eternal." (2 Corinthians 4:16-18)

The promises of God are the medicine to cure the critical ailments of the aging. But...What is the reason for all our suffering?

Mrs. Reagon asked me that. She was crippled with arthritis, 80 years old, in constant pain. I was taking her downtown to do some business. I replied, "I'm not sure, but I have a theory." "What is it?" she demanded. "I'll tell you sometime." "No, I want to know right now!" So I told her my theory. The strength and beauty of youth is physical and the strength and beauty of age is of the spirit. Those who work so hard at trying to stay young and beautiful often neglect the beauty of spirit. The tragedy is that in the end they lose both! They grow weak and aged and are weak and ugly of spirit. Besides, I told her, if we stayed young and strong we wouldn't want to go to heaven. God has planned it so that we lose our physical strength and beauty so we will concentrate on the real, eternal inner person and get ready for our eternal home. I told Mrs. Reagon and she was silent.

Several weeks later she was rushed to the hospital. I visited and had no sooner entered the room than she called out, "It's the truth! Your theory is true! I really want to go to heaven!"

I didn't make up the theory, of course. It's in the Bible. 2 Corinthians 4:16-5:5: *So we do not lose heart. Though our outer self is wasting away, our inner self is being renewed day by day. For this light momentary affliction is preparing for us an eternal weight of glory beyond all comparison, as we look not to the things that are seen but to the things that are unseen. For the things that are seen are transient, but the things that are unseen are eternal.*

Some people don't like to think about the end of the journey, but that's a great mistake. God tells us we'll gain great wisdom by thinking about the end of life: *"Every living man is no more than a puff of wind, no more than a shadow...I am only your guest for a little while."* (Ps. 39:5,12) *"Teach us how short our life is, so that we may become wise."* (Ps 90.12)

The wise person knows that no matter how long he lives, it is short. Just a puff of smoke, a fleeting shadow. And knowing this he uses his short time on earth to prepare for eternity. That is true wisdom.

The grace of growing old, resources for the journey? For the feelings of uselessness, loneliness, bitterness, fear? The promises of God! Trust him! He's strong enough, smart enough and loves you enough to die for you. You can trust him!

September 5
The Worker and the Boss
Deuteronomy 24:14

"You shall not oppress a hired worker who is poor and needy, whether he is one of your brothers or one of the sojourners who are in your land within your towns." (Deuteronomy 24:14)

What are the responsibilities of management? The manager must not threaten. He has power over the welfare and livelihood of his employee; he must not use it to coerce. When an employer demands something unethical or illegal from an employee, such as offering a bribe to a prospective customer or demanding sexual favors, the sins of cheating and immorality are compounded by the use of economic coercion.

Furthermore, all working arrangements, including pay, must be just. Unsafe working conditions in a coal mine or chemical plant are certainly unjust, but so are subminimum wages for immigrant grape pickers.

Finally, this justice includes equal or fair treatment. Justice does not permit an employer to give one person greater or less benefit for unfair reasons—discrimination for family (nepotism), friendship, race, or sex. Is it fair for the pay of executives to rise from twenty-nine times the average worker's pay to forty times his pay within a span of six years? During this time when the U.S. automobile industry was threatened by imports, workers accepted reduction in pay to keep their product competitive in the marketplace, while executive income skyrocketed. Paul says management must be fair.

In addition to Paul's teaching, Old Testament teaching concerning the owner's responsibilities throws light on the *responsibilities of management.* God is totally against slavery and always has been. He did make laws governing the system, not by way of approval, but to protect the slave. The master was not to harm the slave (Ex. 21:20 ff.). There was to be a time limit for holding a fellow Israelite in slavery (Ex. 21:2-6), so that "slavery" was actually indentured servanthood for a limited time (Lev. 25:39 ff.). When the slave was released, he was to be given assets so that he could start his new life of freedom (Deut. 15:12 ff.). Not all these laws are applicable, of course, but principles embedded in the regulations should prove instructive.

Most of the admonitions were for the master, and this is certainly appropriate for any relationship in which one party is strong, the other weak. Management must not defraud, oppress, or harm, and must pay fair wages on time.[55] The established rest day must be given. Management[56] must not despise the cause of the employee (Job 31:13) but should reward and pay him well.[57] In fact, the master was to treat his servant as a son (Prov. 29:21) or brother (Philem. 16).

Responsibilities of labor. The employee, for his part, is not to deceive or be violent,[58] is to honor his employer,[59] be faithful, and be patient and follow orders,[60] even when the employer doesn't deserve it (1 Pet. 2:18-20). He is to work hard and not be lazy (1 Thess. 4:11 ff.; 2 Thess. 3:7).

Let me speak plainly about the implications of this teaching. The employer who pays less than a fair wage (in terms of what others are paid or compared to company profits) is stealing from the worker. The worker who carelessly arrives late, wastes time with small talk, inattentive work, long breaks, or daydreaming is a thief. And both sin against God, their true employer.[61]

Suppose labor does not live up to its responsibilities? Management has almost limitless economic power to enforce compliance. But suppose management does not live up to its responsibilities? Labor has only two possible recourses: protection by a higher authority or collective bargaining.

God is the ultimate higher authority, and one day he will settle all accounts. But in the meantime government is the only higher power, and government is often less powerful than management. Many multinational corporations are far more powerful than some of the nations in which they operate. Some can close down the economic life of a nation. In powerful states, the government can control private corporations but often chooses not to because of blatant or sophisticated corruption. Yet in enlightened and powerful governments, the rights of the laborer are normally protected in minimum ways and broad categories. Safety standards, minimum wages, and nondiscrimination have been legislated.

But for the specifics of how justice is worked out on the shop floor and in the office, or in the case of reluctant government initiative, management cannot always be counted on consistently to pursue fairness and justice in humility, from the heart. I conclude that Scripture demands justice and fairness from management, and the law of love would nudge a manager/owner toward providing all the benefits possible while making the business succeed for the sake of both the employees and owners. Profits for stockholders or management must be in line with benefits for employees. Labor, in like manner, may demand justice and fairness but should not coerce other benefits, especially when they might jeopardize the company's welfare.

---

[55] Lev. 19:13; 25:43; Deut. 24:14 ff.; Prov. 22:16; Mal. 3:5; Matt. 10:10; Luke 10:7; Rom. 4:4; 1 Tim. 5:18; James 5:4
[56] Exod. 20:9-11; 23:12; 34:21; Deut. 5:14; 15:18
[57] Prov. 17:2; 27:18; Jer. 22:13; Matt. 24:45, 47; Luke 12:35 ff.
[58] Zeph. 1:9; Luke 16:10-11
[59] Mal. 1:6; 1 Tim. 6:1
[60] Eph. 6:5; Col. 3:22; Titus 2:9; 1 Pet. 2:18
[61] IBE (2014) p 449-451.

September 6
One More!
1 Corinthians 15:58

"So we do not lose heart. Though our outer self is wasting away, our inner self is being renewed day by day. For this light momentary affliction is preparing for us an eternal weight of glory beyond all comparison, as we look not to the things that are seen but to the things that are unseen. For the things that are seen are transient, but the things that are unseen are eternal." (1 Corinthians 15:58)

Most often we work extra hard to please a particular person: me! I may not be the only one. A person can be driven by a desire to succeed, a fear of failure, a hope of recognition, a sense of accomplishment.

But if my hard work is for the Lord, it will never be in vain. No matter what the visible outcome; no matter what the earthly recognition or rewards, such work will never be in vain. He guarantees it! Maybe it will seem in vain to others, in the home church, in the family. Certainly it will seem in vain to the world, but not "in the Lord"!

Does this mean that results are unimportant? Of course not. Results are very important—that's the end toward which we labor. It's the motive for seeking success in our endeavors that can empty them of lasting value. But if we work hard to produce results that God desires, that glorify him, that fulfill his purposes, such work will be ever full of lasting significance. We want to prepare a royal inheritance for the King.

When do we look for the payoff for our hard work? Both to the Corinthians and to the Colossians Paul points to the final awards ceremony. "From the Lord you will receive the reward," He assures the slaves of Colossae. And after exulting for the entire 15th chapter of his letter to the Corinthians in God's final victory at the resurrection, he concludes: *"Therefore"*— in the light of God's great final victory—*"Therefore, my beloved brothers, be steadfast, immovable, always abounding in the work of the Lord, knowing that in the Lord your labor is not in vain." (1 Cor. 15:58)*

One evening I was at a millennial-end party when the question was raised: "In heaven will there be difference in rank? Will we all be the same in our relationship with the Lord, the same level of godliness?" The general consensus of those who spoke was quite democratic—we will all be the same.

Yet how about Jesus' story of one man receiving 10 cities, another 5 (Luke 19:12-27)? How about Paul's repeated affirmation that each will receive according to works he has done? (e.g. 1 Corinthians:12 ff; 2 Corinthians 5:10)

You no doubt chose others—there are plenty! But on what will those rewards be based?

Last summer at Morrison Academy in Taiwan I was ministering to the annual gathering of missionaries but keeping up on my daily exercise. I'd started the running routine some years earlier. When I resigned my ministry to care for Muriel I thought, *Now I won't have to bother with those annual physical exams the Board forced me to take.* But on second thought, *Hey, McQuilkin, Muriel needs you to stay alive!* That's when I began to exercise seriously!

But it was so hot and muggy that early morning in Taiwan, why wasn't I in bed asleep like those hundreds of my fellow missionaries? I ran three hot, sweaty laps around the soccer field at the Academy and then began to think, *McQuilkin, why are you punishing yourself like this? Why not just peel off at the end of the lap and head for the shower and air-conditioned room?* I decided so to do, when the thought came to me, *Who are you doing this for anyway?* With a surge of determination, I thrust my fist in the air and cried out, *One more for Muriel!*

Weary Christian, I invite you to look heavenward and shout, "One more lap for Jesus!" Your labor will not be in vain! Maybe today you've reached your limit. You've run so hard, but it all seems in vain. Every fiber of your being—body and soul—cries out, *Enough!* Maybe it's time to reflect on whose you are and why you're here at all and then look up and shout, *One more lap for Jesus!*

September 7
Cardiogram
John 3:16

"For God so loved the world that He gave His only begotten Son, that whoever believes in Him should not perish but have everlasting life." (John 3:16)

For some, a cardiogram might be a non-threatening experience but to others it might be a stress test. For those wanting to examine their own insides, let's begin with a chart measuring health, the attached chart of a normal, healthy life.

Our heart examination must be made against this standard or model set by God. How is your heart? Healthy? This is especially important for the leaders because they are the heart of the organism we call the church. If the heart is not healthy, the rest of the body will have problems. Jack Layman would tell us that the "fish rots first at the head!"

MODEL: God
HEART CONDITION: so loved
HEARTBEAT: the world
EVIDENCE: that He gave
STRENGTH: His only son
CAPACITY: whoever believes
OUTPUT: eternal life

How can we evaluate the heart condition? Look at the chart! The evidence is not in the feeling, but in the activities of life. Out of the fulness of the heart, the mouth speaks. By our fruit we are known, by the outcomes, the behavior.

Let the Bible examine your heart in a few action-patterns and let the Holy Spirit trace the profile of your heart condition. Let's begin at the bottom of the chart, the output. What does the standard, the model look like? God's purpose is that people should not perish but have everlasting life. That is God's heart. Is it yours?

The object of God's heart, His HEARTBEAT: He loved the WORLD. Even that half of the world with no one to tell of the good news.

The Lord appointed 70, not just the 12 leaders, and sent them on ahead of him...and he said to them, *"The harvest is great, but the laborers are few; pray therefore the Lord of the harvest to send out laborers into His harvest. Go your way..."*

There were two churches in the same state; one was 40 years old, one was 150 years old. Both gave 50% of budget to missions, both have reputation of being <u>the</u> missions center for their region. The younger church supports 180 missionaries, the older church 61, but the younger church is three times as large. There is a basic difference, however. The 180 supported by the younger church are all sons and daughters of the church. In the church with 150 years of history only one has ever gone to the field; and when I was there she was present. Retired. They did not like to be asked about that, though they had paid me to come and give an examination of church vitality. The pastor especially did not like it. What is your heart condition? Are you participating in sending out laborers, reproducers, pioneers? What proportion of membership would be appropriate for people who love the WORLD? Perhaps a tithe?

10% of the church body? Not just short term for two weeks, but for years—learn their language, their culture, their worldview and love those who do not know of God's love.

Let's go back to the chart, the standard. The evidence of God's heart condition was that he gave and the strength of that giving, the depth of that love was that he gave His only son. Have you thought about the depth of His love?

Sixteen years after I caught this glimmer of truth, God let me experience it in a small way: I have three sons, but what a crushing blow to lose even one of them. And a loss I never chose. What would I deliberately choose to give for another person? Especially for a worthless enemy? And think of it, my son immediately translated into celestial bliss. God's son went to hell. And not one person's hell, but hell for all of us! God so loved that he gave...

Such is the evidence of God's heart, the strength of God's love. Love is measured by the sacrifice it makes. What love for you, what love for me!

September 8
Purposes of the Church
Matthew 16:18

"Jesus said to Peter "And I tell you, you are Peter, and on this rock I will build my church, and the gates of hell shall not prevail against it." (Matthew 16:18)

Notice that Jesus didn't say, *"I will build you and the gates of hell will not prevail against you."* Actually, without church, the gates of hell will prevail! Not only will the Pentagon of hell steadily launch successful attacks to bring us down, but we'll also never make any headway against those powers, no matter how furiously we wage war. The promise is to the church. We're born into family, not as isolated storm troopers. Yet many a Christian has gone down before the enemy onslaught because "church" is not utilized.

When Jesus announced his plan to build "church" what did he have in mind? The best clue we have is how those who heard him understood his meaning. The book of Acts records what they did—they crossed the Roman world, starting local congregations. And they believed Christ was fulfilling that promise to build His Church. There's a Church universal, including all peoples of all ages who have sworn allegiance to the God and Father of our Lord Jesus Christ, the Church on earth and the Church in heaven. But the Church on earth, the Church visible, is actually constituted of local churches and the Apostles took Christ's words to mean that's what he had in mind. Poor enough building blocks, to be sure, but he makes it invincible—all the powers of hell can't defeat it, nor even withstand its assault.

"Church" is ideally expressed, it would seem, in a local congregation. Perhaps there are legitimate substitute relationships with other members of the Body of Christ—the larger Church—to provide the needed nurture and protection of the one deprived of the ideal.

Of the five purposes of the church the first is worship. The church is to worship, meaning corporate worship. The individual worships in private, of course; in fact, his whole life should be worship! But there is a special function of church in corporately seeking God, worshiping him, singing His praises.

The church has other purposes; evangelism and service. Evangelism is what each believer is about, so we partner with all aspects of church in carrying that out. By "service" I mean the salt-and-light ministry of the church, seeking justice, healing wounds, compassionately caring for the hurts of the world.

Of the many possibilities for describing the inward purposes of the church I chose koinonia, accountability, and teaching. By "koinonia" I refer to that family solidarity, that oneness of loving care that takes responsibility for the welfare—spiritual, material, physical, emotional—of other members of the family. By "accountability" I mean the obligation to hold one another accountable for godly living. The extreme would be church discipline if all else fails. By "teaching" I mean leadership in seeing that every member is growing in knowledge of the whole truth of God as found in Scripture.

For years I taught a course on the biblical principles for Christian ministry. When we came to the purposes of the church, I did a little exercise with that large group of graduate students from many denominational backgrounds. I would flash on the screen the name of a denomination or prominent Christian leader and the students were invited to shout out the church function or purpose that first came to mind. It was amazing to see how that variegated crowd would shout the same word in unison, year after year. If I flashed, "Charismatic" the response was "worship." "Methodist" would bring "service." "Independent Bible church" was viewed as "teaching." Do you want to know how outsiders view you? "Southern Baptist" always drew "evangelism."

You may not join the chorus in any given case, to be sure, but the exercise does point up the fact that we tend to major on one or two purposes of the church, and neglect others. Surely we want to work hard at developing healthy "bodies," not cripples or basket cases. Our purpose here, however, is not to focus on the ideal church, but to evaluate what functions of church are strongly present in our own lives, what has been missing.

Let us be church-centered, convinced that the local congregation is what Christ is out to build. Some people seem to thrive with or without other humans in close relationships, though the numbers may not be as large as might appear. But God knows we need human companionship. *"It isn't good for man to be alone,"* he concluded at the very beginning talking about marriage. And church—we really do need one another even if some of us feel that more acutely than others.

September 9
Activity of the Spirit
1 Corinthians 12:7

"Now to each one the manifestation of the Spirit is given for the common good." (1 Corinthians 12:7)

When we consider the activity of the Spirit in our lives, we could become very introspective, even self-oriented. We live in an age of radical individualism and some people might see "spiraling up" as a very exclusive relationship between God and me. But the Holy Spirit won't let that happen! We were born in community, and we were designed to live in community. Furthermore, the more like God we become the more we'll be oriented outward, preoccupied with others, not with self.

And the startling thing is this: God has chosen to do His work in the world through us! So a major activity of the Holy Spirit is to get God's purposes on planet earth accomplished through His people reaching out. "People reaching out," however, does not mean individuals doing God's work independently of one another. God's method is called the church. The Spirit of God works primarily through and in relation to the church.

What are tasks that need to be done in your church? You might name preaching, teaching, serving meals, counseling, ushering, singing, leading, managing money, helping those with physical or material needs, playing a musical instrument, evangelizing, or starting new churches. If you want those tasks in the church to have spiritual results, the Spirit must be involved!

When the Spirit supplies you with some ability to serve, it's called a gift. Spiritual gifts are not just natural abilities, though such talents are also gifts from God and used by him to accomplish His purposes. A Spirit-gift points to something beyond our natural abilities. Think of two jobs in the church. How could we tell if the person doing them has the touch of the Spirit on his or her work? For example, what might result from a naturally gifted person's teaching in Sunday School and what might happen if the Spirit worked through the teacher?

Under a natural ability of teaching, you may have considered things like: people listen, it's interesting, people learn. Under the Spirit's gift you may have put things such as: people understand spiritual truth and begin to act on it; the Bible seems to come alive; people grow spiritually—their lives are changed.

Or let's consider finances. Imagine on your church's finance committee a person with the natural ability to manage money being Spirit-led in exercising that gift, as opposed to the same person operating on natural ability alone. What might be the results of each of the different person's management?

This one is tough. Perhaps you would put under natural ability, things like we don't have to worry about finances—everything is honest, above board, and accounted for; we never get in a jam because our finance committee can project income and expenses and hold us to our budget. The Spirit's touch might be seen in the following ways: our finance committee members are people of faith, they encourage us to give generously and trust God for miracle provision; they are people of vision, making sure that the church invests in what is most important from God's perspective; they are compassionate, seeing needs both in the church and outside as well, and leading us to meet those needs.

Natural talent or spiritually gifted? What kind of results do you see in your life? What about the life of your church? As we grow to become more like Jesus, we live in community and build the body of Christ using our spiritual gifts. There is supernatural fruit, results only the Spirit of God provides.

Why not pray today using the following prayer as a guide? *Holy Spirit, what a wonder You are! Thank You for making me with such high potential—to think and act like Jesus and to be one with You. When I mess up, You don't give up. Thank You for taking my broken model and transforming me into a new kind of person. Thank You for revealing to me what You want me to be and how I can become what You plan. Thank You for growing me up toward greater likeness to Jesus and thank You for all the growth that lies ahead. Thank You for companioning with me daily and for giving me those wonderful weapons to win out in life: prayer, the Word, the church. I want to be a faithful reflection of You. I want to be used by You to the maximum. I want to walk with You all the days of my life. I do trust You and love You. Here's my life—all of it, past, present, and future to do with as You please. I'm Yours, gladly and forever! Amen.*

September 10
Are You Listening?
James 1:19

"Know this, my beloved brothers: let every person be quick to hear, slow to speak, slow to anger..." (James 1:19)

The problem with conflict in the church is that it usually isn't the confrontation of two opinions, as in the world at large, but between perceptions of right and wrong. Each person or group feels they are on God's side, either because "the Bible told me so" or because "God told me so." That's why we start with the principles of yieldedness and trust toward God, not love and humility toward others. Until I yield my right to be "right" and trust God with the outcome, I'm not in a position to confront my opponent at all. And if I do anyway, it won't be in love and humility! When I get those attitudes adjusted, I'm ready to take the initiative.

A fundamental principle in taking the first step of directly talking with the other person is *"Be quick to hear, slow to speak, and slow to anger"* (James 1:19). When you meet, immediately start listening and listen so well that each of you can state the issue in such a way that the other will agree you have understood his or her position. Being slow to speak means waiting to talk until you're not angry, fatigued, or stressed so that you will be fully in charge of your emotions and objective in your reasoning. Quick listening and slow speaking will help put distance between you and the issue and close the gap between you and the other party.

Genuine listening means you're open, honest, and even vulnerable, ready not only to listen to criticism but also to accept it without counterattack. That's the way trust is built. After all, without trust, real solutions will remain out of reach. Jesus said your objective is to win over your brother, not to win the conflict (see Matt. 18:15).

Let's say you haven't won over your opponent, he hasn't won you over, and you haven't found an honorable compromise. If the issue is not one on which you and the other party can agree to disagree and bury the matter, then it's time to bring in others to help persuade and, if that doesn't work, to serve as witnesses to the outcome. Proverbs 11:14 advises, "With many counselors there is deliverance." With more perspectives, corporate wisdom has come to the table.

Compromise may not always be the solution, because some issues are nonnegotiable. Sin and ethical issues belong in that category, but the task force has the responsibility to determine the facts and then discern whether the issue is truly ethical from a biblical perspective and whether it is serious enough to warrant discipline.

Even ethical issues, however, are not always your responsibility. Parents are responsible for their own children but not for others' children. If you are not in a leadership position, you don't have as much responsibility to straighten things out.

Another nonnegotiable is doctrine, again, when you are in a responsible position. When members come into conflict over doctrine, Scripture has already spoken, and the church has already set parameters on church doctrine.

Most differences in the home or church aren't ethical or doctrinal. They are negotiable, and finding common ground is the objective. It will mean compromise, each giving up a little territory so that the two sides can get close enough to meet and move forward together. It takes love and a servant heart to resolve negotiable issues. Which of these do you need today in order to resolve the conflict in which you find yourself?

September 11
Why so Happy?
Isaiah 45:7

"I form light and create darkness; I make well-being and create calamity; I am the Lord, who does all these things." (Isaiah 45:7)

Some people seem to thrive with or without other humans in close relationships, though the numbers may not be as large as might appear. Others can't survive without an abundance of human companionship—touchy-feely relationships are essential. Most of us are probably somewhere in between. But God knows we need human companionship. "It isn't good for man to be alone," he concluded at the very beginning. Marriage. And church—we really do need one another even if some of us feel that more acutely than others. And yet, even missionary Paul felt lonely on occasion because members of his team weren't there. Other members need to be on the alert to reach out to those who are silent in their loneliness, including special care for singles.

But as maturing Christians, we must also be proactive, taking the initiative to find and nurture friendships that are emotionally and spiritual satisfying to both parties. That's one major purpose of church! If you're strong and independent you may not feel the need so acutely, but beware! We really do need one another. Besides, others need you! And if you're "people-addicted," in some measure of pain without plenty of close relationships, don't throw a pity party. Take the initiative to build mutually strengthening relationships.

Colin Green greeted me with a big smile and a cheery "Praise the Lord!" Praise the Lord? For what? Here she was, cooped up in the hospital room with that giant of a man she'd lived with for decades, now incoherent, uncooperative, belligerent, far down the terrifying road into Alzheimer's.

"Why so happy?" I asked. She told me the story of how she found a despondent woman in the hospital corridor, a mother who had traveled from a distant city to watch her son die. Colin, forgetting her own woes, became a friend to her, and led that distraught mother to find hope in Christ. Both were inundated with unexpected happiness as they embraced and mingled their tears. But what about Colin? Bit by piece I dragged from her the story.

Last week her husband broke down the door of their small home to get out of his "prison." Halfway across the front yard he stumbled to the ground and couldn't get up. Colin couldn't lift him, but she was reluctant to call 911 lest they find her beloved in his pitiable condition. He was incontinent and his clothes totally soiled. Colin pulled off his clothes, cleaned him up, and redressed him as he lay there, helpless. Then she called for help!

She spent the night with her man in the hospital, rescuing the nurses from his irrational behavior. The next morning, Sunday, her ne'er-do-well son arrived with bad news: "Mom, your house is going up in flames!" A few hours later I entered that bleak scene, received a warm embrace from that courageous little lady who called me her "family" and whispered in my ear, "Praise the Lord!"

Not everyone responds to trouble like Colin Green. And we need one another in difficult times for encouragement and sharing the burden. Some emerge from the storm better people, some worse. Why?

The crucial thing is not in the circumstances, but in our response to them. Faith in God keeps the circumstances outside, pressing us ever closer to God, and we become stronger, better persons, more like Jesus; unbelief lets the circumstances come inside and put a wedge between God and you or me, and we become a weaker person, less like Jesus than before, perhaps discouraged, despondent, even bitter, or at least a miserable, complaining person. Remember, though, it's not the quantity or even the quality of our faith, but the object of our faith—a trustworthy God. He is the one who can transform our trouble into strength and beauty. And though this means of grace is our least favorite, it can be the fast track to spiritual maturity.

September 12
The Cause of Adversity
Deuteronomy 32:39

"See now that I, even I, am he, and there is no god beside me; I kill and I make alive; I wound and I heal; and there is none that can deliver out of my hand." (Deuteronomy 32:39)

We ended yesterday with the crucial thing, in our adversity, is not in the circumstances, but in your response to them. You saw that faith in God keeps the circumstances outside, pressing you ever closer to God and become a stronger, better person, more like Jesus; unbelief lets the circumstances come inside and put a wedge between God and me and I you become a weaker person, less like Jesus than before, perhaps discouraged, despondent, even bitter, or at least a miserable, complaining person. Remember, though, it's not the quantity or even the quality of your faith, but the object of your faith—a trustworthy God. He is the one who can transform your trouble into strength and beauty. And though this means of grace is our least favorite, it can be the fast track to spiritual maturity.

Sometimes it's quite clear who caused me pain, but often it can be frustrating trying to figure out who's to blame. And the effort can be self-destructive, besides. Some people forever blame others for their troubles—they are victims of others' malice or stupidity. It may be a misguided or evil parent or spouse, the perverse society in which they live, the mission leadership, or the devil himself. Of course, there are others who tend to blame themselves for everything, guilty or not. Have you ever fallen into the "blame-it" trap? The strange thing is this: even if my blame-laying is on target, that truth has little power to deliver me from my problem. Indeed, the blame hunt itself may make me a worse person, less like Jesus.

But there is a way out. No matter where the problem may seem to come from, it always originates in one source. And, surprise, that one source of all trouble is God! Consider Deuteronomy 32:39: *"See now that I, even I, am He, and there is no god beside me; I kill and I make alive; I wound and I heal; and there is none that can deliver out of My hand."* [62] Of course, the awful tragedy in your life that is the result of someone's sin is not God's will. He didn't send it. But he did permit it. And one thing is certain, no harm can touch the child of God unless it passes through those nail-scarred hands. To know that God is behind every grief of mine may create some other problems, but at least it simplifies the search!

Once we understand that basic truth concerning suffering, we no longer need to devote our energies to determining the guilty party and making them pay for it. We can give our attention more to understanding the reason or purpose God has in our suffering. And to discover the purpose in the suffering relieves the deepest agony of it, for meaningless suffering is the greatest torment of all. And that is the distress of every person who doesn't know God. Furthermore, wherever the pain in your life originates, no matter how destructive it appears, no matter how entrapped you feel, there's always a way out.

---

[62] See also Job 1:12; 2:6; Ephesians 1:11; 2 Corinthians 12:7-10; Amos 3:6; Isaiah 45:7; Proverbs 16:4

September 13
Why Me?
Ezekiel 20:9

"But I acted for the sake of my name, that it should not be profaned in the sight of the nations among whom they lived." (Ezekiel 20:9a)

"Temptation," as you know, is a term that could point to any kind of trouble or adversity. One kind of trouble is temptation to sin. When you get down to it, all trouble is a temptation to the sin of unbelief! And the "faith" way could be an escape from that trouble or strength to bear up under it, as the passage assures us. Either way, more profitable than trying to identify the source of your problem, it may help to focus on the purpose God has in permitting it or sending it.

- To bring erring children back to the right way (Psalm 119:67,71; Hebrews 12:5-11).
- God may punish an erring child as a warning or example to others to be careful (1 Corinthians 10:11).
- Sometimes God allows hard times to get us to go somewhere or do something we otherwise might not consider (Acts 4:8; Matthew 10:23).
- Suffering prepares a person to help others (2 Corinthians 1:3,4).

Sometimes it's difficult to be truly comforted by one who hasn't suffered. Suffering is God's great tenderizer.

If you have difficulty in deciding what purpose God has in mind for sending or permitting a particular adversity, it may be that we need to consider the most important purposes in suffering. Sometimes those listed above are God's reason, but often those purposes are difficult to sort out, as you may have discovered. There are two purposes, however, that are always present in every trial. It is simpler to concentrate on those!

- God's Glory
- My Growth

When you respond to trouble with childlike confidence in God, people see it and give God the credit, either when they see a miraculous deliverance (John 9:2,3) or when they see miraculous strength in the midst of suffering (2 Corinthians 12:7-10). Suffering always has that purpose- the glory of God. Consider Ezekiel 20:9; *"But I acted for the sake of my name, that it should not be profaned in the sight of the nations among whom they lived, in whose sight I made myself known."* (See also verses 14, 22, 33, 39).

Suffering also has the purpose of growing me up into Christ's own likeness—the fast track on the spiral up. Do we live for ourselves or for others? Circumstance in our life is designed to make us more like Jesus.

September 14
Difficult Choices
1 Corinthians 10:13

"No temptation has overtaken you that is not common to man. God is faithful, and he will not let you be tempted beyond your ability, but with the temptation he will also provide the way of escape, that you may be able to endure it." (1 Corinthians 10:13)

Practically speaking, how does a Christian, committed to the absolute nature of the whole law of God, face a situation in which these laws seem to conflict? When Christ tells us to preach the gospel and the government tells us to be quiet, what do we do? When spies (such as with Rahab, or Jews in Germany during WWII) who are God's people are in my home and the police come to arrest them, do I betray them or deceive the authorities? When the same God who commands, "Thou shalt not kill" also commands to destroy a whole people, what does the soldier do?

Christ himself tells us that David did *well*—not a bad but forgivable act—in violating the law by eating the showbread in an emergency (Matthew 12:3-5). When the priests profane the Sabbath, Christ does not say they are forgiven, but rather that they are *blameless*. If the Pharisees only understood these things, they would not have condemned the *guiltless* disciples who did on the Sabbath a *lawful* thing that otherwise would have been unlawful. How does one decide when to keep the law and when to violate it?

Define the law carefully. The first step in solving this dilemma is to define the particular activity precisely. Is it truly a sin on *biblical* terms? For example, many people feel that all deception is a form of sinful lying; all killing is a form of sinful murder; all civil disobedience is a form of sinful lawlessness; all work on Sunday violates the Sabbath law. However, these definitions are not only naïve; they are not biblical. When a soldier kills, he is not necessarily committing murder. When the government taxes, taking some of my possessions by force, it is not stealing. It is important to insist that the Bible itself define what kind of deception, if any, is legitimate; what kind of killing is legitimate; what kind of taking by force is legitimate; what kind of civil disobedience is legitimate. We are not free to decide. The Bible itself, giving the command, must be allowed to define the limits of that command.

The faith way of escape. Normally there is a third alternative when we face a moral dilemma. Scripture promises that God will provide a way of escape (1 Cor. 10:13). Often, this is the way of faith. We must choose to do right and trust God with the consequences. As Brother Lawrence said, "I hope that when I have done what I can, he will do with me as he pleases."[63] Such is the utter God-confidence and childlike trust of an obedient child. God who is love, infinite in wisdom and power, can be trusted to handle the outcome of our obedience.

When we define the ethical choice in biblical terms and seek for the third alternative, the way of faith, most dilemmas are solved. I personally have never experienced a moral dilemma that was not resolved by biblical definition and choosing to trust God with the consequences. Beyond this, I am not sure of biblical authority. As a result, in counseling, I would not advise a troubled person to do more than this. However, some have been in positions in which a choice must be made between two actions, both of which they consider wrong. How should the choice be made?

If one feels he *must* make a choice and do what the Bible describes as breaking a law, he should make the choice in line with biblical precedent and confess the sin as a sin.

---

[63] Brother Lawrence, *The Practice of the Presence of God* (New York: Revell, 1895), 36.

1. *Making the choice according to a biblical precedent.* There is a biblical hierarchy of both virtue and sin. So, if a person concludes he must make a choice between two apparently sinful alternatives, he should certainly choose the lesser of the two evils, not the greater.

2. *Having made such a choice, however, one should confess this as sin.* Ask God's forgiveness. This does not necessarily mean that God judges it to be sin. The early disciples disobeyed the law, saying to the supreme court, "We must obey God rather than men" (Acts 5:29). Apparently, God did not consider this civil disobedience sinful. It was not "the lesser of two evils" but the "higher of two goods." Suicide is wrong, but is the soldier in a bunker who clutches the live grenade to his belly to save his comrades guilty of sin? *"Greater love has no man than this, that a man lay down his life for his friends"* (John 15:13).

God may have a different evaluation of a given act, and in the end this "tragic moral choice" that one feels compelled to make may be judged by God as a righteous act, not the lesser of two evils. In the meanwhile, however, it is important, lacking the perspective of God, to confess as sin what one believes may be sin. Whatever is not of faith is sin. In this way, one upholds the law and refuses the situationist's policy of universalizing the procedure as the norm of ethical behavior.

Do not make an exception normative. If one feels in conscience before God that a choice must be made, he should do so only with the firm conviction that this is a rare exception, not to be repeated and certainly not to be made the basis of daily choice. While there are problems to be solved, we must stress the reasons for utterly rejecting the current choices in morality as being untenable, unbiblical, and unworkable. This morality is a meticulously crafted castle founded on sand. It will fall and shatter those who live in it because it was not built on the rock of God's revelation. Our task is to unmask the deception and rescue the deceived.

September 15
Bumper Crop
John 15

"As the branch cannot bear fruit by itself, unless it abides in the vine, neither can you, unless you abide in me." (John 15:4)

    Why don't you read John 15 (vv. 9,10,12,13,17) as we consider the fruit of the Spirit today? Did you discover lots of love-fruit? That's appropriate, for love is at the head of Paul's list of the fruit of the Spirit, too (Galatians 5:22,23) and Jesus tells us love is in first place. In fact, he said that the whole Bible depends on this fruit (Matthew 22:37-40).

    Joy is found in this fruit passage, too (vs. 11). And there you find the "full" word again—he's teaching us about fruit bearing for the specific purpose that our joy will fill to the brim.

    Obedience is sort of a summary of Jesus-fruit. He speaks in many different ways of obeying His commandments—all of them! (Consider John 15:14). That points to all the fruit there could be. Jesus says we must allow His words to take up residence inside us (v. 7).

    Don't you get the image of a vine or tree so heavily loaded that the fruit is pervasive, not just visible evidence but the dominant characteristic? Everyone can tell! Except maybe the person himself... So much Jesus fruit that people will be drawn to Jesus, either to embrace him or to crucify him.

    Paul gives a more complete list of Spirit produced fruit in Galatians 5:22,23: love, joy, peace, patience, kindness, goodness, faithfulness, gentleness, self-control. If these characteristics are the product of the Spirit's activity, they can't be explained by the influence of a person's early environment or present circumstances. That kind of love, joy, or peace, though desirable and beautiful, would be quite natural, not supernatural.

    The Spirit wants to produce a bumper crop of Jesus' characteristics. There's one sure-fire way to know what your crop looks like. Do you have an accountability partner? Remember, Christlikeness is the one meaning of "full" only others know for sure. You need a fruit inspector! Here's a plan you may want to follow. Show your partner, or someone you can trust to be honest about it, the list of possible fruit noted from Jesus' description of fruit and Paul's list and ask for an evaluation. Ask them to underscore any characteristic that is very evident and circle any they feel need cultivating.

    You may not be able to know when you're full of fruit, but you have a pretty good idea when the fruit is sparse, or lacking altogether, so add to your partner's list your own list of fruit that's in short supply. What are the attitudes or actions, responses you want to have more consistently, more often, more fully? Choose personal characteristics that don't remind people of Jesus. In fact, they're your own product, coming right out of your circumstances and temperament. Now ask the Holy Spirit to grow you in each of those qualities. If you keep on praying about those daily it won't be long till people will exclaim, "She sure reminds me of Jesus!" or "Now there's a **real** Christian!" What they mean is, "There's a Spirit-filled Christian." And even a blind man can see it!

September 16
Division Within
1 Corinthians 3:10

"According to the grace of God given to me, like a skilled master builder I laid a foundation, and someone else is building upon it. Let each one take care how he builds upon it." (1 Corinthians 3:10)

Division within the church often comes when the *leader* falls into sin. But it also may come when the leader fails to lead. They may be insensitive to what is taking place among their people, appear to play favorites, give the impression of a domineering approach, fail to fulfill some essential function in the church, or fail to seek and allow someone else to fulfill the function in which they themselves lack strength. All the characteristics of God-like leadership, if neglected or absent, could sow seeds leading to disunity in the body.

Personal failure is the most common cause of division in the church. There can be personality clashes or temperamental differences as in the church in Philippi. There can be personal animosity developing from envy, selfishness, pride, or even from misunderstanding. When this morally cancerous attitude is spoken in criticism or gossip, it can easily become group failure, and schism results.

Someone has said that when Satan fell, he fell into the choir loft. The implication is that music is often the focal point of division in a church. The same might be said of those in charge of the finances of the church. Why should the areas of music and money so often prove the scene of church fights? Perhaps because in these areas a worldly person can succeed whereas in a ministry such as teaching or evangelism, success would not be so common through efforts unaided by the Spirit. Again, there may be those who serve in the areas of music or finance who are motivated by something other than the welfare of the church. At any rate, these two areas are often the scene of conflict and division, so the leadership does well to be on alert.

Structural failure. Division in the congregation can come because of failure in some program. Again, the form of government may enhance or militate against unity. But another factor, less suspected, may be size and geography.

The potential increases for superficial unity and decreases for deep family solidarity with the increase in the size of the church and the distance between the residences of members and/or from the central meeting place. If the church is a large church or the flock is widely scattered, true biblical solidarity will prove impossible unless compensating structures are provided within the larger congregation. Two approaches to compensate have proved popular. The plan to assign each member of the congregation to a small accountability group, geographically based, has been observed more in theory than in practice, perhaps, but the cell group concept has sometimes proved successful. The other approach is to hive off new congregations as a policy rather than simply growing larger. I do not advocate one approach over the other but do advocate that some compensating approach is necessary if members of a mega-church are to have the unity in family solidarity, the caring and responsible relationships necessary to experience God's purposes for the church.

Change. When the leadership decides that change is necessary, that there is some better way to accomplish some particular objective, success in making that change without causing division depends on many factors apart from the merit of the objective. If these other factors in the management of change are not fully observed, division and failure to reach those objectives is predictable.

The *timing* of the initiation of any change and of the various stages in that change is of great importance. Are the people ready for the change, has the education/preparation been adequate? Are all those affected by the change incorporated in the decision, structure permitting, or at least in the communication network?

Not only is timing important, but the *rate* of change has a great deal to do with success in making the change. If the rate of change is more rapid than can be sustained by the group without division or, on the other hand, more slowly than can be tolerated by the group without division, the rate of change must be modified. This is an extremely difficult factor to manage. Ordinarily, one cannot hope to manage the rate of change with perfect success in terms of approval of all members of the fellowship. The most that can be expected is that the pace will be within the tolerance of all members so that division does not result.

The *method* chosen to make a change and the *person* who initiates or who carries through some aspect of the change are major factors in potential for making the change without causing fragmentation of the body. Our school pioneered the concept of distance learning and the man responsible was an unparalleled visionary. But he was not an unparalleled change agent. He so disrupted the unity of the body that the vision was a quarter century in coming to fruition. In that case, the visionary was the wrong person for leading change.

As C.V. Matthew, an Indian educator, puts it, "It may take months or years to build a ministry, but only a moment to destroy it." I don't know exactly what that would look like, but Paul says destroying God's church is very serious business indeed *(1 Corinthians 3:17)*. Which of these do you see yourself doing?

September 17
Greater Harvest
John 15:16

"You did not choose me, but I chose you and appointed you that you should go and bear fruit and that your fruit should abide, so that whatever you ask the Father in my name, he may give it to you." (John 15:16)

Muriel loved cherry tomatoes. One day she had the bright idea of planting one. It soon sprouted and began to climb all over the railing on our back steps. During the summer that vine produced more than a thousand of its kind! A bumper crop. Reminded me of the vine in John 15. But it must have been beginner's luck because the next year there was a sparse crop of a few wizened tomatoes. No matter how we worked those vines, they refused to produce. Reminded me of many Christians.

Did Jesus mean His promise that we could consistently have a bumper crop, year after year? Maybe the vine analogy causes us to expect more "fruit" than is true to real experience? If we were talking of tomatoes or grapes, when we see the seed catalogue photographs of luscious, ripe fruit bursting out everywhere, the vine covering everything in sight, we tend to doubt the reality of it, at least for our own experience. So with Jesus' promise of spiritual fruit. If we doubt the reality of it for our own lives, when we see someone who seems to be producing a great crop we may find it depressing because we can't produce such a crop. Or perhaps we conclude that it's an illusion—it's just the camera angle. If we knew the whole truth about that successful-looking Christian, they aren't really that good. Or—a third alternative—maybe a professional gardener would help...

Jesus' good news is that we have one already: the Father! (John 15.1). And, if we stick with Jesus, the vine-stem, he guarantees an abundant harvest. In that kind of relationship, his life will flow and we will produce His own characteristics. The cherry tomato vine produced cherry tomatoes as the natural outcome of the flow of its own life. So with the fruit of a Christ "plant". And we won't have a minimal crop, either. It is by much fruit that we are fulfilled and he is honored (vs. 5,8). "Much" may mean all the varieties of good characteristics he possesses rather than merely certain ones—self-control but not joy or peace. It surely means producing Jesus' characteristics in large measure—becoming more and more loving, for example.

He identifies two specific characteristics or "fruits," then he identifies all of them as a cluster, and finally he adds the dimension of fruitful ministry. If we believe His promise and desire a bumper crop, we cannot close the series without a closer "fruit inspection."

The fruit or product of our life united with Christ is called by Paul the "fruit of the Spirit" (Gal. 5:22,23). Jesus here specifically identifies the first two in Paul's list: love and joy (Jn. 15.9-17).

We are invited to share a love affair with God himself. Now he tells us this love is to spill over and engulf our relationships with one another: *"My command is this: Love each other as I have loved you"* (vs 12,17). And how did he love us? How do you measure the quality of love, calibrate the depth of it, gauge the intensity of it? By the sacrifice it makes. *"Greater love has no one than this, that one lay down his life for his friends"* (vs 13). Sometimes it seems more difficult to "lay down life" in small increments than in one heroic surge of self-giving. But lay it down we must, if we truly love. So there evolves a way of life in which we habitually say "no" to self-interest in order to say "yes" to the best interests of family, friends, neighbors, co-workers, the lost of the world. "Such beautiful fruit! Reminds me of Jesus," the fruit inspectors in our lives will say.

Jesus promised abundant fruit, increasing likeness to him in character and growing effectiveness in ministry for him. He doesn't promise this to some exceptional super saint, but to everyone who stays close to him. If this is not happening, are you abiding in him? Are you even joined to him? If you do demonstrate the evidence of such a union, but not what could be called a "bumper crop" perhaps you need the gardener to prune a bit. Here's a checklist from John 15 on how he does it:

- Are you abiding in the Word, growing in knowledge of it and obedience to it?
- Are you abiding in loving companionship with him?
- Are you responding in faith to the discipline of adverse circumstances?

As you continue to (abide) in these, your crop will grow greater every year, bumper crops of glorious fruit. He guarantees it.

We ask, "What is fulfillment and how do I get it?" A tomato vine is fulfilled only through bearing tomatoes. And it is really "filled full" when the vine is loaded with fruit. Jesus holds before us, in John 15, a beautiful portrait of ultimate fulfillment: Himself! And he describes in detail how we can have it: Himself! As you stay tight with him, His life feeds into yours and the inevitable outcome is greater and greater likeness to him. Not "falling in love," but growing in love, from one degree of His beautiful character to another. May he ever be satisfied with a bumper crop through us!

September 18
Expectations
1 Thessalonians 1:4-6

"For we know, brothers and sisters loved by God, that he has chosen you, because our gospel came to you not simply with words but also with power, with the Holy Spirit and deep conviction. You know how we lived among you for your sake. You became imitators of us and of the Lord, for you welcomed the message in the midst of severe suffering with the joy given by the Holy Spirit." (1 Thessalonians 1:4-6)

The effectiveness and usefulness of short-term mission was researched and discussed, as short-term international missions reached tsunami proportions, prior to the pandemic. Missions in general was crippled in immediate post-pandemic years due to complications of international travel, acquisition of visas, and other hindrances. Let us take a few minutes to consider, "What may I expect from a short-term missionary experience?" If I expect something that such an experience can't give, I may be setting myself up for a disappointment—or worse—drawing wrong conclusions from that disappointment. What are some unrealistic expectations of short-term missions?

Some young adults wrestle with the question of whether God is calling them into a career of missionary service. Do they have the necessary gifts for cross-cultural missionary service? So they hit on the plan of going for a limited period of time to find out. Sort of a trial run. This is a big mistake. What one tries out in a few weeks or months, or even a couple of years, is not the missionary vocation. It is sort of like trial marriage—the couple is trying out something, all right, but not marriage!

The essence of missionary service is identity with the people, a love that bonds. Just as Christ came to become one of us, so is every missionary who follows in His train—"as the Father sent me...." Effectiveness—success—in missionary work is intimately tied to the level of identification the missionary has and the people sense that he has. This includes understanding, appreciating, and adapting to the culture and, above all, mastering the language. None of this can take place in a short period of time. Therefore, to test one's potential for missionary service would require becoming a missionary! Or at least some years of living and learning among the people.

A leader in urban ministry told us that when he took teams of short termers into the Watts district of Los Angeles, the people would always ask them how long they intended to be there. Not until they moved in with the intent of becoming one with them, did the people begin to accept them. You can't "try out" incarnation, you have to do it.

A second unrealistic expectation is to overestimate the value of one's contribution. Unless the short termer has a special skill that is needed by the people, such as a medical doctor, the contribution to advancing the cause of Christ will be modest. Short term missionaries are not going to save the world, contrary to some of the glowing promotionals surrounding the enterprise. They should not be disappointed if they do not see a seismic spiritual impact. The work of evangelizing a people and planting the church is the task of long-term commitment to such a vocation. Thus, if I expect a short term on the mission field to test my gifts and calling, to make a major contribution, or to fulfil a lifetime of obligation to Great Commission living, I will either be disappointed or misled.

But short-term service can do great things. First of all it can provide an unequalled educational experience. Those who have a thorough preparation for the experience, good supervision in it, and adequate de-briefing will learn a great deal about another culture, about missionary work, and about themselves.

Second only to education is the opportunity for inspiration. For the person who goes into it with the pores of his mind and heart wide open, the short-term experience will infect with the excitement of what God is doing in the world.

This is not only life transforming, that inspiration often infects others upon re-entry to the home base. Since inspiration is one of the great benefits of short-term service, specialists in the field caution us that a term of more than three months and less than two years is hazardous. During the first few weeks and months, the excitement of the new experience is exhilarating, but if they stay beyond the time of initial euphoria, the reality of the spiritual warfare hits home. Since they have not entered the battle with long-term commitment or with cultural adaptation and language fluency, the experience often becomes bitter and short circuits any possibility of lasting inspiration.

As a result of the peerless education and inspiration of short-term experience on a mission field, the greatest outcome for the cause of world evangelism is that short termers provide the major reservoir of recruits for career missionary vocation. It doesn't hurt to go short-term with the idea in mind that it may indeed be a stepping stone toward a life-time investment in the great enterprise of bringing the world to obedience to Christ. One interested in missions should go, invest, and serve well, yet manage expectations for that experience. It may be that God has additional work for us to accomplish for the sake of the Kingdom. How will you find what that is?

September 19
Raiding the Devil's Tackle Box
Part 1
1 John 2:16

"*For all that is in the world—the desires of the flesh and the desires of the eyes and pride of life—is not from the Father but is from the world.*" (1 John 2:16)

I invite you to help me raid the devil's tackle box. What are the lures he uses to catch us? I think we'll discover they aren't evil, repulsive, ugly. Actually, they're very attractive—how else would they lure? And he didn't create them. God did! The devil uses God's good gifts to lure us into a devil's lifestyle. They're God's good gifts: our bodies with the body's appetites, the world around us, our sense of worth. How could the devil use such wonderful gifts to lure us into bad attitudes and behavior?

Let's ask John to help us get started in the raiding party. 1 John 2:15: "*Do not love the world or the things in the world. If anyone loves the world, the love of the Father is not in him.*" The "world" can't mean the people of the world (John 3:16). Surely it doesn't mean God's good gifts. So it must have to do with *how* we love those gifts.

What is it to "love" God's good gifts in a God-displeasing way? Well, surely it would make him sad, dishonor him if we abused His gifts, misused them? And how might that be? He tells us explicitly in verse 16: the desires of the flesh and the desires of the eyes and pride of life.

Consider one lure today and two of these lures tomorrow.

1. **Lust of the flesh**. We can love food too much. It's called gluttony. I don't know how this sin made the list of "the seven deadly sins" because there's not much about it in Scripture. Actually, until 20th century America there wasn't much of a temptation to over-eat—most people throughout most of history were too busy finding enough to eat and working off what they did eat. But since our bodies don't belong to us and since God takes up residence in them, to abuse them is not right. And certainly there has never been a society in history that has committed gluttony like ours. There are other ways we get caught by Satan's lures—athletics, sleep, travel, entertainment, alcohol, or books. Anything that goes beyond God's design for the fulfillment of God-given desires to enjoy, to have or to be. When we go outside God's design, that's to love the world through the lust of the flesh, the appetites of our bodies.

But if there's any lust of the flesh, appetite of the body, that America is devoted to more than food, it would be sex. Now THAT the Bible does talk about from beginning to end! It's God's good gift when used as he designed, but to violate His standard is to love the world. And, says John, if you do that, the love of the Father is not in you. God's exquisite gifts of taste buds, of sex—to abuse them is to devalue them and if we really cared adequately about our own selves, we'd run from every lure to misuse them.

Think of sex. People grab for pleasure and get it. But every illicit pleasure diminishes one's capacity for the maximum ecstasy reserved for those who use the wonderful gift of sex God's way—in marriage. It's a package deal. Split them and you reduce the ultimate pleasure he designed. You get the animal rush. But you abort the potential for bringing a passionate, permanent love relationship to a climax.

Suppose there's a family friend who's very fond of you. He also happens to own the factory in town that makes Porsches and he's promised you a brand new $100,000 Porsche when you grow up and get your driver's license. For your 14th birthday he takes you down to the plant to give you a preview, to show you how it's all put together. Your eyes pop as the different glistening parts roll down the assembly line. Then comes the magnificent engine. You've never seen anything like it. "Crank it up" you shout excitedly. They crank it up and VROOM! You say to your benefactor, "I want that gift. Now." "Are you sure?" he says. "If you'd just wait you could have the whole package. One without the other may be exciting and a bit of fun for a while, but the end product will be diminished. Are you sure you want it now?" "Oh, yes, yes, yes!" "Well, if you insist..." You take it home and every evening you crank up that magnificent gift and listen with rapture as it purrs and roars. What a rush! But you never ride that car, you never really get anywhere near what your benefactor planned. Even after you get your license and he helps you try to put back together his gift for you, it never runs as smooth or as fast.

Maybe you're single and you've already been fooling around with that powerful engine; take it back to the Manufacturer. Give it over to him. And when the time comes he'll put it all together and you can drive that sucker home. It will be worth the wait—trust me!

Sex and marriage are designed for one another. Split them, and you're left with a poorer gift. One without the other isn't the exquisite gift God plans for you. Unless, of course, he has something even better in mind for you. Paul reminds us of that—a special relationship with him reserved for those gifted with singleness. But most of us need to be reminded often, sex without marriage or marriage with a used engine won't be all God intended.

And some of you married folks. Maybe the old Porsche is getting a bit worn, a few dents in her body, maybe some knocks in your engine. You look at that cute little Miata flashing by in the next lane and begin to think, "Now if I put this engine in that baby we could really fly!" Don't you believe it. Oh, you'll get an initial Vroom no doubt—as Solomon tells us, illicit sex has a special kick to it—stolen water is sweet, he says (Proverbs 9:17). But it won't last. It's likely to blow up in your face and if not, it usually ends in a crash. Whatever, it never runs as the Designer planned. If you don't believe me, just read the statistics.

Please—don't mess with God's good gift of your body. Save it, keep it tuned up, run it the Manufacturer's way. But maybe you love the world too much. Then, says John, there's a reason: the love of the Father is not in you. You don't love HIM that much.

September 20
Raiding the Devil's Tackle Box
Part 2
1 John 2:16

"For all that is in the world—the desires of the flesh and the desires of the eyes and pride of life—is not from the Father but is from the world." (1 John 2:16). *"But godliness with contentment is great gain, for we brought nothing into the world, and we cannot take anything out of the world. But if we have food and clothing, with these we will be content. But those who desire to be rich fall into temptation, into a snare, into many senseless and harmful desires that plunge people into ruin and destruction. For the love of money is a root of all kinds of evils. It is through this craving that some have wandered away from the faith and pierced themselves with many pangs."* (1 Timothy 6:6-10)

The three lures of the devil: your body, your things, your significance—God's good gifts. Satan wants you to fall in love with them so he can turn them into the ultimate ugly like himself—lust, covetousness, pride. Yesterday we examined the lust of the flesh. Today let's consider the lures of the *lust of the eye* and the *pride of life*.

2. **Lust of the eye.** When do you pursue covetousness instead of contentment? To covet is to desire, seek, pursue something not yours. Or, not in God's plan for you. Have you noticed that a person doesn't have to be poor to be covetous. If you did have a lot, you might be even MORE covetous—*clinging* to what you have, *guarding* it, *trusting* it. The temptation of a desire-filled eye is a powerful enticement for both the haves and the have-nots. To love stuff is to prove the love of the Father is not in us. At least love for God doesn't dominate our life. Is covetousness a small sin? Surely the 10th commandment is the least of all the commandments? Well...

- It's dumb because it doesn't usually improve anything much, just agitates your own spirit. But it's far worse than dumb.
- Covetousness is so bad, in fact, that Scripture calls it idolatry. Idolatry of things. Not idolizing an admirable person or grand cause, but just plain things. Stuff replacing love and worship of God is so bad, Paul tells us, the covetous will never inherit the kingdom. He even ranks the covetous along with adulterers and thieves (1 Corinthians 6:10).
- You see, covetousness is a cancer of the spirit. Cancer is a good cell in our body gone bad, eating up its brothers. Covetousness is a cancer of the spirit gone berserk, eating away at our love for God, eating away at our love for others with love for self. But note a strange thing about covetousness and contentment, counterintuitive to the contemporary mindset: Covetousness is a great LOSS and contentment a great GAIN! That's what Paul told Timothy (1 Timothy 6:6-10). *"If you love the world—the lust of the eye, stuff—the love of the Father is not in you. And,"* Paul tells young Timothy, *"it will drown you in a sea of destruction and perdition."* Strong words. Not mine—God's!

3. **Pride.** Instead of humility, the servant heart. *"I am among you as one who serves,"* said the King of all the worlds. Then He washed their dusty feet; yes, even the feet of the ultimate betrayer. Then he said, *"Now get on with it—you do the same."* But we are not naturally that way.

Paul said, "Let each consider others better than self." Even when they're obviously not better? Yes—treat them as your betters. A slave might have been much more intelligent, much better looking, much more spiritual than his owner, but as a servant he treated his master as his better. That's the servant role.

Why is pride a particularly enticing temptation? Maybe because fame is not only a lure for the greatly gifted, for those who have earned recognition by performance, but just as much for those who do not have it but want it and seek it.

Why is pride such an evil thing? The trouble with pride is that it's a break with reality. And any break with reality is destructive, not health-giving. Of course a low self-image, evaluating ourselves below what we are, what God has invested in us, what we are in Christ—that is destructive, too, because that low view of self also is a break with reality. But Scripture focuses on our bent toward grasping for the glory, thinking of ourselves more highly than is true and wanting others to recognize our worth. To distort reality does not enhance your value, it diminishes it—doesn't make you more grand but more tawdry. Satan discovered that. He exalted himself, grasping for the power and glory that are God's and became the ultimate ugly, the premier failure. Jesus, on the other hand, came down, embraced the humble, servant role. And displayed the ultimate beauty.

How do you spot destructive pride? Easy—where does the spotlight shine? Who gets the credit? God will take the three root sins—lust, covetousness, and pride—the stench of the world—and change them into the fragrance of Jesus—pure, contented, humble.

September 21
Grief
Romans 5:3-5

*"...but we rejoice in our sufferings, knowing that suffering produces endurance, and endurance produces character, and character produces hope, and hope does not put us to shame, because God's love has been poured into our hearts through the Holy Spirit who has been given to us." (*Romans 5:3-5)

I don't ask why. The truth is for years I've been asking another "why?" When a dear friend is struck down with cancer, I say, "why her, Lord? Why not me?" When I grieve with a friend, whose child is in rebellion, "Why not us?" I often awake in the morning and say, "why me, Lord? Why am I still alive? Why am I in such good health? Why do I have such a challenging role to play? Why do my precious children love me so? Why me?"

How long since you stopped fretting to be treated fairly? To get what you deserve. But here we are in the human condition where people suffer, die and grieve. Why should any be immune? Grace overwhelms us day by day. Why should you not experience occasionally the reality of a fallen world? The truth of Scripture is such a comfort.

Another question that seems inappropriate, another game some people are tempted to play, is second guessing, "*if only.*" If only the new diving wetsuit had arrived on time and my son had not rented a faulty wetsuit. *If only* he had slept well the night before so that he could be alert. *If only, if only.* In the first place, there are no ifs in God's vocabulary. He who works all things after the counsel of His will. How many forks in the road lead to every decision that we make? How far back down the road are you going to trace the *if onlys*? But it's more than impossible, and thus fruitless. It can be very destructive.

Well, they told me some people are angry. Angry at the one gone. Why did he take risks? Why didn't he arrange his affairs better in preparation for such an eventuality? It's so fruitless. That person is out of range. And the only psyche that's going to be damaged by that kind of fire is the person who is asking the question. Besides, did you love that person or someone else? Did you love them who has such a free spirit, with such a verve for life, with such exuberant joy, such living at the edge of potentialities? Then you have to take the package. No need to try to rearrange them now. And even if you could, they wouldn't be the one you loved. Your life could be a long string of regrets, but left to God, there are no regrets.

Some people ask "Why?" David certainly wrestled with it in public. There are so many possibilities. Death is an enemy and we're at war. It wasn't God's idea. Ah, you say, but he permitted it. He could have prevented it. By saying God could have prevented it, you resent it. That if God were smart enough, and strong enough, and loved me sufficiently this would not have happened.

What kind of God do you think you have if he gave His Son to die, not by accident, but by design, for His love of me. What kind of person would you be to call His motives into question? How do we calibrate deep grief? I know it is a great grief. The void and the sense of loss is there. We cannot rank grief, as if this is worse than that. We are ambushed by grief. Out of nowhere the pain comes. Well, the comfort of the Scripture gives hope. Hope for heaven. But a great discovery is the comfort of the Scripture, and the unity of the family—the Body of Christ. And you see, both are given to give hope.

September 22
Inspiration
2 Peter 1:19-21

"…So we have seen and proved that what the prophets said came true. You will do well to pay close attention to everything they have written, for, like lights shining into dark corners, their words help us to understand many things that otherwise would be dark and difficult. But when you consider the wonderful truth of the prophets' words, then the light will dawn in your souls and Christ the Morning Star will shine in your hearts. For no prophecy recorded in Scripture was ever thought up by the prophet himself. It was the Holy Spirit within these godly men who gave them true messages from God." (2 Peter 1:19-21)

    The Bible claims to be inspired by God, and that makes us curious. Exactly what did the Holy Spirit do to the human Bible authors? How did he make sure they wrote what he wanted to say? Since he doesn't tell us, we try to figure it out. Some concluded the Spirit must have dictated the Bible to the authors like executives used to dictate to their secretaries. He obviously did dictate parts of the Bible, as when he gave the 10 Commandments to Moses. Not much of Scripture, however, was dictated. Some, in fact, was written from historical research, like Luke and Acts (Luke 1:1-4).

    On the human side, then, the experiences and writing style of each author are evident throughout Scripture. But in some mysterious way those authors were influenced by the Holy Spirit, so that what they wrote was consistently called "the Word of God." The authors were "carried along" by the Spirit (2 Peter 1:2-21) so that "all Scripture is God breathed." (2 Timothy 3:16) We translate Paul's term for the Spirit's activity in that passage: "inspiration" meaning "breathed-in." Our focus is what he did to the authors, but Paul's emphasis was on the source—God Himself is the origin, it's God-breathed-out. Though we may not know how the Spirit carried out this activity, we know from Scripture itself that he so guided the writing process that the human authors wrote what the divine author wanted communicated. This cannot be said of any other book, no matter how helpful it is. Other books may be called "inspired," in the sense that they inspire the reader, but none can be said to be God-breathed as this Scripture. The Bible alone carries that guarantee. If you do what Jesus Christ never did, that is affirm error in Scripture, then you have put yourself over Scripture. By deciding what to accept and what not to accept as trustworthy, you sit in judgment on the book: your authority becomes superior to its authority. In that way, you would reduce the authority of Scripture to the size of your intellect. And that's not a very impressive "Revelation"! Paul assures us, "All Scripture is inspired." So, we take the step of faith and embrace Jesus's view of the Bible. We are not smarter than he!

    If God had not taken the initiative in revealing things we cannot discover through scientific investigation, how little we would have known about him, about our lost condition, about His will for us! Without His gracious revelation, how could we have experienced salvation, or the abundant life God promises? The trustworthiness of the Bible depends on who said it. If God said it, you'd better believe it. More than that, you had better move out and do what it says! We call this book—and only this book—The Word of God. That is why it has supreme authority for our lives. We believe it; we obey it.

    The power of the human intellect is awesome. It ought to be—it is designed on God's model, but has been so disabled by sin, that unaided, people cannot understand the Bible. It doesn't even make good sense to them. (1 Corinthians 2:14; 2 Corinthians 3:14-15) Even if there were no crazy mirrors of sin to distort reality, our capacities are limited. We were never designed in likeness to God's infinite capacities. We are finite. So, we grope after meaning, the meaning of our own lives, if not the grander meaning of the universe. We probe with our ten-watt brains, short circuited by sin even before the search begins. On this pitiful scene breaks a great light, a mega-burst of eternal truth, truth about God and truth about His plan for our salvation, truth about the meaning of our lives. In the Bible, the Holy Spirit has turned up the lights and revealed God and His will for us. That's why we call the Bible "revelation." God said it, so we believe it. God said it, so we must obey it.

What a magnificent gift the Holy Spirit has given us! In the Bible, He has unveiled the hidden God. And you can know God! And knowing him, you will surely love him. It would be really a mismatched friendship, though, if you did not become increasingly like him. So, to make that possible, the Holy Spirit gave you a fully reliable revelation of God's will for you. Now you look more closely at Scripture as God's revealed will for what you are to think and how to behave. He could have left you to stumble around in the twilight until night closed in, but he broke through with a brilliant light, liberating you with His own truth. That's what truth does—it sets us free (John 8:32). What Love! Hallelujah!

September 23
Purposes
Isaiah 40:28-31

"Hear the sovereign Lord, do you not know? Have you not heard? The Lord is the everlasting God, the Creator of the ends of the Earth. He will not grow tired or weary. And His understanding no one can fathom, He gives strength to the weary. And increases the power of the weak. Even youths grow tired and weary and young men stumble and fall. Those who hope in the Lord will renew their strength. They will soar on wings like eagles. They will run and not grow weary. And they will walk and not be faint. Do not fear. For I am with you. Do not be dismayed, for I am your God. I will strengthen you and help you, I will uphold you with my righteous right hand." (Isaiah 40:28-31)

You may ask, "What shall I do?" or, "I know exactly what I'm supposed to do, but will I ever be successful?" Is that where you're sitting? What's up? Dreams dashed by some influential powerbroker. Why are you uncertain? Why is there apprehension? "Will I succeed? Will I fail?" Well, let me suggest one reason. You aren't God. Well, that's pretty fundamental, isn't it? Actually, there's only one person who can be very certain about the future, who can be absolutely sure of success.

Our text is Isaiah 46:10, *"But God says my purpose will stand."* That's it. *"My purpose will stand."* You'll notice in this where he says that some of the aspects of the sovereignty of God are touched on. For example, he says, *"I make known the end from the beginning, from ancient times, what is still to come."* The Sovereign One has all the information, all the knowledge. Then, he says, "I will do all that I please." So not only all wisdom, but all power. Then in the 11th verse, he says, "what I have said that will I bring about." One of integrity. If he says it's going to happen, it's going to happen. If he says that it's His purpose, that will be achieved. God is sovereign, so you may have uncertainty, but the good news is that there is One with great certainty. Perhaps you suffer from a feeling of guilt, some wrong that whatever you do you can't seem to make right. Listen to the sovereign One, *"Why even I am He who blots out your transgressions for My own sake and remembers your sins no more. I have swept away your offenses like a cloud, your sins like a morning mist. Return to me, for I have redeemed you."* That's His purpose. And remember, His purpose will stand.

Or perhaps you are uncertain about the future. It seems that you are in the midst of a dark tunnel. You don't really see any real light at the end. Or perhaps you are emerging from a tunnel and the road ahead is rough and perhaps unpassable. *"Hear the Sovereign Lord. I will lead the blind by ways they have not known along unfamiliar paths. I will guide them. I will turn the darkness into light before them and make the rough places smooth. These are the things I will do. I will not forsake them."* That's His purpose. And remember His purpose will stand. Who may have fears? Perhaps you fear some circumstance.

Perhaps there is a wavering with a sense of insecurity. Maybe still groping to know what God intends you to be. Does anyone really know me? The real me? Does anyone really care? Hear the Sovereign Lord, *"Fear not, For I have redeemed you. I have called you by name. You are mine. When you pass through the waters, I will be with you. When you pass through the rivers, they will not sweep over you. When you walk through the fire, you will not be burned. The flames will not set you ablaze, for I am the Lord your God, the Holy One of Israel, your Savior."* That's His purpose for you and remember His purpose will stand.

Perhaps you sense a gap between your dreams and your perceived ability. Can you really cope with the problems, let alone with the opportunities that loom, and you are acutely aware of your own weakness? That's His purpose. And His purpose? Welfare. And that's a great relief. You don't need to cringe and be apprehensive. His purpose will stand. You don't need to fret about the attitudes and activities of others. Whatever their purpose, God's purpose will stand. You don't have to strive so feverishly and desperately. You don't have to cower before the enemy. God's purpose will stand, whoever the enemy, whatever the opposition. You don't need to feel all the pressure that keeps you dashing frantically from crisis to crisis, because His purpose will stand. And he will do all that he pleases, so relax. Wait quietly on the Lord. He will bring about His purposes—not yours, but His.

God's purpose will stand. That's what he says of himself. So that you really shouldn't feel it necessary to believe the future, your ministry, or whatever it may be, really depends on you or your health, on your smarts, on your courage. His purpose really will stand. Relax, stop trying to play God. You aren't God. Stop flirting with all those other gods of this world, the strength that you have in your bank account or your money or your whatever. "No," he says, "turn from those gods. There's only one God. Consider the things that I've done," and then in the next phrase he says this, *"I am God and there is none like me. I make known the end from the beginning, from ancient times."*

The only question for you today is whether or not he will somehow identify and prosper your purpose, and whether you will be caught up in His purposes so that what he promises will come true.

September 24
Unrealistic Expectations
Ephesians 4:13

"...until we all reach unity in the faith and in the knowledge of the Son of God and become mature, attaining to the whole measure of the fullness of Christ." (Ephesians 4:13)

What is the result of unrealistic expectations? Boris said that he alone at his work was perfect. But don't ask any of the secretaries about that evaluation. They feared his explosive rage that could be ignited by the slightest thing that didn't go his way. What was his problem? Was he self-deceived? He no doubt considered his anger, "righteous indignation" and thus remained "perfect." That result comes from a difference in definitions and can lead to self-deception. Of course, there may be some who know they have not reached their standard of perfection, yet who still talk like they had. They would be in danger of hypocrisy—not self-deceived but seeking to deceive others.

Linked to one's definition of sin is the definition of perfect. We use "perfect" in many different ways.
- The Smiths' new baby is perfect.
- Gifts of ministry enable God's people to grow up into perfection. (Ephesians 4:13)
- Be perfect as God is perfect. (Matthew 5:48)
- This ice cream is perfect.

There would be no problem among us if people who teach the possibility of perfection in this life meant healthy (like the Smiths' new baby) or mature (as in Ephesians 4:13) or outstanding, really good (like the ice cream). The Bible uses the term "perfect" in all these ways. The problem comes when some speak of sinless perfection, meaning "without flaw in the moral realm." As we have seen, Scripture says a person who says he is without sin is self-deceived or, worse, makes a liar of God. The only way a person can do this is to redefine sin, to make it something less than any falling short of God's moral perfection. Thus when people speak of sinless perfection, the difference is often semantic; the term "sin" defined with limitations. If I'm promised a life free of deliberately choosing to break the known will of God, for example, maybe perfection is within reach. But if I promise a flawless life, free from all wrong attitudes and actions, full of God's perfections, my expectancy is too high. Of course, it's no doubt better to aim too high and fall short than to aim too low and hit the target.

For many, however, the danger is the opposite of self-deception: discouragement in not being able to achieve or maintain what is expected. Many become so discouraged as to drop out altogether. Such are the hazards of unrealistic expectations:
- Self-deception, especially by redefining sin or a particular sin.
- Hypocrisy, knowing that I fall short but professing otherwise.
- Discouragement from expecting perfection and falling short.

We've spoken of too low expectations and too high expectations, but there's a strange combination of the two, not in any church's formal doctrine but common in Christian practice. "I don't do half the bad stuff most people do," people say and feel that's good enough. Another variety of the same syndrome: the Christian who prays, "forgive us of our many sins," but doesn't pause to think of any specific wrong he needs to right. Both may be jealous of a fellow worker, are critical in spirit, for example, but quite satisfied with their level of achievement. Their expectations are too low by biblical standards, but their valuation of themselves is way too high! They too qualify as misguided and expectations, and they too may be self-deceived or hypocritical.

They don't have the third bad result, however. They're not in danger of becoming discouraged about falling short! We've looked at some of the results of holding unrealistic expectations about our potential. But before pressing on, "to lay hold of all for which Christ laid hold of me," I need to accept the biblical limitations on my expectancy. I'll never in this life be absolutely perfect as God is, without sin. Though when I see Jesus, I shall be like him. (1 John 3:2) Hallelujah for that! How can we praise God, for the bad news of limited expectations? Here's my response:

Thank you, blessed Spirit, for releasing me from the drivenness and disappointments of unrealistic expectations. Help me to accept my own limitations and those of others. And please, please don't let me swing in the other extreme and settle for less than you intend. I want to be all a redeemed human being can be. And that's for Jesus sake—not just for mine. Amen.

September 25
Cut it Out!
John 15:2

"Every branch in Me that does not bear fruit he takes away; and every branch that bears fruit he prunes, that it may bear more fruit." (John 15:2)

In the last century, a shift, massive and rapid, occurred. A book by Daniel Yankelovich was subtitled: "Searching for Self-Fulfillment in a World Turned Upside Down." The "old rules," he said, stressed duty to others, particularly to one's family. If someone were selfish and got caught at it, it was embarrassing and it looked ugly, especially in others. But no longer. Now if a person does not put self-interest first it is no longer that he is stupid; he is dishonest. He has broken the rules. In what he calls "the duty to self ethic," your duty to yourself is your primary responsibility and all other relationships and values must fit into that order of priority.

Yankelovich felt that the movement could be liberating, but he was an honest scientist and admitted, after tracking 3,000 people in personal, in-depth interviews with his staff, and analyzing hundreds of thousands of questionnaires, that so far the search for personal self-fulfillment has been futile. It resulted in insecurity and confusion. "What is self-fulfillment?" he asked. And: "When you find yourself, what will you do with yourself?"

The frightening thing is that eighty-three percent of Americans buy into the "new rules," either in whole or in part. But those foolish people are not Christians, at least not evangelical Christians, right? Wrong! James Davison Hunter, in his examination of students and faculty in eight leading evangelical colleges and eight leading evangelical seminaries, used Yankelovich's earlier questionnaire and concluded that evangelicals are not less committed to self-orientation than their secular counterparts, but more committed to personal self-fulfillment as the primary value. [64]

He found them to believe that self-fulfillment is no longer a natural by-product of a life committed to higher ideals

---

[64] James Davison Hunter, *Evangelicalism: The Coming Generation*. Chicago: University of Chicago, 1987, pp 64-75.

but rather is a goal, pursued rationally and with calculation as an end in itself. The quest for emotional, psychological, and social maturity, therefore, becomes normative. Self-expression and self-realization compete with self-sacrifice as a guiding life-ethic.

Is it possible to fill up with all the good in life by concentrating on that pursuit or does Jesus really mean it when he says that is one sure way to get empty? How can "abiding in Christ" provide a key to sorting out this fundamental crisis of the self.

Jesus' longest recorded "sermon" or talk (John 13-17) was given in their favorite indoor rendezvous, the "upper room", perhaps upstairs in John Mark's family home. As Jesus talked, smoke rose from the nearby valley of Kidron Brook where grape vine prunings were burned at that time of year. The disciples may well have watched the smoke and smelled the acrid aroma even as he spoke. Grape vines couldn't be used to build furniture, even to make pegs for hanging clothes. They were good for nothing but burning (Jn. 15.6). So it is, said Jesus, with those who do not stick with him. Life lived apart from him is dead loss.

"Apart from me" means "in your own strength" or "with your own resources" or "on your own" (vs. 4). Life and fruit flow only from Jesus, the vine-stem. So the only way to live and be fulfilled is to maintain that intimate relationship, "mutual indwelling."

"Apart from me" (vs 5) means more than that, however. It is "not simply without My help but separated from Me." There are two kinds of people who are cut—some are cut off (vs 2, 6), and some are cut back (vs 2). For a bumper crop, even vines that stay tight with the main stem need pruning. But one way or the other, everyone is cut.

Years ago, I found illumination of John 15 in—of all places—a travel magazine advertisement! The managers of a well-known California vineyard told the general public the secrets of their abundant grape harvests:

No two vines are identical. Each one must be pruned differently: How old is the vine? How is the vine supported—on its own stump, on a stake, or on a wire? Does it get hot afternoon sun or only the cooler rays? Is it in vigorous health and should its crop be retained this year or sacrificed for the future good of the vine? Precisely where on the vine should spurs be permitted to grow? How many buds on this spur? How many on that spur? A master pruner must know all such things and care for each vine according to its own individual needs.

We, too, need pruning if we are to produce the best possible crop of godly behavior and effective ministry. Jesus introduces us to the Master Pruner—His own Father! (Verse 1). And then he shows us the two methods God uses in cutting back the bad, the unnecessary, and sometimes even good things that sap resources needed to grow and produce more. One method is gentle, the other severe. The gentle method, emphasized in John 15, is the Word; the severe is the sharp knife of God's discipline.

The Lord of our personal harvest, seeking to bring us to maximum fulfillment, cleans out the hindrances with His Word—the entire body of His teaching. It won't do simply to admire or respect the Word, it must abide in us. We must study it, think about it, master it, live in it. Without this relationship to the Bible, one cannot be at one with Jesus. To abide in Jesus, he said, was for His Word to abide in us.

September 26
Ignoring the Unseen
John 16:13-14

"When he, the Spirit of truth, comes, he will guide you into all truth. he will not speak on his own; he will speak only what he hears, and he will tell you what is yet to come. He will bring glory to Me by taking from what is Mine and making it known to you." (John 16:13-14)

Imagine the following: the President of the United States comes to speak at your local high-school auditorium. The band strikes up "Hail to the Chief" as the president strides to the microphone. The spotlight follows his every step. Suddenly the crowd, as one, rises and—what's this? They turn their backs to the stage and, pointing to the balcony, erupt in applause for the fine performance of the spotlight operator! Absurd? Of course, but it illustrates a truth about the Spirit. The Spirit glorifies— shines the spotlight on— the Son. The Spirit points people to Jesus, and Jesus glorifies the Father (John 15:26; 16:13-14). Each member of the Trinity respects the others. They maintain a balance between individual personality and corporate identity. In the same way we need to have balance in our approach to the Spirit. Proper theology and proper living are always a matter of balance. We must not focus so completely on the person and work of the Spirit that we lose sight of the central figure of time and eternity, the Lord Jesus Christ. We must also beware of and avoid the opposite extreme. We must not ignore the person and work of the Holy Spirit. Many churches and Christians treat the Spirit of God as if he did not exist. To ignore the Spirit is a tragic error. We need the Holy Spirit to empower us for daily living. Jesus depended consciously on the Spirit for everything he said or did (John 5:30). We require the presence and power of the Spirit no less than did the Savior. We do not have to go to either of these extremes. We can strive to live in the balanced center of biblical truth about the Holy Spirit.

Unfortunately, many people act as if all that really matters can be bought or sold, enjoyed by the body, or used to make them look good to other people. You might call such people unspiritual, since the realm of the Spirit is not very important to them. On the other hand, to those who are spiritually minded the realm of the unseen is all-important, and God is the most important person in life. Relating to him is the most important relationship. In fact, a spiritual life is one dominated by the Spirit of God. Stop and think about this a moment. In which direction do you tend to actually live out your life—ignoring the unseen or constantly connected?

A primary question relates to the nature of the Holy Spirit. Is the Spirit a person or an impersonal god-force? Consider what the following Scriptures indicate about the nature of the Holy Spirit. *"I will ask the Father, and he will give you another Helper, that he may be with you forever; that is the Spirit of truth, whom the world cannot receive, because it does not behold Him or know Him, but you know Him because he abides with you and will be in you. The Helper, the Holy Spirit, whom the Father will send in my name, he will teach you all things, and bring to your remembrance all that I said to you"* (John 14:16-17, 26, NASB). *"In the same way the Spirit also helps our weakness; for we do not know how to pray as we should, but the Spirit Himself intercedes for us with groanings too deep for words"* (Romans 8:26, NASB).

How do we know that the Holy Spirit is a person distinct from the Father and Son? For one example, read John 15:26, *'When the Counselor comes, whom I will send to you from the Father, the Spirit of truth who goes out from the Father, he will testify about Me."* This verse indicates that the Spirit goes out from the Father and testifies about Jesus.

Romans 5:26 tells us that the Spirit talks to the Father. John 14:17 says that the Father sent the Spirit. You may have drawn from your own Bible knowledge for instances such as Jesus' baptism. All three persons of the Trinity were present on that occasion, but they were separate and distinct (Matthew 3:16-17). From these passages you see that the Holy Spirit is a person, and he is God; yet he is distinct from the Father and Son. Furthermore, a division of responsibility exists between Father, Son, and Spirit. The Holy Spirit's role is that of executive—the one designated to carry out the purposes of God.

Since college days, I have greatly benefitted by keeping a journal. Often my entry will be a prayer telling the Lord how I feel about my situation, praising him for something about him I especially appreciate, or calling on him to help. As I finish, I always pause to tell the Lord my personal response to what he has been teaching me. I share my prayer response with you for today's reading. If you feel the same sort of response and wish to use this prayer as your own, please feel free to do so. Or perhaps my prayer will trigger something you wish to talk to the Lord about. Writing out that response in your own journal will help you. Whatever form your prayer response takes, be sure to close each day's reading by talking directly to God about what you have read. Below I offer my response to today's reading on spiritual realities.

Heavenly Father, thank You that You are real and that Your unseen world, which goes beyond my senses and beyond scientific measurement, is more important than everything I see. Thank You for giving me Your blessed Spirit. May I grow to know Him better and to experience His presence and power. Teach me all I need to know about the Holy Spirit, but especially help me learn to walk with Him all my days. I ask this with confidence because I come in the authority of Jesus' name.

September 27
Individual Faith or Corporate Faith?
2 Corinthians 4:18

"We fix our attention, not on things that are seen, but on things that are unseen. What can be seen lasts only for a time, but what cannot be seen lasts forever." (2 Corinthians 4:18, GNB)

When we study the activity of the Spirit in our lives, we could become very introspective, even self-oriented. We live in an age of radical individualism and some people might see "spiraling up" as a very exclusive relationship between God and me. But the Holy Spirit won't let that happen! We were born in community, and we were designed to live in community. Furthermore, the more like God we become the more we'll be oriented outward, preoccupied with others, not with self. And the startling thing is this: God has chosen to do His work in the world through us! So a major activity of the Holy Spirit is to get God's purposes on planet earth accomplished through His people reaching out.

"People reaching out," however, does not mean individuals doing God's work independently of one another. God's method is called the church. The Spirit of God works primarily through and in relation to the church. How have you seen the latter days of Covid impacting church attendance? Are we still reaching out? Perhaps we've become passive in affirming that "being spiritual" is all we need.

The off-duty flight attendant sitting beside me on the plane was an articulate conversationalist. As we talked, I learned that she was active in her church and occasionally listened to Billy Graham on TV. Yes, she believed what he taught, though she herself was not a member of an evangelical church. What about her husband? "Well, he doesn't have any use for church," she said. "But he is very spiritual." Spiritual? What did she mean? She meant what many people today mean by the word spiritual. She meant that her husband believed in an unseen world and was interested in it. The contemporary fascination with the unseen represents a mega-shift in Western thinking. For several centuries we have concentrated on what can be seen and measured: scientific facts and the competence of the human mind to figure it all out. But now it seems feeling is more important than thinking; unseen forces are center stage. Spiritual is in, and the most ungodly people are said to be spiritual. But is this what the Bible means by spiritual? Biblical spirituality grows out of the nature and activities of God. God is a spirit-being, not material; we were originally created in His image.

Three approaches to understanding the word *spiritual* coexist in our society. Generally, people use the word *spiritual* in one of the following ways:

1. Some people deny that we have a spiritual nature or that a spiritual world beyond the reach of science exists: we might call this the naturalistic worldview. With the dawn of the scientific era, many people embraced the scientific method as the only way to valid knowledge and came to view the unseen world as nonexistent or at least irrelevant. According to this view, the meaning of spirit must be limited to the processes of the natural world.

2. Some people recognize our spiritual nature and dabble in the spiritual world. They choose not to limit themselves to biblical guidelines for dealing with spiritual reality. We might call this the spiritualistic worldview. Today angels, magic, reincarnation, prayer, horoscopes, crystals and the occult, and life-after-death experiences fill newspapers, magazines, and talk shows. Maybe the interest came from the Eastern belief systems with New Age thinking. Some say it came from widespread disillusionment with a sterile, rational approach to life—the scientific outlook. Science, it turned out, wasn't solving our basic human problems. Wherever this new concept of spirituality came from, it influences many people today. This view recognizes the reality of the spiritual dimension but does not always distinguish between the good and the evil aspects of that spiritual world.

3. Others recognize our spiritual nature and the spirit world but choose to deal with the Spirit world only through a relationship with the God of the Bible: I call this the biblical worldview. Those who believe the Bible recognize that the material, visible world is not all that exists in life; it is not even the most important part. To treat what we can see, hear, touch, or taste as if the world we see were everything—or even the most important thing—will sooner or later lead to disaster. Paul reminded the people of Corinth of this truth in 2 Corinthians 4:18. Christians recognize the spiritual world, and they deal with it through obedience to the Triune God.

Only the biblical view of the world can provide a foundation for building a true and effective spiritual life. I am grateful that people are beginning to recognize an unseen, "spiritual" realm, but we need to know just what really is out there. We need the ability to distinguish what part of that unseen world is good and what is not. If we want to understand spiritual reality and to link up only with the good part, we need to get better acquainted with the source of all spiritual good, the Holy Spirit of God. What about you? Do you try to experiment with "the spiritual world" or do you work to understand the spiritual through a relationship with the God of the Bible? Where will you invest your life? How will you know what is good? Take a few minutes and evaluate if you working to reach out in community primarily through and in relation to the church. Perhaps you allowed the isolation of Covid or past disappointments to sever that relationship. Why not commit to pursuing the spiritual world within the context of biblical community?

September 28
Much Power
Colossians 4:2-4

"Continue earnestly in prayer, being vigilant in it with thanksgiving; meanwhile praying also for us, that God would open to us a door for the word, to speak the mystery of Christ, for which I am also in chains, that I may make it manifest, as I ought to speak." (Colossians 4:2-4 NKJV)

A magnificent southern thunderstorm was entertaining me one evening. From my porch, I watched the display of cosmic fireworks when all of a sudden there was a mighty explosion right in our backyard—an extravaganza of sight and sound. Lightning had struck the transformer. In a moment, we lost all light and power—for days we were without power. Yet just a half mile away, giant electrical towers trooped through the fields, bearing unlimited supplies of light and power. The situation reminded me of how many Christians live. Power flows all around them, but they aren't connected.

Holy Spirit power flows through prayer. Prayer forms the human conduit for divine energy. Since the Spirit acts in response to the believing prayer of an obedient people, prayer is the most important part of evangelism. As E.M. Bounds said, "Much prayer, much power, little prayer, little power, no prayer, no power."

If we pray for our missionaries at all, it may be a routine reading over some brief request. But the kind of prayer Paul describes is very different. In these verses he calls such prayer "struggling." He describes it with the words "earnestly," "always laboring fervently." It sounds like a spiritual battle in prayer against unseen enemies that fight to hold captive those we aim to release. Notice that our prayer isn't to be occasional but continuing, regular—daily, at least. Furthermore, our fervent labor in prayer is not only the regular set times for prayer but in-between times. We are to be sensitive to the Spirit's intimations of special need for special prayer. When Paul says, "with thanksgiving," he doesn't mean merely saying thank you when God answers, important as that is.

We are to thank God for the answer even as we ask. In other words, faith-filled prayer. Paul gives instruction on what we're to pray about: (1) the missionary's ministry and (2) the missionary's life. The Holy Spirit must empower both or nothing of eternal significance will be done. He said to pray that doors of opportunity would open up and that the missionary team would have the ability to make the mysterious gospel understandable. That's Spirit-energized ministry.

Paul recognized the need for the fruit of the Spirit as seen in his instruction to believers in that same passage: "Be wise in the way you act toward outsiders, make the most of every opportunity. Let your conversation be always full of grace, seasoned with salt, so that you may know how to answer everyone" (Colossians 4:5-6). Furthermore, Paul tells the Ephesians in a similar passage (Ephesians 6:19-20) to plead with God that he might have courage. Missionaries may have the most glorious, good news; but if their lives don't demonstrate the beauty and strength of Christ, their proclamation will not be as effective as it could be. So we must pray for both the ministry and the life, the gifts of the Spirit and the fruit of the Spirit.

On home leave from service overseas, I had just completed my report on Japan and stood at the door of the church to greet the people. I felt a tug on my jacket. Looking around I saw a tiny, retired schoolteacher who said, "Robertson, I know you're busy, but please don't leave till I have a chance to talk with you for a minute." "Why, Miss Ethelyn," I responded, "I'm not busy; let's talk right now." I knew she prayed for me continually and fervently, one who was combat-ready and fighting my spiritual wars with me. We went to a nearby stone wall, and no sooner had we sat than she began to pepper me with questions about my work. I soon realized she knew more about my work than my fellow missionaries. When she began to ask about the conference I had left in Japan just 48 hours earlier, I said, "Miss Ethelyn, how do you know all this stuff?" "Why, Robertson," she remonstrated, "you're my missionary! I've been praying for you for 12 years. I should know something, shouldn't I?"

Perhaps you don't know any missionaries that well. You need to design a strategy to get involved in God's enterprise as an intercessory prayer warrior. Why not ask your pastor or your denominational headquarters to introduce you to a missionary who works in an area in which you may have an interest? Most missionaries send out regular reports with prayer requests. Ask the missionary(ies) you choose to put you on their mailing list. When missionaries visit the church, invite them home for dinner. And don't spend the time reworking the Super Bowl! Pull their story out of them, learn what their prayer needs are. Then pray! If you don't have a missionary you can call "my missionary," why not make a telephone call to the church office or write a letter right now? Get started!

September 29
Gifts and Fruit
1 Corinthians 12:28-31

"And God has appointed in the church first apostles, second prophets, third teachers, then miracles, then gifts of healing, helping, administrating, and various kinds of tongues. Are all apostles? Are all prophets? Are all teachers? Do all work miracles? Do all possess gifts of healing? Do all speak with tongues? Do all interpret? But earnestly desire the higher gifts." (1 Corinthians 12:28-31)

Surely all gifts are of equal importance to him? Careful! The central purpose of 1 Corinthians 12-14 is to get the church to understand that gifts are not all of equal importance for accomplishing God's will. Some gifts are less important. The church at Corinth was focusing on one of those less-important gifts (speaking in tongues). Furthermore, the church at Corinth should have focused on some very important gifts, but they didn't—gifts like apostle, prophet, teacher. Paul even numbered them: *"And God has appointed in the church first apostles, second prophets, third teachers, then miracles, then gifts of healing, helping, administrating, and various kinds of tongues."* (1 Corinthians12:28), so they wouldn't miss the point. He doesn't continue his numbering system beyond those three, so they may just be representative. But these three give a hint as to what Paul considers more important— roles that seem to have the greatest impact for God's purposes in the church and in the world.

My personal definition of his top three would be pioneer missionary evangelist (apostle), power-filled preaching (prophesy), and Spirit-anointed teaching. These three represent important tasks indeed. If you read chapters 12-14 of 1 Corinthians in a hurry, you may conclude that Paul is contrasting lower gifts with the highest gift, love. If you draw that conclusion, you will miss the point. Paul is teaching the people at Corinth about spiritual gifts, and having exhorted them to seek the higher ones, he pauses for a mid-course correction. "Don't get me wrong," he says. "These gifts, even the more important ones, aren't the most important thing. Love is most important." Love isn't a "gift" in the sense Paul is talking about; he calls it a "way." "I'll show you an even better way"—better than the best gift (1 Corinthians 12:31).

Elsewhere Paul describes love as the fruit of the Spirit. So let's not confuse fruit with gifts. Gifts are Spirit-given abilities; fruit represents Spirit-developed character. Paul's command in verse 31 is to desire Spirit-given abilities to serve God, but his teaching in all of chapter 13 is that love is more important than any gift. The importance of a gift does not imply that one gift is more spiritual than another. Spiritual has to do with fruit of the Spirit, likeness to Jesus, as Paul concludes in 1 Corinthians 13. Also, importance does not equal greater reward. Reward is based on faithfulness, not outward results. To accomplish God's mission on earth, however, some gifts are of greater importance than others.

For 12 years I was a pioneer missionary evangelist. My job was starting churches, a very high calling according to Paul. Today I'm primarily a homemaker, which calls more for fruit than for gifts. My Spirit-given gifts have a limited outlet through some writing and speaking. But I'm not claiming that my role in life is as important as anyone else's. My calling cannot compare with that of others in terms of eternal impact. God only expects that we be faithful to our own calling. Then the whole body can function smoothly. In turn, we will find personal fulfillment, and God will be pleased. We might find security and significance as we use our spiritual gifts. Although we've learned something about what the gifts are by examining the biblical lists of gifts, apparently the Holy Spirit didn't intend to give a clear-cut list of specific job descriptions. Perhaps He intended for us to see what needs doing and trust him to provide people with the abilities needed to do it. Can you describe your calling? Or define your ministry? How does God want to use you in building up His kingdom?

September 30
Seasons
Psalm 92:12-14

"The righteous flourish like the palm tree and grow like a cedar in Lebanon. They are planted in the house of the LORD; they flourish in the courts of our God. They still bear fruit in old age; they are ever full of sap and green." (Psalm 92:12-14)

Some people think the only thing worse than growing old is the alternative: not growing old! I often have occasions to tell an older friend, "Gettin' old ain't fer sissies!" And yet, I recently read a report on research on happiness. You know what they discovered? The oldest Americans are the happiest segment of the population! Yet for many there are feelings of uselessness, loneliness, bitterness, and a fear of possible illness and financial insecurity.

But I don't fear growing old. In fact, I sort of enjoy it. Why? The Bible has special promises for us old folks. Our resources are the promises of God. In fact, the Bible has promises for every one of the problems of aging. Think about it.

As we grow older and are tempted to feel less and less useful, there's something we need to remember: God is much more concerned with who we are than in what we do. At Easter time some years ago I visited two close friends who were growing old. Both were ailing and could do less and less. Both had served powerfully as pastors, one in long years of missionary work, the other in education. They were miserable and had given up on life. Cranky, hard to live with. I tried to persuade them that their value and significance does not depend on what they accomplish but in what kind of person they become. But they couldn't even hear me. They said their role model is Caleb who was still fighting wars in his old age!

Many people are miserable in old age because they can't do things of significance. Their sense of worth is tied to their activity. Even Christians think they must earn God's approval by hard work and can't relax, trust God's grace and enjoy God and His gifts. For all those feelings of uselessness, the Bible has a promise: "The righteous will flourish...like trees...that still bear fruit in old age and are always green and strong." Ps. 92:12-14.

"Aunt" Mary was over 100 years of age. In her prime she was a successful businesswoman when women didn't do that sort of thing. But for her last 25 years she was in a nursing home, the last 10 years abed. No family, alone. Useless, right? No, she was very valuable to many people, including me. She prayed for people, for God's work around the world. Do you want to do something significant? Prayer is the most important work a person can do! And she strengthened all of us who knew her. Instead of feeling sorry for herself and complaining, she was always cheerful, full of gratitude for a lifetime of God's faithfulness toward her. Visitors left her feeling uplifted. Such a useful person!

Our role changes through the seasons of life, as we grow older, but we must not cling to the past or we will destroy ourselves. God has ever new purposes for us to fulfill—a special purpose for each person at each stage of life. "Do not cling to events of the past or dwell on what happened long ago. Watch for the new thing I am going to do." (Is. 43:18,19)

Of course, that new assignment God has for you may be some significant work for him but more likely it may be a quiet ministry of prayer as in Aunt Mary's case. Whatever, it will certainly be to put His glorious character on display, and to be His companion. Useless? We are useful to God and people at any age as we fulfill what God has called us to be and do at that stage. And when we do His assignment we have His assurance that we are very useful. To him, if not to anyone else!

October 1
Downcast
Psalms 42 & 43

"As the deer pants for streams of water, so my soul pants for you, my God..... My soul is downcast within me; therefore I will remember you.... Deep calls to deep in the roar of your waterfalls; all your waves and breakers have swept over me. Why, my soul, are you downcast? Why so disturbed within me? Put your hope in God, for I will yet praise him, my Savior and my God." (Psalm 42:1,6,7,11)

One thing that is fun is to go out on the beach and get out beyond the breakers in an inner tube and get in it and just relax. Don't quite go to sleep, but you just sit out there and relax and it rocks you And then the current takes you a down the beach and to finally you float to land on some gentle, rolling breaker that leads you in. One day I was so relaxed and so happy just sitting and waiting for that exhilarating moment, when all of a sudden it seemed that the whole ocean just went out instead of in, and I dropped into it. And then the most gigantic breaker that was ever created fell on me. Well, it lifted me up, turned me upside down and landed me smack on my head. And then it began to tumble me like a tumbleweed underwater. Which direction I didn't know, but fortunately was toward shore, disoriented. I was aching all over. I was half conscious. I said to myself, "McQuilkin, you seem to have lost control of your destiny."

Have you ever been there? Maybe it's a money breaker, or maybe it's some huge exam and you can just see it, maybe it's some illness and a loved one. Conflict with someone? You seem to have lost control. Life gets so bad, you feel like you're melting inside, just utterly hopeless, almost like your bones are collapsing. You begin to wonder yourself if God has abandoned you. David had the same experience. And in Psalm 42 and 43. He paints this black, black picture. *"Why are you so downcast?"* This form of this verb used, says, "it's not why do you let someone cast you down, but why do you bend yourself down? Why do you bend yourself out of shape?" *"Oh my soul, why so disturbed within me?"* It's a word used of a raging sea within.

My spirit is downcast within me. Perhaps it's the cascading whitewater, or perhaps it's the waterspout - the tornado in the ocean, where the terror of the wind and the terror of the sea meet, and one roars and calls to another- one terrifying experience. God, it's your waves and the breakers have swept over me. *"Put your hope in God, I will yet praise him, my Savior, my God."(Psalm 42:11)*

I say to God my rock, *"Why? Have you forgotten me? Why must I go about mourning, oppressed by the enemy? My bones suffer mortal agony*." (Psalm 43:2) The idea is of a shattering of the bones to bits and fragments.

The pathway home is dark. Treacherous. Like steppingstones through a jungle swamp in the starless night. Why have you been relying on your brains, on your bank account, on your family, on your friend? On some special relationship? David chides himself, "Why do you allow the storms to rage within? Why do you allow yourself to slip off the pathway? Into the bag of dark self-pity. Don't you know God is your rock? He's the solid pathway. Have confidence in him. He has the strength enough for each of us and our small problems. He has the wisdom to lead us on. And he loves us; hope in God."

Here is the secret, praise. Our problem is that we focus our lens on our circumstances. We get it in very sharp focus so that we can see all the details. And God becomes fuzzy and out of focus around the perimeter of our vision. Or perhaps he's off the picture altogether. David says praise him, enumerate His splendor, His glory, His beautiful character. Focus sharply on God and the circumstances will come into focus as need be. Praise not only hoping but resting with patient expectancy.

It's a special kind of praise and it's a special light on our pathway, the singing heart. Is it nighttime in your experience today? Is your spirit dark and foreboding? You are uncertain about the future? Turn your thoughts to Jesus.

How much do you want it? You will have it to the extent that you really want it. How much did David want? He tells us like a deer chased by the animals, hounds hounding his life from him. You can endure hunger for a time. But thirst? And tears will not slack the thirst. Only living water. My thirst pants for you, oh God, send forth your light and your truth. Let them guide me, let them bring me home.

October 2
Connecting
Ephesians 5:18

"And do not be drunk with wine, in which is dissipation; but be filled with the Spirit" (Ephesians 5:18)

Many years ago, when there were thousands of missionaries in India, a study was made of the "casualties"—those who left missionary service for what the mission leadership deemed less-than-satisfactory reasons. They discovered that none of those dropouts were having a daily time alone with the Lord. Alienated from God? Maybe. Spiritual malnutrition? Probably. Spiritually weak or disabled? Some, perhaps. Just too busy in God's behalf, I suppose. This, in spite of the fact that survey after survey indicates the great felt need of missionaries is just such a vital time alone with God. Furthermore, in those surveys the common response was that prayer is the most important factor for success in the missionary enterprise.

I concur. We sense intuitively that God must do God's work and that our link-up with him is prayer. What a mysterious plan for living a godly life and participating in achieving God's purposes in the world! That God the omnipotent, the infinite One, should listen to such as us! Even more, that he should think of us as co-laborers and choose to accomplish his purposes through us.

To achieve His purposes, he tells us, *"Be filled with the Spirit."* This is a command—something I must do—but it's in the passive form, something the Spirit does to me. *"Be being fill*ed" would be an awkward translation but gets at the meaning. So how do I obey if he is the one who does it? I take the initiative and deliberately yield control and then I keep on praying and expecting him to produce the fruit of godliness—*"Be very careful, then, how you live...understand what the Lord's will is."* I expect him to empower for ministry—*"making the most of every opportunity."* He even indicates the inner state of those who are filled—*"Sing and make music in your heart to the Lord, always giving thanks to God the Father for everything."*

Notice another thing about the command. It's a continuous action verb: *"Keep on being filled with the Spirit."* It's a constant in that sense, an abiding relationship. Steady-state filled; you might call it. If I stay tight with him, he'll continually fill me with power to live and serve and to have a singing heart. It won't be like being filled with wine, the counterfeit filling. That's only a temporary high and doesn't change anything for the better. No, no, Paul says, let the Spirit fill you always as a way of life.

The permanent relationship God wants every believer to have can best be described as "full"—fully yielded to the Spirit's control, giving evidence in a life and ministry energized by His own power, and an inner sense of joy in His presence. Then, from time to time, of His grace, he'll blow into your life with gale force and fan the embers into an all-consuming fire of the Spirit's own making. Filled full!

With all the analysis, however, let's never forget that the basic idea of being filled is a relationship. We mustn't focus on theological formulations, important as they are, nor do we focus on experience, exciting as that is. He intends a personal relationship

Part of that mysterious plan is the connection with divine power he provides: prayer. Of course, prayer isn't the only means God has provided. The Spirit has given us other weapons as well, weapons to join him in waging war, tools to participate with him in his remodeling project. "Means of grace" we call them, given to spiral us up toward ever greater likeness to Jesus, to ever more intimate companionship with him, and to empower our life. Among those means of grace, prayer is indispensable.

Into our reflection on our prayer life I'll fold the element of soul food—God speaking to us through his Word. We'll not be considering Bible study for ministry or professional growth, but the devotional use of the Bible. Bible research for ministry can be transmuted into warm personal communion with God, of course, but in those studies often we're preoccupied with what the passage should mean to those to whom we minister. So today we focus on looking to Scripture for a personal encounter with God, hearing the whispers of the Spirit through the love letters he's prepared for us, what he is saying to us as well as what we may say to him. Why not spend some time in the Word asking for an encounter with him, listening for His whisper?

October 3
Intimacy
1 Corinthians 13:13

"So now faith, hope, and love abide, these three; but the greatest of these is love." (1 Corinthians 13:13)

Our next generation is onto something. On a flight to Philadelphia my seatmate was a 14-year-old, right in the middle of that generation. I soon discovered his parents were recently divorced so asked if he'd seen it coming. He choked up, looked out the window and shook his head. I tried to offer hope in Jesus and he took me to mean "church."

"I'm not speaking of church, Kevin. I'm talking about a personal relationship. I understand your generation is after intimacy. Is that right?"

"You mean sex?"

"Well, not just sex, but a caring relationship of intimate sharing, an openness, a vulnerability..."

Kevin spoke quietly, almost to himself, "And trust."

A generation that has had all its trusts betrayed is in quest of someone it can count on. They're not quite as hopeless as the generation before them, so small hopes glimmer around the edges of their consciousness. But the deepest longing of, perhaps, any generation, is an intimate, enduring love relationship.

I tried to explain to Kevin, my partner on the plane, about intimacy with Jesus and I used the expression, "tight with Jesus." Instantly he shot back, "Are you tight with Jesus?" Guess that's the question I'd like to ask you. Are you tight with Jesus? Not every Christian is you know. Trust? Yes. Hope? Yes. But the *greatest of these is love. (1 Corinthians 13:13)*

As we have seen, the ultimate goal of life is not power-packed ministry, exciting as that is. Nor is the Spirit's goal merely to make us godly in character. The holy life is a means toward the ultimate goal, for only as we are like him, God-compatible, can we respond in the kind of loving intimacy he designed us for. Compatibility is the key to a happy marriage. Isn't it so? Sad the marriage where husband and wife have no shared interests, no common values, no passionate commitment to the same goals in life. A miserable co-existence as strangers under one roof. Or divorce. "Incompatibility," the legal documents say.

And so with God and you. He wants you to be like him, God-compatible, so you can be intimate companions. And he empowers for ministry so you can partner with him in bringing about his purposes in the world, bringing others into the family. But above all, the celebration on that Great Day will focus on the climax of a lifetime of intimate companionship, uninhibited union with your forever Lover.

October 4
Lord of the Harvest
Luke 10:2

"And he said to them, "The harvest is plentiful, but the laborers are few. Therefore pray earnestly to the Lord of the harvest to send out laborers into his harvest." (Luke 10:2)

It is easy to predict the future of the missionary enterprise: it will be successful! "I will build my Church," Jesus assures us. And, "*This Gospel...<u>shall be proclaimed</u> in all the world for a witness and then the end will come.*" (Matthew 16:18; 24:14). The only questions are who will do it and when will it be done? The Church will do it, but in what generation? I predict that this generation will not complete the task. Unless, of course, God surprises us with an unprecedented intervention.

He has done that twice in the past. Who would have predicted the end of the Soviet strangle-hold on hundreds of millions of people in the 20th century? And consider China--where communism still reigns. A report from a Chinese government agency, which has never admitted more than ten million Christians, conceded there are 63 million! God did it twice, so let us pray he will do it again—in those countries still and for the worlds of Islam and Hinduism.

There may be an even greater divine intervention needed, however: revival among Christians. Without it, we will never mobilize the task force necessary to complete the job. Yet, some say we are nearing completion of the task. They point out that there is now one Bible-believing Christian for every seven non-Christians. Such is the optimism of statistical percentages. There are two problems with this. Without a radical change of values among believers, the "one" isn't going to reach the "seven." But the even greater error is talking percentages without dealing with the absolute numbers of those still alienated from the Father. The population explosion is so great that, in spite of unprecedented spiritual harvest, more lost people are now living than have lived and died throughout recorded human history. And half of these, at least, live outside the reach of a witnessing church. Thus without special divine intervention we cannot be optimistic about finishing the task anytime soon.

But we are called to faithfulness whatever the situation, and there are certain trends in missionary ministry that can be predicted. The emphasis on reaching the unreached and starting churches among them will continue and increase.

I applaud the emphasis on short term service and "tent-making" ministry. If God's people utilize these two approaches with wisdom, not expecting of them that which they cannot produce and safeguarding short-termers and tentmakers from frustration and failure, they prove to be instruments in the hands of the Lord of the harvest.

Never has there been a time for greater pessimism--the task is impossibly great and the laborers woefully inadequate. But never has there been a time for greater optimism--the resources are here and God is moving in unprecedented ways. Let us cry out to him for other incredible interventions, including the movement of his Spirit in our own lives and churches.

October 5
Bible Study
2 Timothy 2:15

"Do your best to present yourself to God as one approved, a worker who does not need to be ashamed and who correctly handles the word of truth." (2 Timothy 2:15)

The first and fundamental task of Bible study is to determine what the Bible author meant and what that means today. To put it another way, the two-fold task of the interpreter is to determine (1) the meaning the author intended to communicate and (2) the response God desires. The two are intimately related. What the text says to God's people today must be based on and flow directly from what it said to God's people originally or the sermon is no longer an authoritative word from God. So your task is to understand and apply the biblical text authentically.

The problem is that many of us seem not to handle the text well. Paul says that is shameful. We are to study diligently in order to stand before God unashamed because we have handled his Word rightly (2 Tim 2:15). Yet, listening to some Sunday morning sermons, one begins to wonder if he has been watching a smoke and mirrors trick in which Bible words are used as a masquerade for the preacher's inherited tradition, current fad, or personal predisposition. Good and uplifting, perhaps, but did the original author really intend to communicate <u>that</u>? And if it is not demonstrable that he did, can I be sure God expects me to respond the way the preacher says I should?

How can you miss the intent of the biblical author? Perhaps one's Bible study tools have grown rusty through neglect. The rigorous pursuit of the author's intended meaning has been by-passed to get on with the urgent task of telling others exactly what you have been burdened about of late.

Whatever the cause of the deficiency, the result is that we who should be learning how to understand and apply Scripture authentically have, instead, a model of handling Scripture that will be impossible to follow or that might prove disastrous if they did.

The twofold task of Bible study derives from the nature of the Book. It was authored by human beings so the first task is to use the basic tools of understanding human communication to get at the meaning intended by the author. The Bible is more than human in origin, however. It was inspired by God and thus is <u>God's</u> Word, so the second task is to derive from the meaning of the text what response God desires from his people today.

How glorious a responsibility! We live, not by physical nourishment alone, but by the words God has communicated to us. And our people, in turn, live by that same spiritual nourishment, not by our own wisdom. And we will do more than subsist, we will flourish if we feed ourselves. We can feed ourselves the Word of God, however, only if we learn how that Word is to be understood and applied. Our task, then, is not to dazzle people with ideas that no one could ever imagine were hidden away behind the text, but to demonstrate how we read it with understanding and apply it to our own lives with integrity.

Context is king for the meaning of words; the same is true for analyzing the flow of thought. If one has the linguistic tools to trace the grammatical construction, use them. But if one does not, do not use that as an excuse to bypass this critical step in careful study. The structure or flow can be discerned for most passages in a good translation and certainly can be examined.

After thoroughly examining the background of the text, the key words, and the structure or flow of thought in the passage chosen for exposition, the entire context must be examined. Context is still king, so the meaning of a passage must not be studied in isolation. It must fit and flow from the context of the entire chapter, the entire book. In fact, many make it a practice to read the entire context, even the entire book, many times before beginning the detailed analysis of the passage, getting a "feel" for the author's flow of thought.

Why consider these Bible study principles? We must be faithful to God's intent when He superintended the writing of the scriptures. What does He really want us to know and do? That is the question for you today. How well do you handle the Word of God?

October 6
After Start
Matthew 18:19-20

"Again, truly I tell you that if two of you on earth agree about anything they ask for, it will be done for them by my Father in heaven. For where two or three gather in my name, there am I with them." (Matthew 18:19-20)

It cost $35, my first automobile, and I was very grateful to have a friend who would sell his ancient and diminutive 1931 Austin at such a price, but it wouldn't start! After weeks of tinkering and conning the neighborhood kids into pushing me round and round the block, one glorious day it coughed into life. A start is a great thing. But only if it is the beginning of movement. Sadly, the object of my pride and affection soon sputtered to a stop. In fact, like some new Christians who worked so hard to get started, that Austin never did go very far. Start is emptied of significance if it stops!

Has your walk with God proven to be static state-motionless or will it prove to be the beginning of dynamic movement with God for a lifetime? Let's spend a few minutes in thinking about how to keep moving and even accelerate advancing the Kingdom.

To build momentum we pray and plan, as well as plan and pray. Some are better at planning than praying, but they don't get very far in advancing God's purposes, like a well-designed engine with no fuel. Others are strong on prayer but not much for concrete planning, like igniting a tank of gasoline in the street. Lots of excitement but not much mileage. Both prayer and planning are needed, and they are needed together, plans emerging from and effected through prayer, prayer focused on and resulting in action.

When it comes to accomplishing God's purpose of world evangelism we are talking about a particular kind of prayer: intercessory warfare, both strategic and tactical. Strategic prayer is for the whole cause of world evangelism and is most effective when based on a promise of God. "*Ask of me,*" the Father promised his Son, "*and I will give you the nations for your inheritance, the uttermost parts of the earth for your possession*" (Psalm 2:8). How about joining the Son in asking the Father for one specific unreached "nation" or people? And keep on warring in prayer combat till the answer comes!

One of our regular number was missing from our prayer group and we were asked to pray for him as he was in London at a strategy meeting to plan the conquest of Albania. They told me that as freshmen, five of them had banded together to pray for the five most unreached nations of the world and now as seniors they were planning their initial assaults.

Another strategic prayer: "*Pray the Lord of the harvest that he will thrust out laborers into the harvest*" (Matthew 9:39). Pray for the whole enterprise, as we are woefully shorthanded even today, over 2,000 years after Christ said, with broken heart, "The laborers are few." Pray for students preparing for Christian ministry, by name if you know any. Strategic prayer.

But this same prayer can be tactical, praying by name for those we know who might be used of God in some unharvested field. Perhaps someone who hasn't yet caught fire, perhaps someone who had the vision but now wavers, but certainly needs prayer reinforcement. Tactical prayer is not for the whole cause of world evangelism but for one particular battle, one particular person or team. And tactical prayer includes the personal, "Lord, what will you have me to do?" Daily reaffirm to the Lord your commitment, seek to know his assignment for you for that day and for the future, and claim his power for your life and witness.

Not only private prayer, however, is essential to successfully prosecute the war. There is power in united prayer (Matthew 18:19, 20). Pray with a partner, pray with a team of allies who have the same heart, pray regularly and meet on special occasions of extended prayer. God moves in answer to the united prayer of an obedient people. Neglect prayer and the most wonderful start won't move you very far for God.

After starting, where? Keep going! Pray and plan, plan and pray, get involved, and partner with others to make sure that God's will is done on earth as it is in heaven--swiftly, whole-heartedly, fully, to completion--and to make your own life count to the maximum for his purpose of world evangelization!

October 7
Anger
James 1:19-20

"Let every person be quick to hear, slow to speak and slow to anger, for the anger of man does not produce the righteousness of God." (James 1:19-20)

Incredibly, Christ's commentary on the sixth commandment includes a person's inner state. Anger is subject to God's judgment (Matthew 5:22). This was not original with Jesus. Moses had already recorded God's will, "You shall not hate your brother in your heart . . . or bear any grudge against the sons of your own people, but you shall love your neighbor as yourself " (Leviticus 19:17-18). Lack of love, as well as positive hatred, is a form of murder.

Anger is not always wrong. If it were, God would be the chief sinner, for he is angry every day (Psalm 7:11). And note that David does not say God is angry merely at sin. He is angry with wicked people. The wrath of God is seen throughout the Old and New Testaments and is the inevitable result of his holy character exposed to unholy attitudes and behavior.

But is it possible for a sinful mortal to be godlike in his anger? It must not be easy, for the Bible is filled with teaching against anger. Anger is to be put away (Ephesians 4:31; Colossians 3:8); whoever is angry is in danger of judgment (Matthew 5:22); anger is one of the works of the flesh (Galatians 5:19-20); it does not work the righteousness of God (James 1:20); and it is the prerogative of God, not man (Romans 12:19). Proverbs condemns anger repeatedly.

But Jesus was angry (Mark 3:5), and we are commanded in our anger to refrain from sin (Psalm 4:4; Ephesians 4:26), to be slow about it (Titus 1:7; James 1:19), and to get over it quickly (Ephesians 4:26). There seems to be approval of being angry under some circumstances, but the major biblical emphasis is on anger as evil; exceptions seem very limited.

Anger at sin, even anger at the sinner, can be a good thing (2 Corinthians 7:11). Jeremiah was full of the fury of the Lord (6:11), and Paul was angry over the idolatry of the Athenians (Acts 17:16). Yet Christ himself refrained from anger when the offense was against him personally (1 Peter 2:23-24), and "like a sheep that before its shearers is dumb, so he opened not his mouth" (Isaiah 53:7).

Righteous and unrighteous anger can be distinguished by the cause of anger. One should be angry over sin that offends God, harms others, or harms the person sinning. The difficulty with being righteously indignant is that our motives are mixed. Am I distressed over a sin that offends God and harms people, or am I angry over the way I am affected? Since motives are mixed, the safe thing may be to eschew anger altogether when the sin of another directly affects me, as when my child does wrong but the wrong embarrasses me. Better to wait till the anger subsides to be sure the resulting action does not come from a mixture of righteous and unrighteous indignation. Anger is sinful when it is for the wrong reason or results in the wrong action.

To keep this emotion from igniting for the wrong reason or from burning out of control, Scripture gives two ways of control: Take it easy—don't get angry suddenly (James 1:19), and don't let it keep burning—don't let it last till the next day (Ephesians 4:26). Either a "low flashpoint," a quick response without reflection, or a "slow burn," continuing on with the emotion, seem to risk causing even righteous indignation to go astray.

Against the clear teaching of Scripture that most (not all) human anger is wrong, and that the proper response is to control it (Proverbs 16:32), many Christian psychologists hold that anger is morally neutral and must be expressed.[2] To this we respond that anger is neutral in the same way that hatred and killing are neutral: Sometimes they are right; mostly they are wrong. Anger in itself is a wrong emotion to have if it is directed against the wrong object (God, an innocent person, a thing); for the wrong cause (personal offense); or leads to wrong behavior (retaliation, vengeance, physical violence).

Anger under these circumstances should not be denied *or* expressed. It should rather be confessed as sin and the resources of God appropriated to control the emotion itself. We need to be encouraged to evaluate in the light of Scripture whether our anger is godly and, if it is not, to confess our sin, thus removing all guilt. Then we should trust God for his resources in overcoming the temptation.

How is this for you? Perhaps you excuse anger as justified. Are you offended? Is the object of your anger appropriate? Can you maintain self-control? Do you want your own way? Are you protecting yourself or others? What is the outcome of your anger? Take a few minutes and reflect on the impact of your anger and how you might have a reason, action, or outcome that honors God.

October 8
Road Blocks And Detours in Kingdom Work
Matthew 16:24-26

"Then Jesus told his disciples, "If anyone would come after me, let him deny himself and take up his cross and follow me. For whoever would save his life will lose it, but whoever loses his life for my sake will find it. For what will it profit a man if he gains the whole world and forfeits his soul? Or what shall a man give in return for his soul?" (Matthew 16:24-26)

There are many obstacles that test your motives, your character, and your commitment to the cause of world evangelization and Christian service. The most common of these is marriage.

Don't accept the third date! You might ask for or accept a second date with a person to be polite, but the third date may well encourage one or both to get ideas about something more serious. And nothing deflects from God's highest will like emotional involvement with one of the opposite sex, resulting in **marriage to the wrong person**. In fact, the female/male attraction is almost too strong for the Holy Spirit to counter! This is an exaggeration, of course, but I put it boldly to make the point that you should not become emotionally involved with anyone who does not already have the same level of passion for the Lord and the lost world that you find in your own spirit. You wish to engender that spirit in your friend? Ask God to provide someone else to do it if there is the slightest stirring of romantic attraction in your own spirit or the possibility of that stirring in the other person. I have personally seen scores of young people blocked off from God's purposes through a poor choice of friend resulting in a road-block marriage.

Money can block you off from fulfilling God's purposes in two ways--a crushing debt or the fear of raising financial support for Christian service. The best way to get out of debt is not to get into it! Better to take a little longer getting an education than to end up with a debt that makes the day of freedom to pursue service recede beyond the horizon of hope. If you already have a large debt, bend every effort, make every sacrifice necessary to retire that debt and escape the bondage!

The head of the largest mission board in the nation I was visiting was visibly upset as he showed me graphs of the work. Notice, he said, the rapid increase in the number of new missionaries who drop out before completing their first year of service. He assured me this phenomenon was not in missions alone. I asked if there were any explanation, any common denominator. "Well," he said, "They all are of the me generation." He was right and wrong. Wrong in that self-orientation is not new, not limited to any particular generation since Eve made her self-oriented choice. But he was right in that this century is unique in ultimate **commitment to self** as the only honest approach to life. Self-fulfillment is the goal and when the Christian does not find fulfillment he would be dishonest to himself and thus doing wrong to hang tough and pursue what he had begun.

So fallen human nature and contemporary culture conspire to detour us into a dead end. The life that begins with self-affirmation and aims at self-fulfillment, said Jesus, will end in total loss. Rather, true life begins with the opposite-- self-denial--and aims at <u>God's</u> fulfillment. What an incredible paradox! Aim at self-fulfillment and lose it all, aim at God's fulfillment and find your own.

Some Christians flatly **reject** what they know to be **God's will** for them and in rebellion break fellowship and wreck their lives. But far more drift out of vital touch with God through neglecting time with him, his book and his people and through compromising with the values of our age in little choices along the way. Where once he or she was hot for God, going for the fulfillment of God's purpose, a coldness has seeped in. A love for self or for this world grows stronger.

There is only one way to get off this dead-end detour back onto God's mainline and that is to turn around and head back toward God, repenting of all sinful attitudes and actions, and pleading with him to restore the clear vision and the passion for him and a lost world.

What blocks your progress toward maximizing your kingdom effectiveness? Of course, don't divorce your spouse, rather be careful in your choice. True financial freedom is found in spending less than you have. Steward well. Go for fulfilling Go's plan not your own. Obey! Though the stars fall, do right. Pray this for yourself and your children and grandchildren.

Accelerate toward full speed with God, avoiding every roadblock and enticing detour, and finishing the course designed for you with the strength he has pledged to supply.

October 9
Clay Pots
2 Corinthians 4:6 – 5:11

"But we have this treasure in jars of clay, to show that the surpassing power belongs to God and not to us. (2 Corinthians 4:7)

Perhaps your day is beginning. Your blades have been finely honed; you've been polished inside and out till you fairly gleam. But before we begin to think of ourselves more highly than we ought to think, let's be reminded of what we are-humble clay pots! Not diamond-studded golden bowls, just plain old clay pots. But notice an incredible incongruity, an incomprehensible irony. Someone has put in this clay pot a magnificent treasure. So, the value is not in the pot, but in the contents. What is the treasure? The light of the Gospel? The glory of God? The presence of Christ? Yes! And somehow that treasure takes a fragile, insignificant, common clay pot and transforms it. Watch what happens.

Nothing exposes our fragile vulnerability like suffering. *"So we do not lose heart. Though our outer self is wasting away, our inner self is being renewed day by day. For this light momentary affliction is preparing for us an eternal weight of glory beyond all comparison"* (vs 16-17). Sometimes these clay pots are shattered and all of us are shaken. But we don't have the normal response. 2 Corinthians 4:8-9 affirms: *"are afflicted in every way, but not crushed; perplexed, but not driven to despair; persecuted, but not forsaken; struck down, but not destroyed."*

Why do we not have a standard clay pot response? How do we have the response of some magnificent royal vessel? This passage answers those questions--the why and the how. First then, why? Why do we respond so a-typically? Psychologists might say we are suppressing our real feelings and endangering our psychological health. But Paul seems to have another reality that transforms humble, fragile, vulnerable clay pots.

To die is to be swallowed of life. Our son Bob seemed to have been swallowed up in a dark, watery grave when he died in the deep waters of the great lakes in a diving accident Paul says boldly, what really swallowed him that September afternoon was LIFE.

Yet the shattered clay pot doesn't remain a jumble of broken shards. Brian sat in my living room and spoke confidently of his good health, his strong body, his expectancy to life long and serve God well. But at that very moment his clay pot was cracking all over and a few weeks later it was dead. But Paul says, Sunday's coming! Brian will be put together again in a beautiful strong body. Resurrection!

God's life- His power is put on display. This is what happened with my friend Bart. He took in a homeless man, who one night killed him. Those who knew him affirm the character of Christ that was demonstrated in his life. Some who didn't know him have stepped forward to take his place. By living at risk for God's purposes in this world, he joined our Savior in giving his life for lost people. With his blood he indelibly marked our fledgling program in church-starting evangelism. God's power has been vividly put on display.

How can a lowly, fragile, vulnerable clay pot ever hope to respond this way? It is the power of God. Dick Woodward reminds us of the how; "I won't, but he will, I can't, but he can, I don't, but he does."

We give the testimony of our inner condition letting the contents of the pot spill out. During times of suffering, faith turns our world right side up exactly at the point circumstances have turned it upside down. I visited my friend, John Dunlap, in his last days. On the first visit what was seen was the visible which seemed unbearably heavy and never-ending. Paul says whatever these afflictions (and who can compete with Paul!) they are light and temporary. Compared with the unseen, with the invisible realm, which most people consider unreal, is in fact the ultimate reality, the heavy stuff, the permanent. What was happening in John Dunlap's life as his big, strong clay pot disintegrated? A gentleness, patience, kindness his family never knew was in there began to spill out. So, faith works!

Only what's done for Christ will last. Perhaps you have had it all brought into focus by the shattering of the clay pots. Perhaps verses 17-18 will help: *"For this light momentary affliction is preparing for us an eternal weight of glory beyond all comparison, as we look not to the things that are seen but to the things that are unseen. For the things that are seen are transient, but the things that are unseen are eternal."*

October 10
Beautiful Feet
Romans 10:8-21

A frightened jailer who had just been rescued from suicide and execution, cried out, *"What shall I do to be saved?"* and was told, *"Believe on the Lord Jesus Christ and you will be saved."* A successful young businessman asked, *"What shall I do to inherit eternal life?"* and was told, *"Sell what you have, give it to the poor and follow Jesus."* A group of awe-struck Jews called out to a nondescript, uneducated bunch of street-preachers, "What must we do?" They were told, *"Repent and be baptized."*

What did these answers have in common? They were all addressed to particular people in specific historical settings and were never intended to give a theological explanation of how all people in all circumstances are to be saved from sin. But there is a summary statement which is intended to give a more comprehensive, theological definition of saving faith: Romans 10:9: *"if you confess with your mouth that Jesus is Lord and believe in your heart that God raised him from the dead, you will be saved."*

First, one must confess Jesus as Lord. You must be willing to go public with your acknowledgment that you are no longer lord of your life, but that Jesus is Lord. Secondly, you must believe from the heart that God raised Jesus from the dead. In other words, the saving faith of Paul's theology is not in some undefined deity or disembodied philosophical concept, it is in a person, an historical person, a person who through his power over death demonstrated publicly that he is the Savior. His resurrection validates all his claims and as history it is a verifiable fact, not a myth or philosophical abstraction. Thus, reliance on the Savior raised from the dead, and acknowledgement of his absolute authority is what Paul says is "*trusting in him"* (vs 11) or "*calling on him"* (vs 13).

That's how a person gets saved. But how does he get lost? And who is lost? Paul doesn't tell us in this passage, but he has already told us in chapter 3: "*All have sinned and fall short of the glory of God*" and chapter 6, "*The wages of sin is death...*" But, he says here, "*whoever calls on the name of the Lord, will be saved."*

Are there no other ways to life? Are there not, as the Japanese say, "Many paths to the summit of Mount Fuji?"

It is no accident that Paul says, whoever calls on the name. In other words, not just any name will do. Peter said the same thing, "*Neither is there salvation in any other..."*(Acts 4.12). Increasing numbers of liberal evangelicals in our day are saying that people are saved only on the merits of Christ, as Peter and Paul said, but they are saved without knowing about him. They are saved when they are obedient to the light they do have. But Peter said, in the same way Paul says in this passage, "*there is none other name under heaven, given among men whereby we must be saved."* Note that he didn't say, no other person. When you name a name there is no ambiguity, no leeway for conjecture. Christ taught the same thing: "*I am the way, the truth, and the life."* (Jn 14.6). But now we are told people can have the life without going the way or knowing the truth. Jesus seemed to be saying something else: "*No one comes to the Father except by me."* In this passage Paul says that saving "*faith comes from hearing the message, and the message is heard through the word of Christ"* (vs 17).

Some say a person must actively reject the gospel to be lost. But is it fair that people be condemned for not believing something they've never heard of? The answer: they aren't lost for lack of knowledge they don't have. Paul has told us in great detail in Romans 1 and 2 that people are condemned for rejecting the light they do have. And they all have two great lights. Creation and conscience. He hints at this again in this passage; verses 8 and 18.

If people respond to the light they have been given, God has a marvelous plan outlined here: he will get more light to them. Psalm 50:22,23: "*Now consider this you who forget God lest I destroy you: to those who give thanks and seek to do right, GOD WILL SHOW HIS SALVATION."* Psalm 22:26, (LB) "*All who seek the Lord shall find him."* Jesus taught the same thing. He often used the basic principle that those who have will be given more and those who have not will lose even what they have. On one occasion he applied this specifically to spiritual light--those who respond to light with obedience will be given more light, those who reject the light they have will lose even what they had. Paul speaks of this in Romans 1: "*God gave them up".*

When new Christians in Japan asked about the final destination of their ancestors, I responded in the words of Abraham who was debating with God the same issue of righteous people being condemned along with the unrighteous, "*Shall not the judge of all the earth do right?"* (Genesis 18:25).

Does that mean that everyone who lacks knowledge is lost? The Scripture does not directly address this question. So I cannot affirm on the basis of Scripture that every person in every time and place who has not heard of Christ will be lost, but neither can I affirm from Scripture that anyone will be. In other words, since God did not choose to answer our question, we are shut up to speculation. And if we speculate, we are morally accountable for the result of that speculation should it prove to be wrong. On one position, based on the clear teaching of Scripture that all have sinned, and the result is death and that faith in Christ, indeed in the name of Jesus Christ from Nazareth, crucified and risen, is the only way of salvation, one interprets that to mean that all who do not call on that name are lost. The result of that teaching is to put world evangelization at the top of one's priority, to obey the great commission, to find Paul's teaching in this passage life-transforming. Not a bad result.

But consider the outcome of the other conjecture, that many if not most or even all who have not heard of Christ will be saved on his merits because God is loving and fair, a speculation based not on what Scripture anywhere teaches, but on one's deductions from the revealed nature of God. Where is the urgency to point people to the way of life? If fact, would it not logically follow that more would be saved by being left in ignorance and thus not coming under judgment for rejecting light they never had? The nerve of the missionary mandate is cut. And in our day, that is exactly what has happened--more and more of God's people do not believe that people must hear to be saved, as Paul outlines here so forcefully.

Do you believe that people without Christ are lost? Do you care? Does your life demonstrate that you believe and care?

October 11
Pray the Lord of the Harvest
Matthew 9:37-38

"Then he said to his disciples, "The harvest is plentiful, but the laborers are few; therefore pray earnestly to the Lord of the harvest to send out laborers into his harvest." (Matthew 9:37-38)

There's more to great commission prayer than holding the lifeline for the individual missionary. We are commissioned not only to pray for individual missionaries but for the cause at large. The leadership of the church should take the responsibility to set up the link between missionary and prayer partner and, indeed, to mobilize the entire body for in-the-Spirit prayer, personal as well as united.

Jesus commanded, for example, to pray and keep on praying, is the force of the verb, for laborers for the harvest. Because, he said, the unreaped harvest is so very great and the laborers are far too few (Matthew 9:37, 38). I imagine that is the prayer the church at Antioch was praying when God told them to send out their senior pastor and his associate, Barnabas and Paul (Acts 13). And they weren't just offering an occasional "missionary moment" prayer. It says they were fasting and praying and it takes more than 30 minutes of united prayer to be a fast!

For some years I conducted "Great Commission Work Shops" with local church leaders, eight hours of evaluation and planning. Only churches that considered themselves strong in missions would invite me for such a grueling exercise, of course. I discovered a startling thing: the average amount of time devoted to united prayer by some group- large or small- was three minutes a week. And these were the premier missions-minded churches. Even that token prayer was almost exclusively for their own sons and daughters in missions. I found almost none praying as Christ clearly commanded, for laborers for the harvest. Of course, that kind of prayer could be hazardous. Begin to pray that way and God might call the senior pastor, as in Antioch. He might call one of the sons gathered at the family altar should such prayer be made on a regular basis with faith and fervor.

Another strategic prayer is suggested by the Father's invitation to the Son, *"Ask of me and I will give you the nations for your inheritance, the uttermost parts of the earth as your possession"* (Psalm 2:8) We must join the Son in asking the Father for all the nations as an inheritance for the Son. I've long prayed that prayer for Japan and the Bengali. And not just because I had a daughter who labored in Japan for almost two decades and a son who labored for 10 years among the Bengali slum dwellers of Calcutta. I pray that kind of focused prayer because I long for these nations to become part of the Lord Jesus' inheritance. I plead with the Father, "You've answered the prayers of the Son and are giving him China and Korea in unprecedented harvests. Why not just across the water, the people of Japan, and to the south, the largest unreached people group of all "the Bengali?"

We can claim the Father's promise and do what has been called, "adopt a people" for focused prayer until the gift is given. Years after I began that prayer, God began to answer among the Bengali of Bangladesh in which there is unprecedented turning to Christ in one of the most hard-core Muslim nations of the world. Now for the Bengali of India!

We may not understand about spiritual warfare in prayer like Daniel did. He read in Scripture what God's will was for the nations, as we have done, and then, unlike us, he went to his knees for days, for weeks, pleading for the fulfillment of the promise. We read that God heard him and sent the heavenly emissary to answer that prayer, but that Gabriel was detained in mighty combat with celestial evil forces. And Daniel, not knowing that, nevertheless participated in that war through fasting and prayer till victory came (Daniel chapters 8 and 9). We may not understand how all that works, but we know for sure there is powerful resistance by evil powers of spiritual darkness to Gospel advance and that we are called to participate in the battle through prayer.

So the most important part of the missionary enterprise is prayer, individual and corporate, persistent, fervent, untiring. There must be prayer for the individual missionary representative of the church, but there must also be strategic warfare for laborers for the harvest and for the unreached peoples of the world.

"Apostles" are so important in God's program of reaching the whole world because they are the Spirit's point-men (or women), his only strategy for completing the Church and saving humankind. We've seen how all must witness, some must evangelize, some of the evangelists must go to those out of reach of present gospel witness. And we've seen how the "going" will be effective to the extent there is praying.

Are you praying? Fervent, faith-filled, detailed for specific missionaries? Is your church praying for the Lord of the Harvest to send forth laborers? How can you facilitate ever deeper corporate prayer for the missionary enterprise? Why not commit today to deepening your great commission praying and keep on praying? Develop a plan for strategic, specific prayer and fasting for the harvest among unreached peoples of the world.

October 12
Get Moving
Ecclesiastes 4:9-12

"Two are better than one, because they have a good reward for their labor." (Ecclesiastes 4:9)

The missionary enterprise has often moved forward dramatically when God's people have taken leaps of faith. It never moves at all unless individuals take steps of faith in personal involvement.

Commit to give a specific amount of your income--an amount worthy of the sacrificial gift of God's own Son. Share spiritual truth with those outside of Christ whom God puts in your life and lay plans to contact others who don't naturally come your way. If you do not win others to faith now, how can you expect God to use you at some frontier of gospel outreach? And especially get involved in recruiting other believers as world Christians.

The most powerful force for sending out laborers into the harvest is another laborer who invites, "Come with me!" Much more powerful than exhorting, "Go with them!" We need to plan and act aggressively because we are by nature spiritual single focused-we keep focusing on our world, not on his world. Maybe God will enable you to mobilize others and only the limits of your faith will restrict the sphere of influence he will give. Keep moving. By deliberate steps of faith in praying, giving, witnessing, and recruiting others, make decisions for personal involvement.

Go for it, yes, but not alone. Partnering with others is essential or you will quickly lose momentum. A partner of like mind is great, the Bible says, for--if *"one stumbles the other can lift him up. But woe to the one who is alone when he falls "* (Ecclesiastes 4:10). *A three-strand rope will hold when a single strand won't* (verse12). But partnering is not only for support, encouragement, and strength; it provides for accountability. Most of the great heroes who fell had moved beyond accountability for their actions to others who took that responsibility seriously.

Partnering is not only for a team of two or a handful of like-minded warriors. Partnering must be with the church. Otherwise, where is the biblical responsibility demonstrated by Paul and his missionary team? Otherwise, where is the prayer and financial support? Douglas spent five years in a typical church that supported missionaries and had an annual missionary conference. But it seemed half-dead, tradition bound. He tried in every way to seek renewal, but to no avail. They appreciated him, elected him to the Board, but didn't move out in prayer and evangelism. Now it was time for Douglas to leave for the mission field. What sort of spiritual power base would that church be? Even though it would mean a delay in getting to the mission field, he decided to move half-way across the country to identify with a vital church as a support base. He didn't have a job and the church didn't give him a place on the staff. He moved by faith, figuring that would be good preparation for the mission field. The church was delighted to have his volunteer services and he was finally "at home" in a fellowship that shared his heartbeat. The result? A year later Douglas went to the mission field, accountable to a church which took that responsibility seriously and with several scores of partners deeply committed to prayer warfare on his behalf. As a bonus, all his financial support was provided. Partnering is essential for effective life or ministry.

Pray strategically, with whom can you partner? Single? Find a friend or a child of your heartbeat for God's heart. Accountability? Who are you trying to fool? Be authentic in your accountability. No cover-ups. A serious partner or partners keep us on track to keep moving forward in effectiveness and faithfulness.

October 13
The Insiders
John 15:2 & 6

"Every branch in Me that does not bear fruit He takes away; and every branch that bears fruit He prunes, that it may bear more fruit" and *"If anyone does not abide in Me, he is cast out as a branch and is withered; and they gather them and throw them into the fire, and they are burned."* (John 15:2 & 6)

Is there a life filled so full of good things that it overflows? We can discover God's own guarantee of a life overflowing with love and joy, of effective service to God and others (John 15). And the plan was not to provide this fulfillment for some special cadre of super saints, but for everyone who is "in Christ." Yet how that life may be experienced seems to elude most people.

Part of the problem is that many start at the wrong place in their search for fulfillment. One must begin, not with discovering something about God, but something about oneself. We probably don't like that the Bible starts with bad news about us. In fact, it says that apart from Christ we are "like a branch that is thrown away and withers; such branches are picked up, thrown into the fire and burned" (Jn 15.6).

In the verses for today in John 15:2 & 6 was this "branch" in Christ and then got cut off? Or was this person safe in Christ but was merely disciplined? Or was he never in Christ at all? I suggest that the passage is figurative, an allegory, and thus should not be treated as a literal doctrinal statement. To fit the vine-and-branch analogy Jesus was simply saying that people who do not live an authentic Christian life should not consider themselves joined to him, that people who do belong to him will give evidence of it in attitudes and action. Whatever the interpretation, it seems clear that those who are not "in Christ" are in bad trouble. And this is the consistent witness of Scripture.

But we don't like the bad news. Yet the Bible is clear that without Christ I am a worm, a worthless wretch. Indeed, a withered branch fit for burning. We don't like to hear it put that way. Oh, I am an image bearer of the glorious God, to be sure, spoiled and damaged though the likeness is. But the bad news I must confront first is that I deserve hell since I fall so short of God's standard for me.

The law always precedes the Gospel. Paul understood this. The most glorious description of our salvation, of what it means to be "in Christ" (Romans 3-8) follows hard after the very bad news of humankind's moral rottenness and total lostness apart from Christ (Romans 1-3). First the bad news, then the good.

And the good news is good indeed. In fact, when God regenerates or re-creates a person, the transformation is so radical you could compare it to a birth (John 3). The new-born is very like the fetus, but such new potentialities and relationships! The transformation is so radical you could liken it to death (Romans 6). The new entry into celestial bliss is the same person who lately lay immobile on his death bed, but what new capabilities, what undreamed of new dimensions of life! One other biblical expression used to identify this new being is to describe a person as now being "in Christ." Thus, whoever is in Christ is a new creation, the old characteristics and relationships have passed on, all is new (2 Corinthians 5:17). Philip E. Hughes, in commenting on this passage, describes what it means to be "in Christ":

- security in him who bore our sin
- acceptance in him with whom alone God is pleased
- assurance of the future in him who is the resurrection
- inheritance in him who is the sole heir

- participation in the divine nature
- knowing and being free in the truth that is in Christ[65]

This is the first meaning of being "in Christ." It describes the relationship into which one enters by faith at initial salvation, what takes place when God re-creates or does what the theologians call regeneration. This concept does not exhaust the meaning of being "in Christ." What Christ himself teaches us about abiding in him in John 15 includes this, but his teaching goes far beyond that basic entry "into Christ." We shall examine the teaching about "abiding" another day for it holds the key to a life filled full. But Paul, who uses the expression "in Christ" most, emphasizes the basic, start-up relationship when he speaks of it.

Indeed, what you are in Christ, as King James English would have it, is an "exceeding magnifical" creation. You have been chosen as an intimate companion by the all-glorious One. You have been forgiven--the Judge no longer sees you as a stumbling failure but as pure and innocent as the Lord Jesus. You have been adopted so that you now belong to the first family of the universe. You have been re-created, given the capacity for holiness, for wholeness, for growth, for fulfillment. You are no longer an outsider. You are an insider and all those changes took place the moment you moved from outside to inside. That is what it means to be "in Christ."

But that is just the beginning. To "abide in Christ" is something more. Much more.

October 14
Lost
Acts 4:12

"Salvation is found in no one else, for there is no other name under heaven given to men by which we must be saved." (Acts 4:12)

Have you ever experienced the terror of being lost -in some trackless mountain wilderness, perhaps or in the labyrinth of a great, strange city? Hope of finding your way out fades and fear begins to seep in. You have likely seen that fear of lostness on the tear-streaked face of a child frantically screaming or quietly sobbing because he is separated from his parent in a huge shopping center. Lost. Alone. Equally terrifying and more common is the feeling of being hopelessly entangled or trapped in a frustrating personal condition or circumstance: alcoholism, cancer, divorce. Incredibly alone! Lost.

The Bible uses the word "lost" to describe an even more terrible condition. Those who are away from the Father's house and haven't found the way back to him are "lost." Jesus saw the crowds of people surging about him as sheep without a Shepherd, helpless and hopeless, and He was deeply moved.

Worse than being trapped and not knowing the way out is to be lost and not even know it, for then one does not look for salvation, recognize it when it comes, nor accept it when it is being offered. That's being lost.

We are told there are 500 million Christ followers in the world who trust Jesus for salvation and are active in his church. The estimate is optimistic, perhaps no more than an educated guess made by some of those who devote

---

[65] Hughes, Philip Edgcumbe, <u>Paul's Second Epistle to the Corinthians,</u> Grand Rapids: Eerdmans, 1962, p 202.

themselves to analyzing this sort of data. Still, it's a reasonable and widely used figure. If true from God's perspective, that leaves more than five billion—11 out of 12—who do not know Christ savingly. And get this, its 17 times the number of lost people alive when Christ was broken hearted over the large number of the lost (Matthew 9:35-38).

In the 20th century there was an unprecedented expansion of Christianity so that the percentage of both genuine and nominal Christians increased dramatically. Some people focus on this fact almost exclusively in painting a very optimistic picture of the task remaining. But the tragedy of the 20th century is that the population explosion was so great the incredible expansion of Christianity could not keep pace with the growth in numbers of lost people. At the beginning of that century total world population was 1.6 billion people: by the end of the century, more than 6 billion.

So for a moment I invite you to contemplate, not the exciting percentages of growth, but the number of actual lost people. More than half the people of the world have yet to hear with understanding the way to life in Christ, at least 3 times the number in that condition in 1900. And even more tragic, at least a third of humankind *cannot* hear because there is no one near enough to tell them.

They live in a tribe or culture or language group that has no evangelizing church. If someone doesn't go in from the outside they have no way of knowing about Jesus.

But are these people in the half of the world without Christ really lost? What of those who never had a chance, who have never heard- are *any* of them lost? Are *all* of them lost?

Throughout church history there have been those who teach that none will be finally lost. The old universalism taught that all ultimately will be saved because God is good.

There are problems with this position. Philosophically, such a teaching undermines belief in the atoning death of Christ. For if all sin will ultimately be overlooked by a gracious deity, Christ should never have died. It was not only unnecessary but surely the greatest error in history, if not criminal on the part of God for allowing it to happen. This view then demands a view of the death of Christ as having some other purpose than as an atonement for sin.

Scripture teaches clearly that there are those who perish and those who do not. Notice that it those who believe on Christ- not simply whose who, through their encounter with creation and their own innate moral judgement, believe in a righteous creator- who receive eternal life. God's intent is to save the world through him [Christ]" (John 3:17) The word "through" speaks of agency: it is by means of Jesus Christ that a person gains eternal life.

Jesus Christ himself said "No one comes to the Father except through me" (John 14:6). In other words, Jesus is the *only* agency of salvation.[66]

---

[66] *The Great Omission,* Robertson McQuilkin, 1984, Gabriel Publishers, 39-44.

October 15
It's My Move
Matthew 18:15

"If your brother sins against you, go and tell him his fault, between you and him alone. If he listens to you, you have gained your brother." (Matthew 18:15)

Paul wrote, among other things, *that love is patient, is kind, is not selfish, is not provoked, and doesn't keep a record of wrongs.* If I love the other person, I'll refuse to judge their motives or generalize about their character. Just as I don't like it when people take a single act or word of mine and generalize to conclude something about my character, I'll refuse to do that to my opponent. As I do for myself, I'll even try to figure out a good motive for bad conduct.

A lack of love, the irreducible form of killing, ignores potential factors in the case, affixes unworthy motives, and reaches premature conclusions. And then talks about it. Love, on the other hand, seeks the welfare of the loved one, even at personal sacrifice. Do I make excuses for my opponent with the same persistent creativity as I do for myself? For me, that's the hardest thing, but that's love.

Peacemaking requires humility. Most of us don't naturally like being a servant, much less actually considering others better than ourselves (see Philippians. 2:3). Yet if I refuse the servant role—one my Savior took—conflict is inevitable. Servants don't object to washing dirty feet. Bonding in peace, then, begins with love and humility: *"Walk worthy of the calling you have received, with all humility and gentleness, with patience, accepting one another in love, diligently keeping the unity of the Spirit with the peace that binds us"* (Ephesians 4:1-3).

While David was fleeing from Saul (see 1 Samuel 25), David sent his men to request provisions from a rash man named Nabal. Ignoring customs and laws of hospitality, Nabal refused to accommodate David's request and sent his men away, so David prepared to attack in retaliation for this insult. When Nabal's wife, Abigail, heard about the conflict, she had a generous supply of food loaded on donkeys and went to meet David's troops. Falling at David's feet and humbling herself, she apologized for her husband's behavior and asked David to forgive the offense. David accepted her offer. Abigail's wise, humble action prevented unnecessary bloodshed and vengeance that would have best been left to the Lord. Humility defuses conflict and promotes peace.

Attitudes alone won't achieve unity. Actions are needed. The first action needed is usually the last we take. Paul admonished, *"In everything, through prayer and petition with thanksgiving, let your requests be made known to God"* (Phil. 4:6). The result? *"The peace of God, which surpasses every thought, will guard your hearts and minds in Christ Jesus"* (v. 7). Prayer is an antidote for worry or conflict.

The next principle is to take action. If there is a significant difference of opinion, it won't help to let it go, hoping the problem will go away. It won't. Jesus instructed us in the actions to take.

Let's look the first action Jesus said to take in Matthew 18:15-17. *"If your brother sins against you, go and tell him his fault, between you and him alone. If he listens to you, you have gained your brother."* Seek a private consultation. Go to your opponent alone, not to anyone else. It's much easier to reach amicable conclusions if issues are negotiated privately. A gossip or church politician goes to everyone except the offending party, thus revealing a heart bent on verbal killing. But Jesus said first to go alone, seeking reconciliation.

And here's something to simplify life: it's always your move. If the other person sins against you, as in Matthew 18:15, or if you're the one who is wrong, as Jesus earlier described in Matthew 5:23-24, you must still take the initiative. Never wait for the other person to make the first move. Why not take that step today?

October 16
Fear
Daniel 3:17-18

"If this be so, our God whom we serve is able to deliver us from the burning fiery furnace, and he will deliver us out of your hand, O king. But if not, be it known to you, O king, that we will not serve your gods or worship the golden image that you have set up." (Daniel 3:17-18)

Though some may hold that all sin stems from the three roots of lust, covetousness, and pride, it seems apparent that some sin may result from none of these. Just as lust, covetousness, and pride are distortions of basic drives that God gave for our good, so the most basic drive of all, self-preservation, may be pursued in sinful ways. Our minds are armed with the instinct to protect self from harm or death, just as our bodies are "wired" with a defense mechanism of pain sensors without which we would be totally vulnerable.

The fear of danger is a good gift that makes survival possible. In fact, in the Old Testament the fear of the Lord is seen as the basis of all life and good. But when the strong drive for survival becomes obsessive or overpowers other higher obligations, it becomes wrong. There is no moral law that demands preservation of my well-being or life at all costs. On the contrary, a higher loyalty to God and even love for others may well demand self-sacrifice rather than self-protection. In answer to the sin of unbelieving fear stands the strong virtue of courage.

Although all varieties of sin relate to the taproot of unfaith in one way or another, fear seems to be most closely connected to lack of faith and certainly its opposite—courage—is born of faith. Of course, the absence of fear may not come from faith. A fearless person may simply be ignorant of the danger that threatens. Presumption dispels fear quite as effectively as faith. Presumption is confidence misplaced, relying on some person or something that is not reliable. We may fearlessly trust a great leader or a dear friend, only to be hurt badly. A person may receive advice from a godless psychiatrist, rely on it, and rush headlong to destruction. But confidence placed in God will never be betrayed. This confidence produces fearless courage. The lack of it leads to fearful timidity.

Ordinarily we stress the gentler virtues of kindness, humility, meekness, patience, but Scripture stresses the stronger virtues as well: courage, loyalty, discipline, endurance. The champions of the Old Testament were men and women of incredible valor. Consider how even the name evokes a sense of courage: Noah against the world; Abraham leaving his homeland; Jacob and the Angel; Joseph and the temptress; Moses versus Pharaoh; blind Samson; Gideon and the three hundred; Deborah and the weak-kneed generals; David against Goliath; Elijah and the prophets of Baal; Daniel and the lions; Esther and the king. And think of Daniel's friends: *"Our God whom we serve is able to deliver us from the burning fiery furnace; and he will deliver us out of your hand, O king. But if not, be it known to you, O king, that we will not serve your gods!"* (Dan. 3:17-18).

The Christian is called to fight aggressively for right, truth, justice. Valor is the active, aggressive side of courage, but there is a passive side as well: fortitude or endurance. The New Testament speaks constantly of this, but we don't recognize it, for often it is translated "patience." Patience in Scripture is not Milquetoast acquiescence but tough endurance. The one who endures to the end will be saved (Matt. 10:22; 24:13; Mark 13:13). Those who overcome, who endure steadfastly to the end, are the ones who receive a "welcome home" and all the rewards of the victors.[67] Therefore we are enjoined to run with endurance, to stand fast, not to be weary in the battle, to put on the whole armor, to strive mightily, to wrestle, to war. In fact, through him we are more than conquerors in the face of every enemy and obstacle.

---

[67] Revelations 2:7, 10-11, 17, 26; 3:5, 12-21; 21:7

October 17
Growing in Grace
Romans 6:22

"But now that you have been set free from sin and have become slaves of God, the fruit you get leads to sanctification and its end, eternal life." (Romans 6:22)

The basis for successful Christian living, according to many, is a transforming intervention of the Holy Spirit subsequent to salvation. The experience goes by many names—the second blessing, the baptism of the Spirit, being filled with the Spirit, entire sanctification, perfect love, and a host of other labels, but there is one common denominator: to experience the fullness of God's blessing on your life you must have a second encounter. To this, others stoutly object: there is no qualitative difference among Christians. From the new birth on, gradual sanctification occurs in every true believer by the sovereign grace and power of God.

To the first group we would say, "show me your Scripture"; to the second group we would say, "how can you miss so pervasive a biblical teaching that there are differences among Christians?" At the same time, let us say to both, "We commend you for emphasizing an important biblical truth; now let's examine how we may draw closer to one another into the main channel of Scriptural sanctification!"

For now, let us agree with those who insist on a second work of grace. Very few people are like the Apostle Paul who grew from new birth to translation into his Lord's presence with no second experience. To get around this apparent exception, those who adhere to a theologically necessary second work of grace are pushed into the corner of claiming that Paul had both experiences virtually simultaneously. I think it more natural to hold that Paul demonstrated the normal Christian experience available to all—steady growth toward Christlikeness from birth to death. Nowhere in Scripture are we told of a theologically necessary "second work of grace," an omission truly astonishing if indeed the Spirit intended such an experience to be the cornerstone of Christian living.

On the other hand, though Paul's experience may be normative it certainly isn't typical. Practically speaking, most Christians, especially those who came to faith at an early age in a Christian home, desperately need a second work of grace! Or a third, or fourth. In fact, when through rebellion or drift, a Christian begins to spiral downward again, nothing will do but a major turn-around. To failing Christians, the Apostles never mention a new and different experience, a spiritual booster rocket, but consistently point us back to the original contract—*don't you know who you are? Don't you realize the Spirit is in you*? Such Christians need a fresh encounter with God, a crisis, a u-turn. So let me invite us to meet on common ground—an experience of the Holy Spirit in transforming grace is indeed needed by most Christians at some time subsequent to salvation. But please don't insist that such an experience is theologically necessary for all.

Those on the other side of the channel, however, will object to this strongly. "That creates two classes of Christians, and the New Testament knows only one." To these friends I respond, "But of course. There are only the saved and lost. Let us agree." But to hold that there are no distinctions among Christians, that God in his sovereign grace is transforming every true believer whether he cooperates or not, flies in the face of pervasive biblical evidence to the contrary. Some respond, "There are certainly many church members who are not growing spiritually, but they are simply unconverted." The theologians who hold thus must never have pastored a church! Or, for that matter, not read the epistles with open eyes where failed Christians, Christians who behave like worldlings, Christians who have lost their first love, Christians who crucify Christ afresh, Christians who need to present themselves anew as a sacrifice can be found on almost every page.

So let us agree on this: we'll leave the judgment to God as to whether a professing Christian is one in reality. And to any who seem to be failing of promised blessing in their attempts to live the Christian way, let us agree to encourage them to have a fresh encounter of surrender and faith.

October 18
Faith is the Key!
James 1:2

"Count it all joy, my brothers, when you meet trials of various kinds...." (James 1:2)

How do I make sure adversity actually brings glory to God and growth to me?

Faith is the key! When I pass the faith test I become tougher in endurance and that leads to maturity, which, in turn produces more and more the character of Christ in me. On the other hand, if I doubt that God is big enough to handle my problem, that he is smart enough to know what's best for me, or that he cares enough to see me through, I spiral down—I crumple in self-pity and give up or grow hard and cynical or even mean-spirited and hostile. But faith will transform that same trouble from a stumbling block into a steppingstone, God's fast track to spiritual growth. Without the testing we would remain spiritually flabby and quite unlike the One who "learned obedience through the things He suffered" (Hebrews 5:8). When we respond with childlike trust in a loving Father, we can join others in trusting God in our pain, with a child we lost, a job unfulfilled, with a mate's Alzheimer's, a ramshackle little house that just burned down, an only son who never panned out. And I can say from the heart, "Praise God!" Nothing honors him more. Faith is the key that turns tragedy into triumph.

Of course, you may not have that many major problems! This may be a "still waters and green pastures" time of life. Then pause and give thanks. On the other hand, you may need an extra sheet of paper! Now are you ready to take the leap of faith? Here it is: thank God for each one of those problems. You probably can't thank him for the problem itself, for it may be evil incarnate. But stop right now and thank him for how the Spirit is going to transform each of them into glory to God and growth in you. Write out your prayer of thanks in your journal for today, with full detail. Turn it over to God, thanking him that He is wise enough, strong enough, and cares about you enough to use that problem for eternal good.

In a personal retreat at Highlands, NC I wrote the following verse flowing out of my conversation with God:

Why?

Why does God sit idly by while dev'lish men set his world aflame, creating hell before it's time?
And why does God allow good men feel pain unassuaged and unexplained generations unending?
Why?

I'll tell you why: God is love.
Mindless, I labor to create an anti-image of God but ever and always love barricades my way. With pain.
Just as the severe mercies of the trainer discipline the unbridled colt so God's love-wounds— by little and by little— shape me into what the trainer has in mind.
And when I strain to break free of love-bonds meant to hold me close to him, in hot pursuit of some seductive other-love, jealous love flashes warning signs to turn me back again.
Why pain?
Because he loves me so.

October 19
Rationalization Hazard
Philippians 4:8

"Finally, brothers and sisters, whatever is true, whatever is noble, whatever is right, whatever is pure, whatever is lovely, whatever is admirable—if anything is excellent or praiseworthy—think about such things." (Philippians 4:8)

This is our big one. When you suppress the activity of the Spirit when he raises need to the conscious level. The initial instant we are conscious of some attitude that might need be considered wrong, we figure out a way to justify, to make it acceptable, or at least to make the motive clean. Is it a TV program that doesn't pass the 4:8 test? "Whatever is true, noble, just, pure, lovely." (Philippians 4: 8, authors paraphrase). "Well, but I'm so tired," you sigh. "I need a little relaxation; it's not that bad. Besides, I need to know what the people I minister to are being exposed to." You see we are pretty good at rationalization! What's the solution? Eternal vigilance with a good dose of skepticism about your own purity of motive. Most of all, sensitivity to the still small Voice.

There's a practical approach you may find helpful. When the debate starts up in your mind about whether something is right or wrong, cut short the debate by deciding to treat it as wrong, whether it or not it actually is, since you will rarely suffer harm that way, and may well suffer damage if you go with the self-justification.

The person in bondage to an addiction may finally come to the place of recognizing it as a bondage. At that point, for the first time, deliverance becomes possible. Yet it's anything but certain! Still, in seeking victory, the addiction seems to be a twilight zone. When they continue in the destructive behavior, it seems neither "unconscious," on the one hand, nor "deliberate, " on the other. Certainly they are painfully conscious of it, and don't really choose to do it. It's compulsive, almost involuntary. Perhaps, the model may not be that helpful to those with compulsive behavior. Still, there's good news and bad news.

The good news is that the same approach to seeking success in the Christian life has proven effective in this kind of bondage, too. For some, there has been instant deliverance when a person turns in faith and makes an unconditional commitment to God, as in the case of deliberate, voluntary sin. After all, the beginning stages of addiction were deliberate choices. But for most addicts, deliverance comes through the growth pattern for overcoming unintentional sins. Therefore, we can really bypass the question of which category it fits. Furthermore, the strategy for overcoming temptation will prove effective for compulsive, addictive behavior as well as more common temptations.

The bad news is that nowadays, virtually any behavior is dumped into the discard bin of "addiction." Sex, consumerism, anger, lying- you name it! If it's habitual and difficult to root out, define it as an addiction. Isn't that true of all strong temptation, though? Sin is powerfully addictive! I call it the "discard bin" because, by blaming our behavior on an uncontrollable addiction, we deflect the blame from ourselves. After all, we are powerless to overcome. If you are victim, you feel you are not quite as responsible for the personal choices as you once were. That's why, when you look for deliverance from a pattern of bad behavior, resist the temptation to create a special category and call it compulsive or irresistible, consider it more appropriate to reserve the category of "addiction" for some kind of chemical dependency. Otherwise, any kind of habitual behavior can be put in a category that shields us from the responsibility to engage the sin-bully in our lives with the firepower of the Spirit. In any event, there are two things to remember

- You are responsible for your attitudes and actions.
- God can deliver you from any sin.

The weapons of our warfare are the same for this kind of enemy and our responsibility is to grasp those weapons with courage and fortitude, expecting our all-powerful inside partner to win out!

It's all-out war, however, and for that we don't need a "touch of the Spirit. " We need the Spirit full strength! That fullness and how to experience it is our theme. Hopefully you are excited with the realization that you can have total success in saying "yes" to God, and "no" to sin whenever given the choice, and you can expect to "spiral up" in every way in which you unintentionally fall short of Christ likeness. If you are grateful, why not tell him so now?

October 20
Grief
Romans 15:1-4

"We who are strong ought to bear with the failings of the weak, and not to please ourselves. Each of us should please his neighbor for his good, to build him up, for even Christ did not please himself. But as it is written that the insults of those who insult you have fallen on me. For everything that was written in the past, that scripture was written to teach us, so that through endurance and the encouragement of the scriptures we might have hope." (Romans 15:1-4)

"Dad, there's been a terrible accident. Bob is in critical condition." Bob? So, full of life, reaching his prime as a very successful photojournalist. Bob, my buddy, my son, open, loving, generous. Bob had just told me three days before, that God had spoken to him and it was time for him to set sail for God. On a routine underwater photo assignment Bob had run out of oxygen, become disoriented and stayed underwater for 10 minutes.

"Bob is with Jesus." I think the word to describe my Inner state during those days was numb. Solomon said only the person involved can know his own bitterness or joy. No one else can really share it. Each must find his own way. In my case, I realized on reflection there were great therapies at work. One was the love of family and friends, and the other was the comfort of Scripture.

The passage along this line is our verse for today in Romans 15. Here is an underlying principle that requires reaching out to brothers who are weak in faith, and furthermore, perhaps an underlying principle that describes the Christian response to one. There may be weakness for whatever reason, and so I find here this beautiful unity of the Spirit. God gives endurance and encouragement to those who need it, to those who falter and not going to endure, but those are down and needing courage, through a spirit of unity. Among yourselves as you follow Jesus Christ, so that you have one heart and one way. Well, we had this love expressed food and flowers, telephone calls, visits, letters, hundreds of letters. This was a healing balm. There's a unity of the family.

I had all varieties of expression, I'm sure, from those who felt I should be grief free and filled with joy and the strength of the Lord, to those who said they understood well because it was similar loss, to those who said nothing but stood by in silent grief. None seemed inappropriate to me. All were trying to say, "I love you. I care." How can that be inappropriate? And love assuages the grief. It's the unity of the body. My suffering was public.

But as the weeks wore on, I became aware of a great comfort that was at work, the comfort of the scriptures. You see that in verse 4, "through endurance and the comfort of the scriptures we might have hope." There's something in Scripture that brings hope in the most hopeless situation. Well, my problem was that at the time of Bob death, my daily Bible reading was in Numbers and Deuteronomy, and there's not much comfort there. But I didn't change or go on a search mission for more appropriate texts. It gradually dawned on me. That the true comfort of the scripture was in what it had taught me across the years about God, and heaven, and life, and death. By the molding of my mind and directing my thoughts, I had come to see things from God's perspective. So that when the bombs began to fall. We are already safe in the shelter of his truth. There's something basic about just routinely getting all of this into our head. It's sort of like learning the multiplication table. It's not fun. You don't see any immediate application in life. It's pretty much a grinding. You wouldn't do it if the teacher didn't make you do it. But it's sort of undergirds the rest of your life. You find that the comfort of the Scripture comes, and we have the knowledge of God through the Word of God.

Well, the comfort of the Scripture gives hope. Hope for heaven. The void and the sense of loss is there. But a great discovery is the comfort of the Scripture, and the unity of the family -the body of Christ. And you see it was given to give hope. Remember the former things. So it's not wrong for us to remember and to recount the former things about those we have lost, but the text in Isaiah says *"remember the former things, those of long ago, I am God and there is no other. I will do all that I please. My purpose will stand. I'm not like these idols. I'm not like these gods of the nations. I am the God of truth. And I will do all that I purpose."* Remember, *"I am the God, not the one that you have to carry and protect and explain."* No, no, no. It's the other way around, he says, *"even to your old age in gray hairs. I am He. I am He who will sustain you. I have made you, and I will carry you. I will sustain you and I will rescue you, because I am God."* Remember this.

October 21
Church Discipline
Hebrews 12:14

"Strive for peace with everyone, and for holiness, without which no one will see the Lord." (Hebrews 12:14)

In an age when tolerance is the chief virtue and intolerance the chief evil, it comes as no surprise that the church practicing biblical church discipline may be sued in secular courts. So the fundamental issue may be ideological: when is tolerance biblical, when is intolerance demanded?

God is holy and he intends us to be holy. And not just us as individuals- but holiness as a congregation. As a result, the Bible is very clear in teaching that there should be church discipline and that the ultimate discipline is the breaking of fellowship, or separation. Certain people should be separated from the church.

I take it that those who speak of a doctrine of "separation" base the doctrine on this New Testament principle of church discipline. When one does not have power to put out the person who should be put out, the only way to separate is to leave oneself.

How does one identify a congregation that is guilty of unholy unity, the sin of unbiblical compromise? The New Testament clearly outlines a pattern for church discipline- *who* is to be disciplined, *why* they are to be disciplined, and *how* they are to be disciplined. If for any reason such a person or persons is not disciplined, the congregation is sinning against the revealed will of God.

How does one identify a congregation that is guilty of unholy separation, the sin of schism? Since God has told us who should be disciplined, why they should be disciplined, and how they should be disciplined, if that discipline or separation is of the wrong person, of the right person for the wrong reason, or of the right person for the right reason but in the wrong way, the Christian or congregation is guilty of the sin of schism.

1. Who should be disciplined? The New Testament teaches that a person must be disciplined if he is guilty of unrepented, overt, moral delinquency (for example, I Corinthians 5:1, 11) or one who is guilty of teaching heresy (Galatians 1:6-9; 2 John 7-11). It is important to notice that the discipline is not for one who fails in some sin of the spirit or who sins and repents, but for one who sins deliberately and continues in it. Discipline in matters of faith is not for one who has doubts. Jude 22 says clearly that we should show mercy on those who have doubts and save them.

But when one *teaches* heresy, he must be disciplined.

When a congregation does not discipline in either of these cases, it has an unholy unity and is guilty of the sin of impurity, standing under the judgment of God. On the other hand, when a congregation or when individuals discipline for reasons other than moral dereliction or the teaching of heresy, they are guilty of an unholy separation, the sin of schism, and come under the judgment of God.

In the light of this biblical teaching, it does not take much discernment to see that a great deal of ecumenical promotion is uniting the wrong people and a great deal of separatist agitation is dividing the wrong people.

The only point on which Bible-committed Christians can legitimately differ on this clear teaching is the question of what constitutes heresy. I suggest that the biblical example would seem to limit a definition of disciplinable heresy to a denial of one of the great fundamentals of the faith, those doctrines confessed by the Church at large in all ages. Disciplinary action for teaching deviant doctrines of a lesser kind is schismatic.

2. *Why* should one discipline? The primary purpose of discipline in Scripture is to save or restore the person who has sinned.[68] Discipline is designed as a means of grace, not of destruction; as an evidence of love, not of hate or of fear. A secondary legitimate motive is that discipline may serve as a warning to others: it has a deterrent value (1 Timothy 5:20).

We may derive a third legitimate motive from biblical principles in general. Church discipline can be useful in protecting the reputation of Christ and of the Church. It is also useful in protecting other believers from defilement. Jude, who uses stronger words to denounce heretical teaching than any other biblical author, does not end with an injunction to begin disciplinary procedure or to separate from such people but instead exhorts the Christians who were faithful to keep on being faithful (20,21). He then concludes the passage with these words: *And on some have mercy, who are in doubt; and some save, snatching them out of the fire; and on some have mercy with fear; hating even the garment spotted by the flesh (22,23, ASV)*. Following this, Jude again turns to the faithful ones, assuring them that God is able to guard *them* from stumbling and to keep *them* till that day when they will stand in the presence of his glory *without blemish* in exceeding joy (24).

Note that one motive is excluded as a motive for discipline or separation. Church discipline is not to be punitive, retributive. God clearly reserves this motivation to himself- *Vengeance is mine; I will repay, says the Lord* (Romans 12:19)

From this brief outline of biblical teaching on motivation for disciplining an errant brother or sister, when Christians discipline or separate from motives of legalism, vindictiveness, fear, or pride rather than with the basic motivation of saving the brother, they are guilty of the sin of schism.

3. *How* is church discipline to be administered? Before any thought of discipline, of course, there must be prayer and self-examination (Galatians 6:1; Matthew 7:1-5). If a person has not given himself to prayer for the brother or sister and if he or she has not carefully examined his or her own life, they are disqualified because they do not have the love and humility necessary to be God's agent in discipline.

Throughout most of the twentieth century the purifiers who were weak on love and the unifiers who were weak on faithfulness wreaked havoc with the image of God seen by the lost world. Furthermore, those who follow in their train are guilty of something else as well, inside the church. They are in danger of creating a climate that makes growth to spiritual maturity exceedingly difficult. Amid this strong polarization, is biblical balance possible?[69]

---

[68] 1 Corinthians 5:5; 1 Timothy 1:19,20; 2 Thessalonians 3:13-15

[69] The reader is encouraged to seek an in-depth treatise on church discipline in Five Smooth Stones by Robertson McQuilkin published by Lifeway.

October 22
Six Characteristics of Godly Leaders
Luke 22:27

"I am among you as one who serves" (Luke 22:27)

The mode of leadership on the godly model is to serve. Jesus himself is the model, *"I am among you as one who serves"* (Luke 22:27). And with that he took the apron and basin of the slave, telling us that we were to follow his model (John 13.1-17). Notice that in Peter's instruction manual for the leader we have been considering, he calls on us to take the initiative, to humble ourselves. He doesn't tell us to pray for humility or to feel humble or to say humble things. No, the leader is to act in humility. He is joyfully to accept orders from those to whom he is responsible, to serve others, to fit into their arrangements, to confess his sin, to share his leadership role with others, to do the servant thing. Maybe "servant leadership" isn't such a useless term after all! Just be sure to fill it with Peter's meaning.

Whether male or female, in differing roles, some in a spiritual office and many in leadership, we are called be among God's people as one who serves. Without seeking to be exhaustive, let us note some of the major characteristics of God's authoritative leadership. We take our cue from one whom some have called the first prelate, the prince and lord, the pope of the Church- Peter, whom we shall discover did not arrogate to himself those lordly titles. We will consider six characteristics of leaders today and five characteristics tomorrow.

1. **Shared Authority.** *The elders who are among you I exhort, I who am a fellow elder.... (I Peter 5.1)* The Trinity is a beautiful model for what God seems to have intended in human leadership. Although God the Father is preeminent in the relationships of the Trinity, the Godhead is a shared authority. Not only does the Trinity share in authority with one another, God has chosen even to share his responsibility and authority with people, as we have seen, even to exercise his authority through human beings.

Leadership that becomes solitary rather than participatory, drawing all authority to itself, is actually Satan-like rather than God-like. It is marked by unaccountability, inaccessibility, pretensions of infallibility and stubborn immutability. In shared leadership there is often an order of preeminence in role as in the Godhead and in the family, but this does not in any way detract from the Trinitarian model of shared authority and responsibility for leadership.

2. **Loving.** Peter testifies that he is a witness of the sufferings of Christ (vs1) and John gives the same testimony: *...we have seen and testify that the Father has sent the Son as Savior of the world...And we have known and believed the love that God has for us. God is love, and he who abides in love abides in God, and God in him...as he is, so are we in this world. (1 John 4:14-17)*

God is love by nature, the very Trinity itself bound together by living bonds of love. Then, in the overflow of that love we are redeemed and bound together to him (vs. 15). But even more- we are bound by those same love-bonds to one another. If not, says John, we are none of his at all (vs. 20, 21). In the world, strong leadership can be exerted successfully through bonds of fear such as the fear of consequences if one does not obey. God's bonds are bonds of love.

3. **Purposeful.**...*the glory that shall be revealed (vs. 1)*. When God's purposes are brought about in and through his church, what honor it brings him! But let's not be more spiritual than the Bible, thinking God's glory is the only legitimate goal. It is the ultimate goal of course, but there are many contributing goals or outcomes. For example, Peter says that he looks forward to our ***participation*** in that glory. He also says, *you will receive the crown of glory that does not pass away (vs. 4)*.

God's leadership, then, is marked by the dynamic of a great unity of purpose in the Trinity. In the same way,

God-like leadership is goal-oriented. God is active and his activity has an end, a goal, a destination. Some human relationships are not voluntary, as with children in the home. But the church is a voluntary organization. It is the unity of purpose, the shared objectives that challenge to participation and holds the body together. Because of this a leader who follows God's model must have a clear vision of what the group should be and do. This is what the Guidebook is given for- to define and refine that vision.

4. Shepherding. *Shepherd the flock of God which is among you...(vs. 2).*

God himself as the chief shepherd (vs. 4) is our model as under-shepherds. The shepherd role (literally, pastor) hints at what the leader should be-- guide, caregiver, counselor, friend.

5. Strong... *serving as overseers...* (vs. 2). God rules with authority. His leadership is positive, not passive. He takes the initiative. And he is the one who appoints the leaders of his people. In any human organization a strong, positive leadership is essential to success in achieving the purposes of the organization. Weak, passive leadership will not do. Technically speaking, the **office** is that of presbyter and this person **functions** as a shepherd or overseer. This responsibility is assigned by God (for example, 1 Peter 5:2,3) and is a responsibility to supervise, give direction, provide, protect, discipline, and teach. God-like leadership should be positive and with authority.

6. Free of Compulsion. *not by constraint but willingly...*(vs 2). Jesus was under no compulsion to come but did so freely. He gave not only life itself but gifts beyond measure free of charge. That's why we call them graces (*charis* often translated, "gift.") And so the leader is called to give unstintingly of life. Leadership is painful, like crucifixion. Jesus told us on at least four different occasions that we are to take up our cross and that such action is a continual action—daily, he says. We are to give and give of time and energy and emotional resources, not because we're compelled to, nor for the money, says Peter. Willingly. That's the way our Model lived. And that is the way he died.

October 23
Five More Characteristics of Biblical Leaders
1 Peter 5:5,6

Therefore humble yourselves under the mighty hand of God that he may exalt you in due time. (1 Peter 5:5,6)

Yesterday we considered six characteristics of godly leaders. Today let us consider five more characteristics of the leader who follows God's model. You may be the leader, certainly you are around church leaders. The leader we describe will be among God's people as one who serves. Here are five more characteristics of Godly leaders:

1. Eager...*serving...eagerly* (vs. 2). Similar to the "freely" characteristic but adding the positive. Not only should the service not be coerced, it should be with enthusiasm, not reluctant. Jesus endured the cross for the *joy* set before him. He took up the towel and basin in the upper room because of his great love for the disciples. Great love is the seed from which eager serving is the fruit.

2. Non-Coercive *Shepherd the flock of God which is among you, serving as overseers not...as being lords over those entrusted to you...(vs. 2,3).* Although God's authority is absolute, he doesn't use this authority in a coercive way. God goes to great lengths to teach, to persuade, to motivate, yes, to woo. He forces no man to accept his lordship.

Control does not mark the way God works. There is coming a day when all will bow before his sovereign authority, but the model of authority which he presents to us is one of restraint, of persuasion. God created our capacities for thinking, feeling and choosing. He influences but doesn't short circuit or override our capacity for response, even to reject his love and rule.

Peter instructs us to lead God's people in the same way. A domineering relationship is strictly prohibited (vs. 3) To dominate is the great temptation of human leaders. But it is the way of defeat in achieving the purposes of the congregation and also, ultimately, damaging to those relationships which would make success possible.

3. Modeling *..not as being lords, but by being examples to the flock. (Vs 3).* God himself models what he intends for his people to be and do. In fact, revelation is, above all else, the disclosure of God himself. Both the written revelation and the living revelation in the person of Jesus Christ are the models for our individual behavior and for church doctrine and life.

In the same way, the responsibility of the leader in Christian ministry is to set the example. The idea of making oneself an adequate model is not an instantaneous decision or experience but a continuing activity.

The chief emphasis in both 1Timothy and Titus on qualifications for spiritual leadership is the model role, not the ministry role. The leader must be an example of what a person should be and how the work of God should be done. Paul repeatedly told people to follow him, to imitate him. Would people be safe, would the church be healthy, if all were like me? What a startling reminder of the serious nature of the modeling responsibility of leadership!

Leading an exemplary life, by itself, does not make one a leader, of course. Followers have the identical calling. Though godliness alone does not qualify a person for leadership, a breakdown in godliness disqualifies one for leadership. His role model, then, is primarily that of a Christ-like character.

4. Humble *...serving..."Likewise you younger people, submit yourselves to you elders. Yes, all of you be submissive to one another, and be clothed with humility, for God resists the proud, but gives grace to the humble."* The astonishing thing is that this is one of the chief characteristics of God as revealed in Jesus Christ. Remember, humility is not denying the gifting and responsibility to lead. The humble person lives out those God graced realities but does not use that position to aggrandize himself or to gain power over others.

Jesus himself is the model, *"I am umong you as one who serves"* (Luke 22:27). And with that he took the apron and basin of the slave, telling us that we were to follow his model (John 13.1-17). Notice that Peter calls on us to take the initiative, to humble ourselves. He doesn't tell us to pray for humility or to feel humble or to say humble things. No, the leader is to *act* in humility.

It's strange that the word for servanthood, "minister," should have come to refer to one who is many times the opposite, one who is exalted and served by others, whether a minister of state or a minister of the church. Perhaps that is evidence of where we have gone astray. The leader who follows God's model will be among God's people as one who serves.

5. Faith Filled *….casting all your care upon him, for he cares for you... (vs7).* To become, even in partial measure, all that Peter says the godly (read God-like) leader should look like, only God himself can accomplish. Faith is the key, but it must be expressed in prayer. The prayer of faith is the indispensable means of accessing the resources God provides for leaders.

How beautiful that our Model, above all others, models dependency on his Father and a life of prayer. If Jesus Christ needed to pray incessantly, how much more does the leader who would be like him!

October 24
Commendation
2 Corinthians 3:1

"Are we beginning to commend ourselves again? Or do we need, as some do, letters of recommendation to you, or from you?" (2 Corinthians 3:1)

Maybe Paul would say that today many people pedal the word of God for profit. Oh, perhaps that's not their whole purpose, their whole motive, but they're making a good deal out of it. He says in 2 Corinthians 2:17 *"Unlike so many, we do not peddle the word of God for profit."* We are surprised that he said, *"unlike so many"* but as they say, "there's gold in them there evangelical hills." If you're really good at singing, or you're really good at writing, or you're really good at preaching, there's plenty in it.

Perhaps Paul would say that many pedal the word of God for profit. But he says we're not like that. No, On the contrary, in Christ we speak before God with sincerity. Like men sent from God, he comes back to this same theme down in 2 Corinthians 4:2; *"We have renounced secret and shameful ways. We do not use deception, nor do we distort the word of God. On the contrary, by setting forth the truth plainly, we commend ourselves to every man's conscience in the sight of God."* The servant who disseminates the knowledge of Jesus Christ, has to be authentic. And that servant can't distort what they are doing with the Bible. They can't have tricky ways which are a shame to Jesus Christ. Shameful and tricky ways, not with sincerity. What will happen? Well, there are false servants, but how do you know a true servant, the authentic ones? Paul continues in 3:1. *"Are we beginning to commend ourselves again? Or do we need, as some do, letters of recommendation to you, or from you?"* He says, "Do I have to have a diploma from seminary? Or impeccable recommendations from important people? Oh, that's not the authentication of a servant. That's not how you tell the true from the false. No, here's how you tell. *'You yourselves are our letter, written on our hearts, known and read by everybody. You demonstrate that you are a letter from Christ. The result of our ministry, written not with ink, but with the spirit of the living God, not on tables, tablets of stone, but on tablets of human hearts.'"*

The authentication of the servant is spiritual results in his ministry. God, the Holy Spirit, writes that message of Jesus Christ in the heart of somebody else. That's how the servant is authenticated. That's how we know whether the person is a true servant of God. That's how we can tell; there is heart transformation and there is spiritual transformation. And so you might say, "Well, I can't point to many people who've turned to Christ through my ministry. Does that mean I'm not a true servant? Does that mean I'm a fake? Does that mean that I distort the word of God?"

If God did not give you the ability to consistently bring people to faith in Christ, you would want to identify with a reproducing body. And if neither we reproduced nor the body we are with reproduced, we would really begin to question about whether it's authentic. But whatever our specific ministry, Paul is saying that the that the validation of the servant's task, of the dissemination of the knowledge of God, is that something is going to happen. There will be spiritual change. The Spirit of God is going to write something in the hearts of people. Then you say, "oh, that's too much, who is sufficient for these things?"

Our competence comes from God. He has made us competent as ministers. Oh, there's the new covenant. Not of the letter, but of the spirit, for the letter kills, but the spirit gives life. Our sufficiency is of God, and that's why we can be confident.

And the way we disseminate the new covenant is by putting Jesus on display and telling the truth of Jesus Christ, Perhaps, you say well, I'm prepared to follow him and do the job of spreading this good news. But I don't see any results. Am I a fake after all? What was Paul's secret of successful communication? How did he become a success? Paul gives us a little review. He says, *"don't give up, don't lose heart"*.

You know, there's several kinds of Christians. There's one with never any pressures, always prosperous, always healthy, plenty of leisure time, happy, never any perplexities. They have everything under control. Everybody praises him. Circumstances never seem to get to him. What kind of good news is that to me? And what kind of fragrances?

What of the one who was acquainted with sorrow, who was always under pressure, always under attack? Knocked down, but never out. Of course, there's the other kind of Christian, I suppose, always under pressure and whining and complaining and crushed. What sort of fragrances that?

No. Paul says we have the servant's role. We are to disseminate to everyone all the time the knowledge of Jesus faithfully- the good news of life in Christ by putting this life on display. As far as I know, the only way God's light is going to shine out through me is when I'm broken. The only way his lifegiving fragrance is going to flow is when I'm under pressure. Now, I'm not saying you shouldn't ask for delivery. No, no, no. That's not biblical. But pressure is going to be there, that's why God made us clay pots instead of gold-plated steel vats. That's the way he puts his glory on display.

October 25
Purposes
Isaiah 46:8-10

"Remember this and stand firm, recall it to mind, you transgressors, remember the former things of old; for I am God, and there is no other; I am God, and there is none like me, declaring the end from the beginning and from ancient times things not yet done, saying, 'My counsel shall stand, and I will accomplish all my purpose,'" (Isaiah 46:8-10)

What are you about? What drives you? What is your overall reason for living? Are your purposes God's purposes? God is saying, as noted by Isaiah 46:11, *"I make known the end for you."* Do you want to know whether I'm God? Do you remember? Want to know my purposes? Well, look, *"I make known the end from the beginning, from ancient times what is still to come. My purpose will stand."* Now notice who this is addressed to in Isaiah 41:8, *"Remember this and stand firm, recall it to mind, you transgressors, remember the former things of old."* Remember this- fix it in your mind- take it to heart.

Now here He is addressing the people of God, Israel. We might say today, the church members. What's wrong with you? Here you are flirting with materialism as a god. Here you are going after the god of self-fulfillment. Or finding your life fulfilled in pleasure, or the search for it, or your name being recognized, or being accepted and approved. "What are your gods now?" He says, those are not gods. They don't even have a purpose. And if they did, they couldn't fulfill it. Certainly, they couldn't guarantee it. *"I am God ...and there no others ...and my purpose will stand."* So what should you do? Well, this is a great time to climb up into the grandstands and watch God do his thing; if his purpose will stand and who can oppose him? Well, then, let's just watch God do his thing: *"My purpose will stand, and I will do all that I please."*

I don't know what your parents had in mind, but I know what God had in mind; that you were chosen before the foundation of the world. You are redeemed on purpose. Remember what Paul said, he was giving everything, all of his strength to *"lay hold of that for which Christ laid hold of him. God laid hold of him"* on purpose. You were born on purpose. You were redeemed on purpose. You were commissioned on purpose. Isn't it incredible? This particular passage brings together the most profound problem- the sovereignty of God and the responsibility of man.

Let's suppose there's a fourth dimension. Outside of time and space. Timelessness- Spacelessness. If God stands outside and looks down, it's not altogether proper to say that he foreknows what I'm going to do. It's all in the eternal now so that he knows what I am doing. So that he doesn't have to *predict* what's going to happen in the future or *determine* what's going happen in the future and then incorporate that into his purposes that he fixes up ahead of time if there is a fourth dimension. The Bible doesn't try to explain to us. It just boldly says I will do all my purpose and I'm going to do it through you.

If you act as if the outcome really does depend on you. If that's what you act like, so you work frantically and you collapse in remorse when you fail. Then you've gone way out. You've lost hold of the fact that *"My purpose will stand."* If you seek your fulfillment in life, if you do your thing in life. You missed it. You've gotten hold of the idea that you have responsible choice. And if you have some arrogant talk about your free will, you are gone.

He started with the truth, that you're responsible and God's going to do his work with you, but you've taken it out beyond the bounds of Scripture. Or you can go the other direction, depending on your proclivity. You can withdraw into the grandstand of life and presume on God's capability to accomplish everything without your help. Which of course is true, so no exertion is needed. And you say it's over to God, it's up to him. It's all going to turn out the way he wants it to.

So what is my responsibility? They're both true. As Isaiah 26:12 says, *"all that we have accomplished. You have done for us, oh God."* That really does lift a load. It gives perspective. It humbles to reality, that you are an instrument of God. And that lifts up with destiny. That infuses you with hope. It gives direction, it clarifies vision. He's got a purpose. It's going to stand, and you can become identified with it. Not that I would bend down his omnipotence to make to fulfill my dream, but that it's quite possible for me to become an instrument of his purpose and to be caught up in his purpose and to accomplish what he is desired.

That's the will of God. That's his purpose, to provide redemption. *"My purpose will stand."* The only question for us today is whether or not He will identify and prosper our purpose, whether we will be caught up in his purposes so that what he promises will come true. You are under summons of the almighty God to accomplish his purposes in the world. You can't give your life to find fulfillment for yourself. It's his fulfillment of his purpose. You can't spend your life and waste your life and dreaming up dreams independent of his purposes in the world. You're under summons. Is there anything more exciting than to believe that the infinite sovereign God chooses to accomplish his purpose through you?

October 26
Championship Christianity
2 Corinthians 2:15-17

"For we are the aroma of Christ to God among those who are being saved and among those who are perishing, to one a fragrance from death to death, to the other a fragrance from life to life. Who is sufficient for these things? For we are not, like so many, peddlers of God's word, but as men of sincerity, as commissioned by God, in the sight of God we speak in Christ." (2 Corinthians 2:15-17)

Championship Christianity is our theme today as we find it in 2 Corinthians. God has called us to be champions, not one's who are "also rans." Who is a champion who consistently wins? Not necessarily always but consistently. And you and I were born to this; our birthright as a new breed to live victoriously for Jesus' sake. All of us stumble and fail. What then is the need? Life does not have to be that way. We need to get back in a relationship of obedience and faith. But why does God build champions? Is he preparing you and me as a splendid trophy for some celestial museum? He is not. We're not to be static symbols of his power; but working models of his life. We are called to follow hard after him. And so consider that theme; "follow the leader."

If we follow, where does he lead? In two of the passages in 2 Corinthians 2 and in 2 Corinthians 5, we have magnificent presentations of what a victorious Christian life is and how we may be champions; victorious, successful in the Christian walk or the Christian race. How do we follow the leader and what is the purpose of this life? Now there are other purposes. But a chief purpose, according to these two passages, is that we might bring others to faith, that we might bring others to this kind in this quality of life. And these two passages help us also to understand how we can be successful in that. Tells us by demonstration, by proclamation, by reconciliation.

Look again at the 2 Corinthians 2:14 demonstration, as we follow in his triumphal procession. To what end? Through us He defuses the fragrance of his knowledge in every place. For we are to God the fragrance of Christ among those who are being saved, and among those who are perishing.

Everywhere we go we are designed to exude his fragrance, not the essence of self, but the fragrance of Christ. We follow with him, in him, and he makes our life beautiful. Then what happens? People who can't see the invisible begin to see the invisible made visible in you and in me. And when they see it, well, they all run to it and embrace it? Well now, if that's not what happened with the original, how can we expect it always to happen with the reproduction? In fact, the majority of those who visibly saw the original, crucified Him.

And we have here, the strange phenomenon that when the very fragrance of Christ is released upon among us, some are saved through it, and some perish through it. The results are mixed. Now, of course, you move among people and release instead of the fragrance of Christ, the essence of self. We are a caricature of Christ. We are not a legitimate genuine reflection and accurate interpretation of Christ so that they get a false impression of what He is like and yet we bear his name. Oh, what a foul odor. What noxious poisonous fumes that does indeed result in death.

But that's not what this passage is about. This passage is about those who release the fragrance of Christ, or those who are not perfect working models but authentic working models. What happens? Well, there are many who will come to faith in Christ, but there are also many who will reject it. No one who has seen an authentic replica of Jesus Christ will be able to stand before the Judge can say "but you didn't communicate, you didn't tell me. You didn't let me know." It becomes death upon death. Now some feel that when they have lived a reasonably consistent life that their responsibility is discharged. But notice what Paul says in the 17th verse, "we speak" not just demonstration, but proclamation. *"We speak in the sight of God in Christ."* You follow the Leader. He not only demonstrates that beautiful quality of life. But he brought the words of eternal life.

He proclaimed the way to life. If we just demonstrate and not proclaim it wouldn't exactly be considered good news. In fact, the more perfectly a person could demonstrate without explaining how he got that way, it would be bad news.

But the first thing we must do in this proclamation, according to this verse, is to check our motives. Notice what he says. If we proclaim with a false motive, then that motive belies the proclamation and leads people away from the life rather than to the life. Because our Lord Jesus did not speak the truth to serve himself.

The proclamation is aimed at something else, reconciliation. God's purpose is not attained until the aliens and until the prodigals are reconciled to him. If we go out and search for lost sheep but never find them and bring them home. his heart is still broken because his purpose is not merely that we demonstrate and proclaim, but that we bring people to reconciliation. He is taking the initiative. He is making the reconciliation. And we are fellow workers, just to follow on. Fellow runners in the race, reconciling men to God. Where does he go? Out into the highways and the hedges, out to the unreached, to the very ends of the earth. That's where he goes. Are you going to follow him? Follow the leader. He demonstrated his life in proclaiming the truth, in reconciling as a servant, and an ambassador of the King of Kings.

October 27
Lies that Blind and Bind
John 8:44

"He was a murderer from the beginning, and does not stand in the truth, because there is no truth in him. When he lies, he speaks out of his own character, for he is a liar and the father of lies." (John 8:44)

Now, I'm sure you may say, why talk about the devil? Wouldn't it be better to ignore him? Doesn't he prefer that we get preoccupied with him instead of with Jesus? Yes, he would prefer that. But he's a great extremist. And there's something even better than preoccupation.

But as Paul said, we are not ignorant of his devices- of his plots. If we are ignorant of the way he operates he will get the advantage over us to our great loss. Many Christians are defeated today because they are ignorant and try to go through life like tourists on a holiday instead of a combatant in a hot war. What are his devices?

Weapon number one is his deceit. From the very beginning in Genesis 3 when he said, "You will not surely die." All the way through to Revelation 20, when Satan, who deceives the whole world, is released from his millennial prison to deceive the nations that are in the four corners of the Earth. His great weapon is the lie. With a lie he blinds people to the truth. And when they' are blind, he binds them firmly with that lie. He is a cosmic con artist. The final flim-flam. A liar.

2 Corinthians 4:4 says, "He blinds in order to bind,".... in order to control, says the god of this world, the controller of this world. That's one of his most common titles in Scripture, the prince of this world, the god of this

world. His power is in the lie. With what lies does he blind and bind?

Consider the non-Christian. It's easier for us to see his lies in the life of the non-Christian because we have been freed by the truth and we can see. The first lie of the enemy is there is no God. Have you ever contemplated what would happen to the Bible? Then what would happen to salvation if there is no God. The Bible is a hodgepodge of useless if not harmful myths. "Sin is ultimately non-existent. And therefore, salvation is superfluous. God, there is no God, and they are blinded to the truth that from the very beginning, "in the beginning God" and this is the truth that gives meaning to the written word and gives life through the living Word.

But there's another lie for those who would say, "Oh yes, there's a God, and that God is irrelevant." Did you work with people who are unconverted? One lie or the other will be their blindness; God is irrelevant. Now the classical philosophical construction of this was that God is distant and uninvolved. He actually created a master mechanism, which we call the universe. He wound it and he let it go.

Many of the founding fathers of our Republic were deists. And they say that God is irrelevant because he's concerned only with matters that are irrelevant to me. And therefore, he could be ignored without harm. Actually, this is the official position of our government. And the predominant position of our culture, education, media, arts, science. God is irrelevant. Deists are blind to the truth that "in Him we live and move and have our being."

The second great lie is there is no God. Well, maybe there is, but God is irrelevant. Many people don't buy that, and so there's a third lie. And that is God is a Santa Claus. He's too good to punish anyone. Especially me. Now there's an evangelical aberration on this lie of the enemy. It goes like this because of God sovereign grace, there is no need to repent, just believe and acknowledge that He is the Savior. Just acknowledge that you've gone wrong; this is not a harmless innovation.

Another common lie is come to Jesus and you'll be healthy, you'll be affluent, you'll be trouble free. It's all part of this idea that God is a Santa Claus. This position, held by earnest, intelligent, believing scholars, is a lie of the devil. I guess the same way the Lord Jesus could say to the chief theologian and churchmen of the law Peter "get behind me, Satan." Not because Peter was filled with Satan or possessed by Satan, or was consciously giving himself over to Satan, but because he told a lie. It was a terrible notion. It could be used of the enemy to deflect Christ from going to the cross. That's why it's such a fearful thing.

And there are those that say, Oh no, I know that God is not a Santa Claus. In fact, God is so holy that there is no hope for me, and that's the 4th lie. There is no hope. I'm too bad to be forgiven. Or I'm too weak to get my act together so that God could accept me. Sometimes a person means God is so cruel or God is so mean, but it would not do to say that, so we say there is no hope.

Truth that sets a person free is John 3:16 "... *for God so loved the world He gave His only begotten Son, that whoever believes in him should be freed, set free from the body, should not perish, but have everlasting life. For God sent not his Son into the world to condemn the world, but that the world should be saved through him.* "

October 28
Lies
Ephesians 6:13-16

"...put on the full armor of God, so that when the day of evil comes, you may be able to stand your ground, and after you have done everything, to stand. Stand firm then, with the belt of truth buckled around your waist, with the breastplate of righteousness in place, and with your feet fitted with the readiness that comes from the gospel of peace. In addition to all this, take up the shield of faith, with which you can extinguish all the flaming arrows of the evil one." (Ephesians 6:13-16)

Today I want to give you four lies of the devil, and God's great weapons for overcoming. We come to God, in our confusion, in our helplessness and he delivers us out of the power of darkness and transfers us into the kingdom of His dear Son. Hallelujah! Out of the power, the control, the god of this world, out of the power of darkness. That's where Satan's power is, it's in moral darkness. But God has transferred me into the Kingdom of his dear Son, into light and freedom. I was blind and Jesus touched my eye and struck my chains and set me free. Christ announced his program and his purpose to be in the world was that he had come to give light to those who sit in darkness, to open the eyes of the blind and to set the captive free. There's a social dimension of that. There's a political dimension to it in the last day when Christ returned. Can Christians be deceived? Can Christians be bound by Satan? Fooled by his tricks? Remember Paul's great war cry in Ephesians 6!

There are those among us who today who are blind or bound. This is the trick of the enemy. There are many lies that he gives to Christians, I'll just mention four. The first lie is this. "<u>This isn't a sin</u>." We have a fancy name for it. We call it rationalization. For example, I've known people who tell me that divorce is not a sin because their spouse is not a Christian. And the Bible clearly teaches the person is not a Christian, is a spiritual adulterer or adulteress, and therefore they are free to be divorced and remarried. One man said, "listen, God is on the side of happiness, and I've been miserable for 22 years." That's a lie. He is stuck in his chains. Criticism. There are people who are not safe from the mouths of other people- friends, teachers. Why? Criticism. "Well, if it's true. It's OK," and with this, criticism gets a stronghold on us.

What about the lie of materialism? What Satan has done is to con us into thinking that things are important, that things matter. That happiness can be found in things, that a man's life consists in his things.

Certainly, God wants to deliver you. He wants to shake the bonds; he wants to set you free. Not your personality. And Satan's classic word in the garden of Eden where he says. "No, no, Eve, it is far from being a sin. It looks good. It tastes good. It makes you so smart. It makes you free?" That's the first laugh. This isn't a sin. And we rationalize this. Maybe, maybe not. But it doesn't matter.

Here is the second lie to us: " <u>It's an insignificant thing</u>." Little deceptions, cheating on a term paper by not giving credit to the original source or lie- just little white lies about why I did something, a good reason instead of the true reason. Cheating on that girl's future husband, or your own future spouse by doing things together. Or looking at things that are lustful. It doesn't matter. It's such a little thing.

The third lie is "<u>I can't help it</u>." You say you see? Therefore, you're doubly blind, says the Lord Jesus. Now there is a theological, Christian cop- out on this Christian view of this; "All sins, past, present and future have been forgiven." True. So that "you never need be guilty, never feel sorry, never repent, never ask God to forgive you." Oh my friend. It flies in the face of the whole teaching of the New Testament. Get the truth- to sin deliberately is to shame

Christ openly and to treat his death as if it were nothing. That sin of mine that nailed him to the cross and if I can say that it doesn't matter, it's to put him to shame before my brothers and before the world. There is deliverance.

The final lie is the opposite that takes us to the other extreme. "Total victory is possible now." This is Satan's final last-ditch deception and goes to the other extreme. Paul said, "For I am not yet perfect." John says at the end when he was 90 plus years old, "If we claim to be sinless, we are self-deceived." No, not perfection, to say total victory is possible, these are Satan's lies.

Let us end our time with God's great weapons to overcome the blinding and binding:

- Overcame him by the blood of the Lamb. Revelation 4:11- The death of Christ Jesus overcame your enemy. Jesus did it. Son of God destroyed the works of the devil. Jesus crushed the head of the enemy. Confidence in and commitment to Jesus Christ.
- Name of Jesus. Jesus is given a name supreme over every name. Authority, power and salvation is given to Him, there is no other name. He proclaims release to the captives. Freedom from that besetting sin is found in the united prayer of faith and the power of God.
- Word of God. (John 8) If you abide in my Word, you will be my disciples and know the Word.... you shall be set free!
- *Church of Jesus Christ.* I will build my church. The gates of hell will not be able to overcome the church. We will stand together- responsibly stand together.

October 29
Saving Faith
James 2:24

"You see that a person is justified by works and not by faith alone. " (James 2:24)

Some people feel that faith is a miraculous gift of the Holy Spirit that flies in the face of evidence. Others take the opposite view that faith is induced by intellectually impelling evidence such as the Bible, philosophical proof, or experience. Historical evidence differs from mathematical proof or scientifically observed events. Persuasion is based on evidence to be sure, but it is the evidence of testimony- in the case of Scripture, the testimony of the prophets, and the apostles. There are many reasons for considering this testimony thoroughly trustworthy, such as the character of those who gave it, the unity of the testimony, its content, and so on. The evidence alone, however, does not compel acceptance. The work of the Holy Spirit is needed, and thus faith is a miraculous gift that confirms the evidence and even carries one beyond the evidence if necessary. It does not contradict evidence nor is it "sight" based on irrefutable scientific proof.

Faith is at once a gift of God (Ephesians 2:8-9) and our own responsibility. How God's sovereign, autonomous authority and our responsibility to believe relate to one another is not clarified in Scripture. Scripture makes it clear, however, that we must respond in obedient faith in order to receive God's promises of salvation. In summary faith is a choice to commit all of oneself unconditionally to the person of God, who is revealed in the Bible and witnessed to by the Holy Spirit (1 Corinthians 2:14 & Romans 10:17).

Are there degrees of faith? Must it be absolute to be effective? Scripture seems to answer both yes and no. When the disciples asked for an increase in faith, Christ responded that if they had even the smallest amount, it would be quite adequate (Luke 17:5-6). In this sense any faith at all is adequate, since it is not the faith itself that saves but the object of one's faith. One may have strong faith in thin ice and drown but have weak faith in thick ice and be safe.

One may not have an emotion of confident assurance, or heart peace, about a matter. And yet, if he or she chooses to act in obedience to God and launches out in response to what is known to be God's will, this choosing is saving faith or sanctifying faith. Such a person may feel quite unsure and may be fearful and unable to predict the outcome of the step of obedience. But the key question is, "What is the response of the will?"

A person who is living by faith may have – indeed ought to have – an inner tranquility, Christlike behavior, a doctrinally correct confession of faith, and unwavering conviction and assurance. None of these, however, is the key evidence of sufficient faith. A person can have inner peace with confidence in the wrong object – as do some devotees of false gods, as well as those Christian who have confidence in some misappropriated Bible promise. Again, while living by faith produces tranquility, one's emotional state may vary with changes in health or circumstances.

A Christlike character is the result of true faith. On the other hand, not all character comes from biblical faith. It is quite possible for a person in ideal circumstances to develop a commendable degree of personal integrity and good behavior without God's regenerating power. So far as correct doctrine is concerned, even the devils know the truth.

The most important evidence of faith, as we have seen, is *unqualified commitment to doing the will of God.* Obedience may not evidence full or mature faith, but it certainly gives evidence of some faith. Abraham proved his faith through obedience (James 2:21-24), and Israel proved its unbelief through disobedience (Hebrews 3:18-19). The choice to obey is absolutely necessary for birth into God's family or growth as God's child because God does not force a person. Faith frees the Holy Spirit to work. Unbelief, or disobedience, stops that work.

Note that it is quite possible for the will to speak contrary to the emotions, as Christ demonstrated in the Garden of Gethsemane when He initially cried out in anguish for deliverance but in the end chose the will of the Father. Ordinarily, the other two elements of faith – emotional response and understanding – will follow the choice to obey (John 7:17).

As we have seen, it may be possible to be an surrendered Christian, although there is no legitimate biblical ground for assurance of salvation for the one who is deliberately rejecting the known will of God. "If you live according to the sinful nature, you will die" (Romans 8:13). At the least, without this basic confidence of a saving relationship with God, growth in the Christian life is impossible. If there is a longstanding rejection of the known will of God, a person is certainly not living by faith; moreover, the Bible clearly teaches that God is saving those who are believing. Thus, the essential element of faith for one who is disobedient is obedience. The unyielded person must surrender.

Scripture gives many evidences of an surrendered heart: unreconciled personal relations, unforgiving spirit, a complaining attitude, unloving criticism, persisting in a wrong even after realizing one is sinning, grieving more over what hurts oneself than what hurts God, making decisions on the basis of personal benefit rather than promotion of God's purposes, and seeking the praise of other people. Even if you do not display conscious rebellion, behaviors such as these indicate that now is the time to choose to surrender unconditionally to the will of God.[70]

---

[70] Taken from Five Views of Sanctification by Melvin E. Dieter, Anthony A. Hoekema, Stanley M. Horton, J. Robertson McQuilkin, and John F. Walvoord. Copyright © 1987 by Zondervan. Used by permission of HarperCollins Christian Publishing. www.harpercollinschristian.com.

October 30
Insufficient View
1 Corinthians 13:9-12

For we know in part and we prophesy in part, but when the perfect comes, the partial will pass away. When I was a child, I spoke like a child, I thought like a child, I reasoned like a child. When I became a man, I gave up childish ways. For now we see in a mirror dimly, but then face to face. Now I know in part; then I shall know fully, even as I have been fully known. (1 Corinthians 13:9-12)

We know only in part—as a child (1 Cor. 13:9-12). I once came upon my four-year old daughter and a friend building with blocks.

"It isn't chimbley. It's chimley."

"It is not chimley. It's chimbley."

And so the argument went on and on. I smiled to myself and then began to wonder. How often does our Father smile on us and our dogmatic declarations that so often go beyond the realm of our knowledge? The children were both right within their field—how to build a chimney of blocks. But they became foolish when they dogmatized outside the realm of their very limited experience.

The good news is that we will not remain children. We will become adults. We will not become infinite, but we will know more fully, even as we are fully known, when we no longer see dimly in a mirror, but face to face. "They shall see eye to eye, when Jehovah returneth to Zion" (Isaiah 52:8, ASV). When one truly sees his own finitude against the backdrop of infinity, humility is inevitable and dogmatism impossible.

We are fallen. Not only are we finite; we are fallen. Sin has dimmed and warped our understanding of the revelation we do have, and therefore, we are subject to error. We choose the interpretation that lets us do what we want to do. Our sinful desires and our arrogance distort our understanding of God's Word.

These first three elements of humility in Bible study should remind us that humility and love are more becoming than dogmatism. A healthy agnosticism concerning all that goes beyond certain fact will preserve the unity of the Spirit among God's children and peace in one's own heart. Nothing is more likely to disrupt unity among brethren or the calm of one's own soul than a dogmatic difference of opinion in questions of Bible doctrine.

Augustine has said, "In essentials, unity; in nonessentials, liberty; and in all things, charity." The problem comes, of course, in dividing between essentials and nonessentials. If everyone could only be satisfied with the great clearly revealed truths of God's Word and refuse to move any mere opinion from "nonessential" to "essential" standing, what unity and harmony and consequent blessing would result!

Humility in regard to knowledge should be inevitable when one faces the above facts. However, it is not inevitable. It would be if humility were the product of reason alone. But it is not. Humility is a fruit of the Spirit, and rational facing of the facts is possible only to one who belongs to the order of the broken and contrite heart, to one with a totally yielded will.

We see things through the glasses of our experiences, by what we have read and heard, through our way of life, or through a previously settled system of doctrine. That fact is illustrated by an interesting experiment conducted by a research psychologist. He placed two different pictures in a stereoscope. The left eye was to see a bullfighter, the right eye, a baseball player. Then he asked some Mexican subjects and some Americans subjects to peer through the instrument. Most of the Mexicans saw the bullfighter, most of the Americans saw the baseball player. What is behind our eyes often has more to do with what we see than what is before our eyes.

Therefore, we must develop a healthy suspicion of ourselves and of our own ideas, and a view of the Bible that separates it from our own past thinking and experience (insofar as humanly possible) to let it speak not what we already believe or want to believe, but what it says. A suspicion of our own ideas will lead to a willingness to reject even lifelong and deeply cherished opinions, ways of living, friendships, and associations without hesitation, once God's Word has come into clear focus. The surrendered heart wants to know what the Bible says, not what it can be made to mean. The acceptance of the possible, rather than the certain, meaning is often done to make a self-consistent scheme. But the system must not force the Bible into its logical mold. The Bible gives the system all it can legitimately have. If it needs more to complete it, it must wait for the fuller light of eternity.

Think of some area of Christian living in which you are unsure. How are you seeing it? Are you seeing what you are looking for or what the author intended? How do you know?

October 31
Unflagging Love
1 John 4:16-17

"So we have come to know and to believe the love that God has for us. God is love, and whoever abides in love abides in God, and God abides in him. By this is love perfected with us, so that we may have confidence for the day of judgment, because as he is so also are we in this world." (1 John 4:16-17)

My human experience is all the analogy I have. By comparison with God's analogy, mine is so feeble. Yet, I remember when Muriel and I were engaged–she was the passion of my life: my mind obsessed on her all day and most of the night. No sacrifice was too great if only it would bring her joy, words always proved inadequate to express my feelings, though I constantly attempted by letter and phone calls. There seemed no limit to the glories I discovered in her and proclaimed to all who would listen. Indeed, I seemed in danger of worshiping her. And now? Now she lies abed and I care for her every need, feeding, bathing, changing. I love her dearly. The heartache is, she can't love me back. Sometimes our eyes connect briefly in the morning, and she responds with a grunt when I do something that doesn't please her, like cleaning her teeth. That's it. I often think, "Lord, is that the way it is between you and me? You pouring out your love and care so ceaselessly and all you get in return is a brief connection in the morning and a grunt when things don't go my way?" How sad. For him.

I lament with Isaac Watts, "And shall we then forever live at this poor dying rate? Our love so faint, so cold to Thee, and thine to us so great?" And with Pollock I confess and plead:

> We have not loved thee as we ought,
> Nor cared that we are loved by thee;
> Thy presence we have coldly sought,
> And feebly longed thy face to see.
> Lord, give a pure and loving heart
> To feel and own the love thou art.

For this he created me. For this he redeemed me. Oh, that the passionate love affair of my youth would seize me, that my mind would obsess on him throughout the day, my words and actions would ever keep the spotlight on each of his excellencies, that I would listen attentively to his wooing, tell him often of my love. I realize I will not fully experience that loving oneness till I move to his House. But in the meantime, what focus, what delight, what energy it brings to contemplate his unflagging love for me and the ultimate purpose of my life, to love him with all my heart and soul and mind and strength.

November 1
Infancy or Impulse Giving
Luke 12:16-18

"And he told them a parable, saying, "The land of a rich man produced plentifully, and he thought to himself, 'What shall I do, for I have nowhere to store my crops?' And he said, 'I will do this: I will tear down my barns and build larger ones, and there I will store all my grain and my goods." (Luke 12:16-18)

Spiritual maturity. We all think we have it or at least aspire to it. But who actually has it? It may startle us to discover that the Lord Jesus measures spiritual maturity by one's relationship to material things.

Lest we take a jaundiced view of anyone talking about money, remember that Jesus made it a major theme of his teaching. John MacArthur notes that 16 of Christ's 38 parables deal with money; that the New Testament talks more about money than about heaven and hell combined, and five times more about money than prayer. While 500+ verses mention prayer and faith, over 2,000 deal with money and possessions. So the Lord must think our relationship to money is an important indicator of our level of maturity.

Infants are basically self-centered non-givers. Some time ago, I hazarded watching a nursery full of two-year olds. One small male person seemed to take a fancy to me, repeatedly bringing me toys. I said to myself, "Kid, if you don't quit this, you'll ruin my sermon point about infants being takers, not givers." So I tracked the little fellow cruising among the others. An unsuspecting little girl sat alone in a corner with her doll. My generous little friend slipped up behind her, bonked her on the head and snatched her dolly to bring as a gift. "Thank you," I breathed, "for restoring my faith in original sin." An infant is basically a non-giver. Every church seems to have its share of infants-getters, not givers, needing a platoon of the faithful to quell their squabbles, entertain and clean up their messes.

Jesus told us about this stage: *"And he told them a parable, saying, "The land of a rich man produced plentifully, and he thought to himself, 'What shall I do, for I have nowhere to store my crops?' And he said, 'I will do this: I will tear down my barns and build larger ones, and there I will store all my grain and my goods."*

God's response? *"Fool! This night your soul is required of you."*

Actually, the self-centered getter is already dead, spiritually. A sign of genuine spiritual life is often the desire to give.

Luke introduces us to a kindergartner who began to get his kicks out of giving. The wealthy little big-time chiseler, the despised head honcho of the local Roman tax unit, wanted to see Jesus, but couldn't because of the throngs of people. So Zacchaeus - imported brocade robe tucked up under his sash - climbed a tree to glimpse this famed itinerant preacher passing by. Jesus stopped and invited himself to a meal. We know there was birth from above because of the host's announcement: I give half my goods to the poor. And if I have taken anything from anyone by false accusation, I will restore it four-fold. (Lk 19:8) Quite a surge of generosity for an ex-getter! Impulsively he risked bankrupting himself. Most Christians give by impulse.

While I was a student, my wife and I attended an event sponsored by a premier fund-raiser. Following his appeal, it was as if a giant vacuum cleaner swept through the audience, cleaning out every purse. We, too, emptied our pockets-right down to bus fare home. Impulse giving.

November 2
Legalistic vs Honest Management
Malachi 3:8

When a Christian moves from sporadic impulse giving to giving as a way of life, he often becomes a tither. *"Will a man rob God? But you have robbed me." " How do we rob you?" "In tithes and offerings."* (Malachi 3:8)

The kindergarten Christian hears that and says, "That's Old Testament legalism." Jesus, too, had problems with the legalists of his day, the Pharisees. They were so careful to obey the Law - measuring even the harvest of tiny herbal seeds to give God his tenth. But they were not so devoted to the heavy concerns of God. *"Woe to you Pharisees, because you give God a tenth of your mint, rue and all other kinds of garden herbs, but you neglect justice and the love of God".* (Luke 11:42)

Surprisingly, Jesus did not tell them to stop tithing. "What you should do," he remonstrated, "is concentrate on the big ones - justice and the love of God - and don't stop tithing. It's better to give legalistically, apparently, than not to give illegalistically!

Tithing is the elementary, basic level of giving, but the majority of faithful church members do not reach even this stage of giving. After I had spoken on giving at a large influential church, the church business manager called me aside. The church had every sign of dynamic vitality, including a budget of over $3,000,000, a third of which was for missions - a sure sign of clear biblical priorities. "We did a demographic study of our congregation," he said, "and discovered that if every member quit their job, went on unemployment, and began to tithe, we could double our budget!" Tithing moves the Christian from impulse, kindergarten level giving to giving as a way of life.

In a society of excess, luxury, and waste, Western Christians should cultivate a spirit of contentment and learn to say, "Enough!" (Philippians 4:10-13). We should learn to live more simply that others may simply live. At the great Lausanne Congress on Evangelism, several thousand church leaders committed themselves to this simplicity: "We cannot hope to attain this goal without sacrifice. All of us are shocked by the millions of poor and disturbed by the injustices which cause it. Those of us who live in affluent circumstances accept our duty to develop a simple lifestyle in order to contribute more generously to both relief and evangelism." [71]

The incarnation and atoning sacrifice of Christ are the new model for showing generosity (2 Corinthians 8-9), not the Old Testament tithe. Christ became (materially) poor so that we through his poverty might become (spiritually) rich (2 Corinthians 8:9). Jesus, not Abraham or the Mosaic law should be our model.

What then is "excess"? Each one is accountable to one's own master. "Who are you to pass judgment on the servant of another? (Romans 14:4 RSV). But it must mean something, and something that consumer-oriented Americans apparently find difficult to comprehend.

---

[71] IBE (2014),476-477.

November 3
Secondary Giving: Honest Managership
Luke 16

"I tell you, use worldly wealth to gain friends for yourselves, so that when it is gone, you will be welcomed into eternal dwellings." (Lk 16:9)

One of the clearest passages on managership is the story Christ told about the cheating manager. (Lk 16) The story is straightforward: an owner discovered his manager was a cheat. When the owner announced his intention to fire him, the shrewd fellow used his boss's assets to win friends for himself officially cancelling large portions of others' debts. Jesus made a single point: even worldlings are smart enough to use available resources to prepare for their future. So why are the "people of the light," who should know better - acting so stupidly?

Jesus contrasted temporal and eternal wealth: the temporal is very little at best, sort of a test; the eternal, great wealth (verse 10); the temporal, fake, like play money; the eternal, the real thing (verse 11). Then the punchline: Even that small amount of play money you have isn't yours! You are just a manager of some of God's property (ver.12). It's impossible to live for both, to work with equal fervor for temporal and eternal payoffs, "...you cannot serve both God and money" (verse 13). The audience, having a love affair with money, scoffed at his teaching (verse 14). So he told those cheating managers using God's property for their own benefit what their final payoff would be: an eternity in hell (verses19-23). This teaching rocked my life. As a young adult I continued my childhood pattern of tithing. God got his ten percent first. Always. It was like paying taxes. But when it became clear to me that I was not the owner at all, just a manager of another's property, I stood convicted as an embezzler. I was avidly getting, saving and spending 90% of God's property on myself without a qualm. I shrank from managership, fearing to lose the good life. Finally, I concluded that the cost of disobedience was too high and yielded to God's will. Suddenly it was as if my cage door swung open, setting me free! If the corporation is his property, it's his responsibility. And so am I! I no longer needed to worry about finances, that was his concern. My responsibility is simply to be an honest manager. The manager looks at the King's business differently from the tither. Tithers look at their paycheck, calculate the 10% and ask, "Where should I invest this?" The manager looks at the needs of the business and asks, "How can I rearrange my resources to meet this great need?"

> "The angels from their realm on high
> look down on us with wondering eye.
> That where we are but passing' guests,
> We build such strong and solid nests;
> And where we hope to live for aye,
> We scarce take thought one stone to lay."

Jesus says, "That's dumb, really dumb. You should use whatever I have put under your control now to build your eternal estate. Don't squander my possessions building your own petty kingdom here on earth. At least be an honest manager."

November 4
Higher: Love Giving
Luke 21:1-4

"Jesus looked up and saw the rich putting their gifts into the offering box, and he saw a poor widow put in two small copper coins. And he said, "Truly, I tell you, this poor widow has put in more than all of them. For they all contributed out of their abundance, but she out of her poverty put in all she had to live on." (Luke 21:1-4)

Jesus did something few pastors would dare do. During the offering he followed the ushers down the aisle so to speak, and examined each contribution put in the plate!

As God observes our giving today, how does he measure love, calibrate its intensity, or sound its depth? Jesus answers, "love is measured by the sacrifice it makes." Bob, a Bible College student, asked for help with a difficult passage found in Luke 18. I guessed. "You've got problems with the story of the young wealthy aristocrat, right?"

Yes, he responded. "Why did Jesus tell him to sell what he had and give it away?" "Well," I said, "the way to life for that young man was blocked by things, his sin of covetousness. For the woman at the well it was men, not money. Self-righteous Nicodemus needed to hear about a second birth. Jesus identified the key issue, the roadblock, for each."

"I see," said my young friend. "If possessions were his sticking point, would you say there are those today with a similar problem?" I wondered where Bob's questioning was headed. "Yes," I chuckled a little nervously, "Just about everyone, I suppose." "Why then," he asked, "have I never heard a sermon on the subject?" "That is a very good question, Bob, because Christ gave exactly the same teaching to anyone who wanted to be his disciple": *"Sell what you have and give alms, provide for yourselves money bags which do not grow old, a treasure in the heavens that does not fail, where no thief approaches nor moth destroys."* (Luke 12:33)

Does anyone actually do this? Some years ago, I wanted to personally thank two of our graduates for their many generous gifts. When we had special needs, a gift of one or two thousand dollars would come from this couple. I wondered how they could do this being schoolteachers in a poor district of Appalachia. One day I called to see if a visit would be convenient. They were delighted- said they had something to tell me. Meeting me at the highway, they escorted me on foot through the muddy ruts that snaked around the hillside. There nestled in the little mountain cove was their home, a· small log cabin. That's the reason they could give so generously! Or so I thought.

The husband was so excited. "Robertson, isn't the Lord good?" he exclaimed.

"Yes, He is" I replied. "And how has He been good to you?"

"This week we were able to sell land to a government agent who will buy it over 10 years and give us $1,500 a year. So we've decided to take early retirement, go to the mission field, take care of MKs and live on what we get from the sale of this property! What do you think about that?"

"I think you're crazy. What are you going to do when that money runs out?" I asked. "Oh," he answered, "We'll be in heaven by then!"

Love graduates a person from the secondary level of honest managership to the higher level of sacrificial love giving. While watching a television interview with Mother Theresa, I, along with the young woman interviewing her, swelled with pride as Mother Theresa told us how wonderful Americans are. She said, "I don't know if there has ever been a nation that has been so generous. You are such generous people." Mother Theresa continued, "Of course, you give out of your 'muchness.'" She chuckled, "Muchness' is a word, isn't it?" She paused, then added, "You don't really give until it hurts." The young woman's eyes grew large, astonished. "Must it hurt?" The angel of Calcutta responded, "Love, to be genuine, must hurt." Love is proved by the sacrifice it makes ...

November 5
Graduate: Faith Giving
Luke 12: 28

But if God so clothes the grass, which is alive in the field today, and tomorrow is thrown into the oven, how much more will he clothe you, O you of little faith! (Luke 12: 28)

Paul speaks of the gift of faith. There are those George Muellers of the world who trust God for miracle provision - finances far above that which could be provided even by sacrificial giving. I call this the graduate level of giving because this gift of faith is not given to everyone equally.

But in another sense, faith is essential for any level of giving. *"Without faith it is impossible to please him."* The Pharisees were not the only ones who had problems with Jesus' radical teaching about managership and sacrificial giving. The disciples did, too. Jesus' teaching cut across the grain of everything they believed about money and things. So he said: *"If then God so clothes the grass which today is in the field and tomorrow is thrown into the oven, how much more will he clothe you, 0 you of little faith?"* (Lk 12:28)

Faith must validate every level of giving. An impoverished widow living on Social Security must have faith to give 10 percent. Furthermore, when she does so, it is certainly sacrificial love. But if I am unwilling to move up from my present level of giving, is it not because I don't trust God to meet my needs - a lack of faith? Or love? The person who trusts and loves God will be willing to move from kindergarten impulse giving to elementary, lawful tithing; if already a faithful tither, to go on to honest managership; if an honest manager, to graduate to a sacrificial way of life. My relationship to my possessions is, according to Jesus Christ, a clear indication of my faith and love, my level of spiritual maturity.

God himself models this standard. He created me so he is owner. I stole his property - took possession of myself. But in love, at terrible cost, he purchased me just as if he had no prior claim on me, making me twice his. If I will only respond with love in obedient giving he guarantees my livelihood (Lk 12:31); rewards me lavishly in this life as if I were giving what is my own property; and in heaven he rewards me all over again! (Lk 18:28-30). That is God's level of giving - love giving. What is yours?

November 6
The Harvest
Matthew 9:37-38

When our Lord saw the crowds, He had compassion for them, because they were harassed and helpless like sheep without a shepherd. Then He said to His disciples, "the harvest is great but the laborers are few. Pray, therefore, the Lord of the harvest to send out laborers into His harvest" (Matthew 9:37 & 38).

Today we pray for laborers for the harvest. I would like to ask you to consider the harvest and the harvesters and seek answers to the situation in the world and in our own lives, in order to direct your prayer. The first, then, **what is the harvest?** At the time Christ said, "The harvest is great," the population of the entire world was equal to that of North America or Russia today. The harvest was great then, but today it is more than 15 times greater. We are not completely sure of this statistic, but many demographers tell us that if Jesus Christ were to come tonight, there would be more lost people now living than of all the lost throughout history who have already died.

There are six billion lost in the world today. I speak of the lost because of Matthew's analogy here. He says that Christ was distressed because people are harassed and helpless, like sheep without a shepherd. So the word "lost" is a good biblical word. It is appropriate to refer to the five billion without Christ as those who are "lost."

The Lost are the **churched and unchurched.** There is no doubt that the harvest is very great, as our Lord said. However, let us separate the lost into those who are "churched" and those who are "unchurched." I have called those "lost sheep" whose names are on the roll of a church, "churched in name only." For example, a spiritually deadened nation, like Italy, may be "churched," but the vast majority of them still need the good news of life in Jesus Christ.

Within the unchurched peoples are **those within reach and out-of-reach** of the gospel. Today we are particularly concerned with the unchurched, and not even with all the unchurched. We are going to divide the "lost sheep" between those within the reach of the present ministry of the church and present missionary outreach, and those OUT-OF-REACH PEOPLES. Perhaps you would call these the hidden or the by-passed peoples. We care about this group that are presently out of reach of any organized church of Jesus Christ.

We can further divide the out-of-reach peoples into those who are NEGLECTED and those who are ISOLATED. It may not be so much that the church has neglected certain peoples as that the church has been isolated from them for one reason or another, perhaps where it is illegal to preach the Gospel. Another example is the country of Libya, both structurally and ideologically isolated. And then there are others just as ideologically isolated.

There is another great proportion which is simply NEGLECTED. The door is open, but no one has gone in cross-culturally. The harvest really is ripe, such as the indigenous people-groups of Nigeria, where perhaps 25 tribes have been neglected, many of them non-Islamic. Certain areas of Indonesia would be "out of reach," but they are neglected. We simply have not gone there. If God doesn't send them, they won't go. Even in a group of highly motivated people, if God doesn't get hold of them and thrust them out, the chances are they will never get there. We've got to pray that God, the Holy Spirit, will thrust out laborers into the field. Would you do that now? That God would send laborers to the churched and unchurched? To the within-reach and out-of-reach populations around the world? To those neglected; to whom one has bothered to go and share the good news of Jesus Christ with them? Ask for godly, wise, culturally appropriate laborers for the harvest.[72]

---

[72] Seeds of Promise: World Consultation on Frontier Missions, Edinburgh '80 edited by Allan Starling. Copyright 1981. Used by permission of William Carey Library, P. O. Box 128-C, Pasadena, California, 91104.

November 7
The Church
Matthew 16:18

I will build my church (Matthew 16:18)

The whole church....now enjoyed a period of peace. It became established as it went forward in reverence for the Lord and in the strengthening presence of the Holy Spirit, continued to grow in numbers. (Acts 9:31, JB Phillips)

Sheralee insisted, in our seminary course on the theology of doing church, that "church" meant universal and that the purposes I outlined for the local church were actually intended for the church at large. Each local congregation has it's own calling, its own profile of responsibility. For example, her church did evangelism, not foreign missions. And that's OK. "That's our calling." Just as no individual Christian, not even the pastor, has all the gifts- the Spirit distributes as he wills - so the local church has a particular calling or gifting, I couldn't persuade her otherwise.

On the way home from the city where Sheralee and I discussed the issue, I formulated an answer. She had not been convinced by the exegetical answer outlined above, so I told a story. Here is part of what I wrote:

"If a local congregation has it's own profile (like individual Christians) and is responsible for less than all the purposes, what if a person goes to a church and finds no singing, no worship, just offerings and prayers and preaching? "Oh, you want worship? Well, you'll have to go down the street to New Life Charismatic Fellowship." You go there and find great worship, but very little solid Bible teaching from the pulpit so you ask when they do that. They say, "Oh, if you want Bible content, you'll have to go over to Calvary Bible Church." So you head down there and like it for a while, but then discover a lot of hypocrisy, leaders living double lives. You ask why they don't have any discipline and they say, "You want discipline, accountability? You'd better try First Fundamentalist Church over on Main Street." So you go there and, wow, how you begin to long for some caring help, some sense of family belonging, but all you get is hard-edged discipline.

I've been to many churches that are great on evangelism and keep growing and growing but they don't have two thoughts or care two dimes worth about the billions living in the unreached half of the world, outside of gospel light. And I've been to other churches that send lots of folks to the mission field and have big missions budgets but it's the same crowd year after year. No evangelism at home, no growth. So what is the motive, I ask myself that drives them to all local evangelism and no missions or to all missions and little local evangelism?

Sharalee responded graciously: "That scenario helps me to sort this out much better in my brain. I think your example is an excellent one! I believe you have made me see clearer why every local congregation should be doing everything God has commanded us to do." Sheralee experienced the same conversion I had experienced years before: the local congregation is God's appointed means for achieving his redemptive purposes and he expects the full prosecution of *all* the purposes he has established.

If there is a weak or missing purpose in a congregation it must mean some activity of the Spirit in gifting members is being neglected. What are the five purposes of the Church? Fully developed churches balance these purposes; 1. Worship. 2. Make disciples, 3. Member Care, 4. Evangelize, 5. Ministry of Compassion.

So what gift do we seek for ourselves or for our congregation? Pause now and review the purposes of the church. What might be needed in your church to fulfill those purposes. How do you fit into these purposes to bring all God's plan for the church into full effectiveness?

November 8
A Root Sin?
1 John 2:15-16

"Do not love the world or the things in the world. If anyone loves the world, the love of the Father is not in him. For all that is in the world—the desires of the flesh and the desires of the eyes and pride of life—is not from the Father but is from the world." (1 John 2:15-16)

Many theologians hold there is a root sin from which all other sins grow, or a comprehensive sin that includes all others as aspects of *the* sin. What that basic sin might be, however, is a matter of strong disagreement. Since the great commandment is to love, some have held that the violation of this or the opposite of love must be the root sin. But what is the opposite of love? Is it positive hatred, or is it simple indifference? Misdirected love is a summary statement that might qualify as the root sin, but it is so general that it conveys little precise meaning.

Some hold that the opposite of love is selfishness and that this is the source from which all other evil flows. If the choice of self is the supreme end, it must, therefore, be the essence of sin. Others propose that rather than selfishness, as the root of sin, opposition to God's character and will is the root of sin.

Since pride is the idolatry that enthrones oneself in God's place, many, such as Augustine and Thomas Aquinas, have held that pride is the taproot of sin. Is not this the sin that brought down Lucifer?

On the other hand, since the right relationship to God is summarized in the great biblical concept of faith, it should come as no surprise that the Reformers Luther and Calvin held the root of all other sins to be unbelief.

Perhaps idolatry, refusing to allow God to be God in the kingdom of one's life, could be considered the sin that summarizes the other sins. For example, unbelief is failing to acknowledge and trust God as God. Selfishness is replacing God with self, and pride is the same. Again, to fail in love is to fail in a right relationship to God first of all.

Or perhaps we should conclude that sin is so unutterably evil and so grotesquely complex that we shall never sort out all its hidden twistings and turnings. Perhaps our very disagreement serves to underscore the awful, incomprehensible nature of sin.

Sin is so hideous and destructive a force in our lives and in our society, it deserves our fullest hatred. But the sad thing is that none of us by nature hates sin. We may hate it in its final, gross manifestation. We may hate the results when they are painful or distasteful. We certainly may hate it in others. But we do not naturally hate sin in its beginning, enticing forms. And yet, we will never seek the cure until we see sin from the viewpoint of the Great Physician and abhor it.

Lists of sins. The medieval church identified seven deadly sins: pride, covetousness, lust, anger, gluttony, envy, and sloth. Answering to these, the church also developed the seven cardinal (chief) virtues. To Plato's four virtues of wisdom, courage, temperance, and justice were added the biblical qualities of faith, hope, and love.

The Apostle Paul presents eight lists of vices (Rom. 1:29 ff.; 1 Cor. 5:11; 6:9; 2 Cor. 12:20; Gal. 5:19 ff.; Eph. 4:31; 5:3; and Col. 3:5 ff.). Of these sins Paul listed, it is noteworthy that Jesus also condemned fornication, lasciviousness, covetousness, railing, clamor, and deceit.[16]

Basic sins. There is another way to put sins together in "affinity" groups or clusters. Scripture seems to identify certain basic sins of the spirit from which other sins flow. Each of these is the distortion of a good desire that God has put within us. We are created with the desire to enjoy things, the desire to have things, and the desire to accomplish things. When we fulfill these desires in a God-pleasing way, we are satisfied and God is satisfied. However, when we fulfill these in the wrong way, they become sin, sin that God categorizes as lust (the lust of the flesh), covetousness (the lust of the eye), and pride (the pride of life) (1 John 2:16).

When do these desires become evil? Note that temptation is not a sin. Temptation to do wrong is inevitable in the morally polluted environment in which we live. Christ himself was tempted in every way we can be tempted (Heb. 4:15). We should not feel guilty because we are tempted to lust, covet, or to be proud. However, to yield to the thought is to sin. To entertain lustful thoughts, for example, is to "*make provision for the flesh*" (Romans 13:14) and is wrong.

Again, to break God's laws in order to fulfill legitimate desires is wrong. For example, to lie in order to succeed or to cheat in order to possess is sinful. To fulfill legitimate desires in a wrong way, to go beyond God's design, is to sin. Also, when the desire controls us, as in an addiction, that desire has, in a sense, become our God. This, of course, is sin.

Some people seek the solution to temptation by refusing these God-given desires. The desire to enjoy things is denied through asceticism and celibacy. The desire to have things is controlled with vows of poverty. The desire to achieve or to "be something" is controlled through monasticism. However, these are not biblical ways of handling our God-given desires. The Roman Catholic church, Buddhism, and Greek dualism have held that asceticism is the highest and best way. Our human desires are evil and are to be reduced or eliminated. But the great good news of Christianity is that Jesus came eating and drinking, teaching a life-affirming doctrine. These basic human desires are God-given and good. They are not to be suppressed or denied, but enjoyed.

Having said this, however, we must point out the biblical truth that these desires sometimes should be denied in order to demonstrate our love for God and our love for others. This is why the teaching of self-denial in Scripture is so clear and strong. Not asceticism for its own sake, but self-denial, when it is necessary to act in love for God or for others, is the biblical way. Self-denial is not a popular idea in our age or, in fact, in any age. But the way of the Cross is still the way of love. Nevertheless, in the normal flow of life, these basic drives are created by God to be fulfilled. They become sinful when abused or misused. And when this sin is repeated, it can become a habitual characteristic.

When one habitually gives in to the temptation to lust, he descends into a life pattern of sensualism. When covetousness becomes a way of life, one becomes a materialist. When pride reigns unchecked, the character becomes egotistical. Which habitual characteristic marks your life? Sensualism? Materialism? Egoism? How might you go outside God-given boundaries for these human desires?

November 9
Trustworthy Words
Exodus 20:7

"You shall not take the name of the LORD your God in vain; for the LORD will not hold him guiltless who takes his name in vain." (Exodus 20:7)

The primary prohibition of this commandment is the prohibition of breaking contract. It is wrong to invoke the name of God to validate the truthfulness of one's statement when it is actually untrue. It is wrong to call God as witness to a contract, to make a vow before him, and then to break contract or vow. This is the way the third commandment is used in Scripture (Lev. 19:12; Matt. 5:33-34, 37; 23:16 ff.; 26:63). James 5:12 prohibits the using of an oath in any event. It seems that the Christian, by the very name he bears, has validation enough for every statement he makes. His word should be his bond. His yes or no are complete in themselves. For a Christian to break contract or to tell a lie is to break the third commandment, for it is to use profanely the name of God which he bears, whether or not he invokes the name. Though breaking a contract given in God's name is the primary focus of the third commandment, there are other implications.

Did Jesus and James forbid all oath taking? Some have held that it is wrong to take an oath in court or to swear allegiance to one's nation. The first problem with this view is that the Israelites were commanded to swear by the name of their God (Deut. 6:13; 10:20), and it was considered praiseworthy (Ps. 63:11). In line with this, Paul often said, "For God is my witness" and at least once took an oath (Rom. 1:9; 1 Thess. 2:5, 10). God himself takes oaths and swears by his own name (e.g., Heb. 6:16 ff.). Christ spoke under oath in court (Matt. 26:63). How is this apparent conflict to be resolved? Most branches of the church have held that Christ and James are reinforcing the teaching originally intended to prohibit oath breaking, not oath taking.

Of course the scope of prohibition was broader than just the breaking of a formal oath. In the *first* place, a covenant people (Exod. 19:5-6; 1 Pet. 2:5, 9) are name-bearers of God, and, by virtue of that, every word they speak must be trustworthy, every act in conformity with the covenant or oath of allegiance they have sworn to God. Who has broken the solemn vow of marriage in getting a divorce? The Lord will not hold him guiltless who takes his name in vain. Who has broken the solemn pledge given at baptism? The Lord will not hold him guiltless who takes his name in vain.

Sometimes it seems impossible to live up to the promises made, for every promise, even every yes and no of a Christian, is given in God's presence. He is the witness. Difficult to be sure, but God loves the kind of person who sticks to his word no matter how costly (Ps. 15:4). God loves the bankrupt businessman who spends his life attempting to repay his creditors. Integrity, rock-ribbed integrity, is the key idea in the third commandment and in the reinforcement given by Christ and James.

In the *second* place, the custom of invoking God's name to induce confidence in what one says had become so commonplace as to empty it of meaning. They were literally "taking God's name in vain." Today people use God's name without meaning it—mindlessly profaning God's holy name, often just a habit revealing an impoverished vocabulary. Even preachers use God's name flippantly, in a casual way, or in quoting a profane person. Against this both Jesus Christ and his brother James spoke stern words of warning.

Is this the only prohibition of the third commandment? Literally, to "take in vain" means to use in an empty way. Therefore, to use God's name without meaning it is to use it profanely. In a sense, to pray or to sing without meaning it is to use God's name in vain. The great temptation of those in full-time Christian work is to do religious activity professionally, simply to go through the routine of "performing" a church service. This is another way to profane the name of God.

Certainly any sort of irreverence violates the third commandment. To joke about sacred things or to joke with sacred things in such a way as to debase them is to act profanely. To use sacred things or words emptied of sacred meaning is wrong. For this reason, jokes about the Bible or sacred Bible truths, such as baptism, are not fitting for the Christian who holds God's name and God's things in high reverence.

Some people seem to use God's name in vain by repeating it often in prayer without thought. Others invoke God's name on almost every decision or plan they make. "God said . . ." "God told me to . . ." God's name is invoked to validate almost every activity. This may be genuine so far as a person's heart condition is concerned, but there is the danger that this may become profane, invoking God's name when it is not altogether certain that God himself stands behind that particular choice or activity.

What of minced oaths? Do these violate the third commandment? The sensitive Christian needs to be especially careful that he does not judge others too severely in these matters. Nevertheless, a good rule might be for the Christian to refrain from using any term that a standard dictionary identifies as being a substitute for true profanity. Certainly the Christian desires to give no appearance of evil.

What of humorous language? Christ says that we must give account for every idle word that we speak (Matt. 12:36). Ephesians 5:4 seems to prohibit levity of any kind. My understanding of the passage in Ephesians is that Paul is actually speaking of what we might call dirty jokes or impure speech (Eph. 4:29). It can hardly be held a sin to speak with a humorous touch since Christ himself did so on more than one occasion. When he nicknamed James and John the "Sons of Thunder," it can hardly be understood as a dead-serious speech. A log in one's eye or a camel crawling through a needle's eye are not solemn illustrations. Actually, humor can be anything but idle. It can be very productive of good.

Yet there are other standards that must be maintained. For example, humor should not hurt another person. However, humor to relieve tension, to counteract a heavy-handed approach is certainly productive of good. Sometimes a humorous touch will get across a message where the direct approach would be unacceptable. Humor is not necessarily a sin. Does it produce good, or is it idle, nonproductive foolishness? Does it violate the law of reverence or the law of love, or does it spring from love in a spirit of reverence for God?

For the people of God, words have a sacramental character. Jesus is the living Word of God. The Scriptures are the written Word of God. Our mandate is to speak and live the Word of God in the world reverently and consistently. The third commandment charges believers, avowed name-bearers of God (James 2:7), never to profane the name in word or behavior.

November 10
What is Murder?
Exodus 20:13

"Thou shalt not kill." (Exodus 20:13)

Murder is considered the worst of all crimes more universally than any other, and at the same time is the sin most universally practiced. Most practiced because Christ would not let us get away with restricting the law to those who slit throats or blow off heads. Jesus said, "You have heard that it was said to the men of old, '... whoever kills shall be liable to judgment.' But I say to you that everyone who is angry with his brother shall be liable to judgment" (Matt. 5:21-22). Even anger violates the sixth commandment.

FORMS OF KILLING - By including anger and verbal abuse in the category of murder, Jesus did not say or mean that they were as evil as murder. But they are the same variety of sin and may not be excused as mere human weakness. In fact, all sin, including murder, is rather like an onion. Beneath the final act are lesser acts, and beneath all the acts is a corrupt heart. Murder is highly visible, the full-grown sin, but when the outer layer is peeled away, various levels of violence are seen as part of the same "onion," and beneath the physical and verbal abuse is the heart of anger, hatred, or failing to love. If the core of inadequate love is planted and allowed to grow, the hateful activity will follow. And all of it falls under the judgment of God.

Murder. Some vegetarians have held that when God inscribed "You shall not kill" (Exod. 20:13) in stone at Sinai, he forbade the taking of any life for any cause. Some pacifists have held that he forbade the taking of any human life for any cause. But the commandment cannot be taken that way, for Moses, who received the Law, commanded the taking of animal life for sacrifices and food and the taking of human life in war and capital punishment. "Thou shalt not kill," in the context of Old Testament law, meant to deliberately take a human life that the Bible gives no authority to take. But there is one other biblical exception to the law against taking human life: killing in self-defense.

Self-defense. Physical resistance in self-defense seems to be validated in Scripture (Exod. 21:13; 22:2; Num. 35:22 ff.) but not commanded. There is a higher way—the law of love. Christ did not resist evil but gave himself to evil men to provide for their salvation.

Not all actions called self-defense are legitimate, and there is a hierarchy among those that are. Defense of others or even of oneself is certainly of higher priority than the defense of material possessions. But when there is danger of physical harm, a key question is whether or not life is in jeopardy. That is the clearest validation of self-defense.

Another basic question for the Christian is whether the impending harm is crime-oriented or whether it is persecution for Christ's sake. One might choose nonresistance when suffering for Christ but choose to resist in a crime-oriented aggression for the sake of others or even for the sake of the aggressor himself. If the choice is made to resist physical violence, the Christian should ask whether or not physical resistance is the only action available or whether there are other options such as talk or deception. If there seems to be no other option but to resist with physical force, the Christian should discern whether killing is the only alternative or whether lesser violence would accomplish adequate restraint.

Though there are exceptions in which God authorizes the taking of human life, the sin of murder is the ultimate sin against a human being (Lev. 24:17; Num. 35:16-21). Life may not be the supreme value, but it is certainly a critical one for the continued pursuit of other values! And the value of life is probably the watershed issue for any society.

Violence. In a decaying society murder may still be abhorred, but violence short of murder often becomes acceptable. Studies have repeatedly shown that violence in the entertainment media fosters such acceptance. But the ugly end result is a sick society where spouse abuse and child abuse is said to touch one of four people. Violence in the home has been the underreported and largely ignored crime of a society preoccupied with appearances.

Christ's commentary on the sixth commandment emphasized verbal abuse. James (1:26; 3:1-12) and Solomon (Prov. 13:3; 15:1, 4, 23; 17:28; 18:8, 13; 21:23; 29:20) had a great deal to say about sins of the tongue, but the rest of Scripture is strong on the subject as well. James says that the tongue is like wildfire and poison. It not only poisons relationships and burns up the lives of others; it consumes the one himself whose tongue is not disciplined by the Spirit (James 3).

A direct attack on a person with carping criticism or biting depreciation, sarcastic humor, or subtle insinuation can destroy something in that person. But just as deadly is the criticism spoken about a person to others. The law of love seals the lips. Any word that harms another is murder, unless spoken in love to that person or spoken only to another who is responsible to correct the wrong (Matt. 18:15-18). The absent person is just as safe with the Spirit-directed child of God as the one who is present with him.

Neglect. Another way to harm is by doing and saying nothing when a word or an action would keep from harm. Failure to put a balustrade around a flat rooftop brought bloodguiltiness if someone fell from the roof (Deut. 22:8). Failure to do good, when in one's power to do so, is sin (Prov. 3:27-28). So the poor, the helpless, and the starving are my responsibility to the extent I have ability to help. To be silent when another is falsely accused, whether in a court of law or in the presence of private gossip, is to participate in the harm. Neglect, then, is another form of murder (see also Exod. 21:29-31).[73]

Anger murders, but this is so prevalent we will deal with murder another day. As does racism, abortion, suicide and euthanasia. The question for us now is consider which of the manifestations of murder described above do you, or even someone else, see in your life? Perhaps a punishment that is too severe to a child, or verbal abuse toward your spouse. How do you value life? Whose life wins when there are competing interests? How could you appropriately intervene in a culture that neglects the vulnerable? Hard questions, but necessary for the Christian life.

---

[73] IBE (2014), 349-350, 349-355.

November 11
Emergent or Submergent?
Matthew 28:18-20

"And Jesus came and said to them, "All authority in heaven and on earth has been given to me. Go therefore and make disciples of all nations, baptizing them in the name of the Father and of the Son and of the Holy Spirit, teaching them to observe all that I have commanded you. And behold, I am with you always, to the end of the age." (Matthew 28:18-20)

Let's agree right up front that the terms "emergent" and "holistic" are so elastic they can be made to fit whatever the user has in mind. At the same time, let's agree that proponent and opponent alike feel, whatever the meaning, it is of great significance for the future of the churches. And that future will differ from the past. One other agreement one could wish – the discussion should not begin till the discussants agree on what they're talking about!

So let me begin with a statement of what I'm talking about. A growing ("emerging") number of those who consider themselves evangelical wish to combine ("holistic") all the responsibilities of the church toward the world in defining the mission ("missional") of the church.

Who could object to advocating that the church fulfill all of God's purposes toward "those who are without"? Simply put: that depends on how you combine them. Do we prioritize? If so, which purpose receives priority? Or should we keep them differentiated? My objection is to those who combine the churches' ministries of mercy and seeking justice with the historic evangelistic/church starting mission in such a way that the evangelistic mission is diminished, if not dismantled. Increasing numbers do this intentionally for reasons we will shortly examine, but far more seem to be slipping unconsciously into such a mode.

My contention is that this is justifiable neither by Scripture nor by history. I become more distressed and confused as I watch the juggernaut of missions in the last century fade. Numbers of career missionaries shrink, historic mission agencies struggle for recruits, training programs languish in seminaries and Bible colleges designed to prepare Pauline style pioneer missionary church starters.

What happened to the tidal wave of World War II veterans who flooded to the fields for what must have been the greatest foreign missionary advance since the first century? What happened to the vision we saw in 1974 as we sat with 4,000 mission and church leaders from 141 countries in Lausanne, Switzerland? Billy Graham, who convened the convention, said, "We stand on the threshold of a new era. Never before have the opportunities been so great. I believe that God will....direct our strategy toward total world evangelization in our time." At Lausanne we heard Ralph Winter tell us of the "hidden people," the thousands of people groups lying outside the reach of gospel witness. A whole new focus of mission activity was born. Target those as yet unreached people groups, he advocated. And that's exactly what we did. Missions activity was transformed. For example, of the scores of movements that emerged, the most prominent was the AD 2000 movement, a movement that strategized how to get the gospel to every person and a church for every people by the year 2,000.

The result? Well, I'm sure those efforts participated in what became the greatest advance of the gospel in history. But I'm sorry to report that, in spite of that, today probably 4 billion people have yet to hear with understanding the way to life in Christ, and half of those can't hear because there is no witnessing church among them. They live out of reach of present gospel witness. Church-less, Christ-less peoples. Now-a-days missiologists call them the "unengaged unreached people groups."

So what is the response of the evangelical churches of America to this unfinished task? We hear of holistic mission by emerging churches. We hear of missional vision and a focus on finding scientific solutions to the health problems of the world, especially AIDS, our responsibility to protect God's creation from the assaults of modern consumer-driven technology, to educate the illiterate, to correct all injustices, empower the oppressed, alleviate poverty.

Is this bad? Not at all. Just insufficient. Because, if all illnesses were conquered and all people lived strong and healthy to age 100, if all poverty were eliminated so that everyone owned her own home, a "chicken in every pot" and a "car in every garage," if all illiteracy and ignorance were wiped out and every citizen of the planet had a college education, if we could eliminate injustice so that everyone on earth lived free and without fear, but they all ended up in hell, what would we have accomplished?

We would have utterly failed God's purpose for his Church. From Genesis 3 to Revelation 22 the problem is sin, alienation from God. And God's own solution? It's the story of spiritual redemption, reconciling an errant people to himself. And his method? Create a redemptive remnant. To do what? Reconcile the alienated with himself. In a word, provide hope for eternity, not just comfort for one's brief lifespan. God's primary mission from of old - including the 21st century- is John 3:16! God so loved that he took extreme action so that people need not perish but have everlasting life. In summary, my problem is the paradigm shift *from* finding and sending special evangelistic church starting incarnational missionaries *to* holistic mission by everyone to do everything good and calling it the mission of the church.

I saying that humanitarian effort is unworthy? Not at all. If God rewards for even a single cup of cold water given a thirsty person in Jesus' name, what sort of reward can the giant-slayers anticipate? So, yes, do all the good you can to relieve this dysfunctional human race. We're appointed as salt and light for a dark, corrupt and corrupting society. Furthermore, if we don't demonstrate the mercy and justice of God, why should anyone believe our story? I truly believe in holistic ministry. You could say the church has many missions if you mean by that term, "purposes." But to draft the term "mission" to encompass all the church is called to do for a fallen world is misleading in light of what the term has meant historically.

So will it be the Great Commission or The Great Command? The evangelistic mandate or the cultural mandate? Both! And don't just prioritize. Differentiate. Because, when you merge the two and call it "holistic mission," the horizontal, the visible, the cultural mandate has always submerged the evangelistic

This move to merge, of course, ranges all the way from those who simply want to consolidate the purposes of the church toward the world into a whole and who yet maintain a priority for evangelism, all the way to those in the Emergent Church who replace the evangelistic mission altogether and whom their fellows no longer consider evangelical in faith. The commonality among the holistic and emergent of all varieties is the merging of church purposes into one. And how does the Emergent Church movement, not to mention increasing numbers of main-stream evangelicals, justify the leap from the differentiated model to the consolidated? Simply put, by shifting the model for missions from Acts and the example of the apostles, especially Paul, to Jesus himself with a contemporary spin on what Jesus' mission was.

November 12
Sent
Luke 4:18

"The Spirit of the Lord is upon Me, Because He has anointed me to preach the gospel to the poor; He has sent me to heal the brokenhearted, To preach deliverance to the captives And recovery of sight to the blind, To set at liberty those who are oppressed, To preach the acceptable year of the Lord. " (Luke 4:18)

The Emergent Church concentrates on Luke, chapter 4 as the key mandate for us as well as for Jesus. Note that there's nothing here about evangelism unless you spiritualize the language. This was pre-cross, pre-great commission. But this is taken as the answer to the prayer he taught us, "thy kingdom come." Bringing in God's Kingdom, then, is to obey the first of the five versions of Christ's great commission: As the Father has sent me, so I send you (John 20:21).

Since Christ does not expand his meaning of "as," commentators through the centuries have not agreed on his meaning. Was it a simple parallel, "as the Father sent, so I send." Or did he intend the "as" to mean the motive–love? Or did he mean the same job description, as emerging interpreters contend? Surely it would be instructive to consider all his final mandates to understand a term so critical to understanding his final command?

Also the commission in Matthew is used to reinforce this Kingdom mandate: Go...disciple...baptize, teaching them to observe all that I have commanded you..." (Matthew 28:19, 20) . And what did he command? Deliver the poor, the ill, the oppressed. In a word, Bring in my Kingdom.

To make this shift on biblical grounds three major factors must be ignored: (1) Jesus didn't carry out his mandate the way the contemporary Emergent Church advocates, (2) the three other "great commissions" can't be made to sound like that quote from Isaiah Jesus read in the synagogue at Nazareth; and, most significant (3) those who heard him repeatedly give his last, great command, his marching orders for the church, understood him to mean something wholly different from what the Emerging Church is up to.

Consider those three flaws in the new paradigm. (1) Jesus' ministry as our model. Jesus was concerned about illness, poverty, injustice, but he did not work to change the structures of society, he didn't even preach against an oppressive Roman regime. His ministry seemed more like a spiritual implementation of that ancient prophetic word. He said explicitly, when accused of seeking to set up a kingdom, My Kingdom is not of this world. (John 18:19).There's coming a day when it will be fully earthly-- political, if you please. Yes, military. But not when he was here on earth. And not what he commissioned his disciples, his Church to do.(2) The other three commissions are hard to get around, so they're largely ignored by those who advocate the new paradigm: Go into all the world and preach the gospel to every creature (Mark 16:15). And what is the "gospel" they are to preach? He leaves no doubt of his intention. There in the upper room he showed them from the Old Testament Scripture what their mandate was to be:

"Thus it is written ...that repentance and remission of sins should be preached in His name to all nations, beginning at Jerusalem. And you are witnesses of these things." (Lk 24.46-48).

You'll notice the Apostles still didn't get it, because as they left the upper room where he had just spelled out their mission, they were still into Kingdom mission – displacing the unjust oppressors, restoring the messianic reign. But Jesus said, "That really isn't your business. Kingdom restoration is up to the Father – his timing, his action. Your business is to....be my witnesses in Jerusalem, Judea, Samaria, and the uttermost parts of the world" (Acts 1:8). (3) So what did those who heard the great commission, given on five different occasions, hear him say? Read the book of

Acts. Follow the travels of Paul. Surely they healed the sick, yes, they raised funds to care for the poor of their own church family. But the focus of their ministry was to go and go and go to proclaim the good news of eternal salvation and plant local congregations. "I will build my church," Jesus had promised. Not, "I will transform society into God's Kingdom on earth." I will build my church! They finally got it. We seem to be losing it.

So if the new paradigm of holistic mission--merging the two, the evangelistic mission and the ministry of mercy, if you please - is not Bible-based, where did it come from? The leaders of the Emergent Church describe themselves as "evangelical post moderns." For much of the leadership this is self-conscious, but for the vast majority of Evangelicals it's simply the inevitable result of unconscious adoption of some postmodern assumptions.

To the self-conscious postmodern evangelical, Scripture is not taken as objective, unchanging, revealed truth. It is simply the narrative of God's story, his wisdom worked out in the experience of the people of that ancient culture. It's valuable, but never intended to make unalterable mandates. For example, to the postmodern, judgmentalism is out, tolerance is in. You don't impose, you propose. And who knows who has more of God's truth–you or them?

So how does an eternal destiny called hell fit in? Not very well! Thus, even if you suspect there may be some reality to the biblical suggestion of an eternal destiny at stake, you mustn't talk about it, let alone shape your ministry by it. And if you did, you would be doomed to failure because that kind of black-and-white, in-or-out talk is unacceptable to the postmodern.

Yet, because we are true followers of the Jesus way, what do we do? Well, there are parts of our good news acceptable to the postmodern– compassion, caring, personal involvement, relationships. Thus, to maximize our postmodern values in the cause of God's Kingdom, what better way than to focus on those ills in society we can see and, if we're like Jesus, care about. Besides, if we insist on the old paradigm of evangelistic church multiplying, you authenticate that message only by embodying the character of Christ in seeking mercy and justice.

Does the 21st Century missions' enterprise, then, mean bringing in the Kingdom by correcting the ills of society? The answer may well depend on where you live. Do you live in the North or the South?

We spotlight the mega-shift in Christianity from the Northern hemisphere to the Southern. We northerners are in the rapidly shrinking minority of Christians. And what is the mission theology of the South? First of all, it's thoroughly evangelical, biblical., if you please – it flows from Scripture, not from their – often dreadful - environment.. For the Southern hemisphere, missions is defined in Apostolic terms, not by 21st century postmodernism.

Where, then, is the 21st century church headed? I predict continued explosive growth from the Southern hemisphere by a people who believe the Word of God. They're out to win their neighbors – near and far – to reconciliation with God and incorporation into his church. And often, as they go, they ameliorate the ills of their community as well. And in the Northern hemisphere? If we do not correct course we may discover the churches' efforts to save for eternity submerged by the emerging surge of efforts to save for time. So perhaps the answer to where we're headed depends on where we live. How do you define mission? Is it defined in Apostolic terms, or by 21st century postmodernism?

November 13
Part or Central?
Acts 1:8

"You will receive power when the Holy Spirit comes on you; and you will be my witnesses in Jerusalem, and in all Judea and Samaria, and to the ends of the earth." (Acts 1:8)

The students at a leading evangelical seminary wanted to examine the question: What is the place of world evangelism in the life of a Christian and in the life of a church? They wanted to determine what the Bible says about the issue. Being seminarians, they staged a debate. They invited the most influential man in world missions at that time, Donald McGavran. McGavran said, "Missions is a most important purpose of the church."

After the meeting I approached him, "Dr. McGavran, the last time I heard you speak you said it was *the* most important task of the church. Which is it, `a' or `the'?" "Well," he said, "if it's `the' purpose, that includes `a'; and some audiences aren't ready to call it *the* purpose of the church." He obviously ranked world evangelism near the top of his agenda of what the church is about.

On the other side of the debate was a leading evangelical theologian. The task of a theologian is to organize biblical truth in logical order. Most theologians consider missions part of the church history department or the practical theology division along with subjects like Christian education. They usually do not consider missions a proper subject for theology.

Before the debate began, the theologian said, "Dr. McGavran, before we begin I just want you to know that I believe in missions. It's even in my theological system. It's point number D-12 in my theology." By the designation D-12 he meant that missions was a part of the outline but not a central part. It was simply lost in the list. The theologian's statement set the stage, because missions was clearly A-1 in McGavran's theology. After the debate the theologian said, "Dr. McGavran, you're very persuasive and I admire you and your work. But I want you to know that missions is still point number D-12 in my theological system."

For most evangelical churches in America, world missions is point D-12 in the church program, or off their agenda altogether. What about the handful that are committed to world evangelism? Are they misguided, or are they merely obedient to the Lord of the church? Finding an answer to that critical question is important. Today ask yourself: How important to God is world evangelization? How will living for Christ impact my concern for missions? What can I use as a measure of my concern and commitment? If what is central in God's thinking turns out to be peripheral in mine, perhaps I have heart trouble. But God doesn't. God is love, so much so that He gave His one and only Son that no one might perish.

The Old Testament prophecies repeatedly predicted the coming of the Messiah, but He was not for Israel only. He was coming for all peoples. What does the New Testament predict about Christ's second coming? Jesus Himself said: "This gospel of the kingdom will be preached in the whole world as a testimony to all nations, and then the end will come" (Matthew 24:14). Finally, John pulls the curtain on the last act of earth's drama: "After this I looked and there before me was a great multitude that no one could count, from every nation, tribe, people and language, standing before the throne and in front of the Lamb" (Revelation 7:9). From Genesis to Revelation, the Bible is full of promises about God's plan of world evangelization. The Spirit has a global plan, and He is bringing it to pass in our day as never before. The downside of the population explosion - more people are lost today than ever before. Now let me tell you the positive side. God is bringing in a harvest greater than any since the world began. In fact, more people have been born into God's family in the last 25 years than in all the centuries of church history since the apostles' day! God's promises assure us His salvation purpose will be accomplished.

May we remember, more important than where we stand in a debate on world evangelism is to discover where God stands! When we examine Scripture, we find that:

- God's character makes world evangelism inevitable.
- God's activity proves His heart is passionate for the world to know Him.
- God's promises assure a successful conclusion to His plan.
- God's command means we must think as He thinks and act as He acts.

You may agree with John the apostle. He says that a certain characteristic of God is so central to His nature that you could even say He is that attribute (1 John 4:8). John so wanted to get the point across that he repeated the same words a few verses later: "God is love" (1 John 4:16). God didn't create love to give His creatures something to aim at. He is love by nature. As a result, the Spirit created humans in the image of God, so that He could love them and be loved by them. Creating humans with the power to choose was a risky proposition. People might choose to walk away from a loving relationship. They might even defy that love - which is just what our first parents did, and every son and daughter of Adam since.

But that didn't change God's character. He continued to so love the world that He gave His own Son to buy us back (John 3:16). That's the express purpose for His invasion of our humanity - to seek and to save the lost (Matt. 18:11). If love was the reason for Jesus' first coming, love is also the reason He has not come again. People keep resisting God's loving advances to them; and it breaks His heart. The broken-hearted God delays His coming because He doesn't want anyone to perish (2 Pet. 3:9).

Consider the tension in the loving heart of God: longing to return to embrace His bride, the church; but at the same time, distressed over the many who are lost. How many? Just a number doesn't reach our hearts, since we don't have the capacity to love each one as God does. But here's a statistic that should snap into focus what distresses God: the population explosion is so great that one demographer concluded more people live now than all who have lived and already died.

This means that more than 6 billion people today are lost. It's difficult to grasp such numbers and even harder to love those faceless multitudes. But God does love each one - they aren't faceless to Him. The situation is more difficult than numbers alone can tell. Half those lost people are out of reach of any witnessing church. That must break God's heart. Because God is love, world evangelism is central in His thinking. Is it central in yours?

November 14
Spittin' Image
Genesis 1:26-27

"God said, "Let us make man in our image, in our likeness, and let them rule over the fish of the sea and the birds of the air, over the livestock, over all the earth, and over all the creatures that move along the ground. So God created man in his own image, in the image of God he created him; male and female he created them." (Genesis 1:26-27)

"Just look at that boy! Why, he's the spittin' image of Joe!" I'm not sure how the "spittin'" got in there, but we get the picture: the boy is a replica of his father - looks like him, walks like him, talks like him. And so with us. In some mysterious way we were made on the model of God Himself. In a strategic planning session deep in eternity, the Father, Son, and Holy Spirit agreed, "Let us make man in our image."

God created us, in some mysterious way, to be like Him. That likeness we call the image of God. But what does His image look like? Theologians debate the meaning of image. Since the Bible doesn't give a concise definition, we have to draw from various passages of Scripture to find the meaning.

A few scholars suggest that our bodies reflect God's nature in some mysterious way, but most would leave our bodies off the list. God is spirit and not physical, apart from the incarnation of Jesus. Recently, some Bible scholars have added sexuality - maleness and femaleness - to the characteristics of God. They believe that God combines in His being all the characteristics of both sexes, but most would not include sexuality in the list.
Alexander the Great, Caesar, King Nebuchadnezzar, and Herod the Great all had two things in common-each claimed to be God and hated cats. They grasped for supreme authority, and the cats were the only ones who wouldn't obey! Would supreme authority and power represent God's image? Today we are rapidly achieving corporately what some of the ancients futilely tried to achieve as individuals.

With the assistance of computers, we dream of accumulating infinite knowledge. With jets and telecommunications, we think we can be everywhere- omnipresent. But these were not the aspects of God He intended for us to share. Not omnipotence. Not omniscience. Not omnipresence. Of course, we do have high potential for knowing and doing, since we are modeled after God Himself. That's why so much human achievement in the arts and sciences is truly magnificent, but God's infinities are forever beyond us. Yet, in one way God designed us to be just like Him.

Scientists tell us that porpoises communicate with signals; but they've written no dictionaries yet. Pandas make tools - they break off a stick to dig out the food they want; but they've built no automobiles yet. Ants build incredibly complex cities and even keep aphid-cows to milk; but no churches or temples have ever been found in those cities. Monkeys misbehave; but none have been known to blush. When God created a special being in His own likeness, He designed one unlike the animals He had already created - one with a spirit who could communicate, create, know right from wrong, and, above all, love and be loved by God Himself. That is His "image," the stamp of the Designer. We are indeed a "designer model" - modeled after the Designer Himself. That was the work of the Holy Spirit in His first activity, creating us in God's image.

Even the greatest among us fall far short of the authority, intelligence, and strength of God. So, does being somewhat more intelligent, stronger, or having greater earthly authority really make a person that much more like God? God made us to be like Him, not in power or authority but in our moral nature. He designed us to be loving, holy, trustworthy, just, good, peaceful, and joyful. We share, to a greater or lesser degree, some of His non-moral attributes, such as the capacity for abstract reasoning. But He designed us to be exactly like Him in His moral nature: *"Be holy because I, the Lord your God, am holy"* (Lev. 19 :2).

You and I are designed on the model of the Creator. The joy of life comes from glorifying Him. We glorify Him as we more accurately reflect His character. How are you in your modeling? Why not pray and ask God to show you how you can become more like Him in His character?

November 15
Lead Well
1 Peter 4:10-11

"As each one has received a gift, employ it for one another...in order that in everything God may be glorified through Jesus Christ. To him belong glory and dominion..." (1 Peter 4:10-11, RSV).

It seems strange that God who graciously shared his very nature with us, creating us in his moral image and who by his Spirit works to restore that likeness, should also share his incommunicable attributes as well - his authority, his wisdom, his power. Only he distributes those qualities among his people in what we have called the gifts of the Spirit.

What wisdom! There is no limit to his intention for us to advance in holiness. The Spirit's goal is to make us **just like him,** all of us. But he never intended any single person to arrogate to himself those incommunicable attributes. So he distributed them - he gave gifts to each as he willed.[74] His purpose was that through us corporately, together, the ***congregation***, we could do his (supernatural) work in this world.

How sad, then that we, while pursuing holiness, to be sure, also reach in unrighteous pride for his incommunicable attributes, especially his lordship. Perhaps that is why God says several times in slightly different ways, "I resist the proud but give grace to the humble." And following Satan's rebellion we are in danger of falling, of losing it all - both the powers we sought and the holiness we neglected. So what should we do about it?

The first part of the solution is for the leader to demonstrate personally an example of yieldedness to God, obedience to him alone, brokenness over and hatred of sin, openness with the brethren, and unaffected acceptance of the servant role.

Just as important is for the leaders to hold before the people constantly the lordship principle. This must not be preached as a doctrine, merely, but discipleship training in this relationship with the head of the church must characterize the life of the congregation.

Each member must also be discipled in her or his role as a member of the body, recognizing one's own gift and esteeming the gifts of others. *"Don't cherish exaggerated ideas of yourself or your importance, but try to have a sane estimate of your capabilities by the light of the faith that God has given"* (Romans 12:3, Phillips).

An essential element of demonstrating that Christ is indeed lord in a congregation is a heart attitude of humility and love. We must submit in love and humility to the authority above us. We are to be subject to one another (Ephesians

---

[74] 1 Corinthians 12-14, especially 12: 11; 29, 30

5:21), in honor preferring one another (Romans 12:10), giving honor to whom honor is due (Romans 13:7). Those who lead must do so in love and humility, first by example, those for whom they are responsible. The brother or sister's welfare - not one's own - is master of the spiritual leader.[75] Paul says his freedom of choice is freedom to make himself the servant of all. In humility, the leader must count others better than himself (Philippians 2:3), in honor preferring the other (Romans 12:10), not lording it over the flock (I Peter 5:3).

We have noted how organizational structure may adversely affect the lordship principle. One way to ameliorate such negative impact is to follow the biblical pattern of a plurality of elders. Whatever the structure, if the New Testament model is to be followed, the authority and responsibilities of leadership will be dispersed among several, not reserved for a single leader. Another practical measure for promoting the lordship of Christ is to promote interpersonal ties with many people rather than maintaining exclusive relationship in spiritual authority with the pastor alone. It may be hard on one's emotions or ego to find people dependent on other members of the congregation or holding them in high esteem as spiritual leaders. So it may be difficult to permit it, let alone plan for it. But by the same token it is essential. This means a division of labor so that all who are gifted as teachers have ample opportunity to teach, all whom God would gift in counseling would have ample opportunity for a pastoral ministry, and so on throughout all the spiritual ministry of the church.

We have noted the general malaise of the church and some ways to cure it, but we must return to the initial truth that God does indeed exercise his authority on earth through human leadership. This delegated authority, whether in the home, society, or church, is not absolute, to be sure, but it is real - authority not merely to give benevolent advice or to enforce obedience to the ten commandments. It is an authority to make rules and to supervise conduct for the benefit of all members of the group. All human authority is limited by human finitude and warped by human sinfulness, but God has chosen to accomplish his purposes in the world through people in authority. When it comes to church, what that authority should look like may come as a surprise.

But it may surprise us to discover that the role-model for making him lord is the Lord Christ himself! We take our cue from one whom some have called the first prelate, the prince and lord, the pope of the Church - Peter, whom we shall discover did not arrogate to himself those lordly titles. In his first letter, Peter spells out the pattern of godly or God-like leadership:

To the elders among you, I appeal as a fellow elder....: Be shepherds of God's flock that is under you care, serving as overseer, not because you must, but because you are willing, as God wants you to be, not greedy for money, but eager to serve; not lording it over those entrusted to you, but being examples to the flock... Young men, in the same way be submissive to those who are older. Clothe yourselves with humility toward one another, because, 'God opposes the proud but give grace to the humble.' Humble yourselves, therefore under God's mighty hand... (1 Peter 5:1-6)

---

[75] 1 Corinthians 10:23-11:1; 1 Corinthians 9:19-23; Romans 14

November 16
Sabbath Rest
Exodus 20:8-11

"Remember the Sabbath day, to keep it holy. Six days you shall labor, and do all your work, but the seventh day is a Sabbath to the LORD your God. On it you shall not do any work, you, or your son, or your daughter, your male servant, or your female servant, or your livestock, or the sojourner who is within your gates. For in six days the LORD made heaven and earth, the sea, and all that is in them, and rested on the seventh day. Therefore the LORD blessed the Sabbath day and made it holy." (Exodus 20:8-11)

Jesus Christ said both yes and no to Sabbath regulations. Christ said yes to the rest day, but a resounding no to the rabbinical additions. He contended with the scribes continuously over their interpretation of the law, with the complex hedge they built about the law to protect it.

Christ is speaking of himself as being lord of the Sabbath. What does this mean? First, we know that Christ did not come to destroy the law, but to fulfill it (Matt. 5:17-19).

"Fulfilling the law" has several meanings. It means that he obeyed the law. That is why he was in the synagogue on the Sabbath and why he obeyed the rest of the Old Testament moral law although he opposed the rabbinical interpretation.

The rest day as a special day is somewhat similar to nighttime. Man has to have several hours of rest every night. Most normal, healthy people are delighted that they can go to bed and rest at night. They don't feel it is something laid on them that is very hard to do. Even so, some things must be done at night, and in an emergency a person may skip the rest time. In a similar way, Christ indicates some exceptions to the law of the rest day and some emergency situations. He said it was all right to grind grain informally and thus prepare necessary food to eat (Mark 2:23-27). He said also that it was all right to water cattle on the Sabbath (Luke 13:15). In fact, he commanded a man to pick up his bed and take it home (John 5:8). So there are "works of necessity" that must continue on the rest day, and Christ was against a dry legalism that hurt people instead of helping them. Then Christ healed on the rest day (Mark 3:1-5) and was angry with the religious leaders for even thinking he should not heal the man. According to their rabbinical teaching, it was wrong to heal on the Jewish Sabbath. He was angry with them because "works of mercy" are not only legitimate; they are a necessary part of the rest day: healing the sick, pulling cattle out of ditches (Matt. 12:11; Luke 14:5). These then are exceptions to the law of rest: works of necessity and mercy.

Then there is work involved in the service of God (Matt. 12:5). For spiritual leaders the rest day is the busiest day of all. But it is a special service to the Lord of the rest day and to his people, making it possible for them to worship and serve.

We hold that the law of a rest day was established by God at the time of creation both by example and by ordinance. When the time came for him to reveal in permanent form a summary of his moral requirements of man, this commandment of the rest day was included. It was also incorporated in the entire ceremonial system as a special sign of redemption and covenant relationship. In subsequent years, teachers of the law, who were not authorized to write Scripture or give an authoritative revelation of the will of God, created an enormous compendium of obligations for Sabbath observance. When Jesus came, he spoke with authority and cut away all the scribal additions. He faithfully observed the commandment as God originally gave it. He illustrated the kind of work that was permissible in the spirit of the day. Works of necessity, mercy, and service to God are not a violation of his intent in giving the commandment,

437

but rather a part of his intent. This much is clear.

We conclude that a rest day is a good thing, one of God's good gifts for the welfare of mankind. It is a law rather than a recommendation because a recommendation would be no blessing at all. It is the binding aspect of the rest day that releases one for rest and worship. If the rest day is merely recommended, we are not free to rest from the pressures of life and turn without hindrance to joyful fellowship with God and his people. We must still face the pressures and frustrations of mundane obligations. But a required rest day sets us free. To turn away from our daily occupation to spend a day in fellowship with him and service for him must certainly please him even more than offering to him a portion of all our possessions in token of the fact that all belongs to him. The only way the careful observance of the rest day commandment could displease our Lord would be if a person looked to that obedience as a means of earning merit or as a way of salvation.

In light of God's action in resting after work, his setting aside at that time a day of rest sacred to himself, the subsequent commands of Scripture concerning a day of rest, the example and teaching of Jesus Christ in affirming and interpreting the Old Testament standard, and the observance of the first day of the week by the New Testament church as a special day of worship, we must recognize Sunday as a special day of rest, worship, and service to the Lord.

Notice, in brief review, how every topic we have studied centers ultimately in God. We shall see as our studies continue that every standard for life is the same. Note also the outcome when God is not given first place in any standard, how quickly it disintegrates into meaningless and powerless, even destructive half-truth.

True love begins and ends with God. He defines it by his own character, and all other loves reach their potential only when yielding to love for God as supreme. Law is based on God's character—his expressed will that we be like him. Thus, to violate his law is to violate his person. Even human authority derives its authority from God and must give an account to him for how that responsibility has been discharged. Those under human authority owe ultimate allegiance only to God. All sin is, in the final analysis, against God. This is seen in the fact that sin is falling short of God's glorious righteousness, that sins of the mind and heart are crucial, and that sin is, above all, breaking the first four commandments. Lust is God-given appetite gone berserk, and covetousness is, at root, idolatry. Pride is the essence of sin against God, for in it man attempts to usurp the credit due God and establish his own autonomy.

Thus, "God first" is far more than a theoretical, appropriately courteous starting point for Christian living. It is intensely practical and, in fact, the only way to integrate all the other horizontal relationships. God in person is the beginning and ending point of all truly biblical choices.

November 17
What Doubt Says About God
Habakkuk 2:4

"The righteous will live by faith" (Habakkuk 2:4)

The Spirit of God lives inside and has all the resources of heaven to empower me. But what if I don't seem to experience a supernatural quality of life? Everything I say or do, even most of my attitudes and thoughts, could be explained by a good psychologist in terms of what I might have inherited and what my circumstances might have been. What's wrong? I may not have a close connection with the Spirit. The divine current doesn't flow automatically - I have to throw the switch, and the switch is faith. "The righteous will live by faith" (Habakkuk 2:4) must be an important truth: It's the only Old Testament faith quoted three times in the New Testament (Romans 1:17; Galatians 3:11; Hebrews 10:38). Not only are we justified by faith, but we live out the Christian life by that same faith. "As you... received Christ Jesus the Lord [by faith], so walk in him [by faith]" (Colossians 2: 6, NKJV. author's paraphrase). The Holy Spirit within does his work when we throw the switch of faith. But is he really able to give me the victory over my besetting sin? Someone else, maybe, but me?
One day, when I was stumbling down a dark alley of doubt, three Bible stories startled me with what I was actually saying about God.

- The father was distraught. Jesus' disciples had failed to live up to the advertisements. They couldn't heal the father's son of his terrifying condition. Then Jesus came on the scene and the father said, "If you can, heal my son," (Mark 9:22-23, author's paraphrase) "If you can!" What kind of lead-in is that?
- The hired mourners had lots of experience with dead people. They knew dead when they saw it. So they slapped one another on the back and scoffed. As they pointed at the itinerant preacher, they said, "Some healer he is! He doesn't even know the kid is dead. We know better." (Luke 8: 53, author's paraphrase). You know better? What kind of talk is that?
- The wind howled and the waves lashed the little boat mercilessly, terrifying those seasoned fishermen. But there was a passenger on board who had no better sense than to lean back on a pillow in the stern and go to sleep. "Enough of this!" The fisherman shook their leader awake, "What's wrong with you? Don't you care that we're dead men?" (Mark 4: 38, author's paraphrase) "Don't you care? "What kind of question is that?

These were questions of unbelief. The father wondered if Jesus could handle his tough situation, the professional mourners were more confident in their own judgment than his, and the disciples accused him of being uncaring. When those three Bible stories woke me to what I was actually saying about God, I saw my "innocent" flirtations with unbelief as actually calling into question the very character of God. What an insult. When we fail to trust God, we are actually questioning his power (as the father did) or his wisdom (as the mourners did) or his love (as the disciples did). We're saying in effect, "You're not strong enough to handle my rotten boss, to make me victorious with my impatience, to meet my needs while I'm unemployed." Or we're saying, "I'm not sure you're smart enough to figure out how to get me out of this jam, to guide me in the best way. I think I know a better way than yours." Or we're saying, "you're powerful enough, alright, and you're smart enough. You just don't care that much about me." We call into question the character of God. That's the first problem with unbelief. God is displeased when we don't trust him; He has been insulted. And by a family member at that. "Without faith it is impossible to please God." (Hebrews 11:6). When we don't trust him, it makes God sad, just as it makes us sad when someone we love doesn't trust us. But there's more to the tragedy. Not only is God hurt; so are we. Unbelief short circuits the flow of divine energy. The Holy Spirit won't act freely in the life of one who doesn't trust him for salvation, for growth, for success. In the Christian life, for power and ministry, faith is the connector to God-power. How about you? What are you saying to God about your point of need? Is He powerful enough? Smart enough? Strong enough? Does He love you enough? Or do you know better?

November 18
The Purposes of Pain
James 1:2-4

*"Consider it pure joy, my brothers and sisters, whenever you face trials of many kinds, because you know that the testing of your faith produces perseverance. Let perseverance finish its work so that you may be mature and complete, not lacking anything." (*James 1:2-4)

Consider some major adversity in your life and reflect on God's purpose in sending it or permitting it. Here are some possibilities:

1. *Punishment for sin.*[76] No believer will face punishment for sin in eternity. But while here on earth Christians may suffer as a result of sin. In former days when tragedy struck, people ask, "For which of my many sins is God judging me? " Today we tend to ask., "What's wrong with God? Why me, who deserves so much better?" In searching for the purpose of your grief, it doesn't hurt to ask the former question because God still does punish sin.
2. *Chastisement*. The chief purpose of punishment is often to bring erring children back to the right way. (Psalm 119: 67, 71; Hebrews 12: 5-11).
3. *Warning.* God may punish an erring child as a warning or example to others to be careful. (1 Corinthians 10: 11).
4. *Guidance*. Sometimes God allows hard times to get us to go somewhere or do something we otherwise might not consider.(Acts 8: 1, 4; Matthew 10: 23).
5. *Comfort.* Suffering prepares a person to help others. (2 Corinthians 1: 3-4). Sometimes it's difficult to be truly comforted by one who has not suffered. Suffering is God's great tenderizer. If you have difficulty in deciding what purpose God has in mind for sending or permitting a particular adversity, it may be because there two more important purposes in suffering. Those listed are sometimes God's reason, but often those purposes are difficult to sort out, as you may have discovered. There are two purposes, however, that are always present are in every trial. It is simpler to concentrate on those!

---

[76] Jeremiah 11: 10 through 11; First Corinthians 11: 30-32; 2 Samuel 12: 13-14; John 5: 14

6. *God's glory.* When I respond to trouble with childlike confidence in God, people see it and give God the credit, whether they see a miraculous deliverance or miraculous strength in the midst of suffering (2 Corinthians 12:7-10), as we saw. Suffering always has that purpose - the glory of God.[77]
7. *Your growth.* Suffering also has the purpose of growing you up into Christ's own likeness - a fast track on the spiral up. Every circumstance in my life is designed to make me more like Jesus: " the spirit... pleads for God's own people in God's own way; And then everything, as we know, He cooperates for good with those who love God and are called according to their His purpose. For God knew his own before ever they were, and also ordained that they should be shaped into the likeness of his son. (see Romans 8:27-28)

Talk about a powerful spiral up! The Holy Spirit uses everything in the life of believers for the purpose he had all along, shaping us into the likeness of the Son. That includes, especially, the pain.[78]

How do you make sure the adversity actually brings glory to God and growth to you? Watch the spiral carefully. *"When all kinds of trials and temptations crowd into your lives... Don't resent them as intruders but welcome them as friends! Realize that they come to test your faith and to produce in you the quality of endurance. But let the process go on until that endurance is fully developed, and you will find you have become mature and character, people of integrity with no weak spots."* (James 1: 2- 4, author's paraphrase).

Faith is the key! When you pass the faith test, you become tougher in endurance, and that leads to maturity, which in turn produces more and more the character of Christ in you. On the other hand, if you doubt that God is big enough to handle your problem, that He is smart enough to know what's best for you, or that he cares enough to see you through, you spiral down, rumple in self-pity and give up or grow hard and cynical or even mean spirited and brittle. But faith will transform that same trouble from a stumbling block into a steppingstone, God's fast track to spiritual growth.

Remember how to strengthen faith? Faith begins with an unconditional "Yes," to God's will in the matter. Faith surges forth on the wings of praise, is reinforced through Bible promises and the help of fellow pilgrims. All these ways of growing faith are essential. Leave off even one of them, and you stall at the starting gate.

Faith - the alchemy that transforms the most bitter pain into a life giving elixir. The adversity that can poison your whole life is the very thing the Spirit can use to bring God high praise and put you on the fast growth track. It almost seems like we should be grateful for trouble! Well, we are to give thanks always for everything. That does not mean, however, that we must be grateful for the pain itself. It may be evil incarnate that you resist and seek deliverance from. But in the meantime, we trust our all-wise, all-powerful, all-loving God to bring about His purposes through it. And what clearer expression of faith than thanksgiving and praise?

---

[77] Ezekiel 20: 9, 14, 22, 33, 39
[78] 2 Corinthians 12:7; Philippians 3: 10; Hebrews 12: 4-13; John 15: 2-4; Romans. 5: 3.- 4; Psalm 119: 67, 71

November 19
Anger
Proverbs 16:32

"Whoever is slow to anger is better than the mighty, and he who rules his spirit than he who takes a city." (Proverbs 16:32)

Incredibly, Christ's commentary on the sixth commandment includes a person's inner state. Anger is subject to God's judgment (Matt. 5:22). This was not original with Jesus. Moses had already recorded God's will, "You shall not hate your brother in your heart . . . or bear any grudge against the sons of your own people, but you shall love your neighbor as yourself" (Lev. 19:17-18). Lack of love, as well as positive hatred, is a form of murder.

Anger is not always wrong. If it were, God would be the chief sinner, for he is angry every day (Ps. 7:11). And note that David does not say God is angry merely at sin. He is angry with wicked people.[1] The wrath of God is seen throughout the Old and New Testaments and is the inevitable result of his holy character exposed to unholy attitudes and behavior.

But is it possible for a sinful mortal to be godlike in his anger? It must not be easy, for the Bible is filled with teaching against anger. Anger is to be put away (Eph. 4:31; Col. 3:8); whoever is angry is in danger of judgment (Matt. 5:22); anger is one of the works of the flesh (Gal. 5:19-20); it does not work the righteousness of God (James 1:20); and it is the prerogative of God, not man (Rom. 12:19). Proverbs condemns anger repeatedly.

But Jesus was angry (Mark 3:5), and we are commanded in our anger to refrain from sin (Ps. 4:4; Eph. 4:26), to be slow about it (Titus 1:7; James 1:19), and to get over it quickly (Eph. 4:26). There seems to be approval of being angry under some circumstances, but the major biblical emphasis is on anger as evil; exceptions seem very limited.

Anger at sin, even anger at the sinner, can be a good thing (2 Cor. 7:11). Jeremiah was full of the fury of the Lord (6:11), and Paul was angry over the idolatry of the Athenians (Acts 17:16). Yet Christ himself refrained from anger when the offense was against him personally (1 Pet. 2:23-24), and "like a sheep that before its shearers is dumb, so he opened not his mouth" (Isa. 53:7).

Righteous and unrighteous anger can be distinguished by the cause of anger. One should be angry over sin that offends God, harms others, or harms the person sinning. The difficulty with being righteously indignant is that our motives are mixed. Am I distressed over a sin that offends God and harms people, or am I angry over the way I am affected? Since motives are mixed, the safe thing may be to eschew anger altogether when the sin of another directly affects me, as when my child does wrong but the wrong embarrasses me. Better to wait till the anger subsides to be sure the resulting action does not come from a mixture of righteous and unrighteous indignation. Anger is sinful when it is for the wrong reason or results in the wrong action.

Some say that God's anger is merely judicial—he takes a position of judgment against sin. The theory is that God's wrath is impersonal and objective and without any emotion of indignation on his part. But this is not the biblical picture of a God who burns with fury. Judging by the reaction of Jesus to sin against himself, this fury is over what sin does to the sinner and those he sins against rather than over what sin does to God himself. But God's example does imply that some people, if they were filled with the Spirit, would become angry, possibly for the first time. In an age when "there is no sin but the sin of intolerance," some of us need to be stirred to participate with an angry God against the wickedness, oppression, and evil of this world.

To keep this emotion from igniting for the wrong reason or from burning out of control, Scripture gives two ways of control: Take it easy—don't get angry suddenly (James 1:19), and don't let it keep burning—don't let it last till the next day (Eph. 4:26). Either a "low flashpoint," a quick response without reflection, or a "slow burn," continuing on with the emotion, seem to risk causing even righteous indignation to go astray.

Against the clear teaching of Scripture that most (not all) human anger is wrong, and that the proper response is to control it (Prov. 16:32), many Christian psychologists hold that anger is morally neutral and must be expressed.[2] To this we respond that anger is neutral in the same way that hatred and killing are neutral: Sometimes they are right; mostly they are wrong. Anger in itself is a wrong emotion to have if it is directed against the wrong object (God, an innocent person, a thing); for the wrong cause (personal offense); or leads to wrong behavior (retaliation, vengeance, physical violence).

Anger under these circumstances should not be denied *or* expressed. It should rather be confessed as sin and the resources of God appropriated to control the emotion itself.

Lloyd H. Steffen, writing "On Anger," indicates that anger is not always bad: "Sometimes only anger will make us act to address a grievance or change a situation." But, addressing the position common among psychologists that anger must be ventilated, he responds:

Ventilating anger is like ventilating a fire. The environment will only become more heated and smoky, the damage will only increase. Ventilating anger postpones investigation of its causes and the beginning of repairs. . . . Our anger is usually a response to things that we perceive as somehow injuring us, or that keep us from having our own way.[79]

To encourage a person who feels guilty about his anger by assuring him that there is nothing wrong with this perfectly human reaction, and that the only healthful thing is to express the anger and not feel guilty, will simply drive the sensitive Christian's real guilt "underground" and put off the day of biblical resolution. Rather, the person needs to be encouraged to evaluate in the light of Scripture whether his anger is godly and, if it is not, to confess his sin, thus removing all guilt. Then he should trust God for his resources in overcoming the temptation. [80]

November 20
Explosive growth
John 15:16

"You did not choose me, but I chose you and appointed you so that you might go and bear fruit—fruit that will last—and so that whatever you ask in my name the Father will give you." (John 15:16)

During the 1980s and 1990s, something infinitely significant was taking place. On the other side of the world, an explosive growth that dwarfs anything in the 2,000 years of church history – China! When my wife and I were young we planned on going to China where one fifth of the world's population lived. At the time, there were fewer than a million evangelical believers in that vast nation. And by the end of the century? Perhaps a hundred million! How did it happen? In the July, 1980 *Chinese World Pulse,* the dean of China watchers, David Adeney, made a startling

---
[79] Lloyd H. Steffen, "On Anger," *The Christian Century,* 16 January 1985, 47.
[80] IBE (2014), 354-344.

statement. He told why the Three-Self, government approved church in China had made no advances during those years of Communist rule. Then he defined what the Chinese church must be and do if the stagnated churches were to live again. He spelled out what kind of church it must become. It did in fact become just what he spelled out in advance and the rest is history! What essentials did he enumerate at the beginning of this incredible burst of life?

For the church to survive and thrive it must live under the authority of Scripture, not the surrounding culture. Christ's own world view must be theirs, he said.

The church must experience:

- The reality of true fellowship in Christ. Christians cannot stand just as isolated individuals
- They must support one another.
- The experience of the power of the indwelling Holy Spirit and a deep reliance upon prayer.
- An understanding of the true nature of the church and the priesthood of all believers.
- The recognition of the Lordship of Christ over every area of life.

These align with what I call "The Five Smooth Stones," the principles of biblical leadership for every ministry.

Fast forward to 2004. Around the world, church planting movements were exploding. Not the old paradigm of planting individual churches or even planting reproducing churches, but movements of rapidly reproducing house churches that envelop a whole people. Every movement was unique, diverse as snowflakes. Were there any common characteristics? In 2004, David Garrison published the results of thorough research on the common indispensable characteristics among those movements. Without them, no movement. And what were those characteristics? Two were not found in our pouch of five smooth stones, two elements peculiar to church planting movements: (1) local, not foreign leadership, and (2) very rapid reproduction of many churches. I noted that those two characteristics were in fact working, but I could find no theological basis for them.

Here's how I describe the basic biblical principles for doing ministry:
1. The ***Bible:*** making it the functional authority
2. The ***Congregation:*** aligning it with the biblical purposes
3. The ***Spirit:*** releasing his energizing power
4. The ***Plan of Redemption:*** the mission of every disciple
5. The ***Lord Jesus:*** gauging servant leadership

You may remonstrate, "That's so simple. Everyone knows that!" Then why do we flounder and miss the way? Could it be that we simply don't make the commitment to evaluate our work relentlessly by these standards? Or could it be we don't work hard at ferreting out the implications of these principles? I invite you to join me in deep reflection, honest evaluation, and courageous integration of each of these principles into the practice of every aspect of ministry. It will also take commitment to change whatever is necessary to experience the kind of life God intends. How is your ministry? What change needs to happen to see happen with your ministry similar to what happened in China?

November 21
The Absent
Exodus 20:13

*"You shall not murder" (*Exodus 20:13)

The tongue can be a burning fire, can't it? Maybe you have seen hate-filled speech set a relationship or an encounter on fire. The conflict escalates as a malicious tongue rages out of control. It happens in homes, at work, in schools, and in churches. A whole church can become an inferno, set on fire by undisciplined tongues. I've rarely seen a church that didn't have little fires blazing here and there, continuously set or fanned by critical talk. So damaging is the tongue, Jesus warned, that whoever calls someone a fool or a moron "will be subject to hellfire" (Matt. 5:22).

Muriel was teaching school hundreds of miles from the school I was attending, so our courtship was conducted by mail. Enthusiastically I wrote of how we were going to be one in every sense—no secrets, full disclosure. She responded cordially but added a caveat: "But Sweetheart, let's not make our home a garbage dump. Let's agree never to say anything bad about anyone." A high standard! But we committed to it. We didn't follow through perfectly, but we made it our aim and helped each other hold to our agreement.

You can imagine our distress, then, soon after we arrived on the mission field, to have a longtime friend who preceded us to the field begin filling us in on the faults and foibles of our missionary comrades. I guess he thought this was a crucial element in new-missionary orientation! After Jack and Susan left, I said to Muriel, "What shall we do? They're coming back next week, and I can't spend another evening like that. But how can a new missionary rebuke a veteran?"

"Don't worry," she responded. "I'll take care of it." Muriel, an artist, made a small plaque and hung it in the center of an empty wall.

When our senior missionary friends came the next week, the plaque caught Jack's attention. He studied it for a moment, then called his wife to help figure it out. Finally, he called me over. "Robertson, what does this mean?" I read aloud, "'The absent are safe with us.' That means folks who aren't here don't have to worry about what's said. The idea is that the conversation would go just as if they were present." "Oh," said Jack. And we proceeded to spend as boring an evening as I've ever known!

So I ask you, "Are the absent safe with you?" Do others have a concern for what you will say about them when they are not there? No sharing of gossip? No repeating rumors? No trash talk, no making others look less so you can look better. What about judging their motives, or angry invectives? Diminishing another? Exodus 20:13, *"You shall not murder."*

Money and possessions aren't the only things that can be stolen. Perhaps the most common theft we practice is reputation theft. Verbal criticism is a form of murder. With critical talk we violate not only the Sixth Commandment but also the Eighth; such talk kills, but it also steals someone's reputation. The writer of Proverbs warned: Whoever conceals an offense promotes love, but whoever gossips about it separates friends. Purpose today to make the absent safe with you.

Nov 22
Are You Filled with the Holy Spirit?
Ephesians 5:18

"Be filled with the Holy Spirit" (Ephesians 5:18)

Basically, when Scripture speaks of being filled with the Spirit, the term is used in three different ways. So if you asked me if I'm filled with the Spirit, I'd have to respond, "Yes" or "You tell me," or "Sometimes," depending on the definition you had in mind.

In the three different ways listed above there might be a parallel between Spirit-fullness and, for example, Judas being full of the devil, an unholy spirit (see John 13:2). The chief idea seems to be that he was under the devil's control. Although the devil "entered in" to Judas and the Spirit "indwells" our bodies, the idea of being filled is not physical like a tank of gas. We're talking about a relationship between two persons, and in that relationship, one might allow the other to dominate. That kind of "full"—full control—is the first meaning of being filled with the Holy Spirit. If you asked me whether I'm filled with the Spirit and you have that in mind, I'd say,

"Yes, so far as I know my own heart I'm unconditionally yielded to the will of God."

But there's another meaning. When a child is said to be full of mischief, we mean that those characteristics are highly visible. Everyone is aware of the mischief. Most of the Scripture references to being full of the Spirit indicate some evidence, some outcome of that filling. Not just an illness healed or miraculous speaking in an unknown language, however. When the disciples acted courageously instead of fearfully, preached with life-transforming power, sang while chained in a filthy dungeon, met a crisis with faith, people saw that unexpected—even miracle—behavior and concluded, "The only way to explain that is to recognize Holy Spirit power at work." So, if that's what you mean when you ask if I'm Spirit filled, I'd have to say, "You tell me!" People in Scripture do not claim to be Spirit-filled. It's always, "*they, filled with the Spirit*," or "*he, filled with the Spirit.*" The evidence was visible.

But there's a mystery to being filled that defies analysis. It has something to do with an inner surge of feeling. Joy is often associated with being filled with the Spirit, for example (Acts 13:52). That's what some people have in mind when they speak of being filled—an ecstatic inner sense of God's presence. If that's what you have in mind when you ask, I'd have to respond, "sometimes."

If you choose a phrase like, "John is full of whisky." That's a good example of being filled, because Paul seems to tell us not to get drunk on wine but on the Spirit! (Ephesians 5:18) Well, at least he tells us to fill up on the Spirit...

What happens to someone who drinks alcohol? "Under the influence," we say, and the change of control is clearly evident to everyone. He doesn't have to tell you when he's drunk. Not if he's full of it. His talk tips you off, his walk proves it. Isn't that parallel to what happens to one filled with the Spirit? You are under the controlling influence of another so that influence is very evident, it's the dominant characteristic, something others are aware of and it creates powerful feelings.

Notice something about these three meanings. Whether or not I'm fully yielded to the Spirit, whether he or I am in control is something only I may know for sure. The same is true of any feelings resulting from that relationship. But the outward evidence, the result of the Spirit's full control is something only others may be able to evaluate. How would you answer the question, "are you filled with the Spirit?"

November 23
Love Talk
Psalm 34:1

*"I will bless the L*ORD *at all times; his praise shall continually be in my mouth."* (Psalm 34:1)

In an intimate relationship of true love, expressions of love must be what the recipient perceives to be loving, not what the giver thinks the lover should want. How does one's partner wish to be loved? The husband loves his wife so much he works 70-hour weeks to provide her every heart's desire. But the lonely wife's "heart's desire" is to hear her strong and silent man say it. He demonstrates his love the only way he knows how, but his children gradually grow distant. They long for some of his time, some of him, you might say. So in your relationship with God, how would your Lover like you to express your affection to him? Oh, surely with a life that points people his direction and surely with Spirit-energized ministry. But it's much more than being good and doing good. True lovers not only act out love, they say it. Often.

Have you noticed that children aren't naturally thankful? They just expect their parents to be there for them, to provide all they need. And they certainly aren't thankful for any discipline. We have to grow up to a love relationship with Jesus in which our heart constantly wells up in gratitude. Thankful for the big things, yes, and for the little things as well. And thankful, yes, even for the discipline. Did you notice that thanksgiving is me-oriented? We focus on what he has done for us. A great place to begin, but a very unsatisfactory place to end.

So there's affirmation, praise, and adoration. Early in my ministry I hit a dry spell. Things we're going well; I just didn't have what it took to meet the challenges of my responsibilities no matter how hard I prayed. And I prayed hard! But my prayers didn't seem to rise above the ceiling; the line to Headquarters was dead. Finally, I had a crazy idea—go outside and pray where there is no ceiling! But, as you guessed, the skies were brass, too. Suddenly the thought came, "Try praise!" I'm ashamed to admit it, but I was so out of practice on praise I ran out of subject-matter in five minutes! But that was enough. It seemed the reservoirs of heaven were un-stopperved!

I don't suggest praise as a method to bend God's ear to our petitions. No, but I do suggest praise as a wonderful way to connect and express our love, whether or not he ever answers another prayer. Praise for what he has accomplished, adoration for who he is.

Thanksgiving, praise, adoration—we call that kind of communication, "worship." But he intends something beyond worship, something utterly astonishing: intimate companionship. That's what I miss the most with my beloved Muriel – intimate companionship. I can still tell her thank you, praise her, and I do. But no companionship. Someone to share the good news with the bad. Someone to dance away the night with. Gone.

But our never absent, forever Lover always is waiting for us to embrace him in love. I recently reflected on the fact that when I rejoice with him, it's over something he's done for me, when I weep with him, it's over some grief in my life. And I thought, "It gets old real quick when a friend forever dumps on me." So I've begun to exult with Him in what brings him joy, whether or not it impacts me directly at the moment. Nature, for example, church, victories for righteousness. Rejoice with him, laugh with him!

And I try to weep with him over his griefs—the persecuted church, for example. How his heart must break as hundreds of thousands of Christian brothers are slaughtered, and in my own city, the hatred, the brokenness, the rotten infidelities, the oppression, the injustice, the cheating, all those things invisible to me or ho-hum, how painful to him. Or churches divided and impotent when he longs to build the invincible church. Weep with him!

Take a few minutes and note the categories of love-talk you might share with your ultimate Lover. Why not begin that conversation now?

November 24
Contentment
1 Timothy 6:6

"Godliness with contentment is great gain" (1 Timothy 6:6)

It's important to recognize a distinction between being dissatisfied and being unsatisfied. To be *unsatisfied* is to long for more, the eternal longing that is in every human heart. In that sense a godly person is never satisfied with the status quo. As long as we fall short of all the fullness of God, we will strive for the goal. But to be *dissatisfied* is to demonstrate unbelief and ingratitude, one of the most destructive of all sins. This is the condition that brought down God's wrath on the Israelites after they left Egypt. Instead of being grateful for God's deliverance, they grumbled and rebelled, always dissatisfied with their condition (see Exodus 15:24; 16:2; 17:3). Paul taught that dissatisfaction is the natural state of those who reject God and refuse to believe: *"Though they knew God, they did not glorify Him as God or show gratitude. Instead, their thinking became nonsense, and their senseless minds were darkened"* (Romans 1:21).

Covetousness grows from a heart that is dissatisfied with God's provision. It is a state that God will not honor, and it is a cancer that destroys the one who covets. Unchecked, it destroys other people as well. The biblical answer to covetousness is contentment. Contentment is a beautiful and healthful condition the Bible commends.

A pursuit of God brings contentment. Jesus said to seek the Kingdom above anything else, and God will supply our needs. In Philippians 4:13 Paul gave credit to Jesus for his contentment. In his words to Timothy, he related contentment to godliness and warned that money draws people away from the faith. Paul reminds Timothy, *"Godliness with contentment is great gain.* " (1 Timothy 6:6) Standing opposite covetousness are two Spirit-given qualities, one passive, one active: contentment and generosity.

What are the benefits of a contented spirit? First, those possessing the virtue of contentment will likely be generous with their resources. They are not ruled by money and can give generously. Second, in commanding us not to worry but to trust him, God promises the faithful manager and generous giver to supply their needs according to God's glorious riches. Ultimately God will guarantee that investments made for his kingdom are never wasted but are eternal. Third, While Christian should never be dissatisfied, they can justifiably be unsatisfied in certain respects. A godly person can be unsatisfied with the spiritual or moral status quo- as Paul said, *"pressing on toward the goal for the prize of the* upward call of God I Christ Jesus." (Philippians 1:21). Even in material things, Christians may be content but legitimately work hard to improve their condition.

Notice how these wonderful graces reinforce others. For example, humility leads to faith, faith to contentment and courage, which in turn reinforces self-control, and all are motivated by love. Begin with any of them, and like a giant spiral heavenward, each is a step to the other. These graces do something else. Each reproduces a harvest of its own kind. That is, the decision to control self leads immediately to greater strength in self-control. Contentment breeds more contentment; each servant act begets greater humility and a disposition more prone to behave as a servant. Courage produces courage, faith more faith, love more love. We call these the roots that bear the fruit of right thinking, right words, right actions. And they are. But they have wonderful by-products as well: They bear the glorious fruits of joy and peace.

Lay your sources of covetousness before the Lord in prayer. Confess that He is your greatest treasure and the source of everything you need. Thank Him for His faithful provision and ask Him to fill you with Himself when you are tempted to feel dissatisfied. Enjoy fruit today!

November 25
Thanks be to God!
2 Corinthians 1:14-15

"But thanks be to God, who in Christ always leads us in triumphal procession, and through us spreads the fragrance of the knowledge of him everywhere. For we are the aroma of Christ to God among those who are being saved and among those who are perishing, to one a fragrance from death to death, to the other a fragrance from life to life." (2 Corinthians 2:14-15*)*

If someone said the word minister, what would come to mind? Perhaps it would be the chief religious officer in a socially acceptable Protestant church. Or perhaps, having just listened to the news, you would think more in terms of Ministers of State, Minister of Finance or Prime Minister. It's not too likely, that when I say the word minister, you think servant. And yet this role, the servant role, is the theme of 2 Corinthians 2:14*: "But thanks be to God, who in Christ always leads us in triumphal procession, and through us spreads the fragrance of the knowledge of him everywhere."* But. Thanks be to God, but what?

In other words, something has happened for which you ordinarily wouldn't think to give thanks. Well, let's begin somewhere else. Let's try the 12th verse: *"Now when I came to Troas to preach the gospel of Christ, even though a door was opened for me in the Lord, my spirit was not at rest because I did not find my brother Titus there. So I took leave of them and went on to Macedonia."*

Have you ever noticed how the Bible is often not nearly as spiritual as we are? This doesn't look like the way we ordinarily get guidance. Paul went to a city and God opened the door for him, it says. But. He didn't have any peace of mind, particularly because his friend wasn't there. So he went on to the next town with all of this peregrination, all of this wandering around from place to place, God opening doors and Paul was not feeling good about it, about his friend not being there.

But thanks be to God. Why? Because wherever I go, wherever I am, thinks Paul, God always leads us in his triumphal procession in Christ and through us spreads the fragrance of the knowledge of him. For we are to God the aroma of Christ among those who are being saved, and the smell of death to those who are perishing. To one the smell of death, to another the fragrance of life.

So this is the job description of the servant of God. The figure Paul is using here is the analogy of the triumphal procession, in which the conquering general returns home to Rome. Perhaps he has made conquest of a whole area, a whole region. And he comes back in triumph. They have a procession. They built an arch for him. And at the head of the procession, first are the leaders of Rome, and then comes the triumphant general in his chariot. And they tell us, chained to his chariot was the one who was a very special captive followed by incense bearers and soldiers.

And Paul is saying, "I one day bowed the knee to the conquering General Jesus Christ. Then he chained me to his chariot, and now wherever he leads me, I follow him. Then Paul changes the analogy to the incense bearer in the processional and wherever I go, I am the fragrance of Christ. Notice what he says, for we are to God the aroma of Christ. So when something other than the fragrance of Christ comes from us, it not only is a terrible and tragic thing for those who are around us wherever we go, but what a sadness for our God.

So there you have it, the job description of the servant. It's really very simple, and you may not be sure always that you're exactly in the right place, or maybe that you're doing exactly the right thing. But if you, in loyal obedience to him, follow him and disseminate, as it says here, the knowledge of Christ to everyone in every place. Then you're a true servant and God's heart is satisfied. A rather simple job, but awesome, isn't it?

In the Cairo museum, we saw an alabaster jar which had been sealed for 4,000 years. When they opened it the fragrance of the perfume was the same as when it was first put into the jar. After the Museum they took us to a perfume factory. They called those fragrances "essences". They talked me into buying a very small jar of a rare perfume. They told me it was not sold outside of Egypt – Lotus flower. And I thought, "Whenever Deb opens this we will catch the essence of Egypt and our honeymoon cruise down the Nile." And so it has been.

Today, Jesus doesn't want to keep his fragrance bottled up in you. He wants to open you up and let what's inside come out. Maybe the unstopping won't be fun. Perhaps he'll pry you open with a cruel tongue of an evil person, put the squeeze of adversity on you, turn up the heat of an impossible task under you. And when he does–God works the impossible alchemy, the miracle transformation and the essence of Jesus suffuses your world.

November 26
Poverty or Wealth?
Proverbs 30:7-9

"Two things I ask of you; deny them not to me before I die: Remove far from me falsehood and lying; give me neither poverty nor riches; feed me with the food that is needful for me, lest I be full and deny you and say, "Who is the LORD?" "or lest I be poor and steal and profane the name of my God." (Proverbs 30:7-9)

Both Testaments have much to say about poverty and wealth. What is wealth? We shall never agree.

There is a reason is that society and culture how material possessions are secured, used, and viewed. Suppose we agree that poverty is a state in which resources are chronically insufficient to meet one's necessities and that absolute poverty means less than adequate food, housing, or clothing. Immediately our agreement will founder on the definition of *necessity* and *adequate*. Suppose we define wealth as material resources more than necessary for basic livelihood. What is a necessity? What is a basic livelihood? The answers depend, to some extent, on what is considered poverty or wealth in a given community or society.

The second problem is that these questions are very personal and charged with intense emotion. It is difficult to be detached and objective because any definition may threaten my own status. Since Scripture has so much to say on the subject, let us assume the definitions given above and grant in advance that agreement on specific applications of these definitions may not be possible. Also, let us assume that the vast majority of Americans are wealthy if wealth is considered anything more than basic necessities. Let us also assume that the primary emphasis in Scripture on this subject is the loving response of those who have to those who do not.

Still, grave problems remain. A basic problem is the apparently radical difference between what the Old and New Testaments say about wealth. Jacques Ellul says: "Incontestably, in the New Testament wealth is condemned. To my knowledge there is not one text that justifies it. The Old Testament, on the other hand, presents wealth as a blessing, willed by God and pleasing to him. There is no more apparent radical opposition between the two covenants than the one concerning wealth."[81]

How the Old and New are to be reconciled is a matter of continuing debate. Is the Old Testament view of wealth part of the overall this-worldly structure of a (transient) earthly kingdom to be superseded by the spiritual kingdom, the church? Whether or not this is the correct explanation, it must be conceded that the New Testament nowhere teaches that wealth is the evidence of God's blessing but is often stark in its condemnation of the rich.

It is easier for a camel to go through the eye of a needle than for a rich man to enter the kingdom of God. (Matt. 19:24; Luke 18:25) Blessed are you poor, for yours is the kingdom of God. (Luke 6:20)

But woe to you that are rich, for you have received your consolation. (Luke 6:24)

Sell your possessions and give alms; provide yourselves with purses that do not grow old, with a treasure in the heavens that does not fail, where no thief approaches and no moth destroys. For where your treasure is, there will your heart be also. (Luke 12:33-34)

"No servant can serve two masters. . . . You cannot serve God and mammon." The Pharisees, who were lovers of money, heard all this, and they scoffed at him. (Luke 16:13-14)

These passages are merely a sample. I wish the Bible consistently and clearly condemned only the wicked rich, but often it fails to make the distinction. Is that because it is impossible to be both wealthy and godly, or because it is uncommon? Taking all the biblical evidence into account, it seems that the generalized condemnations result from the fact that the temptations of wealth are so strong that few handle them successfully, and therefore rich people as a class are sometimes grouped together in condemnation. But this should not be taken as evidence that there are no exceptions, for the Bible never says that possession of wealth in itself is sinful.

Wealth is, in any event, a temptation—not an evil in itself, but a temptation . . . because it urges us to put our confidence in money rather than in God. . . . It is almost impossible to have many possessions and remain righteous. Righteousness is total dependence on God's action.[21]

How do we fight such strong temptation? The biblical antidote to the virus of avarice or the fatal illness of relying on the phantom of wealth is the act of giving it away.

We have very clear indications that money, in the Christian life, is made *in order* to be given away. Note especially Paul's lovely text (2 Cor. 8:1-15). . . . If among fellow Christians we study Paul's law of equality, we see that money must be used to meet our needs, and that everything left over must be given away.[22]

The Bible does not advocate appropriating the wealth of the rich. And though there are passages that instruct us to sell and give, when the rich are directly addressed, they are not instructed to divest themselves totally, but rather to be rich toward God and toward those in need.

Perhaps rather than taking Abraham as our model and the Old Testament as our instruction in this matter, we would be safer in taking Jesus Christ as our model and New Testament teaching as the norm. If we follow the example of one who, having everything, became poor for our sakes, and if we submit to his sometimes painful teaching, will we not voluntarily divest ourselves of all excess wealth in order to provide for those in spiritual and physical need?

But what is "excess"? Each man is accountable to his own master. *"Who are you to pass judgment on the servant of another?"* (Rom. 14:4). But it must mean *something,* and something that consumer-oriented Christians apparently find difficult to comprehend.[82]

---

[81] Jacques Ellul, *Money and Power,* trans. LaVonne Neff (Downers Grove, Ill.: InterVarsity Press, 1984), 35.
[82] IBE (2014), 474-475.

November 27
Beyond Excellence
Matthew 22:27

"And he said to him, "You shall love the Lord your God with all your heart and with all your soul and with all your mind." (Matthew 22:37)

The former President of Hillsdale College, George Roche authored a powerful book entitled, *A World Without Heroes*. In this brilliant analysis of what naturalism and humanism have done to us, he holds that the reason heroes have disappeared is that such an outcome is inevitable if we're animals and matter is all that exists. Today let us strike a small blow against the prevailing orthodoxy and advocate the ancient virtue of excellence. In fact, beyond excellence. Let us to focus this day on that phrase "with all your heart." We strive for excellence. Excellence in living a godly life, excellence in service to God, and to man. We avoid sin as best we can.

But I wonder if that's excellent? If that's a complete definition of excellent, then who defines excellence? What is excellent? Are we minimalists merely avoiding spiritual or ministry failure? Is that how we define excellence?

Think in terms of going beyond excellence. Now, in Israel there were very influential people. In fact, they were determined. They themselves determine the course of the nation for 40 years. Look at Numbers 13:1,3 where we'll find these people and also find one other for us to think about today. *"The LORD spoke to Moses, saying, "Send men to spy out the land of Canaan, which I am giving to the people of Israel. From each tribe of their fathers you shall send a man, everyone a chief among them." So Moses sent them from the wilderness of Paran, according to the command of the LORD, all of them men who were heads of the people of Israel."*

Now read Numbers 13:30, *"Caleb, quieted the people before Moses, and said "Let us go up at once and occupy it, for we are well able to overcome it." Then the men who had gone up with him said, "We are not able to go up against the people, for they are stronger than we are." So they brought to the people of Israel a bad report of the land that they had spied out, saying, "The land, through which we have gone to spy it out, is a land that devours its inhabitants, and all the people that we saw in it are of great height. And there we saw the Nephilim (the sons of Anak, who come from the Nephilim), and we seemed to ourselves like grasshoppers, and so we seemed to them."*

The majority wisdom prevailed. Often does. But whoever heard of these 10 people in the flow of history? The 10 spies who were leaders and the three million who followed them. They were the losers. But Caleb had a different spirit. Read Numbers 24:14: *"But my servant Caleb, because he had another spirit with him and had followed me fully. Him will I bring into the land where until he went, and his seed shall possess it."* He had a different spirit. How is it different? He wholly followed the Lord. You see, he went beyond excellence.

Well, Caleb stood in the minority. He had faith enough to wholly follow the Lord. He took an unpopular position. And he stuck with his people even though they made the wrong choice. When the final showdown came and he was getting ready to possess his gift, his possession. Notice what he said, *"It may be that the Lord will be with me, and I shall drive them out as the Lord said."*

There was no great macho speech of self-confidence that of course he was going do this. He was really very humble about it. But he moved ahead with faith. He waited 40 years for the fulfillment, but he never gave up. At 85, he was still going for it. Joshua 14:10 -12 says, *"And now, behold, the LORD has kept me alive, just as he said, these forty-five years since the time that the LORD spoke this word to Moses, while Israel walked in the wilderness. And now, behold, I am this day eighty-five years old. I am still as strong today as I was in the day that Moses sent me; my strength now is as my strength was then, for war and for going and coming. So now give me this hill country of which the LORD spoke on that day, for you heard on that day how the Anakim were there, with great fortified cities. It may be that the LORD will be with me, and I shall drive them out just as the LORD said."*

Caleb asked for Arba. You know about Goliath. But Arba? He was bigger and better than Goliath. Arba was the greatest man of the Anakim. Curious that we don't read about the site named for Arba, because the site of Arba was renamed Hebron, where David was later crowned king and reigned there for seven years.

Goliath was 10 feet tall. So what must these people have been? These are the very ones that had intimidated. All the Israelites through the ten spies ten years earlier said, *"they're going to eat us up."* And remember Caleb back then, at that time said *there will be bread for us*. Just a little different perspective.

Caleb didn't choose the easy way out, did he? For God's purposes to be fulfilled in the promised land somebody had to overcome the big boys. Now, I think if I were Caleb at 85 years of age, I would have said I've served my time, I'm an old man. Give me something you've already conquered. I think I would have said that, but not Caleb. He chose the toughest part of the conquest. Not the easiest.

And Joshua blessed him and he gave Hebron to Caleb, *"Therefore Hebron became the inheritance of Caleb the son of Jephunneh the Kenizzite to this day, because he wholly followed the LORD, the God of Israel. Now the name of Hebron formerly was Kiriath-arba."* Why? Because he wholly followed the Lord, the God of Israel. Caleb was faithful and obedient - beyond excellent.

November 28
Body Language
Mark 16:15

"And he said to them, "Go into all the world and proclaim the gospel to the whole creation." (Mark 16:15)

My friend, this world is filled with people on their way to destruction. And it's quite possible just to sing a little louder and drown out their cries. But not if we are in this world as he is - to love as he loved. He's given his marching orders, so we better be intentional about it. Oh, none of us can single handedly change the world. We can't bring the big story to the last chapter, but we can make a difference. Every one of us.

And what is the big story? Well, every tribe, every person, he said. God loves the world. If your life story does not track with His life story, what's your excuse? By the Spirit, he's given the orders, so the only question is, will you obey? Or will your life story be sort of a beautiful footnote to the big story? There are many roles to play, many tasks to do, and all are equally legitimate. Notice they are not equally important. No, some roles are far more important than others. That's why Paul said, "first apostles." (1 Corinthians 12:28)

We don't need to envy others the greater role they have in the story. You may be assigned a bit part, or perhaps a supporting role. Not many play lead roles, even fewer are stars. But your role is legitimate. If it's God's assignment for your part, it's more than legitimate, it's significant. You can make a difference. Whatever your role, your responsibility is to see that it advances God's big story - the evangelization of the world.

On the other hand, don't settle for a bit part if God wants you to play a major role. Maybe God will use you to change the world. Don't shrink back from that. The need of the hour is like it was in the first century; for a Timothy or Barnabas, those who go to the front, to plant the church where Christ is not yet known.

I'm sure someone may say wait a minute, that's all in the past. Now it's over to the Developing World churches. They'll take care of the mopping up operation now. I thank God for the way the younger churches are now taking responsibility for the big story. But do you know that even with all of those commitments from Korea and Brazil and Nigeria, the Philippines, and Southern India combined with all of those who go from this country, we can't finish the task.

We don't know how many people would be needed. Probably 200,000 people to train to go to the yet unreached peoples of the world. You ask how many unreached peoples there are. Nobody really knows. My estimate is it's more than one in four alive today on planet Earth who have not heard the gospel in a way they could understand and savingly respond to. Of course, many of those live within reach of the gospel or of gospel witness. But the scary thing about the unfinished story is this, at least a billion immortal souls live out of reach of present gospel witness. They live in language groups or cultures isolated from the storytellers. So if someone doesn't go from the inside of the church to those places, they have no way of hearing the story at all. Why not aspire to that role?

But in whatever role God puts you, make very sure that God's mission is central. A reported survey on the components of the healthy church cited spiritual maturity, outreach, evangelism, fellowship, relationship community, and mature leadership. The missing ingredient? Missions. A healthy church without God's central passion, the Spirit's first purpose for his church, was last on the list or missing altogether from the healthy church.

Are you going to participate fully and finish the story? Perhaps you will inspire and raise up dozens of storytellers to go where you can't. Perhaps you'll invest at least as much in supporting them as you do in building your own edifice. Will you lead people to stop playing at prayer and get involved seriously with God in finishing the story?

Many people don't like to make commitments, especially long-term commitments. Where would we be if Jesus felt like that? So where are you today? Secure in the familiarity of home. Is it time to consult with him, to see if down the road he has a plan for you to leave home to a foreign realm so God can finish his story there? Well, surely, at least with Jesus to do the Father's will.

But maybe in these days you'll come to your own Jerusalem, set your face toward your destiny. No matter how demanding. No matter how painful. No matter how costly to bring salvation to the world. But perhaps today is Gethsemane- God is calling you. Everything in your life is pointing in the direction of playing out your role at the frontiers. But you shrink back naturally. Jesus shrank back. "Father, must it be? You can do anything. Please give me another role nevertheless. Not my will. But yours be done."

Is God calling you to move your story just a step further incrementally? Not a big leap all at once perhaps. But today, if you're still comfortably at home, not even thinking of anything beyond, you can say "Yes, Lord. I've got to be about your business, your story." Or have you come closer to discovering your destiny? Committing to it. Perhaps it will be your Gethsemane. Maybe you need to commit to full participation by finishing the story as a pastor or leader in a local church. Why not commit to build a truly Great Commission church?

November 29
Life in the Spirit
John 15:16

"You did not choose me, but I chose you and appointed you that you should go and bear fruit and that your fruit should abide..." (John 15:16)

Tsuruta san had a delightful, outgoing personality and an infectious faith. Hardly a Sunday passed in our fledgling church in Japan but Miss Tsuruta would have a fellow university student with her. Many of them came to Christ. For her, Jesus' promise proved true--"*You did not call me, but I called you and appointed you to go and produce fruit...*" (vs 16).

Ijima san, however, was the opposite. She was so quiet and retiring I didn't even see her the first time she came to church. She stood outside the meeting room, hidden behind the crowd. She left a note for me, however: "I like the atmosphere here and will return if you do not call on me to pray." The middle-aged widow had heard me call on a church member to lead in prayer and she didn't want that to happen to her! During the months that followed I carefully safeguarded her desire for unobtrusive participation, never asking her to do anything "public." One day she told me that she was having a luncheon at her home and wanted me to attend. She was inviting some neighbors and friends and wanted me to tell them about Jesus. The occasion was elegant in traditional Japanese style and many women, decked out in their finest kimonos, were seated on their heels around the low table. How could they not be there? She had loved them with constant concern and help. Why, she even cared for their cats! When the time came for what I expected would be the introduction of her foreign male guest, Ijima san reached beneath the table and produced a scroll, written in ancient characters, and with hands trembling, began to read the story of her spiritual pilgrimage.

Did Jesus keep his promise? Several of the women who gathered about her table that day gather still at the table of the Lord, almost thirty years later--"fruit that remains." Quiet, timid Ijima has born more fruit than anyone else.

Winning people to Christ is one kind of fruit, but there are many other ministries as well. According to Paul every believer is given at least one ability to serve God (I Cor 12). For each of these God promises effectiveness, that is, "fruit." More than that--lasting fruit!

In John 15 Jesus promises a supernatural life that overflows with qualities very like his own. And yet, many in our day deny the possibility of such a life. "It's not realistic," they say. I have a problem with that opinion. I've seen the life Jesus promised lived out. I can never get away from the reality of a life that produced a bumper crop right in my own home. At my father's memorial service I told hundreds of mourners that I had - in 25 years - never once seen my father fail in living a Christlike life. To me that is not threatening, something to be denied, explained away. It is wonderfully reassuring to see in living color the reality of Christ's promise fulfilled in a fellow "branch."

We tend to evaluate people, especially Christian leaders, in terms of their giftedness. But God is the judge and he's already passed judgment: fruit is more important! One reason is that the fruit is the more sure measure of our relationship to the Spirit, and that's why our recognition by him on the last day will be based on faithfulness, a fruit. Of course, that faithfulness includes faithfulness in fulfilling our calling, using our gifts for Kingdom advance, but that will be ony one small part of the evaluation. There's another reason conspicuous fruit is more important to God than conspicuous gifting, and that has to do with the relationship between natural and supernatural abilities. Whether God chooses to bypass natural ability/inability, or whether the Spirit lifts a natural ability to a higher power, we may not always know. But if it's a Spirit gift, there will be the Spirit's miracle touch.

But don't be misled. It isn't the strategy for ministry that wins the victory. It's the Spirit! Never forget that the secret of success in the Christian life, including consistent success in ministry effectiveness or of overcoming temptation, does not ultimately depend on a technique, strategy, or your own activity. No matter how skilled you get in wielding the weapons, the Spirit provides as you participate with Him in winning the battles. Ultimately, it's the Holy Spirit within who is the overcomer.

Victory may sound triumphalistic and may grow dim anyway. Even if that were possible, we are not sure we want it. Can we really have enough power to win out over the world of stuff, the fun of the flesh, and the pride of ourselves? Absolutely! We have the power to consistently overcome temptation and grow into greater likeness to Jesus. We have Almighty God in residence to empower us to be all we were meant to be.

November 30
Our First Priority
Exodus 20:3-8

"Thou shalt have no other gods before me. Thou shalt not make unto thee any graven image. Thou shalt not take the name of the LORD thy God in vain. Remember the sabbath day, to keep it holy." (Exodus 20:3-8)

For most people in the Western world the horizontal has totally eclipsed the vertical. Human relationships to each other are all-important; their relationship to God is of secondary or no importance. Even in the church, reconciling people to people, rather than reconciling people to God, has become top priority for many. Christians find it difficult to feel that violating the first table of the law is nearly as serious as violating the second table of the law. We cannot understand the Old Testament prescription of capital punishment for working on the Sabbath, for profanity, or for worshiping another deity.

Why is the command to love God with all our being the first and great commandment? Why are the first four of the Ten Commandments prohibitions of sin against God? Why not put them last, after the important ones like murder and adultery? Obviously Scripture holds that sin against God is of greater seriousness than sin against others.

God is the ultimate reality, the fundamental fact, the integrating factor of the universe. Therefore, to be rightly aligned with him is the most important relationship in human existence. To be in alignment with reality and truth is life; to be out of alignment is destruction and death. To leave God out of the equation of life or to diminish his role is like seeking to build a skyscraper without mathematics or to bake a cake without flour.

God knows this, so his commandments simply reinforce the facts. He treats this relationship as the most important because it *is* the most important.

Yet it is not simply a matter of reality and truth. God *cares* about this relationship. God is repeatedly called a jealous God. That is, it makes a difference to him whether or not we are rightly related to him. This word for jealousy in the Old Testament is the same word used when a husband is jealous of the affection of his wife. This is not a petty envy of legitimate competition. It is a profound caring and total unwillingness to allow any other to replace the prior and ultimate love relationship.

The first commandment has to do with our heart attitude, our thoughts, our personal relationship with God.

But God is also interested in our deeds, what we do about how we feel. Furthermore, he is concerned about our words, how we use his name, what we say about him. Some tend to spiritualize the relationship with God and are careless with the external manifestations of that professed heart relationship. But that God is interested in deeds and words as well as in thoughts is clearly revealed in the first three commandments.

In the light of this, one's trust and obedience, allegiance or love may be quite legitimate and never demand a special, conscious evaluation until the loves or loyalties come into conflict. Then one's god stands revealed. At the point of choice, which love or loyalty we put before the other will determine who or what our true god is.

What is most valuable to me? What do I hold to be most irreplaceable? What would I be lost without? What do I think of with most intensity in the long stretches of my thoughts? What is my incentive for living? What gives my work meaning and purpose? This I worship.

A couple in Japan was at the point of divorce when God rescued them and their home by his grace through Christ Jesus. Unknown to me or to the young wife, the husband did not destroy the photographs of the other woman but put them in the bottom of a bureau drawer. Many months later, his wife discovered these photographs and in anger cut them to pieces. This made her husband so angry that the home was on the verge of breaking again. He said that the relationship with the other woman had been broken off, that there was no continuing contact of any kind, and that the pictures meant nothing. It is very hard for an outsider, let alone a wife, to believe that the pictures meant nothing when he took scissors and shredded her clothes in retaliation. Somehow there was unfaithfulness even though it was merely an outward form. God is a jealous God and will not countenance any competition for first place in our lives or the appearance of it.

December 1
The Measure of Life
2 Corinthians 5:15

"And he died for all," he repeats, "that those who live might live no longer for themselves but for him who for their sake died and was raised" (2 Cor. 5:15).

Jesus fulfilled the law by fulfilling the prophecies contained in the law. His birth, life, and ministry had been predicted in great detail, and these prophecies he fulfilled. Among them all, the great central event in history was his death, by which he simultaneously brought the law to completion and abolished it. He brought it to completion by becoming the sacrificial lamb to satisfy the demands of the law once for all. He "abolished" it by destroying the power of the law to condemn. By enacting the reality foreshadowed in the symbolism of the ceremonial laws, he brought them to an end (Heb. 7:26-28; 9:1, 9-10, 23-27). Jesus Christ fulfilled the entire system of ceremonial laws and thus set them aside.

This explanation of the meaning of Christ's death after he accomplished it fits perfectly with the pattern of his life and teaching. He consistently affirmed the authority of the "law," but his teaching was ever centered in the moral law. He never affirmed the ceremonial elements of the law. Christ's death was more than the fulfillment of the law in the sense of paying the penalty demanded by the law. It is also our example of supreme godlikeness. In fact, he put on display the highest form of love—complete sacrifice of self, even for one's enemy (Rom. 5:8). Never had the world even imagined such love. And it became the foundation for Christian behavior as well as the source of Christian life.

The preaching of Christ and him crucified is the only enduring foundation for sound morality. "For God," Paul insists, "has not called us for uncleanness, but in holiness" (1 Thess. 4:7).

In this fact he finds the motive for holy living. That is why Paul never tires of relating the obligations of morality to the fact that Christ died for us. Is it a matter concerning domestic relationship? "Husbands, love your wives, as Christ loved the church and gave himself up for her" (Eph. 5:25). Is it a matter concerning the weaker brother? "Do not let what you eat cause the ruin of one for whom Christ died" (Rom. 14:15). In fact, he rather did the opposite on occasion. For example, he "declared all foods clean" (Mark 7:19) even before the Cross, thus setting aside all the dietary regulations. Is it a matter of ambitious rivalry? Have this mind among yourselves, which you have in Christ Jesus, who, though he was in the form of God, did not count equality with God a thing to be grasped, but emptied himself, taking the form of a servant, being born in the likeness of men. And being found in human form he humbled himself and became obedient unto death, even death on a cross. (Phil. 2:5-8) Is it a matter of daily living? "And walk in love, as Christ loved us and gave himself up for us, a fragrant offering and sacrifice to God" (Eph. 5:2). Is it a matter of sexual morality? "Do you not know that your body is a temple of the Holy Spirit . . . ? You are not your own; you were bought with a price. So glorify God in your body" (1 Cor. 6:19-20).

The writers of the New Testament consistently appeal to the work of the Cross—to an accomplished redemption—as a ground and a motive of holy living.[83] How do measure yourself? Do you live for yourself or for Him who gave himself up for you? Today ponder what yardstick you use to evaluate your own walk of love. How well do you measure up?

December 2
Purpose Driven
Matthew 22:37-38

"'Love the Lord your God with all your heart and with all your soul and with all your mind.' This is the first and greatest commandment" (Matthew 22:37-38)

Holiness is important because without it no one will see God (Hebrews 12:14). But it's a limited goal. We often use holiness to describe growing away from sinful attitudes and actions. That is hardly the ultimate goal of life. Making holiness the primary goal creates another problem. Striving for holiness can become self-oriented and legalistic. Our ultimate purpose must be God-oriented, not self-oriented.

Focusing on God is certainly biblical and surely all we do should bring Him glory (1 Cor. 10:31). The problem with making the glory of God our ultimate goal is that, like Christlikeness, it isn't very specific. We're left with the task of spelling out in detail how we can best glorify Him. Some people seek to give a more specific focus to our purpose of glorifying God. Worship is a particular form of giving glory to God. Therefore, they make worship the goal of life.

---

[83] IBE (2014), 78-80.

Worship as a life purpose is another exclusively God-oriented choice. Indeed our whole lives should be worship, demonstrating His worth, but making worshiping Him the ultimate goal presents another problem: Why would a God of love be so self-centered as to demand worship as the whole purpose of making and saving His people? Is God selfish?

Five-year-old Kent was trying hard to get our guests to notice him and his talents. "Oh, Kent, quit showing off," I said. He apparently devoted some deep thought to the subject, because early the next morning he had developed his response, "Daddy, why does God want us to brag on Him?"

Many Bible students believe God desires that we conform to the reality of who He is for our own good. To get out of alignment with reality is self-destructive, allowing self to usurp the honor that belongs to God alone. God expects us to recognize who He is and behave accordingly because such recognition and behavior will result in our good.

The term "jealous" applied to God may jar us, but the Bible repeatedly tells us He's a jealous God. Perhaps we get a clue of what God is teaching us by considering the fundamental command of both Old and New Testaments: to love God. When God came in person to reveal His heart purpose, He said, *"'Love the Lord your God with all your heart and with all your soul and with all your mind.' This is the first and greatest commandment" (Matthew 22 :37-38)*. "*First and greatest*" makes clear what God is concerned about. Jesus quoted this commandment from the foundational revelation of God's will in the Old Testament, what the Jews call the Shema (Deuteronomy 6 :5). He then explained its importance. Everything else He said-everything taught in the Bible, "the law and prophets"-hangs on this command, along with the command to love one's neighbor (Matthew 22 :40). Perhaps we'd be safe to make loving God our chief end, except for one thing. Genuine love must be mutual. It's not so much that we love Him, but that He loves us! (I John 4 :10). So we must search for a more complete statement of God's purpose for us.

God is love in His nature (1 John 4 :8,16). From all eternity the Father, Son, and Holy Spirit are bound together in bonds of eternal love. From the overflow of that love, He designed a creature to love Him back. God's purpose all along has been to have a loving, mutual relationship with us. That's why He calls His relationship to us a marriage! When a man "knew" a woman in Bible times it meant they became one in intimate identity. That's why we say the goal of life is knowing God-an identity so close it could be likened to marriage. Closer than that-it could be likened to the unity the Father and Son have with one another. Now we see how being like Christ fits into the ultimate goal! We are intended to be like Him not only in character but in relationship. A prayer of Jesus speaks of our unity with one another (part of being like Jesus) intertwined with our unity with God. This also, we now see clearly, is part of our being like Jesus. Here's the whole passage, including both kinds of oneness-with God as a basis for unity with one another. Why not take a few minutes to read John 17:20-26?

Astounding! The love relationship He planned for us is intimate, exclusive, and permanent. The only way to exhaust its meaning is to say it's like the Father's love for the Son and the Son's love for the Father! That's why the two of them made that greatest of all sacrifices-He died for us so that we, alive or dead, might live in union with Him (1 Thessalonians 5 :10). Jesus' prayer in John 17 speaks of two unities-among believers and with God. The unity among believers shows outsiders whose disciples we are. Such unity has often proved difficult to achieve. Unity with one another is indeed the mark of true discipleship. The basis for unity between believers is our oneness with the Father, the Son, and the Holy Spirit. This second unity is beyond comprehension. It's like trying to explain to a five-year-old the glories of married love. A child doesn't have a clue. It's the same with us. If the unbeliever can't understand the glories of present unity with Christ, no more can we understand the ecstasies of our future union with Christ in heaven. We just don't have the capacity to grasp a whole new dimension of the human-divine relationship. We haven't matured yet. We've not undergone the final transformation into God-compatible beings. One day we will experience God in all His fullness. What joy!

December 3
Eternity
Romans 8:11

If the Spirit of him who raised Jesus from the dead dwells in you, he who raised Christ Jesus from the dead will also give life to your mortal bodies through his Spirit who dwells in you. (Romans 8:11)

Not everyone wants to die. Not everyone anticipates that day. One of my best friends, John, was dying an as agonizing death of bone cancer. When I visited him in his home he said, "Robertson, you probably want to go to heaven, but I don't. I've got too many things planned to get done for God right here on earth."

He declined rapidly, and soon I heard he had made his final trip to the hospital. I rushed to the hospital and found his room. When I entered John said, "Robertson, I've got something to tell you about death. It takes too long." I reached his bedside and groped for words of comfort, but he continued: "I can't figure out the purpose of all this pain and suffering." I responded, "I haven't got it all figured out either. But I do notice one thing it's done for you. A few weeks ago you didn't want to go to be with Jesus. Now you can hardly wait." John grimaced. "You're right, pal." A few hours later he had his desire.

Some understand Romans 8:11 to refer to spiritual rather than physical resurrection. They understand the verse to say Holy Spirit power energizes the spiritually dead to make them alive in Christ. The immediate context of the passage does speak of that regenerating work of the Spirit, but Paul addresses Christians here, not the spiritually dead. He assures them that the Spirit will yet give life to their physical bodies. I believe, therefore, that Paul speaks here of the final resurrection.

A clear parallel and a connection does exist with the already-accomplished spiritual resurrection. But the final resurrection is a major theme of the last half of the eighth chapter of Romans. I believe Paul is inserting a preview of that in our memory verse. Our physical resurrection is the grand climax of all the Spirit's work in us. It is the consummation of all He intended from the start: God's image fully restored, and union with God fully consummated.

WHAT A DAY THAT WILL BE! In a sense we're already married to God, united with Him forever. But in another sense, the consummation of that marriage is yet to be. You might call our present relationship an engagement and the Holy Spirit our engagement ring. God "*set his seal of ownership on us, and put his Spirit in our hearts as a deposit, guaranteeing what is to come*" (2 Corinthians 1:22; see also 5:5 and Ephesians 1:14).

Exciting as the engagement has been, our present experience of God will fade into the dim recesses of memory when the marriage is consummated! The climax of all the Spirit's work is to usher us into the banquet hall to introduce us to our beloved where we shall meet Him "*face to face*" (1 Corinthians 13:12). The Spirit's work will be complete when "*we shall be like him, for we shall see him as he is*" (1 John 3:2).

Many of God's promises about eternity will be fulfilled when we die and are instantly with Him. Others will be fulfilled when the bride, the church, is completed and Jesus returns to take her to the final celebration. Since the Bible doesn't explain all the delightful mystery of it, I'm not sure exactly what will happen when; no one knows. What a glorious anticipation!

As I think about eternity, here are some of the things I look forward to:

- Jesus. Seeing Him, feeling His warm embrace, being united with Him in a union so intimate I don't have the capacity even to imagine.
- The Father. Seeing Him smile and hearing Him say, "Well done." I want to tell Him how grateful I am for

His love for me, so great He let His own Son go for me. In fact, for the first time I'll be able to worship Him as I have always longed to, but never seemed able.
- The Spirit. I want to tell Him in detail how deeply I appreciate all He's done for me.
- Being reunited with my son, my parents, and other loved ones who got there before me, and, especially, my wife.
- All sorrow, pain, sickness, weakness, sin, and failure gone forever.
- Jesus' smile when I give Him my wedding present-my life investment for Him.
- Being in the likeness of Jesus, my transformation complete.

Do you resonate with any of those hopes? What do you most look forward to?

We began our walk with the Spirit in eternity where He designed us to be God-compatible. We've kept "in step with the Spirit" (Galatians 5:25) through His work of transforming us, a spiral up from one degree of Christ's glorious likeness to another. We're headed toward the grand finale when the Spirit will complete His work. But somewhere we must have gotten out of step, because we aren't rejoicing with the Bridegroom in anticipation of that glorious wedding day. If that's your situation, don't you want to get back in step with the Spirit?

I invite you to join me in prayer.

Holy Spirit of God, what a wonder You are! From beginning to end You made it all happen. And You not only do for me, You love me and want to be with me. That I can't understand, but I love You, too, and want to be Your intimate companion always. Hold me close and when I start to drift away, draw me back. I want to become all that a mortal can be, so here I am, Yours to do with as You will. Father and Dear Son, how can I ever express my gratitude for Your great gift at Calvary and Your great gift at Pentecost? I cannot, so I offer You all of me with the hope that it will bring You some small joy. In the authority of Jesus' name I come. Amen.

December 4
Pruning Shears
John 15:3

"Already you are clean because of the word that I have spoken to you." (John 15:3)

We need pruning if we are to produce the best possible crop of godly behavior and effective ministry. Jesus introduces us to the Master Pruner -- his own Father! (John 15:1). And then he shows us the two methods God uses in cutting back the bad, the unnecessary, and sometimes even good things that sap resources needed to grow and produce more. One method is gentle, the other severe. The gentle method, emphasized in John 15, is the Word; the severe is the sharp knife of God's discipline.

The Lord of our personal harvest, seeking to bring us to maximum fulfillment, cleans out the hindrances with his Word -the entire body of his teaching. It won't do simply to admire or respect the Word, it must abide in us. We must study it, think about it, master it, live in it. Without this relationship to the Bible, one cannot be at one with Jesus. To abide in Jesus, he said, was for his Word to abide in us.

The cancerous growth of self-orientation, injected into the life of the Church by popular culture, must be cut out of the believer's thinking or there will be no fruit. The good news is that God's Word will do it, if we allow it to. We do not take vows of poverty, chastity, and humility in some form of legalistic asceticism. But for the sake of a bumper crop, the Master Pruner will cut out false thinking by the instruction of his Word.

Some hold that the cleansing of John 15:3 continues the analogy of pruning. If we respond to the teaching of God's Word with obedience, the pruning knife of harsh discipline may not be necessary. So the word cleans us, day by day.

I called this the gentle method of pruning. But actually, some of his sayings are not so gentle. One of his most repeated sayings is very painful, for it runs directly counter to much of contemporary counseling, preaching, and writing. As we have seen, the contemporary wisdom holds that life really begins with the affirmation of one's self and aims at self-fulfillment. Jesus slashes into our lives with the announcement that life begins at the opposite end: self-denial, saying "no" to self-interest, not "yes." And it aims in the opposite direction, too: not at my own fulfillment, but at God's fulfillment. In fact, Jesus repeatedly warned that those who say "yes" to self-interest, who work to preserve themselves, to enhance their own welfare will lose it all! Whereas those who abandon their own interests for his sake and the gospel's will find exactly what everyone else so frantically and futilely seeks: life, fulfillment.[84]

The pruning knife of the Word is used in two ways. The first is consciousness raising, the second is focus. Those who read through the Bible consecutively, day by day, are exposed to the whole of God's revealed will and areas of unawareness are spotlighted, consciousness of unnoticed teaching will be raised so that it can be used to cut out counterproductive growth. Focus has to do with deliberately searching out all that Scripture teaches on some known temptation. That scripture can then be brought to mind in the time of temptation, just as Christ did in his hour of temptation.

For example, growth may be choked out by things and the "American dream" may have beguiled even the best-intentioned Christian. If the regular reading of Scripture does not raise consciousness about a materialistic lifestyle, a study of what the Bible says about covetousness will start cutting. To find out that covetousness is beguiling, idolatrous, and hell-deserving, for example, could begin the process of pruning!

And if through insensitivity or active rebellion we do not allow him to gently clean us with his Word, he will faithfully cut away at us with adverse circumstances. The analogy of John 15 does not go into detail about the nature of the pruning, but commentators almost unanimously agree that Jesus speaks in verse two of the pruning of discipline.

Suffering, according to Scripture, may come from many sources and may have a variety of purposes, but always there is the purpose of making us more like Jesus. In his skillful hand, every hard experience can be a pruning that will make us more fruitful than we might have been without it.

Growth and greater fruitfulness do not come automatically, however. They come only as we abide in Jesus--trust him, obey him. If we respond to the difficult circumstance with resentment, fear, worry, or retaliation, the circumstance will not prove to be a life-giving pruning knife. That very circumstance will become a hammer, battering us into damaged branches that bear little or no fruit. But if we bring that painful event or relationship to him with childlike confidence that he means it for our good--in other words if we abide in him--he will use it for cutting us back to make us more fruitful than we ever could have been with pain-free, random growth.

The reason is plain. Without the cutting circumstance we might never let go that shriveled, fruitless old twig from the past, that deformed off-shoot that keeps bearing ugly fruit, that out-sized growth that uses up the flow of life to produce a mass of showy leaves, or just that busy sprouting of so many buds that we never produce the full bodied fruit he plans.

To abide in Christ is to accept the daily cleaning action of the Bible and the sharp cut by the Master Pruner's hand in the circumstances of life. Then comes the harvest! But continuing with fidelity in obedience to Christ's words is not the end of "abiding." It is only the starting place. The end is joy beyond telling. And that glorious love story can be our theme each time.

---

[84] Matthew 16:24-26; Mark 8:35-37; Luke 14:26, 27; John 12:24, 25

December 5
Acceptable
Romans 12:2

"Do not conform to the pattern of this world, but be transformed by the renewing of your mind. Then you will be able to test and approve what God's will is—his good, pleasing and perfect will." (Romans 12:2 NIV)

One word Paul uses to describe God's will is acceptable, or some translators have it, *pleasing*. Success and overcoming temptation is pleasing. Alright, but to whom? Who do you think Paul had in mind as being pleased?? God? Yourself? Others? Bible scholars may debate which of those Paul had in mind, but I would say all of the above! To overcome temptation and to do the good thing brings joy all around. It's a victory celebration.! To fail and not do the goodwill of God is pleasing only to unholy men and unholy spirits. To you and to God and to all good people it's distressing.

When you put on display the perfect will of God in your life, you demonstrate your ultimate goal which is to be "flawless, without defect," and to have reached our appointed end goal, and purpose. These are just other ways of saying -to be like Jesus. And we'll celebrate that level one day. But not now. What can we fulfill in this life? His will is that we demonstrate maturity and obedience. And when we do, what a celebration of the glorious will of God! It's perfect! And that's very pleasing and very good.

What a wonder he is! Our inside companion does glorious things in us all the time! But what he does inside isn't all. He prays for us when our prayers fall short (Romans 8:26-27). And He engineers all the circumstances of our lives towards the same goal of transforming us into his likeness (verses 28-29). Furthermore, when it comes to the very weapons of the Spirit, it is He who enables us to pray effectively. It is God, the Spirit who gave us His Word, and it is He who enables us to understand and appropriate that Word in the face of testing. He is the one who gives us the church too, and he who enables us to live in the kind of relationship with other Christians that will make us overcomers together.

In regeneration, "everything" becomes new, that is, the Spirit changed something about every part of you- the way you think, how you feel, and what you choose. Here's a brief checklist of things that change so that you can evaluate what the impact the Spirit has been in your own life:

Your mind- How you think. What viewpoints changed about what is right and wrong? What changed about determining important or unimportant, about who you are, who God is, and what you can become?

Your heart- How do you feel about things? What attitudes changed? what you liked and disliked, and who you like to be around, and who your heroes were? What impact did the Spirit have on your feelings about yourself and about God?

Your will- What is different in your ability to make choices for God and against sin? Is the new you empowered to do what the old you couldn't do-consistently say "yes" to God, "no" to temptation?. Did any bad habits stop, good habits start? Any changes in lifestyle, activities?

You have just described a "Magnifico" new creation., as the Old English word would describe it! The new you. How exciting. It could be likened to a fuzzy little worm, earthbound and slow, transformed into a free, glorious creature of the skies. The transformation from caterpillar to butterfly is so radical that we call it a metamorphosis. Maybe that's a good synonym for "regeneration!" But regeneration is not the end. It's just the beginning of a great restoration project. There's an instantaneous transformation that takes place when we first put our trust in Christ, and this starts a transformation process that lasts a lifetime.

As in all of God's other activities, this "inside job "is assigned to the Holy Spirit as the primary mover. The Holy Spirit not only created us in God's likeness, he not only recreated us as an altogether new people; He takes up residence inside of us. Hallelujah! With such an inside partner, nothing can stop you! A successful life in the Spirit is no fantasyland, Our salvation is no "pie the sky by and by." Now. God, the Spirit lives in you in such a tight relationship that everything he promises is within your reach. Hallelujah! Our inside companion in person is all the resource we need to live out the Christian life successfully, to spiral upward, to spiral ever greater likeness to Jesus and intimate relationship with our Lord. Today may you exalt in the radical recreation that has already taken place! What a glorious gift!

December 6
Best Friends
John 15:5

"No longer do I call you servants, for the servant does not know what his master is doing; but I have called you friends, for all that I have heard from my Father I have made known to you." (John 15:15)

Josh was furious about his Christmas gift. It wouldn't work right. Suddenly he threw it across the room to crash through a valued lamp shade. Josh was only three and in the ensuing years he tried, with varying degrees of success, to bridle that temper. We became good friends. An unlikely friendship. He was very small and our conversations did not rise to great heights. He didn't always agree with me. Sometimes he would use creative epithets like, "You left your brains in Africa!" We would go to the amusement park together but we wouldn't stay together. He would never design to ride on the tame rides and I soon got ill on his favorites. When we returned from the circus he announced to his embarrassed mother that the best act was the elephant poop.

Josh taught me something about God and me. Now there is an unlikely friendship! Our conversations don't exactly reach the heights--at least mine don't reach very far toward his heights. Sometimes I may get angry with a gift he gives, say a bad thing, do a foolish thing, enjoy something ugly, but still he calls me, "friend."

It is hardly remarkable that we should love one so ineffably loveable as God. But that he should love such a person as I--that strains the imagination. And yet Jesus calls us friends (Jn 15.15). Strange that God should love us in such a one-sided relationship. But that we should love him--how could we not! And yet...and yet, how feeble and passionless my love for him. The one who has no good reason to love, loves passionately; the one who ought to love much, languishes in feeble and passionless responses.

A paradox, but not a mystery, for the quality of love depends on the character of the lover, not on the merits of the one loved. Against the backdrop of this lop-sided love affair, Jesus calls us friends. Not slaves or even children, both of which we are. But friends! He gives us an incredible invitation. He invites us to a relationship so intimate it can only be described as he being **in** us and we being **in** him (John 15:5).

Let us turn to the affectional part of abiding: to be in love (vs 9-17). This passage highlights three aspects of that love relationship: choices, communication, companionship.

Choices. I did not choose him to begin with, he chose me (vs 16). To be chosen by some beggar I may have befriended is one thing, but to be chosen by the Lord of the universe whose love I ignored! And not chosen merely to have the judgment against me revoked and receive assignment to some distant island of paradise, but chosen for companionship in a love relationship, more intimate and abiding than marriage. That is not easily believed. It points up an important thing about love. True love, as we have seen, depends on the nature of the one loving rather than on the loveability of the one loved.

God's character is so loving you might almost equate him with love: "God is love" (I Jn 4.8,16). God did not invent love as a moral hoop through which his creatures are enticed or driven to jump. No, God is love. From infinity past the Father, Son, and Holy Spirit have been bound together in bonds of living love. He just is that way. And from the overflow of that love he created a being designed on the model of his own nature that could receive his love and respond in love. A risky plan. What if that created being chose not to respond in love, to walk away from his love or even to reject it? Which is what that being chose to do. And every son and daughter of Adam since has followed that incredible path. But God didn't change in nature, so he reached out to reclaim the ones who chose to fall out of love.

God chose us (vs 16). Then he calls on us to choose, too. Thus love is more verb than noun--first of all what I choose, not how I feel. Notice that obedience and love are used almost interchangeably in the passage: "As the Father has loved me, so have I loved you. Now remain in my love. If you obey my commands, you will remain in my love, just as I have obeyed my Father's commands and remain in his love...You are my friends if you do what I command" (vs 9,10,14). The contemporary mood is to stress love and neglect obedience, but that won't work.

Love is demonstrated by the choices it makes. Choosing to act in behalf of another is to love; without action there is no genuine love. But volitional love in itself is not full love. Note that love begins with a choice. And the ultimate evidence of love is its choice to make a sacrifice: *"Greater love has no one than this, that one lay down his life for his friends"* (vs 13). Without sacrifice, love may be genuine, but there is no proof of it. One could act kindly or generously toward another for the benefit he himself gets from the relationship. So it is sacrifice that proves other-love rather than self-love is supreme. And the strongest love is proved by the greatest sacrifice, life itself.

We are chosen for companionship with the best of friends. So one strand in the three-fold bond of love is choice--his choice of us as his friend and our choice of him as our Lord.

Josh has been my friend, now, for several years. He is especially hard to resist when a smile breaks across that pixie face as he offers a gift of atonement, some well-loved toy, hugs me tight and says, "Sorry, Pawpaw." Recently Josh moved to a distant city and entered first grade. The other day I received a letter, the first from my buddy while we learn to communicate and companion…

December 7
Seek Justice and Love Mercy
Isaiah 1:17

"...learn to do good; seek justice, correct oppression; bring justice to the fatherless, plead the widow's cause." (Isaiah 1:17)

Seeking justice through political activism as a church is another matter to consider. The fact that neither Jesus nor the Apostles pursued justice through political action may not be construed as a prohibition of such activity. The argument from silence is notoriously weak. Simply because a matter is not mandated in Scripture does not mean we may not do it. Much less does the fact that some activity is not reported in Scripture have normative implications-that is, that since neither Jesus nor the Apostles did something can hardly mean that we may not. If biblical silences were mandates, many good things could not be done. For example, church buildings, children's ministry, theological education and many other things would be ruled out. On the other hand, since they are not forbidden in Scripture, polygamy, slavery, pornography, abortion and a host of other things would be acceptable. Our conscience must be governed by the principles of Scripture, not historical precedent or Scriptural silences.

One possible reason for the early church's non-involvement in the "political process" might have been the impossibility of it- they could hardly have done anything "political," living under the rule of totalitarian Rome. Of course, they could have launched a revolution as many attempted. But Christ expressly forbade taking up the sword in his name (Matthew 26:52-53) and his kingdom is not of this world (John 18:36).

And yet, what a poorer world this would be if Christians had not become involved in the rough-and-tumble of politics to rid the world of slavery and other fundamental social evils. My judgment in the matter is, however, that seeking justice through the political process is better done by Christians as citizens when they live in a society where this activity is possible, rather than by the church. To enter the political arena as a church is hazardous because the chief purposes of the church can be eclipsed or suborned. Besides, neither Christ nor the Apostles gave such a mandate nor gave principles that would demand it. Thus, one way the congregations Christ is currently building differ from the nation God built in the Old Testament, is that the people of God bound together in Christ's name can be "planted" in any political, economic, or social context. To say that there is not a mandate for the church to always, in every context, take political action in seeking justice does not mean, however, that the church should not, as church, speak out on moral issues that have become imbedded in the political process. For example, the social reformers in England brought about the end of slavery there through direct political action and the social activists of America today rightly campaign to change the laws concerning abortion. The prophetic voice is not merely permitted, it is demanded. Surely the church should be more than vocal, but active in healing divides and fighting injustice.

But more than seeking justice, the church follows Christ's example when it seeks to "do good to all." Ministries of mercy have been largely left to merciful governments—and thank God for merciful governments!--but still, to be true to its character and to its Lord, the church itself must reach out to the poor, the grieving, the ill of mind and body, the disadvantaged in education, those trapped in addictions. Some dysfunctions in society require both political and mercy solutions. For example, the church that is active in anti-abortion politicking should surely minister to those with unwanted pregnancies and single mothers.

Injustice in our society is pervasive, the needs almost without limit. No local congregation can even attempt to heal all the hurts. But to shrug off all responsibility is surely not the way of Christ. Wise selection of what societal ills a church should address might be the starting point for the congregation that has done nothing for those outside the walls of the church. But start we must if we are to follow our merciful Lord's example and commands.

December 8
Ministry to Society
Luke 14:34-35

"Salt is good, but if salt has lost its taste, how shall its saltiness be restored? It is of no use either for the soil or for the manure pile. It is thrown away. He who has ears to hear, let him hear." (Luke 14:34-35)

Should the Church speak to social issues *only in generalities* or should it speak *specifically?* It certainly has the right to speak specifically. John the Baptist did not address Herod with the general principle that "adultery is wrong." He said, "It is not lawful for *you* to have *her."*

What if the church says the wrong thing? It has certainly done so in theology, and we do not solve the problem by saying the church should not interpret the Bible. The church often errs in evangelistic practices, but we do not cease engaging in evangelism. We simply say, "That interpretation is wrong, and the churchmen who make it do not represent me."

For example, I would speak out in favor of Sunday closing laws, while other churchmen would speak out against them. And the irony of it is that I might be right morally and wrong politically. But this is the risk one runs.

For maximum effectiveness the church should limit its social action agenda to causes that are clearly biblical mandates. The problem with so much of both the religious left and the religious right agendas is that they are often a carbon copy of non-Christian society, whether the change-agent elite on the left or the traditional culture-captive on the right. This means that nonbiblical items are included on both agendas, and thus the moral force of whatever biblical mandates may be on the agendas is greatly reduced. Does defense buildup or the ownership of the Panama Canal really have the same clear biblical mandate as the sanctity of the home or the right to life? Far better to limit our agenda so that we establish battle lines on clear biblical mandates.

This will not only give us God's own authority in the battle for truth, it will also go far toward bringing believers together for a united impact. A graphic illustration of this truth was seen in the experience of Evangelicals for Social Action. The Thanksgiving meeting in 1973 brought together a broad spectrum of evangelical leaders who united in writing "The Chicago Declaration of Evangelical Concern." But the unity was soon dissipated, and the promising movement quickly failed of its potential because the agenda got too long with too many disputed specifics so that the hoped-for powerful, united voice for justice and mercy faded to the weak, if strident, voice of a band of loyalists who insisted on an extensive leftward-leaning agenda dealing with political means as well as moral ends.

May the church make *official pronouncements,* or is this limited to the preacher speaking in private as a citizen? If Billy Graham speaks on a social issue, such as nuclear disarmament, it will have more of an impact as "the voice of the church" than almost any major church council resolution. When any Christian speaks, that is the voice of the church to the people who accept that Christian as a responsible spokesperson of Christianity. The clergyman in the pulpit, the layperson on the street, the church body in council, or the mother with her children—they are "the voice of the church" to those who look to them for spiritual guidance.

The Christian *citizen* should provide the primary fighting force for justice and mercy, and the *church,* through its leaders, should avoid partisan politics and work hard at creating truly Christian citizens and speaking to clearly biblical moral issues. But can morals be legislated? The idea that morals cannot be legislated is usually based on a cultural or ethical relativism that teaches that moral behavior depends entirely on the culture and that nothing is right or wrong for all cultures at all times. This is a difficult position to follow consistently because the culture of a street gang must be granted legitimacy just as much as the Supreme Court.

The truth of the matter is that there are no theoretical limits to the extent to which the law may move against immorality. The truth is that most legislation is based on morality. If morality cannot be legislated, nothing can be. Most sensible people would agree with this in general, though there would be sharp disagreement as to which are private morals and which are public. Homosexual conduct is held by most Americans to be wholly private. But is it? What impact will the beleaguered family sustain as children are indoctrinated in the notion that homosexual relationships are normal and beautiful? How does homosexuality impact the military? These are not exactly private issues. The same might be said of any moral issue.

If the government is representative or democratic, it cannot but reflect the judgment of the society as to what moral standards should be required of all its citizens. If such a society legislates morals that are not acceptable to the majority, or even to a large minority of its citizens, the law becomes unenforceable. It is a bad law because it promotes lawlessness. Therefore, if a Christian is interested in having morals legislated, he must not only ask what is right and what is good for society, he must also ask, what will this society accept? Of course, he may fight for a losing cause on principle. But if he actually intends to impose a minority standard on the majority, he should understand that the legal fabric would be weakened and in the end much more than the specific moral issue would be lost.

In order to fulfill our responsibility in seeking justice and mercy, the Christian should study the Scriptures to determine God's view on any specific issue that arises. The Word of God must be our controlling authority.

The Christian must study the needs of the community—drugs, crime, slums, poverty, migrants, pornography, racism, family life, unemployment, housing, disease, unfair tax policy, discrimination, political corruption. What are the specific facts? What should we do about these problems? When do we begin, and how? What clearly biblical mandates concern you? How can you maximize your influence on individuals and on society in general?

December 9
Communicate and Companion
John 15:7

"If you abide in me, and my words abide in you, ask whatever you wish, and it will be done for you". (John 15:7)

Earlier we examined choosing and being chosen for friendship with God. That was the first of the three aspects of our love relationship: choices, communication, companionship. Today let us consider that friends- lovers - communicate and companion.

Lovers communicate. Our best friend communicates with us as his words take up residence in us (John 15: 7, 15) and we communicate with him in prayer (John 15:7, 16). If we are listening to him, he says, we can ask whatever we wish and it will be given. The Father will hear our prayers because we are abiding, obedient, fruit-bearing friends and because we come on the authority of Jesus' name, not our own.

Those are important qualifications to the glorious promise of answered prayer. If his words abide in us. That is, "whatever we wish" will become exactly what he wishes as we listen to him carefully and obey wholeheartedly. Of course he will grant such requests--they are exactly what <u>he</u> wishes!

<u>If</u> we ask in the name of the Son. I learned something of this at a time of great crisis. I was approaching the age of 40 and I was a failure. As a missionary in Japan I knew I could live among the people, love them to Jesus, and see a strong church established. I knew I could do it because I had done it before--more than once. But this time it wasn't happening. The Nakamuras were my last best hope, the only couple in this fledgling group, and their marriage was coming apart. I was failing as a missionary. I was failing as a father. I was failing as a provider for my family.

I sent the family away for a vacation and stayed behind to fast and pray. I was desperate. I cried out to God to deliver me. He seemed to gently ask, "Son, why do you ask?" I blurted out loud: "Who wants to fail?" In that instant my true self stood revealed and I was revulsed by what I saw. All those years I had been praying "in Jesus name" and "for Jesus' sake" when I should have been saying honestly, "for Robertson's sake, amen." Why ask for success? Well, who wants to fail? Why ask for healing? Well, who wants to hurt? Why ask for my children? Well, who wants to be embarrassed? There is no power in coming for my own sake or asking on my own authority. The qualification is clear: if we ask in <u>his</u> name, the Father will surely answer. I sensed the flow of power as I began to pass all requests through the screen of what would be for <u>his</u> benefit. God gave deliverance from all those woes, but if he had not, I could rest in the confidence that what he did grant was for his glory and my good. To abide in him is to listen and talk with our best friend.

Lovers companion. We have considered in great detail what Jesus identified as the specifics of what it means to abide in him, but the underlying concept seems to be the part least understood and most neglected by Jesus' friends. To abide in him is to abide in his love (vs 9) and John's commentary on this passage makes it very clear: "And so we know and rely on the love God has for us. God is love. Whoever lives in love lives in God, and God in him (I Jn 4.16)."

When Paul speaks of being "in Christ" it is more the judicial aspect of the relationship--we are viewed by God as righteous because of Jesus, "in Christ." But Jesus here is speaking of an intimate identity of life characterized by constant companionship. "The phrase (abide in) is a favorite of John to denote an inward, enduring personal communion"[85] This use of "in" is reinforced by "abide" so that Jesus here focuses on the central theme of this marvelous relationship: loving companionship.

There is a life of uninterrupted awareness of our Lord's dear presence. We cannot converse uninterruptedly--there are other things to do. But we can companion, can joy in the aura of his nearness all through the busiest of days. Just as a small child is well aware of her mother's presence in the room and enters naturally in and out of conversation, so we are invited to companion always with our best friend. Living in love!

Best friends. To abide in Christ, then, is to live in love. We act out love in our choices, especially sacrificial choices. We grow our love through constant conversation. And best of all, we companion with our lover always. The ultimate goal is God--to love him well and receive his love.

---

[85] W.F. Arndt and F.W. Gingrich, ed, <u>A Greek-English Lexicon of the New Testament</u>, Chicago: University of Chicago, 1957, 505.

December 10
Currency of the Kingdom
Matthew 16:21-17

"From that time Jesus began to show his disciples that he must go to Jerusalem and suffer many things from the elders and chief priests and scribes, and be killed, and on the third day be raised. And Peter took him aside and began to rebuke him, saying, "Far be it from you, Lord![e] This shall never happen to you." But he turned and said to Peter, "Get behind me, Satan! You are a hindrance to me. For you are not setting your mind on the things of God, but on the things of man." (Matthew 16:21-17)

Good Friday, we call it. The day Jesus was crucified. But it seems to me like a bad Friday, a very bad Friday. And yet, the only currency that will pass in the Kingdom of God is the cross. That's our theme today: the currency of the Kingdom.

Do you want to see the glory of the cross?
* We were exiles on the lonely island of our life, disinherited, banished from the Father's Home.
* Under sentence of death. Not like the hundreds in death row cells across the country today–they have hope that some appeal might work, that they might live. But in our case there was no hope, no "perhaps." Death was certain. There was only one uncertainty–when it would finally come.
* Further, we were not in some enlightened prison with all the conveniences of heaven's civilization. We were mired in the swamp of our own moral pollution. And worse, we were weak and helpless. There was no way for you or me to work free, to escape.

You remember Paul's pitiful cry, "Who will deliver me from this death-body?" He answers with very good news: "I thank God–through Jesus Christ". He has commuted our death sentence, there is a reprieve. We don't have to die. We can live. "There is therefore now no condemnation." We are justified.

But what if God gave you life and left you alone? What if your life should now be lived out on your own little island–alone, separated, unacceptable to Him? No, no. He LOVED you, forgave you, took you back into his own home, adopted you into his own family, gave you the royal inheritance. You are forgiven and adopted.

But what if he took us back, dirty and polluted, foul smelling? No. He cleaned us up, washed us. To him we are as pure and clean, innocent, and fragrant as Jesus. We are sanctified–set apart. But what if you are viewed by him as cleaned up, but still a weak, stumbling failure, always an infant--self-centered, demanding service, making mischief in the household of faith? No, no. He gives you power. Power to grow, power to succeed, sanctifying power.

How does he do all these glorious things? Only one currency will pass in the Kingdom of God: the cross. You see, God can't simply give you life, accept you, forgive and act as if everything is all right when in reality everything is all wrong. A price must be paid. It costs for you to enter the Kingdom. And that's the meaning of the cross. Otherwise, he would betray his own holy, trustworthy nature. The whole moral structure of the universe would crumble.

Consider the grand exchange, the cross-over.
*He had life, you had death. The only way for you to have life was for Him to take your death–change places. He was wounded for your transgressions, he was bruised for your iniquities; the chastisement for your peace was laid on him, and with his stripes you are healed. To give you life he died.
*He had sonship, we had exile, banishment, alienation. The only way for us to get into the family was for him to leave it, to take our banishment. My God, my God, why have you forsaken me? To his cry we hear only silence. But perhaps the Father whispered to the Son, "for your sake, that's why." To win our adoption he was abandoned.

*He was pure, without sin; we were filthy, rotten, polluted. The only way for us to be clean was for Him to become dirty. He who knew no sin was made sin for me and for you. He was made sin: sin incarnate. He was polluted with our pollution so that we could be clean.

*He was all-powerful, we were all weakness. The only way for us to become strong was for Him to become weak. So He did not count being equal with God a right to be clung to, but emptied himself, became weak, became a servant.

That's the meaning of the cross. The great cross-over, the great exchange. That's why it really is GOOD Friday. His death for your life, his banishment for your adoption; his pollution for your purity; his weakness to give you strength.

It is not Easter, or Christmas quite yet, it doesn't need to be. To understand what Good Friday means for us today, to see the meaning of the coming Christmas, look again at HIS cross.

Without His birth there is no cross, not only the provision for our salvation, but a model for our own responses to the trials of life. Not just his cross, but ours. Notice that on one occasion when Jesus returned to the theme of cross-bearing he added the word "daily" (Luke 9:23). Not a single heroic act, but a daily way of life.

December 11
Love for God and Love for Self
1 John 5:1

"Everyone who loves the Father loves whoever has been born of him" (1 John 5:1b)

All the infinite variety of potential loves can be divided into four groups: love for God, love for others, love for self, and love for things. It is quite possible to love many people and even many things at once without any sense of competition or conflict. But often there is conflict among the "loves," and nothing can be more painful and destructive. Today let us consider two of those loves.

Love for God. Christ tells us that this is the supreme objective: "Love the Lord your God with all your heart" (Matt. 22:37). This is the first command, first in importance, and the greatest, superseding all others as the controlling authority of life. Thus the Old Testament command (Deut. 6:5) identified by the teachers of Israel as the ultimate, comprehensive summary of God's will for man was affirmed by Jesus the Messiah as the most important commandment of all.

How does a mere human being love the infinite God? By the loving adoration of worship, by unceasing thanksgiving, by a life of steadfast obedience, by sharing his companionship and exulting in the endless profusion of his gifts. This is the goal of creation and redemption: to love God. Not so much to find my fulfillment, but to find his, to bring him joy, to seek his purposes, to do his will.

Indeed, to love God is the first and great commandment, but it is not the only commandment. The "law and the prophets" do not depend on this alone. There is another commandment. And, in truth, one cannot obey the first without obeying the second.[86]

---

[86] Matt. 22:34-40; 1 John 3:11-18; 4:19–5:1

Love for self. Contemporary psychology, in seeking to make people whole, is committed to the "cult of self-worship." Apparently in accommodation to this pervasive atmosphere, there is a tidal wave of Christian promotion of self-love as the biblical norm, so that self-discovery, self-affirmation, self-assertion, self-fulfillment, self-actualization, self-worth, self-esteem, self-importance are all advocated as worthy objectives for the Christian. In fact, we are told, we cannot be whole without them. How does this fit with the Bible's injunctions to self-sacrifice, self-crucifixion—indeed, with the command to hate oneself? (See Luke 14:26). Part of the problem is in the definition of "self-love," and part is a basic ideological difference.

The term *self-love* can be used to mean either "self-centeredness" or "self-acceptance." If we have in mind self-centeredness, no Christian would advocate it; if we have in mind self-acceptance, there is something to discuss. Since the term is ambiguous, perhaps we avoid it. But the problem is not just a matter of semantics.

No, we are not commanded to love ourselves—we are built that way. Yet some are so strong on self-sacrifice that they hold self-love to be wrong. Is not self-love a mark of the utter decadence of the end times (2 Tim. 3:2)? Did not Christ himself say that a person should hate himself? We are called upon to deny self or to deliberately choose to reject self-interest in favor of God's interests or even those of another person. The one who "loves" his own life (his own self) is the one who affirms his own rights and self-interest at all costs. In the final analysis, he loses his own life—the very thing for which he was grasping.

The contemporary notion is that wholeness begins with self-affirmation and ends with self-fulfillment, whereas Scripture teaches that wholeness begins with self-denial and ends with God's fulfillment. If one begins with self-affirmation and makes self-fulfillment the primary goal of life, neither he nor God will find fulfillment in his life. But if he makes the fulfillment of God's purposes in this world his goal, God will be satisfied and glorified, and he will find, as a by-product, the fulfillment of the purpose for which God created and redeemed him. That is true self-fulfillment.

If a person actually hates himself emotionally, dislikes himself, he is abnormal. And nonacceptance of self is indeed a great problem. Many psychologists seek to solve this problem by convincing a person that he is truly worthy or that he is not guilty. Building a high view of oneself is never given in Scripture as a solution to any problem. Such a "solution" only compounds the problem, for sooner or later the hurting person will discover that he really is not all that important in the eyes of others and that he truly is guilty.

The biblical solution to this problem is very different. It is the assurance that God forgives and accepts us. We are responsible for what we do and what we have become; we really are guilty. But the guilt has been done away with. And if God accepts us, we can certainly accept ourselves. Furthermore, Scripture teaches that we are created in the image of God and that we were created and saved *on purpose*. Though we may not be important or significant to anyone else, we are that important to God. What a self-image: created in God's likeness, redeemed at infinite cost, and invested with a unique purpose in life by God himself!

This great self-discovery of who I am in Christ then frees me and makes me strong to hate and exterminate the evil in myself and to sacrifice (self-denial) my own rights and even my own welfare for others. Now I can gratefully accept what I am—and what I am becoming—as God's loving gifts.

From this comes a biblical concept of self-image. A "strong" self-image is that perception of self which is true, which is most nearly aligned with the facts, including all the weakness and corruption that is mine by nature and all the glory that is mine by grace.

Self-love, then, properly defined, is recognized by Scripture as the way God made us. To treat self in this way is to be in alignment with reality and thus to promote wholeness.

December 12
Love for Others
Matthew 22:39

"Love your neighbor as yourself" (Matthew 22:39)

Jesus identified two commandments on which all else depends, and the second, he says, is very like the first: *"Love your neighbor as yourself"* (Matthew 22:39; cf. Leviticus 19:18). Both Jesus himself and John the well-loved took pains to spell out in great detail that other-love is the indispensable evidence of love for God. But the demands of other love are not equal for all people. Consider the various levels of responsibility.

When God created the male, he judged that he was incomplete. He had God in daily companionship, yet still God said, *"It is not good that the man should be alone"* (Genesis 2:18), so God created a partner to complement him. Thus the primary human relationship-in-love was God's wonderful idea of a man and woman united as one in marriage. So important is this relationship that the husband is charged with loving to the level of that high-water mark of love: *as Christ loved the church and gave himself for it* (Ephesians 5:25). And wives, in turn, are to *love their husbands* (Titus 2:4).

Then comes love for one's own family: parents, children, brothers, sisters. So important is this relationship that one who does not care for his own family is worse than an unbeliever (1 Timothy 5:4, 8).

But there is brotherhood beyond one's human family. The Old Testament focus of responsibility was on love for fellow countrymen, and the apostolic guiding principle was love for the brethren. For example, in the most exhaustive treatment of the theme of love in the Bible (1 John 3–5), John consistently speaks of love for *the brothers.* Paul concurs: *"Let us do good to all men"*—yes—*"and especially to those who are of the household of faith"* (Gal. 6:10). This is the New Testament pattern (John 15:12, 17; 1 Peter 1:22; 2:17; 3:8). It draws the altogether startling picture of a group of people, the church, that is, a true family bound together by closer blood ties than human blood relations, the blood ties of Calvary. It is the picture of a people bound by love in interdependent responsibility for one another in every facet of life: spiritual, physical, emotional, material. Such is New Testament "love of the brethren." But biblical love does not end there.

The Old Testament theme of "neighbor love" was never restricted in Scripture to fellow Israelites. The foreigner was included (Lev. 19:33). But Jewish people, being human, wanted to restrict the application of the sweeping demands of love. So the lawyer, who demonstrated that he knew the summary command of love well enough, wanted to justify his unloving behavior and asked: *"And who is my neighbor?"* (Luke 10:29). Jesus turned his question upside down (or right side up) with the story of the half-breed Samaritan who understood love better than the credentialed religious leaders and became a neighbor to the one who needed him. So neighbor-love reaches beyond brother-love to anyone at all who is in need.

Neighbor does not really mean "anyone" or "everyone." It is so easy to love mankind in the mass and neglect or even despise the one nearby.

Love is not mere tolerance, a warm feeling for everyone "out there" or even special indignation for the oppressed in some distant place. It must be for one's neighbor—the person within reach. Anyone within reach, to be sure. But love as action must be for someone who needs what I have and can give (Gal. 6:10). Neighbor-love extends to a wider circle than love of the brotherhood, just as love of the brotherhood extends beyond family love. And it is not restricted to worthy neighbors. It includes even one's enemy.

Love for one's enemy was taught in the Jewish law (Exod. 23:5; Job 31:29-30; Prov. 24:17; 25:21), but no one took it very seriously. In fact, Jesus says that tradition held it was all right to hate your enemy (Matt. 5:43). But he taught love of enemy with a force and consistency that startled the Jewish world. He startled the world of Roman law and Greek philosophy as well. This was unique: Love your enemy. If you cannot *feel* all that warm about him, you can *choose* to act lovingly: pray for him, do good to him, speak well of him (Matt. 5:43-48; Luke 6:27-38). But the world-shattering message was not that he *taught* this way of life—incredible as that is—but that he loved his own enemies just that way: "*But God shows his love for us in that while we were yet sinners Christ died for us*" (Rom. 5:8). And we are to love our enemies just that way. [87]

How is your love life today? Why not take an inventory? Love for your spouse? Love for your family? The body of Christ? Your neighbor? What love do you choose to express for your enemy? Do you speak well of your enemy? Difficult? Yes! It would not be commanded if it could not be done. How do you measure love? Its height or depth? By what thermometer do you take its temperature? As Jesus demonstrated for us, love is measured by the sacrifice it makes.

December 13
A Conflict of Loves
John 15:13

"*Greater love has no man than this, that a man lay down his life for his friends*" (John 15:13)

God, others, self, things: One may love all so long as they do not conflict. But what if love for someone else conflicts with the love due God? What if my best interests and those of my neighbor's cannot coexist? How do we handle the conflict of loves?

Most people choose and act from the motive of self-interest. The highest loyalty for unredeemed man is to self. Even in the most altruistic of humanistic ethics, the top priority is mankind, not God. But in biblical love the ultimate, controlling love, the integrating factor of life, the pivotal relationship, is love for God. How can I tell if I love God supremely?

It is futile to try to decide whether we have as warm an affection for God as we do for a parent or child, a wife or husband, but there is a way to tell which love is paramount. The controlling love becomes quite evident when a confrontation comes. When the best interest of another or ourselves and the best interest of God come into conflict, love must make a choice.

Ordinary human love gives for another to a point. But when the cost of acting lovingly gets too high, loving behavior ends. God's kind of love is different. How can I tell if I truly love my neighbor as Christ would have me love? Ask the key question: Does my love for self limit the expression of my love for the other person, or does my love for the other limit the expression of my love for myself? Love is measured, not by the intensity of its feeling, but by the sacrifice it stands ready to make.

---

[87] IBE (2014), 44-46.

Jesus indicated this when he said, *"Greater love has no man than this, that a man lay down his life for his friends"* (John 15:13). Often love is present without sacrifice, but so long as there is a return benefit, there is no *proof* that the love is truly other-love rather than self-love. No matter what our emotional response, if we choose to sacrifice what we perceive to be our own interests for the welfare of another, we have loved as God loved. Sacrifice. That is God's way of loving. And the world finds it beyond comprehension.

Natural man does not ordinarily want to get involved for someone else's benefit. Above all, he does not want to suffer loss for someone else. When Kitty Genovese was brutally stabbed to death in front of her apartment in New York in March 1964, thirty-eight people watched from behind darkened windows. No one did anything to help her, though she cried for help for thirty minutes. Why? The police investigator said, "The word we kept hearing from the witnesses later was *involved*. People told us they just did not want to get involved. They do not want to be questioned or have to go to court." Her case was celebrated because of nationwide coverage, but the story is repeated daily. No one wants to be involved. But godlike love is precisely the opposite: It chooses to get involved, no matter what the cost.

And yet the sacrifices we shrink from are not usually life-threatening: the sacrifice of a parent to allow the child to be childish when he is young and to let him grow free when he is older, the sacrifice of a child to allow his parent to "smother 'im with motherin'," the sacrifice by a spouse of his right to be right—all the small irritations of the daily routine. For the conflict of interests to be resolved, someone must be sacrificed. Who will it be? Will I take up my cross or nail him to his? It depends on whom I love the more.

Shirai was a young Japanese wife whose husband was the traditional lord of the house. When she came to faith in Christ, he was furious. If she ever went to that Christian meeting again, he warned, she would be locked out. Sunday night Shirai came home to a darkened, locked home. She slept on the doorstep till morning, and when her husband opened the door, she smiled sweetly and hurried to prepare the best possible breakfast of bean soup, rice, and raw fish. Every Sunday and every Wednesday the story was the same. Winter came, and with it the rain and cold. Shirai huddled in the darkness as her wet cotton-padded jacket froze about her. Week after week for six months she forgave, freely and fully. No recriminations, no sulking. It was costly—she bore his sin. But her poor husband finally could stand it no longer. Love finally won out. When I met him, he was a pillar in the church, learning to walk the thorny path of sacrificial love. Shirai's example shatters my own complacency with a sharp, clear picture of what it means to deny oneself, take up one's cross daily, and follow Jesus.

"That a man should always be ready to forgive has been called Jesus' most striking innovation in morality."[88] Perhaps one of the most painful sacrifices that love makes is forgiveness. To forgive is costly, for someone must pay the price of wrong. If I choose to treat the person as if the wrong had never been done (forgive), then I may have to pay for it. It is not just the sacrifice of ego—that seems to be painful enough. But if I forgive—truly forgive—the smashed fender, then I pay for it. And I do not make the guilty party pay for it in installments through petty insinuations. When President Ford forgave Richard Nixon, he paid for it, they tell us, in the next election. Even when the relationship is such that discipline is necessary, as with a parent and child, forgiveness means full restoration without the haunting specter of subtle reminders. And sometimes it's not forgiveness at all, but a joint assumption of guilt that is needed.

On the other hand, some people have the knack for making an accusation under the guise of apologetic words. I may say, "I'm sorry to have been so dumb as to say that and tee you off. Please forgive me." The not-so-hidden implication: "I forgot how you are so unreasonably touchy. Too bad you had to sin again with your insensitive tongue." The net result of such an "apology" is a double wound, one for your badness and a second for my own implied innocence.

---

[88] Anders Nygren, *Agape and Eros*, trans. Philip S Watson (Philadelphia: Westminster Press, 1953), 48.

Must I forgive if the other person does not repent, does not ask forgiveness? Jesus said, "If your brother sins, rebuke him, and if he repents, forgive him" (Luke 17:3). So we *must* forgive the one who indicates regret for sin against us. That is when God forgives. But Christ and Stephen both prayed that God would not hold accountable those who sinned against them, even though the murderers had not asked forgiveness. So it is all right to forgive anyway. And since we are not godlike in our knowledge of the other person's thoughts, it may be the best thing to forgive anyway. Usually the other person does not view the circumstances from my perspective and does not sense a need to repent or ask forgiveness. In any event, an attempt at reconciliation is always my responsibility, no matter who the chief wrongdoer was.

December 14
Character of God
1 John 4:7-8

"Beloved, let us love one another, for love is from God, and whoever loves has been born of God and knows God. 8 Anyone who does not love does not know God, because God is love." (1 John 4:7-8)

Agape-love is said to be "the center of Christianity, the Christian fundamental motif *par excellence.*" [12] Is this statement claiming too much for love? I believe Augustine was nearer the truth when he said that the supreme good is nothing other than God himself. Surely the center of Christianity is Christ himself. And yet, what kind of god is God? And what is the character of Jesus Christ? As we have seen, God is loving. Indeed, God *is* love. The supreme importance of love is seen in this: Love is the way God is.

Great and sharp has been the contention over whether righteousness or love is paramount in God's character. And how do his justice and holy wrath against sin fit with his love? Some hold that righteousness is the comprehensive description, and that love is an element of what is right or true. Others hold that love is the comprehensive category and that righteousness is one facet of love. Perhaps we can do no better than rejoice with the psalmist that *"steadfast love and faithfulness will meet; righteousness and peace will kiss each other"* (Ps. 85:10). This they did at Golgotha when God's righteous indignation against sin fell on his own beloved Son because of love for you and me. Certainly it is true that God's kind of right cannot exist without love, and God's kind of love cannot exist without righteousness. Love is of supreme importance because that is the way God is.

Love is not only a primary characteristic of God; it is the imprint of his likeness in human beings, the indispensable family characteristic without which no one can claim membership in the family of God (1 John 4:7-8). Love binds the Trinity into one, and from the overflow of that love came the creation of a being that is not the *"highest of the animals"* but a *"little less than God"* (Ps. 8:5), capable of companionship and loving unity with God himself. Not only is this loving unity the central fact about God and the purpose of creation; it is also the purpose of redemption in restoring the image man marred. He did not restore man merely to prove his powers and defeat Satan. He was out to fulfill the original purpose—nothing less than loving union with himself.

True love is so deep, so broad, so high that it is beyond understanding (Eph. 3:18-19). In fact, somehow it is related to "all the fulness of God" (v. 19). But if Christ indeed lives in us through faith, we can be so established in the experience of love that *we* have the power to comprehend this greatest of all qualities (vv. 17-18).

Not only is love so important because it is characteristic of God and suffuses the origin and destiny of man; it is the foundation of all ethics, God's revelation of what he wills us to be and do.

Finally, the results of loving attitudes and behavior underscore the supreme importance of our theme. God's love for us provided life and salvation and now provides all that we need. "Who shall separate us from the love of Christ? . . . Neither death, nor life, nor angels, nor principalities, nor things present, nor things to come, nor powers, nor height, nor depth, nor anything else in all creation, will be able to separate us from the love of God in Christ Jesus our Lord" (Rom. 8:35-39). How great the results of God's love for us! But what of our love for God?

When we love God with all our affections (heart), with every choice (soul), and with the concentration of all our mental powers (mind) (Matt. 22:37), we not only prove to be his and please him, but we validate all the other loves. Love for God makes love for others and even for ourselves operate at the level he designed. If I fail to hold love for God as the ultimate, I may do more than damage love for others or diminish the worth I have as a person in Christ. I may even invalidate the other loves altogether. For example, when parents put a child on the highest throne of affection and sacrifice responsibilities to God and obedience to his will for that child, the relationship to the child himself becomes warped and grotesque.

I enjoyed visiting the Nakamuras. God had rescued them from a miserable life at the brink of divorce and brought them into the family of God's people. Their six-year-old son, Hideyaki, was a great playmate for our youngest. One day I asked if they had any pictures of him. Did they! The first album, to my amazement, brought me only through the first six months of Hideyaki's life—pages and pages at his birth, pages for the first month "birthday," and then more pages for the first hundred days. The whole closet was full of albums almost exclusively of Hideyaki. What affection for an only son! Gradually the affection crowded out God's place and, inevitably, began to erode the affection of the couple for one another.

But perhaps Hideyaki at least would benefit? The last I heard, he had broken the hearts of those adoring parents, falling deeper and deeper into a life of drugs and crime. The idolatrous affection not only destroyed the relationship with God and other relationships, it participated in the destruction of the very object of supreme devotion itself.

But love for God, when enthroned above all other loves, has the power to anchor the other loves, to give them direction and power, to fill them with meaning, discipline them, and lift them to their highest and best. Above all other results, the person who lives in love actually lives in God (1 John 4:16), the ultimate goal of all our existence.

Why not take a few minutes in this season to consider your love life? What does your love life reflect in your choices to operate at the level God designed? Do you hold love for God as the ultimate? Or perhaps it does not and you damage others or diminish your own worth in Christ? Perhaps your love for God anchors your other loves and you and those you love function at their best. Why not choose today to live in love?

December 15
Poverty
2 Corinthians 9:11

"You will be enriched in every way to be generous in every way, which through us will produce thanksgiving to God." (2 Corinthians 9:11)

There are three main types of poverty in the world. *Collective* poverty (which includes *class* and *regional* poverty) is the semipermanent insufficiency of the material means of life for an entire population and can be applied to nations. *Cyclical* poverty is the widespread but temporary deprivation caused by disease, crop failure, or economic breakdown such as occurred in this country in the 1930s and 1980s- possibly in the 2020s due to the pandemic and war. *Individual* poverty is a condition of want resulting from an individual's misfortune or inability to work, including the widows, orphans, physically handicapped, outcasts, aged, mentally deficient, and alcoholics.

We tend to think of poverty as a personal matter, and we feel better about it when we are convinced that it stems from laziness or lack of discipline. Scripture recognizes that there is such poverty but says very little about it. Rather, the constant emphasis in Scripture is on poverty due to oppression. This oppression can be individual or corporate—a whole people can come under God's condemnation for oppression and injustice. This corporate injustice seems to be a central theme in the great pivotal events in history: Violence was the only specific sin mentioned as a reason for the Flood (Gen. 6:11, 13); oppression and injustice brought judgment on Egypt (Exod. 1–12); Israel and Judah were sent into exile for injustice as well as idolatry as the prophets consistently emphasized in their denunciations. Even the Incarnation had something to do with this theme. Mary sang of it: *"He has put down the mighty from their thrones, and exalted those of low degree; he has filled the hungry with good things, and the rich he has sent empty away."* (Luke 1:52-53)

Christ himself announced his calling: *"The Spirit of the Lord is upon me, because he has anointed me to preach good news to the poor. He has sent me to proclaim release to the captives and recovering of sight to the blind, to set at liberty those who are oppressed, to proclaim the acceptable year of the Lord."* (Luke 4:18-19)

This proclamation of Christ is normally spiritualized, but Christ's own description of the next pivotal event—the Second Coming (Matt. 25)—makes abundantly clear that he will judge people, at least in part, on the basis of what was done to relieve physical need and oppression.

Is there something in societies' structures that is unjust and is the *cause* of suffering? *Something* in the system itself must contribute toward the problem World Bank President and successful capitalist Robert McNamara graphically identified:

> Two-thirds of mankind . . . remain entrapped in a cruel web of circumstances that severely limits their right to the necessities of life. They . . . are caught in the grip of hunger and malnutrition, high illiteracy, inadequate education, shrinking opportunity, and corrosive poverty.[89]

I do not present these comments in an attempt to define any specific systemic cause for the present human tragedy; that lies in the province of specialists. But both Scripture and human history do point toward corporate responsibility as well as individual responsibility and call for corporate action as well as private charity. The solution must begin with the private individual. But each individual is responsible to involve those in his sphere of influence to

---

[89] Robert McNamara, *One Hundred Countries, Two Billion People* (New York: Praeger, 1973), 30.

find corporate solutions, whether a mother with her children, a pastor with his church, a businessman with his policies, or a public servant with his power to change and use the structures of society to promote justice and mercy.

Scripture calls for both broad based action and private involvement. Change must begin with the individual. Take a few moments to examine before the Lord how you can better relieve physical need and oppression. What will you do to break the web of circumstances that limits access to the necessities of life? As we broach the Christmas season, can you purpose to reach out of your abundance to not only meet the needs of the poor for the next weeks, but work to relieve systemic poverty? What might this look like?

December 16
Internal Love
1 John 4:9

"Beloved, let us love one another, for love is from God, and whoever loves has been born of God and knows God. Anyone who does not love does not know God, because God is love. In this the love of God was made manifest among us, that God sent his only Son into the world, so that we might live through him. In this is love, not that we have loved God but that he loved us and sent his Son to be the propitiation for our sins. Beloved, if God so loved us, we also ought to love one another. No one has ever seen God; if we love one another, God abides in us and his love is perfected in us." (1 John 4:7-12)

In the Old Testament, love speaks of a spontaneous feeling that impels to self-giving. This was true both for God and man. When man "loved" God, it meant to have pleasure in God, striving impulsively after him, seeking God for his own sake. From God's side, the warm, strong feeling of affection that characterizes a healthy parent-child relationship is taken as a picture of how God the Father relates to Israel, his son. Love is the foundation of the covenant relationship. If the legal, covenantal aspect of the relationship is strong in the father-son analogy, the passionate loving-kindness of a good marriage is strong in the picture of God the husband and Israel the wife. The climactic revelation of this love relationship is seen in the prophet Hosea and his well-loved harlot-wife. The same analogy of father-son, bridegroom-bride continues in the New Testament, focusing on the warm affection and unfailing bonds between two who love each other deeply.

But the internal aspect of love is more than a feeling. It is a characteristic of life, a disposition. Old Testament scholars seem to have a problem in translating another Hebrew word, *chesded*. Some translations speak of *loving-kindness* (KJV), some of *steadfast love* (ASV, RSV), some of *constant love* (TEV, Today's English Version). Indeed, the love of God is steadfast, unfailing—a basic disposition that never changes and that controls all that he does. This has to do with commitment. God's kind of love is not a sometime thing, tentative and sporadic. It does not run out. His covenantal love is from youth to old age, from generation to generation, from age to age, from eternity to eternity. This unending love is faithful through all kinds of circumstances, even rejection. Biblical love, then, is not a passing emotion, but a way of life, a disposition, a relationship of permanent commitment to the welfare of another.

There is yet another element in the internal aspect of biblical love: loving feelings motivate. In fact, it is not too much to say that love is the only motive. At the root of every choice, every action a person takes, lies love. It may be purely from love of self that a person takes action, or it may be other-love. But always love is the dynamic that propels, the catalyst that transforms thought into action.

Some speak of the glory of God as a motive. But strictly speaking, glory is not a motive. If I seek my wife's glory, for example, my motive may be my own glory. If she is highly thought of, I will be more praiseworthy for having caught her and kept her. Of course, I may seek to put her in the best light before others because I love her, not me. But the *motive* is not *her* glory. The motive is *my* love, one way or the other. In the same way, the great commission is said to be a motive. But I may obey any command of God because I love me—it is the smart thing to do. A pastor may work himself into an ulcer to build his own reputation on earth or in heaven. I may give generously for the impression it will make on others or witness for fear of the consequences if I do not. Thus, I may seek my own glory because I love me. Or I may be totally indifferent to how people think of me. I may prefer pleasure. Or money. But money, pleasure, honor do not motivate; they are the means by which I may seek my own fulfillment. The same is true of seeking God's fulfillment, or my neighbor's. The basic drive, the mainspring, the motive of all human action is love.

Another day we shall see how the Bible treats self-love and other-love and how conflict between them may be resolved. But at this point it is important to identify how biblical love is a feeling, a disposition, and a motive.

Our focus on the internal aspects of love is immediately shifted to the external by the term *motive*. Motivated to what? To act. How do we now turn from love as an inner response to love as the way a love-motivated person behaves. [90] How would you describe how you love as a way of life, a disposition, and a relationship of permanent commitment to the welfare of another? Ready to walk away from a friendship? Your church? Perhaps a marriage? Or that troubled teenager? Love is determined not by the attributes of the one loved, but by the qualities of the one who loves. (*We love because he first loved us.*1 John 4:19) How can you love better today?

December 17
The External Aspects of Love
2 John 6

*"And this is love, that we walk according to his commandments; this is the commandment, just as you have heard from the beginning, so that you should walk in it." (*2 John 6)

The Bible emphasizes what love does more than how love feels. This is no doubt why those who translated the Hebrew Old Testament into Greek chose the colorless *agape* over the strong, vibrant *eros* and the warm, affectionate *philia*. *Agape* had this going for it: It emphasized choice, action. The others did not. *Agape* referred to a free and decisive act determined by the subject himself, not by the drawing power of the object, as in the case of passionate *eros* or warm, but duty-bound *philia*. The primary characteristic of biblical love is action.

In the New Testament, as in the Old, loving is often linked with obeying—the outward response of an inward condition of love. We are *commanded* to love. "You shall love the LORD your God. . . . You shall love your neighbor

---
[90] IBE (2014), 30-33.

as yourself" (Lev. 19:18; Deut. 6:5; Matt. 22:37-39). "If you love me, you will keep my commandments" (John 14:15). "For this is the love of God, that we keep his commandments" (1 John 5:3; 2 John 6). The first question Scripture asks is not, How do you feel about this person? but, rather, What choices must you make concerning this person?

Of course, a human being is a whole and cannot be divided, for example, into knowledge, will, and emotions. However, since a whole person does function both volitionally and emotionally, it is proper for us to say that the will "controlled" one action and the emotions "controlled" another. One can will to act contrary to the impulse of his emotions. Jesus did this when his heart (emotions) cried out, "Father, let this cup pass from me." Yet he chose the Father's will, contrary to what he wanted, or how he felt. From the Bible's viewpoint, the choice to act lovingly, not the intensity of the feeling, is the test and ultimate proof of love. The concept of volitional love overriding affectional love is of paramount importance, for one may not be able to control his emotional response. But by the grace of God he can choose to act lovingly, no matter how he feels.

Some contend that this is dishonest. One must act in conformity with his feeling, it is said; otherwise he is attempting to deceive the other person into thinking that he feels a way he does not. But this line of reasoning emasculates a person, cutting away from him all his functions but one. Not only am I a person with feelings, I am also a person of choice—not to mention intelligence, commitments, and many other facets of my whole self. To be honest to myself I must be honest to my whole self; I must choose to act in conformity to my total being. Above all I must be honest to God, to act in conformity with his will and my commitment to him. This is indeed a liberating truth—I can choose to act for the welfare of another no matter how I feel about him or about the action God desires of me.

To say that acting lovingly takes precedence over the emotion of love does not mean that biblical love is exhausted by acting lovingly. Without the emotion, love can be authentic, but it is not complete. If we act in love, ordinarily the affection will follow. Thus one can love in a biblical, active sense, without liking. In fact, it is required that we act lovingly no matter how we feel.

Love-in-action has both a negative and a positive aspect. Biblical love is positive and active—constantly planning and acting for the welfare of others. To refrain from killing one's enemy is a loving thing, but to give one's life for an enemy is the ultimate act of love (John 15:13).

An emerging definition of love, then, is an affection, or a desire for the welfare of another that moves to a commitment to act in his behalf. Ordinarily, this is the way love moves, from attitude to action. But when the internal aspects are missing, one can begin with loving action, the external, and leave the feeling to tag along as it will. And this is not an aberration, an undesirable last resort. No, *acting lovingly without the feeling of love can be of the very essence of biblical love*—that which causes it to stand out in bold contrast to ordinary human love. We call it sacrificial love. Thus love may flow either direction—joyfully from affection to action or painfully across the bridge of the cross—"nevertheless," no matter how I long for some other way, "not my will but thine be done."

Reciprocal love and nonreciprocal love. Some disparage reciprocal love, calling it "need-love" or even "swap-love." They say it is unworthy to expect or even to desire a return on one's investment of love in another. But it is easy to become more "spiritual" than the Bible .

Indeed, God himself expects a "return on his investment." He longs and desires to be loved (Hos.; Matt. 22:37; John 4:23; Rev. 3:20). But the difference is this: He does not demand it. He does not make a loving response the condition for giving love (Rom. 5:6-8). And, humanly, we always do. *Eros* to the ancient Greek, and to the modern man as well, is passionate love that desires the other *for itself.* We continue to give only so long as we receive—or so long as we hope to receive. But God's kind of love is not preoccupied with the question, How well *am* I loved? but rather, How well *do* I love?

Thus the focus of biblical love is on the quality of the subject, the loving character of the one loving, not on the quality of the object, its worthiness of love, its desirability, its lovableness. Jesus spells this out in great detail with many examples (Luke 6:27-35). He teaches that to love those who love us is nothing great. It is when we choose deliberately to love those who do not deserve it that we have reflected divine love.

Yet the ideal is reciprocal love, each finding in the other abundant reason to appreciate, to feel drawn to, to be overwhelmed by the desire to give. We give because we want to, not because we have to—we delight in the loved one. Then we rejoice in receiving from the one loved. When the object is not lovable, or the emotion is not present, it is then that the character of the giving lover shines in greatest splendor. Biblical love, then, is an affectionate disposition that motivates the lover to consistently act for the welfare of another, whether or not the other deserves it or reciprocates.

We have tried to define love. But the length and breadth and depth and height of it (Eph. 3:18-19) stretch far beyond our reach. What shall we do? Often, to understand an abstract idea or a large concept it is necessary to define by description or demonstration. How good that God has given us both.

December 18
Incarnational living
Philippians 2:1-11

"So if there is any encouragement in Christ, any comfort from love, any participation in the Spirit, any affection and sympathy, complete my joy by being of the same mind, having the same love, being in full accord and of one mind. Do nothing from selfish ambition or conceit, but in humility count others more significant than yourselves. Let each of you look not only to his own interests, but also to the interests of others. Have this mind among yourselves, which is yours in Christ Jesus, who, though he was in the form of God, did not count equality with God a thing to be grasped, but emptied himself, by taking the form of a servant, being born in the likeness of men. And being found in human form, he humbled himself by becoming obedient to the point of death, even death on a cross. Therefore God has highly exalted him and bestowed on him the name that is above every name, so that at the name of Jesus every knee should bow, in heaven and on earth and under the earth, and every tongue confess that Jesus Christ is Lord, to the glory of God the Father." (Philippians 2:1-11)

On a trip abroad to speak at conferences, I saw the results of God's handiwork. When going from one conference in Kenya to another in Egypt, I arranged a stop-over in Ethiopia. For two reasons. Our daughter is serving there among the homeless children, the AIDs victims, the sex victims. I wanted to spend a bit of time with her. But I also wanted to search out some of my roots. From childhood I had celebrated my uncle, Tom Lambie who had given his life there. My guide knew his story well and took me first to the Lambe Café. Outside an attorney waited.. He thought I was his appointment, since I was a Westerner. When I told him I was visiting the work of my uncle Tom Lambie, he exclaimed, "Oh he is the one who brought Christianity to Ethiopia!"

Of course, he forgot, perhaps, that it was some time earlier that Christianity came to Ethiopia! Remember Christ's disciple, Philip, when he was sent to baptize the Eunuch, on his way home to the royal court of Egypt? Perhaps the attorney was thinking of the major Protestant denominations—2 of them, not 1, that Uncle Tom had founded a half century ago. Or was it the immense hospital complex across the street from where we stood, one of several Uncle Tom had established?

At any rate, we entered the little café and found a large photo of Uncle Tom caring for a wounded soldier and the Emperor, Haile Sallaise, standing by. Lambie was personal physician to the Emperor. After coffee we went next door to visit a prestigious girl's school. The principal was delighted to meet the nephew of the founder. How they venerated Uncle Tom and his founding of this, the very first education for women in Ethiopian history. That was 80 years ago, but still they celebrate him. He so loved the people of Ethiopia, that when the Italians invaded and took control, throwing out all Western missionaries, he gave up his American citizenship and became an Ethiopian so he could remain.

Bad move, or, as one of those we met that day in Addis Ababa, put it, he bet on the wrong horse. When the Italian regime ended and the Emperor returned from exile to take control, he expelled Uncle Tom! But the story doesn't end there. Actually, that's where the story leads us to Bethlehem. Uncle Tom refused to retire. Instead he moved to Bethlehem in Transjordon where the people were oppressed, with many suffering from Tuberculosis. So he established a large TB sanatorium near the place Jesus was born. And there he lived out his life. Jesus re-incarnated all over again, you might say.

As we ponder Christmas and perhaps return home or join family, how might you give up your rights and privileges to serve another? Our example? Jesus! Who miraculously condensed all his attributes and perfect character to come in the form of a baby! Why not re-read Philippians 2:1-11 and ponder the miracle?

December 19
The Year I Lost Christmas
Luke 2:4-7

"And Joseph also went up from Galilee, from the town of Nazareth, to Judea, to the city of David, which is called Bethlehem, because he was of the house and lineage of David, to be registered with Mary, his betrothed, who was with child. And while they were there, the time came for her to give birth. And she gave birth to her firstborn son and wrapped him in swaddling cloths and laid him in a manger, because there was no place for them in the inn." (Luke 2:4-7)

Christmas was the happiest time of the year and I never doubted anything about it. Until my twentieth birthday. And then–angels singing in the sky? A baby born to a girl who had no contact with a man? A star that moved around locally?

1015 Gregg Street, Columbia, South Carolina–that's where I was born and that's where I celebrated those happy, happy Christmases year after year. But then I encountered Freud. I was twenty years old with a freshly minted BA and supreme self-confidence. That's when I got acquainted with Freud as the father of psychoanalysis and psychotherapy. Only later did I discover that he was the most influential philosopher of the 20th Century, almost single handedly creating our therapeutic society. He made sense to me. And the more sense he made to me, the less sense the Bible did.

Losing confidence in the Bible stories, before long I lost God. Oh, I wasn't arrogant enough to be an atheist. How could I affirm that such a being didn't exist if I'd never even been to the other side of the moon? But I was agnostic. I didn't know, could no longer affirm God's existence. In fact I found myself committed to a thoroughly naturalistic view of life. Nothing was for sure unless I could put it in a test-tube, under a magnifying glass and prove it. What was to have been liberating freedom from the old superstitions, however, turned out to be a lonely road. If you couldn't believe something unless you could prove it scientifically, then the most important things in life were uncertain–love, for example. With what sonar do you plumb the depths of love, with what scales measure the weight of it, with what tape determine the breadth of it? Or hope–where do you look for it, let alone find it? Especially for the dark void beyond the grave? That Christmas was lonely indeed. I didn't simply lose the tinsel and trees, I didn't merely lose the Bible and God. Nothing in fact was for sure–it all depends, they told me. I was trying to live by that ultimate oxymoron, absolute relativism. Nothing is really for sure except this one thing–nothing is for sure!

Then I had a moment of truth–"If you're so all-fired scientific, McQuilkin, why have you excluded the possibility of a god from your investigations?" Thus I mused. And thus I decided I should be at least honest enough to give that option a try. So I prayed – the first time in a long while – a rather arrogant prayer: "Oh, God, if you do exist, please prove it to me on my terms. Give me evidence in a way I can see it, touch it, evaluate it rationally." I didn't think he could, even if he did exist. But maybe God answers even arrogant prayers...

For me he did! I had in my hands a book I didn't believe. Especially I was bothered by the Old Testament. But I did have it my hands. I could evaluate it rationally, scientifically, so to speak. I knew what the critics disallowed as un-authentic. But as I began my investigation with the residue of what the critics admitted as evidence in their highly programed "court," I found predictions of a coming messiah–when and where he would be born, what he would do, that he would die, how he would die in a criminal's execution, but that he would live forever. Impossible! Hundreds of years before the events (even by the critics' dating)–why, I reasoned, even the most renowned futurist or fortune teller couldn't match that!

Thus I began timidly, slowly to return to the faith of my fathers. Enough to enter into ministry, ultimately as a missionary, yet! But still doubts about the reliability of the Book lurked around fringes of my consciousness. Ten years passed. At last I said to myself, "In or out, McQuilkin–get this thing settled once for all." So I pitched a tent on a lonely beach to spend as much time as I needed to get it settled–"in or out." I decided to read the gospels. As I read I was well aware of what the critics challenged, what "couldn't be so." But as I read a second and third time through, a historic person loomed over all the theories and challenges, over all the critics and detractors, a person who – try as I might -- could not be explained in naturalistic terms. On the third day, as I stood looking over the broad Pacific, contemplating this unexplainable person, there seemed to be a presence with me, almost tangible, and a voice, almost audible. What I heard in my soul was the question, "Little brother, are you smarter than I?"

All the lights flashed on. "Oh, no, no Lord. I'm not smarter than you. And none of those critics–now long gone and forgotten for the most part–are smarter than you." I ran to Jesus and embraced him with my mind. He's smarter than I! Whatever he said about the Book, I accepted. He's smarter than I. Whatever he taught about God and how to find him, about my final destiny, that I accepted. Oh, there are still parts of the Bible I wish weren't there, things I don't understand, but I can wait. In the meantime, I trust the record, I trust *him.* He's smarter than I!

So let the celebration begin! Merry Christmas! There is a God and he does care enough about this dysfunctional old world to reach out in person on a rescue mission. It would be hard to imagine a more beautiful way to begin the Christmas story. Celebrate!

December 20
The Emptying
John 13:3-5 & Philippians 2:5-8

"Jesus, knowing that the Father had given all things into his hands, and that he had come from God and was going back to God, rose from supper. He laid aside his outer garments, and taking a towel, tied it around his waist. Then he poured water into a basin and began to wash the disciples' feet and to wipe them with the towel that was wrapped around him." (John 13:3-5)

I love that story. Jesus, knowing from where he had come--the form of God himself--and knowing where he was going-did what? Took a towel and knelt before his pupils and washed their dirty feet.

He humbled himself even to death. What if he had identified with us in all our humanity, except our death, as the Muslim says? A laughing baby cradled in lovely Mary's arms, a carefree lad playing under gentle Joseph's roof, a strong young artisan caring for his widowed mother and orphaned younger brothers and sisters--exemplary, perhaps even sinless, but surely not death?

The plan in his mind as he left heaven for that smelly stable included death above all else, that nadir of human experience, that farthest point from the image of God, embracing the very judgment of our rebel sin.

The vibrant life of John 1, dead

The mighty creator of Col 1, decomposing

The Eternal One of Heb 1, finished

Not only so--death, Paul says, on a cross. It is one thing to die a hero in battle or even to die of old age or illness. But to die as a criminal, hanging naked and helpless before a mocking world. That's the inside story according to Paul. But why was it told? This is the explosive meaning of Christmas-- *"Have this mind in you!"* (Phillipians 2:5).

Being in the form of God--that's who he was. But who am I? Who being educated, comfortable, busy about important things with certain rights: to my possessions, to my reputation, to my health, to my career, to my ambitions--- what will I do about all that?

"Have this mind among yourselves, which is yours in Christ Jesus, who, though he was in the form of God, did not count equality with God a thing to be grasped, but emptied himself, by taking the form of a servant, being born in the likeness of men. And being found in human form, he humbled himself by becoming obedient to the point of death, even death on a cross" (Philippians 2:5-8).

Jesus emptied himself of his prerogatives--that which was his by right. We have trouble letting go of our pretenses (vs 3). Consider others better?! In church--that hypocritical loudmouth- treat him better than myself? When I am at work--that goof-off who shoves all the work off on me him better than me? Or on the street--treat that road hog like she was driving the presidential limousine? Even at home--that obnoxious kid brother, better than me? TREAT them that way, whether it's true or not. Like Jesus did. In a manner we cannot even imagine, let alone attempt. But Jesus could. And did.

Jesus took the form of a servant. What is that like? See Philippians 2:4: *Let each of you look not only to his own interests, but also to the interests of others.* Be on the lookout, always planning for my own benefit, but always on the lookout, planning for the benefit of the others in my life.

The meaning of Christmas? Oh, it's a multi-faceted star of exquisite beauty. But the inside story is this: Have the same mind-set Christ had when he left heaven for the womb of a Jewish girl--Letting go all pretense and prerogative. Deliberately assuming the role of servant. Pouring out all of life--even death, if need be, for the salvation of people: the people in your life and those to the ends of the earth.

December 21
Birth and a Cross
1 John 1:1-4

"That which was from the beginning, which we have heard, which we have seen with our eyes, which we looked upon and have touched with our hands, concerning the word of life — the life was made manifest, and we have seen it, and testify to it and proclaim to you the eternal life, which was with the Father and was made manifest to us…" (1 John 1:1-4)

"Born in the likeness of men…. obedient even unto death," Paul says in Philippians 2. When James Calvert went out as a missionary to the cannibals of the Fiji Islands, the ship captain tried to turn him back, saying, "You will lose your life and the lives of those with you if you go among such savages."

To that, Calvert replied, "We died before we came here." Died to self-will, self-preservation, self-fulfillment. Died to the old man.

We may not be called on to suffer martyrdom--though more of our sisters and brothers around the world have been martyred in the last years than ever before. But for most of us, what does it mean to take up my cross daily? The daily cross is not some mysterious feeling of self-abnegation. It's to choose someone else's benefit over my own. When my desire or pleasure or rights collide with God's best interests, who gets sacrificed--God or me? If I choose the other person's benefit, if I choose God's, that's to die to my own benefit. Why should I have that kind of mind-set, that life-orientation? It's the only way to follow Jesus.

And when I follow him, where will we go? He came into this world on purpose--to save those who don't yet know Him. And we're to have in us the same mind-set. He leaves us in this world, above all else, to save those apart from Him. So missions really is the bed-rock meaning of Christmas. It may cost me my life, as it cost him. It certainly will cost me a daily dying to my own rights and desires.

Let me tell you about a mighty flood, a new thing, God is doing in our day. Have you heard of the "back to Jerusalem" movement in China? The vision was to go from China on foot to evangelize the peoples of middle Asia, India, the Muslim world–all the way back to where the gospel started: Jerusalem. The vision began to flow through Simon Zhou in the late 40's, but he was arrested by the Communist government in the early 50's and given a 40-year prison sentence for his Christian witness. When Zhou was released in 1983, he began to spread the vision again. Now it has become a flood to reach the nations. A new thing! 1,500 have already gone and their goal is 100,000. Where did they get that number? The leaders decided they should send a tithe of their pastors and since there are a million leaders among the house churches of China, they've decided on 100,000 missionaries. A new thing! Should we not participate in flooding the nations with the gospel in our own small way?

How did China get so many believers? It wasn't always that way. Indeed, persecution of Christians is increasing in China today. In 1950, there were fewer than a million Protestants in that whole vast land. But the communists took over, expelled all missionaries. So what happened? A new thing. A new thing in all of church history since the Apostles were first sent to evangelize. A flood of witnessing Christians in that desert, meeting together in homes, forming small house churches across the land. Flooding, you might call it–a new thing! Today there are 100 times more believers in China than when the communists took over! A hundred million, in fact. A mighty flood! An altogether new thing. Perhaps the new thing would mean sons and daughters in every church flooding out to some dark corner of the world where there is no church, no gospel witness at all. Fully one-half of the world's population live in such places. A new birth and a daily cross- Christmas incarnate for the world!

December 22
Celebrate!
John 3:16

"For God so love the world that He gave His only begotten Son that whoever believes shall not perish but have eternal life."(John 3:16)

One Christmas I had a date. My wife, wanted to attend a musical show, the Trans-Siberian Orchestra. I was apprehensive. The apprehension seemed well-founded when we arrived and saw 12,000 people streaming in. I had to watch closely to see anyone with grey hair, let alone my age.

Actually, it proved to be the most spectacular light show I've ever seen, combined with marvelous music and dance. But what startled me was to find the story they were telling--it was the Christmas story! But the focus of their story would have indeed pleased any Christmas Coalition. They focused on becoming like the story of one born so long ago—the one who cared about the hurting.

What are we celebrating? The wedding of a prince? Like a king-in-waiting at Buckingham palace? No, our celebrant was born in a cowbarn. He was homeless most of his last years on earth, a friend of the poor, the sick, the oppressed, the bad guys. He was unjustly accused and illegally convicted. For what? The crime of embracing the whole world of sinners? He died in public disgrace, hanging naked, nailed to a cross, a death reserved for the most evil of criminals.

Him we celebrate at this season.

And many of you—praise be to God!—celebrate by investing a significant part of your own lives in the very people He cared about so deeply.

Kent was so burdened for the least and lost that he moved to the gates of hell, Calcutta. There he lived in a tiny room, about 10 feet square, slept on a mat on the concrete floor. He had to make room for the cottage industry he was launching for his neighbors. A bucket for a kitchen/bathroom sink, a hole in the ground for a toilet, a single gas burner to cook. That was my son, and other unknown Mother Theresas giving in the most desperate parts of earth. And what about me? I stand convicted of a callus heart and ask God to unleash his love through me. If he does that in me—and in you—how would he go about it? Two ways, I think.

He created us in his own likeness, God-compatible. Why did he create such a being as us? God is love, that's why. And in love he climaxed his creative activity with a being who could love him back. Lovers to be truly one must be compatible. So he created us that way. But that wasn't his only purpose. One purpose of making us on his pattern is to enable us to join him in loving the world of hurting people. So we try to behave in a God-like way toward the homeless, the ill.

But we fall short. So he went into creative action again. And that's the Christmas story. God himself invading our humanity. Since we chose to go our own way, which all too often isn't God's way, he planned a re-hab program, a plan to re-create us more and more into his Son's likeness. And that's the second part of his plan.

The Holy Spirit wants to invade OUR bodies as he did Mary's. Do you remember the Christmas carol, "O holy Child of Bethlehem! Descend to us, we pray, cast out our sin and enter in; Be born is us today." He wants to give us life. Born AGAIN, is the way Jesus put it on one occasion? A fresh start, not just our bodies, life eternal for our inner selves.

So at this season of the year, let us celebrate life—Jesus' life. And OURS! And then through the new me, the new you, he wants to flow life to the hurting, poor, dispossessed in your country, and into to the whole world he loves. *"For God so loved the world that he gave his one and only son, that whoever believes in him should not perish…"*

December 23
Learning Humility
Philippians 2:8

"And being found in human form, he humbled himself by becoming obedient to the point of death, even death on a cross." (Philippians 2:8)

In clear and strong language, Paul holds up the Servant as our model. We are to think the way Jesus thought when he relinquished all his rightful prerogatives as Deity in order to become one of us. He humbled himself, not to a kingly role—as great a condescension as that would have been—but to the role of a servant. And then, as a servant among men—men who actually owed him their all—he stooped to accept a criminal's death (Phil. 2:1-8).

But who can deliberately choose to serve others, to treat others as superior to self, even when truthfully they are not (Rom. 12:10; Eph. 5:21; Phil. 2)? Who can deliberately and consistently choose the menial task all others avoid, forgive the arrogant offender, pick up after the careless destroyer, give to the ungrateful? Who, that is, would deliberately choose to consistently respond as a servant is expected to respond? Only one who loves deeply.

Love is a Great Antidote to Pride.
"Love is patient, love is kind, and is not jealous; love does not brag and is not arrogant, does not act unbecomingly; it does not seek its own, is not provoked, does not take into account a wrong suffered, does not rejoice in unrighteousness, but rejoices with the truth; bears all things, believes all things, hopes all things, endures all things." (1 Cor. 13:4-7, NASB)

1 Corinthians 13 is a perfect description of everything pride is not. Love, as an emotion strong enough to make one a servant, may not be self-produced. But one can choose to take a servant's role whether or not he feels like it, and to this the love of Christ draws us. If we are not drawn, God in his love may bring into our lives that which will press us to our knees, aiding us to become humble even when we neglect or refuse to humble ourselves.

Suffering is God's Gift to Produce a Meek Spirit. Paul often gloried in his infirmities. Why are so many of the Hebrew words for humble rooted in ideas of being crushed, bruised, broken, chastened, afflicted, subjugated? For stiff-necked, arrogant sons of men this is often the only way to a humble and contrite heart. One biblical term for gentleness has the root concept of taming a wild animal. Meekness in Scripture is not weakness but strength harnessed. Is not a great crushing of spirit often the only route to Christlike humility? Even Jesus learned obedience in the school of suffering (Heb. 5:8).

Without tenderness of spirit, the most intensely righteous, religious life is like the image of God without his beauty and attractiveness. It is possible to be very, very religious, and staunch, and persevering in all Christian duties, even to be a brave defender and preacher of holiness, to be mathematically orthodox, and blameless in outward life, and very zealous in good works, and yet to be greatly lacking in tenderness of spirit. . . . We often come across Christians who are bright and clever, and strong and righteous; in fact, a little too bright, and a little too clever . . . and there seems too much of self in their strength, and their righteousness is severe and critical. They have everything to make them saints, except the crushing weight of an unspeakable crucifixion, which would grind them into a supernatural tenderness and limitless charity for others. But if they are of the real elect, God has a winepress prepared for them, through which they will some day pass.

The ways to the great grace of humility, the means to conquer demon pride are to acknowledge reality, concentrate on God with gratitude and praise, trust him actively for the resources of life, assume the servant role, love deeply, and accept God's loving chastening.

As we approach Christmas, consider humility. *"And being found in human form, he humbled himself by becoming obedient to the point of death, even death on a cross."* (Philippians 2:8) Conflict in your home? Consider love and humility. Disappointment? Consider others more important than yourself. Anger? Consider it all loss for the sake of knowing Christ. Love deeply for love covers a multitude of sins (1 Peter 4:8).

December 24
Needing Christmas
Isaiah 9:2

""The people who walked in darkness have seen a great light; those who dwelt in a land of deep darkness, on them has light shone." (Isaiah 9:2)

Do you know what I like about Santa Claus and Christmas commercialism? Or about ACLU and our courts crushing creches? What could I like about the downside of Christmas with the crescendo of drunkenness, murder, suicide? Not to mention the virgin Mary?

Think about Santa. Don't you think it's better to celebrate the benevolent old geezer than, say some dictator's birthday? Or how about Lenin Day for the communist world? Aren't you glad we don't sing carols to that usurper of the throne, of God, "Hail to Caesar"? Why do I say such heresy? Well, what nation in all of history would spend 50% of its annual retail sales for GIVING AWAY? That's why commerce in other lands can't make Christmas fly like American commercialism. Commercialism? Maybe we should re-name it Generosity? Why, generosity is like God! Distorted, in the shopping frenzy of the holidays, to be sure, but surely better than celebrating martyrs who blow themselves up trying to kill people and gain rewards in heaven?

And what could I like about the court battles? Well, think of it this way: why do people make such an issue of saying "Merry Christmas" and bring endless lawsuits to get rid of every manger scene in public? Why fight so ferociously? They don't fight Grimm's Fairy Tales! Because Jesus is threatening, very powerful. The incarnation is not some human, gentle myth, but God's powerful invasion of our humanity. It's hard to stay neutral!

But what of that downside of Christmas? All the drinking and drunk driving, all that increase in the rate of murder, family murder at that? What can be good about that? It's nothing but bad, distilled evil. But it does put into sharp focus what may not be so clear at other times of the year–our empty core without Jesus. And the hostility that breeds on our selfish core? All those failed expectations emerge from the shadows in the bright light of the Christmas season? And in the light of that brilliant star of Bethlehem how dark our lostness stands out. At Christmas people feel acutely what they do not have, in contrast to the high expectations of the special Day. What an opportunity to hold out hope to those who live in darkness! Isaiah 9:2 The people who walked in darkness have seen a great light; those who dwelt in a land of deep darkness, on them has light shone. Isaiah 9:2 *"The people who walked in darkness have seen a great light; those who dwelt in a land of deep darkness, on them has light shone."*

December 25
The Gift
Luke 1:34

"And Mary said to the angel, "How will this be, since I am a virgin?" (Luke 1:34)

Mary, the virgin, so venerated by our Catholic friends, so neglected by us Protestants. But I dearly love Mary. Why? Who is the real Mary? What did she look like? Hair style, clothes? What kind of house did she live in? What sort of family income? Education? What age was she? And was she skinny or not? The truth is, we don't know any of those important things about Mary, do we? Nothing. Except her insides. The REAL Mary. That part of Mary we know intimately.

Read Luke 1.28-38; 46-55. That's the REAL Mary. But we concentrate on the gift wrap, don't we? Was Mary Miss Nazareth? A graduate of Jerusalem Women's College? No indeed!

God's gift to Mary was not just for Mary. She was the Christmas package in which God wrapped His gift for the world. And that is what he designed you for. From eternity: to bring Christ to others, to do a special job for God in the world, something no one else can do.

But what if that isn't happening? Well, maybe your insides, the real you, isn't ready for Jesus. What do you have to be like for Jesus to come in? Strong and successful and smart? No, Mary was a poor girl by our standards, uneducated, unknown beyond the small circle of family and friends. So...What was the REAL Mary like?

When you have the wraps stripped off by cruel circumstances or evil people, what do we discover within? The ugliness of a person self-centered? Or how about self-discovery, self-fulfillment, self-expression, self-indulgence, self-pity, self-assertion. What an ugly little hard core of self-worship. You are god–and there is no room for two gods in the package of you! But what about Mary?

Above all she was humble. *"I am the bond-servant of the Lord."* Whatever you say, is OK. She was surprised by grace–"why me, Lord?" Luke 1:38. This is where heart preparation starts. But I don't naturally incline toward servanthood. How could I get that way if I wanted to?

Mary's obedience came from a trusting heart. Mary had faith in God that he is going to do the best thing and that he can do the impossible. *"How can this be?"* She asks in Luke 1:34. Not the way Sarah questioned the prediction of her pregnancy, not like Zacharias questioned the prophecy of his wife's pregnancy. Think of her faith: a baby without sexual intercourse? and would she lose her most precious possession, Joseph? she would certainly lose her reputation. Which is probably what she did: "we were not born of fornication".(John 8:41), and perhaps she would lose her friends.

But she said, "Yes." What faith!

If you have a yielded and trusting heart toward God and his messenger what will happen to you? The same thing that happened to Mary, in a way: the Holy Spirit will come on you and the power of the Almighty will overshadow you and that holy One formed in you is the Son of God.

Yes, right there in the dirty, smelly, obscure, rejected stable of your circumstances, you can receive the magnificent gift, the Holy One. But perhaps you already have Him. Great, now you can grow ever more like him. And now you can deliver his grace to others. If I only have Mary's heart of humility and faith, with God nothing shall be impossible. Mary's Christmas can be your Christmas: God's magnificent gift of his Son delivered in the package of you to all the people in your life.

December 26
Relationships: A Source of Joy
Psalm 16:11

"You make known to me the path of life; in your presence there is fullness of joy; at your right hand are pleasures forevermore." (Psalm 16:11)

Friendship, marriage, children--marvelous sources, and biblically approved sources, of joy. Invest life here! But human relationships, fraught with such high potential for joy, often bring sorrow instead. To be sure, a son who turns out to be wise, in the biblical sense, brings great joy, as Solomon said, but should he turn out to be a spiritual fool, is there a greater pain? Perhaps the most painful contrast on earth is the joy of a wedding and the agony of a divorce court.

Like things and activity, human relationships can go either way. It is altogether appropriate that when Scripture speaks of joy it emphasizes another relationship--our relationship with God.

"Why are you downcast, O my soul? Why so disturbed within me? Put your hope in God...God my joy and my delight." He himself is the joy. In fact, says Nehemiah, *"the joy of the Lord is your strength."* Why? David tells us clearly: *"Let all who take refuge in you be glad; let them ever sing for joy. Spread your protection over them, that those who love your name may rejoice in you."* So it is from God, his strength extended in our behalf, his protection covering us that brings joy.

In fact, God does many things to give joy. In the Old Testament a major joy theme was the celebration of military victory and this carries on through to the joyous celebration at the final conquest of evil forces at the end of time. *"The ransomed shall return with songs and everlasting joy on their heads; Gladness and joy will overtake them, and sorrow and sighing shall flee away."* So sang Isaiah the prophet.

In the NT the joy theme clusters around two great events: Advent, the invasion of planet earth by God in baby form, and the resurrection when God vanquished the last great enemy. In fact, when Jesus came the celestial beings sang and a fetus in the womb of Elizabeth leaped for joy, and at the resurrection folks were so filled with joy they lost the power of speech! Joy, joy, joy! No wonder Christmas and Easter are the joyous times.

But God does things today to give us joy as well: he answers our prayers--*"ask and you will receive that your joy may be full,"* There's a marvelous purpose for prayer! The greatest joy he gives is, no doubt, salvation: *"God is my salvation; therefore with joy you will draw water from the wells of salvation."* Our salvation is a well-spring of continuing joy. But there is the more down-to-earth joy of giving and receiving gifts. Paul's heart leaped for joy when he received gifts and in both the Old Testament and the New Testament God's people were filled with joy when they emptied their pockets!

Even greater joy, of course, comes when God gives us <u>spiritual</u> fruit--it brings joy in heaven, too, but we rightly are filled with joy when sinners are converted. And when they grow, too. In fact, for John there is <u>no greater</u> joy than to find his children walking in truth.

But actually, more than all the good he sends our way to give us joy, it is his very presence that brings the greatest joy: (Psalm 16:11) *"you fill me with pleasure with your presence, with eternal pleasures at your right hand,"* David assures us.

God the Holy Spirit is the one who gives joy. Not only is joy the natural result of the Spirit's indwelling reign, the "fruit," He Himself is constantly linked with the experience of joy. How often the disciples are said to have been filled with the Holy Spirit and with joy. Perhaps that is why those who emphasize the fullness of the Holy Spirit are noted for their exuberance in worship and in life. Perhaps today you don't feel joy. There is a hole where joy used to exist. Hold tight to Jesus. Joy will return. Perhaps your feel full of joy! Rest deeply in this well-spring of continuing in His presence.

December 27
Love Demonstrated
1 John 4:8, 16

"God is love," (1 John 4:8, 16).

This is the basic difference between the biblical concept of love and our concept of love. The Bible defines love by the nature of God. We tend to define love by the nature of man.

To say that God is love does not mean that God *equals* love. Love does not describe God exhaustively. He has other qualities, such as wisdom and strength; but this does not mean that those characteristics in God's nature violate love. God always acts lovingly, even in judgment.

Again, "God is love" does not mean that *love equals God.* Love is not an entity, having existence as an object, let alone having personality. To say that love and God are equivalent would deify love and make it some absolute concept to which God himself is subject and by which he could be judged. Rather, love gains whatever stature it has because God is that way. He forms the concept by his nature. He is the source of all true love (1 John 4:7, 19). Since God himself defines love, true human love is godlikeness (1 John 4:16).

God was not obliged to love by some external "ought." Loving is the way he is. This is one of the greatest evidences for the Trinity. God the Father loves God the Son and God the Holy Spirit from all eternity. God the Son loves the Father and the Spirit, and the Spirit loves the Son and the Father. Thus by love they are bound, and only out of love for others was that unity broken at the Cross when, by the power of the Spirit, the Son assumed our guilt, and the Father turned away in judicial rejection from part of his very being.

The loving nature of God is the basis for his creative and redeeming activity. He created man because he is love and desired a being designed on his own pattern so that he could love that creature and be freely loved in return. When man rejected this loving approach of God, breaking that relationship, God continued loving because God is love by nature. And so we have the story of redemption. Love became incarnate. Thus all of life finds meaning in being loved by God and loving him.

By his life, Jesus demonstrated flawlessly how godlike love behaves, and in his death he demonstrated the ultimate proof of love. He was our model—we can now *see* how we are to "walk in love, as Christ loved us and gave himself up for us, a fragrant offering and sacrifice to God" (Eph. 5:1-2). We now can *see* what it means to have the kind of mind-set that was his who "being in very nature God, did not consider equality with God something to be grasped, but made himself nothing, taking the very nature of a servant, being made in human likeness. And being found in appearance as a man, he humbled himself and became obedient to death—even death on a cross!" (Phil. 2:6-8, NIV). "By this we know love, that he laid down his life for us; and we ought to lay down our lives for the brethren" (1 John 3:16). Throughout the New Testament Christ's love is given as our model: "This is my commandment, that you love one another as I have loved you" (John 15:12).

All of Christ's life puts on display God's loving character, but the Cross of Christ demonstrates the love of God more clearly than any other act of any other person in all history.

Christ himself is the perfect, living model of God's character; but God graciously re-creates that character in other people who, in turn, demonstrate true love. In fact, "By this all men will know that you are my disciples, if you have love for one another" (John 13:35).

Pastor Son was . . . a mild, little man—less than five feet tall—whose two great joys in life were his two sons, Tong-

In and Tong-Sin. During the war Tong-In, like his father, had refused to worship at the Shinto shrines and had been thrown out of school by the Japanese. After the war, at twenty-four years of age, he went back to high school. . . . In October 1948, a wild Communist uprising swept through his part of South Korea and Communist youths seized the school in a reign of terror. A nineteen-year-old Communist leveled a pistol at Tong-In and ordered him to renounce his Christian faith. But Tong-In only pleaded with him to turn Christian himself and try the Christian way of love. Tong-Sin, the younger brother, rushed up to save him. "Shoot me," he shouted, "and let my brother live." "No," cried Tong-In, "I am the elder. I am the one who should die. Shoot me." The Communist shot them both. . . . Two days later the uprising was smashed and the murderer of the two boys was caught and brought to trial. Pastor Son found him with his hands tied behind his back, about to be condemned to death. He went to the military commander. "No amount of punishment will bring back my two sons," he said, "so what is to be gained by this? Let me, instead, take the boy and make a Christian of him so that he can do the work in the world that Tong-In and Tong-Sin left undone." Stunned at first by the proposal, the authorities reluctantly consented to release the young man into the custody of the father of the boys he had killed, and Pastor Son took him home.

God graciously demonstrates his loving character not only in his eternal Son but in other sons and daughters in every land, in every time.

In summary, love is a warm affection, suffusing a disposition till it concentrates on others whether or not they are worthy of the gifts of love. Is that too theoretical? Then consider the attitudes and activities the Bible describes as godlike and the commands revealing God's will—they describe the loving way of life. Is that overwhelming, perhaps confusing by its multifaceted complexity? Then look at Jesus. He is the complete demonstration, the full incarnation of love. But perhaps you need someone you can see and touch? Then choose an authentic Christian and watch him. Not too critically, of course, remembering that someone may be watching you, too. Consider these things and you will discover that God's kind of love moves beyond feeling to take the initiative and acts to promote the welfare of another.[91]

---

[91] IBE (2014), 40-42.

December 28
Homeward Bound
Psalm 90:12

"Teach us to number our days, that we may gain a heart of wisdom." (Psalm 90:12)

Some people don't like to think about the end of the journey, but that's a great mistake. God tells us we'll gain great wisdom by thinking about the end of life: *"Every living man is no more than a puff of wind, no more than a shadow...I am only your guest for a little while."* (Ps.39.5,12) *"Teach us how short our life is, so that we may become wise."* (Psalm 90.12) And knowing this he uses his short time on earth to prepare for eternity. That is true wisdom. The grace of growing old, resources for the journey. For the feelings of uselessness, loneliness, bitterness, fear? The promises of God! Trust him! He's strong enough, smart enough and loves you enough to die for you. You can trust him!

Let Me Get Home Before Dark

It's sundown, Lord.
The shadows of my life stretch back
    the dimness of the years long spent.
I fear not death, for that grim foe betrays himself at last,
    thrusting me forever into life:
Life with you, unsoiled and free.
But I do fear.
I fear the Dark Spectre may come too soon—
    or do I mean, too late?
That I should end before I finish or
    finish, but not well.
That I should stain your honor, shame your name,
    grieve your loving heart.
Few, they tell me, finish well…
Lord, let me get home before dark.
The darkness of a spirit grown mean and small,
    fruit shriveled on the vine,
bitter to the taste of my companions,
burden to be borne by those brave few who love me still.
No, Lord. Let the fruit grow lush and sweet, a
    joy to all who taste;
Spirit - sign of God
    at work, stronger, fuller, brighter at the end.
Lord, let me get home before dark.

The darkness of tattered gifts,
        rust-locked, half-spent or ill-spent,
A life that once was used of God
        now set aside.
Grief for glories gone or
Fretting for a task God never gave.
Mourning in the hollow chambers of memory,
Gazing on the faded banners of victories long gone.
Cannot I run well unto the end?
Lord, let me get home before dark.
The outer me decays —
I do not fret or ask reprieve.
The ebbing strength but weans me from mother earth
        and grows me up for heaven.
I do not cling to shadows cast by immortality.
I do not patch the scaffold lent to build the real, eternal me.
I do not clutch about me my cocoon,
        vainly struggling to hold hostage
        a free spirit pressing to be born.
But will I reach the gate
        in lingering pain, body distorted, grotesque?
Or will it be a mind wandering
        un-tethered among light fantasies or grim terrors?
Of your grace, Father, I humbly ask…
Let me get home before dark

December 29
Clay Pots
2 Corinthians 4:6 – 5:11

*"We are afflicted in every way, but not crushed; perplexed, but not driven to despair; persecuted, but not forsaken; struck down, but not destroyed. "(*2 Corinthians 4:8,9)

Before we begin to think of ourselves more highly than we ought to think, let's be reminded of what we are-humble clay pots! Not diamond-studded golden bowls, just plain old clay pots.

But notice an incredible incongruity, an incomprehensible irony. Someone has put in this clay pot a magnificent treasure. So the value is not in the pot, but in the contents. What is the treasure? The light of the Gospel? The glory of God? The presence of Christ? Yes! And somehow or other that treasure takes a fragile, insignificant, common clay pot and transforms it. Watch what happens.

Nothing exposes our fragile vulnerability like suffering. Some of the clay pots have been shattered, those we love die, and we are shaken. But we don't have the normal response.

Why do we not have a standard clay pot response? How do we have the response of some magnificent royal vessel? This passage answers those questions--the why and the how. First then, why? Why do we respond so a-typically? Psychologist might say we are suppressing our real feelings and endangering our psychological health. But Paul seems to have another reality that transforms humble, fragile, vulnerable clay pots.

The shattered clay pot doesn't remain a jumble of broken shards. Brian sat in my living room and spoke confidently of his good health, his strong body, his expectancy to live long and serve God well. But at that very moment his clay pot was cracking all over and a few weeks later it was dead. But Paul says, Sunday's coming! Brian will be put together again in a beautiful strong body. Resurrection!

God's life, power is put on display. This is what happened with Bart. Those who knew him reflect on the character of Christ that was demonstrated in his life. Some who didn't know him have stepped forward to take his place. By living at risk for God's purposes in this world, serving in a distant unsafe land, he joined our Savior in giving his life for lost people. With his blood he indelibly marked a fledgling program in church-starting evangelism. God's power has been vividly put on display.

How can a lowly, fragile, vulnerable clay pot ever hope to respond this way? It is the power of God. 2 Corinthians 4:7: *"But we have this treasure in jars of clay, to show that the surpassing power belongs to God and not to us."* Dick Woodward would say "I won't but he will, I can't, but he can, I don't but he does." The treasure in a clay pot.

A broken pot gives testimony of our inner condition, letting, the contents of the pot spill out. I went to visit the hospital room in a Colorado Springs burn unit. Ben's pot had been shattered. He was in a car crash and a young man came every day to help. For long months he came, and Ben spoke of faith. Hardened family members, strangers, this new friend came to Jesus because the faith spilled out. 2 Corinthians 4:11: *"Since we have the same spirit of faith according to what has been written, "I believed, and so I spoke," we also believe, and so we also speak."*

Faith turns our world right side up exactly at the point circumstances turned it upside down. True faith works no longer for the visible, lightweight, temporary stuff, but for HIS happiness, fulfillment. As long as we live for the seen, the light weight, transient stuff, we demonstrate that we do not yet live by faith.

What we live for is all brought into focus by the shattering of the clay pots. What would spill out of your clay pot if it shattered today?

December 30
Love Expressed
Matthew 22:37-40

"And he said to him, "You shall love the Lord your God with all your heart and with all your soul and with all your mind. This is the great and first commandment. And a second is like it: You shall love your neighbor as yourself. On these two commandments depend all the Law and the Prophets." (Matthew 22:37-40)

Some disparage reciprocal love, calling it "need-love" or even "swap-love." They say it is unworthy to expect or even to desire a return on one's investment of love in another. But it is easy to become more "spiritual" than the Bible. C. S. Lewis speaks to this:

We must be cautious about calling Need-love "*mere selfishness.*" *Mere* is always a dangerous word. No doubt Need-love, like all our impulses, can be selfishly indulged. A tyrannous and gluttonous demand for affection can be a horrible thing. But in ordinary life no one calls a child selfish because it turns for comfort to its mother. Every Christian would agree that a man's spiritual health is exactly proportional to his love for God. But man's love for God, from the very nature of the case, must always be very largely, and most often be entirely, a Need-love. This is obvious when we implore forgiveness for our sins or support in our tribulations. . . . It would be a bold and silly creature that came before its Creator with the boast, "I'm no beggar. I love you disinterestedly."[92]

Indeed, God himself expects a "return on his investment." He longs and desires to be loved. But the difference is this: He does not demand it. He does not make a loving response the condition for giving love (Rom. 5:6-8). And, humanly, we always do. *Eros* to the ancient Greek, and to the modern man as well, is passionate love that desires the other *for itself.* We continue to give only so long as we receive—or so long as we hope to receive. But God's kind of love is not preoccupied with the question, How well *am* I loved? but rather, How well *do* I love?

Thus the focus of biblical love is on the quality of the subject, the loving character of the one loving, not on the quality of the object, its worthiness of love, its desirability, its lovableness. Jesus spells this out in great detail with many examples (Luke 6:27-35). He teaches that to love those who love us is nothing great. It is when we choose deliberately to love those who do not deserve it that we have reflected divine love.

Yet the ideal is reciprocal love, each finding in the other abundant reason to appreciate, to feel drawn to, to be overwhelmed by the desire to give. We give because we want to, not because we have to—we delight in the loved one. Then we rejoice in receiving from the one loved. When the object is not lovable, or the emotion is not present, it is then that the character of the giving lover shines in greatest splendor.

Biblical love, then, is an affectionate disposition that motivates the lover to consistently act for the welfare of another, whether or not the other deserves it or reciprocates.

We have tried to define love. But the length and breadth and depth and height of it (Eph. 3:18-19) stretch far beyond our reach. What shall we do? Often, to understand an abstract idea or a large concept it is necessary to define by description or demonstration. How good that God has given us both.

Love is defined by its description. The most well-known description of love was penned by Paul (1 Cor. 13). Notice that he gives examples of the internal but also the external; love's attitude and disposition, but also love's activity. On the one hand love does not boast, is not proud or self-seeking, keeps no record of wrongs, does not delight

---

[92] C. S. Lewis, *The Four Loves* (London: Collins-Fontana, 1960), 8–9.

in evil but rejoices with the truth, always trusts and hopes. On the other hand, love takes action: It is patient and kind, is not rude and quick-tempered, always protects, and always perseveres.

Scripture is filled with many other descriptions of love. Love is without hypocrisy works no ill for others, will lay down its life for another, takes the servant's role, is brotherly.

Though direct descriptions of love are plentiful enough to challenge for a lifetime, the indirect descriptions seem all but exhaustless. Consider the teachings on what have been called the "reciprocal verbs" of the New Testament.

Not only are we told to love one another thirteen times, we are commanded to have the same care one for another, to receive one another, to be affectionate to one another, to greet one another with a holy kiss, to wait for one another, to be kind one to another, to prefer one another, to forbear one another in love, to forgive one another. Furthermore, we are not to judge one another, speak evil of one another, lie to one another, "bite" one another, provoke one another, or complain against one another. Incredible as this listing may be, it is only one of any number of teachings in Scripture that describe the attitudes and behavior of love.

Let us agree that the commands of Scripture reveal God's will for those to whom they are addressed and that his ultimate will is that we be like him in moral character. Since "God is love" it should come as no surprise that the entire Old Testament revelation of God's will for man hangs on the law of love (Matt. 22:37-40). After stating the Golden Rule, Jesus concluded, *For this is [the essence of] the law and the prophets.* Paul repeats the thought: "*For the whole law is fulfilled in one word, 'You shall love your neighbor as yourself'*" (Gal. 5:14). Again he says that this law of love sums up the Ten Commandments (Rom. 13:8-9). This basic fact about the relationship of love to the commandments of Scripture means that every command applicable to Christians is a description of how love will behave. In other words, the instructions for life in Scripture give substance and definition to the basic law of love.

Yet a description can be a lifeless code of ethics, an intimidating statement that lays a heavy hand of condemnation on me, confuses by its complexity, numbs by its impossible demands, blurs my perception by its distance from my own experience. God knows we need an example. We need to have love demonstrated, and this task he took upon himself at infinite cost.

December 31
Choose the Image of God
Matthew 5:48

"You therefore must be perfect, as your heavenly Father is perfect" (Matthew 5:48)

God created man in his own image morally. There are, no doubt, other elements in man's likeness to God, but a morally right character is primary. It is the basis of shared love and fellowship; it is indispensable to demonstrating in human life the glory (glorious character) of God. Mankind has ever neglected this aspect of God's image and worked to attain likeness to God in his attributes of knowledge and power. This was Satan's temptation to Eve: "You will be like God." How? She was already like God in his moral nature. She rejected this likeness in order to reach for God's infinities and from the outset lost both. All her descendants, save one, have followed in her steps. But God's purpose remained the same: He wanted people to be like himself.

This is the purpose of the sovereign Lord, commanded through Moses at the beginning of the Old Covenant and through Jesus Christ at the beginning of the New Covenant: You must be holy as I am holy (Leviticus 19:2; 1 Peter

1:16), you must be perfect as your heavenly Father is perfect (Matt. 5:48). It is not optional. Since it is a divine imperative, we properly call this will of God law. 0

It is wrong not to be like God morally. This wrong is not just a weakness or an unfortunate deviation from the norm. The Bible calls it sin. To be holy is to be separated from sin; to be right is to be in alignment with God's character. This is the holiness required of men. It is an obligation, not mere instruction or advice. Without it no one will see God (Heb. 12:14).

This most important use of the word law is often called the "moral law," God's expressed will concerning what constitutes likeness to God. Does the New Testament use the term in this way? When Paul speaks of the work of the law being written in the hearts of those who do not have the written law (Rom. 2:14-15), he is speaking of God's moral law. This, then, is a common use of the concept of law in the New Testament as well as the Old: God's expressed will that we be like him, commonly called the "moral law."

For anyone who wants to know and do God's will, it is of utmost importance to discover what that will is. Since both Jesus Christ and the apostles taught that some change had taken place in the relationship of God's people to "the law," we must be careful to discover exactly what that law is and what that change is.

All would agree that a change was long overdue from the damning idea that a person can gain acceptance with God through his own efforts. At least some elements of the Mosaic system of law were done away with in Christ's sacrificial death and the institution of the church. But here agreement ends. Some hold that Paul makes no distinctions among laws and that the Christian is not obligated to any of the Mosaic law, including the moral law.

Because law is used in many different ways and often with several meanings overlapping, it is important to be sure from the context which meaning was intended by the author. Otherwise we shall be applying a teaching concerning the law that does not actually apply. For example, if we speak of being free from the law and use this to refer to the moral law of God when in fact Scripture is referring to the condemnation resulting from the law (Rom. 8:1-2) or the Old Testament system of sacrifices, we are making a great error. For the time being, we will use the term law in its primary meaning: law as the expressed will of God that people be like him morally.

This ultimate standard for the Christian is not merely a code of ethics or system of doctrine or a subjective feel for what is right. The standard for the Christian is God himself. This is exciting. It means that the foundation of our moral standard is not man, his wisdom, his fallen nature, his desires, his values, his traditions, nor his culture. These may be the foundation of man-made law, but not of the Christian standard of life. Since God himself is our standard, our standard is not relative, changing with each age or society. God's law is absolute, perfect, unchanging, and eternal. Since God himself is our standard, the standard is universal. The moral character of God as a standard applies to all men of all ages. This standard is personal, living, and visible rather than a dead code. It is not something that God imposes on us arbitrarily. It derives from his own nature.

This truth also means that God's character is not derived from the moral structure of the universe. Some would hold that God behaves rightly and lovingly because he is obliged to do so by ultimate "natural" law. Rather, we say that righteousness and love are good because that is the way God is. We do not, as some theologians, derive our standards from nature, setting up great cosmic moral hoops through which God must jump. Rather, we see these standards flowing out of the nature of our infinite, ultimate, personal God.

Thus, God's will for man is that we be like him. We were created in his moral likeness, reflecting the glory of his character. His purpose in redemption is to restore that image, which has been marred. As you finish this year, which direction will you choose? Where will you go from here spiritually? How will you become transformed from one degree of likeness to another into His image?

Made in the USA
Columbia, SC
05 December 2022